# WANDERINGS

### Ch...
### Histo...

Throughout the tragedy and promise of their panoramic history, the lives of the Jews have been intertwined with the great cultures of Mesopotamia and Egypt, Greece and Rome, Islam, medieval Christendom and modern secular society. The Jews have been exploited, tormented, and, all too often, slaughtered. Yet by making use of their gifts, their wisdoms, their skills and strengths, these cultures have paradoxically helped to create their unique and ineffaceable identity.

---

# WANDERINGS

*Chaim Potok's*
*History of the Jews*

*Fawcett Crest* ● *New York*

*WANDERINGS*

THIS BOOK CONTAINS THE COMPLETE TEXT OF
THE ORIGINAL HARDCOVER EDITION.

Published by Fawcett Crest Books, a unit of CBS Publications,
the Consumer Publishing Division of CBS Inc., by arrangement with Alfred A. Knopf, Inc.

ISBN: 0-449-24270-6

Selection of the History Book Club
Selection of the Jewish Book Club
Selection of the Jewish Publication Society of America

Printed in the United States of America

First Fawcett Crest Printing: March 1980

10  9  8  7  6  5  4  3  2  1

## To the Fathers

Benjamin Max Potok
[1895–1958]

Max Isaac Mosevitzky
[1889–1968]

*I YHWH, in My grace, have summoned you,*
*And I have grasped you by the hand.*
*I created you, and appointed you*
*A covenant-people, a light of the nations. . . .*

*—ISAIAH 42:6*

# Contents

## MAPS

# WANDERINGS

# Introduction

I am an American, a Jew. Early in this century my father came to America from Poland. He had served in a Polish unit of the Austrian army during the First World War and had returned home to a strange reward: a pogrom.

He crossed the Atlantic but underwent no sea change. He never grasped the essential difference between the Christian in America and the Christian in Europe. Though beardless, and garbed as a twentieth-century man, he was a very pious Jew. He saw himself mirrored in the eye of most American gentiles as a Jewish Caliban.

He spoke often about the strange destiny of our people, a destiny chosen for us by the transcendent One God who had created man in His own image, thereby making each and every one of us unique and of infinite worth. For some mysterious reason, God's world was imperfect. Man's task was to help God perfect it.

My father often spoke in military terms: the Jews were the vanguard of mankind, the reconnaissance troops, and therefore prone to taking the highest casualties. But we would succeed one day in establishing the Kingdom of God on earth. Of that he had no doubt. Unlike the English historian G. M. Trevelyan, who regarded history as having no beginning and no end, my father saw history as the path that led from the creation of the world by God almost six thousand years ago to the future coming of the Messiah and the redemption, first of Jewry and then of all mankind. It was the sacred duty of the Jew to lead man along that path; it was the demonic intent of unrighteous gentiles to try to kill us along the way.

In the schools that served me as daytime homes during

the early decades of my life, I was taught my father's Judaism and Jewish history: the taken-for-granted obligation to observe the commandments of God; the story of the creation and the eating of the apple and the first murder and the Flood; I learned of Abraham and the covenant with God; a son was nearly sacrificed by a father in a gesture of ultimate faith (I remember how I trembled the first time I read that chilling story); patriarchs roamed a promised land; strong-willed women loved, quarreled, and connived; brothers fought, and one was sold into slavery and became second in command to the great pharaoh of Egypt; then the long enslavement and the coming of Moses; plagues; freedom; the crossing of a miraculously parted sea and the Revelation on a desolate mountaintop; the wandering in the wilderness; the death of Aaron and Moses; the conquest of Canaan by Joshua; tribal military chieftains labeled "judges"; aged Samuel; tragic Saul; heroic David conquering Jerusalem; wise Solomon building the first Temple; evil Israelite kings and fearless spokesmen for God called prophets; the destruction—because of our own sins; exile to Babylon; return; Ezra and a new covenant with God; Nehemiah and a new Jerusalem; the age of Alexander and the Hellenizing Syrians; the brave Maccabees; then Rome and rabbis and blood and death and the long exile in which my father and mother and sisters and brother and I were now a link in the chain of generations leading to the Messiah.

It was a history rich with ideas, hallowed by martyrs, characterized by a familial intimacy with God and a tenacious fixing of the eyes upon the promised future. I studied it in depth and did not find it difficult to feel myself part of it—especially when I discovered how to cope with its fundamentalism during the years I learned to appreciate and use modern scientific methods of research into ancient writings. I lived at ease in the core of my faith.

Then I entered the American army. I too crossed an ocean. In the shattered villages of Korea, in the exquisite temples of Japan, in the teeming Chinese hovels of Hong

Kong, in the vile back streets of Macao, all the neat antique coherence of my past came undone.

Once we bulldozed a piece of Korean earth on our compound to lay a cement foundation for a Quonset hut and discovered a mass grave of children who had been butchered during the Korean War. We were always finding such graves in Korea. No one seemed to know who had done the killing; no one really cared. We would cover them over and build elsewhere.

My early decades had prepared me for everything—except the two encounters I in fact experienced: a meeting with a vast complex of cultures perfectly at ease without Jews and Judaism, and a confrontation with the beautiful and the horrible in the world of oriental human beings. It was not the anguish of my own people that sundered me—that I had come to accept as part of our destiny—but the loveliness and the suffering I saw in the lives of pagans.

Jewish history began in a world of pagans; my own Judaism was transformed in another such world.

I have spent the subsequent decades in an evolving reshaping of my faith. I have done this by writing novels; that is my personal way of giving shape to thought. The novels are about certain kinds of culture conflicts in the present. This book is about the past that led to this present.

I write this book in Jerusalem and in certain cities of Europe and America. I write it in the bloodiest century in the history of my people; probably in the history of mankind. To be a Jew in this century is to understand fully the possibility of the end of mankind, while at the same time believing with certain faith that we will survive. There is so much about Jewish history that is mysterious and bewildering; I write with no illusions that I will attain to sudden revelations. I have only the hope that somehow in the writing, a small light will be shed on a nagging question: How is it that after almost four thousand years of tense, fructifying, and often violent culture confrontation—with ancient paganism, with Greece and Rome, with Christianity and Islam, and, for the past two hundred years, with modern secularism—how is it that after all this, Jews still exist and are still—as I am here—attempting to understand and interpret their history?

It was Robert Gottlieb of Knopf who suggested that I consider doing a nonfiction book on the Jews. Though I had studied history with great teachers in the Jewish Theological Seminary of America and elsewhere, I hesitated to move from the world of the imagination to the hard country of fact. But the challenge became irresistible when I realized that such a work might help me construct boldly the scaffolding that supports the novels and all my years of commitment to my people. I began to read and study with discipline—and rediscovered the truth of an old axiom I had learned during my years as a doctoral student in philosophy: whatever "history" is, it is not simple. For each sentence in this book, ten more might be added to do justice to the conflicting views of hard-working scholars laboring over their own visions of the human past. But I am writing mostly in narrative form and have had to make choices and decisions which I will not (and could not) justify. Only when my story stumbles into a factual morass will I turn aside briefly to discuss the differing views of scholars.

Jewish history has been involved with the histories of many nations. Out of the rich, quite incredible complexity that is the story of the Jews, I have chosen a number of fundamental themes. These I follow through the sunlight and darkness of my people's past—to locate my own sense of self, to determine what of all that past has deepest resonance for me.

There is a vast library of material on each of the periods I am writing about, and each library is a lifetime or more of reading. I have borrowed freely from these libraries and concede all claims of priority by others for ideas expressed in this book. Among my very close friends are those whose life's work is history, all kinds of history. They have helped me give focus to my reading and to enter into the frontiers of contemporary scholarship where the areas I have been writing about are continually being probed.

I remember with warmth my many conversations with

Jonas Greenfield, Nahum Sarna, Moshe Greenberg, and Yosef Yerushalmi. I remember too the help given me by Thorkild Jacobsen, Solomon Grayzel, Hayim Tadmor, David Weiss Halivni, and Arthur Hertzberg. Specialists will recognize the extent of my debt to these scholars as well as to Samuel Noah Kramer, Henri Frankfort, A. Leo Oppenheim, William W. Hallo, Sir Alan H. Gardiner, John A. Wilson, William Kelly Simpson, Ephraim A. Speiser, W. F. Albright, John Bright, George E. Mendenhall, Delbert R. Hillers, Roland de Vaux, Kathleen M. Kenyon, Avram Malamat, H. L. Ginsberg, Moshe Weinfeld, Raphael Sealey, M. Cary, N. G. L. Hammond, Moses Hadas, E. R. Dodds, Robert Flacelière, Menahem Stern, Jonathan A. Goldstein, Elias Bickerman, Martin Hengel, Victor Tcherikover, Abraham Schalit, Shmuel Safrai, Michael Avi-Yonah, Saul Lieberman, Judah Goldin, Jacob Neusner, Philip K. Hitti, Eliyahu Ashtor, Yitzhak Baer, Gerson D. Cohen, Bernard Lewis, Shalom Spiegel, David Flusser, Roland H. Bainton, Paul Winter, Yehezkel Kaufmann, Bernhard Blumenkranz, Cecil Roth, Isadore Twersky, Normal F. Cantor, Franklin H. Littell, Carolly Erickson, Irving A. Agus, Haim Hillel Ben-Sasson, Bernard D. Weinryb, Shmuel Ettinger, Jacob Katz, Gershom Scholem, Leo Strauss, Peter Gay, Alexander Altmann, Lucy S. Dawidowicz—and others. I leaned hard in certain places on the scholarship in the *Encyclopaedia Judaica,* the *Encyclopaedia Britannica,* and the *World History of the Jewish People*. The staff of the Hebrew University Library was of considerable assistance to me during the time I worked in Jerusalem, as was Nessa Rapoport. Many of the scholars I studied are fine writers, and it was a special pleasure to be able to work not only with their ideas but also with their words. I thank them all.

Knopf set up a special production team for this book: Martha Kaplan, Louise Fili, Ellen McNeilly, Linda Sykes, Bob Scudellari, and Deborah Zwecher. They brought this work with care and skill through the many difficulties that lie between completed manuscript and finished book. They have my deepest gratitude.

# BOOK ONE

*Through Ancient Paganism*

# SUMER

## The Wandering Mesopotamians

When I turn to the Bible, I discover that my ancestor's name was Abraham. He appears to have come from the city of Ur in southern Mesopotamia. He left the sedentary world of Ur—the first civilization created by man—and became a wanderer.

He wandered northward through Assyria, westward through Syria, and southward into Palestine along an uneven arc of mostly fertile land bounded by mountains to the north and east and by a desert to the south. During a famine, he followed the arc to its western end, Egypt, then returned to Palestine. That arc of verdant earth was named the Fertile Crescent by the American scholar James Henry Breasted. It is a region more easily grasped on maps and in the imagination than in reality. Flat, open, occasionally patchy with areas of uncultivated land, and unprotected by natural barriers, it was for millennia the green grail of hungry nomads and conquering armies.

North of the Persian Gulf, into a delta of reedy marshland, flow the Tigris and Euphrates rivers. It is an almost rainless region of scorching summers, whirling dust clouds, sudden torrential winter storms. At times the waters of the gulf wash across the mud flats and salinize the soil to death; the sweet waters of the rivers, running shallow along meandering beds, often flood and leave behind lakes and swamps and devastation. The land has little stone or timber.

But the rivers and the rich silt they bring down from the mountains and deposit on the alluvial plain that is southern Mesopotamia presented the people who lived there about six thousand years ago with two of the necessary conditions of early civilization: water and arable land.

We do not know who those people were; they left no writing. Archaeologists evaluate carefully the artifacts yielded up by the earth of Mesopotamia from Iran to Syria—various styles of painted pottery, tools and weapons of stone and copper, musical instruments made of bone, and sickles, bricks, figurines—and call them the Ubaid people, after the mound, or tell, known as al-Ubaid, a location four miles from the ancient city of Ur. These people established villages and towns throughout southern Mesopotamia from about 4300 to 3500 B.C.E. (Before the Common Era; used by many non-Christians in place of B.C., Before Christ). All the great cities of ancient Sumer rose from those villages. In an Ubaid village the most prominent and best-constructed building was the temple.

Archaeologists discern two additional layers of culture in that region from other styles of pottery, artifacts, and seals. These styles are called the Warka and Jemdet Nasr types; the time span is from about 3500 to 2900 B.C.E.

The people who lived there during the Warka period, from about 3500 to 3100 B.C.E., may have been the Subarians, who moved intrusively downward from northern Mesopotamia for some still unknown reason. They were the region's first farmers, fishermen, cattle breeders, carpenters, potters, smiths, weavers, masons. Some scholars make this claim because the people who followed them—the creators of the first civilization—appear to have used words from a language other than their own for those crafts, as well as for the names of their cities. In a similar way, Americans use words and names like ranch and Dakota today, and Englishmen use London and Manchester—all derived from prior inhabitants who did not speak English.

Jemdet Nasr is the name archaeologists give to the stratum that contains the first indications of a new cultural presence in southern Mesopotamia; it is the name of a mound that covers the ruins of a town between Baghdad asd Babylon whose ancient name we still do not know. The cylinder seal makes its first appearance at Jemdet

Nasr. Tools mark clearly the invention of bronze. The Stone Age has come to an end.

The newcomers, many scholars believe, arrived in southern Mesopotamia sometime around the year 3400 B.C.E. They gradually subdued the native population, then fused with it ethnically and culturally. In their language the word Subarian came to mean slave. But there are other scholars who contend that there never were any newcomers in southern Mesopotamia, that the creators of the world's first civilization were simply there all along, that the strange names of their crafts and cities may come from early dialects of their own language.

It was through language that these cultural newcomers were rediscovered about a century ago after having disappeared from the memory of man for more than two thousand years. Scholars working on the translation of newly found Babylonian and Assyrian documents—in the wake of decades of efforts and ingenuity that resulted in the decipherment of the cuneiform, or wedge-shaped, script of the ancient world—were puzzled by strange words in the texts. The language of Babylonia and Assyria had been Semitic; the puzzling words seemed to be non-Semitic.

Then, in 1855, someone discovered a tablet in southern Mesopotamia that was inscribed in an unknown language. Scholars assumed it was the oldest language in the world. No one was optimistic about the prospects of its decipherment; it had no affinities with any language known to man.

Highly trained specialists are able to read that language today—though not without disagreement among themselves concerning the meaning of many of its terms—because of the help they received from an ancient Assyrian king who, sated with conquest, decided to assemble a library into which would be systematically deposited the written treasures of his world. Archaeologists, digging in the Mesopotamian mound that was all that remained of the magnificent Assyrian capital of Nineveh, discovered the library of King Ashurbanipal, who ruled about 650 B.C.E., and its twenty-five thousand clay tablets. Some of those tablets were lexicons and phrasebooks intended to aid Semitic-speaking students of that unknown language.

But still no one knew what people had spoken the language.

Among the texts dug up out of the earth of Mesopotamia was an inscription to a king who had called himself "king of Sumer and Akkad." One scholar gave the name Akkadians to those mysterious early inhabitants of Mesopotamia. Another called them Sumerians. Still others denied the existence of non-Semitic people before the Babylonians and Assyrians and took the strange language to be the secret writing of Semitic priests.

The controversy was resolved by archaeologists digging in southern Mesopotamia around the turn of the century who discovered Sumerian texts which antedated the very earliest Babylonian records. And the 1928-1931 dig at Warka turned up the vague beginnings of writing: pictographs, the easily recognizable drawing of objects. By that time, scholars already had a fairly good picture of the people who had shaped man's first civilization.

It was a far different picture from the one given by Berossus, the third-century B.C.E. Babylonian priest and historian, who tells of a legendary race of monsters, half man and half fish, that had suddenly emerged from the waters of the Persian Gulf, possessing knowledge of agriculture, metalworking, and writing. They were not monsters but men, an ingenious stock with dazzling technological ability—and to this day we have no clear idea where they came from or what were the origins of the language they spoke.

The Subarians, some scholars tell us, are the people who ought to receive the credit for inventing pictographs. But everyone agrees that it was the Sumerians who turned those pictographs into cuneiform writing. And it is with writing that the obscurity of the past recedes and history, written history, the living record of the cultures of man, truly begins—about one thousand years before Abraham.

We have tens of thousands of their clay tablets, and no one knows how many more thousands are still buried in the soil of southern Mesopotamia. We have much of their statuary, jewelry, tools, weapons; we can reconstruct their shrines, temples, and private dwellings; we know a good deal about their cities, their technology, their gods, kings, laws, wars, and literature. But we cannot be certain that we are correctly interpreting their world; we are seeing it through the eyes of western civilization and across the obscuring haze of millennia. Only interludes of the fifteen-hundred-year civilization of Sumer are lighted by archaeology and tablets. Large patches of ancient darkness still remain. Most scholars soundly urge caution and restraint.

What we see first when we gaze upon ancient Sumer in the year 3000 B.C.E. is a land around the size of Massachusetts or Belgium containing about a dozen cities, many of which are in plain view of one another. Dikes, ditches, and canals have been built to tame the waters of the two rivers and restrain the wash of salt tide that comes from the Persian Gulf—a massive, highly coordinated communal drainage and irrigation effort that has concentrated authority and power in the hands of a few people in a few places. Over the centuries a number of prosperous villages have expanded into large towns; wealthy Sumerian landowners have chosen, perhaps for reasons of protection and prestige, to build their homes near the temples of their gods. The temples, almost always in the past fairly simple structures consisting of a square room with an altar and a niche for the statue of the god—the temples are now huge, well-designed, ornamented mud-brick edifices whose construction has probably been considerably enhanced by the new bronze tools of the Sumerians. At the same time, bronze weapons have made necessary the second feature that distinguishes the early city from the primitive villages that dot the land: fortifications.

Most of the cities are comprised of three main sections. A wall surrounds the city proper, the inner city, which contains at least one and possibly two temples, the palace of the king in which royal officials also reside, and the homes of the citizens. Streets are narrow, winding, unpaved. Large and small houses crowd together. Lanes sheltered by awnings and lined with open booths appear to establish the Sumerian city as the birthplace of the oriental bazaar.

The city is divided into quarters; the administrative area of each quarter is somewhere near the gate set in its section of the wall. There the scribes sit near vessels of clean clayey mud, ready to scoop up a handful of clay, mold a tablet, and, with a stylus cut from a reed, draw up a contract for a business transaction which will be signed by the rolling impress of the hollow, decorated cylinder seal Sumerians carry on a string about the neck. There too judges do their work, citizens assemble—but not too near the judges: "They'll pull you in as a witness, and you'll get involved!" someone warns on an inscription—and the mayor tends to the affairs of the quarter or the entire city during his one-year term of office.

Beyond the wall are the farms, fields, gardens, and cattle folds of the outer city. These supply the city with its raw materials and food. Finally, there is the harbor along the river which serves as the commercial center of the city, its link with the world of Sumer and beyond.

These Sumerian cities are really city-states, for each incorporates within a defended sphere of influence its surrounding lands and villages. Their economic base is agriculture; their social unit is the family. Their population is unknown; estimates range from thirty-five thousand for one city to about two hundred thousand for others. Their size is unknown too. They are the unique, creative, still not fully explicable Sumerian response to the nightmare of wild rivers and uncertain climate that is the world of southern Mesopotamia.

The cities of Sumer are the precise opposite of the diffused, nonsedentary tribal life of the desert or mountain nomad. Tribal and kinship loyalties have been replaced by loyalty to a king who heads the military machine that ensures the continued existence of the city.

Civilization—a term derived from the Latin *civitas*, city—begins with the cities of Sumer: Eridu, Ur, Erek, Lagash, Nippur, Kish, and others. All the subsequent civilizations of the ancient Near East, including that of the Israelites, will be affected by the extraordinary creativity of the city-dwelling Sumerians.

They did not call themselves Sumerians. The word Sumerian is roughly the English pronunciation of what their Semitic neighbors to their immediate north, the Akkadians, called them. No one knows what the word Sumerian means or why the Akkadians used it. The Sumerians called their land Kengir and their language Emegir. The meanings of those words too remain uncertain; the latter has been translated as " the princely tongue." Some scholars conjecture that Kengir may have been pronounced Shumer in Akkadian or in a dialect of Sumerian. But we do understand the term which the Sumerians used when they referred to themselves: Sag-giga, the black-headed ones.

I try to see them amid the artifacts of their civilization. The men are short, thickly built, some of them cleanshaven, others long-bearded, their long dark hair parted in the middle. They wear a kiltlike garment and, on occasion, a lengthy cloak. In later centuries the kilt will become unfashionable and be replaced by a long skirt; a shawl will be carried across the left shoulder and wound about the waist, leaving the right shoulder bare. The hair of the women too is parted in the middle; they braid it into a pigtail and wind it around the head. Their garments are long shawls which cover them from head to foot. The right shoulder remains bare.

Almost everyone I have read on the Sumerians writes with awe about their technological wizardry. Of major importance is their ability to smelt copper and alloy it with small quantities of tin or arsenic in order to make bronze, a metal much harder than copper and capable of being cast from molds. They have invented glass; they have the potter's wheel and ovens for firing pottery; they are using sailboats, animal-drawn plows, wheeled vehicles; they can distill barley beer, which they consume in quantities that will earn them a special sort of reputation in the ancient world. (*Maz* is the expression they use to describe the pleasant, heady fullness that accompanies the drinking of much barley beer.) Their merchants travel along dusty caravan routes throughout Mesopotamia to Syria and the Levant; they probably reach Egypt as well. They acquire precious stones, gold, silver, copper, lead, timber, and spices; they sell grain, dates, onions, and manufactured goods—clothing, carpets, tools, weapons, jewelry.

The Sumerians have also invented writing. All transactions are meticulously recorded on wet clay by the pervasive scribes. The clay dries and hardens in the sun, is kiln-fired to the consistency of stone, and is then stored in an archive which serves as a kind of bureau of records. The scribes are highly trained individuals, persons of authority. Their bookkeeping is a major source of our knowledge of the ancient Near East. There is neither magic nor mystery about early Sumerian writing. A method was necessary by which records of inventory and transactions could be kept with precision and security and not left to the vagaries of human memory. Writing was developed gradually in response to the practical economic needs of record-keeping, as was the computer in our own time. Once developed, however, it served other purposes as well: the codification of laws; the canonization of sacred texts; the preservation of the names and deeds of kings in annals; the setting down of ancient scholarship—mathematics, astronomy, astrology, medicine, divination; the creation of literature.

Near the Persian Gulf, the Tigris and Euphrates unite to form a single river. Where the river empties into the gulf, sweet and salt water mingle indeterminately along a shore of mud and shallow pools. Often in the mornings a mist hangs over the shoreline and banks of clouds cover the horizon. Earth, air, sea, and sky are a vague, watery, opalescent blur.

In the season of summer the sun burns endlessly, the earth shrivels and cracks, vegetation withers and dies. In the season of winter, heavy storms send the rivers rushing across the plain, and the gulf beats against the containing earth. The soil yields nothing.

The Sumerians felt the different parts of their world filled with awesome, life-giving, death-wielding power. Anu, Enlil, Enki, Ninhursag—sky, air, water, earth. These are the chief gods of the Sumerians. There are three additional gods: Nanna, also known as Sin, the moon god; the son of Nanna is Utu, the sun god; the daughter of Nanna is Inanna, a fertility goddess whom the Semites will call Ishtar. Many Israelites will worship her under the name of Ashtoret.

There are other great gods, fifty of them, who seem to

be children of the sky god Anu. Another, less significant group of gods is called Igigi.

These invisible beings guide and control every corner of the cosmos: from sky to abyss; moon, sun, planets; dust storm, lightning, rain; valley, plain, mountain, river; and the creative cultural endeavors of man—farms, dikes, plows, villages, cities.

Scholars conjecture that these deities were originally nature gods and that the Sumerians took them to be identical with the natural phenomena they represented. They were the inner force, the vital, driving element that brought the awesome displays of nature into being. There is a goddess of beer and one of reeds. Nanna in Sumerian is both the visible moon and the name of the moon god; Utu in Sumerian is both the visible sun and the invisible power within it, the sun god. At some point early in their history, the Sumerians performed the mental jump that separated their gods from the phenomena of nature and gave them human form.

It is in their invisible human frames that we first meet the gods of ancient Mesopotamia in the myths, hymns, epic tales and poignant prayers and lamentations that have come down to us from the world of Sumer. They are immortal—else the part of the cosmos run by a god would die with the death of the god. Their abode is a distant mountain where heaven and earth meet. They travel on foot, in a boat, in a chariot, or on clouds through those parts of the cosmos that are under their care. Invisibly, the gods eat, drink, make love, quarrel, sleep, feel jealousy, hatred, rage, are wounded and killed but somehow return to life, become ill to the point of death but always recover. They seem human in all matters save in that which humans dread most: the final darkness that is death can never claim them.

The Sumerians yearn to stave off that darkness. Their great folk hero, Gilgamesh, warleader and lord of Uruk around 2600 B.C.E., goes off in search of immortality. The sole immortality he will find will be in the epic tales about him that are now part of the heritage of Mesopotamian civilization. They love life—the world after death to which the naked spirit descends is bleak and dark. They take pride in material possessions. A rich harvest, bulging granaries, good hunting and fishing, jammed cattle folds—these are to be highly prized. They have a passion for the law which will affect the thinking of all Mesopotamians for the next three thousand years: property lines have to be meticulously marked and recorded, water rights must be distributed equitably, disputes have to be resolved; without law society reverts to chaos. They try to practice mercy and compassion yet are more often than not motivated by an aggressive drive for prestige and success and show little consideration for the restraints of ethical behavior. The Sumerian lives in a world of constant fear. Above all, he fears the gods. He lives in awe of them; at times, he loves them, feels they have brought him good fortune; he worships them, brings them gifts, pours out his heart in prayer to them. But he knows himself helpless before them and confronts them in utter dread. For he knows he was created to be their serf; they are master, he is slave. He was made of clay; his task is to supply the gods with food, drink—beer, much barley beer—and shelter, else they will grow faint and be unable to continue with their divine activities, their running of the cosmos. The Sumerian accepts his status, has no notion of free will. All is ordained by the gods.

Most often the gods are kindly and prefer that a man be true rather than false, just rather than oppressive. But they are also unpredictable; the motives behind their actions remain unknown. Also, they function as an assembly, a council; no one god can go off on his own to perform an unusual deed, good or bad, without the approval of the other gods. Hence even the gods themselves do not know beforehand the destiny they will decree for a man. This democracy in heaven leads to considerable uncertainty on earth.

It is always best to be wary and do nothing that might anger the gods. Be meticulous in the performance of the cult. Bring the prescribed daily offerings of animal and vegetable foods, of wine, water, and beer; participate in the many annual festivals and the monthly lunar feasts, each with its special rites; utter the prescribed prayers;

tend carefully to the temple, for it is the very center of the cult and must not fall into disrepair; obey the gods.

There were so many gods, hundreds of gods.

Each city belonged to a god. The temple, with its huge stage and soaring, stepped tower, was regarded by the Sumerians less as a place for religious services than as the abode of the god whenever the god chose to leave the distant mountains and dwell in his—or her—city for a time, and as a real and symbolic link between the city and heaven. These temples—ziggurats, we call them, from the Akkadian word that means to build high—became as integral to Mesopotamian religious architecture as the cathedral was to medieval Europe. They were prayers in limestone and colorfully ornamented mud brick, a soaring reach by fearful people for their eternal gods.

The gods communicated with you through dreams, oracles, omens. What else could a dream be but a message from a god? How to read it correctly—for that there were special priests, and scribes. We saw the world then not through impersonal cause and effect, but through the pulsing symptoms in things all around us: the curling of smoke, the shape of entrails of animals, the flight of arrows, the casting of dice or lots, the spreading stain of oil on the surface of water. Illness was caused by demons. You prayed to your personal god. If he heard your lament and if your wailing soothed his heart, he would accept your plea and the sickness demon would leave you.

Care of the city's god and temple was the major responsibility of the king. Once in prehistoric times—some scholars strongly believe this—the villages and cities of Sumer ruled themselves through a form of primitive democracy: a council of free men and elders would convene and debate and arrive at all decisions. Then wars over land and water rights broke out between the growing cities. Barbarians came down from the hills, hungry for urban wealth. Debate became a luxury that might lead to death. A city would choose a man from its midst to be the *lugal*, big man, king. He would gather up the strength of the city, lead its army into battle, protect the city's outlying boundaries, organize the digging of its canals.

The office was temporary at first, or was to last as long

as the emergency. Some Sumerian emergencies went on
for generations; and so kingship became permanent. That
is the form it is in soon after history begins.

Each city has its king who acts as the shepherd of his
people—". . . your shepherding has been good for our
hearts" are the words of a grateful hymn; he is the intermediary between heaven and the city; he is the steward of
the god in the running of the city; he guards the unalter-
able laws of the state that correspond to and express the
divine ordering of the cosmos; he is not the source of the
law but its servant and agent; he is as bound by law as is
his most menial subject and is responsible to the gods for
its enactment; he performs the public cult that ensures the
favor of the god as well as gives the god strength to function in the city's behalf. He also helps bring the land back
to life every year by participating in a sacred marriage.

Twice a year the world stands tenuously balanced between order and chaos. In the winter the supply of stored
food dwindles. The growing emptiness of the storehouse is
regarded with horror; it is the emptiness of a freshly dug
grave. For the people of Sumer the dead months of late
winter were laden with shadows of famine and death.
They felt themselves in rhythm with the cycles of nature
and saw the changes of nature as episodes in the lives of
their gods. They and nature and the gods were all intimately interconnected. All things were alive; all things
died. How to revive the dying fertility goddess Inanna;
how to make certain that the spring rains would come and
the rivers would rise and the desert fringes and marshland
would turn green so the sheep could graze and the land
would once again be fertile and receive its seed—this was
the awesome responsibility borne by the king.

Early in the history of Sumer the city of Uruk was
ruled by a king who bore the name Dumuzi. In some
mysterious manner, he became after his death the protec-
tor of herds, the shepherd god Dumuzi, who was also a
god of fertility and vegetation. There are many myths
about Inanna and Dumuzi in the literature of Sumer, their
love and hate for each other, their strange journeys in the
netherworld. With the descent of Inanna to the world of

the dead, winter came to the land. The descent of Dumuzi brought the killing sun of summer.

To revive the land from its winter, the kings of Sumer, each in his own city, would represent the god Dumuzi during the spring Festival of the New Year. Each would participate in a ceremonial sacred marriage to a priestess of the temple, representing the fertility goddess, and in a way not entirely clear to us perform symbolically or actually the act of fructification. Vast festivities would follow. If the gods had decided in man's favor, the spring rains would come, the rivers would inundate the land, there would be the first harvest, the first shearing, the killing of newly fattened cattle for meat.

But the time of spring is brief in Sumer. Soon the summer would advance across the land. Day after day the sun would bake and burn the soil. The land languishes. The watery lacework of delta tributaries dries and disappears. Often the air is brown with dust storms. Everything once green and alive takes on the pallor of death.

In Sumer this was the time of the dying of Dumuzi, the shepherd god. He had descended to the netherworld. Upon his return all life depended. The Sumerians gazed at the burning sky and waited. There were prayers and hymns, public rites to the gods. Women wept over the fate of the dying god. All Sumer felt his dying as its own. In prayer and rite Sumerians joined him in his struggle for revival. There was never any certainty as to the outcome; even the gods would not know until they had assembled and decreed together the destiny of Sumer for the coming year. Life or death? Food or famine? In some cities another sacred marriage would take place.

Sometime in the late summer or early fall the heat breaks suddenly, quite suddenly, in southern Mesopotamia. A cool moist breeze blows down from the far-off mountains. The dry smell of dead earth vanishes from the air.

Festive days would follow the period of mourning and the sacred marriage, to celebrate the anticipated revival of Dumuzi. But it was a temporary joy. The cycle of dying and revival would be repeated year after year. Salvation was transitory in ancient Sumer.

For more than two thousand years, sedentary and nomadic peoples, many of them Semites, would conquer and reconquer Mesopotamia—and be conquered in turn by the culture of Sumer, her myths, tales, hymns, her cuneiform script. Long after Sumer was dead, her heroes and gods continued to wander through the consciousness of Mesopotamian civilization: Enki ate forbidden fruit in a paradise called Dilmun; Ziusudra was saved from the Flood and granted eternal life; the shepherd Etana flew to heaven on the wings of an eagle to receive the precious gift of kingship and bring it down to earth; Gilgamesh sought immortality through fame; Dumuzi languished in the world of the dead. The Semites of Mesopotamia knew Dumuzi under the name of Tammuz. Israelite women lamented his dying. "Then He brought me to the door of the gate of the Lord's house which was toward the north," wrote the prophet Ezekiel more than a thousand years after the decline of Sumer, "and, behold, there sat the women weeping for Tammuz."

The tablets, cylinder seals, and inscriptions given up to our age after two thousand years of concealment by the earth of southern Mesopotamia offer no indication that the Sumerians believed existence might have underlying direction, a distant fulfillment. That kind of unfolding historical process lay beyond the horizon of their thinking. They lived in rhythm with, and entirely in helpless acceptance of, the repeated cycles of change which they witnessed in their sky, air, water, and earth.

Their scribes wrote lists. They made lists of everything around them: birds, animals, fishes, mountains, plants, stars, gods. Lists were to them what encyclopedias are to us.

They kept records of temple construction. They then began to record the military activities of their kings. There is a record of a five-generation war between the city-states of Lagash and Umma over a few acres of arable land. A king wrote a hymn glorifying the prosperity and security that prevailed during his reign. Another king wrote of his social reforms. Scribes wrote not only on clay tablets but also on bricks, vases, clay nails and cones, bowls, statues, figurines, steles. They began to look upon writing as a possible doorway to immortality.

Sometime around 2000 B.C.E. a Sumerian scribe composed a list of his country's kings. To this list someone later added a preamble dealing with a very early mythical age of Sumerian kingship. This Sumerian King List, part legend and part practical chronology, gives us a glimpse into the confused and bloody political history of Sumer:

> *When kingship was lowered from heavy, kingship was first in Eridu. In Eridu, Alulim became king and ruled 28,800 years. Alalgar ruled 36,000 years. Two kings thus ruled it for 64,800 years.*
>
> *I drop the topic Eridu because its kingship was brought to Bad-tibira. . . . En-mengal-Anna ruled 28,-800 years; the god Dumuzi, a shepherd, ruled 36,-000 years. . . .*
>
> *I drop the topic Bad-tibira because its kingship was brought to Larak. . . . One king thus ruled it for 28,-800 years. . . .*
>
> *I drop the topic Larak because its kingship was brought to Sippar. . . . I drop the topic Sippar because its kingship was brought to Shuruppak. . . .*
>
> *These are five cities, eight kings ruled them for 241,-000 years. Then the Flood swept over the earth.*

There is considerable archaeological evidence not for one general flood but for vast local inundations in prehistoric times that could easily have remained in the memory of our species and been gathered together into this one great devastating Flood.

Only one Sumerian tablet has been found thus far dealing with this ancient Deluge, and it is badly damaged. It tells us that the great gods Anu, Enlil, Enki, and Ninhursag fashioned the black-headed people, vegetation, animals. They lowered kingship from heaven. One of the great gods established five pure cities as cult centers and gave each one to a god. Then the gods talk of the Flood. The tablet is damaged at this point and we are not given

the reason for the Flood. We are told that some of the
gods wept over the coming devastation, and one of the
gods took it upon himself to warn a pious king of the Deluge. The king built a boat. He sailed it seven days and
seven nights as the tumultuous waters swept over the cult
centers and the land. Then the storm ceased and the sun
shone and the pious king opened a window of the boat
and Utu, the sun god, shone his rays into the boat. The
king, Ziusudra, whose name means life of long days, pros-
trated himself before Utu, offered sacrifices to the gods.
He was granted eternal life. The remainder of the tablet is
destroyed.

> *After the Flood has swept over the earth and when
> kingship was lowered again from heaven, kingship was
> first in Kish. . . .*

So runs the King List. A period of calm seems to have
followed, with Sumer enjoying unity under the dominance
of the city-state of Kish. The year is 2900 B.C.E. For the
next two centuries Sumer will experience what historians
call her Golden Age of primitive democracy. Kingship
during this period meant rule by temporary leaders,
councils of free men, and elders.

Kish, at the northern end of Sumer, was heavily populated by sedentary Akkadians—the name given by the
Bible, modern scholars, and the Akkadians themselves to
Semitic tribes that had come from the fringes of the Arabian desert into south central Mesopotamia about the
same time the Sumerians had made their appearance in
the extreme south. Many of the names of the leaders of
Kish are Akkadian.

Then populations began to grow, cities expanded, conflicts broke out over the terrain between city-states, there
was an increase in militarization, wars, efforts at conquest.
"Kish was smitten with weapons," the Sumerian King List
informs us, "its kingship was removed to Uruk." Now we
leave the Golden Age of Sumer and enter the period historians call the Heroic Age; the years are 2700-2500
B.C.E.

Cities became large; temples accumulated wealth and

power; in many cities the high priesthood was more important than kingship; the lightning raid by small bands of warriors tied to a chosen leader, the glory of single combat, the swift siege—all of these gave birth to heroes and legends; Gilgamesh is of this time. Then Elamite invaders came from the east and conquered the country. The Heroic Age came to an end. The Elamites were soon expelled by the king of the city of Adab. After his death, the city-states promptly returned to fighting among themselves. The wars continued. Kingship became a fixed institution. We are now in the Dynastic Age of Sumer; the dates are 2500-2300 B.C.E. Cities rose and fell as centers of power. Then the Dynastic Age came to an abrupt end. All of Sumer was conquered by an Akkadian named Sargon, meaning true king, and the first empire in history was born—in about 2300 B.C.E.

"In Agade, Sargon, whose father was a gardener," the King List says crisply, "the cupbearer of Ur-Zababa, the king of Agade who built Agade, reigned 56 years as king. . . ."

It is difficult to separate fact from legend in dealing with Sargon, so awed were later ages by his momentous achievement. He was probably of humble birth. One account of his life, written in the seventh century B.C.E., informs us that he did not know his father. Soon after he was born, his mother set him adrift in a reed boat on the Euphrates. Found and raised by a water-drawer, he somehow wins the love of the goddess Ishtar, the Semitic equivalent of the Sumerian Inanna, though for the Semites Ishtar was also goddess of war. He is appointed cupbearer—a coveted position—to King Ur-Zababa of Kish. Soon after the death of Ur-Zababa, he becomes king of Kish, builds a new city called Akkad, or Agade, somewhere on the Euphrates, and sets out on the course of empire, aided considerably by an Akkadian invention, the powerful long-range composite bow, as revolutionary in its day as gunpowder is to be almost four thousand years in the future.

His successes are stunning. He conquers a huge ring of territory around Sumer and Akkad. He takes the cities of

Sumer only in the last five years of his life and only after they move against him first.

A cultural explosion occurred as the centers of Akkadian and Sumerian cultures fused. Sargon left behind a vision for all future kings of Mesopotamia: a united land ruled by dynastic succession, by a single royal family whose rule had divine legitimation.

The dynasty of Sargon ruled for four generations. Under his grandson, Naram-Sin, the visual arts flourished; there was the serious beginning of Akkadian literature. Much temple construction took place.

Humble at first, influenced by the traditional Sumerian notion of a king as the steward of the city god and of the laws given by the god, Naram-Sin called himself "king of Akkad." Halfway through his fifty-six-year reign, he introduced the title "king of the four quarters [of the world]." Then he had himself called "god of Akkad"—and became the first of only very few Mesopotamian kings who would let themselves be deified.

In his time the king took on greater importance than the gods. And, as if by divine retribution—one Sumerian theologian saw it that way in his poetic narrative "The Curse of Agade"—the empire of Akkad disintegrated soon after his death. Cities rose in rebellion against the Akkadian garrisons to their midst; the inadequately organized empire administrative staff fell to pieces; outside hordes beat against the borders: Elamites, Hurrians, Gutians. The city of Agade was so completely destroyed that its location remains unknown to this day.

"Who was king? What was not king?" asks the Sumerian King List. Anarchy was king. "Agade was defeated, and its kingship was carried off to Uruk."

Uruk was defeated by barbaric Gutian hordes from the mountains. The Gutians were defeated and kingship returned to Uruk. Then "Uruk was smitten with weapons and its kingship carried off to Ur." The year is 2100 B.C.E.

A brief but extraordinary Sumerian renaissance now ensued under Ur-Nammu and Shulgi, the first two kings of Ur. Gudea, the Sumerian governor of Lagash, rebuilt about fifteen temples in his city. The devotion with which he reconstructed the ruined temple of the city god Ningirsu is profoundly moving. We read of it in his many inscriptions—which today are often the student Sumerologist's first serious reading in the language of Sumer.

Ur-Nammu, King of Ur, instituted a vast building program all through Sumer. In Ur he erected a towering ziggurat. He reconstructed the city's port and irrigation works. Trade increased. He won the loyalty of other major cities of Sumer and at his coronation, during the fourth year of his reign, was given the title "king of Sumer and Akkad." He promulgated the first law code in history, collecting legal precedents that could serve as a guide to future generations. The very form of the code— phrases like "if a man" or "if the wife of a man"—set a precedent for all subsequent law in the ancient Near East, including that of the Israelites.

Ur-Nammu, it appears, was killed on a battlefield. Shulgi became king of Ur in 2093 B.C.E. and ruled for almost fifty years. The armies of Ur extended the boundaries of Sumer to those of the once-great empire of Akkad. The economy of Mesopotamia flourished. Ur was rich with trade and industry. Sumer and Akkad were divided by Shulgi into provinces, each responsible for one month's care of the ritual requirements of the temples in the sacred city of Nippur. He founded the scribal schools of Nippur and Ur, great institutions that would influence generations of Mesopotamian culture. At his death, his son Amar-Sin took the throne. Eighteen years later, Ibbi-Sin became king of Ur.

Beyond the urban centers of Mesopotamia lay the northern fringe of the Syrian desert, a vast stretch of semiarid highland. It had been inhabited for centuries by a seminomadic people whom the cuneiform sources refer to as the Amurru, probably after their leading tribe, or some specific location. The word Amurru came to mean westerners, the people to the west of Sumer and Akkad, tent dwellers of the mountains who did not know grain or cooked meat, uncouth, warlike. In the Bible they are called Amorites.

They began a slow infiltration of Mesopotamia sometime around the establishment of the empire of Sargon.

"Subartu rose with its multitudes," writes the author of the Sargon Chronicle. "Sargon made sedentary this nomadic society." The highland Amorites were not made sedentary. They skirmished repeatedly with the armies of Sargon. Urbanized, sedentary Amorites lived in many cities of Sumer in the period of the empire of Ur, the era of the Third Dynasty. At the same time, the warrior sheiks of the seminomadic Amorites continued their plundering raids against the rich cities and pasturelands of urban Mesopotamia.

Soon after the death of Shulgi the empire of Ur began a slow collapse under the pressure of Elamites and Subarians in the east and north, and Amorites in the west. In the twenty-fourth year of the reign of Ibbi-Sin, Ur was sacked, its magnificent temple looted and destroyed.

No greater tragedy could befall a Sumerian city than to have its temple destroyed. Every brick and bit of stone, the fill in the foundation pits, the sacred pegs that moored it to the watery realm of the god Enki, its altar and statuary—all of the temple was alive and numinous with the presence of the city god. To have it destroyed was a horrifying calamity. The god could no longer reside in the city.

Ibbi-Sin was taken into exile by the Elamites. "Ur was defeated and its kingship was carried off to Isin," the Sumerian King List tells us, and after some additional lines comes to an end.

"O city, a bitter lament set up as thy lament," are the melancholy words of the Lamentation over the Destruction of Ur, written decades after the city's fall. "His righteous city which had been destroyed—bitter is its lament; His Ur which has been destroyed—bitter is its lament. . . . O Nanna, Ur has been destroyed, its people have been dispersed."

A century of peace followed. Ur was rebuilt and remained wealthy but unimportant. Amorite incursions continued, and a bitter century of Amorite petty states at war with one another. In southern Mesopotamia Sumer and Akkad were finally conquered by the Amorite king of Babylon. His name was Hammurabi, and his empire lasted from about 1800 to 1600 B.C.E.

Sumer died and its kingship was carried off to the Amorites.

Abraham was probably an Amorite.

The Bible has set the patriarchal narratives in a zone of timelessness—so it would appear. Links between the lives in the Book of Genesis and the teeming world of Mesopotamia are, it seems, gossamer. There is no fixed chronology for the patriarchs. This does not mean that the patriarchs did not exist; few serious scholars will make that claim today. It means only that there is a span of about six hundred years into which they can be placed—from around 2000 to 1400 B.C.E.—and we do not know precisely where in those six hundred years to locate them.

Recent scholarship has recovered some wispy fragments from the lives, movements, and settlement patterns of people in the ancient world that seem to place Abraham between the years 2000 and 1900 B.C.E. I will follow that tenuous chronology here, with full awareness of its fragility and uncertainty and with the knowledge that some contemporary scholars are questioning its conclusions. My intention is to retell some of the narrative of the patriarchs within the ambiance of their own world, against the background that was entirely lost to us until its recovery in recent decades—a loss which often led to much confusion on the part of centuries of commentators as they struggled to understand seemingly bizarre and bewildering events in the lives of the Biblical human beings whom they deeply cherished.

Abraham was probably born in the Sumerian city of Ur in an early decade of the twentieth century B.C.E., four thousand years ago. His distant ancestor was Shem son of Noah. About two hundred years ago a scholar invented a label for the descendants of Shem; he called them Semites.

We do not know what language Abraham wrote or spoke. During the years he lived in Mesopotamia he probably spoke a Semitic tongue—Amorite or a dialect of Akkadian. If he knew how to write, then he wrote Akkadian, as did all literate Semites in Mesopotamia during and after the decline of Sumer, using a cuneiform script based on that invented by the Sumerians.

Abraham had two brothers. One died, leaving behind a son named Lot. Abraham married. His wife was barren. Sometime during the waning decades of that twentieth century, Terah father of Abraham gathered his family together and left Ur.

They traveled northward out of Sumer and Akkad along the crescent of green earth on their way to a distant land. But they halted in the central Mesopotamian city of Haran.

We are not told why they broke their journey and settled in Haran. It is known that both Ur and Haran were major pilgrimage centers of the moon cult. They may have left Ur after the destruction of its temple. Centuries later, addressing the tribes of Israel at Schechem after their successful penetration into Canaan, Joshua is reported to have said, "In olden times, your forefathers—Terah father of Abraham and father of Nahor—lived beyond the Euphrates and worshiped other gods."

The Akkadian word for Haran, *harranu*, means a caravan, a road, a journey. Haran was the Chicago of Mesopotamia. In those days if you wanted to travel from Assyria or from any point along the Tigris River to one of the trading cities on the Mediterranean coast, you had to pass through Haran; if you were part of a caravan that had originated from anywhere along the lower Euphrates, with Anatolia as its destination, you also went through Haran.

You traveled by donkey, for the camel had not yet been domesticated; only in the twelfth century B.C.E. did the camel become widely and regularly used as a beast of travel and burden. The camels in the patriarchal narratives are a scribal indiscretion, an anachronism, like the striking clock in Shakespeare's *Julius Caesar*.

We are told nothing about Abraham's life in Haran; we do not know what he did there. Some scholars have made him out to be a donkey caravaneer. The trade routes were crowded, especially those leading to Anatolia. He might have been one of the "dusty ones," as those caravaneers were supposedly called. Other scholars scoff at that notion and see him in a more pastoral setting, as a sheik, living off his herds in seminomadic fashion.

The area around Haran was tranquil. The city and its surroundings were inhabited by Amorites and by a people called the Hurrians, who had migrated from Armenia. There were many Hurrians in Haran during the decades Abraham lived there. In south central Mesopotamia, the city of Mari was also host to Hurrians.

On the outskirts of Mari lived a seminomadic tribe which cuneiform documents call Ben-Yamini, meaning sons of the right—they probably pitched their tents to the right of the city. They were numerous and frequently troublesome; there was always friction between city dwellers and tent dwellers. Under Hammurabi, who conquered Mari, the city employed a special official to deal with them. He bore the title "secretary of Amorite affairs."

Tablets discovered in Mari before the Second World War contain west Semitic names like Abraham and Jacob. They also mention Habiru—or, more correctly, Hapiru—a widespread class of outcasts, belonging to no particular ethnic group, wandering in bands throughout the Near East. Their relation to the Hebrews—Hapiru and Hebrew look and sound alike not only in English but also in the original Semitic, and Abraham is called a Hebrew in the Bible—has been a puzzle to scholars for a long time. Are the two identical, or was the term Hebrew attached to the patriarchs because of their incessant wanderings? Is the term ethnic or descriptive? The puzzle has not yet been satisfactorily cleared up.

Also found at Mari were texts written in the Hurrian language. Excavated Hurrian tablets tell us a great deal—as we shall soon see—about life in northern Mesopotamia, the cultural homeland of the patriarchs, the region called by the Bible Padan-Aram or Aram-Naharaim. We have been reading the patriarchal narratives all through the centuries without knowing the customs and traditions of the "old country" from which the patriarchs came. That is like looking at Irish and Italian Americans with no knowledge of Ireland and Italy; like trying to understand the American Southwest with no notion of the existence of Spain; like gazing at Plymouth

and Concord and Boston without knowing that there is an
England.

Abraham left Haran in response to an abrupt call from
his God. That was the oral tradition carried down the
generations until it was put into written form by a writer
sometime during or after the period of King David. The
call was a command and a promise: Abraham was to set
out on a journey for a destination that would be made
known to him; he would father a great nation.

"Abraham set out from Haran," writes John Bright,
"with his family, his flocks, and his herds, to seek land and
seed in the place his God would show him. Or, to put it
otherwise, there took place a migration to Palestine of seminomadic peoples, among whom were to be found the
ancestors of Israel. With that, there began that chain of
events so portentous for world history and so redemptive—the believing man would say so divinely guided—
which we call the history of Israel."

Abraham was seventy-five years old. His father and
brother remained in Mesopotamia. Abraham wandered
westward, perhaps crossing the Euphrates at Carchemish,
where it can be forded during a low-water period. On the
right bank of the river were tent-dwelling Ben-Yaminites.
The trail wound through hilly terrain studded at intervals
with sanctuaries. A few kilometers south of Aleppo there
stands to this day a village named Benjamin on the route
leading to the region of hills, valleys, and coastal plain
known in the Bible as the land of Canaan.

Abraham and his family entered Canaan and journeyed
through the land until they reached the site of Shechem.
There Abraham's God appeared to him again, and the
promise spoken in veiled form in Haran was now made
clear. "I will give this land to your offspring." Abraham
built an altar to his God, a mound of rock and earth, a
sign to mark the encounter. Then he moved on with his
family to the hill country between Bethel and Ai. He
pitched his tent and built another altar to his God. From
there he began to wander slowly southward toward the
Negev, the dry, nearly rainless region of the land of
Canaan, where he remained until a famine forced him
once again to gather his family and his possessions and

move on. He journeyed to Egypt, the civilization at the western end of the Fertile Crescent. Then he returned to Canaan.

Famines were frequent in Canaan, a land whose indeterminate borders encompassed at most the area between the Taurus Mountains in the north to the Brook of Egypt (wadi el-Arish), in the northeast corner of the Sinai Peninsula, in the south, the Mediterranean in the west, and the Jordan River in the east. Unlike Sumer, that land had no extensive rivers, only the brief shallow Jordan which barely watered its own thin valley and could not reach beyond the range of hills that pressed closely upon it.

The topography of the land also differed from that of Sumer: no broad alluvial plain here but densely wooded hills, the rift of the Jordan, a long narrow coastal plain, fertile lowlands, and a central range of stony hills shading down into the lunar landscape of the Negev. There was probably more rain in the south during Abraham's time than there is today; the Dead Sea may have been smaller; the woods were thicker. The soil depended for its life upon dew, mountain springs, and rain, as it does today. When the rains failed there was famine. The land lies on the fringes of a vast desert. Rains failed all too often in Canaan.

This reliance upon rain as the sole source of vegetative life, together with the hilly nature of the terrain, resulted in the discovery by the people who lived in the land long before Abraham that terracing could prevent wasteful runoff when the rains finally came. The terraced slopes that you can still see in the land today are the Canaanite equivalent of the dikes and canals of Sumer. Another response to the helpless dependency on rain was the extreme Canaanite emphasis on fertility religion. There was far more danger of famine here than in Sumer; all the more reason to worship the nature gods found in every green grove of trees, in the wheat and corn, in the storm clouds, on every mountaintop near the rain-giving sky; all the more intense the feeling for the dying fertility god during the withering rainless summer and the need, by rites of sacrifice and sacred prostitution, to revive him, re-fructify the god and the land.

For two thousand years little was known about the world of Canaan outside of what the Bible and a few classical authors—Lucian, who was a second-century Greek writer, Philo Byblius, Plutarch, others—had told us. The ancient Israelites engaged the Canaanites not only in a bitter territorial war, which went on for two hundred years, but also in a seven-hundred-year-long culture war, which the Israelites came close to losing many times. The Bible makes no attempt to offer us an objective picture of Canaanite civilization.

Archaeologists and historians, aided by an extraordinary recent find at the ancient city of Ugarit—today's Ras Shamra—on the coast of northern Syria about fifty miles due east of Cyprus, now present us with a picture of ancient Canaan that helps fill in and clarify some of the meager and often harsh details found in the Bible and in classical authors. The city of Ugarit was, until about 1200 B.C.E., a major copper-ore importing center linking the Mediterranean, Canaanite, Egyptian, and Mesopotamian worlds. The excavators discovered temples, many artifacts from Egypt, Mesopotamia, Crete, and elsewhere, and a library containing inscriptions in a wide variety of Near Eastern languages, including a language and a cuneiform alphabet no one knew existed. Several hundred clay tablets were in that library. The alphabet was deciphered. As a result, we are now able to enter and tour—with caution, for many tablets are broken and much information remains spotty and conjectural—the ancient civilization of Canaan.

The archaeologists assure us that a uniform civilization existed from Ugarit to southern Palestine and from the Mediterranean coast to the Syrian desert. Throughout this region the same artifacts and structures were in use from about 1700 to 1200 B.C.E.—pottery, tools, weapons, temples, fortifications, objects of art. The language shows only slight variations among its various dialects. We are further assured by the archaeologists and historians that the tablets of Ugarit, in spite of their having been written about 1400 B.C.E. and directly mirroring an urban culture were the creations of scribes who used ancient material which they either copied or reworked, and that the texts they left us—myths, epics, legends—reflect to some extent the world of Canaan that Abraham, Isaac, Jacob, and the sons of Jacob may have encountered between 1900 and 1700 B.C.E.

There can be no direct link between Ugarit and the Israelite descendants of the patriarchs who invaded Canaan about 1240 B.C.E. Scholars assume that Ugarit mirrors with some accuracy the Canaanite civilization encountered by those Israelites.

In the time of Abraham, the land known as Canaan was inhabited by Amorites. About the people who preceded the Amorites we know almost nothing; they left no writing. They lived by hunting and fishing; the discovery of a skeleton of a dog in a cave tells us they domesticated animals; the discovery of sickles tells us they cultivated grain. They were Semites, for most of the place names—towns, hills, the Jordan and its tributaries—are Semitic in origin. They built villages and towns and used pottery and copper and some gold. They engaged in extensive trade with Mesopotamia, Anatolia, and Egypt. The cities of Megiddo, Lachish, Hazor, Bethel, Gaza, and others had been established centuries before Abraham wandered into the land. Jericho had been in existence for about six thousand years.

Sometime around 2100 B.C.E. the land was devastated by an incoming wave of people—probably the first of the Amorites. We know about that from the archaeologists, who are able to read the destruction levels in the trenched earth. Slowly the land was rebuilt as the Amorites became sedentary.

The Bible tells us that the God of Abraham referred to it as an Amorite land. Amid the smoke and flames of the covenant He made with Abraham after the patriarch returned from Egypt, the land was once again promised to the offspring of the aged wanderer. The Bible frequently also called it Canaan. The Egyptians too referred to it as the land of the Amorites and as Canaan.

The name Canaan was probably used at first of those inhabitants of the land who lived along the Mediterranean.

coast. It may have come from the Hurrian word *kinahhu,* which means purple. One of the land's most famous products was purple wool; the purple dye was obtained from a certain kind of shellfish that inhabited the coastal waters of the eastern Mediterranean. The people along the northeastern Mediterranean coastline were in later centuries called Phoenicians by the Greeks—from the Greek word *phoinix,* which means purple—for the same reason that the people living along the lower Mediterranean coastline were called Canaanites: Canaan and Phoenicia mean the same thing in Hurrian and Greek. We call the entire land today Canaan because that is the name most frequently used for it in the Bible. It was the coastal Amorites, and some of their colonies in the rich valley of the Jordan, who became the great merchants, rebuilt and fortified the lowland cities, invented the alphabet, fought the Israelites, and created the civilization of which only the merest remnants have been found in Ugarit. Scholars of Semitic languages use the word Canaanite today as a linguistic definition that embraces a variety of dialects: Ugaritic, Moabite, Hebrew, and others. The only living Canaanite dialect is Hebrew.

There were other ethnic groups in the land: an amalgam of peoples. The geographic diversity of the land intensified the ethnic and economic differences among its population. The lowlands were flourishing clusters of agriculture and urban life; the hill country and desert fringes were backward grazing areas. Canaanite city-states were independent petty kingdoms with monarchs, merchants, craftsmen, a professional soldiery, and peasants who worked the land as serfs. Those cities, walled and wealthy, had even less inclination to unite than had the cities of Sumer.

A recent excavation in northern Syria near present-day Aleppo has unearthed the ancient city of Ebla, which appears to have been a vast emporium with a population of about 250,000 people and an economic sphere of influence that extended from the Sinai desert to what is now southern Turkey and from Cyprus to Sumer. An archive containing about fifteen thousand tablets—economic texts, a creation epic, myths, geographic and mathematical lists—was discovered there in 1976 and is now being studied. The city flourished from about 2400 to 2250 B.C.E., became a military threat to the empire of Akkad, and was destroyed by the grandson of Sargon. "The god Nergal did open up the path for the mighty Naram-Sin, and gave him Arman and Ebla. . . ." Ugarit and Ebla are indication enough that the land through which Abraham wandered was not a backwoods culture.

The people were all tied to the yield of the soil, for even the wealthy merchant living in a large urban home dreaded the possibility of drought and famine. No city was so large that you could not see the fields and their life-sustaining produce outside the walls. As in Sumer, cities were ringed by the worked soil. A tenth-century limestone plaque found in the city of Gezer, about twenty miles northwest of Jerusalem, contains an inscription that is an account of a peasant's year.

> *Two months of harvest;*
> *Two months of planting;*
> *Two months of late planting;*
> *A month of hoeing up of flax;*
> *A month of barley harvest;*
> *A month of harvest, then festivity;*
> *Two months of vinedressing;*
> *A month of gathering of summer fruit.*

The Canaanites prayed to their gods for long life and a good harvest. They prayed to El, their aged chief god, whom they addressed as the Father of Men, the Kindly, the Merciful, the Creator of Created Things. In the tablets found at Ugarit he is called *kadosh*, holy; scholars transliterate the Ugaritic word phonetically into *adš*— Ugaritic has no vowels, hence we can never be entirely certain about its pronunciation. The Biblical word for holy is also *kadosh*. One of the Biblical terms for God is El. There is a representation of El on a stele. He wears a horned crown, had a beard, and is seated on a throne.

The Canaanites prayed especially to Baal, their young, vigorous god who was eternally locked in battle with the forces of chaos. He was called the Mightiest of Heroes, the Prince. At times he manifested himself as Hadad, god of storm, thunder, lightning. He is described as *rohev aravot (rkb · 'rpt)*, Rider-of-the-Clouds, in the tablets of Ugarit. When Baal appears in the Bible together with a city—Baal-Sidon, Baal-Hazor, and others—he is probably functioning as the god of the city whose name he bears. Baal was worshiped throughout Canaan as the god of fertility.

Athtart (or Astarte) was the goddess of love and fertility as well as of war. The ancient Semites did not easily distinguish between the passions that went into love and war.

There were hundreds of other gods. A god list found at Ebla contains five hundred names.

North of Ugarit was the dwelling place of Baal and the assembly of the gods—Mount Zaphon. It bore the same significance to the Canaanites as did Mount Olympus to the Greeks.

The Canaanites communicated with their gods through prayer, animal sacrifice, and divination. Similar sacrifices are found in the Bible. There were many priestly families, temple singers, sculptors, potters, makers of vestments, slaughterers, launderers. Divination was general throughout Canaan. Priests would read the entrails, especially the liver, of sacrificial animals. No Canaanite document has yet yielded significant mention of prophets or prophecy. (The word prophet comes from the Greek *prophetes*, which means one who speaks forth, one who proclaims a revelation, who brings a message from a god.)

In a myth found at Ugarit the god Baal descends to the underworld after slaying the serpent Lotan. We are not told the reason for his descent. The underworld is ruled by Mot, whose name means death. Then the text breaks off. When we can read it again, Baal is dead. "The prince, lord of the earth, has perished."

El mourns his death by descending from his throne, tearing his clothes, rolling in the dust. "Baal is dead," he laments. "What will become of the people?" Anat sister of Baal goes off in search of Mot and slays him. "She seizes the godly Mot," says the text. "With sword she cleaves him. . . . Birds eat his remnants. . . ." There is another gap in the text. When we can read it again, Baal is alive: ". . . the prince, lord of the earth, exists."

Mot personifies the killing summer; El and Anat are the autumn rains.

The myth was probably recited during a temple fertility rite at the end of summer before the onset of the autumn rains. Some scholars believe that the monarch may have participated in a sacred marriage. Acts of sexual intercourse took place as expressions of Canaanite man's belief that he could aid the forces of nature: his own act of sacred fructification would bring on corresponding powers in the soil and end the dying and sterile time of the land.

Myths and epics unearthed at Ugarit tell of a beginning of things out of dark wind-shaped air and a miry chaos. Baal fights Yam, the primordial sea, for dominion of the world. "The club swoops in the hand of Baal," reads the tablet. "It strikes the head of Prince Yam. . . . Yam collapses, falls to the ground. . . ."

This Canaanite picture of a deity locked in mortal combat with the sea entered the cultural world of Mesopotamia and found literary expression in the great Babylonian creation epic known as *Enuma Elish*. There the chaotic sea was personified as the goddess Tiamat. Marduk, the god of the city of Babylon, engages Tiamat in fierce single combat, slays her, and out of her vast corpse forms the cosmos.

The Hebrew word for the primordial sea is *tehom*. The opening verses in Genesis read, "When God began to create the heaven and the earth—the earth being unformed and void, with darkness over the surface of the deep *(tehom)* and a wind from God sweeping over the water. . . ." No mythology here; no gods spawning other gods or engaged in combat with serpents or seas. The cosmos has been stripped of its gods; the world has been demythologized. All the gods are gone, dead. "God said, 'Let there be light'; and there was light."

The Hebrew creation story was edited in final form probably about the seventh century B.C.E. Between then and the previous centuries during which the patriarchs had wandered across Canaan and Mesopotamia, a vast cultural transformation took place among the descendants

of Abraham and Moses. That transformation found expression through the greatest of Canaan's contributions to
civilization: certain unique literary forms, especially poetry, which the Israelites utilized as aesthetic molds into
which they poured their own moral vision of the world.
Some of these molds are contained in the burnt remnants
of clay found at Ugarit. You can see them in the Louvre
today, ancient literary treasures, most of them chipped
and broken, pale reddish and beige-colored tablets
preserved behind glass like butterflies.

Time has been telescoped; complex events have been
simplified; strong culture-rooted motivations and the assumed Mesopotamian background became blurred. Despite that, details were preserved with extraordinary
faithfulness by transmitted oral traditions which were
canonized—regarded as fixed and sacred—very early in
time and could not be tampered with when they were first
set down. The accounts, simply yet beautifully written, of
events in the lives of Abraham, Isaac, Jacob, and their
clans are almost visible in the cultural air breathed by
western man. And the basic themes of the Hebrew
Bible—covenant, liberation, redemption; the search for insight into a universe assumed to be meaningful—remain
essentially the same no matter which Biblical author we
read.

Suddenly Abraham is a warrior sheik. He leads a troop of
three hundred and eighteen retainers against a coalition of
four eastern kings who invaded the region to put down a
rebellion of five Canaanite kings. The Canaanite rebels
have been defeated, Sodom and Gomorrah sacked, and
Lot, Abraham's nephew, who had encamped near Sodom,
taken prisoner. Abraham races off after the invaders and
defeats them in a mighty battle near Damascus. Lot is
freed; the booty is recovered.

When Abraham returns, he is greeted with gratitude
by the Canaanite kings of Sodom and Salem. The king of
Salem, we are told, was also a priest of El Elyon, God
Most High, whom we now know to have been the chief
god of the Canaanites. "Blessed be Abram of God Most

High," says the king-priest of Salem. Israelite tradition recorded Abraham as responding in the name of his own God. "I swear to YHWH"—possibly pronounced Yahweh, not Jehovah, and never spoken by devout Jews—"God Most High. . . ."

The patriarchs refer to their God by other names as well—El Shaddai (meaning unknown), El Ro'i (God of Vision), El Bethel (God of Bethel), God of the Father, the Awesome One of Isaac. They lived amid the Canaanites as cordial strangers and without religious tension. They worship their own God and see nothing objectionable in the Canaanite's devotion to his various deities. Quite the contrary, Abraham is pictured as arguing fervently with his God in an effort to save corrupt Sodom and Gomorrah from His wrath. If ten righteous men can be found there, "will He who is judge of all the world not act with justice?" A Hebrew sheik pleading with his invisible God in behalf of Canaanite pagans. . . .

Abraham continues his wandering. Now he journeys again to the Negev from the terebinths of Mamre near Hebron, and stops between Kadesh and Shur. Then he settles in the oasis of Beersheba, a few miles inland from Gerar.

Sarah remains barren into old age. She and Abraham have long abandoned hope for a child, despite the promise of their patron God.

A Hurrian marriage document found by archaeologists in the archives of the Mesopotamian city of Nuzi reads, "If Gilimninu bears children, Shennima shall not take another wife. But if Gilimninu fails to bear children, Gilimninu shall get for Shennima a woman from the Lullu country"—a slave girl—"as concubine. In that case, Gilimninu herself shall have authority over the offspring."

Sarah gives her Egyptian maidservant, Hagar, as concubine to Abraham. Hagar becomes pregnant. Sarah is consumed with jealousy. She has obeyed the family law, but this does not prevent her from acting with intolerable abuse toward her maidservant. Hagar flees. God appears to her. She is promised a son. She returns to Sarah's continuing mistreatment and in time bears a son. He is named Ishmael.

At this point in the Biblical narrative, circumcision—a prehistoric rite—is made by YHWH into the sign of the covenant with Abraham. "At the age of eight days, every male among you . . . shall be circumcised. . . ."

To the astonishment of everyone, Sarah then has a child. He is named Isaac, laughter, joy. In a fit of raging jealousy, she has Abraham cast out Hagar and Ishmael.

Though Sarah had legal authority over Ishmael—and, according to the Mesopotamian low code of Lipit-Ishtar, king of Isin around 1850 B.C.E., also had the right to set her maidservant and maidservant's son free and thereby legally remove their future inheritance claims—still her act is cruel. The Bible clearly records Abraham's reluctant compliance. To free a servant in that time meant removal from the protective circle of the clan. Often it would mean death. We are told that the boy, exposed to the wilderness, comes near death. But God appears to Hagar as she sits a distance from the child, in despair, unable to endure watching him die. God promises to make Ishmael father of a great nation. The boy is saved. Arab nations claim descent from Ishmael.

Then Isaac experiences near-death. God orders him sacrificed. Abraham obeys in a chilling act of faith that will be told through the ages and affect all the future of his descendants. We are not informed whether Sarah knows the purpose of their journey. Isaac senses it but goes anyway together with his father. He is bound to an altar on a hilltop and lies beneath the blade in his father's raised hand. As with Ishmael, God intervenes to save the boy; a ram is offered in his stead. And, as in the story of Ishmael, a covenant also follows this narrative: God blesses Abraham and promises that a great nation will emerge from his seed. Abraham and Isaac return together to Beersheba.

Sarah dies. Legend has it that the ordeal killed her.

After negotiations which reflect accurately Near Eastern business practices of the day, Abraham purchases land and a cave in Hebron. There, inside the cave, he buries Sarah.

Abraham is very old now. He sends his servant, Eliezer, to Mesopotamia to find a wife for Isaac. We are told nothing of the long journey to Aram of the Two Rivers, a Biblical name for northern Mesopotamia. By a well outside the city of Nahor, Eliezer encounters Rebekah, daughter of Nahor, the brother of Abraham who remained behind when the patriarch began his wandering. We know the story of that encounter, the thirsty wanderer and his camels given water by Rebekah, the journey back to Canaan.

Abraham dies around the time of the arrival of Rebekah. He is buried in Hebron next to Sarah.

The Bible is strangely reticent about Isaac; little is told of him. He wanders less than his father did. He tries his hand at agriculture. God appears to him and repeats the promise made to Abraham. He has twin sons: Esau, his first-born, and Jacob.

Esau sells his birthright to Jacob. There is a Nuzi record of the sale of a birthright to a younger brother for the price of three sheep. It was a fairly common practice.

Isaac, blind with old age and eager to bless his first-born, says to Esau, "I am, you see, so old that I do not know how soon I may die." A Nuzi text dealing with an inheritance begins with the words, "Now that I am grown old. . . ."

The words of Isaac have both social and legal significance; they will be binding and irrevocable. Esau has sold his birthright to Jacob, but Isaac's deathbed blessing will restore him to the status he bartered away in an impetuous moment. "As regards my son Zirteshup," reads a Nuzi tablet, "I first annulled his relationship; but now I have restored him into sonship. He is the elder son and a double share he shall receive."

But Esau becomes the victim of a cunning plot. Urged on by Rebekah, who favors Jacob over Esau, a reluctant and disguised Jacob steals his brother's blessing from a blind and confused Isaac. Esau, who was asked by his father to hunt some game and prepare a festive dish for the occasion, now returns. The scene that follows is charged with anguish and horror as all the participants begin to realize the enormity of the deceit. Esau bursts into bitter tears. "Bless me too, Father." But the words already spoken by Isaac cannot be reversed; a blessing carries with it a sanctity and a power of will that cannot be called back. "Haven't you saved a blessing for me?" Esau pleads. Isaac says nothing. Esau weeps. Isaac's blessing, when it comes, is all too brief and unsatisfactory. Esau is enraged. He will kill his brother as soon as Isaac dies. Rebekah discovers his intent and urges Jacob to flee to her brother Laban in Haran. "Let me not be bereft of both of you in a single day!" The killing of Jacob by Esau would mean the death of Esau too through blood vengeance or other punishment.

The blessing stolen from Isaac promised Jacob agricultural wealth. "May God give you of the heaven's dew and of the earth's riches; abundance of new grain and wine." Isaac's hope was that the wandering would come to an end.

Jacob flees to Mesopotamia.

Twenty years of exile follow. By a well near Haran, Jacob meets Rachel daughter of Laban. The impulsive kiss with which he greets her was regarded by Calvin as an editorial slip on the part of Moses.

Laban is at first a gracious host, a paradigm of family unity. He embraces Jacob, kisses him, takes him into his house. "You are my flesh and blood," he says.

A few weeks pass. Laban puts into motion a cunning plan. Jacob's seven years of servitude are rewarded by an unwanted marriage to Leah, Rachel's older sister. He is given Rachel in exchange for a promise to Laban for an additional seven years. There are incessant quarrels between the two sisters during six more years of growing hostility between him and Laban. That is the way Jacob is repaid, the Bible seems to imply, for the part he played in the scheme against Esau.

Laban's sons now begin to scheme against Jacob. He gathers together his family and his possessions and flees.

Rachel steals her father's household gods and hides them in her saddle cushion. By the customs of Haran, possession of the house gods could signify legal title to an estate. Rachel knows that her father will not voluntarily give Jacob the images as formal proof of property release.

Jacob and his family cross the Euphrates and head toward the hill country of Gilead. Laban catches up with

hem and plays the part of a wounded man of good will.
But he is interested mainly in those household images.
The search of Jacob's entourage is thorough and, because
of Rachel's cleverness, unrewarding. Laban concludes a
pact with Jacob: Jacob is to take no other wives besides
the daughters of Laban. "And Jacob took the oath by the
Awesome One of Isaac his father."

Laban kisses his daughters and grandchildren and sets
out on his return journey to Haran. The Laban and Jacob
clans will never encounter one another again. The patriarchal link with the Mesopotamian past is broken.

A different Jacob returns to the land of Canaan—a
man no longer a schemer, a man burdened with the
memories of twenty years of exile and servitude. His
transformation of personality is depicted in the Bible
through the still bewildering spectral account of his mysterious night battle with an unearthly figure. Jacob
emerges from that terrifying struggle with his name
changed to Israel—the precise meaning of which remains
unknown to scholars; some think it may be the name of
yet another patriarch who wandered with his clan from
Mesopotamia to Canaan.

And it is a different Esau who now greets Jacob—af-
fectionate, hugging him, kissing him, weeping with joy.
He is accompanied by four hundred retainers and is a
man of obvious wealth. Jacob offers him gifts to mollify
his expected anger. "I have enough, my brother," Esau
tells him. "Let what you have remain yours." Jacob in-
sists. In the end, Esau accepts. They part warmly.

Jacob travels to the city of Shechem. He purchases
land near Shechem from the sons of Hamor, who live in
Shechem. It is his intention to settle on that land, to put
an end to the wandering. But his only daughter, Dinah, is
raped by one of the sons of Hamor. In vengeance, her
brothers Simeon and Levi deceive and kill all the males in
the city and plunder it. Jacob is bitter with apprehension
and remorse. "You have brought trouble on me, making
me odious among the inhabitants of the land."

They leave Shechem and journey to Bethel. There God
appears to Jacob and renews the covenant. "The land that

I gave to Abraham and Isaac I give to you; and to you
offspring to come will I give the land."

They leave Bethel. On the way to Bethlehem, Rachel
dies in childbirth. Jacob erects a pillar to mark her grave.
The baby is named Benjamin.

Then, we are told, Jacob "settled in the land."

The years of his old age are to be no less anguished
than those of his youth. He has yet to endure the
darkness that will follow the horrifying news brought by
his sons of the "death" of his precious Joseph, the first-
born of Rachel.

Jacob is weary with age and sorrow when a long famine grips Canaan. His sons have fathered clans. Many of
the families, dreading the famine, journey to Egypt, as did
Abraham and Sarah, and settle in the Delta region of the
Nile. Others remain behind to wait out the famine in the
promised land.

There are now Hebrews settled in Canaan and in
Egypt. The patriarchal wanderings have ceased.

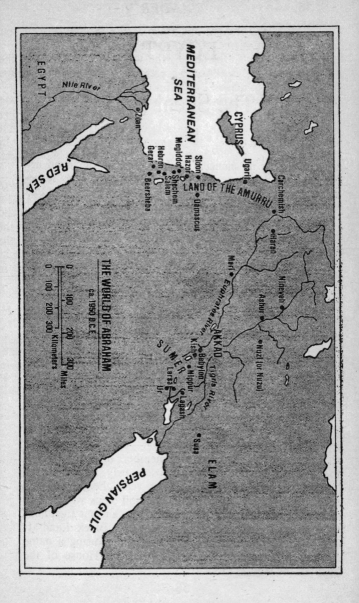

# EGYPT

## The Silent Nile

Centuries pass in silence. The descendants of Jacob appear to be living in peace during their time of early settlement in Egypt, no doubt grateful, as is everyone in that river valley, for the rhythmic benevolence of the Nile.

The Nile runs north for almost two thousand miles from Khartoum in the Sudan to the Mediterranean Sea. It is fed by the White and Blue Niles, which in turn are the creations of the tropical rains of Equatorial Africa. In the hundreds of thousands of years of its existence, the river carved a valley—only one mile wide in some places, no more than thirty miles wide in others—through the sandstone and limestone desert, and then divided into forks—seven in ancient times; two forks today—as it glided through the Delta to the sea. Tall cliffs often mount from the water's edge, leaving no room for agriculture, then recede into the desert and the distant range of pinkish hills. The river brilliantly reflects the deep blue of the sky and the golden color of a pagan sun.

But the running ribbon of river would probably not by itself have created the extraordinary world of ancient Egypt. That world—that civilization—came into existence as a unique response by certain members of our species to the given reality of a river that rose slowly, almost gently, during the same season year after year, then, as slowly, receded and left behind rich alluvial soil black with mountain silt that was a natural fertilizer. The ancient Egyptians referred to their country as Kemet, the Black Land. It was the later Greeks who called it Egypt, using a name for the region of Memphis—Hi-ku-Ptah, House of the Spirit of the God Ptah.

The flooding of the Nile, which commenced in July and began to recede in September, was caused by the annual rain that fell upon the land south of the Nile's Fourth Cataract, the land we now call Ethiopia. The river would slowly swell and push northward. "All of Egypt becomes a sea," wrote the Greek historian Herodotus in the fifth century B.C.E., "and only the towns remain above the water, looking like islands of the Aegean."

In its prehistoric period Egypt was two lands separately ruled. Each land had its gods and its tribes. The ancient Egyptian also called his country Two Lands, for he was always conscious of the difference between the open watery world of the Delta in the north and the long length of sandstone and limestone land in the south. The river valley was filled with marshes in which papyrus and rushes grew taller than a man. Wadis teemed with wild oxen, antelopes, fowl, and carnivores. Archaeologists digging in cemeteries discern various connected layers of culture during the prehistory of Egypt.

From graves we learn that the people were of African stock; later writings tell us that their language contained a strong Semitic element. How a Hamitic people—the African descendants, according to the Bible, of Ham son of Noah—came to have a basically Semitic language remains a mystery, and supports the argument of archaeologists who claim that predynastic Egypt was penetrated by a Semitic people from a still undetermined land or origin; merging with the older inhabitants, they helped turn the land onto the path of civilization.

The people then living in villages menacingly troubled by population increase make a decision similar to the one being made about the same time by the early Sumerians in southern Mesopotamia: they begin to reclaim the marshes and to harness the flooding of the Nile. Basins are made to hold the floodwaters; canals are dug; irrigation ditches bring extended life to the earth as it dries after the waters recede.

Wars are being fought between the north and the south over land and water rights. For a time Lower Egypt—the region of the Delta—may have controlled Upper Egypt. Then around 3000 B.C.E. the entire land is abruptly unified under a single ruler, a southern king named Menes or Narmer—the few Egyptian king lists that have thus far been discovered are not in agreement on this—the probable founder of the First Dynasty. Just as abruptly, writing begins—and Egypt crosses the threshold into history.

About three centuries and one dynasty later, Egypt has brought into being all the major forms of her civilization: a fully organized country, an efficient bureaucracy, a social hierarchy, a conventionalized art, technical skills, writing that will often be incised in pictures on stone and will be maintained almost unchanged by priests for close to three millennia—we call it hieroglyphics, sacred carving—large construction projects, and a ruler who is a god.

The abruptness of the birth is bewildering. Cylinder seals and other Sumerian art forms and motifs—a hero standing between two wild lions; monumental decorated brick architecture—have been discovered in Egypt dating in the period immediately prior to the First Dynasty. Nothing Egyptian has as yet been found in early Sumer. This would appear to make the Sumerians one of the culture catalysts of Egyptian civilization—not through conquest but through trade. By 2700 B.C.E., with the start of the Third Dynasty, all cultural connectedness to Mesopotamia had vanished and Egypt set out on a course of civilization that was to last three thousand years.

The Egyptians did not call their rulers pharaoh until about 1500 B.C.E. when they were halfway through the life span of their civilization. The word means great house, and referred originally to the palace rather than its leading inhabitant. Early Egyptians had various titles for their rulers: Horus, who was the falcon god, a sky deity; King of Upper and Lower Egypt; Lord of the Two Lands; the Son of Re, who was the sun god.

There were other titles. An Egyptian ruler was not addressed directly by the name he had borne as a prince; even to write his name was a sacrilege; hence, when written by scribes, it was enclosed in an oval ring—a cartouche—to separate it from all other words.

Though all of Egypt was under his absolute rule, the king was not a tyrant; the Egyptians were not his slaves.

He was a god who had consented to rule them. By serving him, Egyptians served themselves. No one knows how many centuries it took for this concept of god-king to entrench itself in the core of Egyptian civilization. It is already fully present at the very beginning of the history of the Two Lands.

The early Egyptians left us no written histories; they had no sense of linear history, of time and events moving on into a future. We have fragments of chronicles and annals that deal with one lifetime or reign: they date years by events—"birth of two children to the King of Lower Egypt." Partial king lists have been found on a fragmentary piece of papyrus historians now call the Turin Royal Canon, and on a rock known as the Palermo Stone. Egyptian history is reconstructed out of such bits and pieces of the past.

Sometime around 300 B.C.E., when Egypt was nearing the end of her creative history, an Egyptian priest named Manetho wrote a history of Egypt from the earliest period to the year 323 B.C.E. when the land came under the control of the Ptolemies after the death of Alexander the Great. The work is known as *Egyptian History*, and it did not survive. Fragments of it have come down to us in quotations found in the writings of other ancient historians.

Every book I have read on ancient Egyptian history uses Manetho's neat schematic structure as scaffolding. Thirty dynasties and three thousand years are presented in the following manner. The Early Dynastic Period, starting with Menes, or Narmer, runs from about 3000 to 2700 B.C.E. Then there are three plateaus, two valleys, and a long slow fall: the Old Kingdom (2700-2250 B.C.E.), the Middle Kingdom (2000-1800 B.C.E.) and the New Kingdom (1600-1100 B.C.E.) are marked by monumental building, strong centralized government, and an Egyptian presence either through commerce or conquest, or both, far beyond the borders of Egypt; during the Intermediate Periods that follow the Old and Middle Kingdoms, construction slackens, the centralizing rule of the pharaoh disintegrates, nobles rise to power in local areas and splinter the land, and the international position of

Egypt is weakened; a final eight-hundred-year-long downward glide sets in at the end of the New Kingdom as Egypt is ruled by foreign pharaohs and then is conquered by Persia and Alexander.

Two subsequent events could not have been forseen by Manetho: Egypt is conquered by Rome in 30 B.C.E.; about three centuries later the land is Christian and the civilization of ancient Egypt comes to an end.

It is not only the Nile but also the pyramids, those incredible tombs of dead pharaohs, that we forever associate with ancient Egypt. The monumental pyramids were built by rulers of the Third and Fourth Dynasties of the Old Kingdom, from about 2660 to 2500 B.C.E., during the period when Sumer, at the other end of the Fertile Crescent, was at the very height of her own civilization. Some of the smaller pyramids of the Middle Kingdom, as well as the tombs of nobles found in Siut, Bersheh, and Beni Hasan in the central region of Egypt, were under construction at the time Abraham wandered from Ur to Haran to Canaan and crossed into Egypt to avoid a famine; a tomb painting of an Egyptian nobleman found at Beni Hasan shows Asiatics entering Egypt to obtain food. (The Egyptian term *'A'mu-ḥryw-š* is translated by scholars as the *'A'mu* who dwell in the sand; to the ancient Egyptians the term was a geographic name for Asiatics or easterners; scholars are uncertain about the precise meaning of *'A'mu*.) The pharaohs of the New Kingdom built vast temple complexes in and around Thebes, as well as new cities in the Delta. Much of the construction work on those Delta cities was done by Abraham's descendants, the Hebrews who had settled in Egypt.

We see the Egyptians of the Old Kingdom in arrested motion in museums throughout the world, short, slight of build, with dark hair and eyes, the skin of the men a deep dark-brown color, that of the women a light yellow. We see them hunting game in the desert, butchering cattle, raising fowl. Boys and girls play a game of tug-of-war. In the tomb of a physician there is a scene of youths undergoing circumcision. No pictures depict private prayer by lesser figures than the king; nor are there figures of the gods in tombs other than pyramids. Only the god-king has access to the world of the gods. Others could enter that world only through him.

We see farmers plowing, watering, harvesting. The black earth is so precious they do not use it for permanent roads; they sail the Nile and its canals. Journeys are by boat. Pharaohs and images of the gods sail upstream or downstream, together with nobles, district governors, scribes—and the peasants who live in agricultural villages that are everywhere throughout the land.

Century after century those villages remained on the mounds where they had originally been built; it was wasteful to build them elsewhere and destroy the rich earth. Today they are buried beneath a millennium or more of alluvial silt. Egyptian houses were constructed of Nile mud, wooden supports, and rafters of palm trunks. The walls were thin, often richly colored, with hanging of mattings over the windows. The homes of the wealthy were lightly built, airy, and contained bedrooms, bathrooms, servants' quarters, halls, dining rooms, kitchens, storage rooms. There were shade trees, green plants, and well-kept gardens. The Egyptians loved trees, parks, flowers. Trees were the confidants of lovers.

Flies and gnats plagued the toiling peasants of the Nile valley, as did tax collectors, judges of doubtful integrity, fever at the time of inundation, and locusts. The peasants lived in hovels with their beasts. Throughout the seasons of sowing and reaping, the work in the fields was hard; but even then the peasant could take a drink from a wineskin or doze in the shade during the midday break.

We have dug up the private homes in the cities of Sumer and can walk through them. Egyptian cities were in the main cultic and administrative centers. Temples and tombs were built of quarried stone. Not so the private homes of her people, for whom stone was too costly and prone to retain rather than ward off the summer heat of the Nile valley. The record of the domestic lives of her ordinary people decayed almost entirely in the soil that sustained their daily existence.

We see three thousand years of Egyptian civilization through the dubious optic of tattered scribal documents, damaged art, and chance discovery. That is all we have left of Egypt—official records, ruined temples, looted tombs, and almost no houses, towns, or palaces. Even more than in the instance of Mesopotamia, scholars of ancient Egypt proceed with caution when they attempt to explore the interior of Egyptian civilization.

We must begin with the Nile and the god who predicts and assures its annual rise and fall, the ruler of Egypt, the Lord of the Two Lands.

An Egyptian of the Old Kingdom felt blessed by his gods. No debating assembly of gods here in this unchanging world; no indecision regarding future events. The sun rose and fell every day in a blue sky. The Nile flooded and receded every year, as predicted by the Son of Re. There was much poverty, but no starvation—unless the Nile rose to insufficient height. Indeed, this people had been blessed by its gods.

All depended on the god who reigned over the land from the great house in Memphis. Without him the world would return to the chaos that had been everywhere at the beginning of things. How had he come into being, this god who ruled the Two Lands?

On a hill where vegetation first appeared out of the floodwaters of chaos, Atum, the first of the gods, had emerged. "O Atum-Kheprer, thou wast on high on the primeval hill," reads the text that was used in the dedication ritual of the pyramids of the Sixth Dynasty in the twenty-fourth century B.C.E. Atum created two pairs of gods: Shu, god of air, and Tefnut, goddess of moisture; and Geb, god of earth, and Nut, goddess of the sky. They in turn generated the god Osiris, once probably only a vegetation god, now also king and judge of the dead, and Isis, goddess of fertility, wife of Osiris and mother of Horus, the god who ruled Egypt as Lord of the Two Lands; and the god Seth, brother and murderer of Osiris, whose dismembered body is collected and resurrected by Isis in an Egyptian myth that reminds one of Sumer's Dumuzi; and Nephthys, goddess of women.

In another creation story it was Ptah, god of the capital city of Memphis, who created all the other gods. He created through thought and words. ". . . All the divine order really came into being through what the heart thought and the tongue commanded," reads a document dated 700 B.C.E.; scholars assure us it originates from a text two thousand years earlier. "And so Ptah was satisfied [or "so Ptah rested"] after he had made everything. . . ."

There are myths of quarrels among the gods for the rule of Egypt that reflect the wars waged to unify the land. Later periods produced additional creation stories and different major and minor deities. Three thousand years of Egyptian civilization have given us a mind-numbing pantheon of deities, as pharaohs, priests, cities, nomes, and noble families often vied for power. But that was the future. The Egyptians of the Old Kingdom had no such concerns. They felt themselves chosen by their gods for the gifts and privileges of civilized life.

And life was for them a single continuum, a flowing, harmonious unity. No lines separate nature, man, and the gods. Everything simply is; all are species of the same unchanging substance; there are differences, but they are of degree only; all have the same needs and are to be treated in the same manner.

The gods once lived on earth, experienced joys and misfortune, married, had children, and died. Yet they still live, have needs, and exert power on man; hence they are to be fed, worshiped, and placated. The word for temple in Egyptian, *het-natjer,* means the castle of god.

A living prince too has needs. He is a god. His palace was called *per en ankhyw,* house of the living.

The liquid grace with which an animal moves, the awesome ferocity of the lion, the power in the jaws of a crocodile, the fecundity of the ram—clearly the animal is closer to the natural order of reality, to the world of the gods, than is stumbling and ungainly man. Many Egyptian gods wore the faces of animals familiar to the land of the Nile. The animal has needs. Live animals lived luxuriously in certain temples: crocodiles, cats, bulls. When they died they were mummified.

By the time of the First Dynasty, shortly before 3000 B.C.E., the Egyptians began to give human form to their gods. But traditions sometimes die, if indeed they die at all, with the slowness of a melting glacier; and so Egyptian tomb paintings are crowded with gods that are part human and part animal. Why should it not be so? All the world was a single reality.

And no line divided life from death and death from afterlife. The dead too have needs. The ancient Egyptian often described a man's tomb as a *het ent enheh,* a castle of eternity.

The gods, men, nature, the dead—different faces of the same flow of life.

The living require food and clothes; so do the dead. For to die is simply to pass from one state of life to another. You made the passage with the help of special *hemu-ka,* priests or servants of the soul (the highest class of priest was called *hemu-natjer,* servants of the gods), who brought you to your new life through the recitations and magical movements involved in the *wep-ro,* the opening-of-the-mouth ceremony. But you could not depend on anyone else to concern himself with your needs. Hence the Egyptian spent much of his life preparing his tomb for his death.

The Egyptian had no overwhelming fear of the dead; nor did he worship his ancestors. He sensed that his second life would not be the same as the one he had lived on earth. But he also believed that he would be subject to all the needs he had experienced in his first life. He lived in dread of somehow not making a proper transition from one life to the next, and, once having made it, of going hungry and thirsty and unclothed. To allay that fear, he prepared his tomb. A well-equipped tomb afforded happiness in both lives. With the record of his deeds on its walls, his body prepared for eternity, and papyrus scrolls containing magic formulas, the tomb was the vital point of focus in the process of transition from one realm of nature to the next, from death to life after death.

In that afterlife the Lord of the Two Lands would join the company of the sun god or become Osiris, ruler of the dead; the two notions would not disturb a prelogical Egyptian mind that was like a storage house piled high with diverse and startlingly contradictory ideas and beliefs troubling neither each other nor their owner. The king's nobles in this life would continue to serve him in their own afterlives. Peasants would serve their masters. There were upper-class Egyptians who hoped they might continue the lives they had enjoyed on earth. Tomb pictures depict their longed-for world after death: boating on the Nile, picnicking with relatives and friends, enjoying a good wine in a cool garden. Others yearned to join Osiris in his form as vegetation god and take part in the eternal spring resurrection of the earth. Still others would become stars.

But even after Anubis, the jackal-headed god of mummification, or Horus, or Osiris—it depends upon what tomb picture you are viewing—weighed the heart against the hieroglyphic sign for truth and aided in the entry to eternity, the Egyptian would continue to dwell in his tomb. His preserved, jewel-decked, mummified body, the product of a lengthy secret process—if the body fell to pieces, it would be as if he had never existed—must forever serve as the physical base of his eternal nonearthly existence. And so the tomb was built to be as beautiful as a home and, to prevent it from being robbed, as inaccessible as a blocked cave. Some tombs of Second Dynasty nobles had bathrooms. A wealthy tomb would be endowed; contractual arrangements would be entered into with *ka*-priests who would regularly utter the prayers necessary to ensure permanent transition to the next life and periodically bring food offerings to the hungry dead. No Egyptian could depend on his relatives for such loyal piety.

The dead could be addressed; often they were asked to intercede with the gods on behalf of the living. A dead enemy was the darkest source of dread. He could return and wreak havoc, invisibly. There were special incantations against such terrors, but they were not always effective.

Despite this preoccupation with death, it was not a somber world. If the tomb pictures are to be believed, the Old Kingdom Egyptian lived in a surfeit of self-confidence and prosperity, in an arrogance born of the satisfaction of achievement, and with a sense of insular security afforded him by the deserts that kept foreign marauders at bay.

There was so permanent army. When an army was needed for a raid or a campaign against Nubians or Asiatics, it was raised by a levy. Scribes went through the provinces collecting young men. Women moaned and wept. The gods, of course, were everywhere—village, city, national gods—but the Egyptian was in harmony with them all. He had no abstract notion of ethics save the principle of *maat,* a term difficult to translate and changing in meaning as the millennia went by; but in Old Kingdom Egypt it had reference to the proper, created, changeless relationship of things—pharaoh to gods, ruler to ruled, man to nature, servant to master. Everyone knew his proper place in the order of reality; but ability, shrewdness, and hard work could bring advancement, power, and wealth. And with wealth one could build a great tomb, endow it, and gain eternal life. The scribal class, open to all of ability and crucial to both ruler and noble in the smooth functioning of the vast complexity that was unified Egypt, was an especially inviting doorway to the highest levels of wealth and power. To learn to write was to make oneself different from, and superior to, all other men.

The ancient Egyptian linked his temporary existence to the timelessness of religion, magic, and the harmony of the cosmos. He felt assured that his imposing tomb, mortuary endowment, earthly success, and the favor of the god-king had bought him immortality. If a final resting place in the British Museum or the Louvre is a mark of immortality, then some of those purchases can hardly be equaled for contractual tenacity.

About the year 2700 B.C.E., an Egyptian named Imhotep—priest, magician, author of wise proverbs, physician, vizier, and architect to Djoser, who was Lord of the Two Lands and the probable founder of the Third Dynasty—designed and built a stone edifice within a rectangular enclosure that was over a mile in perimeter. It is the earliest large stone structure known to have been built by our species. A rectangular granite chamber beneath the structure was to serve as the royal tomb. There were underground apartments for the king's spirit. The terraced sides of the structure rose to a height of about two hundred feet. It still stands today in the desert west of Memphis. Architecturally it represents a transition between the old form of burial, which took place in a bench-shaped tomb called a mastaba, and the level-sided pyramids that were yet to come. We call it the Step Pyramid. With its construction the Age of the Pyramids begins.

About a century later, Khufu—known to us as Cheops, after the Greek name given him by the historian Manetho—a king of the Fourth Dynasty, constructed the greatest pyramid of all: 481 feet high, consisting of more than two million blocks of yellowish limestone, each weighing about two and one-half tons. The laborers—peasants conscripted during the flood season of the Nile when the land could not be worked—would float the blocks on boats from the quarry to the pyramid site. Herodotus reports that one hundred thousand men worked for twenty years to build that pyramid. But he is probably telling us what his tour guide told him. A more accurate figure would be four thousand laborers working in gangs of eighteen to twenty for a period of three months a year, which was the duration of the Nile flooding. Taking into consideration the fact that Egyptian technology at that time had only the lever, roller, inclined plane, and possibly long copper saws to cut the blocks of stone, the physical labor involved in the construction of this tomb challenges the wildest imagination. Yet the laborers supposedly worked with joy. A foreman later reported that they worked "without a single man getting exhausted, without a man thirsting, and came home in good spirits, sated with bread, drunk with beer, as if it were the beautiful festival of a god."

They probably had good reason for joy. They were participating in the sacrament of immortality that was the destiny of the god under whose rule they lived. At the same time, their sense of unity and nationhood was being strengthened by this massive organized effort on the part of the entire people. Local tribal loyalties were weakened. Pyramid construction may have served as a calculated means of accelerating the nation-building process in ancient Egypt—which may explain the strange construction

activities of Snofru, founder of the Fourth Dynasty, who
appears to have had three pyramids built for himself. It is
uncertain in which of the three he was eventually buried.

For almost two hundred years, through the period of
the Third and Fourth Dynasties, giant pyramid after giant
pyramid was built. Each was the center of a vast cemetery
complex in which there also stood a temple where prayers
were said and offerings were made on behalf of the entombed ruler, who was also worshiped now as a god. The
pyramids of later dynasties were smaller; many were built
of mud brick. Once a crowded line of pyramids stretched
from the Delta, near today's Cairo, southward to Khartoum, a distance of more than fifteen hundred miles. It is
not known with certainty how many pyramids were constructed. Eighty have survived.

About the year 2250 B.C.E., Egypt began to break
apart into locally ruled districts and cities. The Old Kingdom came to an end, crippled by a series of weak Sixth
Dynasty rulers and by the economically wasteful concentration of national wealth upon pyramid construction and
maintenance. Embalmers, coffin manufacturers, priests of
the dead, stonemasons, builders, artisans, sailors to handle
the boats that carried the stones along the Nile, caretakers
for the cattle yards and storehouses, tens of thousands of
laborers who had to be fed and housed—the death of a
god-king was expensive in ancient Egypt. The two elements that had helped create the Old Kingdom ultimately
destroyed it: the god-king and his tomb. All records
ceased. Egypt entered darkness.

The Nile turned to blood. Men thirsted for water. Plague
stalked the land. The life-giving river ceased its flooding
and became dry. Men went by foot across the dead river-
bed. The sun no longer shone. Crops failed. Men slew the
children of princes. Wild beasts roamed the land; no one
could scare them away. Anarchy was rampant. People
fled from towns for the security of cemeteries.

This was how later Egyptian literature described the
two broken centuries that followed the disintegration of
the Old Kingdom. Literature has license to exaggerate in
order to make a point: human chaos was projected into a

felt chaos in nature. The Nile continued flooding; the sun shone. But the anarchy was real. The Eighth Dynasty in Memphis had collapsed. New and simultaneous dynasties arose in Thebes and in Herakleopolis. The land had god-kings at the southern and northern ends of Upper Egypt. There was intermittent civil war.

"Who was king? Who was not king?" the Sumerian King List asked of the horrors occurring at that same time in southern Mesopotamia after the breakup of the empire of Akkad in 2100 B.C.E.

Chaos was king.

In the year 2000 B.C.E., a new dynasty assumed power is Thebes. The Twelfth Dynasty entered Egyptian history with a king who worshiped the god Amun of Thebes, whose name he carried as part of his own. He called himself Amenemhet, Amun-Is-Foremost, and added the words Wehem-Meswet, Repeater-of-Births, to his royal title, thereby indicating that he saw himself and his era as heralds of a renaissance—about one hundred years after Sumer had entered her own renaissance under the Third Dynasty of Ur. The god he worshiped, Amun, meant hidden—an invisible god sometimes believed to be the breath that gives life to all beings.

The new king, realizing the difficulty of ruling his large land from a city in its southern corner, moved his residence from Thebes to an area south of Memphis. He was wise, wily, and he ruled well and into old age, reestablishing trade and the authority of the throne, and consolidating the borders of Egypt against Nubians in the south and Bedouins and sea-raiders in the north. The period of the Middle Kingdom begins with his rule. The chaos had come to an end.

In the thirtieth year of his reign, while his eldest son was away on a campaign in Libya, he was assassinated in a harem conspiracy by a rival claimant to the throne; harems were not only nesting places of voluptuous maidens but also pits of viperish mothers, each hungry to see her son become king.

Amenemhet's son, Sesostris, who had been co-regent with the king for a decade, was returning from Libya with the army when messengers reached him with the news of

his father's death. A young man named Sinuhe, who was
an official of the royal household, had overheard the
message. Seized with terror at the looming civil war between the factions now claiming the vacant throne—we
do not know the precise reason for his fear; he may have
been involved in the conspiracy—he deserted the army
and fled southward across the Nile and the sand and stone
wilderness called Deshret, the Red Land, by the Egyptians, the home of evil spirits and the dead. He reached the
land of Canaan from Egypt in the year 1962 B.C.E., a few
decades before Abraham probably entered it from Mesopotamia. The account of his adventures, found on papyri,
enables us to gaze upon the world of the Amorites through
the eyes of an Egyptian.

He was helped by a sheik.

He lay dying of thirst somewhere in the wilderness near
the Great Bitter Lake north of the Gulf of Suez. Asiatic
Sand-Crossers came upon him. Their sheik, who had been
to Egypt, recognized him, gave him water and boiled
milk. He took the Egyptian into his tribe.

Sinuhe moved from one region to another and settled
finally in a nomadic land somewhere in northern Palestine; the location cannot be fixed precisely. It was an agricultural land, with herds, and a desert not too far away
where he could go hunting, and a road nearby that was
traveled by Egyptian couriers. He described it as "a good
land, named Yaa. Figs were in it, and grapes. It had more
wine than water. Plentiful was its honey, abundant its olives. Every kind of fruit was on its trees. . . ."

He tells us that he lived with an Amorite tribe whose
sheik had taken a liking to him and had given him his
eldest daughter in marriage. In time Sinuhe became commander of the sheik's army. The Amorite tribes in the
area were restless. They skirmished constantly with the
chieftains of adjacent territories, and Sinuhe joined them
in their battles. He referred to those chieftains as *hekau-
khasut* or *hik-khase*—written Egyptian has come down to
us unvocalized, and we cannot be certain we are pronouncing it correctly. The term means chieftains or rulers
of foreign countries. "Every foreign country against which

I went forth, when I had made my attack on it, was driven away from its pasturage and its wells. I plundered its cattle, carried off its inhabitants, took away their food, and slew people in it by my strong arm, by my bow. . . ."

He engaged a powerful opponent in lengthy single combat—a story that brings to mind David and Goliath, Marduk and Tiamat, and the littered beach before the walls of Troy. He spent much of his life shortening the lives of others.

In his old age he grew fearful of dying on foreign soil. How could an Egyptian who loved his country and yearned for the promised life after death not be buried in a castle of eternity?

He had been wrong about civil war in Egypt. Sesostris had crushed the conspiracy and ruled Egypt with skill and energy. He extended the southern border of the Two Lands to the region between the Second and Third Cataracts, kept his western border secure against the Libyans, maintained strong diplomatic relations with the tribal chieftains and petty kingdoms of Canaan, traded extensively in much of the Near East, worked the diorite and red granite quarries of his land for sixty sphinxes and one hundred statues, mined gold near Koptos, north of Thebes, improved or enlarged almost every temple in Upper and Lower Egypt, and built for himself a magnificient funerary complex—pyramid and temple—that was a close approximation to the castles of eternity constructed during the Old Kingdom. He was a great king, and most of the kings of the Middle Kingdom who followed him were no less great than he; the statues that boldly show the careworn face of one of the kings, Sesostris III, may be indicative of the depth of their concern for their people.

Sinuhe was pardoned by Sesostris. He returned to Egypt and was restored with honor to the court of the king. His story was one of the most popular classics in the rich literature of ancient Egypt.

The Egypt of the Middle Kingdom was a land of power without excessive cruelty, benevolence without effete weakness, influence without undue callousness. The breakup of the Old Kingdom had democratized the world

of the hereafter. Funerary procedures once reserved only
for the god-king were first taken over by the nobility and
then by any Egyptian who could afford to pay the price
for the necessary texts and equipment. The great tombs of
the nobility of the Middle Kingdom have almost been
picked clean by historians, museum directors, and thieves.
Inscriptions on the tomb walls of provincial rulers show
clearly that their loyalties were first to their provinces and
then to the king.

Amun, the invisible hidden god of Thebes, home of the
god-king, was elevated to the head of the Egyptian pantheon, where he would remain for most of the remaining
two thousand years of Egyptian history. He was fused
with the sun god and given the name Amon-Re.

Beyond the borders of the land, there were Egyptians
moving about almost everywhere. They were strongly
present in southern Sinai, working the copper and
turquoise mines. Their good relations with the Asiatic
sheiks of that wilderness peninsula are preserved to this
day on monuments depicting proud chieftains of the
Bedouin. The names of the sheiks were written in hieroglyphics—and we may have here the link between Egyptian writing and what ultimately became a Semitic
alphabet.

Artifacts of the Middle Kingdom—scarabs, which were
inscribed stone amulets in the shape of dung beetles, creatures regarded as self-generating representatives of the
sun god, and which were used as seals; statues of Egyptian officials; sphinxes of kings; statuettes of men and
women of moderate means; the seal of the Scribe of the
Vizier; the seal of a Steward, Accountant of Cattle; the
scarab of a Scribe of the Troops; much else—have been
found all over present-day Palestine and Syria. These findings indicate either political domination or strong diplomatic and commercial relations. No one is certain, because
the ruler of the Middle Kingdom seem to have left no
direct inscriptional record of their activities in Asia.

There were Egyptian officials at Megiddo in central
Canaan, in Ugarit and Byblos on the northern coast of
Syria, and in Qatna in central Syria—and no one really
knows why they were there. Diplomats? Trading mis-

sions? A military presence? There is no feel of thundering Egyptian armies during the Middle Kingdom. One has the impression of a great and serious nation making its presence felt in ways often other than blood and battle.

Many Asiatics settled in Egypt during the Middle Kingdom. They worked as servants in private homes and in the service of temples. We do not know how they came; perhaps the source was a slave trade, or captives taken during clashes with Sand-Crossers, or an occasional military campaign against the Sand-Dwellers. We are reminded of the story of Joseph.

In those days Egyptian rulers practiced a ritual that had come down from the Old Kingdom and was to be used as well by the Greeks and Romans. It was probably practiced routinely and involved the making of a clay figurine of a captured and bound enemy on which curses were written in red ink. Sometimes the curses were written on small pottery bowls. The figurines or bowls were thrown to the ground and smashed. The fragments were then buried near the tombs of the dead at Thebes in the south or at Sakkara near Memphis in the north.

Some of those shattered bowls and figurines have been found and put back together. Scholars now call the curses they contain execration texts. The red-ink writings have been deciphered.

The texts are about one or two hundred years later than the time of Sinuhe. They contain lists of people and things regarded as dangerous to the king. Dead Egyptians are included; their spirits might return and cause malevolent mischief. The names of foreign kings, tribes, and peoples are included; anyone or anything of possible menace to the Lord of the Two Lands is included in these ceremonially smashed bowls and figurines—may be enemies of the king be broken! It was a kind of magic believed to be of help in dispelling the evil plots, thoughts, and acts of real or imagined foes.

The kings of the Canaanite cities of Shechem, Beth-shemesh, Acco, Tyre, are cursed. Jerusalem, mentioned for the first time in history, is cursed: "The ruler of Jerusalem, Yaqar-Ammu, and all the retainers who are with him . . . who may rebel, who may plot, who may fight, who may talk of fighting, or who may talk of rebelling in this entire land." Nubians and Libyans are cursed; rebellious members of the royal family are cursed. Egyptian men and women, nobles and commoners, anyone "who might rebel, weave intrigues, make war, plan to make war, or plan to rebel, and every rebel who plans to rebel in this entire land" are cursed.

The pottery bowls name twenty different countries in Canaan—the region that is today, roughly, southern Syria, Lebanon, and Israel; the figurines name sixty-two. There are no doubt others that went unnamed; the entire world of Canaan could not have merited being cursed by the kings of Egypt. Often a country or a territorial unit is simply referred to by the name of its dominant town: Ashkelon, Hazor, and others. The picture we are given is of a land of seminomadic tribes and small city-states, many of them not entirely loyal to the god-king of Egypt. Some names refer to countries in one text and tribes in another. It is a land whose configuration is being changed by the movement of nomads and seminomads. Urban life declines in some areas, then is quickly reborn. Broken bowls and smashed figurines are the only records Egypt has left us of her view of the Amorite penetrations into the Fertile Crescent, the turbulence and devastation brought about by tribes on the move, and the process of adaptation to sedentary life.

We know they were Amorites; the names on the curse lists are west Semitic and of the same sort found in the cuneiform texts of Mesopotamia that talk with loathing of the Amurru, the Westerners. Their gods too are the gods of nomadic and sedentary west Semites: Hadad, El, Shamash, Anat, Baal, and the mountain god Har, whose name is borne by many of the members of a people who will soon help bring down the Middle Kingdom of Egypt.

The Egyptians are becoming nervous. These bowls and figurines enable us to see the extent to which the tribes of the Amorites have spread westward from Sumer after conquering the last of her city-states. In less than a hundred years Hammurabi will occupy the throne of an Amorite dynasty in Babylon. Somewhere in this turmoil of moving tribes and shifting territorial units are the wandering patriarchs and their families.

The Middle Kingdom began to break up around 1800 B.C.E. The two hundred years of the Second Intermediate Period forever changed the nature of Egypt.

First there were a number of weak kings. Once again the land broke into two parts. The frontiers could not be held.

Ancient Egypt had three traditional enemies: Nubians in the south, Libyans in the west, Asiatics in the east. Nomadic Asiatics came across the frontier in small raiding parties or to graze their herds; other Asiatics came as traders.

Sometime during the reign of Sesostris II (1897-1878 B.C.E.), governor Khnumhotpe of Beni Hasan had received as guests an Asiatic named Abisha and his retinue. The reception is depicted in a painting in the tomb of that governor, with the inscription, "The arrival, bringing eye-paint, which 37 Asiatics bring to him." Their leader is called "sheik of the highlands, Abisha." His name could as easily have been Iburum or Yakub.

Now, less than two hundred years later, the Asiatics penetrated the Delta in large numbers. They had the horse and chariot, the composite bow, a heavy curved sword, and body armor. We do not know where some of those new forms of weaponry originated; perhaps in distant Asia. But the people who were now using them in Egypt were from Syria and Palestine. They bore Semitic names like Yakub-har and Samuken. The Egyptian militia, fighting almost in the nude, with weak bows, small axes, and cumbersome shields, simply disintegrated.

"God was displeased with us," Manetho is quoted by another ancient historian, "and there came unexpectedly men of ignoble birth out of the eastern parts, who had boldness enough to make an expedition into our country. . . . And when they had got our rulers under their power, they afterwards savagely burnt down our cities, and demolished the temples of the gods, and used all the inhabitants in a most hostile manner, for they slew some, and led the children and wives of others into slavery. . . ."

By 1700 B.C.E. a Semite sat on the throne of the god-king. The land of Egypt, chosen of the gods, was now ruled by foreigners. The extent and nature of their rule—how far south it extended; whether it was benign or as cruel as later Egyptian sources and Manetho make it out to be—is much debated by scholars.

The Egyptians called them *hik-khase*, Hyksos—chieftains of foreign countries; the term was used from the Middle Kingdom on to designate Bedouin sheiks. They thought the Hyksos to be an arrogant barbarian horde, hated them, and were so ashamed at having been conquered that no record contemporaneous with the period of conquest has come down to us. No Egyptian scribe would have felt the need to leave behind an account of his country's humiliation at the hands of miserable Asiatics.

They were not barbarians. They were Semites who easily accepted much of Egyptian culture. They adopted hieroglyphic writing. Their kings took on Egyptian names. They were skillful merchants, and they operated a vast fleet of cargo ships. Archaeologists have discovered objects with Hyksos names all through the Near East.

Many scholars believe that this is the time Joseph was in Egypt—about 1660 B.C.E. A Hyksos king would not have hesitated to appoint an able Semite as his vizier and invite his father and brothers to come from famine-plagued Canaan and sojourn in the rich pasturelands of the Delta. There is no mention in Egyptian texts of either Joseph or Israelites in Egypt.

The land was ruled by Hyksos kings for more than a century. Once again, for the third time now, an Egyptian from the south attempted to unite his broken country. About 1600 B.C.E., a Theban king, finding the presence of foreign conquerors unendurable, began a war of liberation. His name was Kamose—Ka-Is-Born. A stele discovered in 1954 recounts his words to his council of nobles. "No man can find respite from being despoiled by servitude to the Asiatics. I will grapple with him, that I may cut open his belly! My wish is to save Egypt and to smite the Asiatics!"

The Hyksos yielded slowly. But the Egyptians by now had also mastered the horse and chariot, the composite bow, the curved sword. "My valiant army was in front of me like a blast of fire." Kamose drove the Hyksos into the northeast corner of the Delta. His brother and successor, Ahmose, captured Avaris, drove them out of Egypt, and reunited the land. With that was born the Eighteenth Dynasty and the New Kingdom—the period in which "a new king arose over Egypt, who did not know Joseph."

The war against the Hyksos continued for decades. Theban troops and Nubian mercenaries raided Hyksos strongholds in Canaan. Egypt had not been won back from the Asiatics by the militia of the individual provinces but by the army of the king of Thebes. It was a strong army: an infantry with new weapons, a chariot force with its own officers, and mercenary troops with their chiefs. When the Hyksos were finally driven out, Egypt found herself in possession of a war machine.

The Eighteenth Dynasty, which ruled Egypt from about 1570 to 1300 B.C.E., owed no debts to the local rulers who in the past had contended for power with the kings of the land. A professional army stood alongside the throne of the New Kingdom. By the end of the Eighteenth Dynasty, there was virtually no private ownership of property in Egypt. About one-fifth of the land was owned by the temples; the remainder was in the possession of pharaohs. Peasants worked the soil almost as serfs.

Humiliated by the Hyksos, stripped of her old sense of security and self-confidence, possessing a military force that gradually began to pervade the land—the "chief of soldiers" supervises the digging of a canal; a charioteer officer oversees the transport of royal monuments—Egypt transformed itself into a disciplined nation with a permanent store of shameful and angry memories, an ongoing nightmare of menacing Asiatics, and a powerful growing army. A national cauldron seething with the ingredients of collective shame, a common enemy, the specter of border insecurity, and the sharp spice of a mighty army will often boil over into an effort at empire.

In the decades that followed the victory over the Hyksos, Theban kings—Amenhotep I, Thutmose I, and

Thutmose II—restored internal order and secured absolute control over the land. They exercised some measure of dominion over Canaan through sporadic raids and military campaigns. Thutmose I ventured across the Euphrates, scooped up much booty, and enjoyed an elephant hunt in Syria on his way back to Egypt with his army.

There was at first much opposition inside Egypt to any effort at empire; many preferred the old ways of diplomatic, cultural, and commercial domination. In one of the most extraordinary episodes in Egyptian history, the wife of Thutmose II seized the throne after his death. "The Two Lands were under her control." wrote an official of the court; "people worked for her, and Egypt bowed the head." Her name was Hatshepsut, and she ruled as godking—posing and dressing like a man—from about 1485 to 1470 B.C.E. She had the support of anti-imperialists, and when she died and her son, an ardent imperialist, ascended the throne, he had her name chiseled out of all the buildings, monuments, and the great temple she had constructed—a practice not uncommon in ancient Egypt: vengeance against one's relatives after they were entombed. In death they were made eternally silent.

The new pharaoh was Thutmose III. In an attempt to quell a rebellion, Thutmose invaded Canaan. His intent was "to overthrow the vile enemy and to extend the boundaries of Egypt in accordance with the command of his father Amon-Re." A coalition of about three hundred princes—rulers of city-states—met him on the field of battle, each with his own little army—a telling picture of the splintered state of affairs outside Egypt. Thutmost proved to be a daring commander, a clever tactician and conqueror.

The son of Thutmose III was Amenhotep II, who ruled from about 1440 to 1415 B.C.E. He continued the imperial tradition of his father. "He ruled the Two Lands, and every foreign country was bound under his soles." When he returned from his second campaign into Asia, he brought with him "princes of Retenu [Canaan]: 127; brothers of princes: 179; Apiru: 3,600 . . . Kharu: 36,300 . . . total: 89,600 men. . . ." Scholars suspect that the figures are inflated.

The word Hapiru now appears for the first time in Egyptian records—written by scribes as Apiru. It remains unclear whether the term was meant as an adjective to describe widespread groups of wanderers, adventurers, and brigands detached from city and tribe, or as a noun to designate a specific people. The Egyptians clearly regarded them as a separate, countable entity. But the enigma about the relationship between the Hapiru and the Hebrews is not eased in any way through the efforts of those Egyptian army scribes who made lists of the booty brought back to the Two Lands by the plundering troops of their pharaoh.

Some prisoners became servants in the houses of wealthy families; others were put to work as slave laborers on temple and mortuary projects. It is probable that among those prisoners were descendants of the tribe of Jacob whose ancestors, about two centuries earlier, had decided to remain behind in Canaan. Already in Egypt, in the north, lived the descendants of the families that had made the journey to the Delta.

Gold, precious stones, cattle, costly produce—from Nubia and Asia, from Phoenicia, Crete, and Mycenae— flowed unendingly into the glittering city of Thebes. Not only goods but also art, architecture, literature, the gods themselves, moved back and forth with ease through the empire carved by the Egyptians. Asians worshiped Egyptian gods; Egyptians worshiped Asiatic gods. The name of Baal—we have already met Baal, the Canaanite god of the heavens, the mountaintops, thunder—was used of the pharaoh: "His battle cry is like that of Baal in the heavens." Baal had his own priesthood in Egypt. Astarte and Anat were adopted as war goddesses. Thutmose IV was described as "mighty in the chariot like Astarte." A byproduct of empire was this domestication of Asiatic gods in a land that had once loathed foreigners. Egypt, her pharaoh, his queen and nobles delighted in the cosmopolitan luxury earned by conquest.

The land was orderly, disciplined. When you died now, it was not so much your meritorious life that got you entry into the next world as the magic and religion worked by the priests. You were buried with the Book of the

Dead in your tomb. You recited from it when you met the forty-two gods who were to judge your worth. "I have not cursed my local god. . . . I have not stood in the path of a god on his procession. . . . I have not stolen. . . . I have not killed men. . . . I have not been covetous. . . ."

The Egypt of empire was the pharaoh, the army, the priests, peasant-serfs, artisans, shopmen, and, as in all ancient lands, slaves.

Amenhotep III died in old age, surrounded by wealth, and a harem of the sisters and daughters of friendly or frightened kings from everywhere in his empire, and deep in a correspondence with the royalty of the Asiatic world. The language of international diplomacy in those days was Akkadian, written in cuneiform script on clay tablets. The diplomatic correspondence of Amenhotep III and his son would be discovered in 1887 of our era by a peasant woman scratching about for fertilizer in the ruins of El Amarna, a village about 190 miles south of Cairo. Amenhotep III was buried in a fine but not exceptional tomb. For some reason, his mummy was transferred to the tomb of his father three and a half centuries later by a high priest. Archaeologists found it and learned that the old king had suffered acutely from toothaches.

The new pharaoh, Amenhotep IV, came to the throne around 1365 B.C.E. He had a long thin neck, which supported a peculiarly shaped elongated head, and a narrow face with a large nose, thick lips, and a long roundish jaw. His stomach bulged as if he were permanently with child; his shoulders were narrow and his chest was sunken. He had slender effeminate legs and heavy thighs. In sculptured reliefs he sits loosely on a cushioned chair or reclines on a couch, his misshapen body an indolent arabesque of seemingly jointless limbs. The backs of his elbows are as delicately pointed as those of his beautiful wife, Nefertiti. He seems weak and ill. But huge standing statues in Karnak show him with the fixed hot look of the fanatic.

The religion of the land he ruled was now more than fifteen hundred years old. I have tried in my reading to find some order and shape in Egyptian polytheism, and am unable to do it. The land grew gods as it grew grain after a Nile inundation. As a city rose in influence, its god washed across the land; as it faded, its god receded, leaving behind here and there ghostly echoes of its former greatness, cults tended by tenacious adherents of a vaguely remembered past. Ancient tribal gods, dynastic village gods, city gods, provincial gods; a cat goddess, a cobra goddess; folk gods that protected against illness and evil spirits and ensured fertility and safe childbirth; gods with a male body and the head of a heron, a falcon, a jackal, a donkey, a crocodile, a baboon; the falcon god bearing different names in different towns; Hathor, deity of dance, music, and love, was a cow goddess in one town and lived in a sycamore near another; Shu, the god who held heaven and earth apart over one town and was a warrior god in another; and on and on, dizzyingly—all lived together in a vast cluttered attic of nature-dominated faith.

The oldest national gods of Egypt were probably the solar deities, all of them—Re, Horus, Atum, Osiris—different aspects of the golden disk that eternally travels the heavens: the sun. It is the bearer of life; it disperses the night, perishes in the evening, and returns from death with each dawn. All of Egypt recognized the timeless sanctity of the sun god. Hence Egyptians often fused their local gods, which they would not abandon, with the god of the sun. A neutral, everyday word that referred to the sun simply in its shape as a disk was in use: the Aten, the disk of the sun. No resurrected god, no animal-headed anthropomorphic host—only the disk, the basic elemental shape of the life-giving fire in the sky, a shape pure and empty of myth. There was a cult to Aten in Thebes during the days of Amenhotep III, and it is probable that the Aten had been worshiped for two generations before Amenhotep IV. Inscriptions indicate a stirring in the god-smothered air of Egypt, an eagerness to bring order and unity to the stifling multiplicity of deities.

That a city god, unique and all-powerful, would be identified with the gods of other towns is an indicator of the monotheistic yearnings that had begun to make themselves felt here and there in the land. At the same time, there were powerful conservative forces that insisted upon the retention of the separate local identities of the gods. As Egypt rested from the efforts of conquest, she was hosting deep within herself the fungus growth of violent and fanatic religious revolution.

The fanatic was the new pharaoh.

For five years he reigned in Thebes, keeping his given name and showing no sign of dissatisfaction over the mounting power of the priests and the army, power that was openly encroaching upon the divinity of the god-king. His name, Amenhotep, meant Amon is satisfied. The young pharaoh too seemed content.

Sometime in his fifth year of rule, while worshiping Amon-Re in a sandstone quarry from which stones were to be taken for temple construction, he alluded to himself as "the first prophet of Re-Harakhti Rejoicing-in-the-Horizon in his name Shu [the sunlight] which is Aten." When depicted as Re-Harakhti, the sun god had the head of a falcon and a human body; he had been worshiped in this form since earliest times in the cult of Heliopolis. Above the head of the falcon was the solar disk. The king is shown worshiping this god in the fixed pose of past pharaohs.

Abruptly the art of this period undergoes a transformation. One of the depictions of the falcon-headed Horus usually contained a solar disk with wings. This winged disk now disappears. In its place is a golden sun. The rays of the sun shine gloriously over the king and queen. In these new depictions, the pharaoh and his queen and courtiers are invested with an intense vivacity, a flow of life that is in utter contrast to all the past centuries of Egyptian art. And all the subjects of the pharaoh are given the strange form of their king, as if what is emphasized here are peculiar nonhuman—divine—qualities inherent in the very physical shape of this pharaoh. All that can be determined from these depictions, some of them on the tomb of the vizier Ramose at Thebes, is that the revolution has begun and court artists are already giving expression to the personal aesthetics of their king. The reactions of the Amon-Re priests of Thebes to the new cult and its art may have brought on what next occurred.

Sometime in his sixth year the king journeyed from

Thebes. About halfway between Cairo and Luxor the mountains east of the Nile move back from the river's edge and leave behind a plain in the shape of a crescent moon, eight miles long and three miles deep. To the west stretches a broad area of agricultural land. On the eastern shore, Amenhotep IV set up his magnificent tent. In the morning, riding a golden chariot, he journeyed northward. At a certain point, he offered a sacrifice to his god. Then he drove southward. The shining rays of the sun guided him to the spot where he stopped and swore an oath. He had set the boundaries of a new city. He swore to his father the Aten that he would never step outside those boundaries and the others he would soon set up to the east and west. He addressed his courtiers, many of them newly appointed, and military commanders. It was the desire of the Aten that the new city be constructed. It would, therefore, be the city of the Aten and belong to no other god, no other priesthood. The courtiers and commanders swore loyalty to their pharaoh.

The city that was built on that Nile plain was named Akhetaten, The Horizon of the Sun Disk. The horizon was regarded as the dwelling of the sun god in the sky. The pharaoh changed his name to Akhenaten, It Is Well with the Sun Disk. The rupture with the official Amon-Re priesthood was complete—but we have no sources that tell us precisely how or why this break with a state religion of such awesome power took place, an unprecedented act in the ancient world. What is clear is that in the mind of the pharaoh the cults of Amon-Re and Aten could not coexist.

The first step in the process of separation was the creation of the new city—a great new temple, smaller sanctuaries, a palace for the royal family, administrative buildings, military quarters, storehouses, residential quarters for workmen and artisans, and sites for the tombs. Priests were appointed, a chief physician, a captain of police, overseers of the royal harem, a commander of the army, and the overseer of the treasury.

The apostle of the new faith, a sickly man made strong by the conviction that he alone possessed the true faith, rewarded his new courtiers with gifts of golden necklets and fed them from the royal table. We do not know whether they followed their king through convenience or conviction. Some were clearly convinced. A tomb inscription of that time—one among many—reads, "How prosperous is he who hears thy Doctrine of Life, and is sated with beholding thee, and unceasingly his eyes look upon Aten every day."

In the tomb of Ay, superintendent of all the king's horses, was found the celebrated Hymn to Aten. It was probably written by Akhenaten, and portions of it remind many of Psalm 104, though a direct connection between the Egyptian and the Hebrew is unlikely:

> *Thou appearest beautifully on the horizon of heaven,*
> *O living Aten, beginner of life. . . .*
> *How manifold are thy works!*
> *They are hidden from the face of man.*
> *O sole god, like whom there is no other!*
> *Thou didst create the world according to thy desire. . . .*

The new god was not given human shape. Unlike Amon-Re, the invisible god who was worshiped deep within the darkened recesses of his temples, the Aten was worshiped in the open as the universal supporter of all mankind and of all life. Atenism made no ethical demands upon the worshiper other than loving gratitude. It was a deeply felt worship of one aspect of nature: the sun. Scholarly debate about the precise nature of Atenism—was it a pure or rudimentary monotheism?—still goes on. It appears to have possessed a striking feature of later monotheism: intolerance. Akhenaten sent workmen throughout the land to obliterate with hammer and chisel the names of the many gods of Egypt.

The king worshiped the Aten; the courtiers and people are often shown worshiping the king. It is not known how deeply Atenism penetrated the masses. There is little doubt that it spread to much of the upper levels of Egyptian society. Hand in hand with Atenism came the return of pharaonic centrality. Akhenaten was supported in these efforts by the army. The priests and civil bureaucracy in Thebes seethed. There were riots. The land wavered on the brink of civil war. The army maintained order cruelly and with difficulty. Bodies floated down the Nile into the jaws of crocodiles.

It has been said of this Aten-intoxicated pharaoh that in his obsession with his god he threw away the great empire of Egypt. Desperate pleas on the part of friendly princes for Egyptian help against attacking enemies indicate that the land of Canaan appears to have fallen into chaos.

"Let . . . the archers of the king, my lord, go forth," wrote the ruler of Jerusalem. "No lands of the king remain. The Hapiru plunder all lands of the king. . . ."

And in the distance, beyond northern Canaan and the buffer kingdom of Mitanni, preparing, waiting, were the Hittites, a mountain people who had migrated into the region that is now Turkey from somewhere in the north before 2000 B.C.E. Now they began to move—a mighty army of chariots and foot soldiers. They were a hardy, fearless people, and they looked upon every neighboring nation as a natural enemy. Their king was an absolute ruler, a high priest, and a god. Ten thousand Hittite cuneiform tablets were found by archeologists in the first decade of this century. Most of the tablets were historical in nature; their decipherment threw a floodlight onto a vast dark stretch of history—the decades after Akhenaten when Horemheb, the commander of the armed forces, became pharaoh, and was followed by a new dynasty that had to face the sudden iron change of the Hittite bid for empire. A slave escape took place at one point during that period of tumult and went unrecorded by Egyptian scribes.

The last years of the reign of Akhenaten are lost in obscurity for lack of historical documents. He died about 1350 B.C.E. and was succeeded for a brief time by his eldest daughter's husband, who now lived in Thebes and abandoned the heretical cult of Aten. His successor was Tutankhamun, the famous King Tut, whose tomb was discovered by Howard Carter in 1922. He was about nine years of age when he ascended the throne and eighteen when he died. Grateful Amon-Re priests gave him a glorious entombment for reaffirming the centrality of Amon-

Re and acknowledging Thebes as the main city of the land.

Akhetaten was abandoned and fell into ruin. The burial site of Akhenaten remains unknown. Some time ago scholars believed his mummy had been discovered. Careful examination of the skull showed the mummy to be that of a man younger than Akhenaten. It is conceivable that the body of Akhenaten was torn to pieces by raging Amon-Re priests and thrown to the dogs.

Then around 1315 B.C.E. a new dynasty arose in Egypt, the Nineteenth Dynasty. Ramses I, Seti I, Ramses II—northerners. The founder was Ramses I—Re-Is-Born—vizier to Horemheb. Their devotion was to the gods of northern Egypt: Re of Heliopolis, Ptah of Memphis, Seth of the Delta.

The pharaohs of the Nineteenth Dynasty have restored order to the land of Egypt. Plundering campaigns into southern and central Canaan have returned much of that land to Egyptian control, including Megiddo and the coastal cities, and swelled the ranks of slave laborers with additional Hapiru and other Asiatics. Bloody battles have been fought with the Hittites, most of them inconclusive—though Ramses II returns home around 1280 B.C.E. from a crucial battle at Kadesh on the Orontes River, trumpeting victory. Egypt and the Hittites sign a covenant—a peace treaty—to respect one another's borders.

We are now in the decades between 1300 and 1270 B.C.E. Ramses II is pharaoh. Egypt has not yet fully recovered from the religious revolution: art, literature—the general culture of the land—have deteriorated; ancient texts are carelessly copied; tomb paintings stress the dangers of life in the next world, the tremulous judgment of the heart before Osiris; much of the lightness of the past is gone. Temple walls are crowded with scenes of war. Priests are wealthy and powerful. Ramses II is building all through Egypt, from the Delta to the deserts of Nubia; and what he is building is, of course, being built by slaves.

There are by now many tens of thousands of slaves in

the Delta—Bedouin, Hapiru, Canaanite; a vast horde of Asiatics originating from many different tribes. Caught in the violent tide of empire and impressed into slavery are the descendants of the patriarch Jacob, who entered the Delta centuries ago, retained their tribal ways, and did not vanish into the civilization of Egypt. At some point in the early history of the New Kingdom those Hebrews were swept into slave labor gangs that were constructing the magnificent cities and temples which even in decay and ruin remain astonishing to this day. Whether these descendants of Jacob are treated as war booty—the lowest form of slave—or as a human pool dwelling in their own houses under military control and heavily called upon as dictated by need or whim is difficult to determine.

Slaves—those who work in the fields as well as the quarries; those who make bricks and build temples and cities—are state property, belonging to crown or temple as do cattle and land. They are regarded as part of the army, are led by standard-bearers chosen from among the soldiers, and are branded with the seal of the government department known as the House of Silver. Their officers are often chosen from their own ranks and are of varying grades. Slaves are mustered and marched to their labors in a military manner.

Whether they are poor Egyptians or Asiatic prisoners of war, slaves are despised by the scribes, who regard them as being without understanding and therefore to be driven like cattle. A poem on a papyrus reads:

*The poor child is only brought up*
*That he may be torn from his mother's arms;*
*As soon as he comes to man's estate*
*His bones are beaten like those of a donkey;*
*He is driven, he has indeed no understanding in his body.*

Under Ramses III artisans in Thebes will often strike because they are not paid their wages of food and oil on time. "We have been starving for eighteen days," was their cry, according to a document that describes one such strike. During that strike they march upon the temple of Ramses II and penetrate into the building. Priests attempt to pacify them. But the workmen are enraged. "We have been driven here by hunger and thirst; we have no clothes, we have no oil, we have no food. Write to our lord the pharaoh on the subject, and write to the governor who is over us, that they may give us something for our sustenance." They are paid, and return to their labors.

Ramses III reigned a century later than the time I am now writing about. But if artisans were in difficult straits during the reign of Ramses III, then I find it difficult to conjure up the hunger, the level of existence beyond poverty, the endless back-breaking toil, the utter hopelessness that is the lot of the slave as he labors beneath the Delta sun to build the cities of Seti I and Ramses II.

In the days of Seti I, the pharaoh who preceded Ramses II, the Nile received a wicker basket caulked with bitumen and pitch in which lay a three-month-old boy. The Hebrews, we are told in the Bible, had "multiplied and increased very greatly, so that the land was filled with them." Seti I, afraid "lest they increase and, in the event of war, join our enemies in fighting against us," had decreed the death of all newborn Hebrew males. The child was given over to fate.

Children were often abandoned to the waters of the Nile—by the poor who could not feed them, by the wealthy to whom they might have been born in adultery, by slaves who had not the heart to slay their own offspring and so consigned them either to death at another's hands or to good fortune. The rivers of Mesopotamia too carried abandoned children—we recall that in the account of the life of Sargon of Akkad his mother set him adrift on the Euphrates soon after he was born. And in an Egyptian myth the mother of the infant god Horus conceals her son among marsh reeds to protect him from the murderous rage of the god Seth. Tales of infants left to the mercy of rivers were common in the ancient Near East. The tales mirrored the truth, and truth gave credence to the tales. There is no reason to disbelieve either the story of Sargon or of Moses.

A princess of the royal house discovered the child, had it nursed by a Hebrew slave woman—unknown to the princess, she was the mother of the child—then took the boy into the palace and raised him as her own son. Egyptian women nursed their children until the age of three; Asiatic women, probably less. In the New Kingdom period, childhood ended at four; then boyhood, the time of education, began.

The boy—all that remains of his original name is Mosheh, which is Egyptian for "born of" or "is born"; the Hebrew word *mashah*, "draw out," from which his name supposedly originates, was taken from later tribal tales or is the touch of the skillful writer who attempted, with the help of oral and written traditions at his disposal, to mold into final literary form the various accounts of the origins of the savior of his people—the boy, this adopted son of the Egyptian princess, would have been educated in the palace together with other royal children and children of the upper class. "Give thy heart to learning and love her like a mother," an Egyptian father counseled his son, "for there is nothing so precious as learning." And he added, "It is only the learned man who rules himself." The Egyptian valued education because it could be used as a means for advancement; it separated him from the mass of the unlearned, the ruled, the ignorant who were like "a heavily laden donkey."

The boy Mosheh—or Moses, as we know him in English—would have learned to read and write. He would have become adept in gymnastics, swimming, the manners of the court. The average life span in those days was about twenty-five; at the age of twelve or fourteen an Egyptian boy who was studying the scribal arts had already mastered enough to be of real use to the authorities. A prince would eventually have become a member of the inner circle of courtiers and would have known of wars, treaties, intrigues—the swirl of royal affairs around the divine, all-powerful throne.

The young man Moses—educated, a prince of the royal court of Seti I—would have been assigned to temporary military duty at the quarries or as army overseer of "his kinsfolk" working in the Delta. The narrator of the Book of Exodus reminds us that the Hebrews are his kin; we have no way of knowing if Moses was aware of that.

What follows is the result of sudden uncontrollable fury, compassion, horror, and outrage. He slays a cruel Egyptian. Burial of a dead body in the Delta earth is accomplished with ease.

A Hebrew slave informs Moses that he witnessed the killing. The young prince experiences a trembling upon all his limbs, for he knows that pharaoh will not countenance murder. The dead Egyptian too may well have been a member of the royal household or the son of a high official. Brutal retribution is exacted for the killing of Egyptian officers, tax collectors, imperial messengers.

The prince Moses gives a road to his feet and flees south and east, slips across the frontier—or probably crosses it with ease in the special garb of a prince, as the guards may not yet have been alerted and do not know to detain him. He does not travel to Canaan, for he knows the land crawls with Egyptian troops. Instead he enters the wilderness of northern Sinai and wanders to the land of Midian, which is in the region of today's Elat near the south of modern Israel.

He could not have made that journey without the help of Bedouin along the way. They would have helped him out of either friendliness or fear, or in the hope of receiving gifts. The Midianites, descendants of Abraham through his wife Keturah (Genesis 25), offer him shelter; he is accepted into the clan of a priest, who gives him his daughter as wife.

These Midianites are Sand-Crossers, Bedouin of the desert, with a vague claim to pasturelands in the peninsula of Sinai. We are told nothing of the god or gods of the priest, whose name, Reuel, evidences connection to the Canaanite deity El. Moses lives with the clan of this Bedouin sheik-priest, tending flocks in the wilderness. In time his wife gives birth to a son. The Egyptian prince names the child Gershom, a word meaning "I have been a stranger in a foreign land." The name is comprised of two Semitic words, *ger*, stranger, and *shom*, there. We are being told of Moses' loneliness and his gradual adaptation to this barren world, so different from his Egypt of wealth and power.

"I am even so a foreigner whom no one loves," wrote

Sinuhe the Egyptian of his exile among Amorites in another time, "any more than a Bedouin would be loved in the Delta."

He tends the flock of his father-in-law in the desolate wilderness. Now we are told that his father-in-law is named Jethro. The commentaries try valiantly to reconcile the contradiction by making Reuel the grandfather. In actuality we have stepped across a threshold into another tradition, a second source or literary document, yet another account of the life of Moses among the Midianites. It is the story of the burning bush.

Years have passed since the flight from Egypt. The prince is a Bedouin now, in the dusty desert garb of the Sand-Crossers. The inexhaustible black soil of the rich Nile valley, the vast temples, the many gods, the golden palace of the pharaoh, the opulence of his youth—all are a vanished dream in the hot, dry, mountainous wilderness with its violent sunlight and shadows, burning days and chilling nights, and the flock that picks at the low leaves of scrub brush and occasional wild grasses that grow in the reddish earth.

I do not pretend to understand the mystery of human transformation, the moment when the response of a man to the world about him throws upon his mind a new and wondrous light concerning the nature of our species and binds him to a vision of the future to which he gives over his life. About a century before Moses, the pharaoh of an Egypt swollen with the spoils of empire envisioned a single god, one natural force at work upon the suffocating multiplicity of gods and men. Sickened by unyielding priests and filled with revulsion toward Amon-Re, the blood-soaked god of the Egyptian empire, he abandoned his world, retreated to a city of his own creation, and turned to the sun and its image as a disk for strength to sustain his vision. The vision died with him. His name was cursed; his god was obliterated. There can be no connection between that pharaoh and the man tending a flock in the wilderness—other than that both are of the same species, both reached for unity beyond the wearying kaleidoscope we wake to every morning.

I accept the following elements of the early life of Moses as truths: he was born a Hebrew; he was raised in the household of pharaoh as a prince; he slew an Egyptian in a fit of temper; he fled and lived with the Midianites. I accept them because there could have been no reason to invent them, and because each is an element at the core of a personality; the absence of any of these elements makes the actions of the man incomprehensible— as we shall see.

Accepting them, I find myself besieged by questions. Why did Moses murder the Egyptian? In a single moment of uncontrollable rage, he not only took a life—and no matter how cruel that Egyptian might have been, the prince Moses could have had no justification in slaying him—but he also threw away his entire future with the royal household. Further, not once during his stay among the Midianites does he engage in combat, join the men in skirmishing with other tribes, do anything that reminds us of his prior military training, his ability to kill. In this, he is entirely unlike Sinuhe, who reveled in fighting and killing. He is man enough to have two sons—but all he appears to do as a Bedouin is wander the wilderness tending the flock of his adopted clan. Why? Among the Bedouin it is women and children who regularly see to the flocks; the men are warriors.

The most horrifying fate that could befall an Egyptian was to die and not be entombed; even the poorest of Egyptians sought mummification and a tomb that would offer protection against the prowling jackals of the desert. Without the body, the spirit would vanish into an eternity of nothingness. The Egyptian slain by Moses and buried in the sand has by now been devoured, his bones scattered and bleached. If we accept as true the account of the two quarreling Hebrew slaves whom Moses attempts to pacify and the manner in which one of them turns upon him, "Who made you chief and ruler over us? Do you mean to kill me as you killed the Egyptian?"—and why should we not accept it; as an invention it adds no glory to the Hebrews, so why should it have been invented; but as truth it helps us better to understand the nature of Moses—if we accept that story, then the horror of the murder deepens into an endless nightmare of the soul. The killing was senseless. The scribes are correct. Slaves are creatures without understanding, to be driven like cattle, like the herd he now tends for his father-in-law. A man whose mind is clouded with a miasma of such nightmarish misgivings cannot be a warrior, cannot kill. He can only tend flocks like children and women.

This happens: a man will perform a sudden unthinking act of heroism or horror, and then spend much of his life in an effort to penetrate into himself and search out the hidden source of his deed. Often there is no source other than the irrationality that is the underground ocean upon which our species floats. Often he will invent a source, and that will be his frail raft of reason. But on occasion he will discover feelings and ideas buried deep within himself, frightening ideas, for they are at odds with everything he has been taught to hold dear—and yet somehow they seem to him burning and blinding with truth—and he will try to see the shape of them, but they may yet be without form though he senses their power and is alternately attracted and repelled by their luminescence. Then he will haul them out of himself and stare at them in fear and astonishment—as does Moses now in the wilderness.

He has arrived at the conviction that the world that raised him is the horror—not his act of murder; that slaves, no matter how callous their behavior, are not like the flock he tends but are as human as the young Egyptians with whom he was schooled; and that slavery is an abomination and all the gods that support it are abominations. He will gaze at this truth that he has discovered at the source of his act of murder. Then, because he lives in a world that knows only of the divine as the source of new ideas, he will experience the religious correlate of that sudden vision. A sense of the inhumanity of slavery has as its religious correlate the feeling of the sanctity of all men and the divine imperative to free slaves. A sense of revulsion toward the visible and multiple gods who support such slavery has as its religious correlate the conviction that all such gods are false.

Perhaps I can be permitted the freedom of the novelist at this point. Moses lived for decades among the Midianites. There is no way we can penetrate the turns of his mind during that time except through an act of the imagination. With an awareness of doing violence to reality but with the hope of performing some service to clarity, I present this simplified and schematic account of his thoughts, straightening the curves and convolutions and making of decades of lost trails and new paths a single straight road.

In the world of that time the feeling that slavery is wrong can only have come from a god. What god? Certainly not the gods of Egypt. A Canaanite god? El and Baal haters of slavery? A new god then. A god who despises Egypt; a god who so detests the Two Lands that he will implant in a man the impulse to kill Egyptians on his behalf. Where is that god? How is he to be called? And why has he chosen me as the instrument of his action? Clearly Egypt is an abomination in his eyes—her preoccupation with death and tombs, her vast temples, her multitude of gods. He must be a god of life if he so abominates death; he must be a god of freedom if he so abominates slavery. But what is his name. . . ?

An Egyptian inscription of the fourteenth century B.C.E. refers to "a land of the Bedouin of YHW" near Edom, the region of the Midianites. The Bible preserves echoes of a deity named YHWH dwelling in that region: "YHWH came from Sinai; He shone upon them from Seir; He appeared from Mount Paran . . ." (Deuteronomy 33:2); "YHWH, when You came forth out of Seir, When you marched out of the field of Edom . . ." (Judges 5:4); "God comes from Teman, And the Holy One from Mount Paran" (Habakkuk 3:3). Paran and Seir are in the general region of the Midianites. Moses seems not to know that the place he has wandered to is sacred. Still some faint link with a Bedouin god is indicated. But whatever that deity might have meant to those Bedouin, it could have had little to do with the way he is to be conceived of and experienced now by Moses.

This is the point where the mind of a man might turn a corner and come upon new and luminous awareness—an act of creation as mysterious as life itself. Some call it an epiphany, a moment of revelation; others call it an inductive leap; still others describe it as the work of the imagination. It cannot be denied that members of our species have shown themselves able to feel or think their way across old thresholds—and that we still do not comprehend how this is accomplished.

In the case of Moses, the response to his questions has been handed down to us by tradition as the story of the burning bush. In the shimmering heat of the wilderness, beneath the burning sun, the leaves of a bush catch the fierce glow of the sunlight and appear to burst into flame. The bush glows and burns and is not consumed. The God he has been seeking is YHWH, the God of his father, the God of Abraham, Isaac, and Jacob. Yes, slavery is a horror. This God will rescue the Israelites and bring them to the land of Canaan. "I will send you to pharaoh and you shall free My people. . . ."

The reluctance of Moses to take on this task, and the literary form it is given, moves the dialogue into the bargaining arena of an oriental bazaar. God promises "various wonders." Moses is skeptical. God produces proof. Moses pleads poverty of speech. God becomes angry. Aaron, brother of Moses, will do the talking. Moses reluctantly accepts the call and leaves Midian—taking his wife and children with him, according to Exodus 4:20; leaving them behind, according to Exodus 18:2. Pharaoh Seti I and all who sought to kill Moses are now dead. But this apostle of God gives no indication of being overjoyed by the job he has been given.

Akhenaten had a vision and retreated into egocentric solitude. The vision died with him. Moses has a vision and now, with fear in his heart, makes of it a teaching with which to engage a hostile world.

The core of the burning bush experience is the call by God, which is at first resisted and then obeyed. It is an overpowering call to a mission. Future prophets will be similarly called, will resist, and obey. The name YHWH is derived from the Hebrew verb *hvh*, "to be"; perhaps for Moses the name takes on the meaning God of life, affirmation, existence; He who causes to be—the polar opposite to Egypt's world of tombs and death.

Aaron succeeds in convincing the elders of the Israel-

ites that God means to free them. But the first attempt
ends in disaster. The new pharaoh, Ramses II, has never
heard of the God of the Hebrews. "Moses and Aaron,
why do you distract the people from their tasks? Get to
your labors!" The Hebrews are deprived of straw for
making bricks. But the quota of bricks is not reduced.
The Israelites turn in anger upon Moses and Aaron. And
Moses turns to God. "Why did You select me? . . . You
have not delivered your people at all."

Now God speaks to Moses in a most curious way. "I
am YHWH. I appeared to Abraham, Isaac, and Jacob as El
Shaddai, but I did not make myself known to them by My
name YHWH. . . . Say to the Israelite people: I am YHWH,
I will free you from the burdens of the Egyptians . . .
through extraordinary chastisements. And I will take you
to be My people, and I will be your God. . . ."

There can be little doubt that a new beginning is being
made both here and in the story of the burning bush—a
beginning between the God YHWH, His apostle Moses,
and the Israelites. This is the start of the history of Israel.
Occurrences of the name YHWH in the patriarchal narratives are anachronisms. This was already sensed by the
Jewish medieval commentator Ibn Ezra and alluded to by
him in his words on Exodus 6:3. "The patriarchs did not
reach the height of merit that would have enabled them to
attain to the Name in the same manner as did Moses,
whom God knew face to face and who was able to alter
the history of the world. . . ." We are now in the age of
the God of Moses, YHWH, a passionate God who loathes
Egypt, who out of love will redeem a slave people with
"various wonders" and "extraordinary chastisements,"
and who will set into motion a chain of events that will
result in the emergence of a new civilization in the Fertile
Crescent—the only civilization of that world that survives
today and continues to affect the lives of a good portion
of our species.

When it came time to put into final literary form the
nature of the events that made possible the slave escape—something of a chaotic nature must have occurred
in Egypt for the escape to have succeeded—it was written

that the Nile turned to blood; frogs, vermin, and wild beasts swarmed over the land; boils afflicted men and beasts (this is absent from the lists of plagues in Psalms 78 and 105); animals and crops were destroyed; the sun no longer shone; first-born children were slain. A multitude of slaves made good their escape into the Red Land and, at the Sea of Reeds, miraculously evaded pursuing Egyptian chariots—the first mass slave escape we know of in history.

We know of it only from the Bible. Egyptian scribes tell us nothing of such an escape. It is not likely that they would have felt any need to record it.

The escape seems not to have affected the completion of Per-Ramses. A student scribe writes ecstatically of the city to his master: "I have arrived at House-of-Ramses-Beloved-of-Amon and have found it flourishing exceedingly. . . . Its field is full of all good things. . . . Its ponds are full of fishes and its lakes of birds. . . . One rejoices when one dwells in it. . . ."

But about the flight of those slaves, about their success in eluding a pursuing Egyptian force, about these first birth pangs of a future nation through its experience with extraordinary events rather than with rivers and floods—about all this the land of the Nile is silent.

# CANAAN

## The Rival Covenants

They were a pitiful rabble, a mass of frightened, quarrelsome Asiatics wandering through the merciless sand and stone wilderness somewhere east of the Nile valley. Their ranks were comprised of descendants of the sons of Jacob. Israelites they are abruptly called, beginning with the last two chapters of Genesis. The transition from Jacob to Israel is unclear. Was Israel a fourth patriarch? We do not know. The suffix "ite," *ites* in Greek, means adherent of a party, member of a tribe. Together with these Israelites came a mixed multitude of other Asiatics —Canaanites, Hapiru, members of various Bedouin tribes, possibly some Hittites and Mesopotamians.

We are told there were among them more than six hundred thousand males capable of bearing arms—but that is perhaps a flourish a people permits itself when it remembers a glorious and terrifying moment in its early history. A force of that size, even if poorly armed, would have had little to fear from the chariots of Ramses II; and the total, including women, children, and the aged, would have numbered more than two million souls and taken up much of the wilderness through which it wandered.

How many slaves made that escape? Three thousand? Thirty thousand? We shall probably never know. There were enough to bring to the event and its aftermath so resonant a response that out of it a people was fashioned.

We are also told that they traveled from the Delta to the Sea of Reeds (not the Red Sea; the Hebrew words *Yam Suf* mean Sea of Reeds), then on through the desert of Shur to Rephidim, where they fought a bitter battle with marauding Amalekites who saw them as easy prey.

After defeating the Amalekites, they journeyed to Mount Sinai.

They did not go directly up the coastal road to Canaan—The Way of the Land of the Philistines, as the Biblical writer calls it, directing himself to an audience centuries after the event when the Philistines were indeed in the land; they were not yet there during the slave escape. The coastal road—the Via Maris—had been heavliy fortified by Pharaoh Seti I. We do not know the actual route the runaway slaves traveled. The stopping points mentioned in the Bible were temporary encampments whose locations cannot be identified today.

If they journeyed north, they turned toward the coast of the Mediterranean and left the chariots of the Egyptians mired on a sand bar in Lake Manzala west of Port Said or in Lake Sirbonis, today's Bardawil. I have seen Bardawil and watched the narrow strip of earth that separates the lake from the sea vanish as east winds sent the Mediterranean rolling across it. Reeds grow near both lakes. To have been saved in this manner from those chariots would have been a most extraordinary event indeed in the eyes of the terrified people running for their lives on a narrow sand bar between two bodies of water. Then they turned south and east toward Mount Sinai, possibly today's Jebel Halal, near the large oasis of Kadesh-barnea, which is about fifty miles south of Beer-sheba.

If they journeyed south when they left Egypt, they turned toward the Gulf of Suez where about six feet of water mark the difference between low and high tide; but there are no reeds in that region today. After crossing the Sea of Reeds—perhaps the narrow northernmost finger of the gulf—they journeyed southward along the eastern shore deep into the Sinai Peninsula to a mountain which is now called Jebel Musa. A Byzantine monastery hugs the eastern slope of that mountain. The Greek Orthodox monks are bearded and kind. The mountain is a pilgrimage site. I climbed it early one morning, starting in darkness and swatching the golden disk of the sun slide over the shoulder of a nearby peak as I went carefully along the steep path. Later I stood on the level top, no more than about sixty square feet of stone beneath my feet and a twenty-foot-high boulder at one end of the pinnacle, and gazed at the clear blue sky and the expanse of sandy valley below and the granite mountains all around and a vast yellow desert off in the distant east. You can feel lifted out of yourself in such a moment, raised above the world—but you are sobered by the thought that this mountain may not be Mount Sinai, despite the assurances of the friendly monks who sell you postcards after you have made it back down to the monastery.

If the fleeing slaves took a central route, they traveled almost due east from Lower Egypt to the Bitter Lakes, a body of water that lies between the Delta and the Gulf of Suez. Reeds protrude from the moist shore, and a narrow muddy rise can be seen at times dividing the water just above the surface—enough to enable a crossing by foot and to bog down the wheels of a chariot. Mount Sinai might be the tall peak called Jebel Sinn-Bishr about thirty miles southeast of the city of Suez. The region of the Bitter Lakes is where, in another time, Sinuhe the Egyptian lay dying of thirst after having fled from his homeland, and was saved by an Asiatic chieftain.

About 1280 B.C.E., shortly before or after the slave escape, the Egyptians and Hittites signed a treaty—a covenant of nonaggression in which they vowed to respect each other's borders. We also have covenants or peace treaties between the Hittites and people they succeeded in conquering. These are called suzerainty treaties—agreements entered into between a political overlord and a dependent state.

During the time of the slave escape, the Egyptians and Hittites were the two major powers in the central and western regions of the Fertile Crescent; between them they dominated and pillaged much of the then known world. Raised as an Egyptian prince in the palace of Pharaoh Seti I, Moses would have known of the Hittite suzerainty treaties.

Treaties are as old as history. A city-state could enforce its law upon its citizens through threats of punishment or exile. People living together in community depended for their existence upon the fulfilling of contracts or covenants, upon law. "When a citizen has committed robbery and has been caught," reads the Code of Hammurabi, "that citizen shall be put to death." And, "When a citizen has had intercourse with his daughter, they shall make that citizen leave the city." To be sent away from your city was to be deprived of communal protection and to be made an outcast, a Hapiru.

But what of crime between city-states? What of war and peace, diplomacy, international relations? These were regulated by treaties or covenants.

In some languages of the ancient Near East, the term for a treaty or a covenant was, literally translated, oaths and bonds. Treaties contained two sections: a promise to do or observe something, and an oath which was intended to bring the vengeance of the gods upon the one who broke the promise. Sumerian treaties dating from about 2500 B.C.E. contain these sections.

The Hittite suzerainty treaties were almost invariably made up of the following parts, not always in the same order: (1) the preamble; (2) the historical prologue; (3) the demands or stipulations; (4) provisions for the deposit of the text and for its periodic public reading; (5) a list of divine witnesses to the treaty; (6) blessings and curses.

The decipherment of the Hittite texts yielded samples of their suzerainty treaties. And those treaties have been shown to have remarkable bearing upon certain crucial sections of the Bible.

PREAMBLE. "These are the words of the sun-god Mursilis, the great king, the king of the Hatti land, the valiant. . . ." It is the Hittite ruler who is the "great king." The one offering the treaty, the Hittite king, states immediately that he is superior in rank to the one who is expected to accept it.

HISTORICAL PROLOGUE. "Aziras was the grandfather of you, Duppi-Tessub. He rebelled against my father, but submitted again to my father. . . . When your father died, in accordance with your father's word I did not drop you. . . . I sought after you. To be sure, although you were sick and ailing, I, the sun-god, put you in the place of your father and took your brothers and sisters and the Amurru land in oath for you." It was no small matter for this ailing prince to have been made king in place of his ambitious brothers. The benevolent acts performed by the Hittite king for the vassal are greatly emphasized. It is more than likely that true events are recalled; only such events would bring about the sense of profound obligation on the part of the vassal which this section was intended to evoke. The vassal had no right to expect those benefits; but he received them anyway. Hence he cannot escape being obligated to the superior power. The Hittite king refers to himself as "I" and to the vassal as "thou." This treaty form expresses a personal relationship rather than a formal statement of law which would have been put impersonally—perhaps "the king" and "the vassal" instead of "I" and "thou."

DEMANDS OR STIPULATIONS. This section is a detailed statement of the obligations which the king imposes upon the vassal, and which the vassal accepts. Some of these obligations prohibit relationships between the vassal and any foreign power other than the Hittites: "Do not turn your eyes to anyone else!" A call to arms by the Hittite king must be answered immediately and "with all your heart" by the vassal. The vassal must trust the king absolutely and without hesitation. The vassal must never utter an evil word against the king; such an act is the beginning of rebellion and a breach of covenant. "If anyone utters words unfriendly toward the king of the Hatti land before you, Duppi-Tessub, you shall not withhold his name from the king. . . ."

DEPOSIT OF THE TEXT AND PUBLIC READING. The treaty was sacred. It was to be deposited in the sanctuary or shrine of the leading god of king and vassal. Its contents were to be made known to the vassal populace. "At regular intervals shall they read it in the presence of the king of the Mitanni land and in the presence of the sons of the Hurri country." It was placed in the shrines so that the gods would read it and remember its provisions and the oaths sworn before them.

THE DIVINE WITNESSES. People served as witnesses to contracts; the gods served as witnesses to international covenants—Hittite and vassal gods. "At the conclusion of this treaty we have called the gods to be assembled and the gods of the contracting parties to be present, to listen and to serve as witnesses. . . . All the gods and goddesses of the Hatti land, the gods and goddesses of the country of Kizzuwatna, the mountains, the rivers, the Tigris and the Euphrates, heaven and earth, the winds and the clouds. . . ."

BLESSINGS AND CURSES. The treaty is sacred law. The gods will curse and wreak vengeance upon the vassal who breaks it, and bring blessings upon the vassal who upholds it. And the Hittite king will march against the vassal with a punishing army—perhaps as a rod of divine chastisement, though this is left unsaid. "The words of the treaty and the oath that are inscribed on this tablet—should Duppi-Tessub not know these words of the treaty and the oath, may these gods of the oath destroy Duppi-Tessub together with his person, his wife, his son, his grandson, his house, his land and together with everything that he owns. . . ."

The vassal would take an oath to uphold the covenant. This oath was part of a ceremony in which the parties ate together, drank together, smeared oil on themselves, or sacrificed a young donkey. The vassal might drink water in order to have the curse enter his body. Most often an animal was cut up, and the one who took the oath was identified by a gesture of some kind—perhaps a finger across a throat—with the bloody pieces. May he be cut up as this animal is cut up if he breaks his oath. . . .

Sometime around the year 1280 B.C.E., in the late spring, the rabble of Asiatic slaves—six weeks' journey out of Egypt—arrived at the foot of a mountain somewhere in the wilderness of Sinai. There they encamped, and waited. The mountain, we are told, was wreathed in a dense cloud.

A cloud obscures the mountain; words obscure the event. The narrative of the Revelation on Mount Sinai is a labyrinth of dark passages that wind through abrupt turns and lurch across sudden chasms. We proceed with increasing bewilderment. The Bible seems helpless before the event, at a loss to shape it with words. We are in the presence of either the uncanny or a ruin of failed literary creativity, or perhaps both.

What are we to make of the narrative?

The people are encamped at the foot of a cloud-covered mountain in the barren wilderness of Sinai. Moses climbs the mountain. "You have seen what I did to the Egyptians," God says to him, "how I bore you on eagles' wings and brought you to Me. Now, then, if you will obey Me faithfully and keep My covenant, you shall be My treasured possession among all the peoples. Indeed, all the earth is Mine, but you shall be to Me a kingdom of priests and a holy nation."

Moses goes down the mountain and repeats the words of God to the elders of the people. All the people answer as one, saying, "All that the Lord has spoken we will do!"

Moses climbs back up the mountain and tells God what the people have said. God informs him that the people must now be purified; clothes must be washed; they must abstain from sexual relations. On the third day "the Lord will come down, in the sight of all the people, on Mount Sinai."

The people are warned not to touch the mountain. Then they are told to come up to the mountain when the ram's horn sounds a long blast.

On the third day the mountain, covered in boiling smoke, trembles violently. The horns blare louder and louder. Moses speaks. God responds in thunder and comes down to the mountain. God calls to Moses from the top of the mountain. Moses goes up to Him. God tells Moses to go down and warn the people not to "break through to the Lord to gaze, lest many of them perish." Moses tells God that the people cannot come up to Mount Sinai, "for You warned me, saying, 'Set bounds upon the mountain and sanctify it.'" God then orders Moses to bring Aaron up the mountain; but we are told nothing more about this.

Moses will climb up and down the mountain many times. The precise number of times remains obscure.

Moses now descends and speaks to the people. The narrative then continues, "God spoke all these words, saying,"—and the Decalogue follows.

Moses returns to the mountain and disappears into the thick cloud. The admonition against the making of graven images, which was spoken in the Decalogue, is now repeated by God; added to it is a brief passage regarding the proper construction of an altar.

A lengthy law code follows, more suited to sedentary village life than wilderness wandering. Scholars call it the Covenant Code and consider it the earliest law collection of the Israelites. Opinions differ as to whether or not it is to be included, together with the Decalogue, in the content of the Revelation at Sinai, or is to be dated in the desert, conquest, and premonarchy period, sometime between 1260 and 1000 B.C.E. The humane treatment accorded the slave and the stranger in this code forms a stark contrast to the experience in Egypt. The structure and wording of the code ("When a man . . . he . . .") have much in common with the codes of Mesopotamia, especially that of Hammurabi. But there are singular differences in content: unlike the Hammurabi code, the Covenant Code does not punish any crime against property by death; unlike the law codes of Assyria and the Hittites, the Covenant Code does not allow any act of murder to be paid for in property or by substituting the life of another man for that of the murderer. It is not possible for the murderer to avoid the death penalty. In Hittite law, a murderer may be pardoned by the king. No such provision exists in Biblical law. "Whoever sheds the blood of a man, by man shall his blood be shed; for in the image of God was man made," reads Genesis 9:6. Cuneiform findings show that Mesopotamian law was linked to the value of property, the strength and wealth of the community; life is replaceable by sufficient goods. In Biblical law the basic assumption is the infinite worth of human life. God is the sole author of law and of life. Hence the demand of the death penalty for murder.

The Biblical recognition of a slave as an individual with rights, though he still lacks the status of a free man, has no parallel in the laws of Mesopotamia. The preoccupation of the Covenant Code with social and moral values sets it off sharply from all of ancient Near Eastern law. It is in most ways the reverse of the codes of its own time and a clear response to the remembered Delta years.

At the conclusion of the code, God requests that Aaron and the elders of the people join Moses on the mountain; they are permitted to bow low from a distance; only Moses may stand near God. The people may not come up at all.

Moses repeats to the people the commandments of God. The people respond with one voice. "All the things that the Lord has commanded we will do!" Moses then writes down all the commands of God.

The following morning he sets up an altar at the foot of the mountain. Delegates selected from the people sacrifice bulls upon it. Then Moses reads the covenant aloud to all the people. And the people answer, "All that the Lord has spoken we will do and obey!" Moses takes some of the blood of the sacrifice and dashes it upon the people, saying, "This is the blood of the covenant which the Lord now makes with you concerning all these commands."

Then Moses, Aaron, and the elders climb up the mountain; "and they saw the God of Israel: under His feet there was the likeness of a pavement of sapphire, like the very sky for purity. Yet He did not raise His hand against the leaders of the Israelites; they beheld God, and they ate and drank."

Then God orders Moses to go back up the mountain for "the stone tablets with the teachings and the commandments which I have inscribed to instruct them." Moses climbs the mountain—with his attendant Joshua. For six days the mountain is concealed by the cloud. We are told nothing more of Joshua. Moses remains on the mountain forty days and forty nights.

There follows a lengthy passage containing the instructions of God about the building of a portable sanctuary and an ark. Moses is told to deposit in the ark the Pact which God will give him. He is further instructed in the making of sacral vestments for Aaron and his sons, who are now advanced into the priesthood.

God then gives the two tablets of the Pact to Moses, "stone tablets inscribed with the finger of God"—tablets which Moses shatters in a fit of rage when he discovers that, during his absence, the people with the help of Aaron fashioned a golden calf, which they are now worshiping. He orders those still faithful to God to take up their swords and slay as many of the reveling calf-worshipers as they can, though he himself had earlier argued before God on behalf of the people and prevented God from destroying them in His wrath over the calf.

There is a tent in the camp called the Tent of Meeting. Moses has it pitched outside the camp. Whenever Moses wishes to speak to God he enters the tent. "The Lord would speak to Moses face to face, as one man speaks to another. . . ."

A conversation is reported between Moses and God, apparently on the mountain, for to Moses' request, "Let me behold Your Presence," God replies, "Station yourself on the rock and, as My Presence passes by, I will put you in a cleft of the rock and shield you with My hand, until I have passed by. Then I will take My hand away and You will see My back; but My face must not be seen."

Moses carves two new tablets of stone and returns to the mountain. God says to him, "I hereby make a covenant. Before all your people I will work such wonders as have not been wrought on all the earth or in any nation. . . . Beware of making a covenant with the inhabitants of the land against which you are advancing. . . . No, you must tear down their altars, smash their pillars, and cut down their sacred posts; for you must not worship any other god. . . . You shall not make molten gods for yourselves. . . ."

Finally we are told that Moses was "with the Lord forty days and forty nights; he ate no bread and drank no water; and he wrote down on the tablets the terms of the covenant, the Ten Commandments."

When Moses returns from the mountain his face is so radiant with light the people cannot gaze upon him. . . .

Indeed, what are we to make of this narrative?

How do you relate to an invisible God who has saved you from slavery and avenging chariots? That God acted not because of any particular merit on your part but out of His own goodness. Your cries stirred Him to compassion. Clearly you are deeply obligated to Him. What form should that obligation take?

How do you mold a rabble into a people? You have with you in the burning wilderness an undisciplined host of recently escaped slaves quarreling over food and water, restless, marching together fearfully for mutual protection—especially after the encounter with the vulturous Amalekites. How do you link them together? What form should that binding take?

The response to the event of freedom from Egypt was the Mosaic covenant—the suzerainty treaty of Sinai. We have no way of knowing if the response was developed over a period of time—which does not depreciate its radical originality—or immediately and spontaneously at the mysterious mountain. Nowhere in Jewish sources is there any alternative to the traditional belief that the events at that mountain were supernatural. The entire wilderness period was seen as a time of extraordinary acts, wondrous moments charged with numinous power—the birthing time of the Israelite people. At the center of that time, set within it like a flame, is the drama at Mount Sinai. There, under the leadership of a man called Moses, a rabble covenanted together to give expression to their gratitude to the God who had saved them. With Moses serving as the intermediary between YHWH and the people, or as the divinely inspired author—the difference between the two views is vast, and we must each of us decide how we see this event—the covenant took the form of a suzerainty treaty. There must have been quarrels; covenants were not lightly entered into by clans and tribes. Moses prevailed. After all, the God YHWH had fulfilled His promise. He had delivered them. Moses went off to be alone with his God.

Did the people afterward remember those tedious scenarios so often called upon by scholars, volcanic eruptions—such activity still occurred in that region in the middle of the thirteenth century B.C.E.—or a sudden dark boiling of thunderclouds, strange for this time of year in that wilderness? Are the cloud, the fire, the thunder, a dramatic touch of a later teller of the event? We shall probably never know.

Moses returned with the text of the covenant. Written in what language? With which signs? Hieroglyphics on stone? Amorite in cuneiform? A dialect of Aramean? Again, we shall probably never know.

The text was the Decalogue—a suzerainty treaty, with YHWH as suzerain and the people as vassal:

PREAMBLE. "God spoke all these words, saying. . . ."

HISTORICAL PROLOGUE. "I am the Lord your God who brought you out of the land of Egypt. . . ."

DEMANDS OR STIPULATIONS. "You shall have no other gods besides Me. You shall not. . . ."

DEPOSIT OF THE TEXT AND PUBLIC READING. There are no provisions for this in the Decalogue itself. But later, in Exodus 25:16, we read, "And deposit in the ark the Pact which I will give you." Exodus 40:20 reads, "He took the Pact and placed it in the ark. . . ." In Deuteronomy 10:5, Moses is reported to have written, "Then I left and went down from the mountain, and I deposited the tablets in the ark that I had made, as the Lord had commanded me; and there they remain."

THE DIVINE WITNESSES. There are no other gods besides YHWH—this is a fundamental transformation in thought and belief, and an abrupt turn by our species toward a new horizon. YHWH is beyond man and nature, yet compassionate and caring for His people, concerned with the welfare of slaves and strangers. I have found no way of connecting this new vision of man and his relationship to the cosmos through a chain of evolutionary causality, a link of logic with past ideas. It is an epiphany, an inductive leap of extraordinary seminality, or a vaulting of the imagination—call it what you wish. The people at the foot of that mountain, as well as millennia of their offspring, believed that the covenant had been given to them by YHWH. And neither YHWH nor His people could have other gods as witnesses. Still, in Deuteronomy 30:19, heaven and earth are invoked as natural witnesses to a later covenant code, "I call heaven and earth to witness against you this day"; and, in Deuteronomy 32:1, the Song of Moses begins, "Give ear, O heavens, let me speak; Let the earth hear the words I utter!" We remember the words in the Hittite treaty, "All the gods and goddesses of the Hatti land . . . the mountains, the rivers . . . heaven and earth. . . ." Mesopotamian treaties carried similar terminology long after the Hittites had disappeared.

BLESSINGS AND CURSES. Perhaps the words "I the Lord your God am an impassioned God, visiting the guilt of the fathers upon the children . . ." constitute a form of curse. The covenant code in Deuteronomy 30:19 reads, "I have put before you life and death, blessing and curse."

THE FORMAL OATH. "We will do and obey!"

THE SOLEMN CEREMONY. The sacrifice of the bulls; the sprinkling of the blood. And the brief scene in which the elders "beheld God, and they ate and drank."

The clans covenanted to become vassals of YHWH and to be joined to one another by a sanctified treaty. They retained the freedom to govern their inner lives. No clan had dominion over another.

The first five commandments are unique to Biblical religion and are present at its beginnings in the wilderness in Sinai. There are differences of view regarding their precise enumeration. The second set of five ("You shall not murder . . .") are common to other ancient Near Eastern civilizations. "I have not been covetous. . . . I have not stolen. . . . I have not killed men. . . . I have not committed adultery," reads the Book of the Dead, the mortuary text that was used throughout Egypt when the young prince Moses was educated in the palace of Pharaoh Seti I and the people now at Mount Sinai were slaves.

We do not know if the Decalogue that has come down to us in the text of Exodus was actually the one transmitted by Moses or was given final form in a later time. It differs in some respects from the Decalogue in Deuteronomy 5:2-18. Both Decalogues may have had their origins in a third, older, briefer version suggested by scholars: "These are the words of YHWH: I am YHWH your God who brought you out of the land of Egypt. You shall have no other gods besides Me. You shall not make yourself a graven image. You shall not take the name of YHWH in vain. Remember the Sabbath day. Honor your father and mother. You shall not murder. You shall not commit adultery. You shall not steal. You shall not bear false witness. You shall not covet."

Nor do we know how the Decalogue was transmitted through the generations until it was given final literary form in the narrative of the Revelation we find in the

Book of Exodus. There is so much we do not know. . . .
The rabbinic commentators struggled to reconcile the various passages. Some moved passages from one section of
the text to another. There was among them considerable
discussion and disagreement as they attempted to penetrate this sacred moment of Israelite history.

The writer who gave final literary shape to the event at
Sinai found himself unwilling or unable to discard any of
the variant traditions he had before him. He treated them
as the writers of the final version of the Bible did the legal
texts. All regional legal traditions that were not pagan
were included—to give the widest latitude to law and to
free the writer of the ominous responsibility of choosing
which tribal or regional law was right or wrong in the
eyes of God. No attempt was made to smooth over the
rough edges of diverse legal traditions by editing the text,
as was often done with narrative texts. Similarly, all versions of the Revelation were included with no effort at
blending—to permit and make valid the widest range of
response to that momentous event.

The construction of the sanctuary and the ark, the
making of the sacral vestments and the advancement of
Aaron and his sons to the priesthood—these were basic
elements in the early history of the Israelites. Surely they
originated at Sinai! The writer, working with narratives
and documents at hand—and only vaguely can scholars
perceive some of those early documents through the finished ones; and how they contend among themselves
about their findings, as do all serious scholars of any
people's origins—the writer placed those narratives too
into his word sculpture of the Revelation, the version we
have today, whose date of composition remains unknown.

There was no doubt a tradition that Aaron too climbed
up the mountain; the writer included it in his narrative.
There was a tradition that Joshua and the elders were on
the mountain; that too was added. Aaron, Joshua, the
elders—these were figures of great authority, leaders of
the people together with Moses; certainly they participated in that moment of fire and thunder when YHWH revealed Himself to His people and bound them to Him by
an eternal covenant whose form was that of a suzerainty
treaty and whose content, most particularly its first sec-

tions, was directly the creation of—YHWH? Moses? The people? All three, at Sinai? All three during the desert wandering? Later history? All the traditions available to the writer connected that covenant to Sinai, and that was the way he wrote it, giving them all equal validity. What right had he to choose among them which was true and which was not? He offered us not a straight narrative but a prismatic, almost surrealistic one filled with splintered, uneven, broken sequences, repetitions, elisions, contradictions, attempting with words to trap the elusive heart of the event, to convey somehow its infinitely mysterious dimensions—and probably failing, as I am failing now in my attempt to describe his effort. That is all I can write at present of that long moment in the wilderness.

From Mount Sinai the covenanted families and clans journeyed to the oasis of Kadesh-barnea at the southern tip of the land of Canaan.

They traveled as donkey nomads through a great and terrible wilderness of rugged mountains, crossing valleys bounded by immense granite cliffs. Often the floor of a valley would be littered with stones and boulders torn loose from the hills by winter rains and washed down by torrents that formed sudden rivers—each a charging Tigris or Euphrates, rushing with enormous power through the crevasses, gouging the hills and gullying the earth of the valleys. It was late summer when they set out. A dry relentless heat burned up the days. The sun carved the landscape into geometrical patterns of light and shadow. The nights were chilling. There was little water. They arrived at the oasis of Kadesh-barnea, with its sweet springs and fertile plain, eleven days after they left Mount Sinai, as Deuteronomy 1:2 seems to indicate. Numbers 33:37-38 informs us that they arrived at Kadesh about forty years after they left Egypt. The wilderness trek was understandably the source of varying traditions.

That was a time when all along the fringes of the Fertile Crescent nomadic tribes from the infinite sand oceans of the Arabian and Syrian deserts were growing increasingly restless. Population growth? The insatiable lure of settled cities and green earth working upon the sun-glazed eyes of hungry Bedouins? We do not know. Tribes had begun to move northward—Arameans, they are called. A thousand years earlier another wave of seminomadic tribes had engulfed the Fertile Crescent and swallowed the world of Sumer, Akkad, Canaan. Those had been the Amorites. Abraham and his family had entered Canaan in the wake of that Amorite movement. Now the Amorites lived in settled cities on green earth. And the Arameans had begun to press forward. In the midst of this Aramean restiveness were the people now encamped at Kadesh-barnea, the clans of the Israelites.

They lived a seminomadic existence, worshiping their God, pasturing their flocks—as Bedouins do to this day. They gazed hungrily at the rich land that had been promised them by their new God. Spies were sent out. An attack was launched, an effort to penetrate the land from the south. It was met by the Amorite inhabitants of the city of Arad. Led by their king, they came out against the inept Israelites like bees. The battle was a disaster. The Israelites returned to Kadesh-barnea, buried their dead, probably in crude graves covered with a few stones—the same practice exists today among the Bedouins; and they waited.

It is not clear how long they remained in that oasis. But there is little doubt that the fertile plain of Kadesh-barnea served as the assembly point for the clans and the nurturing ground for the early institutions of Israelite civilization—with the exception of the monarchy. Here, with the wilderness around them and the springs and pasturelands enabling them to live, the covenanted rabble slowly shaped itself—not without bitter quarrels when water became scarce even in that oasis or an occasional harsh testing of the authority of Moses—into a clan and tribal confederacy, loosely organized but dedicated to the worship of the God who had redeemed them from slavery and whose vassal they had willingly become. Here, in the person of Moses, was developed the paradigm of the Israelite prophet, the individual through whom God speaks to and acts upon man. The sanctuary; the ark; the priesthood; the tribe of Levi dedicated to assist the priests and guard the sanctuary; forms of worship; festivals and sacrifices—these were the beginnings of ancient Israel in this oasis fifty miles south of Beersheba.

They were probably joined by outside families and clans which they absorbed. Their ranks grew. Under the leadership of Moses, who no doubt remembered his military training as an Egyptian prince—how many years ago? forty? sixty?—they were organized into military units according to clans. The same restlessness that had seized the Aramean world now descended upon them. They left Kadesh-barnea and commenced a trek through the wilderness. A long wandering is part of the saga of many peoples' beginnings.

They wandered south and east. At one point early in the wandering some of the clans left the main body and struck northward along the trade route, the King's Highway, that ran through the still-unformed lands east of the Jordan. They encountered no difficulty along the way, according to Deuteronomy 2:2-14; their resting camps have been identified with sites inside the territory of Moab. These clans too would later insist they had been led by Moses. That is why the Bible contains two accounts of the Israelite march through Transjordan. It is not known which clans they were or when they entered Canaan.

The other clans remained with Moses. When they felt themselves prepared to attempt the conquest of Canaan, enough time had passed for other wandering tribes east of the Jordan to have formed lands of their own whose borders were now heavily protected. The Edomites came out against them in force. The Israelites shied away. Then Aaron died and was buried in Mount Hor on the boundary of the land of Edom. Miriam sister of Moses had died years before and lay buried in Kadesh-barnea.

According to Numbers 20:17-21 and 21:4-11, the wandering Israelite clans circled the lands of Edom and Moab, fearful of contact. But north of Moab was an Amorite land under a weak king with a small band of professional soldiers. In their first battle since Arad, the Israelites fought and defeated the king of Heshbon. Then they fought and defeated the king who ruled the land north of Heshbon, King Og of Bashan. They now possessed pasturelands, on which some of the clans chose to settle, and a staging ground for the invasion of Canaan. They stood poised on the eastern bank of the Jordan. The year was about 1240 B.C.E.

Then Moses died.

He was buried somewhere east of the Jordan in the plains of Moab. His tomb is unknown. Some years later, about 1230 B.C.E., Ramses II died, an old man. He was mummified and entombed. His mummy still exists today. In the spring of 1977 of our era it was returned to Egypt by French museum specialists who had been asked to cleanse it of its garden of fungus growths.

The Israelites mourned Moses for thirty days. Centuries later, in the period of the monarchy, an Israelite writer would conclude the Book of Deuteronomy with the words, "Never again did there arise in Israel a prophet like Moses, whom the Lord singled out face to face, for the various signs and portents that the Lord sent him to display in the land of Egypt, against Pharaoh and all his courtiers and his whole country, and for all the great might and awesome power that Moses displayed before all Israel."

Then the period of mourning came to an end. The Israelites, led by Joshua, marched across the narrow Jordan and invaded the land of Canaan. It was the season of spring. They marched as the army of YHWH.

So we are told in the Book of Joshua. They marched, fought, conquered, settled—swiftly, with ease, aided by their God.

Today Jericho is a languid city without fortifying walls, a viridian mirage in a hot sandy plain not far from the bluish haze of the Dead Sea in the south and the pale brown hills leading to Jerusalem in the west. The Bible informs us that it had a significant stone wall in the time of Joshua, for we are told of subterfuge, marching, trumpeting, and then "the wall fell down flat." Populace and cattle were put to the sword. The city was burned. Looting was forbidden. The city was proscribed and dedicated to YHWH as an offering of the first fruits of conquest.

The Bible also tells us that Joshua marched inland and destroyed the city of Ai. He slew its inhabitants, looted it, burned it to the ground, and impaled its king on a stake.

Then strangers in tattered clothes suddenly appeared in the Israelite camp, claiming to be from a distant land.

They had heard of the might of the Israelites and their God; they were eager to "cut a covenant"—the Hebrew term *lichrot brit* is used for treaties between man and man, and man and God—with the fearsome Israelites and to bring themselves under their protection. The covenant was made. Three days later the Israelites discovered them to have been Gibeonites, inhabitants of four cities, one of them Gibeon, all in a crucial region in their path of conquest. They honored the covenant but made of the Gibeonites "hewers of wood and drawers of water" in retribution for their deceit.

Then five southern Canaanite cities formed an alliance and marched against the Gibeonites. They wished to capture Gibeon, punish the Gibeonites for their alliance with the Israelites, and at the same time protect the south from the Israelite advance. Joshua, honoring his covenant with the Gibeonites, swept down upon the Canaanites after a grueling night march to Gibeon from his base camp at Gilgal near Jericho. Apparently he feared he would not make it in time for his planned dawn attack; hence the exclamation, "Sun, stand still upon Gibeon; Moon, in the valley of Ayalon!" Gibeon is in the east near Jerusalem, and the valley of Ayalon is in the west not far from the Mediterranean coast. Since the sun does not set in the east, Joshua was asking it not to rise, to let the moon remain over Ayalon so he could complete the night march to Gibeon and launch his early dawn attack. It is not clear to me how later writers and commentators confused the geography of the land and turned the words of Joshua into a late afternoon utterance.

The battle ended in total disaster for the Canaanites, who went fleeing for their lives along the mountain passes. The five kings of the Canaanite cities who had formed the alliance were discovered in a cave. They were slain by Joshua; their bodies were impaled on five stakes. As in the case of the king of Ai, the corpses were taken down in the evening and buried.

Surprise attacks, clever stratagems, careful planning, the ruse of drawing combatants out of their city into an Israelite infantry ambush, avoiding confrontation with the deadly chariots of the Canaanites—this was the war waged by Joshua and the Israelite clans he led, according to the Bible. They were aided by the inability of the chronically suspicious and independent Canaanite kings to form permanent alliances among themselves. It was a brutal territorial war. The Israelites wanted land—as had the Amorites one thousand years earlier around the time of Abraham. The twelfth chapter of the Book of Joshua lists thirty-one Canaanite cities captured by the Israelites under the leadership of Joshua.

"So Joshua took the whole land," the writer of the eleventh chapter of the Book of Joshua assures us, "according to all that the Lord spoke to Moses; and Joshua gave it for an inheritance to Israel according to their divisions by tribes. And the land had rest from war."

But there are puzzles. Tribal movements were rarely neat and orderly. Sometimes tribes would penetrate peacefully into a new area, then inundate it slowly in a rising tide of population increase. Most often, however, such movements took the form of waves of armed predators who came to steal and to stay. If they had the power, they succeeded; if not, they were driven off. If there was any morality in such rearrangements of human geography, it came from the human need to put an end to wandering, to work the earth in order to feed one's family, and to utilize one's newly acquired sedentary security against the preying of other wanderers. But what of the immorality involved in the horrors inflicted upon the previous population? Tribal movements, like earthquakes, appear to have no anxieties about their reputation. The Israelite conquests were reduced to swift, tidy battles by some writers who were far removed from the grime, confusion, and naked brutality of the events.

But the more sober-minded writer of the material that is now the thirteenth chapter of the Book of Joshua has God say to Joshua, "You are old and well stricken in years and there remains yet very much land to be possessed. . . ." The list that follows is long.

There is an additional puzzle. The Book of Judges—the work immediately following Joshua in the Bible—describes an entirely independent act of conquest by the tribes of Judah and Simeon, who crossed the Jordan north of Jericho, defeated a Canaanite army at Bezek, a town situated between Shechem and Beth-shean, then advanced southward to the hill country between Jerusalem and Hebron—and captured cities whose conquest the Book of Joshua attributes to Joshua. The tribe of Simeon settled in the sandy region of Beersheba. A number of clans that were possibly related to or were later absorbed by Judah—the Kenites, Calebites, Kenazites—came up from the wilderness in the south, took the region of Arad and probably also Hebron and Debir. Judah conquered the hill country and some of the coastal foothills south of Jerusalem but "could not drive out the inhabitants of the valley, because they had chariots of iron." Joshua is not mentioned in these conquests by Judah.

There are still more puzzles. Archaeologists inform us that Jericho had no stone wall at the time of the conquest; in fact, it was not a city at all but a small settlement with perhaps a mud wall; no trace of that level of the town's history remains for archaeologists to sift through. Rain and wind have erased all signs of the Israelite battle that was fought there. The stone wall that we see in ancient Jericho today is from an older time, millennia before the coming of the Israelites. Where then is the origin of the marching, the trumpeting, the tumbling wall? Tribal tales? The invention of a writer who saw the ruin of the old wall and attributed it to Joshua and miracles? We do not know.

The city of Ai was burned to the ground—but not by Israelites. Archaeologists tell us that Ai had been a ruin—the word Ai means ruin—for more than a thousand years before the coming of the Israelites. But Bethel, a mile or so to the west, was destroyed during the assumed period of the Israelite invasion by a fire that left several feet of debris and ash. Perhaps later tribal traditions simply attributed both destructions to Joshua. Again, we do not know.

Archaeologists further inform us that a vast upheaval shook the land during the period historians believe the conquest to have taken place. Major cities—Lachish, Hazor, others—were devastated, and on the rubble were erected what appear to be small crude settlements of seminomads making their initial entry into sedentary life. Who destroyed those cities? Egyptian troops? Israelite tribes? A mysterious people raiding from the sea? Canaan

is in a strange dark age from about 1320 to 1200 B.C.E.
Archaeology, yielding up few artifacts of any significance
for this period, is of little help in establishing the presence
in the area of new tribes.

How does one put together the bits of the puzzle?

It is probable that Joshua led a major tribe, the house of
Joseph, in an invasion of the land of Canaan. That tribe
may have had, probably did have, clans or smaller tribes
attached to it. Scholars refer to this group as the Rachel
tribes. In the patriarchal period Joseph and Benjamin had
been the sons of Rachel, Jacob's second wife; Ephraim
and Manasseh had been the sons of Joseph. The crucial
battle against the Canaanite coalition at Gibeon and the
stunning Israelite victory enabled the Joshua-led tribes to
fan out and occupy much of the region north of
Jerusalem, the Mount Ephraim area. Some of the tribes
moved northward and took part of the Galilee up to
Gilead. They were unable to conquer the rich valley of
Jezreel with its powerful bloc of Canaanite cities. Though
elements of these tribes were like islands in a Canaanite
sea, peaceful passage through the lowlands was not entirely impossible. There is little reason to doubt that some
of the Canaanite cities whose ashes for this period have
been uncovered by archaeologists were put to the torch by
Joshua.

The tribe of Judah, joined by the tribe of Simeon,
crossed the Jordan north of Jericho and took the hill
country south of Jerusalem. The city of Jerusalem was
captured by Judah; then, for some unknown reason, the
city was abandoned. A tribe known as the Jebusites took
the city—when and how remain not known. The Judah-
led tribes—there may have been others besides Simeon—
are called the Leah tribes by scholars. Leah had been the
first wife of Jacob.

Still other tribes may have come in a third wave and
settled deep in the upper Galilee and in sections of the
west. Some of the clans of the house of Joseph may have
broken away after the invasion and become separate
tribes; this appears to have been the case with Benjamin.
A few of the tribes may have moved in peacefully and
settled in unpopulated areas of the land.

Scholarly debate has as yet given us no clear picture regarding the sequence of the invasions. Some say Joshua invaded first; others claim it was Judah. Most appear to agree that the invasions were not far apart in time.

The ease with which some of the Canaanite cities fell may have been the happy result of help given the Israelites by people inside them who had no stomach for battle—or who were Hebrews, descendants of the families who had not gone to Egypt and who saw in the attacking tribesmen their own kin. This conjecture would explain why so many cities are listed as captured for which there exists no record of a battle.

There was no mass slaughter of the Canaanite population. Some cities were burned; many inhabitants were slain. That was what you did in those days to establish your right to territory; in this regard our species has not changed. Then you wearied of it and settled down and either covenanted or lived in tension with your new neighbors.

The Israelites settled in the hill country, where they cleared the forests and built their first towns. In the northern and central valleys the large, still unconquered Canaanite populace continued to live behind the thick walls of their powerful cities, protected from enemies by their chariots and professional soldiers.

An almost solid ridge of hills stretches straight across the land from Jerusalem to the city of Gezer, about fifteen miles from the Mediterranean coast. Much of this hill country and all of the main mountain passes together with the coastal plain and Gezer remained firmly in Canaanite hands. This separated Judah from the northern tribes and was to prove fateful in the ensuing history of the country—for it virtually made the country from its very beginning into a nation of two lands.

One piece of evidence exists outside the Bible that indicates the presence of Israelites on the soil of Canaan during this period. Around the year 1220 B.C.E. an Egyptian scribe composed a hymn of victory to Merneptah, the pharaoh who had taken the throne of the Two Lands after the death of Ramses II. The hymn, discovered in Thebes and published in 1897 of our era, contains a list of enemies destroyed by the troops of the pharaoh. It refers to the Israelites as a foreign people or a foreign tribe, not as a foreign nation; this might mean that though they were present in Canaan—precisely where is not clear—they were not yet sedentary, an apt fixing of the twilight status between successful incursion and final settlement.

This is the only mention of the name Israel in all of ancient Egyptian writing and probably reflects a skirmish between Egyptian troops and Israelite infantry somewhere near the coastline of Canaan. The Nile broke its silence. The words in the hymn that refer to Israel read, "Israel is laid waste, his seed is not."

About a decade or so before 1200 B.C.E. an aging Joshua called the elders, judges, and officers of the tribes to the city of Shechem. That city, built in a pass between two lofty hills and looking out upon a fertile valley, is nowhere claimed to have been conquered by the Israelites and may have been a Hebrew enclave all through the centuries of the enslavement in Egypt. The words of Jacob in Genesis 48:21—". . . which I wrested from the Amorites with my sword and bow"—are possibly an echo of a Hebrew conquest in the region of Shechem during the patriarchal period.

A grateful leader and his people will now covenant with their God who fulfilled His promise to give them the land of Canaan. The covenant takes the form of a suzerainty treaty. It reaffirms the Mosaic covenant and adds to it certain elements which only this new covenant can contain.

THE PREAMBLE. "Thus speaks the Lord, the God of Israel."

HISTORICAL PROLOGUE. "In olden times, your forefathers . . . lived beyond the Euphrates and worshiped other gods. And I took your father Abraham from beyond the Euphrates and led him throughout all the land of Canaan. . . . And I sent Moses and Aaron, and I plagued Egypt. . . . And I brought your fathers out of Egypt. . . . And I gave you a land whereon you had not labored, and cities which you had not built. . . ." No mention was made of the patriarchs in the Mosaic covenant, for that covenant was directed solely at those

who had undergone the slave experience. Here at
Shechem the entire people was being fused together—
those who had remained in Canaan and possessed strong
memories of the patriarchal traditions, and those whose
ancestors had once been slaves and who now brought
with them tales of Egypt, memories of Moses and a long
wandering, and wilderness traditions.

DEMANDS OR STIPULATIONS. "Now therefore
fear the Lord, and serve Him in sincerity and in truth;
and put away the gods which your fathers served beyond
the Euphrates, and in Egypt; and serve the Lord. . . ."
Only YHWH was God. Other gods had no role to play in
the cosmos; they were nongods, bits of wood and stone.
The Yahwist Israelite could not comprehend the radiant,
eternal connectedness the pagan felt certain existed between the images he worshiped and the awesome cyclical
forces of nature they represented; the believing pagan
found utterly incomprehensible the Israelite faith in an
imageless, transcendent God who participated in human
events and had chosen a small, helpless, and not particularly worthy people to be His instrument in an unfolding
purposeful history directed by Him and Him alone. It
seemed there could be no common meeting ground between these two views of the world.

DEPOSIT OF THE TEXT AND PUBLIC READ-
ING. We are told in the twenty-fourth chapter of the
Book of Joshua, in which the final literary version of the
making of this covenant is found, that Joshua "wrote
these words in the book of the law of God." The contents
of this book—its additional covenant stipulations and
laws—are unknown. Scholars believe that it was kept at
the sanctuary in Shechem and read periodically as part of
a religious ceremony.

THE DIVINE WITNESSES. "And Joshua said to the
people: 'You are witnesses against yourself that you have
chosen the Lord, to serve Him.' And they said: 'We are
witnesses. . . .'" This is a curiously innovative move in a
monotheistic situation where no divine witnesses are possible. Joshua also constructed a stone to serve as witness,
"and set it up there under the oak that was by the sanctuary of the Lord. And Joshua said to all the people: 'Be-

hold, this stone shall be a witness against us; for it has heard all the words of the Lord. . . .' "

BLESSINGS AND CURSES. "If you forsake the Lord, and serve strange gods, then He will turn and do you evil and consume you. . . ."

THE FORMAL OATH. "And the people said to Joshua: 'The Lord our God will we serve, and to His voice will we hearken.' "

THE SOLEMN CEREMONY. None is recorded.

Then the people went away, "every man to his inheritance."

The response to the events of the conquest was the Joshua covenant.

The adoption of this form of treaty to express a unique and growing relationship between a people and its one, invisible God was to become the most distinctive element of the civilization of ancient Israel. The treaty would change its form in order to respond to radically new events. But the basic response, no matter how extraordinary or traumatic the event, would always be—a treaty between God and Israel. The suzerainty covenants of Moses and Joshua were based upon gracious favor and persuasion rather than naked force. The people were given the dignity that comes with freedom of choice, for they could have chosen not to accept the covenant. At the same time, God retained His freedom and sovereignty; He took no oath; He could not be called to judgment. Not until the Book of Job, written about a thousand years after Joshua, is the God of Israel called to justice by a member of the civilization of ancient Israel—at a time when that civilization was being transformed into what we today call Judaism.

Sometime after the gathering at Shechem, Joshua died and was buried in the hill country of Ephraim, the territory of his tribe. We are told that the bones of Joseph, carried by the Israelites all through the wilderness trek, were buried in Shechem in the parcel of earth purchased by Jacob centuries earlier. A circle was thereby completed—no, not quite; more a spiral, a point that circles and returns to itself on a plane higher from where it began; for the Israelites now in Canaan were related to but, at the same time, were quite different from the Hebrews of the patriarchal period.

The wandering of the Israelites had come to an end. They settled into their newly conquered land. They built hill towns, terraced the slopes, farmed, grazed their herds, worked at crafts. The towns—hamlets and villages, really—were small; each was populated by a few hundred people; each could have fitted into Trafalgar Square. There was little material culture. In all matters material and spiritual the Israelites were a frontier society. They constituted a loose confederation of families, clans, and tribes voluntarily bound together by the Mosaic and Joshua covenants to the worship of YHWH.

In the central and eastern regions of the Mediterranean, two or three decades before 1200 B.C.E.—at about the same time that Joshua was addressing the representatives of the tribes of Israel in Shechem—volcanic migrations of northern tribes of still uncertain identity and origin began to obliterate the advanced and luxurious civilization of late Bronze Age Mycenaean Greece, which had come into existence around 1600 B.C.E. in the Peloponnesian city of Mycenae. Turmoil engulfed the whole of Greece, and in two generations it was transformed from a land of stone palaces to a thinly populated region of hamlets and villages. Vast populations were dislodged. Land migrants moved through Asia Minor. Others took to seagoing craft in search of new homes. A tidal wave of sea nomads approached the shores of Asia Minor, Egypt, and northern Canaan. Their first invasion of Egypt in 1220 B.C.E., from the direction of Libya, was beaten back by Pharaoh Merneptah. To the east of the newly settled Israelites, some decades after the death of Joshua, seminomadic Aramean tribes from the frings of the Arabian desert proceeded to batter at the world of Mesopotamia.

The Hittite empire stretched across the Anatolian plateau to the headwaters of the Euphrates above Carchemish, and from the Taurus Mountains to Damascus. There is some indication that Troy was part of that empire and that the Trojan War, misty with Homeric legends, was a trade war fought to open the Dardanelles to Mycenaean ships; but there is still much scholarly contention on this matter, and the Hittite records thus far discovered make no mention of such a war. Troy may have been sacked during this movement of northern tribes across Anatolia.

The Hittites were superb warriors and adroit statesmen. They tended toward leniency in their laws and toward kindness—if that word can be used of international relations—rather than cruelty in their dealings with conquered nations. It was a civilization that made much of cultic purity, was obsessively worried that corporeal or spiritual contamination during the performance of cultic rites might anger the gods and result in human misery. It utilized a cuneiform script borrowed from Mesopotamia as well as its own native hieroglyphics. During its empire days it developed an objective, realistic style of writing history—a record of the deeds and achievements of the king presented to the gods, to whom he was responsible for his actions. Hittite art and literature were much influenced by the Hurrians, whom we encountered in the days of the patriarchs.

Around 1230 B.C.E. famine struck the land of the Hittites. Pharaoh Merneptah sent grain. His gesture was less an act of benevolence than a move to maintain the Hittites as a buffer between Egypt and the looming nightmare from the north.

The mysterious tribes which had begun to move downward from somewhere north of Greece, thereby pushing the Mycenaean world into the Mediterranean, may themselves have been driven by vast cyclic changes in climate that produced drought and widespread famine. In 1200 B.C.E.—not 1500 B.C.E., as was once thought—a massive volcanic eruption shook Thera and sundered that Mediterranean island, located about fifty miles north of Crete, breaking it into three fragments. The terrifying noise of the explosion, the ash that darkened the sky for hundreds of miles around, the tidal wave that ensued, over five hundred feet high in some places—all this can only have added to the general condition of chaos then prevailing in the Aegean region of the Mediterranean.

In the year 1200 B.C.E. the land of the Hittites abruptly ceased to exist. Written records come to an end. The royal palace at Boğhasköy, capital of the Hittite world, was demolished. The invading horde—they have no names, no faces—moved southward. Slaughter and

destruction were general throughout the land. The great
port cities of northern Canaan—Ugarit, Arvad, Sidon,
possibly Tyre—were sacked and burned. These northern,
coastal Canaanites—the Phoenicians, as they would be
called by the Greeks—probably survived the destruction
of their cities by taking to the sea in their ships and returning when the raiders, apparently disinclined to settle,
had gone off in search of further plunder.

Carchemish, the city that controlled a major crossing
point of the Euphrates—the one probably used by Abraham in his journey from Haran—fell to the invaders, as
did Hamath and Tarsus. The powerful nation of Amurru
disappeared forever.

When history began again in Anatolia, about a century
or so later, the newcomers who now lived there were
called Phrygians by the Greeks in the west and Mushki
and Tabal by the Assyrians in the east. The origin of
these Phrygians remains unknown. They appear to have
been partly nomadic; now they lived in crude settlements.
The base of their economy was agriculture. They were a
military people with a fondness for horses. One of their
future kings would be named Midas.

The horde rolled relentlessly across Asia Minor and the
Mediterranean in the direction of Egypt. It was made up
of a complex and changing alliance of many different
peoples—nomads, barbarians, plunderers, displaced populations. The Egyptians gave that entire mass of human
movement a single all-embracing name. They called them
the Sea Peoples.

An inscription of the eighth year of the reign of
Ramses III describes the coming of this confederation of
peoples. "The foreign countries made a conspiracy in
their islands. . . . No land could stand before their
arms. . . . They were coming forward toward Egypt. . . ."
That inscription provides us with the only written
evidence we have of the destruction of the Hittite
empire. "No land could stand before their arms, from
Hatti [Hittites], Kode [Cilicia, north of Cyprus], Carchemish. . . ."

At the head of this alliance of Sea Peoples were the
Peleshet. We know them from the Bible as the Philistines.
The Egyptians depicted them as tall, brawny, clean-

shaven. They wore a distinctive plume-crested leather helmet with a decorated band around the brow and a chin strap. They carried spears, long swords, round shields. On land they fought from chariots with crews of three, two warriors and a driver. Their families followed behind them in wooden ox-drawn carts with solid wheels.

This confederation of peoples attempted a massive invasion of Egypt about the year 1185 B.C.E. The Sea People were stopped, at great cost to themselves and the Egyptians. Many were captured. Some of their warriors entered the army of Ramses III as mercenaries. The Peleshet were deflected northward and around 1180 B.C.E. began to settle along the coast of Canaan in a number of cities that had been previously destroyed in their southward movement and that of the other Sea Peoples. These cities—Gaza, Ashkelon, Ashdod—had been under Egyptian domination, and it is not clear whether the Peleshet simply took them of themselves or were given them by treaty with Ramses III or by his tacit and weary consent. When he died around 1150 B.C.E. the Egyptian empire, bled by endless war, went with him into permanent entombment.

The weapons and tools of the Philistines were made of iron. They brought with them the technology of ironworking, which they may have learned and mastered sometime during their ravaging of Asia Minor; the Hittites had known of iron, but had never produced it in quantity. With the advent of the Sea Peoples in 1200 B.C.E., the Bronze Age initiated in the Near East by the Sumerians around 3000 B.C.E. came to an abrupt end, and the Iron Age began.

They absorbed the Canaanite language and Canaanite gods and quickly became Canaanite in all things save their manner of waging war. Each of their cities was led by a king, called a *seren* in the Bible, the Hebrew rendering of the Greek word *tyrannos*, which meant ruler or king. The Philistines were probably from Crete. Their kings were bound by covenant or ancient tradition to meet together in council and decide by majority vote upon a course of military action. Then all would act together. Their warriors were heavily armed, in the manner of Homeric heroes.

In the distant east the Arameans crossed the Euphrates and penetrated into Mesopotamia. They conquered, plundered, settled, splintering the Fertile Crescent into a dark barbaric confusion of petty kingdoms. Assyria and Babylonia fought them for decades that stretched into generations. The Arameans did not have writing. They had succeeded in massive domestication of the camel, and were the first to utilize the mobility and long-range striking power of that animal as instruments of war.

From somewhere in the region of the Euphrates came a king named Cushan-rishathaim. He had gathered an army, and about 1200 B.C.E., during the chaos that was changing the ethnic face of the ancient Near East, he cut deep into Canaan with the possible intent of subjugating Egypt.

Beaten by the pharaoh, leading his army back through southern Canaan, King Cushan-rishathaim—a bizarre name probably given him by the Israelites, for it means Cushan of Double Wickedness—may have sought consolation in further pillage. Othniel son of Kenaz, a member of the Calebite clan of the tribe of Judah, suddenly felt called upon to act. "And the spirit of the Lord came upon him and he judged Israel; and he went out to war. . . ." Apparently he was forceful enough to be able to rally a tribal army. The king from the region of the Euphrates lost his taste for plunder and hurried home.

This brief episode in the Book of Judges, still puzzling and elusive—the text says nothing about Egypt; but why is a king from as far away as the Euphrates raiding the clans of Judah?—this episode introduces the first of the Israelite judges.

It is not known with certainty what laws were in practice in the Israelite tribal league. The account of the Joshua covenant describes how Joshua "set them a statute and an ordinance in Shechem" and then "wrote these words in the book of the law of God." The Covenant Code in the Book of Exodus contains a section, 21:1-22, which seems to suit a rudimentary society of peasants and shepherds. Those may have been the earliest laws of the tribes.

Whatever the laws, there is little doubt that there were

judges who dispensed justice. These judges could be tribal elders, or men and women whose wisdom was highly regarded, or individuals who had shown extraordinary courage and powers on the field of battle; swift, correct decisions in combat sometimes signaled a mind that could make just decisions in matters of law.

In later years the Israelites would look back upon their first two centuries in the pagan world of Canaan as the testing time for the tribal league. They would say of those early tribesmen that they did "evil in the sight of the Lord, and served the Baalim and the Asheroth," and they were probably right. The first contact with the high culture of Canaan, its material wealth and complex cult, was seductive, and much cultural borrowing no doubt followed. When you descend from your wandering donkey and become tied to a plot of ground upon whose fertility your life depends, you might not hesitate to invoke a pagan god or goddess as added security against the dread of famine. Also there were pre-Mosaic Hebrews in the land not yet accustomed to the imageless worship of YHWH. Many a pagan practice was doubtlessly performed at local shrines by those who found it difficult to follow all the demands of the covenants of Sinai and Shechem. And so later Israelites would say that "the anger of the Lord was kindled against Israel." The Lord would give them over to their enemies. Then they would cry out to the Lord, and the Lord would raise up a savior to the children of Israel. These saviors were called judges.

All the saviors in the Book of Judges were judges in the normal sense of that word: dispensers of justice, magistrates; but not all the judges were saviors. The Hebrew word for judge in the Book of Judges—*shofet*—means an arbitrator or a court justice as well as a deliverer.

In the absence of centralized authority or institutions, each tribe was ruled by its judges. Under certain critical conditions some of those judges became extraordinary leaders—deliverer judges, charismatic rulers. They would suddenly, inexplicably, be filled with the spirit of the Lord. They would feel themselves called upon in a time of crisis to act against an enemy of the people—either

alone or by convincing one or more tribes of the need for
military action. If the action proved successful then the
tribesmen would be convinced that the spirit of the Lord
had indeed descended upon that judge.

Not all the judges were of the same character. One was
a brigand; another was a roguish prankster who enjoyed
pagan parties and prostitutes. But all, at one point or another in their lives, were tribal judges, magistrates, interpreters of the Covenant Code.

In Egypt pharaohs in the guise of gods were attempting
to roll back the endless waves of Sea Peoples. In Assyria
and Babylonia kings who were representatives of the gods
were trying to stave off the Aramean flood from the Arabian desert. In the Israelite federation of twelve tribes
there were judges—individuals of varying quality, character, and background—who would suddenly rise to leadership and successfully fight back Moabites, Canaanites,
Midianites, Ammonites. They failed in their fight against
the Philistines.

The period of the judges was not a blood-filled darkness of unending crises. The idyllic Book of Ruth,
written during the early period of the monarchy, reflects
much of the gracious and genteel quality of life that was
probably the backdrop to the outbursts of violence. The
crises were not everywhere at one time; there was peace
here while there was war there.

No judge succeeded in marshaling all the tribes for any
one cause; either there was no cause strong enough or no
judge so highly regarded that he could call out all the
tribal levies at one time. That was where the ultimate test
of leadership lay: How many of the clan and tribal
chieftains could you persuade to call out their *sarim*, military leaders, and troops? There was no standing army; if
you could not rally the military leaders of the clans and
tribes together with their troops, you failed; and the enemy plundered your crops, raided your villages, killed
your people.

A double-edged dagger was a rare weapon in those days;
the usual weapon, aside from the spear or javelin, was the
curved sword. This dagger, fashioned by a man named
Ehud son of Gera for a specific purpose, was short and

could be easily concealed beneath one's garments. He strapped it to his right thigh.

On the east bank of the Jordan, the Moabites had conquered the tribe of Reuven, then had crossed the Jordan, captured Jericho, and reduced the tribe of Benjamin to vassalage. We do not know the date of these events, but it was probably early in the twelfth century B.C.E.

Ehud son of Gera was no doubt a member of an important family, for he is described as leading a delegation of Benjaminites who came to Jericho in order to present the annual payment of tribute to their conqueror, King Eglon of Moab. They were searched for weapons, but no one thought to look at the right thigh of an individual; weapons were worn on the left side of the body to facilitate swift drawing with the right arm. Ehud son of Gera, skilled in the handling of weapons with both arms, asked to have a private word with the king.

Wielded by a knowing arm, the double-edged dagger could do its deadly work swiftly and efficiently for it was a superb stabbing instrument. King Eglon of Moab was a fat man and presumably Ehud thrust the dagger deep into his flabby belly, the haft going into the skin after the blade, in order to prevent immediate external bleeding that might be discovered too soon. He left the presence of the king. The attendants entered the chamber, thought the king asleep, and retreated quietly. Ehud son of Gera was far away when the killing was discovered.

In the hill country of Ephraim he blew a ram's horn, "and the children of Israel went down with him." The suddenly leaderless Moabites retreated in confusion across the Jordan. We do not know if they also retreated from the territory of Reuven. Sometime during the period of the judges the Reuvenites were so decimated by invasion that they ceased to exist as an effective tribe.

Ehud son of Gera was a judge.

Rain is a weapon of doubtful worth in war, but a deadly one against chariots. The chariots of the Canaanites were manned by two warriors and drawn by well-trained horses. Each chariot was armored with metal plates and could be a merciless scythe against tribal foot soldiers.

Sometime around 1140 B.C.E. Canaanite kings determined to put an end to the central and northern Israelite tribes in their midst. They assembled a large army spearheaded by nine hundred chariots in the valley of Jezreel near Megiddo. The Israelites called out their warriors. Most of the tribal militia took up positions in the hilly terrain near the rim of the valley, safe from the Canaanite chariot squadrons. The Israelites were led by a man named Barak and a woman named Deborah.

The Israelites waited. A heavy rain began to fall. The Israelites attacked. The earth of the valley turned to mud in the rain, bogging down the chariots and making maneuverability impossible. Behind the Canaanites the wadi Kishon suddenly filled with water from the spilloff that cascaded down the hills. "The wadi Kishon swept them away, that ancient wadi, the wadi Kishon," reads the Song of Deborah. Never again was there a serious Canaanite threat to the tribes of Israel.

Deborah was a judge.

Ram's horns, torches, and pitchers seem not to be weapons at all. They were used by a man named Gideon son of Yoash, of the tribe of Manasseh, to destroy a marauding host of nomads. Year after year they would ravage the land at harvest time—nomadic eastern and southern desert clans, Amalekites, Midianites, Bene Kedem, acting as a tribal confederacy and using camels, which terrified the sedentary Israelites. Leading a carefully picked force of three hundred tribesmen, Gideon used the torches to light the way as they climbed the hills in the night. Then, as they approached the vast encampment of the marauders in the valley below, with its silent tents and restless camels, he ordered his men to conceal the torches inside the pitchers. They advanced from three sides, blowing the horns and breaking the pitchers to stampede the camels, shouting, "The sword for the Lord and for Gideon!" and setting fire to the tents. The panicked marauders fled for their lives, were later trapped by a large Israelite force, and ceased raiding the Israelites.

Gideon was a judge. Some wanted to make him king. He refused. "I will not rule over you . . . the Lord shall rule over you." One of his sons, Abimelech, made himself king over Shechem. The people rebelled, and he burned the city in a bloody battle, but lost his life during a battle for another city. The weapon that slew him was a millstone tossed down on his skull by a woman. The land was not yet ready for a king.

Judges are listed who "arose to save the land"—but we are not told of their exploits.

A vow is a strange weapon to use against an enemy. A man called Jephthah was the son of a harlot. His half-brother threw him out so he would not share their inheritance. He roamed about with vain fellows and became a brigand, a Hapiru.

The Ammonites, desiring the lands once captured by Moses from Sihon and Og, gathered an army. People appealed to Jephthah for help. "The spirit of the Lord came upon Jephthah." He vowed to the Lord that if he succeeded against the Ammonites in battle, he would offer up to the Lord for a burnt offering "whatever comes forth from the doors of my house to meet me." The Ammonites were defeated. Jephthah returned in triumph to his house, and "his daughter came out to meet him with timbrel and with dances; and she was his only child. . . ." The commentators do not like this story and try every which way to dilute its intent. But the text is clear. He "did with her according to the vow which he had vowed. . . ." No further details are given.

Jephthah too was a judge.

The jawbone of a donkey is a bizarre weapon. It was used by a powerful Israelite of the tribe of Dan to slay Philistines. He was young when "the spirit of the Lord began to move him. . . ." In times of tranquillity he partied with the Philistines, married one of their women, slept with their prostitutes. In times of tension he burned their fields and slew their men.

Who does not know of Samson? Who has not heard the tales of this long-haired man of enormous strength slaying a lion with his bare hands, carrying the gates of a city on his shoulders, deceived by Delilah, blinded by Philistines grown wary of costly pranks, chained, shamed, and finally bringing down upon himself and a Philistine multitude a vast temple with the cry, "Let me die with the Philistines!"

Samson too was a judge.

Apparently some of the tribes specialized in certain

types of weapons. The Benjaminites were especially adept with the sling; the Judites were skilled with spear and shield; the tribe of Zebulun was expert in all kinds of weapons.

A bloody war broke out in which the tribes used their various skills with weapons—against one another. The tribe of Benjamin would not give up for punishment some of its members who had molested and murdered the concubine of another tribesman. The bereaved man had cut up her corpse and sent the parts to the tribes throughout the land, with a cry for justice. The horror was universal. When the Benjaminites refused to yield up their guilty kin, war was declared against them by the other tribes. Bloody battles ensued. Benjamin, successful at first, was in the end almost destroyed.

There were no judges in that bitter civil war. It is told in the Book of Judges in order to present us with a picture of the tribal league in disarray and to prepare us for the coming of the monarchy.

Samuel was a judge, a seer, a priest—and, according to some scholars, the founder of the prophetic movement in ancient Israel. In his time the Philistines began to take the territories of the tribes. They conquered Judah in the south, the valley of Jezreel, and parts of the central mountain country. They had gained control of the sea routes to their coastal cities; now they sought and attained control of the overland trade route that went from Egypt along the sea coast and inland to Megiddo, Hazor, Damascus, then deep into the north, and east to Mesopotamia. Israelite clans in the Galilee and across the Jordan were beyond the range of Philistine interest and remained untouched by the iron sword. But the Philistines extracted taxes from the conquered Israelites and established a monopoly of the manufacture of metal by instituting control over all the smiths in the country. They raided Israelite granaries, garrisoned Israelite towns, and set up fortresses at stategic locations. They were a martial people, superb fighters, well equipped and skilled with the chariot, and the inept Israelite troops could not stand up to them in combat.

About 1500 B.C.E. the Israelites attempted to stop the Philistine advance. They engaged them in a brief battle, lost, and brought the ark from its central sanctuary in Shiloh into the area of combat, hoping that their God would come to their aid. Near Aphek, about ten miles east of Jaffa, the Philistines cut the tribal army to pieces, killed the two priests who accompanied the ark, and captured the ark. Later they destroyed Shiloh and the sanctuary.

At that sanctuary in Shiloh, a little village in the hills of Ephraim between Bethel and Shechem, the tribes had met periodically since the conquest to worship YHWH, celebrate festivals, renew the covenant, recount the miraculous deeds of their God, tell of the time of the patriarchs and the deliverance from slavery and the long wilderness wandering. Perhaps they recounted too the epic of Creation and the legend of the Flood brought by the patriarchs from Mesopotamia—but in this new telling it became YHWH who created and brought the Flood. So we are informed by some scholars. The ark had been the focus of the tribal league. Crushed beneath the relentless pressure of the Philistines, the ark now captured, the sanctuary destroyed, the judges helpless—the Israelite federation of twelve tribes began to disintegrate.

An aged sorrowing Samuel, who had returned to his home town of Ramah north of Jerusalem after the destruction of the sanctuary, now yielded to tribal elders and anointed a tall young man of the tribe of Benjamin king over Israel.

In one version of the anointing, the young man, whose name is Saul son of Kish, leaves his home town of Gibeah near Jerusalem, wanders through the hill country of Benjamin in search of his father's stray donkeys, encounters Samuel along the way, and is secretly anointed by him. Later when Samuel assembles the tribes at Mizpah, a town south of Bethel, and announces the selection of Saul, the young man is acclaimed by the people; but some among them, bitter antimonarchists zealous of tribal independence and fearful of royal power, mock him and leave in anger.

In another version Saul behaves as a deliverer judge. The Israelite city of Jabesh-gilead across the Jordan is besieged by Ammonites, whose terms for surrender are horrifying: "That all your right eyes be put out." Saul is plowing when he hears of this, and he reacts in explosive charismatic fashion. He hews into pieces the oxen with which he has been plowing and sends them off with messengers to rally the clans. "Whoever does not follow Saul and Samuel into battle, this shall be done to his cattle!" Those clans that are able to respond send troops. The Ammonites are beaten. The people are then convinced that Saul is filled with the spirit of the Lord. They bring him to the shrine in Gilgal, where Joshua and the Israelites of the conquest once encamped, and there they acclaim him king. It is about 1020 B.C.E.

Saul was an anointed judge with charismatic qualities whose task it was to lead the Israelites in battle against their enemies. Anointing was a sacred act designed to indicate that the spirit of God had entered the anointed one, that his leadership was not merely for the duration of the crisis but for the length of his life. This was the first time in the history of Israel that an individual had been anointed leader of the people. Anointment of kings was fairly common practice in Canaan and among the Hittites, but not in Mesopotamia. The Egyptians anointed vassal kings and high officials of the pharaoh, never the pharaoh himself. Before Saul only sacred objects used in the sanctuary were anointed, and possibly priests—there is some scholarly controversy on the matter of priests. The words "anointed" and "messiah" are synonyms—the first is the translation and the second is the transliteration of the identical Hebrew word, *mashiach.*

Many enemies confronted the first anointed one of Israel. He spent his entire reign in combat. He fought Philistines, Moabites, Ammonites, Edomites, Amalekites. He broke the ancient covenant made by Joshua with the Gibeonites—for a reason not known to us—slew many, drove the others out. He lived in his home town of Gibeah in what was more a crude fortress—measuring one hundred by two hundred feet—than a palace, had no harem, no court, no administrative machinery. His chief officer was a kinsman named Abner, who commanded the Israelite levies. The power to call out the levies had once belonged only to the tribes; now it was given to Saul—though it is doubted that this power included the right to rally the many clans of Judah. It was a nation of two lands from the beginning.

The tribal army could not be kept permanently in the field. Each soldier equipped himself at his own expense, brought his own food and arms—ox goads, bludgeons, axes, lances, wooden bows, and a quiver of flint-headed arrows; it was an army of peasants and craftsmen. The few wealthy landed proprietors brought fine weapons. But the earth had to be plowed and sown. After a specific campaign the levies would return home. But the wars were endless.

Saul began to recruit mercenaries. Slowly he built a small cadre of young professional soldiers. When he saw or was told of a courageous man, he asked him to join his service. He could not take too many. There was little money. In the end they numbered three thousand men.

He preferred his own tribesmen, Benjaminites, whom he favored with gifts of land from the territories he took from the Philistines—a new practice among the Israelites, but a royal privilege hoary with age in the ancient Near East. But he would hire men from other tribes as well. He also took on foreigners. A mercenary named Doeg was an Edomite; a hired young officer named David came from the tribe of Judah.

The wars continued. There were occasional successes against the Philistines—they were driven from much of the central hill country—but none was a crushing victory. During a raid against Amalekites Saul took booty in defiance of Samuel's command to destroy everything—an early spark in centuries of crown fires between prophets and kings. The aged seer broke with the king, publicly denounced him, and went home to die. But Saul continued to rule, his military successes reinforcing his popularity.

The years of war dragged on. A brooding melancholy settled itself upon Saul, a darkness of the soul fed by the growing certainty that he would never succeed in these wars, that too much was being asked of him. Out of the darkness would erupt sudden raging fits of jealousy directed at those around him whom a battle might have rewarded with success and renown. Early in his career the Israelites had called him *nagid*, commander; then they had called him *melech*, king; now they saw him as a torn, flawed human being.

And that was what an Israelite wrote of him: commander, king, flawed human being. That Israelite, unknown, as are most writers and scribes of the ancient Near East, used the script of the Canaanites, which had been in existence for about three hundred years before the conquest and which the Israelites adopted soon after they settled into the land, along with Canaanite, Mesopotamian, and Egyptian literary forms—poetry, psalms, proverbs, annals. He wrote on wood, leather, or papyrus, with a stylus or a feather pen and colored ink. He wrote in his own language, Hebrew, a mixture of the language of the land and the language, possibly a relative of Aramaic, which the generation of the conquest had brought in from the wilderness—thereby making Hebrew a dialect of Canaanite. He may have borrowed the historical narrative form or he may have invented it; we do not know. But he was the first writer to realize that character too is destiny.

This account of Saul that we have in the Bible was written during or soon after his reign; there is about it a relentless mirroring of truth, an almost cruel beat of authenticity, as if the writer himself had witnessed the battles and the rages, seen the javelin hurled in jealousy, sensed the silent melancholy of defeated greatness, witnessed the unsuccessful pursuits through the southern wilderness of the young officer accused of wanting to steal the throne, watched the encroaching madness take slow possession of an embittered man who had once been tall and young and had gone on a walk through the hills and valleys of his tribe in search of his father's donkeys and had returned as a king.

This is the first portrait in the history of our species of the humanity of a king—the qualities of his character that make him not of the gods but of mankind.

The straight double-edged iron sword was one of the standard weapons of the Philistines. The Israelite sword was a single-edged bronze weapon curved like a scimitar. It is not known what kind of sword Saul carried. At the foot of Mount Gilboa, his tribal army drawn into unwilling battle by clever Philistine strategy and being decimated by deadly archers and chariots, a desperate and defeated Saul threw himself upon the point of his sword. Three of his sons died with him that day, as did the tribal league. It was shortly before 1000 B.C.E.

The Philistines cut off his head and paraded it about their cities. They hung his body on the wall of Beth-shean alongside those of his sons, letting them rot and wither shamefully in full view of passers-by.

The tribal army was crushed. What remained of it scattered and returned to the towns and villages of the defeated Israelites. The Philistines ruled the land unopposed and seemed intent upon putting an end to the Israelite presence in Canaan.

The federation of twelve tribes had been in existence for two hundred years. Crisis events had been met by deliverer judges. The defeat near Aphek around 1050 B.C.E. had shaken the tribal league and brought it under vassalage to the Philistines. Then bands of Israelite ecstatics had suddenly appeared in the land, roaming about and prophesying in dervishlike frenzy to the accompaniment of timbrels and pipes. We do not know where they came from or why they appeared at that time; perhaps, encouraged by Samuel, they stepped into the emptiness that came in the wake of the burning of the sanctuary at Shiloh, an emptiness that was not filled even when the Philistines returned the captured ark, less than a year after it had been taken by them at the battle near Aphek, because they attributed to it a plague that had broken out in their cities. Similar bands of ecstatics are known to have roamed about Canaan, Anatolia, and Mesopotamia. Among the Israelites they served as one kind of response to the Philistine conquest and as a direct continuation of the line of charismatic judges. These early ecstatic prophets kept alive the will of the people and their resistance to the Philistines. We do not know the contents of those prophecies. Often their ecstasies led them to enraptured dance and song and rolling about unclothed on the earth.

The line of leadership forked in a second direction—toward the judge-king anointed by a priest-prophet and acclaimed by the people. Now the first of the kings was dead, and the land lay helpless before the people who had come from the sea. Only one small army of six hundred men was left in all of Israel, a private army of brigands that roamed the southern wilderness of Judah. It was led by an outcast, a Hapiru, named David.

He had been hunted for years by the half-mad Saul, who had accused him of treason against the anointed one of YHWH.

His father, Jesse, had been an elder of the tribe of Judah when the boy David had been secretly anointed by an embittered Samuel, whose disillusionment with Saul had led him to prophesy that the first anointed one of Israel would not establish a dynasty. There were few more dismal divinations one could convey to a king.

It is not clear how David entered the service of Saul. One account has him brought to the attention of the king as a skilled musician who can soothe the despondency that clouds his eyes; the lad plays and sings, and the king's mood is eased. A different account brings him to the field of combat in the valley of Elah, where he slays a gloating Goliath in single combat reminiscent of Sinuhe the Egyptian and his years among the Amorites, David enters the service of Saul, becomes an officer of mercenary troops—not of the tribal levy—involved in the constant border fights against the Philistines, and is so successful that the king, hearing him acclaimed for his bravery in combat, begins to regard him as a threat to the throne. The friendship between the young officer and the king's son Jonathan deepens the suspicion in the brooding mind: the officer is plotting to steal the throne from his naïve and kindly son, who is too blind to see the cunning machinations of the son of Jesse.

Saul attempted to have David slain by the Philistines. In exchange for the hand of his second daughter, Michal, he asked of David a bizarre dowry: the foreskins of one hundred Philistines. "For Saul thought to make David fall by the hands of the Philistines. . . ."

It may have been Saul's intent to send David to certain death by having him practice upon Philistines he slew the same kind of mutilation used against the Sea Peoples by the Egyptians. Further, Saul wanted to be certain that only Philistines would be slain by David—another reason he demanded to see their uncircumcised genital members.

You did not kill one hundred Philistines easily or at one time; you killed ten in this raid, twenty in another, in hacking and sweaty hand-to-hand combat. David was certainly aware of the dimension of danger added to his battles by the king's demand. How the Philistines must have raged and fought once they saw their mutilated dead and realized the humiliation being visited upon them! And what a blunt and unspoken rejoinder it was to Saul's effort at indirect murder when the young David presented him with two hundred Philistine foreskins! From that moment on it was Saul himself, broken to utter madness whenever he thought of the son of Jesse, who sought to slay his son-in-law.

David fled for his life when Saul sent his own agents to kill him, slipping out the window of his bedroom, aided by his wife, Michal daughter of Saul, and running off into the night, weaponless. Then began the years of flight and wandering, from Gibeah to Ramah, where he met the aged Samuel in the company of ecstatics; from Ramah to the court sanctuary at Nob, where the priest Ahimelech, unaware that David was being hunted by the king, gave him food and the sword of Goliath, which had been placed behind the ephod—some kind of oracular garment or image about whose nature scholars can make no clear determination. David did not know that the sword of Goliath was in the sanctuary—which is strange. One imagines him wearing it all through the years of wandering and freebooting that follow; and one begins to understand how it was that the name of Goliath became associated with David and why in the end David was credited with slaying him when, according to II Samuel 21:19, it was actually an obscure soldier named Elhanan who engaged in that act of heroic single combat only to have his name eclipsed by a later accident of history.

The priest paid for his unwitting generosity. Saul ordered him and his family and the entire village of Nob—a village of priests—slain. The Israelite soldiers refused to obey the command of their king. The task was carried out by the Edomite mercenary Doeg.

In desperation David fled to the Philistine city of Gath; but he was recognized and, fearing death, played the role of a madman, froth staining his red beard, fingers scratching at walls, so that when he was brought before the king, who had the then customary dread of the insane—they were thought to be possessed of the gods—he was ordered sent from the city.

The wandering continued. Deep now in the hill country of Judah, he came to the cave of Adullam, a few miles northeast of Hebron. There, his family and a group of malcontents—"everyone that was in distress, and everyone that was in debt, and everyone that was discontented"—joined him. "And he became captain over them; and there were with him about four hundred men."

He took his father and mother across the Dead Sea to Moab to prevent them from falling into the hands of Saul. Then he returned to the land of Judah.

He wandered with his followers through the wilderness of Judah between Hebron and the Dead Sea, a land of shale-covered hills and burning heat. Saul pursued him relentlessly. The clans of Judah, loyal to Saul, would not support their own kinsman. In the midst of this, "Samuel died, and all Israel gathered themselves together, and lamented him. . . ."

David and his men fled to the wilderness of Paran deep in the south, the land through which fugitive slaves had wandered more than two and a half centuries before. He and his band lived by offering protection to the clans of Judah against the raids of Amalekites. He took wives from some of those clans. Finally, David offered himself as vassal to King Achish of Gath. The delighted Philistine took him on. What better way to divide Judah from the rest of Israel than by adding one of her renowned soldiers to his own army—together with four hundred other Israelites, most of them from Judah!

He gave David and his little army the southern town of Ziklag to live in and to use as a base. David's task was to guard the Philistine southern border against the clans of Judah and the marauding Amalekites while the Philistines attended to the more serious business of killing Israelites in the army of Saul.

For more than a year David performed his task with relish and cleverness. He raided the Amalekites, protecting thereby both the Philistines and the clans of Judah. Wisely he shared his booty not only with Achish of Gath but also with the leading families of Judah. His army now numbered six hundred hardened fighters, and Achish planned to use it in a Philistine campaign against Saul. But the kings of the other Philistine cities were loud in their doubts about David's loyalty, and he and his men were sent back to Ziklag. Good fortune danced merrily about David during much of his life; the Sumerians would have said that he had a personal god. We are left to wonder what choice he would have made had he been forced to confront the army of Saul as a Philistine vassal. That was the battle in which Saul died and the tribal army disintegrated.

When David learned of the death of Saul and Jonathan, he gave expression to his mourning in a dirge of moving lyric quality. "Thy beauty, O Israel, upon thy high places is slain! How have the mighty fallen! . . ." Then he gathered up his troops, their wives and children and possessions, and, no doubt with the approval of his Philistine overlord, moved to Hebron, the chief city of the tribe of Judah. There he camped, and waited.

We will never know if he actually coveted the kingship during the life of Saul; doubtlessly he did; just as doubtlessly he would have done nothing against the king to obtain it. He was a profoundly devout man and would never have raised a hand against the anointed one of YHWH. But he possessed an uncanny ability to read events, to anticipate the future, to move toward it and patiently await its coming. As he waited now in Hebron.

The elders of Judah—and, we may assume, those of the small tribe of Simeon and other southern clans as well—gazed northward at the void left by the death of Saul. They gazed at Hebron at the small army of David. One imagines the meetings of those elders, the talk as each spoke his mind. Should they take the unprecedented step of ignoring the elders of the northern clans and seeking separate leadership? In the end they offered David the kingship of Judah, and he accepted. The Philistines looked on untroubled. Their own man had now become king over the troublesome tribe of Judah and the various other clans in its territory.

In the north ruled a surviving son of Saul, Eshbaal (as he is properly called in First Chronicles 8:33); he was forty years old, and he ruled from the town of Mahanaim across the Jordan. He had been made king by Abner, Saul's commander of the tribal levies, who had managed to escape from the carnage of the battle near Mount Gilboa. But the north was a floundering wreckage of tribes, and Eshbaal was an inept weakling. Inevitably war broke out between those who were the followers of David and those still loyal to Abner and the house of Saul.

After two years of civil war, which the Philistines no doubt regarded with delight, quiet negotiations were begun between Abner and David. In the midst of these negotiations, David's commander, his nephew Joab, a brutish, unfeeling, superb leader of troops, slew his potential rival Abner on a blood-vengeance pretext: Abner had earlier slain Joab's brother in battle. The elders of the northern tribes were enraged. David condemned Joab, disclaimed any part in the affair, buried Abner with honor in Hebron, lamented him publicly—and waited.

Two men in Mahanaim slew Eshbaal and brought his head to David, expecting reward. Horrified, he condemned their deed and had them struck down. The head of Eshbaal was buried near the grave of Abner. David waited.

Negotiations resumed between David and representatives of the elders of the north. At the end the elders came to Hebron and covenanted with David, "and they anointed David king over Israel."

He was thirty years old. He had reigned in Hebron over Judah seven and a half years. Now north and south were united in his person; he was king of the two lands of Judah and Israel.

He had attained kingship not through any charismatic action that might have shown him to be possessed of the spirit of the Lord but through the sordid realities of political and military power and the adroit use of diplomacy. For the many clans that dwelt in the extensive territory of Judah, charismatic leadership ended when kingship was given to David. It is not entirely certain that it came to an end as well for the tribes of the north.

At this point events begin to blur in the Biblical narrative—as if the heart of the account was really the rise of David and all that is about to happen is of little significance. The richness of detail, the deft touches that made the early history of David an unforgettable encounter with human beings and their emotions—the horror of unfulfilled existence; the rise to glory of a charmed life; love and hate; heroism, courage, fame, and death—now fade behind a chronological haze. Clarity returns only with a cycle of events involving new characters: Nathan the prophet, Bathsheba, Amnon and Tamar, Absalom, Adonijah, Solomon. . . .

The land had two capitals, Hebron and Mahanaim, a politically divisive situation. The range of hills that had been the physical barrier between north and south now beckoned David into a daring move. He brought his small army northward, and in a sudden maneuver that remains unexplained despite the claim of some that they understand how it was done—a swift scaling of the walls; a surprise attack through an underground water channel—he captured the Jebusite city of Jerusalem. Archaeologists tell us that it measured around twelve acres—about 1250 feet from north to south and 400 feet from east to west. Its small houses were crowded together; its streets were narrow and crooked. What mattered most in an ancient city was not the comfort of space but the protection of walls. Jerusalem was thick-walled and perched on a mountain ridge in the shape, roughly, of a V. David permitted the surrendering Jebusites to remain in the city and brought his retinue inside. It was his city, taken with his own troops. It controlled a vital mountain road that linked the northern and southern regions of the land. He was obligated to no tribe for its capture. It was renamed the city of David. He made it the capital of the united monarchy of Judah and Israel.

The Philistines awoke. A united Judah and Israel was a threat. It is not clear whether they marched against their vassal David before or after he took the impregnable city of Jerusalem. They advanced into the valley of Rephaim south of Jerusalem, with the intent of severing the northern tribes from Judah. Two major battles were fought in that valley. After their first defeat the Philistines returned, fought, and were defeated again. They retreated to their cities. Some kind of peace treaty was no doubt arranged between them and David. They retained their independence but were never again a serious threat to Judah or Israel. Philistines joined the army of David as mercenaries.

The ark of YHWH had remained neglected all these years in the village of Kiriath-jearim. Now David had it brought in joyous procession to Jerusalem. He himself led the procession and danced before the ark in uncontrollable ecstasy. The city of Jerusalem—his city—was raised to the rank of cultic center of the united monarchy. City, clans, ark, and kingship were now linked.

David had a powerful army, a capital city, a united land. He proceeded to take the remaining Canaanite regions in the coastal foothills, in the plain of Sharon between Jaffa and Mount Carmel, and in the northern valleys; they may simply have fallen into his hands without resistance after the collapse of Philistine power. One assumes that the Canaanite intellectual class, whatever it may have been at that time—scribes, courtiers, high-level officials of various kinds—embraced the suddenly vibrant and expanding culture of the people of YHWH. I would assume too that these Canaanites brought with them their scribal archives, which now passed into the hands of the Israelites: diplomatic correspondence, myths, epics, Egyptian and Mesopotamian literature. Canaan ceased to exist inside the territory of the tribes. The Canaanites were not absorbed by the tribes but became subjects of the crown. In time many would become state slaves. Nowhere is the Bible explicit about this conquest; but it is inconceivable that David would have embarked upon the course of empire with enclaves of hostile Canaanites in his midst.

The impetus of conquest went on as if by its own momentum. There was no one to interfere: Egypt was in domestic turmoil, and distant Assyria, whose brief bid for empire under Tiglath-pileser I, from about 1115 to 1075 B.C.E., had come to a halt, was now being pounded back to the walls of Ashur, her chief city, by invading Arameans. David took Moab and cruelly massacred her army. There was an Aramean kingdom in the north at the time whose territory reached to the Euphrates. He defeated it and became ruler of this vast region. The king of distant Hamath sent him gifts to acknowledge his supremacy. David conquered Edom and Elat. He now controlled and could tax the users of the two main trade routes passing from Egypt and Arabia through his land: the coastal Via Maris, over which fleeing slaves had once feared to pass, and the inland King's Highway, which some of those slaves and their children had later traveled and still others had avoided on their way to the land promised them by the God with whom they had covenanted at Sinai. He also took distant Tadmor, later called Palmyra, a dusty town halfway between Damascus and the Euphrates that was an income-yielding caravan stop.

Moab, Ammon, Edom, Aramean Zobah, and Aramean Damascus lost their independence—the precise order of conquest is unclear—paid heavy tribute to David, and were reduced to the status of vassals. About twenty years after the death of Saul, the united kingdom of Judah and Israel, led by King David son of Jesse, was the greatest empire in the ancient Near East.

He lived in Jerusalem in a new palace whose walls were lined with cedar. Canaanite kings too had once lived in such palaces of cedar. During a respite in the wars, he inquired of the prophet Nathan if it was not now time to build a permanent dwelling place for the ark of YHWH.

That night the prophet had a vision, which he quickly communicated to the king. Somewhere in the busy court of the king—a center of empire teeming with troop commanders, administrators, scribes, ambassadors, a large harem, many children, and with high offices like those of royal herald (*mazkir*) and royal scribe (*sopher*) probably copied from the civil service structure of Egypt—somewhere in that court was a writer who recorded the account of the vision. We have no way of knowing if the narrative in II Samuel 7 is his or went through additional hands; it probably received very close to its final form early in the period of the united monarchy.

The vision has come down to us as a private covenant between YHWH and David. No, it is not David who will build a permanent dwelling place for the ark of YHWH; memories of the sanctuary at Shiloh and the wandering ark are still too fresh even after two centuries of settled living. It is the heir to the throne who will build the dwelling place of YHWH. "I will set up your offspring after you, one of your own issue, and I will establish his kingship. He shall build a house for My name, and I will establish his royal throne forever." YHWH obligates Himself to David in an eternal covenant. "I will be a father to him, and he shall be a son to Me. When he does wrong, I will chastise him with the rod of men and the affliction of mortals; but I will never withdraw My favor from him as I withdrew it from Saul. . . . Your house and your kingship shall ever be secure before you, your throne shall be established forever." David responds with poignant humility. "What am I, O Lord YHWH, and what is my family that You have brought me thus far? Yet even this, O Lord YHWH, has seemed too little to You; for You have spoken of Your servant's house also for the future. . . . There is none like You and there is no other God but You, as we have always heard. And who is like Your people Israel, a unique nation on earth, whom God went and redeemed as His people. . . ."

The Israelites saw each of the crucial encounters between God and man through the filtering vision of covenant relationships. God covenanted with Noah never again to destroy the world by flood. God covenanted with Abraham to give his offspring the land of Canaan. In similar fashion, God now covenanted with David to grant him an everlasting dynasty. Neither Noah, Abraham, nor David incurred any new obligations as a result of God's promise. To the contrary, God obligated Himself to remember. The rainbow is a sign of the covenant with Noah, as circumcision is a sign of the covenant with Abraham. Ancient Near Eastern royal land grants may have served as models for this kind of covenant relationship.

It is an altogether different sort of relationship from the one that acts as scaffolding for the Mosaic covenant and its later Joshua echo in Shechem, with its deep anchoring in historic events, its demands, its warnings and threats, and its collective acceptance by a grateful vassal people forever obligated to their suzerain, YHWH, for saving them from slavery and murderous chariots.

Each Israelite family could participate of its own choice in the Mosaic covenant; fathers transmitted memories and obligations to sons; elders recounted it at clan assemblies;

public avowals of continued covenant loyalty took place during festivals. The Davidic covenant was a private promise. It was probably proclaimed by prophets as an oracle and celebrated as part of the cultic rites before the ark in Jerusalem. Psalmists wrote of it, invoking the poetic imagery of pagan myths instead of the wondrous history of saving events (Psalms 89, 110); history was public and given to all the people, but this covenant was private and had been given to one family. True, it was the royal family, upon whose continued stability depended the future of the nation. But the people were at best onlookers; they could participate in the covenant only through the king. The Mosaic covenant required of each family that it establish a certain relationship with YHWH; the Davidic covenant was a move in the direction of making the king and the state intermediate between the people and YHWH. It became dogma in the south and a target for loathing and derision in the north.

And now suddenly, with the covenant given and the dynasty established, the narrator turns away with almost ironic contempt from David the golden lad, the composer of exquisite lyric poetry, the adventurous bandit, the king and conqueror. We are offered a David of brittle fleshly weakness. Distant states are his vassals and doorstep follies are his undoing. From his palace rooftop in crowded Jerusalem he spots a woman bathing. Their adulterous affair leads him to arrange for her husband's death in battle. The man, Uriah the Hittite, was a loyal officer, selflessly devoted to David. Perhaps the successful king recalled that a failed king had once sent him after Philistine foreskins. Uriah the Hittite died in combat, and the first son of David and Bathsheba, born out of their adulterous relationship, died in childhood. The second son of Bathsheba was named Solomon.

We have now entered the cycle of events that will lead to the succession of Solomon. David's oldest son, Amnon, rapes his half-sister, Tamar. Her brother, Absalom, second in line for the throne, has Amnon slain, then flees to the distant city of Geshur east of the Jordan, the land of his mother, where he remains for three years. David is heartbroken by the rape and the death, but longs for

Absalom, whom he deeply loves. To love and to be
loved—these were the greatest needs and the deepest
faults in the lyric and granite nature that was David. He
had Absalom brought back to Jerusalem but banished
him to his home and would not see him for the horror of
his deed. It was two years before the king and his son
were reconciled.

The empire of Judah and Israel prospered. But there
was much discontent. Tribal elders bitterly resented their
loss of authority to the powerful magnetic force of the
kingship. The basic unit of a tribe is the family: the father, his wife or wives, unmarried children, married sons
with their wives and children, and servants. A group of
families is a clan, which is led by its family heads or
elders. A group of clans form a tribe, with one chieftain,
who always acts together with his various clan heads.
Blood kinship, real or imagined, unites the members of a
tribe. Beginnings in a common ancestry, also real or imagined, bind clans together. When your world is a wilderness of sand and stone, a wasteland of scorpions, jackals,
serpents, and enemy tribes, you need a close social organization based on ties of blood in order to stay alive
and protected. In the time of the judges, many tribes did
not have a chieftain; elders wielded authority. That was
already one step removed from wilderness organization;
the tribes had begun to disintegrate. In the time of the
monarchy, the authority of the elders started to wane.
With David in Jerusalem, loyalties were directed toward
court and throne—and elders seethed.

Absalom, fair Absalom, would rise early and stand in
the gate of the city to meet those coming to see his father.
They would come from everywhere in the land. "Your
cause is good and right," he would say to those bringing
grievances. "But there is no one deputed of the king to
hear you." And he would add, "If I were made judge in
the land, then every man who has a lawsuit or a cause
might come to me, and I would do him justice." Grum-
bling elders listened. He bowed to them and "stole the
hearts of the men of Israel."

There were those whose loyalties were still with the
house of Saul and the one remaining male descendant of
that tragic king, the lame son of Jonathan. They would

have eagerly witnessed the end of the kingship of David. Others were angered at the census conducted by David, which had tightened his control over the land for the purpose of taxation and conscription. Resentment was now general in the land—north and south.

After four years of careful planning—winning favor, feeding grievances—Absalom went to Hebron, had himself anointed king, and marched on Jerusalem at the head of a large tribal army. An astonished aging David, caught completely by surprise, thought it wiser to flee than to fight.

He fled east across the Jordan to the canyon city of Mahanaim, from which a son of Saul had once weakly ruled the north. His mercenary troops swiftly rallied to him while Absalom sported in Jerusalem with his father's concubines, one of the traditional ways of displaying newly won authority. That cost him his life, for David's own army was fully organized by the time Absalom felt himself ready for battle. David publicly ordered his commanding officers not to kill his son. The battle was a disaster for the outclassed levies. David wept bitterly when he learned of the death of Absalom, coldly killed by Joab.

Another rebellion followed almost immediately upon the first, fanned suddenly by bickering between northern and southern forces about who would lead David in triumph to Jerusalem. David favored the people of Judah, staking his rule now once and for all upon a permanent base of power in the south. The northerners reacted with rage. Led by a Benjaminite named Sheba son of Bichri, they raised the standard of revolt. David sent in his professional troops. The revolt, such as it was, collapsed. The Benjaminite was pursued to a town deep in the north, whose inhabitants had no stomach for rebellion. They tossed the rebel's head over the wall, and the troops went home.

The aged king seemed incapable of choosing his successor. Perhaps he loved all his sons; perhaps he dreaded losing the love of those he would not choose. The empire was controlled by his troops; the tribal territories, divided into twelve districts, were efficiently administered; but the court, the home of the king, seethed with intrigue.

He was old now, confined to his bed, chilled and withered—this feeble man who had once been a fighter and poet, the remnant of the greatness called David. A palace intrigue almost put another son, Adonijah, on the throne. But Nathan the prophet favored Solomon—and it was Solomon whom David finally designated as his heir in a countermove that put an end to the plotting that fouled the air of the court.

David died about 965 B.C.E., and Solomon ascended the throne. The people may have cheered, but few could have attributed an inspiring nature to this new monarch. It is not recorded that he was separately anointed in the north. He had the army and the empire. He was king. It is estimated that there were somewhat fewer than one million Israelites in the land at the time.

Now these are the achievements of Solomon son of David, king of Judah and Israel.

He sent away or slew all who were a threat to his throne. Adonijah was executed for a final, desperate, and inept attempt to gain the throne: he expressed his desire to marry the concubine who had nursed and slept with the aged, dying David. Abiathar the priest, a supporter of Adonijah, was banished to his village north of Jerusalem. Joab, who also had favored Adonijah, was pursued into the sanctuary and slain at the altar by order of Solomon. A man named Shimei, a follower of the Saul faction who had hurled curses at David during the flight from Absalom, was confined to his house in Jerusalem and later put to death. "And the kingdom was established in the hand of Solomon."

He had been handed an empire by his father. There is no indication that he ever took part in a military campaign. He saw it as his task to maintain and exploit the Israelite peace won by his father's troops. This he did by establishing alliances with near and distant nations and by turning the empire into an emporium.

Alliances were made not only by covenant but also by marriage. The harem of Solomon swelled with the wives who came with political unions. Most distinguished among his many wives was the daughter of Pharaoh Siamun—an indication of the high international status of the king of Judah and Israel and the fallen prestige of the king of Upper and Lower Egypt. Not even kings of Babylon and the Mitanni had been given royal daughters from the land of the Nile. The dowry was the city of Gezer, which the pharaoh presented together with his daughter, thereby bequeathing to scholars another puzzle to ponder. When did the Egyptians take Gezer? From whom? Philistines? Canaanites? It was a key city between the north and south of Israel near the coast. Why did they give it away? Solomon had a private palace built for the daughter of the pharaoh outside the city of David as well as a temple where she could worship her Egyptian god.

David had made an alliance with Hiram, king of Tyre. It was renewed and deepened by Solomon. Most of the coastal cities of northren Canaan—let us call it Phoenicia from now on, though the Greeks who will give it that name are still centuries away—were rebuilt after the locusts of Sea Peoples had completed their ravaging and gone elsewhere. Those coastal cities were all that was left now of Canaan; in the coming centuries they would expand westward and found colonies on the islands of Sardinia and Cyprus, in Spain and North Africa. One of those colonies would be Carthage.

Solomon sent Hiram of Tyre olive oil and wheat and received from him timber from the forests of Lebanon for his building projects. Thirty thousand Israelites were conscripted by Solomon into work gangs to help fell the trees. "And he sent them to Lebanon in monthly relays of ten thousand." So we are told in the Bible. "The men spent one month in Lebanon and two at home."

He transformed the battered ruins of ancient cities—Hazor, Megiddo, Gezer, and others, some of which were crude shanty towns—into powerful fortifications that faced his potential enemies and discouraged the temptation for rebellion or invasion. To the professional army he now added a Canaanite feature—a permanent chariot corps. "He had one thousand and four hundred chariots and twelve thousand horsemen. . . ." He no longer needed the tribal levies for warfare; instead he used them for the corvée, impressed labor gangs, that rebuilt the cities and fortified them.

The empire secure, he pursued the classic goals of powerful ancient Near Eastern kings: wealth, luxury, culture. In those days most foreign trade was a royal monopoly—merchants were rarely able to pool enough capital for risky international ventures. Aided by the Phoenicians, Solomon constructed a merchant fleet which went on regular voyages to distant Ophir, somewhere along the coast of southern Arabia. The voyages lasted longer than a year and broke the Midianite monopoly of the caravans bringing goods from Arabia along the King's Highway; at the same time, Solomon taxed the caravaneers who used the long stretch of the highway that was under his control. The ships of Solomon plied the blue-green waters of the sea and gulf from Ophir to the port city of Solomon called Ezion-geber, located somewhere in the region of modern Elat; they brought back gold, rare timber, precious stones, silver, and monkeys for his private zoo—royal zoos were common monarchical pleasures in many lands of the ancient Near East.

It is not known what Solomon shipped to Ophir—perhaps the copper and iron mined deep in the lunar wastelands of the southern Negev by state slaves. Biblical law refers only to domestic slaves, not to this class of perpetually enslaved individuals whose ranks came from captives of war. In this regard, of course, Solomon was no different from any other monarch in the ancient Near East. The class of state slaves in ancient Israel remained in existence until the destruction of the Judean kingdom about three centuries after the death of Solomon.

He collected tolls for the use of the many major trade routes under his control. He acted as middleman for the enormously profitable trade in horses that came from Cilicia and the chariots made in Egypt. "And a chariot came up and went out of Egypt for six hundred shekels of silver, and a horse for a hundred and fifty. . . ."

The visit of the queen of Sheba from distant southeastern Arabia—the land of the Sabeans, roughly the area of today's Yemen—was a business trip. She had spices, jewels, and gold; Solomon controlled the caravan routes; kingdoms in Mesopotamia and Anatolia wanted those spices and jewels. Queen and king no doubt came to a lucrative trade agreement.

All was well in the land. "Judah and Israel," wrote the Biblical historian of Solomon's reign, "were many as the sand which is by the sea in multitude, eating and drinking and making merry."

With his wealth and the help of Phoenician artisans, Israelite labor, and material sent by Hiram of Tyre, Solomon extended the walls of his father's city and constructed a temple to YHWH. Seven years went into the construction of the temple. It was the last—not the first—Israelite temple built during the period of judges and kings. About twelve temples—structures with altars on sacred sites—had been erected earlier, in Dan, Bethel, Shiloh, and elsewhere. They were all eclipsed by the temple in Jerusalem. Its architecture was similar to that of the Canaanite temple discovered in 1957 by Yigael Yadin in the Lower Bronze Age level (1550-1200 B.C.E.) at Hazor. It was about one hundred feet long, thirty-four feet wide, and fifty feet high; its exterior was of quarry-dressed white limestone; its interior was lined with cedar. It faced east and was fronted by two tall freestanding pillars of bronze. A vestibule and a large sanctuary lighted by high small windows made up the edifice, at the rear of which was a small darkened room in the shape of a cube, windowless. There, in the shadows, the sacred ark was placed, and the presence of YHWH resided enthroned upon two huge, human-headed, lion-bodied, winged creatures called cherubim. In other cultures of the time, where those figures were also found, they were called by different names. We know them too as sphinxes.

The Israelites who came on pilgrimages to Jerusalem from their hill villages in the north probably stared in awe and bewilderment at this house of YHWH. The temple was a visible focal point of culture confrontation. Its architecture and decorative motifs were expressions of the core of Canaanite paganism, the living reality of Canaanite cult and myth: the cyclical lives of their fertility gods; the battles and passions that pervaded their pantheon; their view of creation, man, life, death; the inextricable union with the living, terrifying, divine, pulsing world of nature. Canaanite culture was rich in art forms borrowed from Egypt and Mesopotamia; the port cities of cosmopolitan Phoenicia served as culture conduits for the Mediter-

ranean world. Much of Phoenician and Egyptian art—
carvings of open flowers, palm trees, pomegranates, oxen,
lions, sphinxes—populated the cedar walls of the temple
in Jerusalem, placed there by the skillful craftsmen from
Tyre, who then overlaid the walls with gold.

In its encounter with the core of Israelite faith, the
Canaanite cosmos was emptied of divinity; the heavens,
until now studded with gods, became the handiwork of
YHWH; the gods died; living myth became poetic meta-
phor and decorative motifs; forms were filled with new
content. So we are told by many scholars. But it seems to
me there is no way we can understand what an Israelite
of that time thought he saw as he stood gazing at the
huge basin called the "molten sea"—about fifteen feet in
diameter and seven feet high—inside the temple; it had
been cast to stand upon the figures of twelve oxen; its
brim was shaped like the softly curving rim of a lily; "it
held two thousand baths." Did he see Yam, the primeval
waters of Canaanite myth, or did he see—a large water
basin constructed so that visitors could cleanse themselves
upon their entry into the sanctuary? When he looked at
the tall freestanding pillars, did he envisage matzevot, the
standing stones—fertility symbols, perhaps—of Canaanite
paganism, or did he see only beautifully designed pillars?
We have no way of knowing.

This we do know: the Solomonic temple was devoid of
images. Israelites were called upon to offer sacrifices to
their all-powerful and invisible God, who had covenanted
with their ancestors in Canaan and at Sinai, and whose
promise to the patriarchs had clearly been fulfilled—as
evidenced by the empire of the united monarchy and the
glittering splendor of Solomon's new Jerusalem. They
were to offer their sacrifices in Jerusalem in times of famine, drought, war; for sins; during festivals. The temple of
Solomon was a religious and political undertaking that
deepened the relationship between the city of David and
the people of Israel. Nothing of that temple has survived.

He built a palace for himself in Jerusalem; its site is
uncertain. It took thirteen years to build the palace. The
throne was of ivory and gold. The palace may have been
located close to the temple and could not have been too
far from the palace of his most prestigious wife, the

daughter of the pharaoh. Nothing remains of either palace.

Wealth poured into the city and brought with it refinement of taste, courtly behavior—wisdom, the Bible calls it; the calculated, mannered use of one's skills in the attainment of success. The once small mountain fastness was now an opulent international center of culture and commerce. The united land, divided by Solomon into administrative districts, not all of them given the same boundaries as the old tribal territories, functioned smoothly under high officials appointed by the king. Each district was required to supply the food and funds for one month's maintenance of the royal court—a staggering burden. There was trouble in some of the outlying areas of the empire; Damascus apparently managed to shake off its Israelite overlord. But there was no interference with the caravan routes. "So King Solomon exceeded all the kings of the earth in riches and in wisdom," our Biblical historian wrote. "And all the earth sought the presence of Solomon, to hear his wisdom, which God had put in his heart. . . ."

His father was reputed to have been a gifted lyric poet; the writing talents of Solomon appear to have been of a more earthy nature. He set down practical advice in a flat aphoristic style, possibly taking as his model the *Instruction of Amenemope*, an Egyptian book of wisdom. The Egyptians enjoyed collections of wise sayings, works that directed one to a successful life. That was the meaning of "wisdom" to them. The oldest of these collections of sayings went back to the Fifth Dynasty in the Old Kingdom period. They took the form of an aged councillor instructing the son who is to succeed him on how to act in a manner that will be of greatest benefit to himself and the pharaoh: "If a son accepts what his father says, no project of his miscarries. . . ." "Hear, my son, the instruction of your father," we read in the section of the Book of Proverbs attributed to Solomon.

Wisdom literature was part of the cultural air breathed by much of the ancient Near East. Whether it came to the flourishing civilization of the Israelites directly from Egypt or indirectly from the crossroads culture of Phoenicia is still being debated by scholars. There is little doubt that under Solomon the small nation of one-time wanderers entered deeply into the mainstream of ancient Near Eastern culture.

That culture contact yielded rich fruit. Serious Israelite literary creativity began in the period of the united monarchy. What started with writers and scribes under the patronage of the merchant king of Judah and Israel would in time become a tidal wave of creativity, the special genius of the Israelites, as if all the power of their artistic abilities, restricted from finding full expression in the plastic arts because of the covenanted stipulation against the making of images, channeled itself in another direction—creation with words. And creation of a certain kind—narrative history structured so as to yield meaning and render with clarity the ongoing relationships between YHWH and His chosen people. The people had been born out of a historic event—the exodus from Egypt. In the time of the united kingdom, when ancient Israel began to sense its oneness, it began to shape with words the complex patternings of its past.

Much of what we now call the Books of Joshua and Samuel was written then, as was the account of Solomon's succession to the throne. And somewhere in the land a writer of incalculable genius, gifted beyond measure with a purity of narrative style and a sharply focused vision of the moral interplay between YHWH and man, began to summon up remembered and often diverse tribal traditions of patriarchs, wanderings, and conquests, ancient accounts of creation, a garden of the gods, a vast flood, undying memories of the miraculous exodus from Egypt, the escape from chariots, the convenant at Sinai. In all these he saw clearly, through the magnifying power of his personal vision, the guiding hand of YHWH. These remembered events, the collective experience of his people, were the raw materials of his creativity. To give them expression, he used every available literary form at his disposal, gathered from all the world of the ancient Near East. At times he consciously repeated lines from ancient myths, replacing the nature-rooted, cult-demanding, and often whimsical callousness of the gods with the moral and ethical imperatives of YHWH; at other times he utilized the outlines of old tales and filled them with Israelite content. Often, as in the account of the sacrifice of Isaac, no prototype is known to us and we are presented with what appears to be an original narrative of endless dimensions of meaning and a power to grip the imagination of the most varied members of our species.

We do not know the name of that writer. Except for Egypt, where the names of scribes may be found in tombs, and the occasional Mesopotamian and Phoenician scribes whose names we have, writers in the ancient Near East wrote not as individuals but as members of a community. Israelite writers in particular felt their task to be tribal in nature; their words echoed the pure faith of the people of YHWH; they wrote for the people, for shepherds, farmers, craftsmen. The writer who shaped the segments of the Bible which scholars refer to as the Yahwist documents may have been a scribe, a shepherd, a farmer, a woman. He or she wrote for all the people out of a sense of unity of the Israelite experience that was reflected in the united kingdom and the centrality of Jerusalem and the temple of YHWH. The Yahwist account of Israelite history was probably written to be recited aloud periodically, perhaps at pilgrimage festivals, in the Jerusalem temple. We cannot be certain that was its initial purpose. If it was, then it still functions today on each Sabbath, festival, and holy day when the Bible is read in synagogues throughout much of the world, twenty-five hundred years after the first Jerusalem temple was burned to the ground.

But the price paid for the grandiose world of Solomon was very high. There was a point where he simply ran out of whatever it was he used for money, and could not pay King Hiram of Tyre for construction material. He ceded to the Phoenician a section of Israelite coastline near Acco which included about twenty Galilean towns. It appears that no one inquired of the Israelites in that region how they felt about suddenly becoming subjects of Phoenicia. To my knowledge nowhere in the Bible is Solomon reprimanded for giving away a portion of the promised land.

The price grew steeper in the later years of his reign. It was always so when monarchs ruled: only a few shared the wealth and culture of a royal court. Among the Israelites resentment over the humiliation of forced labor, the high taxes, and the leechlike bureaucracy was deep, especially in the north where old tribal loyalties and the allegiance to the Mosaic covenant in which only YHWH could be king were remembered and would not wither away before the glittering magnificence of Solomonic kingship. There is some indication that the south received favored status—kings could do that—and an easing of the burdens of corvée and taxes; this would have set northern resentment smoldering.

There was one attempt at rebellion, led by an officer of a northern corvée. It did not succeed, and the officer, Jeroboam son of Nebat, an Ephraimite, the most powerful of the northern tribes, fled to Egypt, where he was warmly received. A new pharaoh now ruled Egypt. Unlike his predecessor, he gazed with a malevolent eye upon the empire of Judah and Israel.

In the end Solomon himself fell prey to the pagan world he had brought to Jerusalem. "His wives turned away his heart after other gods; and his heart was not whole with the Lord his God, as was the heart of David his father." So we are told by the Biblical historian.

These then were the achievements of Solomon son of David, king of Judah and Israel. He died about 925 B.C.E. and was buried in the city of David his father.

The mother of Solomon's eldest son had been an Ammonite princess. Now the son, Rehoboam, a vain and totally inept fellow, became king of Judah. He journeyed to Shechem to accept the kingship over the north.

Elders from the north, meeting with Rehoboam in solemn assembly at Shechem, the site of the Joshua covenant, asked for a relaxation of the corvée and taxes. With biting mockery, Rehoboam refused. Tempers flared. They had come, these elders, willing to accept this heir to the dynasty of David. But his words of contempt, uttered as a slick proverb—"My little finger is thicker than my father's loins. . . . My father chastised you with whips, but I will chastise you with scorpions"—incensed them. They raised the ancient cry of independence and revolt. "What portion have we in David? . . . To your tents, O Israel!" Rehoboam's commander of the northern levies was stoned to death. The son of Solomon fled to Jerusalem in a chariot.

In 922 B.C.E. the nation split into two lands: Judah in the south, the eleven tribes of Israel in the north. Jeroboam son of Nebat had returned from Egypt and was now acclaimed king of the northern land. Benjamin, located between Judah and the large tribes of the north, became an arena of intermittent war; much of its territory was absorbed by Judah, leaving ten tribes in the north.

The empire disintegrated as rapidly as it had been created about sixty years earlier by David. Vassals, tugging at their chains and finding their former overlords preoccupied with internal affairs and preparations for civil war, simply ceased paying tribute and regained control of their trade routes.

About five years after north and south became two lands, Pharaoh Shishak of Egypt, a Libyan, invaded Judah and Israel and left behind him a wide swath of plundered towns, from Ramat Matred above Kadesh-barnea in the south to Shechem and Megiddo in the north. He destroyed Ezion-geber in order to break up the trade link between Judah and Arabia. He threatened Jerusalem and was offered tribute; he took away with him "the treasures of the house of the Lord and the treasures of the king's house," and effectively prevented the launching of the war planned by Rehoboam to reunite the land.

Jeroboam made Shechem his capital and fortified it. He turned the towns of Dan and Bethel, located near the northern and southern borders of his kingdom, into cult cities to rival Jerusalem. In each of their sanctuaries he placed a golden calf or bull—not as objects of worship but as pedestals for the invisible God of Israel; no ancient Semitic people ever represented a high god in animal form. He could have done this in the Mosaic north only if there existed some kind of tradition permitting this form of worship—and we have preserved for us a clear indication of such a tradition going back to the desert period in the account of the golden calf at Sinai. We have that event now as a moment of apostasy, just as Jeroboam's calves were regarded with horror by the historians of the south. But a tradition of the calf as a legitimate form of worship must have existed, else it would not have been countenanced in the sanctuaries of the north.

Jeroboam instituted an autumn harvest festival to counteract the festival in the south which was strongly associated with the Davidic monarchy. With these tactics he made northern dependence upon the south unnecessary and successfully drew the northern tribes away from Jerusalem. The city of David stepped out of stage center and slipped into the quiet shadows of a mountain culture only remotely in touch with the culture of western Asia and at odds with the seething world of hill, valley, and coastal plain beyond. Judah was poorer and smaller than the north; her population was homogeneous; she was relatively isolated geographically. The north was large, wealthy, closer to the heart of the ancient tribal ways; but it had a large Canaanite population. The full shock of culture confrontation shifted to the Mosaic north, with its many ethnic and tribal groupings and its borders right up against the world of Phoenicia and Mesopotamia.

Jeroboam, an able king hated by the south and its writers of Biblical history—we have only the southern version of northern history; virtually no official documents can be claimed with certainty as having come down to us from the north—Jeroboam died. The principle of dynastic succession had not been established in the north. The son of Jeroboam, Nadab, became king in 901 B.C.E. and was assassinated about two years later. His assassin, a military man named Baasha, took the throne and slaughtered the entire family of Jeroboam.

King Rehoboam of Judah had died in 915 B.C.E. and was peacefully succeeded by his son Abijah. He died in 913 B.C.E. and was followed by his son Asa, who, unlike his father and grandfather, zealously prohibited Canaanite practices, according to the Biblical historian. He ruled until his death in 873 B.C.E.

In the distant east, above the faded worlds of ancient Sumer and Akkad, Assyria had begun to stir herself into new life after her long struggle with the roving Arameans, who were by now settling down into independent states, engaging in commerce, growing rich off the caravan routes they controlled all around Assyria, and fighting one another.

\* \* \*

Who was king? Who was not king? In the north usurpers were king.

Rebellion against the united monarchy of Solomon had been encouraged by prophets who had loathed Solomon's disregard of tribal independence and viewed his culture contacts with the outside world as a corruption of Israelite faith and a breach of the ancient covenant with YHWH. They were not mystics, these prophets; they made no claim to direct and intimate union of their being with the being of God. They were spokesmen of YHWH, ordinary mortals upon whom the divine spirit descended inexplicably, turning them into messengers of the word of God. They are called ecstatics by scholars, from the Greek word *ekstasis*, which was used in classical Greece to describe any sudden change of mood, any abrupt departure from normal behavior. The prophets were possessed by the spirit of YHWH; in that sense only were they ecstatics. As mysteriously as it had come, that spirit could leave them, and they would return to their normal lives, often with a sense of relief. These prophets in Judah and Israel—Gad, Nathan, Elijah, and others—bear some resemblance to the *apilum*, answerers, described in the cuneiform documents found in the city of Mari: they deliver the word of the god to the king and demand that he fulfill it. Unlike the later, classical prophets of Israel, however, the message of the Mari prophets is cultic and political and entirely empty of ethical or social content.

When King Jeroboam of Israel died and his son Nadab was murdered, kingship passed to Baasha; he was from the tribe of Issachar, and he ruled the north for almost twenty-five years. He warred against King Asa of Judah, recovered some northern territory lost in a previous campaign, and even took the southern fortress of Ramah. Baasha died and kingship passed to his son Elah, who ruled for about two years.

Baasha had been designated king by the prophet Jehu; that same prophet had, in the end, rejected him, thereby once again preventing the establishment of dynastic succession. In the north, a land of conflicting loyalties, the old tribal tradition of leadership by men or women filled

with the spirit of YHWH now wore the garb of monarchy: if you were moved to become king you had to remove the one who stood in your way.

A chariot corps commander named Zimri wished to become king. Elah was drinking himself drunk one day, and
Zimri killed him, took the throne, and slaughtered the
family of Baasha. He reigned in the town of Tirzah, a few
miles north of Shechem. But Zimri had neither prophetic
designation nor the support of the people. The commander of the army, a man named Omri, led troops
against Tirzah and captured it. Zimri set fire to the house
of the king and perished in the flames—seven days after
he had taken the throne. Rival army factions struggled for
the kingship. Four years of fighting followed as the Omri
faction fought a faction loyal to someone named Tibni,
probably another general.

Who was king? Who was not king? Usurping generals
were king. In the end kingship passed to Omri. He took
the throne in 876 B.C.E., three years before King Asa of
Judah died. It is not known if he had prophetic designation.

He established the first dynasty in the north. He left so
powerful a mark upon the land that for a century and a
half the Assyrians referred to the north as "the land of
the house of Omri." Yet the southern writer of the First
Book of Kings recounts the accession and reign of Omri
in a terse passage of thirteen verses. We are told simply
that Omri emerged victorious from a battle of army commanders, took the throne, and moved the capital from
Tirzah to a hill which he purchased from its owner for
two talents of silver. He built a new city on the hill, six
miles northwest of today's Nablus, named it Samaria after
its owner, Shemer—a dubious etymology. Finally we are
informed that Omri "did that which was evil in the eyes
of the Lord," passed on, and was buried in Samaria.

The fact is the southern writer did not intend his work
to be a political history. The focus of loyalty and identity
in such a history would have been tribal chieftains,
priests, kings, cities, nations, empires. He was writing a
history of the culture confrontation between the faith of
YHWH and the world of paganism. His focus of loyalty

was YHWH; his interest in political power was secondary to his fixed vision of the battles won and lost in that confrontation. The reign of Omri was a battle lost, "for he walked in the way of Jeroboam son of Nebat . . . and made Israel to sin. . . ." He was writing a philosophy of history, winnowing out of the facts in the northern court annals at his disposal a pattern of meaning which seemed to him brilliantly clear: whenever Israel broke the covenant, YHWH invoked its curses. He refers us constantly to his sources: "Now all the rest of the acts of Omri which he did, and his might that he showed, are they not written in the book of the chronicles of the kings of Israel?" How could he have envisaged that the court annals, the surface record of how it really was, would not survive?

Omri made the north a stable nation. He brought an end to the wars with Judah, which were ruining both lands. He renewed trade relations with Phoenicia. Tyre was then at the very height of her power, ruled by Eshbaal, priest of the goddess Astarte. King Omri sealed an alliance with King Eshbaal by marrying his son Ahab to Eshbaal's daughter Jezebel.

His new capital, Samaria, was a glittering counterpoint to Jerusalem, as archaeologists have recently discovered. From another archaeological discovery made in August 1868—an inscribed slab measuring about four feet high, two feet wide, and ten inches thick, which has come to be known as the Moabite Stone and is dated about 830 B.C.E.; its language is almost identical with Biblical Hebrew—we learn that Omri reconquered Moab: "Omri, king of Israel, he oppressed Moab many days. . . ." Some refer to Omri as the David of the north.

In the south King Jehoshaphat of Judah reconquered Edom. Now Israel and Judah together once again controlled a vital length of the King's Highway.

Very early in the reign of Omri, the distant land of Assyria had come fully awake. For two centuries, from the days of Tiglath-pileser I until now, the western arc of the Fertile Crescent had not felt her presence. During the first of those two centuries she had suffered defeat and disaster as Aramean tribes had swarmed across Mesopotamia. At roughly the same time, Babylonia was successfully invaded by Chaldeans, a Semitic tribe connected with the Arameans. The invasions came in ceaseless waves. The old centers of Mesopotamian civilization were devastated. Babylonia sank into chaos. Assyria barely managed to survive. It was another century, during which the invasions ceased and the tribes became sedentary, before Assyria was able to reassert her power. That was the century—1000 to 900 B.C.E.—that saw the rise to international greatness of the united kingdom of Judah and Israel.

Assyria had always been a land without the gift of great natural resources, struggling endlessly with beasts and men, given to gloom, superstition, dread of evil spirits, divination, and a fanatic dedication to a religion rooted in fear. Her laws were her own, and punishment was often harsh—slitting of noses and ears, castration. Married women went about veiled. Her god, Ashur, was a solar deity who led the nation and the king in peace and war and to whom captives were sacrificed. The symbol of Ashur was a winged disk inside which the god is shown leading troops in battle or investing the nation's chosen king with authority to rule.

Now, strangled by numerous Aramean kingdoms that were allied by blood and divided by political and tribal lines, Assyria found her position disastrous. The entire Euphrates valley was blocked to her caravans; she could not trade with the west, for that trade was now in the hands of the commercially sharp Arameans. Assyria's main products, metals and cloth stuffs, could not be moved. The country was no longer in military danger, but her borders had been reduced, her commerce was tenuous, her people suffered great poverty.

Then a series of strong rulers appeared who gradually extended her borders. By the end of the tenth century B.C.E. great construction works were under way. In those days you financed the construction of your own cities by plundering the cities of others and by establishing your control over trade routes. From about 910 to 890 B.C.E. King Adadnirari marched and plundered. Slowly the borders widened; the lands around Assyria became increasingly larger hunting grounds for the almost annual ravagings of her growing army.

Subsequent rulers followed a consistent policy of plunder and conquest. Nearly every year for sixty years the Assyrians mustered their army, usually in the spring, and marched over the hot, dusty, summer roads of Mesopotamia or up and down the perilous mountains that were the home of wild tribes.

In 876 B.C.E., two centuries after Assyria lay near death at the hands of the Arameans, an Assyrian army, organized into units according to their various weapons, spearheaded by a powerful chariot corps, and led by Ashurnasirpal II, marched unopposed across northern Mesopotamia to the city of Carchemish, taking tribute and levying troops from kingdoms along the way. Then the army skirted the powerful kingdom of Aramean Damascus, with which it apparently did not yet wish to fight, and came to a halt at the shores of the Mediterranean north of Sidon and Tyre. "At that time I seized the entire extent of the Lebanon mountain and reached the Great Sea of the Amurru country," boasted Ashurnasirpal. "I cleaned my weapons in the deep sea. . . ." He claimed to have received tribute from the cities of the western coast. "The tribute of the seacoast—from the inhabitants of Tyre, Sidon, Byblos, Mahallata, Maiza, Kaiza, Amurru, and of Arvad, which is an island in the sea: gold, silver, tin, copper, copper containers, linen garments with multicolored trimmings, large and small monkeys, ebony, boxwood, ivory from walrus tusks. . . ."

He had first subdued the Aramean hill people near his own borders. Rulers whose resistance was stubborn were flayed alive—a torture meted out by Ashurnasirpal to anyone who caused him difficulty. Terror and brutality—impalement, flaying, beheading, burning masses of captives to death—were made basic state policy by this Assyrian king. The humanitarianism that we at least make a pretext of practicing during wars in our time had not yet been conceived of in those days, but Ashurnasirpal appears to have outdone everyone in brutality and terror, and made a point of gloating over his achievements. "I built a pillar over against his city gate and flayed all the chiefs who had revolted, and I covered the pillar with their skin. . . . Some I impaled upon the pillar. . . . And I cut off the limbs of the officers. . . . Many captives from among them I burned with fire. . . . From some I cut off their noses, their ears and their fingers, of many I put out the eyes. . . ."

After his triumphant march to the Mediterranean he returned home, bloated with wealth but leaving behind no lasting conquest. Nevertheless a chill dread had fallen across the entire ancient Near East.

Omri died in 869 B.C.E. His son Ahab peacefully succeeded him to the throne.

The queen of Israel was Jezebel daughter of Ethbaal, once priest of the goddess Astarte and now king of the Sidonians. Her husband, Ahab, while completing the construction of Samaria, making it an exquisite city filled with buildings decorated in ivory, and replacing the Solomonic fortifications at Hazor and Megiddo with massive walls that might better withstand the new siege techniques being developed by the Assyrians, found money, slaves, and Tyrian craftsmen to build a temple in the royal quarter in Samaria to Baal Melqart in which the queen could worship. Baal Melqart, whose name means Baal ruler of the city, was the god of Tyre. The term Sidonians is a Biblical name for Phoenicians.

Jezebel was of that rare breed of pagan—a fervent missionizer for her god. I have encountered only one other like her in all my reading—Pharaoh Akhenaten. Coming from Tyre, that most cosmopolitan of cities, that coastal island which served as a rich meeting ground of commerce and culture, Jezebel regarded with contempt the austerity and simplicity of imageless YHWH worship. It was her intent to convert the court of the king to the cult of her god. The rest of the land, she believed, would soon follow, and Baal and his consort Astarte would reign supreme in Israel.

She succeeded. She brought to Samaria priests of Baal whose foreign ways and pagan life style were quickly imitated by the high officials of Israel. Her husband did not resist her efforts, though he himself remained, at least on the surface, a follower of YHWH. The north, populated with descendants of Canaanites conquered by David, was full of hesitant followers of YHWH. Many now slipped with ease into the fertility cult of Baal and Astarte. Most fused YHWH with Baal and worshiped both simultaneously, either regarding YHWH as Baal or Baal as YHWH.

Some resisted. Prophets traveled about the land, preaching against the pagan queen. Jezebel, enraged, had some of them slain. For the first time in the history of the land prophets were being killed for preaching loyalty to YHWH. Many were stricken with fear. The prophetic movement splintered. Prophets, out of weakness and dread, entered the service of the court and spoke only what the king and queen wished to hear. They are the prophets condemned as false by the few who remained true to the ancient vision of the covenant. This bitter antagonism between the prophets of the court and those individuals who claimed to be the sole spokesmen for YHWH continued until kingship came to an end in Israel.

Sometime during the latter half of the reign of Ahab, a drought struck the land. The records of Tyre too speak of a drought at this time. We are told by the Biblical historian that the lack of rain had been prophesied by the fiercest opponent of Queen Jezebel, a prophet named Elijah of the family of Tishbi, which had settled in the Gilead region across the Jordan near the fringe of the desert. Wearing a mantle of hair and a girdle of leather about his loins, he ranged through the land like a specter, appearing suddenly at one time here and at another time there. Everywhere he went he denounced the paganism that had spread across Israel from its center in the royal court and now threatened the existence of the faith of YHWH.

The drought raged on and brought famine. Many sold themselves into slavery to avoid starvation. At the height of the famine, in the third year of the drought, Elijah suddenly appears before Ahab on Mount Carmel. Four hundred prophets of Baal are there, probably in a natural amphitheater near the top of the hill, together with a mass of Israelites. The prophet denounces them all. "How long will you halt between two opinions? If the Lord be God, follow Him; but if Baal, follow him." It is a declaration of war by YHWH against the pagan world of fertility cults and images—and we are reminded of that distant time when clans led by Joshua stood poised for the invasion of Canaan. The response of the multitude is silence.

Elijah mocks the prophets of Baal, taunting them, urging them to offer a bullock as a sacrifice and to pray to their god to fire the wood on the altar. They dance about the altar and cry aloud and, as is their manner, "cut themselves with swords and lances until the blood gushed out upon them." But the fire does not come.

Nearby is an altar to YHWH, which was thrown down. This is now repaired by Elijah and the people. Elijah prays to YHWH for a fire to burn the wood upon which he has placed pieces of a bullock; "the fire of the Lord fell and consumed the burnt-offering." The awestruck people proclaim, "The Lord, He is God! The Lord, He is God!" They haul the prophets of Baal to wadi Kishon, fifteen minutes by foot, and Elijah slays them. "The wadi Kishon swept them away," the judge and prophetess Deborah had once sung after a victory against Canaanite chariots bogged down in a sudden rain. "That ancient wadi, the wadi Kishon. O my soul, tread them down with strength. . . ."

Now on Mount Carmel Elijah prays for rain. "Make ready your chariot and get down," he tells Ahab, "so that the rain does not hinder you." A tiny cloud forms over the sea, grows, and darkens the sky. Suddenly there is wind and a great rain. Ahab rides in the rain to the city of Jezreel, north of Shechem, and, in one of those brief Biblical vignettes that imprint themselves forever on a reader's mind, Elijah, his loins girded up, runs like a vassal before the royal chariot in the wind and rain until the entrance to Jezreel as a mark of his respect for the king and kingship of his land.

We have journeyed through a tale filled with enigmatic tonalities and sudden miracles. Many of the stories about Elijah and his successor Elisha have that chilling quality of the miraculous, abrupt flashes of lightning in a black sky. Miracles in the Bible are often barometers of the anguish of the people of YHWH.

The victory of Elijah on Mount Carmel was small and temporary. Jezebel, on learning of the death of her prophets, threatened his life. He fled south to the hill country of Judah, and then journeyed deep into the wilderness to the mountain of YHWH, Mount Sinai. There, stricken with helplessness and despair over the power of the queen, he lived alone in a cave and rediscovered YHWH, not in awesome manifestations of nature, like a devastating wind, an earthquake, a sudden fire, but in the still small voice that is the unyielding strength of every man of vision. Not the external world of nature but the inner, intangible, unseen groping of man toward spiritual and moral awareness—that is where YHWH is to be found. We are reminded of Moses, alone, in the wilderness, searching for the God who he believes bade him slay the Egyptian, and the bush glowing fiercely in the sunlight. Now the Mosaic covenant is renewed and sustained by this fierce, almost eerie, mantle-clad man of YHWH.

We do not know how long he remained in that wilderness. When he emerged he journeyed northward, found a farmer named Elisha son of Shaphat, a burly bald-headed man, plowing a field. He cast his mantle upon him, thereby designating him as his successor. Then, followed by Elisha, he continued northward. The rest of the deeds of Elijah—including his reverberating admonition when he learned how the queen had expropriated from a man named Naboth a vineyard coveted by her husband after she had caused the man to be perversely condemned and murdered—are they not to be found in the Books of Kings? At the time of his death the war against Canaanite paganism remained unresolved.

During the reign of Ahab the Assyrians felt themselves strong enough to march against the heartland of what is today's Syria, a region they had previously avoided. They were checked by a coalition of twelve kings who fought a decisive battle against them in 853 B.C.E. at Qarqar deep in the north above Byblos and Hamath. The Bible tells us nothing of this. An Assyrian inscription lists Ahab as bringing to that battle two thousand Israelite chariots and ten thousand infantry. It is clear from this list that Ahab and Jezebel had created a powerful state.

Nineteen years after he assumed the kingship, Ahab was killed by an arrow on the field of battle in an engagement against the Aramean kingdom of Damascus, with which he had been at war off and on for most of his reign. He was buried in Samaria.

The son who ascended the throne, Ahaziah, died two years later after an accidental fall out of a window. A second son, Jehoram, proved inept, lost Moab, and was slightly wounded in a battle. He returned to Jezreel to recuperate from the wound. Jezebel, ruling as queen mother, was the true royal power and controlled the land through her son.

The prophet Elisha, who roamed up and down the Jordan valley and was as familiar with royalty as he was with farmers, abruptly sent one of the members of the band of prophets to the headquarters of the army. There, in a private room, the messenger anointed the commander, Jehu son of Nimshi, king over Israel. "Thus said the Lord, the God of Israel: I have anointed you king over the people of the Lord. . . . And you shall smite the house of Ahab your master, that I may avenge the blood of my servants the prophets. . . ."

The messenger fled.

The officers accepted Jehu with acclamation. A sense of revulsion had begun to settle over the land toward the queen and the dynasty of Omri.

Jehu mounted a chariot and raced to Jezreel. He slew Jehoram with an arrow. Jezebel, learning of what had occurred, coolly painted her eyes and stood gazing out her window. When Jehu appeared below she mocked him contemptuously. "Is it peace, you murderer of your master?"

Jehu had her thrown from the window. She lay in her blood and was trodden by horses. She had reigned for thirty years and had exerted a powerful cultural and political influence over the land. Her body was eaten by dogs.

A blood purge ensued. Jehu slaughtered the entire family of Ahab, destroyed the pagan temple and its priests, and cleansed the land of worshipers of Baal. It was the bloodiest act in the history of the north, which, unlike the conservative south, always swung wildly between the extremes of rampant paganism and zealous worship of YHWH. Jehu took the throne in 842 B.C.E., about four hundred years after Joshua had crossed the Jordan.

One year later he was bowing low on the ground before

the feet of King Salmaneser III of Assyria and offering him tribute.

The Assyrian army had marched through Mesopotamia, destroying cities and taking tribute, and had come to a halt on the Mediterranean coast either at Mount Carmel, which was at that time the southern border of the Sidonians, or at a promontory north of today's Beirut, the northern border of the Sidonians. "I received tribute from the inhabitants of Tyre, Sidon, and from Jehu son of Omri," are read in the annals of Shalmaneser III. Then the Assyia army withdrew.

An almost seven-foot-high, four-sided black limestone obelisk was erected by Shalmaneser III in the main square of the Assyrian city of Calah, today's Nimrud. One of its panels depicts Jehu's humiliating submission to the Assyrian conqueror. The cuneiform engraving reads, "The tribute of Jehu son of Omri: silver, gold, a golden bowl, a golden vase, golden cups. . . ." Jehu is clad in a sleeveless mantle over an ankle-length tunic. He is bearded. On his head is a pointed cap or turban, its peak bent. It is the only ancient picture in existence of an Israelite king. The monument is known today as the Black Obelisk of Shalmaneser III and can be seen in the British Museum.

The land of Israel was in a torpor, drained by its blood purge. The entire court and most of the high officials had been slain, leaving the country perilously bereft of effective administrative leadership. We may assume that trade links with the Sidonians were disrupted or possibly broken—even the money-minded merchants of Tyre would not have disregarded entirely the death of Jezebel and the obliteration of the cult of their god. But the Mosaic covenant had been vindicated; the land was purified. Prophets no doubt exulted.

The dynasty of Jehu lasted a little less than one hundred years. Of his three descendants who took the throne in succession after his death in 815 B.C.E., the first, Jehoahaz, ruled until 801 B.C.E.; the second, Jehoash, ruled until 786 B.C.E. and almost lost Samaria to besieging Arameans; and the third, Jeroboam II, Jehu's great-grandson, took advantage of a period of Assyrian weakness and, together with King Uzziah of Judah, recaptured lost territories and trade routes until the land was as it had been in the time of David. He brought forty years of wealth and stability to the land, during which he became one of the best customers of the merchants of Tyre. The wealth that flowed into the country from trade and cities in tribute widened the breach between the rich and the poor. The ruling elite wallowed in wealth, the ruled poor became increasingly mired in degradation. At the same time, pagan worship and the fertility cult were rampant; shards found in the region of Samaria and dated to this period contain almost as many personal names that are combined with Baal as with YHWH. It was now the pagan purpose of the state cult to placate YHWH by repeated ritual and sacrifice so as not to incur His anger.

It was in the reign of Jeroboam II that a shepherd journeyed northward from a town in the south and condemned with a raging heart the corruption he saw all around him as king, priests, and the wealthy class paid lip service to the cult of YHWH and ignored the sufferings of the masses—and nothing was ever the same again in the history of the people of YHWH. He appears suddenly before the multitude assembled during a festival at the sanctuary in Bethel, this shepherd—some say he was a cattle-breeder—from Tekoa, in the hill country of Judah south of Bethlehem near the Dead Sea. I see the startled faces of priests and the assembled throng as he interrupts the carefully orchestrated sacrificial service. "Hear this word that the Lord has spoken against you, O children of Israel, against the whole family that I brought up out of the land of Egypt, saying: You only have I known of all the families of the earth; therefore I will visit upon you all your iniquities. . . . I hate, I despise your feasts, and I will take no delight in your solemn assemblies. . . . Take away from Me the noise of your songs, and let Me not hear the melody of your psalteries. But let justice well up as waters, and righteousness as a mighty stream. . . ." To the vulgar popular belief that there will come a Day of the Lord when Israel will rule supreme and untroubled, the prophet responds with bitter sarcasm. "Woe unto you who desire the Day of the Lord! Wherefore would you have the Day of the Lord? It is darkness, and not light. . . . You that put far away the evil day, and cause the seat of violence to come near; that lie upon beds of ivory, and stretch themselves upon their couches . . . they shall go captive at the head of them that go captive. . . . The Lord God has sworn by Himself, said the Lord, the God of hosts; I abhor the pride of Jacob and hate his palaces; and I will deliver up the city with all that is therein. . . ."

Amaziah, the priest of Bethel, goes before King Jeroboam and accuses Amos of sedition. We are not told the reply of the king. The priest then orders the prophet out of the land of Israel. "Prophesy not again anymore at Bethel, for it is the king's sanctuary, and it is a royal house." We do not know how that confrontation between priest and prophet terminated.

Hosea, a near-contemporary of Amos, preached a similar message. He saw the covenant as a marriage between Israel and YHWH. Israel, in worshiping other gods, had committed adultery and faced divorce, ruin, catastrophe. The curses of the covenant would be inflicted upon the nation for breaking its oath of loyalty to YHWH. And yet another prophet, Micah, prophesied, "I will make Samaria a heap in the field, a place for the planting of vineyards. . . ." They could not have made pleasant listening, those prophets. They are a bur in the back, a fire in invisible places within us we prefer to leave dark and forgotten.

Amos was the first to give voice to the threat of exile as punishment for breaking the covenant; and though the covenant as such is not mentioned by him, it is implicit in all his words. He vacillates agitatedly between prophecies of utter doom for corrupt Israel and hope for a surviving remnant who will seek the Lord and be rescued. He is the first to stress the importance of social ethics; and though he condemns the cult, he nowhere says YHWH is not to be worshiped through ritual and sacrifice. But he is convinced that worship of YHWH can never be separated from compassion and justice. Further, the very fate of the people of YHWH is determined by its moral behavior. Amos made explicit what had been implicit in the Mosaic covenant; there is no break here with the past, but a powerful shift in emphasis that would be picked up and accentuated by virtually every prophet who followed him and would in time become the keynote of a new Hebraic civilization.

Amos was neither an ecstatic nor a member of a prophetic guild. He marked a new development in prophecy, a unique Israelite response to corrupt faith and the social horrors of the time. He was the first prophet to set his words down in writing, though the work that now bears his name has undergone much editing and may be only a fragment of all he wrote. Probably he wrote out of hope as well as despair; perhaps a future generation would read and take to heart the words that his generation refused to hear. Others probably wrote before him; his forms and images are too sharply polished and defined for him to have been entirely without precursors. We do not know who they were. Where did he learn to write? Tekoa was well known for her wise men; perhaps he was taught by one of them. We err if we regard every shepherd as an empty-headed illiterate. He was presumably buried in Tekoa, and during the Byzantine period devout Christians built a church there in his honor. Its remains can be seen to this day.

In the year 746 B.C.E. King Jeroboam II of Israel died. About that same time, Tiglath-pileser III seized the throne of Assyria. He built the Assyrian empire.

Some scholars believe that Tiglath-pileser III was an Assyrian general named Pul before he usurped the throne. Later Assyrian kings would remember his act and mutilate his annals—an extraordinary desecration and a mark of the hatred between two powerful families who fought to rule this land.

Now the new king set his face toward empire. The Assyrian army was made up mainly of slaves and peasants given the king by landholders for the duration of a campaign. Now the conscripted army became a permanent one, its ranks drawn from peoples that came under Assyrian dominion; Iranian horsemen, Arabian camel drivers, Anatolian foot soldiers. Tiglath-pileser III was not satisfied merely to take tribute. He marched, conquered, accepted payments of tribute from those who yielded, devastated those who did not, and left behind garrisons and administrators to make permanent his conquests.

Rebellion was punished by the normal horrors in the Assyrian arsenal of brutality and by the practice of mass deportation devised to break up old alliances and repopulate areas devastated by war. Conquered regions were turned into provinces as punishment against those who, in the words of Tiglath-pileser, "forgot my covenant."

In 732 B.C.E., Tiglath-pileser turned his army against Samaria. The death of King Jeroboam II of Israel had brought a banana republic instability to kingship in the land. During the ten years that followed, five kings sat on the throne of Israel, and it would all be a comic opera of kingship were it not for the suffering of the people. Each time an army marches and cities are besieged and regions are subdued, people are maimed, mutilated, killed, a stone of destruction rolls across our planet, and the stench of death fills the nostrils. There is nothing comic about the last years of Israel, except perhaps the incredible stupidity of some of her kings. We look on with a blackness of dread in the heart, for a civilization is coming to an end.

King Zechariah son of Jeroboam II ruled for six months and was murdered by Shallum son of Jabesh, who was murdered after one month by Menahem son of Gadi, who paid tribute to Tiglath-pileser in 738 B.C.E. when the Assyrian king led his army into the west. Menahem died and kingship was transferred to his son Pekahiah, who was quickly assassinated by Pekah son of Remaliah, an army officer. He took the throne and rebelled against Assyria by refusing the annual payment of tribute. His act is as incomprehensible as the reaction of the Assyrians is predictable. They marched and conquered the Galilee, Jezreel, the Sharon plain, Gilead. Hazor and Megiddo were destroyed. I must remind myself that these words really mean that thousands suffered, died. Archaeologists have discovered a three-foot layer of ashes at Hazor, which they date to this time. The city must have burned for days. Only the region around Samaria was spared. The prophet Hosea announced the death of the degenerate state. But an act of God would restore Israel. "I will allure her, and bring her into the wilderness, and speak tenderly to her. . . ." And, "I will heal their backsliding; I will love them freely. . . ."

Then King Pekah of Israel and King Rezin of Aramean

Damascus sought an alliance with King Ahaz of Judah against Assyria. Ahaz refused. They joined in war against him, thinking to replace him with a puppet king whom they could manipulate with ease. Attacked and besieged on all sides, a desperate King Ahaz turned to the Assyrians for aid. He sent Tiglath-pileser a handsome gift. The Assyrian king, who now knew he could only retain control over Syria by achieving suzerainty over Israel, marched against Samaria. King Pekah was murdered by Hoshea son of Elah, who immediately surrendered and saved the city and its surroundings.

Then Tiglath-pileser died. It had taken him only eighteen years to create the Assyrian empire. Hoshea withheld tribute from his successor Shalmaneser V and looked to Egypt for help in an alliance against Assyria. The Assyrian army trudged over the roads of Mesopotamia and besieged Samaria.

The city held out for three years. During the siege Shalmaneser V died or was murdered.

A usurper, about whose origin little is known, took the throne of Assyria. He named himself Sargon II, after Sargon, the legendary Akkadian conqueror of Sumer.

Then in 722 B.C.E. Samaria fell.

Much of her population—officials, scribes, army personnel, craftsmen—was deported to scattered regions of the Assyrian empire and replaced by conquered peoples from Babylonia, Hamath, Midian, by distant nomadic Arabs of the desert. These would in time fuse with the remaining indigenous Israelites and become the people we know today as the Samaritans.

Who was king? Who was not king? In Israel no one was king. The land was a province of Assyria. Israel ceased to exist, and her kingship was carried off to the Assyrians.

Some have said that she was merely one of many minor kingdoms in the path of a great empire and was swallowed as a shark takes a minnow. Others had a different view. "This happened because the Israelites sinned against the Lord their God, who had freed them from the land of Egypt, from the hands of Pharaoh king of Egypt. They worshiped other gods. . . ." So we are told by the

Biblical historian. Israel broke the covenant. YHWH invoked the curses.

About twenty miles to the south of this newest province of Assyria lay the city of Jerusalem.

In 738 B.C.E., when King Menahem of Israel had paid a heavy tribute to Tiglath-pileser III, there were probably close to eight hundred thousand people in the north. Many thousands were slain in battle and in the Assyrian reprisals for rebellion. Additional tens of thousands were deported. Others probably fled to the cities of Phoenicia. Archaeologists tell us that Jerusalem, which had remained a relatively sleepy town since Solomon's death, abruptly began to grow after Samaria's death. I take no dangerous leap of the imagination if I assume that northerners poured into the city while the Assyrians savaged Israel.

Many no doubt had been members of the ruling elite, ruined heirs of the families of callous wealth once condemned by Amos and Hosea. Some were craftsmen, scribes; others were farmers whose lands had been laid waste, homes burned, trees torn out by the Assyrians. I see them wandering about the crowded, narrow streets of Jerusalem and through the spacious royal quarter where they gaze at the white limestone temple of Solomon, the glittering palaces and government buildings. I find it not too difficult to conjecture that some brought with them the annals of their kings and other northern writings. The ten tribes of the north vanished—into the empire of Assyria and the kingdom of Judah.

Now, after the fall of Samaria, the kingdom of Judah was all that stood between the empire of Assyria and the land of Egypt: the one vast, insatiable; the other aged, doddering, yet somehow awesome if only because of her antiquity and her occasional surprising ability to spring back to life. The Davidic dynasty had existed unchallenged for two centuries save for a brief period when the queen mother Athaliah had seized the throne in 842 B.C.E.

The dynasty of David had deep roots in Judah. Subsequent kings, whether weak or strong—Joash, Amaziah, Uzziah, Jotham; the reign of Uzziah, 783-742 B.C.E., was a glorious one in the history of Judah—sent those roots deeper still. The dynasty remained unshaken even after King Ahaz journeyed to the army encampment outside the recently captured city of Damascus in 732 B.C.E. to take an oath of allegiance to Tiglath-pileser III and accept a suzerainty treaty for the help given him by the Assyrians.

In Damascus he saw a bronze altar that intrigued him. He had a replica of it made and sent to Jerusalem, and a duplicate altar made and placed in the temple. At this pagan altar he worshiped YHWH; it was for his own use alone and stood near the bronze altar built by Solomon upon which priests continued to offer the regular sacrifices to YHWH. For the first time in the history of the land an element from the core of Fertile Crescent paganism had penetrated to the core of the religion of Judah. Yet no one raised a hand against the king, the legitimate heir to the throne of David.

King Ahaz of Judah introduced the world of Aramean and Assyrian paganism into his land. Scholars are now reasonably certain that the Assyrians never forced their gods upon the peoples they conquered. It can only be assumed from this that Ahaz willingly embraced paganism and was probably supported by an influential faction of the ruling class—entire families thinking and acting alike—who hungered for culture contact with the world that lay beyond the hills of Judah.

The culture of the conqueror will inevitably seep into the culture of the conquered. It is probable that the Aramaic language, which was displacing Akkadian as the international diplomatic language of the Assyrian empire, had already begun to penetrate Judah. By the time of Tiglath-pileser III, Assyrian and Aramean cultures had so fused that the Assyrians regarded the Arameans as Assyrians; rarely are they called Arameans. This fused culture was pervasive. The author of the Books of Chronicles informs us that Ahaz worshiped the gods of Aram. "And he said: Because the gods of the kings of Aram helped them, therefore will I sacrifice to them, that they may help me."

Archaeologists recently discovered in Jerusalem two caves which give every sign of once having been storage areas for a flourishing cult center dating to about the time of Ahaz. They contained fertility figurines and fragments of little sculptures of horses with disks on their foreheads. The animals were probably miniatures of the Horses of the Sun, which were harnessed to the chariot of the sun god Shamash, who was worshiped by the Assyrians. "White horses . . . went out with the chariot," reads an Assyrian text that describes the cult of the sun god. One estimate places the cult center at about nine hundred feet from the southeast corner of the enclosure around the temple of YHWH.

Ahaz died in 715 B.C.E. His son Hezekiah ascended the throne. He was a reformer. Bad days soon set in for the pagan gods of Judah.

Sargon too had some bad days early in his reign and some horrifying ones at its close. Each Assyrian king had to plunge the empire into a bath of blood when he took the throne. Vassals, bled white by payments of tribute, thought they had little to lose by testing the strength of a new Mesopotamian monarch.

The prophet Isaiah felt that the little kingdom of Judah would pay too high a price in a bid for freedom. He had begun his prophetic career in the year of the death of King Uzziah of Judah, around 742 B.C.E. He was apparently of the royal family, for he came and went with ease in the court of the king. He had been ignored by King Ahaz, who had turned to Assyria for help, a move that brought Judah into the strangling status of vassal. How Isaiah loathed the indolent wealth he saw all around him; how deeply he felt the pain of the poor; how he despised the mechanical observance of the cult of YHWH, deeds without depth of heart, a soulless morality! Assyria was the rod of the anger of YHWH; evil was being used to punish evil. Judah should neither rebel against Assyria nor make alliances with Egypt or others. The excessive evils of Assyria would ultimately be punished; YHWH would destroy her on the mountains of Judah and all the world would recognize the God of Israel as the lord of history. A renewed and prosperous Judah would be ruled by an ideal king. The prophet Micah spoke of the doom of Jerusalem, the plowed field that would one day be Zion, because of the detestable immorality of her people and the vile routinized observance of the cult. He urged the people of Judah "to do justice, and to love kindness, and to walk humbly with your God." But Isaiah believed Jerusalem to be inviolable and urged that she remain free of foreign entanglements.

Ahaz, the passionate admirer of pagan ways, had paid little attention to Isaiah. But Hezekiah, the adherent of YHWH, was inclined to listen. And so the prophet urged the king not to join the rebellion planned by other kingdoms in the western arc of the Fertile Crescent. Hezekiah wavered, then heeded the counsel of Isaiah, and was spared the vengeance of the Assyrian army, which suddenly appeared in the west in 712 B.C.E. after subduing Babylonia and Urartu.

In 705 B.C.E. Sargon was killed in a battle against barbarian hordes on the northern border of Assyria. At first his body could not be recovered—a dreaded omen. The empire erupted in rebellion, from Babylon to Jerusalem.

Sargon was succeeded by his son Sennacherib, who, as an Assyrian inscription puts it, "in wrath of heart" marched his army out of the city of Ashur on the twentieth day of Shevat, our February, and the eleventh month of the Assyrian year. The city of Babylon quickly surrendered. Booty was taken, but the populace was spared. Then Sennacherib marched south, devastated the Chaldeans, took eighty-eight of their fortified towns and all the large cities of Babylonia. He left untouched the city of Ur.

Judah had been cleansed by Hezekiah of Aramean and Assyrian gods. In order to prevent further fusion of YHWH with pagan gods, local altars were ordered eliminated, a new policy whose effect in the time of Hezekiah is not known. Casting out pagan gods and casting off the yoke of vassalage were the religious and political sides of a hand raised in rebellion.

During Hezekiah's fourth year as king, Sargon II had destroyed Samaria. Now Sargon was dead, Sennacherib was king. Hezekiah "rebelled against the king of Assyria and served him not," no doubt urged on by the strong anti-Assyrian faction in his court.

He had new fortifications constructed around Jerusalem. Millennia in the past the city had been built on this hill because underground streams sent endless water to a spring, called Gihon in the Bible, that lay in the valley immediately to the east. Now two teams of diggers started toward each other on opposite sides of the hill and cut their way through about twelve hundred feet of solid rock, one man on each team cutting and chopping, the others hauling the broken stones out in baskets. The narrow tunnel proceeded in meandering fashion through the hill, indicating to us today corrections in the angle of the dig. After six or seven months the two teams, working without a compass or sophisticated directional aids of any kind—perhaps they followed a fissure through which the water may have trickled from one side of the hill to the other—the two teams met in the heart of the hill. It is one of the most astonishing feats of engineering in the ancient world. The tunnel diverted the exposed spring east of the hill to what must have been then a concealed or fortified point just outside the city's western wall. It lies open today to the sun and the sky and is called the pool of Siloam.

One of the workers left behind an inscription describing their labors. It was incised in Hebrew in the cursive Phoenician alphabet, and a young student architect discovered it one day in June 1880 when he slipped inside the darkish tunnel of knee-high water. As he rose to his feet, he spotted the inscription on a smoothed section of wall about three feet above the tunnel floor near its western end. "Now this is the manner of the breakthrough. . . . While three cubits still remained to be tunneled, the voice of a man was heard calling to his fellow, for there was a fissure in the rock on the right. Now when the tunnel was cut through, each of the excavators hewed through to meet his fellow, axe against axe, and the waters began flowing from the source toward the reservoirs. . . ." I saw the inscription recently in the Museum of the Ancient Orient in Istanbul, two and a half feet of text cut into smooth-surfaced whitish stone. It lies behind glass. In a nearby case you can see the small inscription that is the Gezer Calendar, a schoolboy's account of a farmer's working year written about the time of Solomon on soft limestone, probably as an exercise, and discovered in 1908. "Two months of harvest; two months of planting; two months of late planting. . . ." These and about one hundred other small-sized inscriptions, consisting mostly of ostraca—shards that contain writing—are all the written material from the Biblical period that has been yielded up until now by the earth of Israel and Judah.

In the year 701 B.C.E. Sennacherib marched against the west. Babylonia had been silenced. Now the vast Assyrian army—cavalry, chariots, battering rams, scaling parties, archers, slingmen, spearmen, shield-bearers—moved down the coast of Phoenicia. Vassal kingdoms that had trumpeted rebellion when Sennacherib had come to the throne now yielded and offered tribute as his army approached Tyre. Ammon, Moab, and Edom surrendered. He marched into Philistia and took Jaffa. Ashkelon surrendered after holding out briefly, and her king was deported with his entire family. Sennacherib besieged Ekron. The Egyptians, who had promised the rebels support, now appeared with an army.

A few miles east of Gezer is the valley of Eltekeh. There the two armies met and fought an inconclusive battle. The Egyptians—Nubian troops mostly—withdrew and were not pursued.

Sennacherib took Ekron, killed the officials who had engaged in the rebellion, and impaled their bodies on poles surrounding the city. Then we read in his annals, a clay prism upon which his scribes wrote in cuneiform,

> *As to Hezekiah, the Jew, he did not submit to my yoke. I laid siege to forty-six of his strong cities, walled forts, and to countless small villages in their vicinity, and conquered them by means of . . . battering rams . . . combined with the attack by foot soldiers using mines, breeches, as well as sapper work. I drove out of them 200,150 [scholars regard this as an error for 2,150] people, young and old, male and female, horses, mules, donkeys, camels, big and small cattle beyond counting, and considered them booty. Himself I made a prisoner in Jerusalem, his royal residence, like a bird in a cage.*

That war against Judah resulted in one of the most monumental and chilling works of art in the ancient world: the depiction of the siege of Lachish, a fortified city southwest of Jerusalem which offered the most stubborn resistance of all the cities in the west. An Assyrian artist used the siege as a subject for a series of vivid bas-reliefs in the palace of Sennacherib at Nineveh. I saw them one rainy London morning in the Assyrian Salon of the British Museum, wall after wall of stone panels on which the artist and his aides trapped the horror, brutality, and grim efficiency of an Assyrian war. An epigraph on one of these reliefs contains the words, "Sennacherib, king of the world, king of Assyria, sat upon a throne and passed in review the booty taken from Lachish." A large pit was recently uncovered near Lachish containing the remains of fifteen hundred corpses and the bones of pigs. It was the garbage dump of the Assyrian army.

Jerusalem did not fall. The Assyrian annals tell us Hezekiah surrendered and gave much tribute, including his own daughters for the harem of Sennacherib. The Bible tells us that the Assyrian army suddenly withdrew. A plague? Trouble in the distant east? We do not know. The discrepancy has given scholars another puzzle to ponder. Inhabitants of Jerusalem, gazing over the wall in astonishment at the suddenly vacated valleys below, saw it as a miracle of YHWH. The prophet Isaiah, who had assured Hezekiah that the city would not be taken, expressed his revulsion over the levity and celebrating that followed the Assyrian withdrawal.

We know little about the remaining years of the reign of Hezekiah. He died in 687 B.C.E. and was quietly succeeded by his son Manasseh. In the third week of the Assyrian month of Tevet, our January, 681 B.C.E., Sennacherib was murdered in Nineveh. Civil war broke out. Esarhaddon, the younger son in line for the throne, overcame his adversaries, and in 680 B.C.E. began to rule as king of the world, king of Assyria.

King Manasseh had ascended the throne in Jerusalem at the age of twelve. He reigned for about fifty years and became the most loathed and cursed king in the history of Judah.

Assyria was then at the height of her power. All the world of Mesopotamia and the west lay subdued before her. In 671 B.C.E. she would conquer the Egyptian Delta as well, and Esarhaddon would die in 669 B.C.E. during another military campaign against the land of the Nile.

In Judah, Assyria ruled not only politically but also culturally. Her cults, gods, and fashions were introduced into the land by Manasseh. This was the golden age of astrology and divination in Assyria, and during the reign of Esarhaddon priests and astrologers filled the court with their omens and predictions. That was the way we saw the world then—through the perambulations of planets and the permutations in livers and entrails, through oracles and the toss of sacred dice—before we began to see it, not very long ago, through cause and effect. The Aramean-Assyrian gods were clearly superior to the gods of all other lands, for all kingdoms were vassals of the god Ashur. The astral gods of Assyria—Ishtar, Shamash, Adad—were worshiped on rooftops everywhere.

Assyrian cultic texts carefully describe the rituals. "You clean the roof before Ishtar, sprinkle pure water, you set up an altar of incense, you pour out flour, you place honey and butter, and libate wine." "You clean the roof, you sprinkle pure water, you place four bricks . . . you pile up cuttings of poplar trees, you put fire on them, you pour out juniper, you libate beer, prostrate, and do not look backward." "I have set for you, Ishtar, a pure . . . cake baked in ashes. . . ."

Prophets, condemning the vile contagion that infested the land during the days of Ahaz and Manasseh, told of "them that worship the host of heaven upon the housetops" and described how "the children gather wood, and the fathers kindle the fire, and the women knead the dough, to make cakes to the queen of heaven." The southern writer of the Second Book of Kings tells of those who "offered incense to Baal, to the sun, and to the moon, and to the constellations, and to all the host of heaven."

Manasseh paganized Judah with a tenacity fed by conviction and will. He slaughtered influential followers of YHWH. There is a persistent tradition that the prophet Isaiah, fleeing from the troops of Manasseh, concealed himself in the hollow trunk of a cedar. The tree was sawn through with the prophet inside.

Manasseh relished the superstitious, the debased, the

obscene in the culture of the outside world. Whole elements from the core and periphery of the Assyrian world washed across the hills of Judah, leaving behind gods and goddesses beneath leafy trees, on tall hills, in groves, on rooftops. The southern historian tells us, "He built again the high places which Hezekiah his father had destroyed; and he reared up altars for Baal . . . and worshiped all the host of heaven and served them. And he built altars in the house of the Lord. . . . And he made his son pass through the fire, and practiced soothsaying, and used enchantments. . . ."

Less than a mile from where I write these words is the valley of Hinnom outside the walls of the old city of Jerusalem. There, to the din of drums, with smoke and flames rising through the air, children were offered to the god Molech, another name for the king of heaven. The Greeklike word Gehenna, hell, comes from that place: *ge* (pronounced *gay*)—valley, in Hebrew—of Hinnom. In Assyria too the ceremony of burning was outside the city, on a site called the *hamru*, the sacred precinct of Adad. "His eldest son will be burned in the *hamru* of the god Adad. . . ."

Within the temple of Solomon the fertility cult and sacred prostitution—acts of intercourse with priestesses to bring on the fructification of the land—flourished as integral elements of the state cult practiced by the people of YHWH. In the countryside the populace too worshiped YHWH along with pagan deities. It is probable that this would in time have made YHWH the head of a pantheon, like El in the tablets of Ugarit. The sins of Manasseh were never forgotten.

All through his long reign there was peace between Judah and Assyria. The passage in the Second Book of Chronicles which tells of Manasseh hauled off in chains to Babylon remains incomprehensible to most scholars.

The death of Esarhaddon in 669 B.C.E. brought Ashurbanipal to the throne of Assyria. He too ruled for a long time—until 627 B.C.E. His early years were troubled by rebellions, which he put down. He completed the conquest of Egypt, taking Thebes in 663 B.C.E. When Egypt rebelled and broke away in 651 B.C.E. he seemed unconcerned; she had been too much even for Assyria to swal-

low, and the wealth she was to have yielded as a conquest
or vassal proved to have been exaggerated and was not
worth the effort necessary to keep her under control. Instead the two countries appear to have signed a covenant
of peace to respect each other's borders and come to each
other's aid.

After more than a decade of war the Assyrian empire
under Ashurbanipal was at peace; all the Fertile Crescent
rested for nearly thirty years.

The king of the world, king of Assyria, now turned his
attention to the creation of the treasure that was to make
possible the recovery of the civilization of Mesopotamia
twenty-five hundred years after his death—a library.

He had been taught to read and write. He took special
pride in his ability to copy as well as compose in cuneiform on wax-covered tablets. Other kings had collected
texts before him, but he had his empire scoured for its
literary creations; some were read to him. This vast collection of tablets gathered at Nineveh—there were actually two libraries—so much bore the stamp of his own
tastes, as did the art in his palace, the finest achievement
of Assyrian art, that many historians have given the name
of this king to his age—the Age of Ashurbanipal, one of
the landmarks in the history of culture. Little wonder then
that the small kingdom of Judah was caught up in the
oceanic swell of this great empire.

Then something went wrong; we are uncertain as to
precisely what it was. The last years of this king were
filled with sadness. We have one of his prayers. "Why
have sickness, ill-health, misery, and misfortune befallen
me? I cannot away with the strife in my country and the
dissensions in my family. Misery of mind and of flesh bow
me down; with cries of woe I bring my days to an
end. . . . How long, O god, wilt thou deal thus with
me?"

King Manasseh of Judah had died in 642 B.C.E. His
son Amon was mysteriously slain after two years, and the
son of Amon, eight-year-old Josiah, became king of
Judah. He was fourteen when Ashurbanipal died in 627
B.C.E.

In Assyria civil war broke out as two brothers fought
bitterly over the succession to the throne. The war raged

on for years, splitting the empire into two lands. The awesome Assyrian army began slowly to devour itself. One son and then another seized the throne.

Babylon rebelled and broke away, followed by Phoenicia and Media. Now Babylonians and Medes joined together and turned with fury upon the empire that had held them in humiliating vassalage for more than a century.

In the land of Judah, King Josiah, now about twenty years old, quietly and without bloodshed absorbed a section of the southern region of Samaria, including Bethel. The province had apparently been given up by Assyria. A movement for national reform broke out into the open in Judah. The young king began to cleanse the land of the pagan cults introduced by his grandfather. He was in his late twenties when he ordered that the temple, damaged by age and siege, be repaired.

On the other side of the Fertile Crescent, the Scythians, a strong nomadic tribe from the vast plateau north of Mesopotamia, now allied themselves with the Babylonians and Medes. In 614 B.C.E. the Medes took Ashur, the first time in the history of Assyria that her ancient capital fell—and the last. Archaeologists have uncovered evidence of the savagery with which that city was sacked. In 612 B.C.E. the Scythians joined the Medes and Babylonians in the assault on Nineveh. After three unsuccessful attacks the city fell—the city whose name had been legendary for wealth and power. "In the month of Abu," reads the Babylonian Chronicle, "the city was seized and a great defeat . . . inflicted upon the entire population. On that day . . . many prisoners of the city, beyond counting, they carried away. The city they turned into ruin-hills and heaps of debris." Less than three hundred years later the army of Alexander the Great would march by a few miles away, and no one would remember that Nineveh had existed.

About ten years earlier in Jerusalem, during the repair work on the temple, Hilkiah the high priest had discovered an old scroll somewhere in the temple precinct. He read it and brought it quickly to Shaphan the royal scribe. He too read it and brought it immediately to the young king.

\* \* \*

The scribe read the scroll to the king. The words were those of Moses as the tribes stood poised on the bank of the Jordan. "Hear, O Israel, the laws and norms that I proclaim to you this day! Study them and observe them faithfully! The Lord our God made a covenant with us at Horeb. . . ." The scroll reminded the listener of the historic obligation incurred centuries ago. "I am the Lord your God who brought you out of the land of Egypt. . . ." Certain stipulations followed from this obligation. "You shall have no other gods besides me. You shall not make for yourself a sculptured image, any likeness of what is in the heavens above or on the earth below, or in the water below the earth. . . ." The event of the Revelation was retold, briefly and without the tortuous stops and starts we find in Exodus. There then followed a lengthy code of law preceded by the exhortation that

*You must love the Lord your God with all your heart and with all your souls and with all your might. . . . Revere only the Lord your God and worship Him alone, and swear only by His name. Do not follow other gods, the gods of the people around you. . . . If, then, you obey these norms and observe them faithfully, the Lord your God will keep with you the gracious covenant that He made on oath with your fathers. . . . What is it that the Lord your God demands of you? It is to revere the Lord your God, to walk only in His paths, to love Him. . . . Love, therefore, the Lord your God, and always keep His charge, His laws, His norms, and His commandments. . . . You must destroy all the sites at which the nations you are to dispossess worshiped their gods, whether on lofty mountains and on hills or under luxuriant trees. Tear down their altars . . . and cut down the images of their gods, obliterating their names from that site. Do not worship the Lord your God in like manner, but look only to the site that the Lord your God will choose amidst all your tribes as His habitation. . . . Take care not to sacrifice your burnt offerings in any place you like, but only in*

*the place which the Lord will choose in one of your
tribal territories. . . . But whenever you desire, you
may slaughter and eat meat in any of your settlements. . . .*

Laws concerning forbidden foods, certain forms of taxation, and the observance of festivals were then carefully
enumerated. An additional set of laws concerning civil
crime, punishment, conduct in war, and other matters followed—and concluded with the words:

*But if you do not heed the word of the Lord your God
to observe faithfully all His commandments and laws
which I enjoin upon you this day, all these curses shall
come upon you and take effect: Cursed shall you be in
the city and cursed shall you be in the country. . . .
The Lord will let loose against you calamity, panic, and
frustration in all the enterprises you undertake. . . .
The Lord will make pestilence cling to you. . . . Your
carcasses shall become food for all the birds of the sky
and all the beasts of the earth. . . . The Lord will drive
you, and the king you have set over you, to a nation
unknown to you or your fathers. . . . All these curses
shall befall you; they shall pursue you and overtake
you, until you are wiped out, because you did not heed
the Lord your God and keep the commandments and
laws that He enjoined upon you. . . . The Lord will
bring a nation against you from afar . . . a ruthless nation, that will show the old no regard and the young no
mercy. . . . The Lord will scatter you among all the
peoples from one end of the earth to the other. . . .
These are the terms of the covenant which the Lord
commanded Moses to conclude with the Israelites in
the land of Moab, in addition to the covenant which
He had made with them at Horeb.*

When the scribe was done reading, the king reacted to
the scroll with dread and horror. His entire effort at reform had been misdirected. The Davidic dynasty was not
eternal but conditional upon the obedience of the king
and the people to this newly discovered second Mosaic

covenant. YHWH not only wanted images destroyed; He also wanted the centralization of His worship in Jerusalem. Only by closing down the outlying shrines could the war against paganism be won. King Josiah had unwittingly permitted the shrines and high places to remain as local centers of worship. He had erred. YHWH would invoke the curses! The king tore his clothes and ordered that the scroll be read to Hulda the prophetess. Her reaction was vehement. "Tell the man who sent you to me: Thus said the Lord: Behold I will bring evil upon this place, and upon its inhabitants, even all the words of the book which the king of Judah has read. . . ."

King Josiah convened an assembly of the elders of Judah in the temple. He read the scroll. "And the king stood on the platform, and made a covenant before the Lord, to walk after the Lord, and to keep His commandments. . . ." The people accepted the covenant. According to Exodus 20:21-23, the multiplicity of local altars was accepted tribal practice. But this was a new vision of the relationship between YHWH and His people, a response to the seemingly endless and futile war against paganism. Centralize all worship in Jerusalem. Forbid ritual sacrifice anywhere except in the temple. Permit the eating of meat in local areas without the need to sacrifice any portion of it to YHWH—a significant and necessary innovation. Above all make the cult the exclusive responsibility of the temple. And make idolatry a crime clearly punishable by death.

The local shrines were destroyed throughout Judah. Their priests were invited to come to Jerusalem and serve in the temple. In Bethel the sanctuary with the calf images was torn down and the priests slain. Centralization of worship in Jerusalem further deepened the loyalty of the people to the city of David.

The origin and author of the scroll are unknown. There are in it echoes of the zealous compassion of Amos and the reformers from the north who were his followers. How do you give shape to your absolute conviction that a new relationship is necessary between the people and YHWH if the people is to survive? What words do you use? How do you formulate your ideas so that they have coherence and are understood by all? Surely this new relationship to YHWH must take the form of a covenant, for all relationships between YHWH and His people are covenantal. Which covenant form would most truthfully express this new relationship and convey it to the people with greatest effect? And who in Judah would be in a position to be sufficiently familiar with literary and diplomatic documents which could be used as models for such a covenant? Only the royal scribes had access to this material. When we read that Shaphan the scribe was a key figure in the discovery of the scroll we cannot be too far off the mark if we see the hands of the scribes as one of the guiding elements in the movement for reform.

In the time of Hezekiah, when the reform began, ancient documents from the past—codes of law, an account of the Revelation, poems—began to be shaped into unique form on scrolls of papyrus or leather. These were concealed in the terrible days of Manasseh, and then discovered—whether by design or accident remains unstated—when the movement for reform once again came out into the open in the time of Josiah.

The words in the scroll resonated with compelling and familiar echoes. They were words from international treaties. "You shall love YHWH your God with all your heart" is a stipulation in the Deuteronomy covenant. "You will love Ashurbanipal as yourselves" is a stipulation in an Assyrian suzerainty treaty.

The form was easily recognizable from international treaties—historical introduction, stipulations, blessings and curses—that prevailed in the ancient Near East for over one thousand years. This was a common heritage of that world, forms and expressions used by all peoples and nations in the making of treaties—and it was now used by the scribes of Judah.

The curses were in suzerainty treaties made by the Assyrians—an Esarhaddon treaty discovered in 1956 of our era states, "May they [the gods] make your ground like iron. . . ." Deuteronomy states, "The earth under you shall be iron." "May a foreign enemy divide all your goods," reads the Esarhaddon treaty. "A nation which you have not known, shall eat up the fruit of your ground," reads Deuteronomy. "May Sin, the lantern of heaven and earth, clothe you with leprosy. . . . May

Shamash, the light of heaven . . . deprive you of the sight of your eyes," reads the Esarhaddon treaty. "The Lord will smite you with boils . . . and scurvy," reads Deuteronomy. "The Lord will smite you with . . . blindness. . . ."

The people of YHWH shed their vassalage to Assyria by publicly accepting this new vassal treaty with YHWH.

And new it was, for this treaty forever changed the relationship of the people to YHWH. The contents of the scroll, which scholars now identify as chapters 5-26 and 28 of the Book of Deuteronomy—the introductory and concluding chapters are later additions—became the constitution of Judah. It was during this period that a writer shaped the history of his people, molding the annals and documents at his disposal through the vision of things found in Deuteronomy—and left us the work that became the basis for the Books of Kings. An entire school of literature was created by these scribes and their followers— the Deuteronomic school, an unfeeling name (Deuteronomy is Greek for "the repeated law") invented by academicians. It hardly conveys the passionate turning point that was now experienced by the people of Judah.

The cult was centralized in Jerusalem. Israelites could no longer offer sacrifices to YHWH outside the temple. Cultic allegiance began to shift from the local sacrificial altars, which were everywhere in the land, to the temple in Jerusalem. Since most of the tribe of Judah lived outside Jerusalem, this reform made possible the ultimate allegiance to a mode of worship whose focus was a book, the covenant, and a liturgy devoid of the act of sacrifice.

The scribes of the Deuteronomist movement did not believe that YHWH lived in the Jerusalem temple. Pagans believed their gods lived in their temples. YHWH lived in heaven; His name, His spiritual essence, was in the temple. The edifice represents YHWH; it is not His dwelling place.

The code of Deuteronomy veers away from the magical to the rational. The Sabbath has been stripped of its early origin in creation; it is not the rest day of God but the rest day of man, so ordained because God freed the Israelites from slavery; hence they and their servants must rest on that day. History penetrates the holy seasons of the Israelite year. The paschal sacrifice preserves nothing of its ancient quasi-magic elements—blood daubed on lintel and doorposts; the lamb to be roasted whole, with head, legs, innards; no bones of the lamb may be broken, and it must be consumed inside the home; all of these the marks of a magical rite. The new covenant made of the Passover ritual a communal sacrifice to be offered in Jerusalem like any other sacrifice.

The festivals that were celebrated at local shrines before the reform of Josiah and now could also be celebrated in Jerusalem—harvest festivals with processions of fruits and plants and sheaves—are mentioned by name in Deuteronomy; but the rituals that could take place only at local shrines—the willows and flowers that were part of certain celebrations could not be brought on a three-day journey through hot Judean hills to Jerusalem without withering on the way; hence such celebrations could only center around local shrines—these rituals go entirely unmentioned.

The laws of Deuteronomy, those governing human relations, are singularly more humane than their parallels in previous sources. They contain the highest religious principles of the people: unceasing war against paganism, together with a gentle, almost dreamlike, utopianism that pervades the entire work. Do not muzzle the ox as it treads corn; do not remove from a nest the mother bird together with her young; protect the poor, the helpless, the sojourner; debts are to be canceled every seven years; leave gleanings behind on your field for the poor and landless. The individual is protected, as is the family and family dignity. The people are to be holy through separation from other nations and the performance of the ethical and ritual laws stipulated by YHWH. Much is said directly to the conscience of an individual. And great stress is laid upon teaching the covenant to children—in the manner used by wisdom literature, the humanism of the ancient world.

The scroll found in the temple fused together two ancient covenants that had been in tension: the Mosaic covenant with its stipulations and the Davidic or Abrahamic covenant with its unconditional promise: "It is not because you are the most numerous of peoples that the Lord set His heart on you and chose you," Shaphan the scribe read to King Josiah that day; "indeed, you are the smallest of peoples; but it was because the Lord loved you and kept the oath He had made to your fathers that the Lord freed you with a mighty hand and rescued you from the house of bondage. . . . Know, therefore, that only the Lord your God is God, the steadfast God who keeps His gracious covenant to the thousandth generation of those who love Him and keep His commandments, but who instantly requites with destruction those who reject Him. . . . Therefore, observe faithfully the Instruction, the laws, and the norms, with which I charge you today." There is much emphasis on material reward for the observance of the commandments.

The scroll was discovered in 622 B.C.E., and Judah as well as the territories it had taken—from the region of Megiddo in the north to beyond Beersheba in the south, and from Gilead in the east to the coastal cities of Jaffa and Dor—all were cleansed. The fall of Ashur, Nineveh, and Haran during the ensuing years seemed a miraculous destruction of a hated foe. In 609 B.C.E. remnants of the Assyrian army retreated to Carchemish and waited for aid from their Egyptian ally.

The Egyptian army kept its word and set out, led by Pharaoh Necoh. Its route of march took it along the Via Maris and then inland through the plains near Megiddo. It was not in the interest of Judah that Assyria receive aid of any sort. King Josiah assembled his army and met the Egyptians near Megiddo. In the battle that followed he was wounded by an arrow and taken in his chariot from the field of combat.

He died. The stricken people of Judah buried him in Jerusalem. He was in his thirties then, and the bereaved populace could not comprehend the death of the king who had walked so righteously in the ways of YHWH. In the end they blamed it on the evil deeds of his grandfather Manasseh. The southern historian writes, "The Lord turned not from the fierceness of His great wrath . . . because of all the provocations wherewith Manasseh had provoked him. . . . "

The Egyptian army marched on to Carchemish, where it was defeated by the Babylonians. Additional battles— the Egyptians went back again and again, for they were in greater dread of an empire of powerful Babylonians than weak Assyrians—were fought at Carchemish and Hamath in 605 B.C.E. The Egyptians were defeated.

Assyria died. All her people were enslaved. The empire vanished, leaving no discernible lasting influence on the civilizations of our species.

There is increasing evidence of a rise in literacy throughout Judah during the period of Assyrian domination. The ability to read appears to have been fairly widespread in ancient Israel, but only scribes and priests mastered the skill of writing. This changed in Judah during the Assyrian period. Archaeologists are discovering shards dated to that period upon which stonecutters, farmers, vineyard tenders, and others have left evidence of growing literacy in the cursive alphabet of their nonprofessional writing. Nothing of this kind appears to have been found elsewhere in the Fertile Crescent.

The new international brigand was Babylonia. Prophets had said nothing about her abrupt coming to power, and the people of Judah were dismayed. King Nebuchadnezzar of Babylonia roamed at will through Syria, Phoenicia, Philistia, plundering and taking tribute. The Fertile Crescent had traded one royal thief for another. Unlike the Assyrians, the Babylonians did not engage in population exchange. Areas from which the populace was sent off remained vacant rubble.

When King Josiah died his son Jehoahaz was placed on the throne by "the people of the land," the dominant group in Judah, landowners who strongly supported the Davidic dynasty. The Egyptians, simply to display their power over the tiny kingdom, replaced him and sent him off to exile in Egypt. The new king was Jehoiakim, an elder brother of Jehoahaz.

The prophet Jeremiah dictated a prophecy to his scribe Baruch. Nebuchadnezzar was the instrument of the anger of YHWH. The Chaldeans would punish the lands that had mocked the Lord. Jeremiah urged surrender. The scribe read the words to the king, who tore the scroll from his hands, cut it with a knife, and threw it into the fire. Jeremiah, fearing he would be slain for treason, went into hiding. Even those in his own town Anatot, just north of Jerusalem, turned angrily upon him. Against his will, YHWH had touched his lips and given him scathing words to speak, words that condemned the chilling, soulless manner in which the reforms of Josiah were technically obeyed—and his life had become a mire of dread and loathing, dense with accusations of treason and crowded with those who sought to silence him.

Jehoiakim probably accepted vassalage to Babylonia; we cannot be certain. He was firm in his faith in the power of Egypt; Babylonia seemed to have come upon the world too abruptly to be assured of permanence. Using forced labor and earning thereby the hatred of Jeremiah and the people of Judah, he built a magnificent palace outside Jerusalem for the garrisoning of a large military force to protect the capital. When the Babylonians suffered a defeat at the hands of the Egyptians in 601 B.C.E. he threw off vassalage.

In 598 B.C.E. a Babylonian army appeared before Jerusalem. Jehoiakim died at the onset of the siege, possibly murdered. His son Jehoiachin, eighteen years old, ascended the throne and immediately surrendered. The Babylonian Chronicle of Nebuchadnezzar tells us, "In the seventh year, the month of Kislev, the king of Akkad [Babylon] encamped against the city of Judah, and on the second day of the month of Adar he seized the city and captured the king. . . ."

The price of rebellion was high. The king, together with his court and about ten thousand others—scribes, soldiers, artisans, prophets, priests—was deported to Babylonia. I do not know the road they traveled. I assume they took with them certain writings they regarded as significant. The uncle of Jehoiachin, Zedekiah, was made regent.

Zealots for independence continued their militant advocacy against Babylonia. Jeremiah urged loyalty to Babylonia and was followed by many of the leading families of Judah. Hananiah, another prophet, urged rebellion and foresaw the destruction of Babylonia.

In 594 B.C.E. there was a scurrying about of envoys from kingdoms in the west as word came of a rebellion within Babylonia. They met secretly in Jerusalem and de-

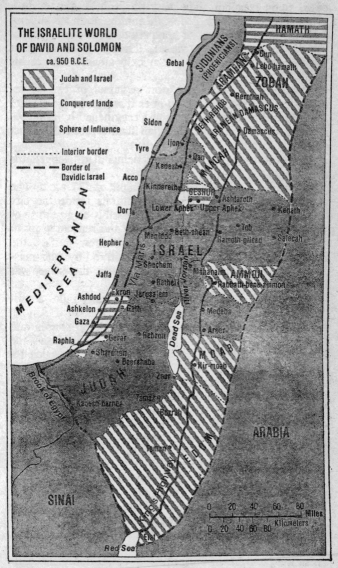

THE ISRAELITE WORLD
OF DAVID AND SOLOMON
ca. 950 B.C.E.

Judah and Israel

Conquered lands

Sphere of influence

........... Interior border

— — — Border of
Davidic Israel

HAMATH

SIDONIANS
(PHOENICIANS)

Gebal

ARAMEAN

ZOBAH

Dan

Lebo-hamath

Berothah

Sidon

BETH-REHOB

ARAM DAMASCUS

ARAMEAN DAMASCUS

Damascus

Tyre

Ijon

Kedesh

Dan

MAACAH

Acco

Kinnereth

GESHUR

Ashtaroth

Dor

Lower Aphek

Upper Aphek

Kenath

MEDITERRANEAN SEA

Hepher

Megiddo

Beth-shean

Tob

Ramoth-gilead

Salecah

ISRAEL

Via Maris

Shechem

River Jordan

Jaffa

Bethel

Mahanaim

AMMON

Ashdod

Ekron

Jerusalem

Rabbath-bene-ammon

Ashkelon

Gath

Gaza

Medeba

Raphia

Gerar

Hebron

Dead Sea

Aroer

Sharuhen

Beersheba

Zoar

Kir-moab

MOAB

Brook of Egypt

JUDAH

Kadesh-barnea

Tamar

EDOM

Bozrah

ARABIA

Yeman

King's Highway

SINAI

0   20   40   60   80
Miles

0   20   40   60   80
Kilometers

Elath

Red Sea

cided upon rebellion. The new pharaoh, Psammetichus, firmly promised help. Zedekiah entered into an alliance with Egypt, now in one of her periods of revival—probably even became her vassal. Then Nebuchadnezzar marched westward. Zedekiah quickly assured him of his loyalty.

The ruler of Judah was now a vassal of two sovereigns—as impossible a situation as it was to be a vassal of YHWH and Baal. Feeling himself strengthened by promises of support from Egypt, Zedekiah finally rebelled against the Babylonians.

In 589 B.C.E. Pharaoh Psammetichus died. Nebuchardnezzar invaded Judah.

Jerusalem was besieged in the winter of 587 B.C.E. The walls could not be breached. Conditions inside the city deteriorated. Slaves were released, possibly as a gesture of piety. The Egyptians kept their word and sent an army to relieve the city. The Babylonians withdrew to face the Egyptians. The freed slaves were recaptured by their masters. The Egyptians were defeated and the siege was resumed.

The city of Azekah, located about twenty miles southwest of Jerusalem, fell to the Babylonians. Among eighteen inscriptions written in black ink on shards and found in 1935 and 1938 in the ruins of Lachish—the heavily fortified border city of Judah which had been rebuilt after its destruction by the Assyrians and was about to be destroyed again by the Babylonians—is one that tells of the fall of Azekah and the dying of its signal fires. "Let my lord know that we are watching for the beacons of Lachish, according to all the indications which my lord has given, for we cannot see Azekah. . . ." Azekah was about ten miles northeast of Lachish.

Jerusalem continued to withstand the siege. Jeremiah persisted in urging surrender; better an Aramean or Chaldean suzerain than an Egyptian ally. He was imprisoned. Plague and famine struck the city in the summer of 586 B.C.E. The wall was breached and the city was taken in the Babylonian month of Duzu, our July.

Zedekiah fled and was captured near Jericho. He was given the punishment prescribed by vassal treaty: his children were slaughtered before his eyes; then he was blinded and led off to Babylon in chains, where he died.

About three weeks later the king of Babylonia ordered Jerusalem put to the torch. A general named Nebuzaradan arrived in Jerusalem from Babylon. He stripped the temple of its treasures, broke down the "molten sea" and the two tall bronze pillars, and sent it all off to Babylon. On the ninth day of the Babylonian month of Abu, our August, "he burned the house of the Lord, and the king's house, and all the houses of Jerusalem. . . ." Whatever remained in the royal archives—legal texts, commercial records, literary treasures—no doubt burned as well. The city's walls were torn down. The remaining populace, except for the poor and the peasants, was deported to Babylonia.

The population of Judah had numbered about two hundred thousand people. In all, about twenty thousand were left in Judah after the 586 B.C.E. deportation. Thousands had previously fled to Ammon, Moab, Edom, Egypt, Tyre, Sidon, Asia Minor.

No mention is made of the sacred ark, which had been in the temple since the days of Solomon. The humiliation of its loss may have been so painful it could not be shaped in words. We never hear of it again.

Jeremiah was permitted by the Babylonians to remain behind. The Babylonians appointed Gedaliah son of Ahikam and grandson of Shaphan the scribe to be governor in Mizpah over what remained of Judah. Mizpah was the small town near Jerusalem where Saul had once been acclaimed king. Gedaliah was a leader of the moderate faction that had sought peace with Babylonia, and sometime after his appointment he was assassinated by Ishmael son of Nethaniah, a zealot who probably regarded him as a traitor.

Fearing Babylonian retaliation, many among the remaining populace now fled to Egypt, taking with them an aged and reluctant Jeremiah and his scribe Baruch. Jeremiah lived long enough to hear Jerusalem women in Egypt blame the destruction of the temple upon the wrath of Astarte because her image had been destroyed during the reform of Josiah.

A near-contemporary poet lamented the loss of the city of David. "Lonely sits the city once great with people. . . . Bitterly she weeps in the night, her cheeks wet with tears. . . . Jerusalem has greatly sinned, therefore she is an outcast. . . . See, O Lord, my misery. . . . See, O Lord, and behold, how abject I have become!"

Jerusalem was a heap of roofless buildings infested with rats. Jackals prowled through her dead streets. Large areas of Judah were devastated.

A wretched rabble scratched about in the ruins of the destroyed land. Seven hundred years had passed since the time a different rabble had fled from slavery in Egypt.

# BABYLONIA

## The New Mesopotamians

They were desolate and could not be consoled. Foreign lands were regarded by them as unclean, and they felt defiled, these new Mesopotamians who had been brought from Judah to Babylonia. They had come in three groups. The first, taken to Babylonia together with King Jehoiachin in 597 B.C.E., had the conviction that their status was temporary and anticipated an imminent return to their land. In 568 B.C.E. news came of the destruction of Jerusalem. The second group of captives then arrived. A third deportation occurred in 582 B.C.E. There were about fifteen thousand individuals in all. Fifteen thousand. The remnant of Israel and Judah. It was a new bondage. They lived in Mesopotamia and dreamed of Jerusalem. The despair was overwhelming.

They were not dispersed throughout a vast empire, as had been the northern tribes of Israel. They lived in compact groups. Some were settled on the Chebar, a canal leading from the Euphrates, in an area called Tel-Aviv not far from Nippur and Ur. Others lived in the city of Babylon.

Through that resplendent city flowed the Euphrates, a wild Nile spanned by six bridges. All through the centuries Babylonian kings had looked upon themselves as the guardians of the civilization of Sumer and Akkad; now Nebuchadnezzar was reaping the harvest of empire and building up the cities of southern Mesopotamia, especially his chief city Babylon. It was a huge city, as cities were measured in the ancient world: five hundred acres, more than one thousand temples, a population of over one hundred thousand people, a massive inner wall around the city itself and a ten-mile-long outer wall protecting the immediate countryside. Eight gates led through the inner wall into the city, one of them, the Ishtar gate, magnificently decorated with blue enameled bricks into which were set red and white depictions of bulls and dragons. An avenue of extraordinary loveliness led from the gate—sixty-three feet wide and paved with white and red stone. Two thick walls decorated with sixty large blue ceramic lions bordered the avenue. The palace of Nebuchadnezzar, an enormous edifice comprising five successive courtyards, stood near the gate. South of the royal palace, set in a large open area, was a towering ziggurat, the temple of the city god Marduk, an ancient obscure deity elevated to prominence when Hammurabi the Amorite became king of Babylon in the eighteenth century B.C.E. and made the city the permanent cultural heart of Mesopotamia. The people of Judah wandered about the city, gazed at its power and wealth, sat on the banks of the river, remembered Jerusalem, and wept.

In time some were swayed by the splendor of Babylon and the power of her gods. Had those gods not conquered YHWH and reduced His city and temple to rubble and His people to captives? For them Jerusalem dimmed and faded.

Most could not forget. They were allowed to build homes, engage in agriculture, practice their crafts, earn a living as they saw fit. Many worked on the construction projects of King Nebuchadnezzar. Those settled in Tel-Aviv on the Chebar farmed the rich soil of the southern Mesopotamian plain. Others began to enter trades. The Babylonians permitted them to assemble. I imagine them meeting often in small groups and talking of the world they had lost by angering their God. That was how we all saw it then: the good and the bad were caused by the gods in reaction to the way we behaved. The Babylonians had explained the destruction of Babylon at the hands of Assyrians in 689 B.C.E. as having been caused by the anger of Marduk over the sins of his people. They had neglected the cult, the god had left the city, the city was destroyed. The remnant of Judah now pointed to the sins of King Manasseh as the cause for the destruction of

Jerusalem. The convenant warning had been clear: children could be punished for the sins of their fathers to the third and fourth generation. The destruction had not come as a total surprise; they had been repeatedly warned by their prophets. But the actual sight of the burnt, gutted temple and the shattered ruin of their city had been a numbing, horror-filled shock. Now they felt their plight to be hopeless.

Among the captives lived a man named Ezekiel. He had come from Jerusalem with the first group of captives. He was of an important priestly family. In Babylonia he lived as a recluse in a house in Tel-Aviv on the banks of the Chebar. For five years he did not venture out, saw almost no one, and was silent. One day on the shores of the Chebar, seven years before the final fall of Jerusalem, he felt a sudden north wind and saw a great cloud and flashing fire and had a vision of the sapphire throne-chariot of God and its attendant winged creatures. That was his call to prophecy.

He prophesied the destruction of Judah and Jerusalem. All through the years preceding the siege he warned of the doom that would befall the land because of the idolatry and pollution brought to it by the people. "Wherefore as I live, says the Lord God, because you have defiled My sanctuary with all your detestable things . . . therefore will I also diminish you. . . . I also will have no pity." In a trancelike vision he is transported to Jerusalem He sees its ugly abominations. Women are bewailing the death of Tammuz, the fertility god whose origins are lost in the world of early Sumer. Men move about stealthily in darkness, worshiping images. He witnesses the presence of God departing from the temple and the city. "Therefore prophesy against them, prophesy, O son of man."

He is a watchman, a lookout, warning his people of the punishment that follows sin and urging repentance. Men will not be saved through the good of others, nor will they be punished for the evil of others. Each will be requited according to his own merit. Ezekiel rejects the Mosaic claim that children may be punished for the sins of their parents; only those who sin are punished, and repentance will bring forgiveness even to them. Nebuchadnezzar of

Babylon is to be the scourge of the people of YHWH. But the dry bones of the people would return to life. His vision of the reestablished sacrificial cult of a new Jerusalem is so bewilderingly different from the priestly code found in the Pentateuch that it almost caused the omission of the Book of Ezekiel from the Hebrew canon, and has left a still unresolved puzzle. He is a prophet of gasping extremes and near-apocalyptic visions: nymphomaniacal adulteresses, giant eagles, depressive silences; a cake baked on hot ashes and human excrement is consumed by the prophet to symbolize the unclean food eaten in captivity; he shaves his head and disposes of the hair to symbolize the destruction of the people of Judah. His wife dies. He does not mourn. His abstention from mourning symbolizes the paralyzing shock that will strike at the captives when they learn of the death of Jerusalem. When Jerusalem is restored, the people will never again suffer the contempt and mockery of her neighboring enemies. They will all have been annihilated. God will redeem Israel even if He must force His laws upon the people. Redemption is a divine necessity, more for the sake of the name of God than the well-being of the people of God. The Babylonian captives will be redeemed although they are as stubborn as the generation of the exodus and the wilderness wandering.

Ezekiel, fiercely patriotic and theocentric, zealous for a pure cult, complete repentance, a cleansed land—Ezekiel urged the people to turn inward, was contemptuous of the world, saw separateness and the exclusiveness of holiness as the only path through the desert of captivity. He seems more priest than prophet. The cult is predominant, morality and ethics secondary: this was what millennia of pagans had said before him, save that he uttered it regarding the worship of the imageless God of history.

Among the exiles was a man who had a different response to the tragic suffering of his people. We do not know who he was. He has no name. But because his words were added by later editors to those of the prophet Isaiah, he is called Second Isaiah. His vision of the task of his people and of the unfolding future planned for man by God is one of the most sublime dreams in the history of our species. He soared beyond the broken days of shame to a future time of tranquillity not only for his people but for all the world. It is awesome and sobering to realize that this vision was attained on the soil of dead Sumer by a new Mesopotamian from Judah.

Take comfort, take comfort, he urges his despairing people. The guilt of Jerusalem has been paid for by her tribulation; her suffering will soon be at an end. A path will be cleared between Babylon and Judah, and the exiles will return to Zion, as fleeing slaves were once brought through a wilderness to a promised land. It is God who directs events; the nations are as nothing before Him. He has chosen Israel to be His servant. "I YHWH, in My grace, have summoned you, and I have grasped you by the hand . . . and appointed you a covenant-people, a light of the nations . . ." This tiny fragment of a people will one day help establish a treaty of peace among the nations of the earth. Soon Babylonia will be destroyed by a foe from the northeast. The worshipers of the false gods of wood and metal do not yet know of this, for their idols are without worth and can tell them nothing. Jerusalem will be redeemed; her exiled people will return; all the nations will render her honor and glory. Not because of her own worth will God do this but for the sake of His own name.

I see him wandering about the flat, alluvial world of Babylonia, through ancient cities and along rivers and canals, prophesying to small gatherings of the exiles. They are unable to accept his words of consolation; their despair is a bog from which they cannot extricate themselves.

He rebukes them angrily. Trust in the name of the Lord, he urges, or you will find yourselves in a place of pain. Remember Abraham and Sarah, whom God blessed and made many. Take comfort. The destroyed land will become like Eden. God has said, "You are My people." The cup of staggering is to be taken from exhausted Jerusalem and given to her enemies. Awake, awake, shake the dust from yourselves. Egypt enslaved you; Assyria degraded you; both have been humbled by God. So will Babylon now be broken by the rising power of Persia.

He paints a picture in exquisite words of the triumphant procession of the exiles to Zion, the loveliness of the mountains of Judah, the exultation of the people. The wasted land will break into song over the redemption of Jerusalem. He describes a radiant Jerusalem in terms that make us wonder if for him a rebuilt city of David is not of greater significance than a reestablished dynasty of David. Do not corrupt yourselves with idolatry and wickedness, he pleads. Do not forsake the Lord. Act justly; keep the Sabbath; refrain from evil; accept the proselyte and the alien who keep the laws of God, "for My house is a house of prayer for all peoples." God rewards and punishes only according to a man's deeds. The enemies of Judah will soon be recompensed. "And a redeemer will come to Zion," and all the world will acknowledge the sovereignty of the Lord. "And as for Me, this is My covenant with them, said the Lord; My spirit which is upon you and My words which I have put in your mouth shall not depart out of your mouth nor out of the mouth of your offspring . . . from now and forever. . . . And it shall come to pass that from one new moon to another, and from one Sabbath to another, all flesh shall come to worship Me, said the Lord."

What an astonishing vision! What audacious words! Impossible of attainment! It was the very impossibility of the vision that set it as a hope and a goal for the despairing captives. They listened. This radiant vision of a future world made sense of their suffering. They had been among the finest of Judah. I do not see them lost for too long in a swamp of self-pity over their burned past. They went about their new tasks—crafts, trade, agriculture. It is clear from the outcome that they did not permit their despair to dictate to them the idea that their God had ceased to exist.

They clung together. They maintained family and clan allegiances and loyalty to elders. They were careful in their observance of the Sabbath and the covenantal sign of circumcision; they rigidly forbade intermarriage—to do otherwise would have meant being swallowed by the pagan world in whose very midst they now lived. They

made of their places of assembly little sanctuaries—not
for sacrifice but for words.

All they had left now were words, the oral traditions
and the scrolls they had brought with them—whatever
those scrolls may have been; we have no way of knowing.
But that they brought with them oral and written traditions we may be certain, else there would have been nothing to begin to shape into what is now the Hebrew Bible
when the dark nightmare of the captivity came to an end.
Scribes who had once worked in the court of the kings of
Judah now copied scrolls in their homes in Babylon. One
of those scribes applied the synchronized form of history
writing used by the Babylonian Chronicles, which list side
by side the reigns of Assyrian and Babylonian kings, to
the separate annals of Israel and Judah, unifying and syn-
chronizing the centuries of those now dead kingdoms.
They changed their script from old Hebrew to Aramaic
cursive, the script of the Babylonian empire. The names
of the Babylonian months of the year replaced the serial
counting—first month, second month, and so on—that
had been used in the period of the monarchy.

Some took Babylonian names. They selected elements
from the periphery and core of Babylonian culture that
would ease and enhance their lives; but nothing pagan
from the world of Babylonia touched them. This small
group from Judah reached sufficient critical mass to begin
a process of transformation from which a new civilization
would one day emerge. There, in Babylon, in the midst of
a thousand pagan temples and the power of Marduk, in
the world that was the birthplace of civilization for our
species, paganism died for the people of YHWH.

The new king of Babylonia was Nabonidus. He was sixty
years old when he usurped the throne in 556 B.C.E. Nebuchadnezzar had died in 562 B.C.E. Two kings ruled
during the next six years, each reign tenuous and brief.
Nabonidus was probably an Aramean, not of royal blood.
His mother was a priestess in the temple of the moon god
in Haran.

He was a dreamy scholar with a great love for antiq-
uities. Whenever he found a relic from the past after ex-

cavating a foundation stone he was very happy. He was devoted to the moon god and saw to the magnificent restoration of the temple in Haran.

It was a strange time in Babylonia. The present was dying and there did not seem to be a future. The weary land was struggling toward a new vision which it could barely see. Inscriptions tell us that god lists were growing shorter. Nabonidus attempted to elevate the moon god to the leading position in the Babylonian pantheon. This infuriated the priests of Marduk. There was an uprising. Nabonidus went to live in the oasis of Teima in the Arabian desert southeast of Edom, leaving behind in Babylon the crown prince Belshazzar, who ruled as regent.

King Cyrus of Anshan was one of many vassal rulers in the enormous empire of the Medes northeast of Babylonia. Cyrus was a Persian, and Anshan was located in what is today southern Iran. He rebelled against his suzerain. He defeated the Medes in 550 B.C.E. and took over their empire. He marched across northern Mesopotamia and conquered Syria and much of Anatolia. Then he conquered Hyrcania and Parthia, today's Afghanistan. He spread like a green vine across the earth. All this took him less than ten years. No military power of any significance existed in Phoenicia, Philistia, and Judah, so he conquered them too, though the date is uncertain. His son Cambyses would conquer Egypt. This was the time that Second Isaiah was prophesying in Babylonia. Stirrings of hope were felt by the exiles. Cyrus was the rod of punishment sent by YHWH to destroy the Babylonians.

Persian armies crossed the Babylonian frontier in the summer of 539 B.C.E. Nabonidus had returned to Babylon, and he thought to concentrate all his resources on the defense of the city. To ensure the spiritual strength of the city, he had the images of all the city gods throughout southern Mesopotamia brought to Babylon. This ensured the complete demoralization of the people in those cities. They opened their gates to the Persians. A battle was fought on the Tigris, and the Babylonians were crushed. The Persian army occupied Babylon without a struggle. It is thought that Marduk priests opened the gates of the city. They had had enough of their king and his moon god. Nabonidus fled, was captured, and was sent off to end his days in a distant land.

The civilization of Sumer and Akkad died quietly of enormous old age. It left us epics, law codes, legends, the twelve-month year, the week, the zodiac, a bleak view of frightened man, a vast pantheon of immortal gods, an enormous religious literature of incantations, poems, prayers, observations of the stars that laid the foundation for modern science and the occult searchings of astrology, a systematic practice of medicine, a profound knowledge of herbs and drugs, and words like sack, camel, sesame, poppy, and hour. Here and there one comes upon a remnant pool of that ancient world as I did one hot summer afternoon outside Antioch in southern Turkey when, climbing the hills of Daphne with its leafy trees and the sparkling falls that burst from the rocks and spill across the earth, I found myself in the midst of a joyous celebration. The hill was thronged with old and young enjoying sumptuous meals on tables set amid the rushing streams and luxuriant greenery. Once pagans had worshiped Daphne on this hill. Now Muslims were eating a festive meal. It is a wedding, they said. A wedding. But I could see no bride and groom. Did they know that they were celebrating the resurrection of the Mesopotamian god Tammuz?

On the third day of the Babylonian month of Marcheshvan, our October-November, King Cyrus, the newest of Mesopotamians, entered Babylon. The people spread green branches before him and hailed him as their true king. Second Isaiah called him the shepherd of YHWH— the term shepherd was used by Assyrians and Babylonians of their rulers. Cyrus was the servant of YHWH, His friend, His anointed. The prophet promised a new exodus. Cyrus worshiped in the temple of Marduk. He ordered all the gods returned to their cities and warned his soldiers against oppressive treatment of the population.

He was tolerant of all religions. He believed that if the conquered people could worship as they wished and enjoy cultural autonomy within the framework of his empire it would ease the burden of rule. All through his empire he encouraged the reconstruction of ancient temples. Whenever he issued an edict for a new temple he would respectfully use accepted tradition and claim that the god of the temple had charged him to rebuild it. When he issued the edict to the exiles from Judah in 538 B.C.E. permitting them to rebuild their temple in Jerusalem he was not certain what part of the universe they believed their God ruled. He called Him YHWH, the God of Heaven.

# BOOK TWO

*Through Classical Paganism*

# GREECE

## War on the Margin of the Map

Then came centuries of morning twilight, the interface between two Jewish civilizations.

The Babylonian bondage was at an end. Almost all who had gone into captivity about fifty years before were no longer alive. Their sons and daughters, and some of the very old, made the difficult journey through the Mesopotamian heart of the Persian empire back to Jerusalem. Probably some few thousands went; the precise number is not known. Most remained behind in the comfort they had fashioned for themselves in Babylonia.

Those who undertook the journey regarded it as a second exodus. They were led by Sheshbazzar, a man in his sixties, whose father had been King Jehoiachin of Judah. One imagines them entering the land in dreamy exultation. Pagans lived in the north, descendants of those who had once been transplanted there by the Assyrians. Peasants lived in the hill country of Judah—called Yehud by the Persians; their parents had been left behind on the land by the Babylonians. The newcomers from Babylonia, regarding themselves as the only true Israel and proud of the purity of their genealogies, would have nothing to do with the indigenous population. Hostility grew and deepened between those who had lived on the ruined land and those who had come to reclaim it. In the years that followed there was crop failure and famine. The attempt to rebuild the temple ended in failure.

A second wave of Babylonian Jews arrived, led by Zerubbabel, nephew of Sheshbazzar. The date of their arrival is not known. In 525 B.C.E. Cambyses son of Cyrus conquered Egypt. When his throne was usurped by Darius, a member of the Persian royal family, in 522 B.C.E., he committed suicide. Rebellions erupted throughout the empire. In Jerusalem the prophets Haggai and Zechariah saw the coming of the day of YHWH and exhorted the newcomers to build the temple. In 515 B.C.E. a small temple was completed and dedicated with joy and weeping. Darius crushed the rebellions and ruled the greatest empire the world had yet known.

Zerubbabel was the last of the Davidic line. With his death the dynasty of David failed and faded from existence.

Those who had made the initial journey from Babylonia to Jerusalem in 538 B.C.E. would never know that just as the first exodus about eight hundred years earlier had brought on a culture war between their ancestors and the Canaanites so would this second exodus bring on a similar war between their descendants and the civilization of tribes that had settled in a distant land along the north central rim of the Mediterranean—the tribes that comprised the villages and city-states of Greece.

In the latter half of the sixth century B.C.E. Athens and Jerusalem and their surrounding territories were similarly small in size, about one thousand square miles, and in population, about thirty or forty thousand people. Beginning in 540 B.C.E., both lands experienced generations of creative cultural achievement and bitter political failure. The relationship of Greece and her conqueror, Rome, to the second civilization of my people—a civilization molded by scribes and by new leaders called rabbis, a word meaning masters or teachers—is similar to that first of Sumer, then Egypt, then Canaan, to the civilizations of the patriarchs, the federation of twelve tribes, and the monarchy. Whole landscapes of this second civilization—rabbinic Judaism—remain deserts of obscurity if we neglect a proper understanding of Greece and Rome.

When I was young, the cultural specter I was taught to look upon with revulsion as I made my way painstakingly through labyrinthine passages of Talmud—the sprawling legal and literary creation of the second civilization of my people—was the Greece of Dionysus and Aristotle. None of my teachers ever uttered the words used by the medieval Jewish thinker Nachmanides, who wrote of Aristotle, "May his name be erased." But similar words, spoken and unspoken, floated through the corridors of my school. Greece was the idolatrous menace we most despised and feared.

Greece for us was Athens, Macedonia, and ruthless Hellenizers. In later years I read of nymphs and fauns gamboling through woods and streams; philosophers probing the cosmos for permanence behind appearances; silken hedonistic loveliness, penetrating godless rationalism; cities that were a testament to wise self-government; a heroic striving for excellence as the assurance of fame and immortality; poetry, prose, and art that were a glory of our species—and discovered how alluring pagan Greece could be. I had to keep reminding myself that this civilization had once attempted to destroy my people. Worse, most of my people had never encountered her rich heart, only her Hellenistic periphery. That was the most sorrowful failure of all in that twilight time between the vanishing Biblical and the not-yet-born rabbinic civilizations of the Jews.

Wandering northern tribes brought a latent genius to a certain configuration of southern soil and sea, and after centuries of silence Greek civilization was born. We can never know if a different people on this same Mediterranean soil would have created this same civilization.

The first wave of Greek-speaking invaders consisted of seminomadic tribes that penetrated the Balkan mountains about 2000 B.C.E. They came under the influence of a civilization that flourished on the island of Crete from about 2000 to 1450 B.C.E. The origin of that civilization is as mysterious as its abrupt disappearance. Arthur Evans, who uncovered its art and writing at about the turn of our century, named it the Minoan civilization, after the legendary King Minos of Crete, husband to the daughter of the sun, father of the monstrous Minotaur who devoured an annual sacrifice of Greek youths and maidens and was finally slain in its labyrinth by Theseus.

The Cretans lived in coastal towns and villages. With their knowledge of bronze tools they built spectacular

palaces; the most remarkable of them, constructed in the
town of Knossos about 1900 B.C.E., remains a wonder to
this day.

The palace in Knossos was destroyed, probably by
earthquake, about 1700 B.C.E. It was rebuilt. Crete was
then in the full flower of its civilization. About 1450
B.C.E. it all came to a sudden end with the destruction of
most of the Minoan centers of culture. A volcanic eruption? An earthquake? Did invaders from the mainland
take possession of the palace and the town at some point
after the disaster of 1450 B.C.E. and hold them until the
final destruction about 1180 B.C.E. by a new tribal inundation from the north? There are no certain answers as
yet about the death of the ancient civilization of Crete.

The Greek-speaking tribes that wandered down into
Attica and the Peloponnesus about 2000 B.C.E. soon
ceased their wandering and built villages and towns. One
of those towns, Mycenae, became the chief stronghold of
the civilization that was eventually created by these
Greeks. Archaeologists date the origins of the acropolis of
Mycenae—the fortified high point—to the Bronze Age.
The palace of Mycenae was built about 1600 B.C.E. by
these Greek-speaking invaders. It was a little city set in a
recess of hills at the northeast rim of a plain. Two hours
away by foot lay the sea. The limestone wall of the acropolis was very high; it followed the contours of a steep
rocky slope. The summit was the center of the acropolis.
The city contained a stone-enclosed circular burial
ground, a palace complex, a boulevard, enormous blocks
of stone used as lintels and in the surrounding fortifications—so huge that in later times they were believed to
have been put in place by the Cyclopes, a mythical race
of giants. The Mycenaeans buried their royal dead with
breastplates and face masks of gold in deepcut shaft
graves. The faces appear stocky and bearded. On the
walls of the buildings were frescoes: ladies carry small
caskets in a frozen procession; trees look like tennis rack-
ets; demons with the heads of donkeys carry mysterious
long poles on their shoulders. The Mycenaeans enjoyed
depicting scenes of battle and the hunt. The art is child-
like.

Mycenaean civilization was at its height in the fifteenth century B.C.E. It was the creation of a small people made wealthy by trade, and it spread across the Greek mainland and many of the Aegean islands. It established colonies on the eastern coast of Asia Minor; its ships took over control of the Aegean from Crete. That was the time when early Hebrew clans, descendants of wandering Amorites, lived peacefully in Canaan, and other Hebrews lived in New Kingdom Egypt and were soon to be made state slaves.

Mycenaean civilization had writing, probably borrowed initially from Asia Minor merchants. Its pottery was popular from the peninsula of Italy to the coast of Asia Minor. The civilization of Mycenae was part of a single culture continuum that stretched from southern Mesopotamia through fertile river valleys, backland hills, fringes of desert, Asia Minor, the eastern Mediterranean, and coastal land bridges to the Egyptian Delta. It was a semifeudal society of warriors, craftsmen, and serfs managed by bureaucrats and ruled by kings. For some reason still unknown to us it appears to have raided and besieged a city on the northern coast of Asia Minor with which it had carried on extensive trade. Perhaps the city controlled the narrow waterway to the Black Sea and raised the price of passage. Mycenae, given casually to brigandage even under normal circumstances, may have preferred war and the prospect of plunder to peace and the certainty of high tolls. The city was Troy, or Ilium, and the raid probably occurred about 1230 B.C.E.

A decade or so later, great waves of illiterate Greek-speaking tribes came down from the north. They had knowledge of iron. The Bronze Age came to an end in Greece and Asia Minor. In the Fertile Crescent, Israelite clans had completed a long wilderness wandering and were burning cities in Canaan. In Greece the palace in Pylos was burned about 1200 B.C.E., around the time Joshua and the conquering Israelites covenanted at Shechem with the God they believed had redeemed them from slavery and given them a new land.

Then Mycenae was destroyed. Writing ceased in Greece. The Mediterranean world was thrown into chaos as the wandering Sea Peoples, hungry and dislocated, plundered and pillaged and searched for new homes. Darkness descended upon Greece; what we know of that land for the next four centuries comes to us mostly from bits of pottery. The first civilization of the Greeks vanished and was lost to memory until its discovery by Heinrich Schliemann and others in the last hundred years.

For the Greeks themselves that civilization and its truths underwent transformation to saga and myth. Bards wandered through villages and into the crude palaces of chieftains and told in powerful rhythmic speech of the curiously human doings of the gods, of heroic kings, their passionate regard for honor and glory, their strivings for excellence in all things and most especially on the field of combat, their scorn of danger, loyalty to friends, and their absolute conviction that fame born of heroism in battle burned one's name forever into the minds of all men and led to immorality. These recently arrived tribesmen saw heroic greatness in the past—which they populated with warlords not unlike themselves and set in an anarchic social order similar to their own—because their present was swollen with brutality and violence. For the Israelites that was the time of bloody raids on their villages by border people and marauding nomads, the period of the judges.

Archaeologists gaze at shards and ruins and detect a slow settling of the turbulence in the Aegean about 1000 B.C.E., at the time David became king of Judah and Israel. Scattered villages began to grow together around high defensible points, the birthing process of the later Greek city-states. Sometime in the ninth or early eighth century the greatest of the bards, someone whose name, Homer or Homeros, means hostage, took the material of four centuries of oral transmission, tales repeated in a traditional manner that utilized stock phrases and formulas, and molded it all into an oral tale of a short period in the siege of Troy, transformed from an act of brigandage to a legendary ten-year-long war of honor. That tale, told through subsequent centuries and written down in definitive form about three hundred years after Homer, became the work we know as the *Iliad*. Utilizing another series of oral tales, Homer or someone else created the *Odyssey*. The Viking heroics of the men in these tales mirror more the time after the breakup of Mycenaean civilization than they do the settled bureaucratic palace life of that first Greek world. The siege of Troy as described in Homer was the first historical memory of this Greek civilization, just as the call of God to Abraham was the first remembered fragment of history for the Biblical author and his audience of Israelites. Modern scholarship has helped augment both histories.

In the second half of the eighth century the new Greek tribes were brushed by the culture of the Fertile Crescent. The rigid geometric patterns of their pottery, typical of peasant cultures, became more naturalistic. Animals, winged creatures, battle scenes, myths began to populate their pottery, freeing it of its rigidity. The Greeks acquired the Semitic alphabet, probably from merchants in the port cities of Phoenicia, and swiftly adapted it to their own needs. They invented signs for the rich vowel sounds of their language and in the end transformed the alphabet almost completely while retaining some of the original names for the letters: alpha and beta are merely the names of letters in Greek; aleph and bet are letter names in Semitic and also mean ox and house.

That contact with the Semitic culture of the Fertile Crescent appears to have sparked the creativity of these northern tribes. Settled now on southern soil, they began to utilize their alphabet not only for commerce but also to preserve and create poetry. Early writings are scanty and fragmentary—worn and chipped stones, isolated quotations by later writers of works now lost. But there is enough left us to enable it to be said that in the eighth century B.C.E. Greece reentered history.

For some, the opening date in Greek history is 776 B.C.E. A fifth-century Greek named Hippias studied the inscriptions on certain monuments and records and discovered that they extended back to that date. The monuments and records studied by Hippias were lists of victors, and 776 B.C.E. is, according to the Greeks, the date of the first Olympic Games. In ancient Israel that date falls into the successful reigns of King Uzziah of Judah and King Jeroboam II of Israel and into the period of the prophesying of Amos.

The people who attended those first Olympic Games were united by a common language and religion. Sometime during the eighth century B.C.E., population increase led to land hunger. The Greeks began to colonize the rim of the Mediterranean from Italy to the coast of Asia Minor, from southern France to North Africa. They colonized Sicily, Libya, Thrace, the Black Sea. We do not know precisely how those distant Greek cities were established, how the new settlers were selected, how the indigenous populations of the colonized areas were treated. Probably selection was by lot; a few hundred individuals would be sent out from the mother city, the metropolis, often under compulsion. The settlers took with them their families, the gods and institutions of the city, and sacred fire and embers from the public hearth. The new city was independent of the mother city. Sites were chosen at the recommendation of sailors, traders, or scouting parties, and were located in fertile coastal plains, in the region of a natural harbor, near land that could be mined for its minerals. The indigenous populace was driven away, subdued, or absorbed through intermarriage.

A little over one hundred miles south of Rome a small tribe called the Graii was among the settlers of Cumae, a city founded about 750 B.C.E. The Romans called them Graeci. The people the Romans called the Greeks called themselves Hellenes and their land Hellas, after their mythic ancestor, Hellen. When we are finally able to gaze fully upon these descendants of Hellen in the full light of history we see their cities sprinkled throughout the world of the Aegean. It is immediately apparent that the home of this Greek civilization was not merely the Peloponnesus, central Greece, and Attica; that was the west coast of Greece. The coastline of Asia Minor was the eastern seaboard. The Aegean was a vast Greek lake, and the numerous puzzle-shaped islands—the peaks of drowned hills—were way stations along its surface. Crete was the southernmost boundary of that watery land.

Tall marble and limestone mountains; small hard-earthed valleys; brief patches of arable soil; a dominating blue-green sea visible from almost everywhere on land; a clear Mediterranean light that flattened distances and dissolved all possibility of soft mist-filled perspective and blurry tonalities of shape; hot unbroken summer sunshine; winters of rain and snow which the stony earth could barely absorb—that was the hard land of ancient Greece. The Greeks used the sea as the Semites used the sand; they wandered back and forth across it. The little islands were oases for their ships.

There were hundreds of Greek cities. In time there would be Greek cities in Egypt and throughout the Fertile Crescent. Jews would attempt to turn Jerusalem into a Greek city.

At first, they were small cities. Streets were narrow, tortuous; houses were shabby. Populations rarely attained or exceeded ten thousand. The Greeks lived in fear of large families, for that could mean starvation. Custom and law condoned homosexuality, abortion, and the exposure of infants in woods, mountains, or garbage dumps.

The cities controlled their surrounding territories and were really city-states. Sparta conquered much of the Peloponnesus and was the largest of the city-states, with a territory of 3360 square miles, about one-third the area of Vermont. Argos ruled an area of 560 square miles; Corinth 352; Thebes 400. The medium-sized islands of the Aegean—many had only one city—ranged from the 2¼ square miles of Delos to the 331 square miles of Chios. The 3440 square miles of Crete contained more than fifty cities.

Often these cities were set in valleys and sloped upward to the high point of a hill, the polis, or, as it was soon to be called, the lofty high point, the acropolis. In time the word polis came to mean the city, and acropolis referred only to the citadel. The high point contained the main temples of the city; nearby, not on the acropolis itself, were the palace of the king with its public hall, where the sacred fire of the communal hearth would be kept burning, and the building where the council met. A wall protected the area of the acropolis. Below the acropolis were the dwellings of citizens and slaves, the shacks of peasants who worked the soil, and the homes of those who owned land and were privileged to fight the city's wars. Beyond the city were villages, fields, groves, olive trees, and often a stream and a beach and port on the sea. There were no navigable rivers. It was to the high point that the townspeople would flee in case of attack by another city or by pirates.

In some cities the mass of citizens had no political rights; in other cities they possessed all rights; but every city had a public meeting place, the agora, where information, goods, ideas, and gossip could be exchanged. The building block of the city was the family and its god, and the hearth and sacred fire around which the clan gathered. Duty existed only between kinsmen. The possessions of the clan—livestock, slaves, land—passed from the dead of one generation to the living of another in a chain no one dared break; to do so, for whatever the reason, meant to be cast out into a world where a man without family was a nameless prey of death.

The Greek city was an experimental station for the practice of politics—how to live in a polis, where family self-interest and the public need were in constant tenuous balance. To maintain this balance various kinds of governments were tried throughout the centuries of Archaic (800 to about 490 B.C.E.) and Classical (490 to 336 B.C.E.) Greece, from dual kingship in Sparta to near-rampant democracy in Athens. In the end it was the city, the very glory of Greece, which led to the destruction of Greek civilization: like the Sumerians, the Greeks too could not look beyond their city walls toward nationhood. They were a proud, independent, mercurial people who seemed unable to grasp the concept of unity. Ancient Greece remained a cluster of independent cities bound together by language, custom, and a common faith in the same gods, especially in Zeus, god of heaven. No doubt the mountains made effective prisons of the small valleys of the land, and the bonds of language and religion could not cross the hills save for special festivals and once every four years when all wars would be suspended so athletes could compete in the Olympic Games.

There were two additional features of the Greek city: the theater, at first the scene of ancient fertility rituals that celebrated the birth and death of Dionysus and later the site of some of the greatest artistic achievements—Attic drama and comedy—of our species; and the gymnasium. This latter was a spacious building where athletes would train and men would go to keep themselves trim. The athletes rubbed their bodies with oil and performed their calisthenics in the nude. Calisthenics means beautiful strength. The Greeks thought the nude body of a healthy youth to be one of the most beautiful of sights. The word gymnasium means a place where one trains naked. A gymnasium would be one of the causes of a twenty-five-year war between the civilizations of Zeus and YHWH.

When I was very young I read a book containing the myths of ancient Greece: Prometheus stole fire from the gods to give to mortals; Perseus slew Medusa; Jason sailed in search of the fleece; Heracles succeeded at his twelve labors; all the storied world of Greece came as a marvel to my imagination. In later years I studied the pre-Socratics, Plato, and Aristotle. What a miracle of the human mind was Greece!

But there was another Greece, a fearful world of magic rituals and charms, miracle workers and half-mad prophetesses, ecstatics, and wandering shamans, hysterical religious frenzies in which animals and sometimes children were torn apart and eaten. No one ever taught me that Greece. I knew nothing of the dark irrationality in the heart of Greek civilization.

Old religious beliefs are seldom erased when new ideas appear; both dwell side by side in the same culture that gave them life, often in the same person, like geological layers of living tissue. Gilbert Murray calls these strata of belief the Inherited Conglomerate. Future centuries saw as exemplary the bright pinpoints of rational light in Classical Greece and ignored or were unaware of the stark presence of earth religions—scholars call it chthonic faith —and the sense of the supernatural that permeated all of Greek life and evoked responses hardly more reasoned than those that characterized the fear-ridden civilizations of the Fertile Crescent.

The Greeks were a profoundly religious people. Their earth and sky, woods and fields and streams, cities and hills were dense with gods. I know of no Greek who denied the existence of deity. Protagoras, who came from Abdera to Athens in 450 B.C.E., declared that man was the measure of all things, and announced that "with regard to the gods I cannot feel sure either that they are or that they are not"—Protagoras was at most an agnostic. Xenophanes, a sixth-century B.C.E. poet-philosopher who spent much of his life wandering back and forth through the Greek world, said that if cattle and lions had hands they would depict the gods in their own images. Yet he firmly asserted the existence of a supernatural power: his god was a single entity, constant, unmoving, without physical form, who moved the material world by effortless thought. To attack a conventional theology is not necessarily to deny the existence of deity. If there were articulate atheists among the Greeks their writings are lost to us.

The pantheon was large and complex, the result of the fusions of many cultures. Successive tribal inundations and their subsequent civilizations made available to the Greeks a bloated family of gods who frequently lived in a murderous relationship to one another. In those days, when a conqueror's gods replaced the gods of the conquered, myths were born that explained the transformation—born not artfully but through the folk imagination that saw in the deeds of the gods reflections on a monumental scale of the acts of man. Men take power from other men by means of war. How could gods replace other gods except through titanic struggles?

The people who lived on the Mediterranean peninsula of Greece before the land was invaded by the earliest of the wandering Hellenic tribes appear to have worshiped a great mother goddess and to have had a matriarchal order of society. Fertility in nature and man was the first concern of these pre-Hellenic people. The Hellenic tribes who poured into Greece from the cold north brought with them a patriarchal order of society and their own clashing gods—Uranus, Cronus, Rhea, Zeus.

The myths about these gods were suppressed by Homer when he shaped the oral traditions available to him into the *Iliad*. The Olympic gods, neatly arranged in a modest pantheon and bestowed with clearly outlined personalities, bear little resemblance to the earth-rooted, child-devouring gods of prehistory, to a social order obsessed with fertility, tribal ties of blood, a preoccupation with sentiment.

The Olympians are cool, rational, remote. Zeus, Apollo, Athena, and the others on that lofty mountain are not monstrous in appearance but the handsomest of men and women, elegant, well bred—so close in form to the warring nobles on the beach before Troy that it is with an effort that we must sometimes remind ourselves how unbridgeable is the chasm between them: the gods are immortal. The only immortality available to man is the fame born of excellence.

The men who worship the Olympian gods are keenly aware of the capacities of man; they display heroism on the field of battle, a vaulting pride of self, a deep sense of honor, and a horror of being shamed in the eyes of others. Public approbation and esteem is the highest good in the world of Homer, not the quiet pleasure that comes from a tranquil conscience. That is why the anger of Achilles and his refusal to join his comrades in battle—a treasonous act in today's world—was perfectly clear to the Greeks: he had been dishonored by Agamemnon, leader of the Greek forces, who had taken away his concubine. Often we know a culture best through its fears: the Greek nightmare was an act of cowardice that would shame one in the eyes of one's fellows; the Israelite nightmare was a sinful deed that would cause one to be found guilty in the eyes of God. The Homeric world is tumultuous with brave men in dread of shame.

The writings of Homer were regarded by the Greeks as sacred texts. When Greeks scattered and went into exile after the fall of Rome in the fifth century C.E., among the first institutions they established in each of their new communities was a school to teach Homer.

Yet even the Homeric world was not without intrusions

of the irrational. Sudden inexplicable changes in normal behavior—an uncontrollable temptation, a mysterious burst of energy, an extraordinarily brilliant or foolish idea, a flash of memory about a long-forgotten event, an abrupt insight into an omen—these were indicators of psychic intervention by the gods into the affairs of man.

The world of Homer throbs with such departures and interventions. A bowstring breaks, and the warrior cries out in terror that a demon is thwarting him; Penelope's refusal to remarry is explained with the words, "the gods are putting it into her chest"; Agamemnon explains his theft of Achilles' mistress by claiming that "not I was the cause of this act, but Zeus and my portion and the Erinys [the divine agent who sees to the fulfillment of a person's lot] who walks in darkness: they it was who in the assembly put wild *ate* [divine temptation or infatuation] in my understanding, on that day when I arbitrarily took Achilles' prize from him. So what could I do? Deity will always have its way."

It had its way in all areas of Greek life. Apollo could bring on prophetic madness; Dionysus, ritual madness; the Muses, poetic madness; Aphrodite and Eros, erotic madness. Mental disease was of supernatural origin: a man was touched by Zeus, seized or attacked by demons—from which we get words like stroke, seizure, attack, touched, which indicate the ancient belief that madness and certain illnesses were the result of divine or demonic possession of one's being. Certain dreams are sent by the gods: a priest is ordered by a diety to build him a temple because he is weary of dwelling in lodgings.

There were yet other elements of the irrational in Greek civilization—the belief held by certain cults in the reincarnation of souls, in the powerful magic of shamans who could stop the winds, restore the dead, leave the body and journey to distant parts of the worlds of men and spirits, in men who could vanish from this world and become gods. The irrational was not peripheral to Greek civilization; it pervaded its very heart.

The Greeks revered not only Homer but also Hesiod, a farmer who lived shortly after Homer and witnessed the hardships of the archaic period. He saw no glory in war, despised men obsessed with pride and power, and thought the age in which he lived the least significant of times—he called it the age of iron and believed it had been preceded by the more glorious ages of gold, silver, bronze, and heroes. He urged upon men the values of truth and justice. He loathed bribe-devouring, folk-killing kings who consumed the world of the weak. Zeus had so arranged matters, Hesiod wrote, that animals should devour one another; but man must act in accordance with the right. He envisioned thousands of spirits roaming the earth at the behest of Zeus. Clothed in mist, they kept invisible watch on the doings of men. Justice is the daughter of Zeus; she informs him of a man's evil deeds, and Zeus inflicts the deserved punishment. Man's own sense of justice and the justice of Zeus are in perfect harmony—a position not unlike that of the Deuteronomist. "Often even a whole city suffers for a bad man who sins . . . and the Son of Cronus lays great trouble upon the people, famine and plague together, so that the men perish away . . . through the contriving of Olympian Zeus." So wrote Hesiod, the farmer from a poverty-stricken village in Boeotia on the mainland of Greece.

Much of our knowledge of the oral traditions suppressed by Homer comes to us from the poems—*Works and Days,* the *Theogony,* the *Catalogues*—of Hesiod. That impoverished farmer had notions about man and the gods quite different from those of Homer. He wrote of Zeus, "For easily he makes strong, and easily he brings the strong man low; easily he humbles the proud and raises the obscure, and easily he straightens the crooked and blasts the proud—Zeus who thunders aloft and has his dwelling most high."

Hesiod's was not a lone voice. Pindar, that most aristocratic of fifth-century B.C.E. Greek poets, was a Dorian who lived in Thebes. His odes shimmer with the aristocratic brilliance of his world. Gods, heroes, and the mythological past were real to him; all were part of the living world. Individual talent was a gift of the gods and an inheritance from one's ancestors; one must use it in the pursuit of excellence. But a man had to know his limitations. The gods punished arrogance; no man ought attempt to scale the heavens. His efforts should be balanced and undertaken not for his own glory but on behalf of his family or city. His true reward would come later: ". . . immediately after death, on earth, it is the lawless spirits that suffer punishment—and the sins committed in this realm of Zeus are judged by one who passeth sentence stern and inevitable; while the good, having the sun shining for evermore, for equal nights and equal days, receive the boon of a life of lightened toil . . . but, in the presence of the honored gods, all who are wont to rejoice in keeping their oaths, share a life that knoweth no tears. . . . "

An altogether different strand of faith from that displayed by the gods and heroes of Homer found expression in obscure cults in Greece. It is called Orphism, after its apparently mythical founder, a shaman who was a magician, poet, teacher, musician, and giver of oracles. It held the soul to be separate from and imprisoned in the body; it emphasized guilt and retribution, good and evil in human nature. The revelations of Orpheus, if followed—abstinence, renunciation, asceticism, certain rites—promised to free the soul from its tomb of flesh and bring it to the divine abode. There were also secret cults—mystery religions—whose rites remain unknown to us. Some preached a personal afterlife utterly different from the ghostly underworld found in Homer.

Unlike the blissful life-after-death of the good man envisaged by Pindar, the real world of a fifth-century B.C.E. Greek knew many tears. We know much about the life of the Athenians of that century. It crackled with magic and the supernatural, with frenzied festivals and fertility celebrations, with the horrors of war, disease, death. Gods and demons were everywhere, to be placated, worshiped, and gladdened with gifts of burnt meat and fat. In much of this the Athenians differed not at all from any other civilization of antiquity save that of the Israelites who worshiped YHWH.

If you were a fifth-century Athenian you participated in the many official festivals of the city. You celebrated on the twelfth day of the first month of the year, our July, a thanksgiving for the safely gathered spring harvest; families held banquets in their homes for all members of the household, including slaves. On the sixteenth of that month you joined in the celebration that marked the unification of Attica accomplished in the misty past by the legendary Theseus. At the end of that same month there took place the national festival of the patron goddess of the city, Athena. Other festivals celebrated the god Apollo, the fertility god Demeter. There were numerous festivals; they were filled with sacrifices, processions, various rites, and athletic competitions. During the lengthy festival of Dionysus three days were set aside for the presentation of tragedy in the theater on the southern flank of the Acropolis. At the start of the day's performances there always took place a ceremony of purification with the blood of a suckling pig.

If you sought a more private and personal faith, one that might respond to your feelings of dread and your desire for happiness in the afterlife, you joined one of the mystery cults. You inquired into the will of the gods by means of divination. Thunder and rain, the abnormal birth of an animal or child, a sneeze, a buzzing in the ears, the rustle of the wind in certain oak trees sacred to Zeus, the flight and cries of birds, the entrails and liver of a freshly slaughtered animal—everywhere you turned you saw the will of the gods; you had only to go to a seer for a proper explanation of the signs. Certain dreams were clearly divine revelations; you went to a skilled dream interpreter. For a miraculous cure you journeyed to the great sanctuary in the Argolid on the Peloponnesus. You spent the night, and in a dream you would see the god of healing, Asclepius, touch the diseased part of your body or hear him prescribe a cure. The will of Zeus might be revealed to you by prophets or prophetesses in a state of ecstasy. In the sanctuary of Apollo at Delphi was a peasant woman who lived a simple and chaste life during the time she responded to the queries put to her by individuals and city-states. She would enter a state of ecstasy or enthusiasm—divine possession—and proclaim in a babble the will of Zeus revealed through his son Apollo. Priests would interpret her words. Anyone could ask a question of the oracle. You had only to pay a fee. If the goat you were about to offer as a sacrifice shivered when it was sprinkled with the purifying waters, you knew Apollo was willing to prophesy. The woman uttered the oracle of Apollo, her words almost always ambiguous. The Delphic oracle had enormous influence upon the world of fifth-century B.C.E. Greece.

There was of course much superstition: you did not walk on a grave or go near a corpse or a woman in labor; if you went outside and heard an owl hoot you immediately said, "Athena protect me"; if you came across an insane person you spat into your robe, spitting being a quick form of water purification. There were also magic rites which could compel the gods to use their power in your behalf. The Greeks of the Classical Period did not favor such practices; they thought magic to be a foreign import, an alien gift of doubtful worth from the barbaric east. By the first half of the fourth century B.C.E., however, after the long nightmare of the Peloponnesian War and the conquest of Athens by Sparta, magic began to spread in Attica. Then you could harm your enemy, particularly one with whom you were involved in a court case, by writing his name and mentioning or drawing various parts of his body on a clay tablet which you placed in a small container. You scratched a curse on a second tablet, rolled it around an iron nail, and buried it and the container in the earth, thereby dedicating your enemy, nailing him down, to the gods of the infernal regions. In the meantime, of course, your enemy was no doubt working that same kind of magic on you.

We cannot know with certainty if rationalism would have been preserved in Athens on the strength of Homer alone. Perhaps reason is the gift of Athens because a mortal threat against rebelling Greek cities in Asia Minor by the barbarian enemy, Persia, sent Ionian philosophers from the shores of Asia Minor to the heart of Attica. It was the peculiar bent of these Ionian philosophers to search for intelligible and natural explanations of phenomena. They were to Attica what many Europeans who fled across the Atlantic from Hitler in the decade of the thirties were to America: leaven for creativity.

The Persians gave indirect impetus to the rationalism of Athens and, for a while at least, forced Athens, Sparta, and twenty-nine other city-states to shape themselves into a league with a single administrative body which had the power to decide general strategy, punish those who favored the cause of the Persians, appoint envoys to negotiate with other states, and raise troops and money. It was the closest the Greek world ever came to unity. The Persians were to the Greeks what the Philistines had once been to the Israelites.

Almost nothing is known about the history of Athens before 600 B.C.E. You were a citizen of Athens if you were the free son of parents who had been born in Athens—which meant that you were descended from one of the four ancient Ionian tribes who had founded the city. Everyone else was a resident foreigner or a slave.

The usury and debt that followed like jungle scavengers in the wake of coinage, adopted by the Greeks about 600 B.C.E., brought ruin to many small farmers. Often a debtor, together with his family, paid for a loan not only by loss of land but also by being sold overseas as slaves. Discontent among farmers threatened the aristocracy, families of wealth, land, and political power. In a display of wisdom of the sort that would save Athens repeatedly, aristocratic families agreed to elect as a ruler a man of royal descent and moderate wealth who had traveled widely as a merchant and had written poetry attacking the dangerous greed of the wealthy. His name was Solon, and he came to power about 592 B.C.E. with full authority to reform the constitution.

The state became more important than faction and clan; all citizens had to participate in its affairs. Citizens took an oath to obey the laws of Solon. He was a deeply religious man who believed in the just decree of Zeus, although divine justice differed from human justice and often punished whole groups for the sins of individuals. The wrath of Zeus is like a storm: often guilty and innocent alike are splashed by his anger. A group must understand the harmonious relationship between its parts if it is to survive and prosper. So he believed as he viewed the sadness and glory of human life.

Athens began to prosper and grow. Slavery for nonpayment of debts was abolished. Those sold abroad as slaves for unpaid debts were brought back with public funds. All free men were now members of the Assembly, which was empowered to double as a people's court to arrive at a judgment in complaints against or for individuals. Power began to pass into the hands of the many.

Solon influenced the Athenians to make his laws binding for one hundred years. Then he left Attica for ten years. Almost immediately aristocrats, merchants, peasants —the factions that tore at the institutions of Greek life— came awake and began to claw at one another for power. Constitutional government broke down.

Solon returned and bitterly condemned the Athenians for "foxy ways and foolish wits." Only revolution could break the power of the aristocrats and their supporting clans, and Solon was too rational a man to resort to that. His constitutional reforms were another of the political failures of that period. But Athenians continued to use his ideas as the standards by which they measured their achievements.

Urban strife invariably led to tyranny and often to civil war. In 561 B.C.E. in Athens a nobleman named Peisistratus, whose family owned estates in the coastland area, seized power. He ruled Athens and controlled all the resources of power—weapons, mercenaries, executive posts, the fleet revenues. State festivals and cults were lavishly celebrated. Competition in tragic drama was instituted in Athens about 534 B.C.E. Drama would become the highest form of Attic poetry.

Peisistratus ruled as tyrant of Athens until his death in 528 B.C.E., about ten years after the first of the Israelite exiles had returned to Jerusalem from Babylonia. The tyrant Hipparchus son of Peisistratus gave particular attention to the arts. A definitive text of Homer was now edited in Athens. Hipparchus instituted the recitation of the poems as an integral part of the festival of Athena. At the festival of the year 514 B.C.E.—one year after the dedication of the rebuilt temple in Jerusalem—Hipparchus was assassinated.

Strife and slaughter followed as the rule of the descendants of Peisistratus became increasingly harsh. A rival aristocratic family urged Sparta, head of a major alliance of city-states in the Peloponnesus, to intervene. In 510 B.C.E. a Spartan force invaded Attica. Thirty-six years of tyranny came to an end in Athens.

Many noble families had been in exile during those years; their influence upon their followers had weakened, The tyrants had placed state above clan, had strengthened the guilds, increased the maritime trade of the city, advanced the cause of the small man, the demos, the ordinary members of the people. They had placed a value upon the individual. Athens had a sense of unity in 510 B.C.E. which it had not had in 600 B.C.E. It buzzed with artists and poets. The people had been disarmed by the tyrants; life was graceful, leisurely. This was the time when a man's sense of his individual worth began to clash with the insistent claims of family and clan. Attic drama would explore the dimensions of these rival claims with a resonance and depth never accomplished before and rarely duplicated since.

Solon had given Athens personal liberty and equality of rights in judicial procedure. A new aristocratic ruler, Cleisthenes, gave Athens that same equality in the electoral sphere. All male Athenians, regardless of wealth or birth, could now vote as individuals without any sense of outside obligation or pressure. The old institutions of government—the Areopagus, the Council, the Assembly—remained basically unchanged. But the criterion of blood for citizenship was abolished. Athens entered the fifth century B.C.E. with all its people feeling themselves deeply involved in the destiny of their state. Ten years later, in 490 B.C.E., Attica was invaded by the Persians.

It was the intention of the Persians to annex Greece and secure the western frontier of their empire, and also to punish the Athenians for their support of the Ionian city-states of Asia Minor during a futile revolt against King Darius in 498 B.C.E. In 490 B.C.E. at the beach in the bay of Marathon, twenty-three miles northeast of Athens, a Persian army consisting of cavalry and infantry disembarked from a fleet of ships lying close to the shore. The Aegean was now a Persian sea. The Athenian Assembly sent a runner to Sparta, a distance of about one hundred forty miles. The runner returned with the news that Sparta was in the midst of a festival and would be unable to march until the full moon, six days ahead. No one blamed Sparta; a city could not violate its sacred tenets. The Athenians met the Persians on the plain of Marathon. For some reason, the Persians began to withdraw their cavalry to the ships. The Greek general Miltiades responded immediately. A sacrifice was made to the gods. The omens were interpreted as favorable. Ten thousand Greek hoplites advanced rapidly against twenty-five thousand Persians. The thin Greek center yielded and the Persians poured through; but the dense hoplite wings folded inward upon the Persian rear. It was a long battle. The Persians broke and fled to their ships.

The Spartans arrived the next day. They had marched about one hundred forty miles in three days. They went to the battlefield at Marathon and viewed the dead—192 Athenians, 6400 Persians. Seven Persian ships had been destroyed. The Spartans congratulated the Athenians, and returned home.

Ten years later, in the summer, a vast Persian army, probably numbering about one hundred thousand men, crossed the Hellespont on a pontoon bridge built across ships anchored fore and aft and lashed in line a few feet apart. The army, led by King Xerxes, moved like a monstrous, turgid swarm across the land, ravaging cities that resisted and drinking rivers dry. A naval force of about six hundred ships followed carefully alongside the treacherous line of coast. Gales blew up; ships were lost. Three hundred Spartans died in the narrow pass at Thermopylae in an effort to stop the Persian advance.

The Athenians abandoned their city, taking to the sea in ships, and watched the Persians loot and burn their sacred Acropolis and the temple of the goddess Athena. They had built a large fleet in the years since the last invasion; but it was easily outnumbered by the Persians. In the narrow bay of Salamis was fought the naval battle that stemmed the Persian advance into Europe. The Greek fleet outmaneuvered and outfought the crowded, unwieldy formations of the Persians. King Xerxes sat on his golden throne on a hilltop and watched the battle. It was late September. Greece was lean and could not sustain his entire army in a winter campaign. He left behind a general with an army of occupation and sailed home. He also left behind his golden throne, forgotten in the surprise and anguish of defeat.

In the spring of the following year the Persians entered Athens, which was still evacuated, and burned to the ground every building yet standing. Then, on the field of battle near the town of Plataea, the Greeks destroyed the Persian army. That was the finest moment of Greek unity —and the last.

Athens, possessing the most powerful navy in all of Greece as well as a good army, now did precisely what Egypt had done after expelling the Hyksos and what the Israelites had done after defeating the Philistines: Athens began to build an empire. Athenian ships ranged throughout the Mediterranean.

In the closing decades of that century, Sparta grew fearful of the expansionist aims of Athens. There began in 431 B.C.E. the long bloody series of raids, pillagings, and draining campaigns known as the Peloponnesian War. It was a war filled with horror and outrage and great disasters for the Greeks. Both Alliances, the Spartan and the Athenian, practiced against each other the sort of brutality one is more accustomed to reading about in Fertile Crescent wars. In one horrifying instance, recorded by Thucydides, the Greek historian of that war, the Athenians staged an unprovoked attack upon the neutral island of Melos, butchered the men and enslaved the women and children. The war went on for almost thirty years and finally came to an end in 404 B.C.E. The army of the Spartan Alliance occupied Athens.

That city, the teacher of all Hellas, home of Aeschylus, Sophocles, Euripides, Socrates, and so many others whose names we speak with pride—that city was nearly destroyed by her conquerors. The Corinthians, who had come from the Peloponnesus and now occupied the city together with the Spartans and others, hungered for vengeance. The war had cost them the very finest of their people. Plague and misfortune had helped reduce Athens. But the Athenians should be made to pay fully for the horror their pride and thirst for power had brought to Greece. They had slaughtered prisoners, massacred adult males, enslaved women and children. Now Athens should suffer the same fate: kill all the men, make slaves of the women and children. But the Spartans refused to destroy the city that had rendered such noble service to Greece in the Persian wars; perhaps they feared the anger of the gods. Athens was spared for another century of creativity. That was the century of Plato and Aristotle.

In the second half of that century Athens was spared again by the conquering army of King Philip of Macedon. A few years later the Persian empire was destroyed by the son of Philip, the young golden-haired Alexander, who scattered the seeds of Greek cities as he passed through the world, encountered the core of Persian culture in Babylon, and to the disgruntled amazement of his troops, transformed himself in garb and manner into the king whose armies he had destroyed.

Alexander encountered another civilization during his course of conquest, but only peripherally. He had brushed by the hill city of Jerusalem in the summer of 332 B.C.E., no doubt glancing at it as one does at the margin of a map. It was a mountain town, away from the paths of armies and of little interest to a busy conqueror.

In later centuries Jerusalem pictured him as bowing low before the Torah in respectful homage to the true God. But that was in the imagination of another time, when war had come to this margin of the map and one longed to consider better ambassadors of Greek civilization than those now killing Jews.

In 458 B.C.E., as Athenian hoplites were dying on the soil of Egypt in an effort to help that land rebel against Persia, a scribe named Ezra journeyed to Judah from Babylon. Judah was part of the enormous Persian satrapy—provincial district—known as Beyond the River, the region west of the Euphrates. It measured about thirty-five miles north to south and about twenty-five miles east to west. It was hill country, extending from the Dead Sea to the lowland near the shore of the Mediterranean.

Ezra was accompanied by fifteen hundred people—

priests, Levites, singers, and others who could participate in the maintenance of the cult of YHWH. In his hands he carried official authorization from King Artaxerxes I of Persia to appoint judges and enforce the law of the God of Heaven.

We do not know how he obtained that authorization; he may have been the highest official of the Jewish community in Babylon and represented his people before the king. Moses had derived his authority from the revelation of YHWH at Sinai. Ezra arrived in Jerusalem as the Royal Secretary for the Law of the God of Heaven; we today might call him Minister of State for Jewish Affairs. He brought with him a royal letter that placed the law of YHWH on the same level as the law of the Persian monarch. Offenders were threatened with imprisonment, seizure of possessions, exile, death. The authority of the Jewish scribe Ezra was derived from a pagan king.

In Babylonia he and other leaders of the Jewish community had no doubt been involved in the preservation of the scrolls on which was written the law of Moses—the Greeks would one day call that law the constitution of the Jews. He took part in the codification of that law and now probably brought it to Jerusalem. Moving about the city—with its broken walls it seemed more an exposed village than a city—he attempted to persuade those who had experienced the exile to separate themselves from the indigenous populace, the people of the land, as he called them in derision. He seemed to regard strangers as a polluting element. Only those who had undergone the exile were the true congregation of Israel.

The people of Jerusalem decided to rebuild the walls of their city. According to the Biblical record, Ezra approved of this effort. But the people of Jerusalem were opposed by a group in the north, descendants of Babylonians and Elamites exiled to Samaria two hundred years before by King Ashurbanipal of Assyria. These people feared a walled Jerusalem and wrote to the Persian court, warning that Jerusalem had always been a rebellious city, and once its people felt secure behind new walls they would cease paying their tribute to the king. The northerners were granted permission to appear in Jerusalem and stage a show of force. Construction was halted.

The mission of Ezra the scribe gives every appearance of having ended in failure. Fourteen years went by. We know nothing of Ezra during that time.

In 445 B.C.E. a Jew named Nehemiah, once cupbearer to the king of Persia—a high office in the court of an oriental potentate—arrived in Jerusalem with authority to rebuild the walls of the city.

He tells us in the book he wrote—the Biblical work that bears his name—that he had learned of the failure of Ezra and, with fear in his heart, asked his king for permission to go to that distant land of his people and rebuild the ruined city. The king, suspicious and hesitant, finally sent him on as governor of Judah, with troops and royal letters. The Persians may have seen some wisdom in having a strengthened Judah act as buffer between Mesopotamia and troublesome Egypt.

Sometime after his arrival in Judah he arose in the night, mounted his donkey, and rode slowly toward the city, surveying the broken walls and the burned gates. The donkey found it difficult to make its way through the rubble. Nehemiah tells us that soon afterward he assembled the people, informed them of his authority, and urged that they rebuild the city walls. They reacted eagerly, formed work teams, and completed the labor in fifty-two days.

In the decades before the coming of Nehemiah prosperous nobles, officials, and priestly families had increased their wealth at the expense of peasants and small farmers. The land had been struck repeatedly by drought and famine. Farmers mortgaged their lands for loans; some mortgaged their bodies. Lands were forfeited; enslavement was common. Some now lamented to Nehemiah. He called all the people to Jerusalem. A great throng gathered. The poor outnumbered the rich. Nehemiah spoke persuasively. The people agreed to his reforms: cancellation of debts and restoration of property to previous owners. The nobles took a public oath that they would carry out the reforms as soon as the assembly came to an end. It would have been injudicious to do otherwise in the midst of that throng of the poor. We are vaguely reminded of the reforms of Solon.

The tenuous existence of this small restored community—continued harassment from the Samaritans in the north, sporadic drought, increasing intermarriages that resulted in children who knew nothing of YHWH—had brought on a mood of fearful uncertainty, a dread of mixing with outsiders, a hunger to win back the favor of YHWH by rigid obedience to covenant law. The golden world promised by the prophets became a distant vision; the real world was gray, bleak. YHWH remained displeased with His people. Only by doing His will could the people bridge the silence between themselves and their God.

Abruptly in the year 444 B.C.E. Ezra the scribe appeared again in Jerusalem after fourteen years of silence. Either he had been in Jerusalem all this time, working in the background to complete the editing of the sacred scrolls of the law of Moses, or he had gone back to Babylon and now came to Jerusalem when he learned that the walls had been rebuilt. The Persians encouraged codification and publication—one of the ways you published something in the ancient world was by reading it aloud before people—of religious laws throughout their empire; they were tolerant of all faiths but wished to have them disciplined by law so as to lessen the possibility of quarrels and insurrection. Even the Egyptians, for whom pharaoh was god and law, codified their laws at about this time.

Now, on the first day of the Jewish New Year, sometime in the late summer or early autumn of 444 B.C.E., a vast assembly of people gathered together before the rebuilt water gate of Jerusalem near the spring Gihon, whose course had been diverted in a distant time by the engineers of King Hezekiah so the city could withstand an Assyrian siege. We are not told who convened that assembly; it may have been Nehemiah.

In the early morning of that day Ezra began to read aloud from the scroll of the law of Moses. He was probably an old man now, and though he stood upon a raised platform of wood built for this purpose, many in the crowd must have been out of earshot. Levites circulated among the people, helping them understand. We are told that the people stood while Ezra read from the scroll. He read until the heat of midday. We do not know what he read. Nehemiah announced. "This day is holy to the Lord your God." The people acclaimed the law of Moses and bound themselves to it by renewing the covenant with YHWH. Some days later they proceeded to celebrate together the seven-day festival of Sukkot. Every day of that festival Ezra read to them from the scroll. After a final day of assembly and celebration the people went home. That is all we know of Ezra the scribe. Five years earlier, in 449 B.C.E., the Romans too had codified and published their existing law—on wooden tablets that came to be known as the Twelve Tables.

Sometime during the fourth century B.C.E. a writer composed a work of history that has come to be called Chronicles. He lived in Judah and appears to have been the only historian of the ancient oriental world who was not afraid to alter the traditions with which he worked: he cannot believe that Solomon transferred Israelite cities to King Hiram of Tyre (I Kings 9:11), so he changes the text and has Hiram giving the cities to Solomon (II Chronicles 8:2); he ignores the northern kingdom; he uses the term Israel when he refers to Judah; the entire people sinned against God, not only the kings and noble families, hence the entire people was punished by exile. He is not reporting facts but using facts, often clearly distorted, in order to offer us his vision of the workings of God in history and to emphasize the idea of personal responsibility: fathers will not be put to death for their children, or children for their fathers. An individual who is punished has sinned. The process of transformation of Biblical history has now begun.

Prophecy faded and died in Israel. Nehemiah had insisted upon the observance of the law of Moses, especially the Sabbath. Malachi was the last of the prophets. His closing words were, "Remember the law of Moses My servant. . . ." YHWH would one day break the silence between Himself and His people. Prophecy would revive.

Until that time the law of Moses would be obeyed. It was the only link left between the people and their God.

We know nothing of what went on in the land of Judah during the century after Nehemiah; there are no records. In the sort of silence that enveloped the Greeks after the fall of the Mycenaean world, a second Jewish civilization was being formed in the hill country of Judah—and we are unable to witness the early stages of its birth.

We can assume that exiled Jews continued to drift toward Jerusalem and the tiny district of Judah. There were Jewish communities scattered throughout the vast empire of Persia. It was to be the only time in its history of exile that all the many fragments of this people would be found in a single world obedient to a single ruler. But it was the beginning time of the exile, and the unity of the empire enabled the people to work out a sense of unity-in-dispersion that deepened as the civilizations of Greece and Rome dominated the world. Each community retained its autonomy; at the same time, all communities looked to Jerusalem as central to the whole people.

In 419 B.C.E. a problem about worship arose in the Jewish community of Elephantine near Aswan in Egypt. The origin of that community is obscure. It now consisted of a regiment of mercenaries known as the Jewish force; probably it had been sent out by a sixth-century B.C.E. king of Judah to serve in the army of the pharaoh. Their descendants, in the service of the Persians, sent an inquiry about some details of Passover observance to the temple authorities in Jerusalem. As far away as it was from Judah, it regarded Jerusalem as the center of Jewish faith.

That Elephantine community was involved in business transactions, brought its claims to local civil courts, intermarried with native women, and had its own temple, in blithe violation of the injunctions in Deuteronomy against the offering of sacrifices outside Jerusalem. In 411 B.C.E. Egyptian priests bribed the Persian governor to arrange for the destruction of that temple. Some historians see that as the first anti-Semitic outbreak. The temple was not rebuilt. The regiment was ultimately absorbed into the army of Alexander.

In 332 B.C.E. King Alexander of Macedon conquered

Judah. Judea would soon be its name, a word that simply means the nation of Jews in Greek. That act of conquest removed Judah from the umbrella civilization of Fertile Crescent paganism. The Jewish world pivoted westward and entered the civilization of Europe.

The Jews had so appreciated the tolerant Persians that they carved on a gate of the temple a picture of Susa, the capital city of that empire. I know of no record of the Jewish reaction to the fall of the Persian world. One wonders how the Jews of Babylon felt on that hot June day in 323 B.C.E. when they heard wailing spread through the densely populated streets and learned that inside the royal palace ·of the city Alexander had just died.

At the time of his death all the world save Rome seemed tranquil and Greek. What the Greeks themselves had barely succeeded in doing, their warrior neighbors to the north accomplished splendidly: Greek customs, the Greek language, Greek money, cities, and ideas had enveloped the lands conquered by Alexander.

He was a founder of cities. A short time before his death he had gone sailing downstream from Babylon. He sailed with his engineers to see how the Euphrates, which meandered uselessly into swamps and stagnant lakes, might be harnessed to provide irrigation for farmers. On the way back he spotted a site that seemed fine for a city, and he ordered that one be founded there. Often soldiers who had fought in his armies were settled in those new cities after they were pensioned off from active duty. The channels Alexander sailed that day were fetid with the sewage of Babylon. Soon afterward he took ill and died of a raging fever that was probably malaria.

Nine years earlier he had destroyed the city of Samaria; the Samaritans had revolted against Macedonian authority and burned alive their governor, Andromachus. It was ordered that Macedonian veterans be settled on the soil of Samaria. A Greek city sprang up about forty miles north of Jerusalem.

Greek pottery, Phoenician amulets, and Egyptian idols have been found in Palestine dating to the fourth century

B.C.E. Oedipus converses with the sphinx on a Greek cup. Six miles north of Jerusalem was found an Attic cup with a sphinx. A Jerusalemite shopping in a coastal city for pottery would return home carrying a drawing from Greek mythology on shaped glazed earth. Coins from Athens were the main currency for trade in fifth-century Palestine. They bore the figures of gods and sacred birds. But these were essentially the peripheral elements of Greek civilization. Neither Pythagoras nor Plato ever met Ezekiel; the Chronicler never met Herodotus; Ezra never met Aristotle; Euripides would have had no Jerusalem dramatist to converse with, for drama was an extension of pagan ritual and could have no place as yet in the sacred city. With the founding of the Greek city in the north and the settlement of Macedonian soldiery, there began the full shock of culture encounter between the worlds of Zeus and YHWH.

Destroyed forever was any possible union between Samaria and Jerusalem, and between Samaria itself and the people in the countryside nearby. Those people had once felt themselves close to the returning exiles, had offered to aid in the rebuilding of Jerusalem, but had been repeatedly turned away by the leaders of the exiles who saw them as semipagans. Now the city of Shechem became their center; there they worshiped the God of Israel in their own fashion—as they do to this day—and ignored the claim of Jerusalem that only on Mount Zion could the God of Israel be worshiped with sacrifices. Judea was a self-governing entity with a garrison of royal troops but with no royal governor; it was an autonomous ethnic-religious unit. The only city of the Jews was Jerusalem.

Jewish soldiers had served in the army of Alexander. When the empire of Alexander disintegrated after his death and was divided among his quarreling generals, Palestine came under the control of the general Ptolemy, who ruled Egypt; a Jewish regiment of cavalry served in the army of Ptolemy. The political unity of the world of dispersed Jewry was broken.

In 200 B.C.E., around the same time that the Romans defeated Carthage despite Hannibal's astonishing invasion across the Alps, King Antiochus III of Syria, a descendant of the general Seleucus, took Jerusalem. Parts of the city were damaged in the seesaw fighting. Taxes now went to Syria.

Jerusalem was ruled by a council of elders made up of priests and aristocratic laymen. The high priest was the intermediary between the royal government and the Jews. He was appointed by the king for life. The common people would sometimes be called to the temple court to listen to official reports and decisions, which they would accept by acclamation. There was political strife between two leading families, the Tobiads and the Oniads. The land had been fought over by descendants of Ptolemy and Seleucus; it had enjoyed about a century of relative tranquillity and prosperity as part of Ptolemaic Egypt despite the fact that it had changed hands five times. Judah exported olive oil to Egypt as well as asphalt from the Dead Sea. Now, in 198 B.C.E., Judea was part of Syria.

In 175 B.C.E. a new king, Antiochus IV, ascended the throne of Syria. He had spent some years in Rome.

Two years later Jerusalem began to take on the appearance of a Greek city. Since the days of Ezra and Nehemiah it had remained a backward mountain town, its people dedicated to the law of Moses as interpreted and taught by the prophets and Ezra. Now priests exercised naked in the gymnasium that had been built near the temple on the sacred mountain of God.

The high priest was a man named Jason, a member of the wealthy aristocratic Oniad family. For generations the high priesthood—the most powerful and prestigious office in the politically insignificant state of Judea—had been passed down in that family from father to son. But Jason, whose brother had held the office, bought the high priesthood from King Antiochus IV with a fat bribe. That was the first time that powerful hereditary office had been sold.

Jason then asked for the honor of founding a gymnasium in Jerusalem and for the right to draw up a list of privileged individuals who would be citizens of the new polis. He accompanied his request with a promised payment of 150 talents of silver—about $450,000—in addition to the 440 talents with which he had bought the priesthood. There were about thirty Greek cities in Palestine at the time. The privilege was granted. A gymnasium was built in Jerusalem. It stood very close to the temple, on Mount Moriah, where, we are told in commentaries to Genesis, Abraham once nearly sacrificed his only son to his patron God.

Jerusalem, the city of David, was now host to Greek sports. Naked Jewish youths tossed javelins, wrestled, ran races. Jerusalem sent young athletes to participate in the international athletic contests in Tyre, once the kingdom of Hiram, who had helped Solomon build a temple to YHWH. The backward mountain city of Jerusalem entered the Hellenistic world, the umbrella civilization of that time. The words Hellenism and Hellenistic refer to the civilization of Greece which Alexander marched from the shores of the Aegean and offered to the barbarians of the Fertile Crescent. Those words are also used of the influence of Greek civilization on areas of the world untouched by Alexander—India, Carthage, Rome.

What he offered the ancient world of Asia Minor, Mesopotamia, Egypt, Syria, Phoenicia, and Judea was a civilization whose representatives were for the most part Macedonian soldiers, Greek mercenaries, and money-hungry merchants. Wherever the Greeks went they took with them the elements of their civilization: language and literature, gods and games, and the basic political ingredients of their unique invention, the polis. The Greeks who emigrated from their homeland—they were mostly single young males—found themselves in a world which they regarded contemptuously as devoid of culture and ripe for exploitation. They struggled hard in this new world to maintain their existence, and the struggle changed the civilized Greek individual into a rapacious Hellenistic man. To survive in a world where power determined whether you lived or died, a man needed to be cunning, clever, and strong. Greedy, hungry for wealth and power, a man shaped by an alien world far from the valleys and the sea that had nourished his early life—that was the kind of Greek most often seen by natives of the Fertile Crescent.

Scholars, philosophers, and writers also came from

Greece as immigrants to the world of the Fertile Crescent. Mostly they settled in the new city of Alexandria, founded by Alexander in 332 B.C.E., the capital of Ptolemaic Egypt, which they helped transform into a great center of culture. There were no other such centers in the Hellenistic world. The first public library in the history of our species was built in Alexandria. The Hebrew Bible was translated into Greek for the large Greek-speaking Jewish community of Alexandria, probably during the reign of Ptolemy II, 285 to 246 B.C.E.—the first major translation project in the history of our species.

The Hellenistic city, whose population consisted of Macedonians, Greeks, and natives, served as the meeting ground of east and west. Greek was the official language of the polis. Any urban native who dealt with Greek merchants or administrators needed to learn Greek. Jews learned Greek. Knowledge of the language made possible an entry into the literature of Greece.

Sports were at the very heart of a polis, an expression of the religion of Greece. The great games were dedicated to the gods. Sacrifices were offered at the start of the games. The very best of the youth of a polis would be sent to participate in the games. A gymnasium would contain statues of the gods. Scholars are uncertain whether or not the Jerusalem gymnasium contained statues.

Jerusalem was now an international city. It was granted permission to mint its own coins. The fifteen hundred priests of the city, along with most of the aristocrats and merchants, were no doubt pleased. Prosperity was a certain promise to the leaders of a city participating in the exported civilization of Greece. But there were those who did not share the eagerness of the Hellenizers, who cared little about having Hellenism serve as the link between Jerusalem and the world. They despised the abominations of paganism. These were the pious masses of the city and the farmers of the countryside who observed fervently the law of Moses. Others among the masses were attracted by certain importations of this new paganism: astrology, superstition, magic.

Then Jason lost the high priesthood to someone called Menelaus, a member of a priestly family whose name is unknown. Some scholars believe the name of the city was changed to Antioch. Popular leaders emerged who preached devotion to the Torah. They called themselves Hasidim, Pietists. Street fights broke out in Jerusalem. Jason fled across the Jordan.

Rome too had in her midst those who despised the way of Greece.

Some saw depravity in the young naked male bodies racing and wrestling in the great games and on the earthen floors of gymnasiums. Others suspected the brewing of insurrection in the words of philosophers and the meetings of a Greek cult known as the Dionysiac Bacchanalia. The members would assemble furtively for worship during the night; initiates swore an oath of loyalty to the cult after the priest read it from the sacred text. Romans dreaded cults whose members were secretly bound together by oath to a god; such cultic oaths seemed to unite invaders from the dark places of conspiracy. In Rome the Bacchanalia had attracted angry elements of the populace. Rome violently persecuted members of this cult, often with torture.

The Syrian king Antiochus probably witnessed this persecution during the years he lived in Rome as a hostage—from about 189 to 175 B.C.E. The legions of Rome had united Italy by 275 B.C.E., defeated Carthage in 201 B.C.E., and crushed the kingdom of Macedonia in 197 B.C.E. The defeat of his father's army in 191 at Magnesia had put an end to Syrian attempts to halt the expansion of Rome.

After the death of his father and brother, Antiochus came to the throne of Syria. He remembered well the might of Rome and the extent to which it was based upon her alliance with the different peoples of Italy. Many non-Roman Italian towns had been granted Roman citizenship but retained their own institutions of local government. It was a privilege to be granted citizenship in a powerful state; it also entailed civic and religious obligations: you had to support the state in its wars, you had to worship its gods, participate in its festivals. Antiochus determined to model his own kingdom after Rome. He sought to strengthen his kingdom, which stretched from Asia Minor to Babylon, Susa, and beyond, by the unifying powers of citizenship and religion. This would give his empire the inner strength to withstand Rome. Far from being the half-mad king some make him out to be, he was a man of profound vision. That vision clashed with a few thousand Jewish Pietists in the backyard of his world. They had an alternate vision of reality and were prepared to die for it. Many did die, many; they were the first martyrs to faith known to our species.

King Antiochus IV probably regarded these Pietists as the Jewish parallel to the Bacchanalia. They prayed at night, they assembled in congregations, they swore an oath of loyalty known as the Shema, and a reader read to them from their sacred text. They recited a blessing over wine. Was not Dionysus the god of wine? On one of the nights of a festival they called Sukkot they engaged in wild, joyous dancing with burning torches in their hands during a special ceremony having to do with water. Did not Dionysiac worshipers dance about too in orgiastic frenzy?

The Syrian monarch set out upon that rarest of pagan practices: religious persecution. He acted as he did against the Pietists because he took them to be conspiratorial philosophers—they were followers of scribes who taught orally but with a copy of a text before them, as did the Greek philosophers who asked dangerous questions about the existence of the gods and the nature of man. He also saw these Pietists as a revolutionary Jewish Dionysiac movement.

There followed decades of blood and war as Jews clashed with Hellenizing pagans in a religious confrontation that became the first successful revolution known to our species. That revolution was a crucial triggering event in the formation of the second civilization of my people—rabbinic Judaism. It was to the second civilization of the Jews what the wars of Saul and David against the Philistines had been to the first.

Who was king? Who was not king? Now, in the late autumn of 175 B.C.E., after the death or murder of Seleucus IV, Antiochus IV was king of the Seleucid empire.

Imitating the Roman republic—according to a persuasive reconstruction of events offered recently by a scholar—he proclaimed an Antiochene republic and invited individuals and communities in his empire to accept citizenship. It was then that Jason purchased the high priesthood from the king and offered additional funds for the privilege of establishing an Antiochene community in Jerusalem. A gymnasium and educational institutions were built. Citizens of the Antiochene republic came under the protection of the king and were exempt from the observance of Jewish law, which had been the law of Judea since the time of the Persians.

Jason wanted the city to become part of the world beyond the Judean plateau. He did not want the abrogation of the law of Moses. He believed Hellenism and Hebraism to be compatible.

About two years after Menelaus acquired the high priesthood he robbed the temple treasury in order to make his promised payment to Antiochus IV.

Pietists saw this as an act of desecration. They despised the Hellenized Antiochene community of Jerusalem. They remembered the doom visited by God upon Israel and Judah when their ancestors broke the covenant. "You must not worship any other god" was a covenant stipulation, and though there is no evidence of actual idolatry in Jerusalem before the onset of the religious persecutions, to the Pietists the goings on in the gymnasium and the looting of the temple treasury were abomination enough. And did not the covenant also stipulate, "If your brother . . . or your son or daughter, or the wife of your bosom, or your closest friend entices you in secret, saying, 'Come let us worship other gods . . .' do not assent or give heed to him. Show him no pity or compassion, and give him no protection; but take his life." To prevent God from invoking the dreaded curses in the covenant—as He had in the past—the Pietists, in obedience to covenant law, began to kill the Hellenizers. A riot broke out in Jerusalem. Some members of the Jewish Council of Elders brought charges against Menelaus. He bribed, bowed, and scraped his way to acquittal and remained high priest of the Jews.

In the autumn of 170 B.C.E. Antiochus IV invaded Egypt. Alexandria resisted siege. All the rest of Egypt fell. Hearing a rumor that Antiochus had been killed in battle, Jason returned from Transjordan sometime in the middle of 169 B.C.E. and led his followers in an attempt to capture Jerusalem. Pietists fought against the troops of both Jason and Menelaus. Antiochus approached Jerusalem with his army. The gates of the city were thrown open to him. Antiochus remained loyal to Menelaus. He punished the city for its rebellious breach of faith by looting its treasury. All opponents of Menelaus were now regarded as rebels.

In 168 B.C.E. Antiochus learned from Menelaus of continuing attacks upon the citizenry by Pietists. He sent twenty thousand troops to Jerusalem under the command of Apollonius, the general of one of his mercenary units. A massacre of Pietists took place. A heavy tax was imposed upon the city. The citadel north of the temple—called the Akra—was fortified and manned by Syrian troops for the purpose of policing the city and protecting its Antiochene citizens.

The foreign troops came as colonizers. Parts of the city were divided among the new settlers. The soldiers no doubt brought with them their gods. Probably acts of looting and rape occurred. The new colonists would want to worship their gods in the temple of the city. Pietist turbulence intensified. Many pious Jews fled to the wilderness.

Sometime between April and December 167 B.C.E., Antiochus IV, confronting the specter of rebellion in Judea and convinced more than ever that the Pietists were rebellious philosophers and Dionysiacs, decreed that the Jews must terminate their loyalty to their Torah, cease observing its stipulations, and adopt the pagan cult he would impose upon them. The penalty for disobedience was death. His adviser in the matter of which gods to impose upon the Jews was an Athenian, perhaps an anthropologist from one of the philosophical schools, who recommended a cult close to that of the Phoenicians, stripped of what he took to be prophetic and scribal pollution. We begin to witness a darkly echoing reenactment of the violent years of Jezebel, Ahab, and Elijah.

Even Antiochene Jews had not thought the king would go so far; they too now hesitated, fearful of the wrath of their God. Royal officials began to institute the decree. Objects of worship the Jews called the abomination of desolation—either images or sacred stones representing the gods of the pagan cult—were placed upon the altar of the temple. The sacrificial service to God was terminated. Sacred prostitution was introduced into the temple precinct. Beyond Jerusalem royal troops used force to compel Jews to violate the Torah.

Insurrection spread to the countryside. Many Pietists were martyred; they would not fight on the Sabbath, for they interpreted literally the convenant stipulation to rest on the seventh day.

In the dusty hill village of Modin, about six miles east of the coastal town of Lod, an old priest named Mattathias, of the highly respected Hasmonean family, killed a Jew who was about to obey the command of a royal official to sacrifice to Zeus god of heaven. Mattathias fled to the hills together with his five sons.

Word spread quickly. The sporadic, unplanned attacks of the Pietists, which Antiochus IV had regarded as the activities of a small group of fanatics, now became a mass rebellion as the Hasmonean family began to organize the people who rallied around them. They were joined by pious villagers and countryside farmers. They waged a nagging guerrilla war, raiding villages, harassing royal soldiers, destroying pagan altars. Mattathias decreed that the covenant stipulation regarding the Sabbath did not prevent their defending themselves from attack. Many Pietists agreed to this imposition of reality upon the word of God.

Mattathias died in the spring of 165 B.C.E. His son, Judah, took command of the rebel force. Astonishingly the poorly armed rebels defeated an army led by Apollonius, who was then governor of the region. He was killed in that battle. Judah took the dead governor's sword and used it as his own from then on.

Two additional attempts to crush Judah and his rebels were turned back with severe losses to the Syrians.

Then the sacred mountain of the temple was taken by the rebels. The decree of religious persecution was rescinded by the Syrians. On the twenty-fifth day of the month of Kislev—then October 16, for the Hebrew lunar calendar had not been intercalated since 167 B.C.E.—in the year 164 B.C.E., the Jews celebrated the rededication of the temple sacrificial service. A new sacrificial altar had been built; the images or stones had been destroyed. New vessels were prepared. The golden candelabrum had no doubt been melted down and sent off to Antioch at the start of the persecutions more than three years before. The troops of Judah—he had been nicknamed Maccabeus, possibly meaning the hammer—may have used the hollow ends of their metal spear shafts for a candelabrum at first, the fresh pure oil poured into the hollows and left to burn as a makeshift eternal light until the new golden candelabrum was completed. The celebration continued for eight days and was made into an annual observance—the first festival not sanctioned by Biblical law. It was another of the many changes that the onrush of events was imposing upon the Jewish vision of the past.

Then Antiochus IV died of wounds in Persia in the late fall of 164 B.C.E. Kingship was transferred to Antiochus V, a child. The Seleucid empire began to disintegrate as generals, ministers, and courtiers contended for the throne. The inner weakness of Syria and repeated incursions from a new enemy in the east, the Parthians, prevented the Syrians from sending their entire army of seventy thousand men at one time against the Hasmoneans.

The war of liberation dragged on. Bitter seesawing battles were fought in hills and mountain passes, tough farmers against trained troops and war elephants. Slowly the Hasmoneans began to extend the borders of the land to absorb Jewish populations outside Judea. Idol-worshiping Jews joined the Maccabees, seeking liberation from the house of Seleucid. The cultural-religious war had become a political and territorial struggle. At one point a

Jewish army fought in Antioch on the side of a contender for the Seleucid throne against rebel soldiers and civilians.

One after another the sons of Mattathias died—two, Eleazar and Judah, in battle; a third, John, at the hands of unfriendly tribesmen; the fourth, Jonathan, took over command, was made high priest in 152 B.C.E. by a contender to the Seleucid throne, and was then lured to a meeting with another contender, who saw him as too powerful a threat and had him executed.

In 142 B.C.E. Demetrius II, king of Syria, exempted Judea from paying tribute and acknowledged her independence, twenty-five years after the start of the war. The Jews counted their sovereignty from this year. Four hundred and forty-four years had passed since the destruction of the Davidic monarchy at the hands of the Babylonians.

Simon, the last of the brothers, was honored at a vast assembly of Jews in Jerusalem in September 140 B.C.E. They covenanted to give him and his heirs the power of high priest and king.

In the east the Parthians, invaders from the grasslands of central Asia, had taken Media and much of Babylonia the year before. The Seleucid empire fell apart. Greek cities seceded and achieved political independence. In the west Rome waited and watched as the Jews and Syrians played out their cultural and political confrontation. Rome had signed a treaty with Judah Maccabee in 161 B.C.E., which marked the recognition of Judea. The treaty promised mutual defense and friendly neutrality.

In 134 B.C.E., in the city of Jericho, the aged Simon and two of his sons were assassinated. The slayer was Simon's ambitious son-in-law, who failed to kill the third son, John Hyrcanus.

Who was king? Who was not king? In Judea, John Hyrcanus son of Simon was high priest and king. He hesitated to call himself king and preferred the term prince. He conquered most of Palestine and took Idumea in the south. He forced the entire pagan population of Idumea to convert to Judaism, the first such mass conversion in history. He conquered parts of Transjordan and destroyed the Samaritan temple in Shechem. He maintained friendly diplomatic relations with Rome, Sparta, and Athens. He died in 104 B.C.E.

His son, Judah Aristobulus I, conquered the rest of the Galilee and forced the Ituraeans—Arameans who had begun to move into the region south of Mount Hermon during the time of the judges—to convert to Judaism. He reigned only one year. In 103 B.C.E. kingship was transferred to his brother Alexander Janneus, who continued to conquer areas of Palestine lost since the destruction of the Solomonic temple. The land began to thrive. Sea trade flourished. Import duties were collected. He died in 76 B.C.E., and his wife, Salome Alexandra, become queen of Judea. She ruled over a kingdom almost as large as that of David and Solomon about nine hundred years before.

By now the Hasmonean court bore the trappings of Hellenistic and oriental royalty: ministers, courtiers, a bureaucracy, a private bodyguard to protect the monarch. The Council of Elders receded somewhat in importance and was given the name borne by all Hellenistic councils to the king: Synhedrion or Sanhedrin.

The nature and origin of this early Sanhedrin remain unclear. Ancient sources offer conflicting accounts, and modern scholars offer a variety of theories. It may have been a single council with a number of committees—one of priests and aristocrats, another of sages—or dominated now by one group, now by another. There may have been a Sanhedrin of sages and another of priests. It may have been a political as well as a legislative and judicial body. Only after the destruction of the second temple was there clearly a Sanhedrin up only of sages.

Queen Alexandra died in 67 B.C.E. Rome annexed Syria. Judea now lay along a border of the Roman empire—as Israel and Judah had once bordered upon Assyria.

Civil war broke out in Judea as the sons of Alexandra, Hyrcanus II and Aristobulus II, fought for the throne. The Roman general Pompey came to Syria and indicated that he favored Hyrcanus—the weaker of the two men, and therefore more easily controlled by Rome. Aristobulus yielded reluctantly to Pompey. The gates of Jerusalem were opened to Roman soldiers by Hyrcanus and his followers. The uncle of Aristobulus, Absalom, refused to yield and held out on the sacred mountain of the temple.

The mountain was taken by the Romans after a three-month siege. They built ramps along northern and western sections of the wall, positioned their catapults and siege engines, and attacked on the Sabbath. Thousands were slaughtered. The priests conducting the temple service were slain at their posts. Pompey entered the darkened interior of the temple, the Holy of Holies, the Residence of YHWH. He left the temple and its treasures untouched.

Kingship was removed from Judea. The Jews were divested of the territory of Samaria and other conquered areas. The Jewish Galilee was separated from Jewish Judea. The land became two lands.

There was unrest and rebellion all through Judea in the years that followed. A brief period of peace ensued while Julius Caesar ruled Rome, for he showed high regard for the Jews scattered throughout his empire—Jews constituted about one-tenth of the total population, five million out of fifty or sixty million people—and treated them as allies. He was assassinated in 44 B.C.E. Civil war engulfed the Roman empire.

Two years later the murderers of Caesar were defeated. Then the Parthians invaded Syria. Thousands of Jews loyal to the Hasmonean house rushed to the side of the Parthians. The Parthians marched down the seacoast and turned inland to Jerusalem.

A young man named Herod was then in Jerusalem. He and his brother, Phasael, had been appointed rulers of Judea in 42 B.C.E. His father, Antipater, an Idumean who had converted to Judaism and a loyal follower of Rome, had been administrator of Judea during the high priesthood of Hyrcanus II. Herod was despised by the Jews; they called him the Idumean slave. The people of Jerusalem revolted against the sons of Antipater and opened the gates of the city to the Parthians.

Phasael was taken prisoner and subsequently committed suicide. Herod and his family managed to flee south into the wilderness. Herod went on to Rome. The Parthians, bloated with conquest, left Judea and returned to the land beyond the Euphrates.

In the summer of 38 B.C.E. Roman legions invaded Judea. In the winter of 38–37 B.C.E. the legions began a siege of Jerusalem. The city fell in the summer of 37 B.C.E. Thousands of its defenders were slain. At the order of Mark Antony, the last of the Hasmoneans, Antigonus, son of Aristobulus II, was executed.

Who was king? Who was not king? Herod son of Antipater, the converted Idumean, was king of Judea—by order of the Senate of Rome.

The periphery of Greek civilization had moved across the map of the Fertile Crescent. Geographers of the ancient world would write notes on the margins of their maps stating that beyond this lies nothing but sandy deserts full of wild beasts, deadly bogs, mountains of ice, a frozen sea. A culture map of that world would have shown Judea edged up against the margin. The mighty Hellenistic civilization of the Seleucid empire had brushed up against the sleepy mountain city of Jerusalem—and nothing was ever the same again for both civilizations.

The Seleucids broke their armies against the iron will of pious Jews. Judea came beneath the umbrella civilization of Hellenism. Those first affected by this culture confrontation were the upper-class urban Jews—priests, aristocrats, government officials—who were most likely to come into contact with outsiders from the world of Hellenism. They learned Greek. The upper class attracted the merchant class, and the merchant class was followed by the masses. The Greek language spread; many learned it well. It was used in the synagogue and the marketplace. "Lord, let much rain fall," uttered in Greek, was the first verse of a prayer for rain.

Before its final editing about six centuries after the last of the Hasmoneans, the Talmud itself, the seminal creation of the second civilization of the Jews, though written in Hebrew and Aramaic, would also contain about three thousand Greek words. One of the greatest of the rabbis, Judah the Prince, the editor of the vast compendium of oral Jewish law known as the Mishnah, would urge his people not to use the Palestinian dialect of Aramaic. "Talk either Hebrew or Greek," he said. He lived at the end of the second century of the Common Era when Jerusalem had been reduced to rubble by Roman legions and the pagan world seemed triumphant and indestructible.

Synagogues constructed at that time have inscriptions in Greek and often are decorated with pagan motifs on their floors and walls. It is not possible to know if a third-century c.e. Mesopotamian Jew gazing at the art in the synagogue in Dura-Europos, the ancient city on the Euphrates, saw the masks and felines as elements of the cult of Dionysus, and the fruit and grain as fertility symbols, or regarded them all as mere decorations.

For the most part, it was the surface peripheral elements of Greece which were absorbed by the Jews of Judea. In a culture confrontation the superficial elements—costume, language, superstitions, technology, and such—are absorbed first; the core elements—patterns of thought, world view—come last, if at all. Plato and Aristotle were never mentioned by the rabbis; they spoke only of Homer. But almost everyone knew of Homer then, even the village housewife who prepared her family's food in an earthen vessel decorated with drawings that echoed the clash of bronze weapons on the misty beach of Troy—just as almost everyone knows of Shakespeare today, even those who have never read him. Little if anything of that vital heart of Greece touched the core of Judean Judaism.

That heart was cold and shrunken. Tiny city-states in which citizens had participated and individuals had counted were of the past. The Hellenistic city was dominated by giant monarchies, mercenary armies, professional bureaucrats, palace intrigues. Previous knowledge was collected and systematized. In place of the cults of city gods came the cults of deified kings. For the people to be heard they had to riot.

Even the urban sophisticates who walked about Jerusalem displaying their wealth and erudition aped a Greece grown pale and weary, her golden years faded to dross with only an occasional flicker of her ancient grandeur emanating from the world of Alexandria, the greatest center of scientific and historical studies in the centuries after Alexander. Elsewhere Euclid composed his work on geometry and Aristarchus offered us his heliocentric theory of our solar system, which everyone chose to ignore until Copernicus wrote his treatise and Galileo spotted a new star in the fixed heavens. Alchemy was discovered. Astrology became a flourishing enterprise. The practice of bleeding invaded medicine, where it remained until the nineteenth century.

Under the impact of this echo of Greece the Judean world splintered into factions as Jews sought to confront the cultural specter that had invaded their mountain world from across the sea. The upper classes embraced it; many of them were priests, deeply involved in the ruthless maneuverings of geopolitics. Because the priestly class claimed descent from Zadok, the high priest in the time of King David, that faction—rich, powerful, urban, aristocratic, formed about 200 B.C.E.—came to be called Zedukim, Sadducees. Not all the priests were Sadducees, but all the Sadducees were priests, aristocrats, or wealthy merchants. They were eager to confront the Hellenistic world, absorb its beauty, share its power, bend to it if need be. They believed fully in the Torah, the written law, and regarded with contempt the interpretations and oral accretions heaped upon the text by generations of scribes. They believed God could be described in human terms and worshiped as one does a human king or ruler. They believed in the centrality of sacrifice and opposed scribal and Pietist services consisting only of prayer and study. Everything we know of the Sadducees comes to us from the ancient Jewish historian Josephus, who witnessed the destruction of the second temple, and from their opponents. The writings of the Sadducees have not been preserved.

From the ranks of scribes and Pietists, around the start of the Hasmonean revolution, came the first of a new breed of religious teachers who drew their support from the lower classes of the city and countryside. Because they were forced out of—separated from—the Sanhedrin by John Hyrcanus, because they held themselves aloof from pagans, and tended to be exceptionally careful in matters of ritual purity, withdrawing from contact with anyone suspected of being ritually defiled—as a result of touching, say, a menstruant, a woman after childbirth, a corpse, a dead reptile, a leper, and other such—this faction came to be known as Perushim, Pharisees, after a word meaning to be separated.

These Separatists held as their fundamental doctrine the belief that an oral law had been revealed to Moses at Sinai together with the written law, and that they were the rightful teachers and interpreters of that oral law. They believed that all of the stipulations of the covenant should be performed, even those that seemed of only minor importance. They believed that God guided human events providentially and meted out reward and punishment in a world to come. They believed in the resurrection of the dead, in angels. Those doctrines had evolved during the critical centuries after the return of the exiles from Babylonia and were now regarded by the Pharisees as rooted firmly in the sacred written text. In none of these doctrines did the Sadducees believe.

Scholars estimate there were about one million Jews in Palestine during the time of Herod and four million in Syria, Asia Minor, Babylonia, and Egypt. The Pharisees numbered a little more than six thousand, the Sadducees even fewer.

Numerous Pietists had looked with despair upon the Hellenism that had come to pervade the Hasmonean court and had gone off to the wilderness to live their own lives with God, away from the raised voices, civil strife, and elaborate temple cult. They longed for the Day of God, an end to strife. Many of them lived a monastic existence in a community they founded on a rocky rise some few miles south of Jericho between an azure sea of undrinkable water and tall hills pocked with caves. They came to be known as the Essenes—the word probably means the healers, after an Aramaic verb, *asa,* to heal: they sought to heal what they thought was illness caused by the sinful passions of man; or it may come from *hasin,* the Aramaic equivalent of the Hebrew word *hasidim,* the pious ones. We know of their world and their lives through the writings of their scribes hastily concealed in the nearby hillside caves as the Romans came down the road after destroying Jerusalem. Those writings are known today as the Dead Sea Scrolls.

There was much civil strife in Judea during the era of the Hasmoneans. Many expected an apocalyptic end of days as the wars—this time for territory, power, trade routes, the normal activities of a land that has entered the arena of international bloodletting—continued. Others, especially the Pharisees, grew increasingly embittered as they watched Alexander Janneus, who came to the throne in 103 B.C.E. and waged endless expansionist wars, perform the duties of high priest in the sacred, silent precincts of the temple, moving softly about the huge altar, offering the sacrifices that linked the people to God. How could hands bloodied by conquest offer sacrifices to the Lord? They saw their land being transformed into merely another Hellenistic state, hungry for wealth and power, the leaders indifferent to the law of Moses as taught by the scribes. On one occasion, when Janneus performed ineptly—whether by accident or with mocking intent is not entirely clear—a libation ceremony during the festival of Sukkot, enraged Pharisees pelted their king with citrons, one of the yields of the earth used ceremonially at that festival. The libation ritual is not found in the Bible and was Pharisaic in origin. Many paid for that act of outraged piety with their lives when the Jewish king called out his Cilician mercenaries, troops from Asia Minor, to slay Jews. At one point open revolt broke out against the king, led by Pharisee extremists. The revolt lasted from about 90 to 85 B.C.E. Jewish troops as well as mercenaries were used by Janneus to put down the revolt. The Jewish historian Josephus tells us that about fifty thousand Jews lost their lives in that civil war.

The Pharisees were repeatedly defeated, but they stubbornly fought on; they wanted sole power over the religious destiny of their people. They saw themselves as martyrs for the Name. God was no longer called YHWH; that name was too sacred, too awesome for normal utterance. They died for the glory of the Master of the Universe, for the sake of Heaven, for the covenant which the people were pledged to uphold else the dread curses would be invoked once again.

One day Janneus sought to make peace with the Pharisees. He sent a herald to ask of them what terms they wanted. They asked for his death—so deep was the hatred of these Jews toward their own king.

It is an error to see these Pharisees as gentle old men with flowing white beards; see them rather as passionate followers of scribal teachings, many adept with sword and spear as well as with texts of the law, quite willing to kill for the sake of their God. We are talking of a time when men easily took up the sword for what they held dear. Pharisees killed for God rather than for plunder. It is to be doubted if those who fell by Pharisee swords were thereby consoled. The Pharisees were to the Hasmonean kings what the prophets had been to the kings of Israel and Judah.

The first scribe to emerge from obscurity since the time of Ezra is Ben Sira, who lived about 180 B.C.E. The personality of the individual teacher now became discernible, a clear result of the influence of Greek custom. The master-disciple relationship that became characteristic of Jewish learning appears to have had its roots in the academies in Athens, in the schools of Stoics and Epicureans. That was the way organized thought was transmitted then—from a master to disciples. Masters would meet together with their disciples and talk of matters pertaining to the personal and communal life of the Jew. They would meet in the temple precinct or in special houses of study. The words bet midrash, house of learning, and yeshiva, seat, the location of the master, are found for the first time in the writings of Ben Sira. The scribe, the master, the disciple, unconnected with court and cult—this was the new kind of leadership. Its beginnings were in the centuries when Hellenism came to Jerusalem.

Some of the masters were poor and worked as laborers; others were wealthy and could have been members of the Sanhedrin together with aristocratic landowners and priests. They formed the elite of the Pietist masses and wanted peace, for only under settled conditions could the people be educated effectively into a life in accordance with the law. In the tranquillity of urban and countryside homes, against a distant background of clashing weapons and bloody conquest, they taught the importance of law and study. "Let your house be a meeting place for the wise," said one sage. "Take a teacher and acquire a companion," said another. All believed and taught that Moses received the Torah from Sinai and transmitted it to Joshua, and Joshua to the elders or judges and the judges to the prophets, and the prophets transmitted it to the members of the Great Assembly, about whom we know almost nothing save that they were regarded by tradition as having been contemporary with Ezra the scribe. The men of the Great Assembly were reputed to have taught the importance of care and patience in the dispensing of justice, the need to raise up many disciples, and the importance of surrounding the covenant stipulations with a fence of precautionary measures in order to ensure that the stipulations themselves would never be breached.

The finest minds of the land were attracted to these Pharisee masters, the sages. Anyone with a gift of will and mind—rich man, poor man, convert—could rise to the status of a sage. As masters and disciples met and studied together, they would talk of festivals, ritual purity, marital relations, civil and criminal law, behavior toward the poor, treatment of children and parents, responsibilities of government authorities—every aspect of the people's life came under the sacred canopy of the law. The oral law was not a secret doctrine but one the sages wished to make known to all the people. Hence while John Hyrcanus and Alexander Janneus were conquering and Judaizing vast stretches of Palestine with sword and spear and non-Jewish mercenaries, the sages were spiritualizing every bright and shadowed corner of existence.

The beginnings of the oral law go back a long way before these sages and are lost to history; but the main development of that law began when Greece brushed Jerusalem and the text of the covenant had to be made vital for this new confrontation with an alien reality. New customs needed to be rooted in the covenant. This was done through a newly developed system of text interpretation which was itself believed to have been given to Moses at Sinai but which had much in common with the way Greek scholars in Alexandria were then reinterpreting embarrassing passages in Homer. All the civilized world at that time held in common the sanctity of ancient writings; all wanted to preserve that sanctity and ensure the continued life of those writings by reinterpretation. We keep alive creations of the past by infusing them with resonance for the present.

In the time of Alexander Janneus, when Pharisees fought their king and thousands were slain, many Pharisees fled from the land. Some went to Alexandria, where they encountered a city of straight wide streets, canals, temples, libraries, a museum and theater—a glittering Greek city in the midst of the wealth and bloated alluvial decay that was Ptolemaic Egypt. No doubt they met with the Jews of the city, who spoke Greek and knew no Hebrew, were eager to obtain citizenship, were producing poets, playwrights, and historians who wrote in Greek, and would soon produce the philosopher Philo, who was raised in a home devoted to the Jewish faith, probably knew no Hebrew, and would become one of the most important thinkers in the development of western civilization. They witnessed the absence of Jewish schools for children; there were schools only for Jewish adults on the Sabbath; Jews were eager to enroll their children in Greek gymnasiums. The Pharisees would have seen that the Alexandrian Jewish community now had the Greek translation of the covenant, the version known as the Septuagint, that the Jews had built many synagogues, one so large the voice of the reader could barely be heard in the back rows, had become thoroughly assimilated to Greek ways and thought, and were fierce in their loyalty to Jerusalem and the temple.

When Salome Alexandra became queen of Judea in 76 B.C.E. she invited the Pharisees to return to the land and the royal council, the Sanhedrin. She was weary of the civil strife that was weakening the land.

An extraordinary period of Pharisaic creativity followed. The queen ran the foreign policy of the land; the Pharisees controlled religious affairs and what we might today call the Department of the Interior. The Sadducees were removed from positions of leadership because of the part they had played in advising Janneus to wage war upon the Pharisees. One of the Sadducees, an adviser to Janneus, was tried by a Pharisee court and sentenced to death, along with many other high-ranking Sadducees. Pagans had no monopoly on the brutalizing effects of power.

The land lay washed in a haze of economic prosperity in the time of the only queen in the history of the Hasmonean dynasty. There was an abundance of rain and revenue. During this time of plenty lived a poor man, a dealer in flax who constantly walked the roads. He was Shimon ben—son of—Shetah, the most influential Pharisee of his day. Legends grew around him. It was said of him that he hanged eighty women for witchcraft in Ashkelon, in keeping with covenant law. But Ashkelon was too briefly in the hands of the Jews during the reign of Salome for that tale to edge into truth. Almost nothing is known of his life save that he treated the Sadducees harshly, instituted an ordinance that mortgaged the property of a husband to the divorce settlement of a wife, thereby protecting the interests of the woman, and created the institution of the public school.

Prior to that time, from Ezra to the Hasmonean period, a father taught his son the convenant law, for that act of teaching was itself a covenant stipulation: "And you shall impress them upon your children." Now the Pharisees, controlling as they did the internal affairs of the land, created a system of public schools. "All children must go to school," stipulated Shimon ben Shetah. A later Pharisee, Joshua ben Gamala, spelled out this general rule by specifying that each district and each town should have a free school for children. The covenant and its oral traditions could be transmitted most effectively only in schools.

That was a brief but important time in the history of the land, that nine-year rule of Queen Salome. Then the land broke apart into two lands, and now in 37 B.C.E. a king sat on the throne who was not of the Hasmonean line and whose power derived from the blood-spattered standards of the Roman legions.

In the centuries when a weary Athens met a reborn Jerusalem and Jews all through the world encountered the full force of Hellenistic civilization, the people who had once created the Pentateuch—the first five books of the Bible—and works of history and prophecy in part as a result of their culture confrontation with Fertile Crescent paganism had turned to face the impact of a new paganism from the west. Writers living in that period and participating in that confrontation recorded their visions of it. Before the full impact of Hellenism was felt, perhaps with the resonance of the Persian period still in the air, the books of Judith and Tobit were written, Bible-like tales of courage and faith. In the middle of the third century B.C.E. writers told of their ideological encounters with universal situations: the Book of Job, with its eternally echoing denunciation of the pious Deuteronomist's theology, the only book of the Bible which dares attack the God of the covenant; Jonah, with its loving embrace of all moral peoples; Ecclesiastes, with its seemingly part-Stoic, part-oriental resignation to the grayness of existence. Job and Ecclesiastes are instances of an attack literature, works written by wisdom teachers who recorded their reactions to what they felt was the hollowness of life and the conventional morality taught by tradition.

Then out of the confrontation with Hellenism came apocalyptic literature—the word apocalypse means revelation in Greek. This literature flourished from the second century B.C.E. to the second century C.E. and gave expression to the Jewish yearning for the renewal of prophecy at the end of days, which each generation of writers believed would come very soon. It was a time beyond history when awesome cosmic forces would wage a terrifying war, the natural world would suffer upheavals, and the redeemer would come, a superhuman being who would assure the final victory of good over evil. The Book of Enoch told of the ministering angels who greet the Lord every morning with song and of the preexistent Elect One, the Messiah, who would judge all mortals on the final day of judgment. There were other such works: Daniel, Jubilees, Testaments of the Twelve Patriarchs, the Dead Sea Scrolls. Still others—among them the Apocalypse of Abraham, the Assumption of Moses—were written during the Roman period. Apocalyptic literature reflected the anguish of blood-filled centuries, despair in man's ability to put an end to suffering, and absolute faith in the miraculous redeeming intervention of God. This stream of literature, a unique creation of Jews in confrontation with Hellenism and, later, with Rome, would affect directly the development of Jewish mysticism and the vision of the world held by the apocalyptic Pharisees who would one day create Christianity.

It was an explosive period of literary creativity, in Palestine, Alexandria, Antioch. Jews painted and sculpted the culture confrontation of their time with words rather than with pigment and stone. What remains is a fraction of what was created. I have little doubt, for example, that Job is all that is left us of an entire genre of literary probing into the problem of evil in a world that believes in a good God.

Herod ruled in Jerusalem, a tool of Roman foreign policy. He slew forty-five members of the Sanhedrin who had supported the Hasmoneans, and the Sanhedrin was left with only religious judicial power. He ruled most of the regions previously controlled by the Hasmonean kings. He was one of the most powerful monarchs of the east under the patronage of Rome. He was given absolute authority over the internal affairs of Palestine. He treated the land as his private property. He encouraged immigration into Judea of aristocratic Babylonian families whose wealth and position depended upon continued peace with Rome. He was the center of turbulent court intrigues. His many sons by his many wives became bitter rivals for his throne. Beneath the splendor of his court was the fungus growth of suspicion and fear. He had three sons executed for conspiracy. At the urging of his sister Salome and on a vague charge of infidelity, he slew Mariamne, the only one of his ten wives he truly loved. Her death left him crippled with grief and on the border of madness. He made of Judea a Hellenistic state: diplomacy, the army, the bureaucracy, the education of his sons—all was in the hands of Greeks or those who lived as Greeks. He himself never publicly violated the Jewish faith. His court was opulent; its atmosphere was Greek, its allegiance was to Rome.

He was hated by the masses in Judea despite the costly improvements he lavished upon the temple and Jerusalem. He loved to build palaces, fortresses, country homes. Rome sent him engineers, designers. He enjoyed being his own architect. He built a magnificent palace on Masada, a massive 1300-foot-high butte overlooking the Dead Sea. He built a hippodrome and a theater in Jerusalem. He placed the Roman eagle on the façade of the temple, a mark of his loyalty to Rome. It enraged the people.

I stood recently inside the ruins of one of his summer palaces near Jericho at the narrow outlet of the waters of a towering, boulder-strewn wadi. It had been built so that the waters would flow through the palace. There was room for a spacious garden with colonnaded paths and trees and exquisite plants. An outdoor pool lay near the garden with stone steps leading down into the water. There, someone who had earned the king's displeasure had been drowned by courtiers. He slew many in his day, that despotic king of the Jews. The most dangerous thing you could be during his reign was his near or distant relative. "It is better to be Herod's pig than his son," Augustus is reputed to have said.

The sages continued their teaching. The range of Jewish thought was so vast it is diffcult for us to label any group normative. The Talmud, reflecting the Pharisaic world view, reports the existence of twenty-four heretical sects. Herod showed regard for the Pharisees and respected the Essenes, thinking this would gain him the favor of the angry masses. But he was too connected to Rome, too much a cruel hedonist, to win the people to his side.

The efforts of the sages during this time remain somewhat obscure. We know that at the head of the Sanhedrin sat two sages; they would share the duties of leadership.

Sometime during the reign of Herod a young man wandered from Babylonia to Jerusalem and joined a house of study. In time he became a good student and then a great teacher. His name was Hillel. He became a member of the Sanhedrin.

Herod died in 4 B.C.E. The margin of the map grew turbulent. The people demanded a different form of government and a lowering of the crippling annual taxation that was the tribute paid to Rome. The demands were not met. In the final months of that century there were riots in the land. The riots continued as our species turned the unseen bend in time that brought us into the year 1 of the Common Era.

# ROME

## Legions From Rome

That was a century of blood and horror and the birth of new dreams. The sage Hillel, head of the Sanhedrin, taught a new method of applying the ancient law of Moses to the realities of everyday life; he founded a dynasty of scholar leaders that would last four hundred years. A young teacher named Joshua son of Joseph was executed by the Romans for fomenting rebellion; but so many thousands were executed during that century, and he slipped out of life almost unnoticed. A Jew named Saul, who changed his name to Paul, wandered through the Mediterranean world, preaching a new faith, writing letters to distant communities, annoying the suspicious Romans. The Jerusalem temple was destroyed by Roman legions. And the long twilight centuries between the two civilizations of the Jews drew to an end with the coming to full life of rabbinic Judaism.

An incident that occurred in the closing years of the previous century appears in the perspective of history as a dark intimation of the conflict between Rome and Jerusalem. During the last year of the reign of Herod, some young Pharisees climbed the façade of the temple upon which had been fixed the eagle of the Roman legions. They pulled down the eagle. Zealous Jews turned upon the legionaries of the Jerusalem garrison. The short swords of the soldiers swiftly quelled the riot. Herod, slowly dying and half-mad with the memories of those in his family he had slain, ordered the execution of the Pharisees who had desecrated the Roman eagle. They were burned alive.

Herod died. He left a will. His kingdom was to be divided among three sons. One of these sons, Archelaus, inherited Judea, Idumea, and Samaria. He proved a callous and inept ruler.

Augustus was emperor then, a frail, cautious man, plagued by chronic ailments—colitis, eczema, bronchitis—and strengthened by a tenacious sense of purpose, a creative energy, and an ability to get along with others which had enabled him to overcome his enemies and become the first emperor of Rome. He listened to the bitter complaints against Archelaus conveyed to him by Jews and Samaritans. He thought the land too insignificant to be made an imperial province requiring many troops and too distinct in its religious practices and ethnic makeup to be attached to Syria. Augustus removed Archelaus in 6 C.E. and turned the territories which the son of Herod had ruled into a single senatorial province named Judaea or Iudaea. Such provinces were governed by prefects or procurators, men of knightly rank drawn from the lower nobility, the wealthy merchant class, rather than from the aristocracy, whose members could often trace themselves back to the early founders of Rome. The Galilee and Peraea—the latter roughly comprised the old kingdoms of Moab and Ammon—remained under the vassal rule of the second son, Herod Antipas, who built the city of Tiberias; parts of northern Transjordan were retained by the third son, Philip. The kingdom of Herod, acquired with blood and ruled with terror, had fallen to pieces.

A delegation of Jews had petitioned Augustus to rid Judea of the hated family of Herod. Now most Jews welcomed the direct rule of Rome. But some looked upon the Romans with hate; only God could be their master.

The Romans called the new province Judaea because the Jews were the majority of the population. Its official Roman name would not be Palaestina until the reign of Hadrian in the second century, though that name was often used in the first century by Greek writers and by Jews like the philosopher Philo and the historian Josephus, both of whom wrote in Greek.

The Jews of Judea—I will continue to use the simplified spelling adopted by many scholars—spoke Aramaic and Greek. Pagans lived in their midst. Jews had little to do with them, would rarely enter their homes, would not drink their wine or milk, eat their bread, or purchase meat from their butcher shops. Three days before a pagan festival Jews would cease their business transactions with pagans; they wished to contribute in no way, directly or indirectly, to pagan rites. Many Jews would not enter a pagan city during a pagan festival, not even to pass through. Jewish workers would not participate in construction that was in any way connected to pagan worship; they would not work on government buildings. Resentful and uncomprehending pagans mocked the Jewish rite of circumcision, the observance of the Sabbath, the abstention from pork.

But it was not possible for Jews and pagans to be entirely separated from one another. They shopped in the same marketplaces, rubbed shoulders on city streets, traveled the same roads. "We support the poor of the pagans along with the poor of Israel, and visit the sick of the pagans along with the sick of Israel, and bury the dead of the pagans along with the dead of Israel, in the interests of peace," reads the Talmud. "We should greet the pagans on their festival days, in the interests of peace," said a sage. "One who steals from the pagan will eventually steal from the Israelite," said another sage. "It is forbidden to deceive a pagan because of the profanation of the name of God," says the Talmud. A pagan wronged by a Jew might curse the God of the Jews. "The pious of all nations have a share in the world to come," said yet another sage. These were regarded as semiproselytes, individuals who had renounced paganism and accepted monotheism and the moral laws but were not yet converted to Judaism and felt themselves unable to accept its ritual laws. Proselytes were welcomed as Jews in all matters.

The Romans respected the gods whose peoples they plundered. Often local cult sites were guarded by legionaries. The temple in Jerusalem was policed and protected by the Roman army, as were the roads traveled by Jewish pilgrims who came from all over the empire to Judea to celebrate the festivals.

Rome conquered the east with her legions; the east conquered Rome with its gods. Thousands of gods inhabited Rome, and she was respectful to all save those she suspected of seeding rebellion. Asiatic gods trekked westward over land and sea routes, accompanying fresh slaves from newly ravaged lands and free men who saw Rome as the center of the world and a mine of opportunity.

There were about fifty thousand Jews in Rome in the early decades of the first century. The city was rich with temples, forums, triumphal arches, commemorative columns, statues, enormous theaters, amphitheaters, circuses, public libraries and museums, public baths, parks, athletic grounds, large markets, lovely shops. Scholars estimate that the population numbered about one million people. About two hundred thousand were unemployed and received their food from the government. Because they would not worship the gods of Rome, the Jews of the city were exempt from attending pagan festivals and from serving in the legions. Rome watched with tolerance but not without concern the flow of money from everywhere in the empire to Jerusalem as Jews voluntarily paid their annual half-shekel tax—about $10—to the temple. In the time of Augustus, Roman legionaries would leave their standards in the Judean port city of Caesarea, so that the images drawn upon them would not offend the sensitive Jews. The Jews mentioned the emperor in their prayers and offered a daily sacrifice on his behalf in their temple.

The Romans wanted the land tranquil. Destroyed cities and a countryside reduced to dust yielded no tribute to the government and no possibility of wealth to thieving procurators. Riots were embarrassing and might bring on questions no matter what influence a provincial governor had with the emperor or the Senate.

The Jews worked hard in their fields and farmed them well. Clay pipes, aqueducts, man-made channels carried water to irrigate the land. Grain was of high quality in Judea. The wheat of Samaria and the Galilee earned praise. Barley grew in great quantity. The land yielded fruit, vegetables, dates, figs. Wine was abundant; some wines were marketed abroad. The Jews raised cattle, sheep, goats. Work was honorable. The sages urged every father to teach his son a craft. There were stonecutters, carpenters, tailors, bakers, tanners, cooks, cattle fatteners, surgeons, barbers, smiths, weavers, bee-keepers fishermen, hunters, potters, glass smelters. Neither the Bible nor the Talmud makes mention of sculptors in Judea. There were painters, but they would not paint portraits for fear of violating the second commandment. Market days were on Mondays and Thursdays. You brought your produce, the work of your hands, to the market of the nearest town or large village. Thousands entered from the dispersion—the Jewish communities outside the land of Israel—to celebrate the pilgrimage festivals. Trade was stimulated. Every purchase of produce, every transfer of goods, every sale of slaves, every bit of land—was taxed by the Romans.

The collection of taxes was farmed out to bidders. You put in a bid with the government in Rome on the commission you wanted for collecting the taxes in a region of the empire. If your bid was lowest, the region would be given to you for a period of five years. Whatever you collected above the taxes stipulated by the government was yours to keep, in addition to your commission. You might accept a bribe to let a rich man off from paying his proper share of taxes, and you would squeeze the unprotected poor for as much as you could get without provoking them to riot. The tax farmer was called a sinner by the Jews and was hated. You could become wealthy as a tax farmer; many became very wealthy.

In the time of Augustus there was a long peace. The legions rested. The borders of the empire were secure. The barbarians along the distant frontiers of Gaul were quiet. Rome governed and maintained order. "Were it not for the government," a sage remarked, "people would eat each other alive." Roman fleets patrolled the seas to keep down piracy; the Mediterranean has been called a Roman lake. Roads were well maintained. Cities and towns throughout the provinces were permitted considerable municipal autonomy.

In Judea the temple, enhanced by the construction efforts of Herod, was a magnificent edifice. Archaeologists tell us that Jerusalem was a prosperous and fully inhabited city. The Sanhedrin, the great court of the Jews, convened regularly to discuss and settle matters of Jewish law. It tried civil cases, announced the time of the New Moon, thereby controlling the dates of festivals, and proclaimed the leap year, which brought the Jewish lunar calendar into synchronization with the seasons and the sun. Its administrative authority extended only to the borders of the land; its religious authority was accepted by most Jews throughout the Roman empire.

There were regional and local courts as well. No Jewish court had the authority to issue the death sentence; only the procurators could do that. They did that often. At times the countryside around a city would seem dark with the stench of the dead and the dying on those crossed wooden beams, a form of execution the Romans learned from the city they had once hated with brutal passion—Carthage. That city had been leveled by Roman legions in 146 B.C.E., its land plowed and sowed with salt, its population slaughtered or sold into slavery. Rome was the model of disciplined, tireless patience when she confronted an enemy. It had taken her more than a century to destroy Carthage.

The Jews of Judea did not wish to arouse the anger of Rome. They would pay their taxes, submit to their conqueror, if they were left to worship their God in peace. The Jews would tolerate much from the Romans save a pagan act that inserted itself between them and their God.

Tiberius died and was succeeded by Caligula in 37 C.E. The new emperor had grown up in constant dread of losing his life in the palace intrigues that swirled all about him. His companions had been young Hellenistic princes, effete and utterly corrupt. Somehow he had managed to survive all his brothers. His reign was well accepted at first; he seemed popular. Then he began to show signs of mental derangement. He demanded that he be accorded the honors due a god and that his horse be elected consul, one of the highest offices of the empire.

Pagans in the city of Jamnia, some miles south of Jaffa, built an altar to offer sacrifices to the emperor. The city was in the territory of Judea where an ancient ban against idolatry had been respected by every Greek and Roman ruler except Antiochus IV. Jews threw down the stone altar and broke it to fragments.

Caligula was enraged when he learned of this act against his divinity. He ordered that a giant statue of gold be built and placed in the Holy of Holies within the temple. The colossal statue was to have the face of Caligula and represent Zeus.

By the end of the second century B.C.E. the Roman republic had been in existence about four hundred years. Its victories had gained it the awe, fear, and admiration of the world. Rome teemed with slaves, freedmen, unemployed peasants, aristocrats of noble blood, merchants of knightly rank, craftsmen, circuses, gladiatorial slaughter, practitioners of a thousand esoteric cults, prostitutes, criminals, astrologers, magicians, philosophers, diviners. At the same time, the city seethed with tension as plebeians and patricians, citizens and strangers, generals and senators vied for influence and power.

The vast manpower pool of Rome could no longer meet the demands of the legions, a powerful professional army fighting everywhere and garrisoning distant provinces. In 107 B.C.E. the consul Marius revoked the qualification of property ownership as a condition for service in the legions. He created a volunteer army, then he hit upon the idea of giving the legions regimental standards.

The professionalization of the army led to the rise in importance of generals who commanded the loyalty of their troops. One such general, Sulla, became dictator of Rome after a decade of civil war. He died in 78 B.C.E. Pompey became consul in 70 B.C.E. It was he who set out to eliminate piracy in the Mediterranean and in so doing conquered Syria and Jerusalem. Soon he too was looked upon with dread as a possible dictator. Rome boiled with disorder in the streets, and assassination, corruption, and venality in the Senate.

In 59 B.C.E. Julius Caesar, nephew of Marius, was elected consul. He was given command of the legions of Gaul for five years. He completed the conquest of Gaul in the allotted time, and was now a wealthy man with a loyal army. He was clearly a rival of Pompey. Caesar asked that his consular power be extended another five years. This request was granted. A consul was required by law to return to Rome without the provincial army. In January 49 B.C.E. Caesar crossed the Rubicon, the narrow river separating his province from Italy. He crossed it with a legion and thereby committed treason.

Civil war followed. Caesar defeated the legions of Pompey in Spain, Thessaly, and Egypt. In 46 B.C.E. the Senate appointed him dictator for ten years. Then, early in 44 B.C.E., it appointed him dictator for life.

It was Caesar who introduced the Julian calendar of 365 days with an additional day every fourth year. The calendar was suggested to him by an astronomer from Alexandria and went into effect on January 1, 45 B.C.E. On March 15, 44 B.C.E., Julius Caesar was assassinated.

The Jews of Rome mourned him deeply and joined his funeral procession, for he had been a friend to Jews throughout the empire. Soon after his death he was proclaimed a god. His images were sold in marketplaces. People prayed to him. He was assured by the state of an eternal afterlife with the great gods of Rome.

Those who slew Caesar did so in the vague hope of preserving the republic. But the republic died with Caesar. A long civil war followed out of which Octavian, nephew of Caesar, emerged victorious. Soon Octavian was emperor and in 27 B.C.E. an awed Senate renamed him Augustus, a term which seems to convey the notion of power willingly given to one who has done right in the eyes of the gods and men. Then, in 14 C.E., came Tiberius. He was a reserved, passive, introverted man, somewhat too timid an emperor for a military autocracy like Rome. And now, in 38 C.E., a demented Caligula sat on the throne of Rome waiting to receive word that the giant statue of himself as Zeus had been erected and placed in the temple of the Jews in Jerusalem.

The land was in turmoil. It had been in almost constant turmoil since the arrival of the first procurator, Coponius, in 6 C.E. He had ordered a census of the population. Many saw that as a prelude to increased taxation; others recalled the Biblical account of the plague that followed the census taken by David and were terrified. Open revolt was averted through the intercession of the high priest. The census was held, but Coponius managed to earn the high regard of the Jews. One of the gateways of the temple was named after him. There is no record of any other general census in Judea.

Out of that brief confrontation with Coponius was born another party, the Zealots. It became a powerful party, and it was uncompromising in its hatred of Rome.

Coponius returned to Rome in 9 C.E. Six procurators ruled Judea during the next thirty-two years. Pontius Pilate was procurator from 26 to 36 C.E. Venality and a frequent resort to executions have earned him a singular immortality. He brought Roman army shields and standards into Jerusalem, issued coins with pagan symbols, and treated Jews and Samaritans alike with utter contempt. There were riots. He was recalled one year before Caligula became emperor.

Previous emperors had been friendly toward the Jews. Caligula himself had at first continued that policy by placing his friend Herod Agrippa, grandson of Herod, as king over the territories of Philip that lay across the Jordan, and of Antipas, who had ruled in the Galilee and Peraea. In 41 C.E. he would be given Judea.

The Jews were elated. Though he had been educated in Rome and had spent his youth among the young nobles of the Roman aristocracy, Agrippa gave every appearance of being an observant Jew, at least within the borders of his kingdom. He was respectful of the clashing factions and the religious sensibilities of his people. He was especially considerate toward the Pharisees.

Caligula took ill a few months after he became emperor. He emerged from the illness with an uncontrollable lust for power, a crazed tyrant.

The governor of Syria was Publius Petronius. He marched at the head of some Syrian legions into the coastal city of Ptolemais, about twenty miles north of Mount Carmel. He had been given the responsibility of carrying out the statue project. He knew the Jews, was in fact their friend, and was aware that there would be opposition to the command of his emperor. For him to disobey the emperor would be an act of treason.

He had not anticipated the extent of the opposition. Jews flooded into Ptolemais from all over the land, pleading for a rescinding of the decree. These were not zealous fanatics. The entire people was united in its opposition to the statue of the emperor. When he marched to the city of Tiberias, farmers abandoned their fields—it was the time of the autumn sowing—to plead with him not to desecrate the temple. Judea would become a sea of blood.

Agrippa was trying to persuade Caligula to change his mind. Petronius hesitated, delayed, wrote Caligula of the difficulties he was encountering. Both were endangering their positions and probably their lives. There is some indication that Caligula planned to have a statue made in Rome, shipped to Judea, and placed in the temple in time for a visit he was planning to the east in the spring.

One day Caligula insulted an officer of the palace guard, mocking him over his sexual habits. Enraged by the insult, the officer trapped Caligula in a secluded corner of the palace grounds and stabbed him to death with repeated thrusts of his dagger. The threat to the temple was averted. But it was not forgotten by the Jews. Madmen could rule Rome and indulge their insanities with all the might of the empire behind them.

Agrippa was in Rome when Caligula was murdered. Claudius, the stuttering, crippled uncle of Caligula, was found behind a curtain by guardsmen looting the palace. He was hauled off to their camp. His dead brother Germanicus had been a favorite of the legions. Now they urged Claudius to accept their support for the throne. Claudius, wiser than his idiot stutter made him out to be, hesitated, accepted, and offered rewards—the first of many times the seat of emperor would be bought by a promise of bounty to the legions. Here Agrippa played a crucial role as intermediary between the Senate and the forces supporting Claudius, and probably helped avert another Roman civil war. The emperor Claudius was bountiful in his gratitude to the grandson of Herod. He gave him Judea and confirmed his rule over the territories given him by Caligula. Agrippa now ruled all of Palestine

—much to the dismay of the many pagan cities within that territory. Claudius restored freedom of worship to Jews throughout the empire, but in 41 C.E. he forbade the Jews of Rome to practice proselytizing, and in 49 C.E., as a result of some disturbance, he ordered the expulsion of the Jews from Rome. They were soon permitted to return.

The reign of King Agrippa I has been called by some historians the last golden age of the Jews in antiquity. We have had such few good periods that we label almost any time of tranquillity and creativity as golden. The kingdom ruled by Agrippa was about the size of the territory of the Hasmonean dynasty at the period of its greatest strength. Jews in Judea and all through the dispersion looked upon him with love and pride. He cared deeply for the interests of his people, protected them tenaciously, maintained friendly relations with neighboring pagan cities.

Christianity had begun its slow early spread during his reign, and he was severe toward it. He ordered the execution of James son of Zebedee, one of the leaders of the sect, and the imprisonment of the apostle Peter.

He died suddenly in Caesarea during a celebration in honor of the emperor. He had reigned seven years, from 37 to 44 C.E. He was fifty-four years old when he died. He may have been poisoned by Romans who feared his popularity with the Jews. Jews mourned him deeply. Pagans rejoiced. Roman troops in Caesarea cursed his memory, broke into his house, attacked his daughters, and celebrated his death publicly with wine and feasting; so we are told by Josephus. Claudius made Judea, the Galilee, and Peraea a Roman province and sent a procurator named Cuspius Fadus to govern it.

He ruled from 44 to 46 C.E. The land grew increasingly turbulent. There were disturbances between Jews and pagans in the Hellenistic cities within the province. The Romans tended to favor the pagan populace.

Fadus was succeeded by Tiberius Julius Alexander, an apostate who had abandoned his Judaism for a career in the Roman world. His family were noted Alexandrian Jews; his uncle was the philosopher Philo. He was detested by the Jews of Judea. Disturbances intensified. Rob-

bers made the roads unsafe. The two sons of a noted
Galilean Jew were crucified for instigating disturbances.

During the rule of Ventidius Cumanus, from 48 to 52
C.E., there was a near-riot during a festival in Jerusalem
when a Roman soldier pulled back his garment and, as
Josephus puts it, "turned his breech to the Jews and
spoke such words as you might expect upon such a pos-
ture." Stones were hurled at the soldiers. Cumanus called
for reinforcements. A riot ensued. Many died. Then a Roman soldier found a scroll of the law of Moses, ripped it
up, and threw the pieces into a fire. The entire land
seemed to pour into Caesarea, headquarters of the Roman
government, to demand that the soldier be punished. To
avert certain revolt, Cumanus ordered that the soldier's
head be cut off.

The burden of Roman rule grew intolerable. Disturbances were not directed by a central leadership—there
was none—but were local, spontaneous. The chasm between the concept of Israel as the chosen of God and the
bitter reality of Roman oppression gave rise to apocalyptic visions, messianic hopes, prophecies of sudden salvation from the heavens by the hand of God. Messianists
roamed the land, gathering followers, preaching sedition.
Many were crucified, many. Among the Zealots there developed a small group of political assassins called the Sicarii—the Latin word *sica* means curved dagger—whose
skillful, silent work against anyone sympathetic to Rome
became a particularly horrifying form of terror. Brigands
attacked villages. Roman rule in Judea seemed rudderless,
bankrupt. Law and order began to break down all
through the land. Assassins went about their deadly work.
Messianists preached of the coming redemption. Jewish
leaders, priests, and Pharisees urged order, warned of the
destruction that would follow rebellion against Rome. In
the end Cumanus was recalled from Judea. Antonius Felix was appointed procurator in 52 C.E. He was a Greek.
The Roman historian Tacitus says of him that he indulged
"in every kind of barbarity and lust" and "exercised the
power of a king in the spirit of a slave." Two years after
the appointment of Felix, Claudius died and Nero became
emperor of Rome.

The large cities of the land were filled with debtors who had lost their land and with refugees from border regions of the province who had fled their villages as a result of incessant brigandage and clashes with pagans. They formed an angry mass eager for the preaching of messianic leaders and political extremists. Their rage was directed at the Romans and at the Judean upper classes who had for years collaborated with Roman rule. A man claiming to be a prophet suddenly appeared from Egypt, brought thousands of disciples to the Mount of Olives, and promised to destroy the walls of Jerusalem and overthrow the Roman garrison. The hill was still crowded with his expectant followers when the Roman legionaries charged. A massacre followed. The prophet escaped.

There was violence in Caesarea where Jews and pagans clashed over the status of the city and the civil rights of its Jews. Jews claimed it was a Jewish city, for it had been built by a Jewish king, Herod. Pagans argued it was a pagan city, that its previous name had been Strato's Tower—a tiny settlement founded by pagans—and that Herod could not have intended it to be a Jewish city, for he had built temples in it and put up statues of gods. There were street fights. The Roman garrison, made up of Syrians, sided with the pagan populace. Angry Jews roamed the streets with swords and clubs. Felix came into the marketplace and ordered the Jews home. They refused. He turned his soldiers loose, many Jews were killed. The disturbances continued. In the end the case was brought before Nero, who ruled against the Jews, relegating them to the position of second-class citizens. Jews seethed at the decision, gained as a result of Syrian influence in the court of Nero.

The land was in a condition of near-chaos. Jerusalem was being terrorized ay the Sicarii. Messianic visionaries clouded the air. Zealots preached rebellion. Priests fought one another for positions of privilege. Pharisees looked on helplessly, torn between their hatred of Roman oppression and their dread of the consequences of revolt.

A new procurator, Albinus, arrived in 62 C.E. Before the arrival of Albinus, a high priest took control of the Sanhedrin and proceeded to try cases using Sadducean law. One casualty among many of this sudden loss of Pharisaic power was James, the brother of Jesus, who was head of the community of Christians in Jerusalem. He was condemned to death and executed.

Pharisees protested vehemently against the trial of James and sent a delegation to Albinus, who at the time was on his way to Jerusalem. They reminded the new procurator that a Sanhedrin had no authority to deliver a sentence of execution without the authority of a procurator. The high priest was removed from office.

The deadly work of the Sicarii intensified. Many were captured by Roman legionaries, imprisoned, executed. Then the secretary of the son of a former high priest was kidnaped by Sicarii, who announced they would free him if ten Sicarii were released. This former high priest, Ananias, worked closely with the new procurator, was in fact his closest ally among the Jews. The Sicarii were released. This method of gaining the release of prisoners now came into frequent use. Albinus made a fortune out of the release of prisoners; he would free those imprisoned by previous procurators upon the payment of a ransom by relatives.

The last procurator of Judea was Gessius Florus, an Ionian Greek. He ruled from 64 to 66 C.E.

All the procurators of Judea before Agrippa had been of Italian stock. Judea, an insignificant appendage of the empire, a sliver of land attached to the great province of Syria—Judea had been ruled since Agrippa by men of low ability and garrisoned only by auxiliaries, Syrian soldiers to whom Roman citizenship would be granted only after the completion of their term of service. The garrison consisted of three thousand men, twenty-five hundred infantry and five hundred cavalry. The immediate superior of the procurator was the governor of Syria. These were ex-consuls, men who were high in government and prominent in Roman society. They had at their command in Syria itself the power of four legions—about twenty thousand superbly trained professional soldiers.

Florus appears to have been the most debased of all the procurators. Roman law made it possible to bring provincial administrators to trial on charges of corruption, though it was a time-consuming and costly procedure. Josephus tells us that Florus provoked the Jews into rebellion in order to make it impossible for them to initiate a request for an inquiry into his administration.

The oppressive taxes, the administrative corruption, the widespread street fighting between pagans and Jews, the Sicarii and their deadly daggers, the apocalyptic Messiahs, the urban poor who looked with hate upon the Romans and the landed and merchant rich, the sages who sensed the horrors rebellion would bring, the high priests who sought peace with Rome at almost any cost, the Zealots whose hatred of Rome went beyond all reason, the Essenes who lived serene monastic lives along the edge of the Dead Sea, the men and women who believed with absolute faith that God would miraculously redeem His people from the slavery of Rome—this was Judea during the reign of Gessius Florus.

I remember a day in Rome one summer some years ago. The air was golden with Mediterranean sunlight and the streets were clogged with the frenetic mayhem of Italian traffic. I crossed a large boulevard, dodging the endless hordes of darting cars, and entered the vast ruin of the Colosseum. There amid the worn stone seats, the disemboweled masonry beneath the vanished wooden floor, and the deep chill shade of arched passageways, I heard the roar of the ancient Roman mob, fifty thousand voices within the ellipse of stone, and imagined the pageants of blood that had fed the idle hours of the people. How many men and animals perished here for the pleasure of those members of our species? Yes, I know that many Romans worked hard and the good emperors worked hardest of all, waking before sunrise and laboring into the night. Julius Caesar and Marcus Aurelius would take official papers to study at the gladiatorial games.

Later I walked through the tumble of carved stones and ghostly columns along the Forum, the stone-paved heart of ancient Rome where senators, emperors, merchants, and mobs had once moved, and stood beneath the Arch of Titus, built to commemorate the victory of the Romans over the rebellious Jews. "The Jewish people is alive," someone had scratched in Hebrew across the stone panel depicting the booty taken from the Jerusalem temple as it went up in flames.

I know that Rome created Europe and that her law, language, literature, architecture, and engineering are part of the heritage of western man. I know she served as the conduit through which th warm-weather civilizations of the Mediterranean and the Fertile Crescent were passed to the dark worlds beyond the Alps. But I see her through my Jewish eyes; I have no love for Rome. Of all the peoples in her vast empire, she understood the Jews least. "Things sacred with us," writes Tacitus, "with them have no sanctity, while they allow what with us is forbidden. . . . The Jewish religion is tasteless and mean." And of the many culture encounters that crowd the history of my people, we learned least from the Romans. We learned what the Greeks already knew; the word Roman in Greek meant power. Rome and Jerusalem met in a periphery-to-periphery confrontation that ended in blood and fire.

Recently I came across a passage in Seneca. He is describing the wealthy, self-indulgent Roman. "People set out on journeys with no particular objective in view. They wander down the coast. In a purposeless way they go by the sea, they go by land, always wishing they were doing something else. 'Let us go to Campania.' 'No, smart resorts are a bore. Rough country is the thing to see.' . . . 'No, let us go back to Rome.' It seems a lifetime since they last heard the applause and din of the games. 'It might be rather nice, too, to see somebody killed.' "

It started on a Sabbath in Caesarea in 66 C.E. "A certain man of a seditious temper," writes Josephus, "got an earthen vessel, and set it, with the bottom upward, at the entrance of the synagogue and sacrificed birds. This thing provoked the Jews to an incurable degree, because their laws were affronted, and the place was polluted. . . ." Street battles followed between Jews and pagans, which the garrison could not control. A delegation of Jews went to Florus, who was then in Sebaste—the city of Samaria, which had been rebuilt and renamed by Herod. He ignored their plea for help.

News of the incident reached Jerusalem. The city grew turbulent. Florus chose that moment to raid the temple treasury for seventeen talents he claimed were wanted by the emperor. People thronged toward the temple. Some passed around a basket in a brazen act of mockery, urging that funds be collected for their impoverished procurator. Instead of marching to Caesarea to quench the riots in its streets, Florus brought troops to Jerusalem to avenge the insult to his name.

The city was tranquil when he arrived. He insisted that those who had insulted him be delivered up for punishment. The high priests and others of influence in the city begged forgiveness. They were unable to distinguish the culprits, they said, and pleaded that the innocent populace not be harmed for the actions of a few guilty ones. Florus, enraged, turned his soldiers loose upon a section of the city called the Upper Marketplace. The area was viciously plundered, its inhabitants slain—3600 died, according to Josephus.

The priests and elders of the city sought to pacify the people, who were incensed by the wanton killing. They succeeded, and the crowds dispersed. Florus then ordered the populace to greet with respectful salutes a troop of soldiers he was ordering to Jerusalem from Caesarea. The priests prevailed upon the people to comply. The soldiers were met with respectful silence. At the appropriate moment, the people saluted. The soldiers, under malicious orders from Florus, did not respond.

This was a taunting public insult to the dignity of Jerusalem and her people. The city at this time was a heavily populated metropolis, famous for its magnificent temple. It was the capital of world Jewry, the center of great Pharisaic academies of learning, the residence of priestly families and the elite of the social and intellectual life of the people. Here lived the finest craftsmen of the Jewish population of Palestine. Merchants came and went from everywhere, as did pilgrims, converts, and pious pagans who felt themselves attracted to the Jewish God. The Roman statesman Pliny regarded Jerusalem as the best-known city of the eastern world. Tacitus tells us that the population of Jerusalem numbered six hundred thousand "of every age and both sexes." There is no way of determining the accuracy of Tacitus, since no population records of this period of Judean history have yet been discovered.

The people, watching the mute soldiers march by, murmured sullenly at their insulting lack of acknowledgment of the salute. Some in the crowd suddenly called out against Florus. The soldiers charged. People fled, trampling one another as they sought to get away from the clubs and swords and horses' hooves. The soldiers began to cut their way through the crowd toward the temple. But the people blocked the way with their bodies while others raced toward the temple to form a line of defense. Then stones rained down upon the soldiers from rooftops, and they withdrew. Florus left the city and returned to Caesarea.

Then Zealots seized the mountain fortress of Masada near the southern rim of the Dead Sea, slew the Roman garrison, and left a number of their own people to guard it. At the same time, the son of the high priest, "a very bold youth," as Josephus puts it, "who was at that time governor of the temple, persuaded those that officiated in the divine service to receive no gift or sacrifice for any foreigner." The temple sacrifice on behalf of the emperor of Rome was terminated. "And this," adds Josephus, "was the true beginning of our war with the Romans."

The high priests and Pharisees could not prevail upon the young governor of the temple and his many supporters to relent and offer the sacrifice to Nero. It was then that serious fighting broke out among the Jews. The high priests seized the upper city, the wealthy area on the higher of the city's two hills; it lay to the west of the temple. The lower city—the crowded section of the poor and the center of Jerusalem's commercial and industrial life—to the south of the temple, and the temple itself were in the hands of the Zealots. The Zealots and Sicarii set fire to the house of the high priest and burned down the archives where records of debts were kept, hoping thereby to gain as allies the poor of the city. The

Roman garrison surrendered and was slaughtered. People began to flee the city. The Jerusalem community of Christians left in 68 C.E. and fled northward to the town of Pella across the Jordan below Tiberias.

On the day of the slaying of the Jerusalem garrison a riot broke out in Caesarea. Jews were massacred. Riots jumped like crown fires from cities to villages throughout Palestine and Syria. Disturbances reached as far as Alexandria, where an entire section of the city was forcibly taken by the Jews. They were thrown back by two legions and suffered heavy casualties. All through Syria and Palestine Jews and pagans burned down each other's villages and fought bloody battles in city streets. The governor of Syria, Cestius Gallus, marched a full legion and some units drawn from other legions through Palestine to Jerusalem. He encountered no opposition.

It was autumn, during the festival of Sukkot, and Jerusalem was crowded with pilgrims. The Jews rushed to their weapons. Days of heavy fighting followed. Cestius Gallus realized he had not enough men to mount a siege of the city. The Romans staged an orderly withdrawal and were trapped in the mountain passes near Beth-horon between Jerusalem and Lod. A rain of spears, arrows, and stones turned the withdrawal into a disastrous rout. This was the Twelfth Legion, known as Fulminata, the Thundering One. Josephus tells us that Cestius Gallus lost more than five thousand infantry and almost four hundred cavalry. The legion left behind all its siege equipment and lost its eagle.

The incredible defeat of that legion turned the revolt into a general rebellion. The Jews, elated with victory, made a brief peace among themselves, set up a government in Jerusalem, struck silver coins, and divided the land into seven districts, each with its own military commander. The commander of the Galilee was Joseph son of Mattathias, of a priestly family. He would later surrender to the Romans, go over to their side, and become the historian Josephus Flavius. When he was appointed military commander of the Galilee he knew nothing about organized warfare. Many Jewish communities in the Galilee were opposed to the rebellion.

Early the following year the Romans returned to Palestine. Instead of training an army, the Jews had spent most of the intervening months fighting among themselves. They were still fighting when Nero's best general, T. Flavius Vespasianus, arrived in Palestine with three legions. By the end of 67 C.E. all of the Galilee and the coastal region south of Jaffa were back in the hands of the Romans.

The Romans did not make the error of Antiochus IV. They took the rebellion of the Jews seriously, prepared patiently to crush it, and marched with ponderous care from one strategic point to another, subduing the land. The Jews did not have a leader around whom the nation could rally. Zealots fought among themselves and fought together against the moderates. Many Pharisees went over to the Zealot camp. Sicarii ran wild, killing anyone they suspected of sympathy toward Rome. Jerusalem was filled with Jewish dead long before the legions of Rome marched along the dusty roads of Judea and encamped before her walls in 70 C.E. By then the empire had become enraged over the misrule of Nero, legions had revolted in Spain and Gaul, civil war had broken out, Nero had committed suicide, three emperors had come and gone in a period of one year—69—and Rome herself had experienced chaos.

During the period of uncertainty in Rome, in 69 C.E., Vespasian had ceased his campaign in Judea and waited. It was sometime during this pause that a sage made his way out of Jerusalem—possibly in a coffin, for Zealots had sealed the city and were permitting no one to depart—to the camp of Vespasian, declared that he had been held in the city against his will and had wanted no part in the fighting, and requested asylum. He was sent off to a refugee camp in the town of Yavneh—also known as Jamnia—where a pagan had once built an altar to sacrifice to Caligula and had caused a riot that had almost resulted in a statue of Caligula being placed in the temple. The name of the sage was Rabban—our master or teacher—Yochanan ben Zakkai.

Then the legions of Vepasian put forward their own commander as emperor. After a brief and bloody civil war, during which the temple of Jupiter in Rome was destroyed by fire, Vespasian became emperor of Rome. That was in late December 69 C.E., 822 years after the traditional date of the founding of the city. He sent his eldest son, Titus, to complete the campaign in Judea.

The conflicts among the Zealots finally ceased. The armies of the Jews numbered about twenty-five thousand men. The four legions camped around Jerusalem, together with their auxiliaries, were a force of eighty thousand soldiers.

The walls of the northern section of the city were breached by May 30. The Romans built a siege wall around the city in the first days of July to starve out the remaining defenders. The city became a horror of famine and death. The dead were thrown over the wall into the valleys below and lay unburied.

The legions had siege machines capable of hurling stones weighing fifty-five pounds for a distance of seven hundred yards. They had battering rams, mobile towers with bridges or drawbridges, iron-pointed wall-borers, hooks, crowbars, and iron-plated mobile screens to protect their attacking force.

On August 6 the daily sacrifice ceased in the temple. It had been offered every morning for more than five hundred years save for the period of Syrian persecution when an abomination had occupied the Holy of Holies. It would begin after dawn with the cry of the herald that awakened the sleepers: "Priests to the service and Levites to the platform. . . ."

In the middle of August the porticoes of the temple were burned. In the last week of August the temple was penetrated by legionaries. The pitiful remnant of Jewish fighters fought on inch by inch, certain of the saving miracle from God that would come at the last moment.

The temple caught fire. It was about the ninth day of the Hebrew month of Av, around the same day as the destruction of the first temple nearly seven hundred years before. Modern historians do not know if the fire was an accident or was set on the order of Titus.

Inside the temple was the scroll of the law that had served as the master, which scribes would use when they wrote and corrected copies. Scrolls of the Torah and the prophets and many other books were preserved in the temple. The master scroll was probably part of the booty taken by Titus to Rome along with the sacred vessels that had been used in the offering of sacrifices.

The temple continued to burn. It took another month of fighting before the remainder of the city was captured. Titus ordered all the surviving population taken captive. The city was leveled house by house. Titus returned to Rome and was given a triumph—a victory procession accorded a Roman commander who had slain more than five thousand enemy soldiers and brought back booty and captives who would become slaves or augment the reservoir of victims for the games. *Judaea capta* read the exultant inscriptions on the coins minted by Rome to celebrate the victory.

The last stronghold, Masada, the towering plateau on the edge of the Dead Sea, fell in 73 C.E. Its defenders—almost a thousand men, women, and children—chose to commit suicide rather than fall into Roman hands. Two women and five children survived.

The rebellion was crushed. Jerusalem lay silent beneath a long deadly night, her ruins guarded by the Tenth Legion.

The Jewish state came to an end. The Sanhedrin was abolished. The high priesthood ceased to exist. The Sadducean party disappeared. The Romans would not permit the temple to be rebuilt. Jews throughout the empire were ordered to continue to pay the temple tax—for the service of the new temple of Jupiter on the Capitoline hill in Rome.

In the town of Yavneh a group of masters and disciples met daily to study the law. They met with Rabban Yochanan ben Zakkai. "Why was the second temple destroyed?" someone asked. Someone responded, "Because of blind hatred."

# PALESTINE

# Rabbis from Yavneh

The Jews of the land were dazed with grief and horror. Some withdrew to caves to await the end of days. Others refused to drink wine or eat meat. The pain of the loss seemed unendurable.

The years went by. Despite the casualties, Jews were still the majority of the population in Palestine. There was much poverty. In the Galilee and along the terraced hills of Judea farmers worked their fields and replanted their vineyards. From hilltops in Judea one could see the hollow ruins of Jerusalem ghostly in the summer sun and embowered with weeds and wild flowers after the winter rains. Some returned to live along the fringes of the dead city.

Kings and priests were of the past. Zealots and Sicarii were gone. Only the quietist Pharisee teachers were left.

People continued to gather in synagogues—houses of assembly. They gathered for prayer and study and the public reading of the law instituted by Ezra and Nehemiah. In the town of Yavneh, Rabban Yochanan ben Zakkai met with his disciples in an attic or near a pigeon house in a vineyard. He had been one of the leading Pharisees in Jerusalem and deputy to the head of the Sanhedrin. He distrusted messianists and religious enthusiasts and is reported to have remarked, "If you are holding a sapling in your hand and someone says to you the Messiah is here, plant the sapling first and then welcome the Messiah." Now he was an old man. Most of his life had been spent in the study and teaching of Torah. "If you have learned much Torah, do not ascribe any merit to yourself," he had once said, "since it was for this that you were created."

There was a court at Yavneh and a family of sages. In that town, under the influence of Rabban Yochanan ben Zakkai and his disciples, sages met and gave the canon of the Bible final form. Discussions were heated. Decisions were made by majority vote. Books were chosen—and we read them today; others were omitted and have disappeared or live in the twilight world of marginal literature. The precise time of those meetings is not known.

Enactments were proclaimed. Matters of law were settled. The calendar was intercalated. In those years the court that made the decisions regarding the Jewish calendar—the dates of the New Moon, festivals, holy days— was in essence the central power of all Jewry. There was some dissension from sages who could not forgive the surrender of Rabban Yochanan to Rome. But he prevailed. Gradually the court at Yavneh began to replace the dead Sanhedrin of Jerusalem. In time it would become the new Sanhedrin.

Once someone lamented the destruction of Jerusalem and wept that it was no longer possible, without the sacrificial system, to atone for one's sins. "No, my son," Rabban Yochanan replied. "We have a means of making atonement. And what is it? It is deeds of love. . . ." With him began the full flowering of rabbinic civilization and the turning of the energies of the people away from futile hate-filled wars against a pagan world and toward study, sanctity, and the performance of the will of God as interpreted by centuries of scribes and sages.

Yavneh began to attract sages and pilgrims. In later years, when the town had become a great city, the city of scholars and rabbis, pilgrims would journey from Asia to Yavneh to celebrate the festivals. Rabban Yochanan ben Zakkai died about ten years after the destruction of Jerusalem.

Yavneh scholars traveled throughout the land, teaching and founding schools. In the towns and villages of Judea and the Galilee, people listened to scholars from Yavneh weave out of the real or imagined meanings of sacred texts a world resonant with God to which they could respond with determination and hope. Slowly the second destruction of the Jerusalem temple became a grim interlude in a long history rather than a darkness that ends existence.

The sages claimed for themselves the right to judge and teach. The authority to interpret the word of God, they said, had come down to them from Moses through Joshua, the judges, prophets, the members of the Great Assembly in the time of Ezra, and the scholar-high priest Simon the Just, who probably lived in the third century B.C.E. Then the authority had passed to the zugot—the word means pairs—Pharisaic sages who had shared the leadership of the Sanhedrin, one as president—or patriarch, as the Romans called him—and the other as head of the court. Hillel had been the greatest of the patriarchs before the destruction of the temple. He served as patriarch—*nasi*, in Hebrew—from about 10 B.C.E. to 10 C.E. Then leadership by zugot was abolished, the patriarchate became dynastic, and descendants of Hillel ruled Jewish life for more than four hundred years.

He was a gentle, thoughtful scholar, a man of patience and tact. He thought it necessary to expand the law and apply it with fresh vision to each new generation. The customs and traditions of the past were vital; it was of utmost importance that a jurist possess a superior memory. But reason was of equal importance, as were new methods of deriving meaning from the sacred texts that would enable the law to be applied to unforeseen realities. He was a poor man, and all his life he had in mind the needs of the masses of his people. He founded a great school—as did his adversary, the wealthy scholar Shammai, a very proper, impatient conservative, who could agree with Hillel on practically nothing and whose legal viewpoint tended to represent the moneyed class. The intellectual controversies that rang through their schools set a style for liveliness in learning that one can still see today in a traditional academy of Jewish studies.

Rabban Yochanan ben Zakkai left Yavneh before his death, perhaps to clear a path for new leadership. A descendant of Hillel, Gamaliel II, became head of the

Yavneh academy of learning and patriarch of the reconstituted Sanhedrin. His father had been Simon ben Gamaliel, one of the leaders of the revolt against Rome. The
house of Hillel was suspect in the eyes of Rome.

The empire was still ruled by the dynasty of the Flavians. Vespasian died in 79 C.E. and was succeeded by his
son, Titus, who had destroyed Jerusalem. Titus died very
suddenly after a reign of only two years. The younger son
of Vespasian, T. Flavius Domitianus, became emperor.
He was a taciturn man, self-assertive, despotic, whose
tyrannizing was soon felt not only in Rome, but throughout the empire, and in the crippled land of the Jews.

The Flavians would not permit the official reestablish-
ment of a controlling institution of Jewish life. From their
headquarters in Caesarea, provincial administrators gazed
with suspicion upon the activities at Yavneh. The sages
did their work quietly. As long as the Jews were politically servile, Rome would grudgingly recognize Yavneh as
a necessary reality—for a people requires some measure
of inner leadership—rather than as a sanctioned center of
authority. The burden of Roman taxation was heavy. The
Jews paid.

Domitian was assassinated in 96 C.E. by a palace servant who stabbed him while he was reading a report
about a conspiracy. The servant had acted on the instructions of the emperor's wife, who had reason to fear for her
own life at the hands of her vicious husband. The Senate
ordered that the name of Domitian be erased from all
public monuments. The Flavian dynasty came to an end.

All through the decades of the Flavian dynasty, whose
great pride had been the destruction of Jerusalem and the
crushing of the Jewish rebellion, the sages of Yavneh re-
shaped the nature of the Jewish tradition, cutting it loose
from dependence upon the Jerusalem temple and the
sacrificial system. In the time of Rabban Gamaliel II the
text of obligatory and communal prayers was fixed. The
canonization of the last of the Biblical books may have
been accomplished during this period. Christians were
taken to be a heretical sect, and contact with them was
forbidden. It was declared that Passover could be celebrated without the sacrifice of the paschal lamb. The

order, *seder*, of the Passover eve ritual was transformed; one could eat the unleavened bread and bitter herbs without the meat of the lamb—contrary to the clear stipulation of the Bible. A new text was developed to explain and accompany the Passover evening rituals. That text is called the Haggadah. The Passover molded at Yavneh out of the debris of the destroyed temple is still celebrated by Jews today.

The most important activity of Jewish life became study. To establish some semblance of order out of the decades of oral disputations between the schools of Hillel and Shammai, Rabban Gamaliel ruled in favor of the school of Hillel in most cases. He favored the liberal humaneness of Hillel over the conservative propriety of Shammai. This did not sit well with all the scholars of Yavneh. There was murmuring. When he continued his high-handed method of establishing order, of cutting down debate and forcing decisions, the sages rose up and deposed him. Undaunted, he continued to attend the sessions of the court, participating in its discussions as one of its ordinary members. Years later the sages reinstated him as patriarch.

The sages of Yavneh were called rabbi—literally, my master—a title that marked one as having received ordination, smicha—the actual or symbolic laying on of hands that serves as public acknowledgment by peers and masters that a student may now teach the oral law, render legal decisions, and even serve as a member of the Sanhedrin. Not all who studied at Yavneh became rabbis; some remained disciples and became itinerant teachers, journeying throughout the land. Often they would teach in marketplaces or out in the fields beneath an olive tree or a fig tree.

The new crisis leader was now the rabbi—unpaid, for he would accept no remuneration for his labors as teacher and judge; often poor, working at some craft or another; often a wanderer from town to town as he taught the Bible and the law, and settled communal problems; on occasion he was a man of means if his family was wealthy; sometimes he journeyed to the lands of the dispersion, Egypt, Cyrenaica, Rome, Gaul, Asia Minor, Syria, Mesopotamia. He might go to Rome and wander through the city that had enslaved his people. He might journey as an emissary to the Jewish communities of Alexandria, Antioch, and Babylon to raise funds for the schools of Judea and the Galilee. Always he studied and taught. He taught the halachah, the fixed rules, the life style based on the word of God to Moses at Sinai and interpreted by the sages. He taught religious law, for it was only by living out the law of God that the Jewish people could show itself still bound to the covenant stipulations. Sometimes he would tell a story, fashion a parable, preach a moral and ethical message, as he turned sacred words this way and that to expose all their possible meanings.

The Sanhedrin of Yavneh was finally recognized as the official leadership of the Jews by the emperor Nerva, who followed Domitian. The patriarch was acknowledged as the representative of the Jewish people to Rome. Nerva died in 98 C.E. His successor, Trajan, continued his policy toward the Jews. The date of the death of Rabban Gamaliel II is unknown. It was probably shortly before 115 C.E.

The Yavneh era came to an end in a torrent of blood. Jewish messianic hopes had not died out entirely. They were nurtured in many rabbinic schools and exploded abruptly in 115 C.E. during the reign of Trajan. While the emperor busied himself in an effort to conquer Parthia—this necessitated the partial withdrawal of the Roman garrisons from Palestine—Jews all through the dispersion, and probably in parts of Palestine, suddenly rose up in simultaneous rebellion. It took Rome two years to put down that movement, which had pinned down Roman troops in Egypt and Palestine. The Jewish populations in the various centers of the revolt had massacred pagans; now pagans massacred Jews. The Jews of the dispersion never again gave serious trouble to Rome.

Hadrian became emperor in 117 C.E. Toward the end of his reign he thought—as had Antiochus IV—to strengthen the faltering empire by uniting all his subjects beneath a single dominant culture. He would solve the awkward problem posed by the constant otherness of the Jews through enforced assimilation. In 131 C.E. he issued an edict against circumcision. He is reputed to have been one of the finest and most versatile of Roman emperors; many regard him as coming closest to Caesar in ability. Circumcision offended his sense of civilized behavior. Declarations such as the Shema Yisrael—Hear, O Israel—he probably regarded as an oath of allegiance to a subversive and barbarous brotherhood. He forbade under penalty of death the public reading of the Torah, the observance of the Sabbath and festivals, the teaching of the law, the ordination of rabbis. He founded a Roman colony, Aelia Capitolina—his name was Aelius Adrianus—at Jerusalem and placed a shrine of Jupiter on the site of the destroyed temple. He saw it all as a way of ironing out a minor and distant wrinkle in his empire. The Jews of Palestine saw it as an end to Judaism.

The land erupted again in 132 C.E. The Jews carefully conscripted an army. Jewish Christians who refused to serve were treated with severity and contempt. It was the bitterest and bloodiest of wars Rome had fought in a very long time. The Jews fought for survival; the Romans fought for the prestige of their emperor and his legions. Out of a blurred mass of Jewish fighters who aspired to the role of leader at the start of the war, there emerged a giant of a man whom many, including the great scholar Rabbi Akiva, regarded as the Messiah. Rabbi Akiva called him Bar Kochba—Son of the Star—one of the names then used to designate the messianic king.

For two years the Jews held off the Romans. The Tenth Legion evacuated Jerusalem and withdrew to Caesarea. The Jews entered Jerusalem and reinstituted the sacrificial system. They struck coins to celebrate the liberation. The Roman Twenty-second Legion advanced into the interior of the land from Egypt and was entirely wiped out. The Jews fought with careful planning and under the unified command of Bar Kochba, a domineering and sometimes cruel leader. Most of the great scholars of Yavneh died in that war, fighting against the Romans or tortured to death for teaching the law.

Rabbi Akiva was arrested and imprisoned. He had been born about ten years before the destruction of the temple in the previous century, had been an ignorant

shepherd until about the age of forty; then, encouraged by
his wife Rachel, he had entered school with little children
to study the alphabet. Fifteen years later he was one of
the greatest scholars of his time. He arranged in logical
order the vast body of oral law so as to facilitate its transmission to students; previously it had been organized by
various mnemonic devices, artificial aids to memory. He
insisted that every word, every letter of the sacred text
was capable of profound meaning, thereby expanding the
range of possibilities open to interpretation. He was a
scholar, a passionate lover of God, a believer in man's
freedom to choose his own way in a world guided by a
providential Deity. He was a mystic. He died slowly for
all these things that he was—drawing out the words of
the Shema Yisrael with his last breath as the iron combs
tore the skin from his body, dying with a look of such exultation on his face that his astonished executioner asked
him in awe, "Are you a sorcerer?" No, he was not a sorcerer, he said. He was rejoicing over having been given
the opportunity to show his full love for his God—by
dying.

Many scholars were arrested and tortured. One was
burned alive with the scrolls from which he had taught
wrapped around him; another was beheaded; yet another
was pierced through like a sieve. Roman brutality burned
these deaths into the folk memory.

The war dragged on. The Romans turned it into a
manhunt in which a large part of the Jewish population of
Palestine was exterminated. Once again, as in the time of
Antiochus IV, the entire people, not only individuals, lay
exposed to martyrdom. When it was done and the legions
brought in from other points of the empire had finished
methodically cutting off and starving out one district after
another and had cleansed and sheathed their weapons—
when it was all done, and Bar Kochba was dead, and the
land lay beneath a film of blood—the Romans reported
that 50 fortresses had been reduced, 985 villages had
been leveled, and 580,000 Jews had been killed in skir-
mishes and battles in addition to countless others who had
perished of starvation, fire, disease. The legions had suffered such heavy casualties that Hadrian, in his report on

the war to the Senate, omitted the traditional salutation, "I trust you and your children are well; I and my troops are well. . . ."

The war ended in the summer of 135 C.E. The religious persecutions continued. Jerusalem became a Roman city, a gleaming model city dedicated to the god Jupiter. There were a number of such cities throughout the empire. A broad street ran through the heart of the rebuilt city, bordered by wide colonnaded walks. The Jews who had survived the war were forbidden to enter the city except on the ninth day of Av. Judea lost its name and became Syria Palaestina. Two legions garrisoned the land. A dusty Jerusalem street was recently uncovered by Israeli archaeologists. I remember standing on its stone paving in the heart of the old city with Arab boys on donkeys and young bearded Jews moving by. The street had been narrow and fronted with Arab markets. An archaeologist sank a shaft and hit the stone of ancient paving. Scholars think it may be the broad street of Roman Jerusalem. It will be excavated now to its original width and some portion of its length. The old paving will be retained. I have heard that Israelis will build shops on it and sell their wares to tourists.

Hadrian died in 138 C.E. Some of the edicts against the Jews were rescinded by his successor, Antoninus Pius, in particular the prohibition against circumcision. The surname Pius was conferred upon him by the Senate and means a likable person.

The land was devastated. Jews were no longer the majority of the population. Pagans began to filter into the land from adjacent areas. The remnants of the rabbis at first remained underground, meeting in caves and isolated village. Then they returned to the sunlight and wept at the desolation of the land.

Many members of the Sanhedrin had fallen. Much of Judea was empty of Jews. After a time the Sanhedrin moved from Yavneh to the Galilean city of Usha.

The fields and vineyards of Judea, which had seen some of the heaviest fighting, were burned and torn. Villages remained uninhabited. There was much emigration

to Babylonia and its wealthy Jewry, with its own organized community led by the exilarch, the head of the
exile, whose family claimed descent from the house of
David.

Rabbi Akiva had left behind a number of great disciples who had somehow survived the war. Despite the
numbing poverty of the land, study was resumed. "The
commandments were given for only one purpose," a rabbi
would say in the next century, "to purify the hearts of
men." The disciples of Rabbi Akiva—Rabbi Meir, Rabbi
Simeon bar Yohai, and others—continued to teach in the
face of the bloodied darkness around them.

The new patriarch was Rabban Simeon ben Gamaliel.
In the academy of his father there had been a thousand
students. Five hundred had studied Torah, five hundred
had studied Greek subjects. Only two had survived the
war—Rabban Simeon and his brother's son. The land had
been through an orgy of blood; it had broken itself
against the stone heart of Rome for the final time. Now
the people would turn their energies inward and engage
themselves fully in the most important of the commandments—study. Slowly, through the efforts of Rabban Simeon, the Sanhedrin reestablished its contacts with the
communities in the dispersion and reasserted its authority
over the religious affairs of Jewry.

In the decades that followed the revolt a silence of exhaustion blanketed the land. Rome had made a desert of
Judea and had thereby gained peace. Though here and
there an academy of learning still flourished in Judea, the
center of scholarship had shifted permanently to the more
populous Galilee, which had escaped much of the horror
of the war.

Roman emperors came and went—Marcus Aurelius,
Commodus, Septimus Severus. The Sanhedrin wandered
from town to town until, in the next century, it settled in
the capital of the Galilee district, the city of Tiberias,
built by one of the sons of Herod. There, during the benevolent oriental policies of the Severan dynasty in Rome,
from 193 to 235 C.E.—probably a result of the African
origin of Severus and his marriage with a Syrian wife—
Palestine underwent considerable economic recovery.

Emigration ceased. Rabbi Judah the Prince, who was the son of Rabban Simeon and had replaced him as head of the Sanhedrin, began the task of editing into final form the work known as the Mishnah, the vast collection of centuries of oral law and tradition. The word Mishnah means, literally, review; it is a record of most of the legal material of the period of the tannaim, the earliest of the scholars, as the sages who lived from the time of Hillel to Judah the Prince are called.

The precise part played by Rabbi Judah the Prince in the systemization of the Mishnah in slowly becoming clear as a result of recent scholarship. He wanted to create a legal canon. Working with editions of the Mishnah used by various academies, he appears to have collected the traditions of the past, added to them the rulings accumulated during his own and his father's generations, altered the original language when it obscured a matter of law (he and his court would decide upon the proper law and that would be made the language of the text), and organized this vast body of material into six major divisions: *Seeds* deals with agricultural matters; *Festival* contains laws pertaining to the Sabbath and holidays; *Women* has to do with family life, marriage, divorce; *Damages* is concerned with buying, selling, injuries, real estate, courts, witnesses, idolatry, the effects of erroneous legal decisions; *Sacred Matters* covers such subjects as sacrifices, dietary laws, the temple service; *Purifications* consists of laws regarding ritual uncleanness. The text of the Mishnah, once thought to be fairly simple and straightforward, has been shown by modern scholarship to be enormously complex, a living weave of fluid traditions. The language is a clear, laconic Hebrew, the Hebrew of the scholars of the second temple period. A variety of Aramaic dialects was then the language of common everyday life, along with some Greek (the extent of the knowledge and use of Greek by the sages is the subject of considerable debate among contemporary scholars); but Hebrew was the language of the developing legal texts in the academies.

It was an extraordinary achievement, accomplished by a man who had wandered from academy to academy in his early years because his father had been in hiding and he himself had to remain on the move in the face of Roman persecution. As a result, he had mastered the traditions of various academies, learned how the various methods of deriving law from Biblical verses were used by different masters, chose what he thought to be the best of these traditions and methods, and fused them into a text of his own.

But the text was not a written scroll, and the handbook contained no parchment. In the very ancient world you published a work by reading it aloud in public or by inscribing it on a stone which you placed in a public area. In the time of the scribes and the rabbis, you published a text by giving it to a publisher who employed professional copyists. The text would be dictated to these copyists; or they would make copies from other copies. In this manner, hundreds or thousands of copies of a work could be produced quickly. Or you deposited the original authentic copy in a special archive, a library, a temple. This would guard the text against forgeries. If a controversy arose as to the authenticity of a text, the master copy could be consulted. A book that was placed in the temple was considered published. We do not know how many such published books were forever lost to us when the temple was burned.

The Mishnah was probably published in a different way. A repeater or reciter—also known as a tanna, the same term that is used of the early great sages but with an entirely different meaning—the tanna memorized certain portions of the Mishnah. These reciters were students chosen for their phenomenal memory. They were not always particularly intelligent; often they were mumblers who spoke without understanding what they said. There are such minds. The tanna, the reciter, was a living book, a basketful of books.

The term tanna for academy reciter probably came into use around the time of Rabbi Akiva. A master like Akiva had his own Mishnah. His students would accumulate notes on the discussions in the academy. When a mass of interpretations accumulated, the master would sift through his students' notes and shape them into some new configuration. He would teach the new Mishnah to a tanna, then he would teach it to another tanna, then a third, and a fourth. . . . The first tanna would recite it in the presence of all who had learned it, then the second, then the third. . . . The memorizers would repeat the Mishnah in the academy, with the master present. He would correct their recitation, thereby giving the text its final form. This was the method of publication used for the Mishnah of Rabbi Akiva, and it probably holds true as well for that of Rabbi Judah the Prince. The multiplicity of versions of Rabbi Akiva's Mishnah—the result of avid and divergent student note-taking—made necessary a new edition.

Rabbi Judah the Prince died in 217 C.E. Alexander Severus became emperor of Rome in 222 C.E. Three years later the grandson of Judah the Prince became patriarch. During his term in office the Sanhedrin was moved to Tiberias.

In most of the semiautonomous academies of the land, and in all the academies of Babylonia, the Mishnah of Rabbi Judah the Prince became the prime text of learning. A living book, a tanna, would speak a passage. "All Israel have a portion in the world to come, for it is written, 'Your people are all righteous; they shall inherit the land forever, the branch of My planting, the work of My hands, that I may be glorified.' " He would pause. Master and disciples would engage in discussion. "What of the righteous among the nations of the world?" someone might ask. "Do they not have a portion in the world to come?" The master might explain that the Mishnah does not come to exclude the pious heathen but to teach us that even Israelites executed by a court of law have a share in the world to come. "How do we know this?" a disciple would certainly inquire. Because the Mishnah follows a lengthy section that deals with four modes of execution, the master will respond.

Then, at a signal from the master, the tanna would utter another passage. "But the following have no portion therein: He who maintains that resurrection is not a Biblical doctrine, the Torah was not divinely revealed, and an epikoros. Rabbi Akiva added: 'One who reads noncanonical books.' "

The tanna stops. The master turns to the disciples. "How is resurrection derived from the Torah?" someone might ask. "What does Rabbi Akiva mean?" someone else might ask. "That noncanonical books may not be read in public or may not even be studied alone?" "What does the Mishnah mean by epikoros?" a third might ask. "A follower of the Epicurean philosophy or one who disparages the Bible and its adherents?"

At the same time, in another academy, a tanna might be reciting the words of a different Mishnah, "From what time in the evening may the Shema [prayer] be recited?" And the discussion of the text might begin immediately with the question of a quick-minded disciple. "Why does the Mishnah start with the evening and not the morning prayer?"

Again the notes of the students begin to accumulate.

Alexander Severus was murdered by mutineers during a campaign against the Germans in 235 C.E. The empire plunged into fifty years of anarchy.

Who was king? Who was not king? During the next fifty years eighteen emperors, made and unmade by different legions, ruled Rome. Three died natural deaths.

Parthians pressed upon the eastern borders; Teutonic peoples invaded and could not be repelled. Life in towns and villages grew insecure. The economy of the empire deteriorated. The great roads leading to Rome were unsafe. The endless civil wars, battles between legions for favored commanders, and the wars along the frontiers resulted in crushing increases in taxation. Many began to leave Palestine for distant Jewish communities.

There were great scholars in the land—Simeon ben Lakish, Hanina, Yannai, and others—but the iridescence of original creativity was gone now. The land seemed weary, ill. Even the weather had altered its pattern. The rains diminished. There were drought and famine. Disease and poverty invaded the land like starved nomads. In Persia a new dynasty rose to power, the Sassanid. All through the middle decades of the third century Rome and Persia were at war. A Roman emperor, Valerian, was taken prisoner by the Persians and died in captivity.

Antioch was sacked a number of times. Goths were raiding Thrace and Asia Minor.

In 274 C.E. the emperor Aurelian, searching for a way to unify the weary empire, introduced a sober-minded worship of the sun. He took the sun to be a universal god of whom all local cults were individual manifestations. Rome was groping toward monotheism. Diocletian became emperor in 284 C.E. and brought some stability to the empire and a temporary end to its civil wars.

In 313 C.E. Christianity was recognized by the emperor Constantine as the official religion of Rome. The successor of Constantine, his son Constantius, regarded the Jews as a "despicable sect." That term would soon become a permanent addition to the vocabulary of western man.

In 364 C.E. the brothers Valentinian and Valens amicably divided between them the empire of Rome. Valentinian took Italy and the districts in the west; Valens received all the provinces in the east.

The patriarchate in Palestine remained an important institution until the end of the fourth century. But it angered the church to have a semiautonomous Jewish body in somewhat regal guise occupying a seat of honor and power in Palestine. The last patriarch was Rabban Gamaliel VI. When he died sometime around 425 C.E. the patriarchate was abolished by the emperor. The Sanhedrin came to an end.

The accumulation of Palestinian discussions and interpretations centering around the Mishnah of Rabbi Judah was collected and put down in writing during the decades preceding and following the turn of the fifth century. Much of the compiling and editing was done by scholars in Tiberias. The final work contains two centuries of Palestinian rabbinic thought. Tales, parables, homilies, and strikingly imaginative interpretations of Biblical verses for the teaching of ethical behavior were also collected and edited in separate volumes about this time. The scholars of this era have come to be known as the amoraim, expositors. Their legal discussions, together with the Mishnah, are known in published form as the Palestinian or the Jerusalem Talmud. It was all done hurriedly, as if they knew they were running out of time. The last two of the six divisions of the Mishnah—*Sacred Matters* and *Purifications*—have no additional material at all, and parts of other tractates are missing.

In the cold distant north the endless migrations and raids of tribesmen from the darkness of northern Europe and Asia continued to batter against the borders of the empire. Northern Gaul was taken by the Franks between 406 and 419 C.E. A smaller tribe called the Burgundians took eastern Gaul. In 408 C.E. the Visigothic chieftain Alaric penetrated into central Italy, demanding and receiving tribute; in 410 he sacked Rome. In 451 the Romans beat back the terrifying incursion of Attila the Hun. That was the final great victory of Roman arms.

Britain fell to Saxons, Picts, and Scots. Central France and Provence were divided between the Franks and Goths. In 455 C.E. Rome was invaded from the sea by the Vandals and so violently plundered that it became a semiruin.

In 476 C.E. a German captain of mercenaries named Odoacer mutinied, killed the ruler of Rome, Orestes, deposed his son, Romulus Augustulus, and declared himself king of Italy. Few noticed this at the time, for Italy had long ceased to matter as a power in the west. Historians now mark that date as the end of the western Roman empire.

Eastern Rome continued to rule at Constantinople. The law code of Justinian originated there in the following century. The empire of eastern Rome became a Greek kingdom with a Roman law code and a Christian faith.

There was a Jewish community and an academy of learning in Rome all during this time of chaos, but we know almost nothing about it. Alexandrian Jewry, decimated by the revolt of 115 C.E. against Trajan, had never recovered its old vitality. Egyptian Jewry too had not overcome the cost in blood exacted from it by Roman legions for its participation in that same revolt. There may have been small Jewish communities in Spain and Gaul, but their activities are concealed behind dreamy folk tales. Palestinian Jewry was in decline.

Along the Tigris and Euphrates, in the forgotten land

of Sumer from which a patriarch had once wandered to a promised land, lived the only remaining vital Jewish community in the world.

Now scholars were the wanderers.

We know very little about the Babylonian Jewish community from the time the exiles left in 538 B.C.E. to rebuild the temple until the coming of the Parthians about four centuries later. Jews were well treated by the Parthians, rose high in government, and were an autonomous cultural unit.

For reasons that are not entirely clear, the Jews of Babylonia did not participate in the Maccabean wars or in the 66-70 C.E. revolt against Rome. They had not anticipated the burning of the temple. The Jewish historian Josephus carefully explained to his readers that the fire was set by a zealous soldier "hurried on by a certain divine fury" and not at the order of Titus: the Romans had no wish to have a raging Babylonian Jewry rising in revolt.

Until the destruction of the temple most of Babylonian Jewry had been outside the sphere of influence of Pharisaic Judaism. As a result of the Bar Kochba revolt, a number of disciples fled from Palestine to Babylonia. Some remained and educated the first of the native-born-and-raised scholars of Babylonia. These scholars and their disciples maintained strong contacts with the academies in Palestine. In most of the cities of Babylonia, Jews were a well-organized minority community. They were proud of the purity of their lineage. Learning was somewhat shallow; traditions were diffused, localized. The leader of the Jewish community took eagerly to the idea of a single authoritative work—the revealed oral law codified in the Mishnah of Rabbi Judah the Prince—that would serve all of Babylonian Jewry. He welcomed Palestinian scholars who were eager to enforce the Torah as understood in the Pharisaic tradition. He used them to create a strong central administration for the Jewish community.

After the Bar Kochba revolution, Palestine and Babylonia were connected not only by geography—by the ranges of hills upon which beacons could be lighted to signal that the New Moon had been sanctified in Palestine and all festivals in Babylonia were to be celebrated accordingly—but also by the transmitted learning of generations of Palestinian sages. We do not know how many Jews lived in Babylonia at this time. Josephus writes that they were of "countless myriads of which none can know the number."

By the time of Rabbi Judah the Prince there were probably about a million Jews in Babylonia. Now messengers were traveling from Palestine to Babylonia to announce the New Moon, for the Samaritans had taken to lighting beacon fires to deceive the Jews. Eight centuries had passed since the destruction of Jerusalem by the Babylonians, and most of the Jews of that exile had maintained their identity and purity of lineage. They had a highly developed and well-organized community, with schools, synagogues, courts, charitable institutions. There were Jews in offices of government and in large commercial institutions. The leader of the Jewish community, the exilarch, an office initiated by the Parthians about 100 C.E., was the political representative of the Jews to the royal court, a major figure in government circles. Most Jews were poor. But everyone was poor then save the very few who were extremely rich. Jews were engaged in agriculture and crafts. They were farmers, shopkeepers, clerks, middlemen, cattle dealers, sailors, peddlers. Taxes were very high, and the result of nonpayment was slavery. Life was not without joy, especially during festivals.

In 219 C.E., about two years after the death of Rabbi Judah the Prince, a man named Abba returned to Babylonia from Palestine. He had spent many years in the academy of Rabbi Judah the Prince and was a young scholar of extraordinary ability. The exilarch appointed him an inspector of markets. He began to travel throughout the country. In time people would come to call him, simply, Rav—master.

His journeys through Babylonia caused him to realize that there was a crucial need for additional institutions of higher education. He chose a region almost entirely neglected by scholars, and there he founded a school in a town about fifty miles north of the ancient Sumerian city of Ur.

The town was called Sura. It was located on the rich soil of southern Babylonia where the Euphrates branches into two tributaries. Fields yielded wheat and barley. There were vineyards and orchards. Some of the farmers of Sura tended their fields and came to listen to the words of Rav.

The academy of Sura is the first bet midrash, house of higher learning, we know about with certainty in Babylonia; there may have been others founded by the scholars who fled Palestine during the 132 C.E. revolt, but we know little about them. The inhabitants of Sura were not familiar with Pharisaic Jewish laws until the coming of Rav. He trained thousands of students. He opened a court; its legal decisions affected profoundly the life of Babylonian Jewry. He taught law, preached sermons, established firmly the authority of the Mishnah of Rabbi Judah the Prince, opened the world of that Mishnah to scholarly discussion, and created the momentum for the future generations of Babylonian Jewish scholarship that would one day produce the extraordinary, unique, and quite indefinable literary creation we call the Babylonian Talmud.

In 224 C.E. the ruling house of the Parthians, the Arsacids, was abruptly displaced by another Persian royal family, the Sassanids. The alliance, centuries old, between Persia and Babylonian Jewry came to an end.

The Sassanids were of a priestly family, fierce in their devotion to the classic gods of Persia. The ancient fire-worshiping religion, Zoroastrianism, became the official religion of the new state. That state was bent on restoring the political and religious glory of the days of Darius. "The bond is broken," Rav commented sadly when the Sassanids came to power.

Jewish life in Babylonia now entered upon centuries of uncertainty as different rulers set conflicting and often contradictory policies concerning the degree of autonomy to be given the Jews in the running of their religious and civic affairs. "Let the law of the government be binding," said Samuel, another scholar, who may have been a disci-

ple of Rabbi Judah the Prince and had opened an
academy in Babylonia. He was referring to imperial
decrees of taxation, which Palestinian Jewry had refused
to accept as legitimate. He urged political submissiveness
as part of the religious way of life. In all other matters of
civil law, Jews were instructed to bring their cases only to
Jewish courts.

Christians and other religious groups were severely persecuted by the Sassanid priests; the extent of Jewish persecution is unclear. Often the Sassanid kings protected the
Jews against their own priests. We know of at least one
instance of mass martyrdom as a result of persecution by
the Magi, the priests, of Ahura Mazda, god and creator,
pure good, sovereign knowledge. His opponent god, with
whom he was locked in eternal battle, was Ahriman, pure
evil. Zoroastrianism seemed uncertain about the outcome
of the conflict between the two gods.

Through it all the rabbis continued to teach, great
academies of learning were opened and attracted thousands of students, and a unique institution was developed,
the kalla. Rav wanted more than an academy for scholars; he saw the need to reach masses of people. In the
early spring and fall of every year, when there was little
work to be done in the fields, he held a kalla, a study assembly—month-long gatherings in which thousands of
Jews from all over Babylonia participated. Alumni whose
work kept them away from the academy for long periods
of time during the year would spend an entire month with
their teacher in the spring and fall: Adar, February-
March, and Elul, August-September. Mostly they studied
the Mishnah; the text had become inviolate for all of Babylonian Jewry. And the festival seasons that followed
were reserved for the masses of Jews. They would stream
into Sura, inundating the town, sometimes making it impossible for all to be housed. They too studied the
Mishnah and also listened to popular lectures.

Samuel was the second of the great native-born Babylonian scholars. He was an astronomer, a folk doctor, and
a teacher of the law. He founded an academy in his home
town of Nehardea, upriver from Sura and not far from today's Baghdad. It was the seat of the exilarch. The Jews

of Nehardea—it was almost entirely inhabited by Jews—believed that when the Presence of God left the burning first temple it settled in the synagogue they built with the earth and stones of Jerusalem which they had taken with them into exile. After the death of Rav in 247 C.E., Nehardea became the most important center of learning in Babylonia until its destruction in 259 C.E.

An academy of learning was founded in the city of Pumbedita along the Euphrates, a few miles northwest of Nehardea. Until the middle of the fourth century that school and its court of law served as the central religious authority for all of Babylonian Jewry. Pumbedita was a large commercial city. The scholars of that academy were given to special sharpness of mind and casuistry. "They could draw an elephant through the eye of a needle," the Talmud says.

Two of these scholars, Abbaye and Rava, were the Pumbedita counterparts to Hillel and Shammai in their zeal to disagree with each other over almost everything. When Abbaye was young he would water his fields in the night to enable him to study Torah in the day. Later he became a wine merchant. Rava established an academy in Mahoza, a town on the Tigris situated along a major caravan route. The Jews were farmers and merchants. They ate well, drank much wine, and were inclined to hedonism. The women were somewhat indolent and overly jeweled. Rava owned fields and vineyards. When he taught he emphasized logical reasoning and inference.

I remember the hours I used to spend as a child marveling at Abbaye and Rava, the agility of their minds, the nimble way they responded to insuperable problems of law, contradictions between various texts of a Mishnah, conflicting traditions attributed to the same individual. "Abbaye said. . . . Rava said. . . . Abbaye said. . . . Rava said. . . ." How many thousands of times I must have spoken those words during my years in the yeshivas I attended.

There were other academies in the land during these centuries. But they lived in the shadows of Sura and Pumbedita. Disciples wandered from school to school, searching for masters to their liking, remaining for a while, wandering on—until they found one with whom they could live and from whose hands they wished to receive ordination.

Some of the scholars at Sura, under the leadership of Rav Ashi, head of the academy, began to assemble and edit the mass of material that had accumulated as a result of the decades of discussion on the Mishnah. There is an old tradition—much debated by modern scholars—to the effect that Rav Ashi worked on that material for more than fifty years, from 375 to 427. At each kalla session the accumulated material belonging to a specific Mishnah was examined orally and given shape and order. This enabled him over the years to systematize the vast accumulation of interpretations that had taken place over the past generations of Babylonian Jewry. He is reported to have gone through his material twice, an astonishing achievement.

His labors were continued by the last of the Babylonian amoraim, Ravina II, who was head of the Sura academy during the final years of the fifth century. Redactors brought together the remembered argumentation of anonymous schoolmen discussing the views of the great masters—the leisurely flow of disputation linked together more by a stream-of-consciousness association between subjects than by the sense of structure we are accustomed to seeing in the writings of the Greeks, a sheer Talmudic delight in meandering legal conversation that may have been the Jewish reaction to the rigidity of Roman law. These redactors also left us seemingly disconnected comments by the rabbis on Mishnaic passages as well as pieces of conversation engaged in by the rabbis as they walked along a road, went through a marketplace, moved among the people; the rabbis take on the appearance not only of teachers but also of wonder-workers, healers, mystics—somewhat similar in function, though certainly not in faith, to the Magi.

We do not know who these redactors were or what criteria they used to make their selections; nor do we know clearly how discussions in the academies were preserved and transmitted through the generations. Two additional generations of rabbis—they are called saboraim, explainers—are traditionally believed to have completed the task of editing. Modern scholarship has been gradually uncovering the complex nature of this centuries' long editing process.

The Babylonians had more time and suffered little persecution, and so their work is livelier, richer, more elaborate, more voluminous, more diffuse—the spoken word set down in writing—more casuistic than its Palestinian counterpart. Its language is eastern Aramaic, a dialect somewhat different from the western Aramaic of the Palestinian Talmud. With only a few exceptions, the Babylonian scholars left us none of their discussions on the first and sixth divisions of the Mishnah—*Seeds* and *Purifications*. Perhaps they found those divisions not entirely pertinent to their own way of life and expended little energy analyzing them. The Palestine-created Mishnah of Rabbi Judah the Prince had been tested in the exile—and most of it worked.

The Babylonian Talmud contains not only legal sections but vast amounts of material born of the flow of the unleashed imagination spinning itself out in zestful and joyous meanderings through verses of the Bible: folk superstitions, astrology, preoccupations with demons, here and there a hint of the doings of magic. These are the aggadic or midrashic portions of the Talmud, much of it originating in Palestine—aggadah is one-sixth of the Palestinian Talmud—the nonlegal, narrative sections that are like windows of dancing light through the solid columns of reasoning that are the halachic sections of a Talmudic text. Their intent is to teach man the ways of God through the faculty of the imagination. They comprise about one-third of the Babylonian Talmud and were always a source of embarrassment to my teachers. We would skip them, and go on worshiping God through the faculty of the mind.

The Babylonian Talmud contains about two and one-half million words on 5894 folio pages. Our goal as students was to master all of this precious literature, the Babylonian Talmud. And any of our people who had not the time or the ability for Talmud had other literature to study: the Mishnah without its amoraic discussions or the many anthologies of parables and homilies. From these anthologies he would learn of the things that preceded the creation of the world: the Torah, the Throne of God, repentance, the Garden of Eden, Gehennom. He would learn that the Master of the Universe first created light and did this by wrapping about Himself a white prayer shawl and letting the radiance of His glory shine from one end of the world to the other. He would learn that the trees and grasses were created for the pleasure of man; that every creature was given life for a purpose, that each fulfills some task given it by the Holy One Blessed Be He, even the frog, even the mosquito. He would learn that before the Master of the Universe created man He consulted with His council of angels. They were divided in their opinions, quarreled long among themselves. The Holy One Blessed Be He went along and created man—then said, "Why are you all still discussing the matter? Man has already been created!" He would learn that when the Master of the Universe created Eve, He dressed her as a bride and brought her to Adam. He would learn that the serpent grew wild with jealousy when he saw the angels of God ministering to Adam in the Garden of Eden, that the sun set after the apple was eaten and the darkness filled Adam and Eve with dread until the sun rose and they realized that this was the nature of the world; that the Holy One Blessed Be He patiently warned evil mankind for one hundred and twenty years before He unleashed the Flood; that there were ten generations from Noah to Abraham, and the Holy One Blessed Be He spoke to no one until Abraham; that Abraham taught himself the entire Torah while he was yet a child; that during the years Abraham lived in Haran he would invite passers-by to his tent, feed them and show them love and convert them and bring them beneath the wings of the Holy Presence; that when Isaac was born all the universe rejoiced, the heavens and earth, the sun and moon, the stars and constellations; that Sarah cast out Hagar and Ishmael because one day she saw Ishmael build an altar and hunt locusts and sacrifice them to idols; that Abraham rose very early to bring his only son to be sacrificed so as to slip away unnoticed by Sarah; that Satan tried repeatedly to thwart him as he journeyed to the sacrificial mountain but was overcome each time by the determination of the patriarch; that Isaac carried the wood for the altar as one who carries his own cross on his shoulders; that as Abraham was about to slaughter his son, the Holy One Blessed Be He appeared to His angels and parted the heavens, and Isaac raised up his eyes and saw the chambers of the Chariot and was terrified, and the angels stood in rows lamenting and weeping and saying to one another, See one slaughters and one is slaughtered. Master of the Universe! What will become of Your promise to multiply his seed? Immediately the Holy One Blessed Be He said to the angel Michael: Why do you wait? Restrain him! And on the day when Abraham our father died, all the great nations of the world stood in the line of mourners and said: Woe to the world that has lost its leader! And woe to the ship that has lost its captain!

And if he continues to read he will discover that Jacob and Esau fought one another while still in their mother's womb. Whenever Rebekah passed a synagogue or a house of study Jacob would push to get out; whenever she passed a pagan temple Esau would attempt to thrust his way out; that Esau grew up evil, a hunter, and in a flippant moment of ravenous hunger threw away his birthright and the Holy One Blessed Be He helped Jacob receive the blessing from his old and blind father by sending Satan out to delay Esau in his hunt for the food Isaac had requested. He would learn of the flight of the fearful Jacob and the wiliness of Laban, of the loveliness of Leah and the modesty of Rachel, of their children and the death of Rachel. Why did Jacob bury Rachel in Ephrath? Because he saw in a vision that all the exiles would pass by there, and he buried her along the road so she could weep and plead for mercy for her exiled children. . . .

Now in Babylonia in the latter half of the fifth century of our era much of the Jewish population of Isfahan, a city on the route from Teheran to the Persian Gulf, was slaughtered on a charge of killing two Magian priests. An exilarch was slain by a Sassanid king. In 468 C.E. many synagogues throughout the land were destroyed, children were abducted into the Mazdean priesthood, the study of Torah was prohibited.

Persecutions continued into the next century. There was a respite of nearly fifty years under the monarch Noshirwan, from 531 to 579 C.E. Then the Sassanid dynasty found itself in a disastrous war with the Byzantine empire, the still intact Hellenized Christian sister of dismembered Rome. In the following century there was a long war between the Sassanids and Byzantium. The Persians took Jerusalem in 624 C.E. and invaded Egypt. Jews served in the Persian armies fighting the Byzantines. Local Palestinian Jewry, persecuted under the rule of Byzantium, welcomed the Persians. Jerusalem was retaken. In 628 C.E. the Sassanids were defeated.

In the end the incessant efforts of the Byzantines and Persians to expand their empires mattered little. Deep in the world of endless sand and sun nomadic tribes of central Arabia had achieved political unity and became the bearers of a burning religious vision. Now they exploded northward upon the world. In 634 C.E. they invaded Palestine. In 636 they took Syria. In 637 they overwhelmed the Sassanids. In 638 they captured Jerusalem. In 641 they invaded Egypt. In 647 they captured Alexandria. These were Arab Muslims. They were already in possession of the sacred words of their prophet Mohammed. They had no need for the writings of pagans. They burned the libraries of Alexandria.

# BOOK THREE

*Through Islam and Christianity*

# ISLAM

## Nightingales in a Sandstorm

I was taught when I was young that the Arabs burned the libraries of Alexandria. You will find it repeated today in scholarly works: they destroyed much of the recorded heritage of a thousand years of pagan creativity.

We have some notion of the treasures that were lost because the authors of works that somehow survived the millennia that separate us from the classical world are constantly citing works and authors that no longer exist. We have ghosts—the mention of a title, the name of an author, a fragmentary passage quoted and given disembodied life in the eternal limbo of another's creation to which it owes its incidental existence. We gaze in anguish at the ruin of a world.

Somehow we would expect them to have done that; the act fits the picture we have been given of those sword-waving, monotheistic, fanatic nomads who moved like a blinding sandstorm across the world from the scorched moonscapes of the Arabian peninsula. They had their God, Allah; they had their prophet, Mohammed; they had their sacred book, the Koran. What need was there for the writings of the barbaric unfaithful? And so they fed the furnaces of the many bathhouses of Alexandria for six months with the seven hundred thousand scrolls in those libraries.

But there is something odd about that story of burning. The great libraries were no longer part of the urban landscape of Alexandria when the Arabs captured the city. During the fighting that took place in Alexandria in 47 B.C.E. between the armies of Pompey and Julius Caesar, the great Ptolemaic Library went up in flames. A later li-

brary, known as the Daughter Library, was destroyed at
the order of Emperor Theodosius I about 390 C.E.—a pious act of purging by a realm newly come to Christianity.
Scholars now tell us that what caught fire in the fighting
between Caesar and Pompey was not the Ptolemaic Library but probably a quayside dump of books for export.
If so, then it was Theodosius I who burned the libraries,
with some possible help earlier from the emperor Aurelian, who crushed a revolt in Alexandria about 273 C.E.
that had been instigated by a Greek merchant named Fir-
mus, razed the walls of the city, and no doubt caused
some damage to the libraries. The walls were rebuilt.

One morning in 641 C.E. an Arab army approached the
walls and towers and stood gazing at the city's temples, at
the cathedral of Saint Mark, at the two red granite
needles erected by Pharaoh Thutmose III, the New Kingdom empire builder who took Gaza and Megiddo and advanced with his armies to the banks of the Euphrates. "I
have captured a city," read the message of the triumphant Arab commander to the caliph, "from the de-
scription of which I shall refrain. Suffice it to say that I
have seized therein four thousand villas, with four thousand baths, forty thousand head-tax-paying Jews, and
four hundred places of entertainment for the royalty."

The city rebelled and had to be taken again in 647 C.E.
This time the walls were torn down. Perhaps the angered
Arabs now burned some small library that had been built
since the time of Theodosius. We do not know.

An Arab historian named Abd-al-Latif al-Baghdadi,
who died in 1231, appears to have been the originator of
the library-burning tale. Why? No one seems to know.
Perhaps he was a pious Muslim chronicler who wrote
what he believed ought to have taken place. He invented
a moment of history—as did the Hebrew author of the
Books of Chronicles when he reversed the clear truth of a
passage in the Book of Kings and wrote that Hiram of
Tyre gave cities to Solomon. Perhaps both chroniclers
sought to express fully their deepest vision of the will of
God.

This much is certain. Sometime in the early centuries
of the common era a new theme was being added to the

history of our species. Now the ashes of books would become, together with the remains of men, part of the crust of the earth upon which we tread.

The very Muslims to whom legend attributes the burning of pagan books built some of the finest libraries in the time that followed the collapse of paganism. They filled those libraries with pagan works translated into their own language, Arabic, the tongue of the angels, the sacred medium for the word of Allah revealed to Mohammed—the name is also spelled Mahomet or Muhammad—and transcribed in the Koran. The word Koran means récitation, discourse, lecture.

When I was very young I was told by a white-bearded man I revered that Muslims were desert barbarians who had somehow stumbled upon the God of our fathers and had taken Him for themselves, distorting His worship to suit their whims. This man, gentle and very old, was deeply pious and sealed within the world of Torah. Beyond that world lay the poison fruit of alien civilizations. How easily we label unknown worlds barbaric. Everyone is a barbarian to someone.

Islam did not originate in the deserts of the Arabian peninsula but in one of its cities. Mohammed was not a wilderness nomad but an urban merchant. Early in the seventh century, at the same time that he was experiencing his revelations, the editing of the Talmud was being completed in the academies of Babylonia. For the next three hundred years, as Arabs conquered much of the pagan and Christian world for Islam, the heads of the academies of Sura and Pumbedita conquered much of the Jewish world for the Babylonian Talmud.

The greatest of these academic leaders was Saadia Gaon, who was born in Egypt in 882 C.E. and was appointed to the academy in Pumbedita in 922 C.E. He was a scholar both of Torah and of the secular sciences. In 928 C.E. he became head of the faltering academy in Sura. He was a man of enormous learning and energy, impossible to intimidate and with no inclination to bow to the political authority of the exilarch when he thought it was wrongly used. There were quarrels between him and the exilarch. During the period of forced retirement that followed, Saadia wrote his philosophic work, *The Book of Doctrines and Beliefs*. Aristotle, Plato, and the Stoics haunt the treatise like benevolent shades as the author presents his theories of the universe, of knowledge, his doctrine of the soul, his concept of divine revelation. It is Judaism interpreted in the light of reason. "It may be asked," he wrote, "how we can undertake to pursue knowledge by means of speculation and inquiry with the object of attaining mathematical certainty seeing that our people reject this manner of speculation as leading to unbelief and the adoption of heretical views. Our answer is that only the ignorant speak in this way. . . ." The book was written in Arabic, which had by then replaced Greek and Aramaic as the language of daily affairs.

Earlier he had written extensively on the subject of Hebrew grammar. He wrote handbooks of Jewish law. He translated the Bible from Hebrew into Arabic, often translating freely, paraphrasing entire chapters, in order to make the work intelligible to the average reader. He wrote commentaries on Biblical books. He composed magnificent liturgical poetry in Hebrew, as well as philosophical poems. He established the genres, one might say, of all the future centuries of traditional Jewish literary creativity. He was the first great literary figure produced by the second civilization of the Jews.

He spent much of his time polemicizing against and beating back a powerful eruption of schismatics known as Karaites, people of the Scriptures, that came into being at the start of the eighth century. These Jews—many of them scholars, theologians, and grammarians from Persia and Jerusalem—recognized only Scriptures as the source of religious law and regarded rabbinic oral law as without foundation. In essence they denied the validity of a thousand years of Jewish creativity, and were bitterly attacked by Saadia and other geonim. (We do not know when or why the title gaon, plural geonim, came into use for the head of an academy. The word means excellence.) The geonim made the Babylonian Talmud the authoritative literature of rabbinic Judaism. They were the highest rabbinic authorities of Babylonia from about the end of the sixth to the middle of the eleventh centuries. They wrested authority from the weakened rabbinate of Palestine; it was to the academies of Sura and Pumbedita that Jews all over the world directed their questions in letters and sent their contributions. The replies of the geonim to these inquiries concerning legal and ritual matters—often they were read out at a kalla—form a responsa library consisting of tens of thousands of letters. Saadia died in 942 C.E.

The Arabs were then experiencing the same process of law by letter. The still undeveloped Mohammedan law with its many traditions made it necessary that questions be directed to experts in each community. These experts issued responsa, usually brief answers to questions, law given in correspondence. The expert was called a mufti.

It would be expected that Jewish civilization, which had faced westward toward Greece and Rome for so many centuries, would now turn back to its Semitic home and enter the new umbrella civilization of Fertile Crescent Islam. But that was not what occurred. The creative energies of Babylonian Jewry went into decline after the year 1000. The Babylonian Talmud had made a safe sea journey and was now the possession of the two major Jewish communities of Europe. We shall discuss these communities later. One originated in Spain, the other in parts of what is today France and Germany. For the next five hundred years these Jewries would undergo diverse experiences and emerge similar in many ways and at the same time so much a reflection of their separate geographies and culture confrontations as almost to be two distinct peoples.

A vast segment of the second civilization of the Jews confronted Islam upon soil alien to both Jew and Muslim. On the third and most distant peninsula of the Mediterranean world, in the glittering castles and villas of Spain, amid private libraries, splendid conversation, and political intrigue, these two civilizations met in a core-to-core confrontation, and at the same time confronted together the core of Greek civilization. Out of that iridescent mingling came gold that is still being mined today.

\*    \*    \*

Sand, swords, desert poets, and the songs of birds were in
the mixture that produced the gold. Their origins were in
Arabia, the largest peninsula in the world, a little more
than one million square miles of white and red sand, huge
volcanic tracts of corrugated lava, a jagged ridge of
mountains that parallel its west coast, and deep scars that
are the land's network of wadis. Occasional winter rains
cover the northern desert—a wasteland sparsely jeweled
by oases—with a gossamer coat of young grass quickly
nibbled by the sheep and camels of the Bedouin. The
southern desert too—six hundred miles of terrifying
reddish sand, more than twice the size of its northern
counterpart and void of oases—receives brief rains, and
the Bedouin lives upon it during its few verdant months
before the summer sun scorches its surface and drains it
of life.

The Bedouin of the north, who had no writing until
just before Mohammed, seems indigenous to the desert,
his origins lost even to the reaches of myth, saga, and folk
tale. Some of the peoples in the southern regions of the
peninsula—Sabeans and their famous merchant, the
queen of Sheba; Mineans and others; civilizations that
have left inscriptions on tablets of bronze and temples to
Astarte and the sun; civilizations that were commercial
and not military in nature, that came to an end at the
close of the fifth century of our era, and about which we
know almost nothing—some of these southern peoples
may have originated in Africa. So the archaeologists and
anthropologists tell us as they gaze upon the shapes of
skulls.

It is in so many ways the cruelest of lands, dry, hot,
without a single river of any importance, with no navigable bodies of water, with systematic cultivation of the
soil possible only in valleys near its southwestern corner
and in the occasional oasis with subterranean streams. Its
eastern and western seas are too narrow to send across
the land sufficient moisture to break its African heat; and
the southern ocean, though it brings rain, has its cool
touch withered by hot seasonal winds.

The harsh desert yields various trees whose ability to
store water or send roots deep into the dead soil for un-

derground moisture was once explained to me during a
Sinai trek by an Israeli with a passion for the desert.
There are various species of acacia, including the tama-
risk. There is the grape vine. The oases grow apples, al-
monds, oranges, watermelons, pomegranates, lemons,
bananas. The date-yielding palm tree is regal both in appearance and in the regard accorded it by the Arab.
Dates and camel meat are the only staple solid food of
the Bedouin. The land has leopards, panthers, hyenas,
wolves, foxes, and lizards. There are eagles, falcons, and
hawks. Lions are extinct. Crows are plentiful. There are
locusts, which the Bedouin roasts and eats with much
pleasure; there are vipers and snakes; there are pigeons
and larks; there are nightingales.

Arab desert existence appears unthinkable without the
camel. The Bedouin drinks its milk, eats its meat, burns
its dung for fuel, uses its skin and hair to make clothes
and tents, and its urine as medicine and hair tonic. The
camel is the gift of Allah. It can go without water for
about twenty-five days in the winter and five days in the
summer. A Bedouin brought to a halt by a violent sandstorm or caught up in some emergency can thrust a
branch down the throat of a camel and find its regurgi-
tated water drinkable if it is not older than a day or two.
There are about a thousand names for the camel in Arabic, almost as many synonyms as are used for the sword.

The geography of the land penetrated deeply into the
grain of the thin culture of its inhabitants. Little in the
deserts of Arabia encouraged sedentary existence; the
wanderer developed a cultural world of his own. Jews and
Christians who entered the peninsula during the early centuries of the common era settled in the few oases of the
land and cultivated the soil. The Bedouin remained a
wanderer. His goal was pastureland for the flocks of
sheep and goats that kept him alive. He was as lean and
sinewy as the sparse desert through which he moved. His
clothes were scanty: a long shirt, a belt, a flowing upper
garment, a head shawl held to his brow by a cord. His
concern was for his own welfare and the needs of his
family, clan, and tribe. The tribe, united by blood and the
common ancestor whose name it bore, was led by its

sheik, who was senior in age, took counsel with elders, and was exemplary in courage and generosity. He was not a king. He remained sheik as long as he retained the respect of the tribe.

Hunger made brigandage an institution of Bedouin culture; hence the razzia, the lightning raid upon a neighboring tribe or village, whose purpose was plunder with a minimal shedding of blood. Christian tribes of the Arabian desert also practiced it with no hesitation. A poet who lived during the early period of Islamic conquest writes: "Our business is to make raids on the enemy, on our neighbor and on our brother, in case we find none to raid but a brother."

Together with the manliness and fortitude that accompanied the deadly game of razzia went the gentleness and grace of Bedouin hospitality. The sparsity of pasturage and water splintered the peoples of the desert into warring tribes; the sense of helplessness in their daily confrontation with the indifferent face of nature made of hospitality a duty invested with sanctity. You gave shelter and food to another because one day you might need another's shelter and food. In a land without public inns every man's tent was a beckoning haven against the relentless heat and aridity of the long season of the sun.

In the century before the coming of Islam the tribes of the peninsula were caught up in a series of wars caused by border disputes, arguments over cattle, water holes, pasturelands, and petty personal insults. There was much single combat, plundering, and raiding. Legends and poetry tell of that century and its heroes in a manner not unlike the tales that recount the deeds of Achilles.

That was the heroic age of the Arabian peninsula, a time of widespread disorder, individual prowess, and oral poetry. The Arabians created no art form save speech, eloquence, the flow of language from the tongue. To these sons of the desert the weaver of language seemed possessed of unique grace and power. The poet, the orator or tribal spokesman, and the soothsayer were able to sway hearts and minds with words and appeared to command an exceptional gift, one that could at times strengthen or weaken the wielder of sword or bow. Often the poet himself was the oracle, guide, and spokesman of his tribe, its historian, the possessor of its collective wisdom. Poetry, rhythm, rhyme, and music produced effects upon tribesmen that were regarded as lawful magic. The origins of Arabic poetry are uncertain—perhaps the rhymed prose of soothsayers and the song of the camel driver keeping pace with the rhythmic motion of the animal carrying him across the sands.

The Bedouin poetry of the Arabian peninsula, especially the ode, set down in writing about two hundred years after Mohammed, gives the appearance of having sprung suddenly into existence during the century of wars.

Archery, swordsmanship, horsemanship, and eloquence—the ability to express oneself elegantly in prose and poetry—were the marks of the perfect man in the period before Mohammed. Islam would forge these desert qualities into a power that would conquer a world greater in size than the Roman empire.

The pagan Bedouin looked upon arable land as a benevolent deity and dead land as terrifying and demonic. Wells and trees were sacred; they maintained life; they became objects of worship. Caves were the dwelling places of underground deities and were holy. The god of springs and underground water was named Baal.

The high god of the Bedouin was the moon, by whose silver-white light he grazed his flocks and whose benevolence cooled the air and moistened the ground. Once I saw a full moon rise over Arabia on a chill April night; no, it seemed to leap from its underground cavern. The strange magic of optical illusion gave it a sky-filling vastness, and I could sense how it might be worshiped as a god, this life-giving lamp that replaced the killing sun of the day.

Sedentary agriculturists worshiped the sun; the pagan Bedouin worshiped the moon. The desert was filled with demons or jinns. Someone who had gone mad was called *majnun*, one possessed by the jinn.

Along the west coast of Arabia lay a plateau known as al-Hijaz. Al means the, and Hijaz means barrier. The range of mountains south of the Hijaz reaches a height of nearly ten thousand feet. To the east the Hijaz recedes in a languorous decline from its four to five thousand feet of elevation; to the west it plummets steeply to a sandy shoreline about fifteen miles from the green-blue African waters of the Red Sea. The region is plagued with frequent drought, sudden torrential rainstorms of demonic violence, and burning heat. There are a few oases, the largest about ten square miles in size. Five-sixths of the people are nomads.

Mecca was at the time a small oasis town in al-Hijaz. It was located near the western coast of the peninsula. The word Mecca probably means sanctuary. The town of Yathrib lay about three hundred miles to the north of Mecca. In the time of Mohammed it would come to be called al-Medina, the city.

South of al-Hijaz is the coastal region named Yemen. It is the only area of the peninsula where inhabitants can cultivate soil watered by rain rather than by underground streams.

In the centuries before Mohammed, the chief god of Mecca was named Allah. The word Allah—*al-ilah*—means the god. It is an old name and is written in the form HLH in south Arabic inscriptions that date to the fifth century B.C.E. We can recognize the affinity of this south Semitic god to his west Semitic counterpart, El.

There were female deities, the daughters of Allah. Al-Lat was the sun goddess. East of Mecca was the cult of al-Uzza, the most mighty one, Venus, the morning star. Al-Manah was the goddess of destiny. Some worshiped ancient totemic deities like the vulture. The Bedouin buried his dead in the desert in graves piled with stones. We know of no early Bedouin belief in a future life.

In Mecca was the Kabah, a simple primitive structure housing a black meteorite which the Arabs worshiped as a fetish, and to which they brought sacrifices and came on annual pilgrimages. Some also worshiped Allah and the goddesses at the Kabah. The building that housed the sacred meteorite was in the shape of an enclosed square; its name, Kabah, gives us our word for cube.

Allah was the patron deity of the Quraysh, a tribe that made its home in Mecca. His sanctuary, deep in a barren valley, made al-Hijaz the most important religious center in northern Arabia. Mohammed's father was named Abdullah—*abd-Allah*—the slave or worshiper of Allah.

The main caravan route that ran north and south through the Arabian peninsula lay on the Hijaz. The mountain region was a center of pilgrimage and trade. In the nearby northern oases were Christian and Jewish tribes, descendants of those who had fled from Palestine over the centuries as well as indigenous Arabs converted to Judaism and Christianity. Many Arabs at the time were dissatisfied with idol worship but could not bring themselves to take up with either Judaism or Christianity.

Mohammed was born to the Quraysh tribe at Mecca about 571 C.E. His original name is unknown. His tribe called him al-Amin, the believing one. Mohammed, which means highly praised, is the name he bears in the Koran.

His father died before his birth and his mother when he was six. He was raised by a grandfather and, later, by an uncle. Little is known of his early life. He was a caravaneer. At the age of twenty-five he married a wealthy widow fifteen years older than he was, and entered into her thriving affairs. His wife's cousin was a Christian. We know almost nothing about the next fifteen years of Mohammed's life.

There was a cave in a hill outside the city. On occasion Mohammed would seclude himself in its darkness. It was a little cave set in a barren, rocky mountainside.

He was almost forty years old when he received his call. We are told that a voice called to him, "Recite!" The frightened man could not respond and felt himself being strangled. He mustered the strength to ask what it was that he should recite. The commanding voice, that of the angel Gabriel, answered, "Recite!" three times, and then said, "Recite in the name of your Lord who created all things, who created man from clots of blood. . . ." It was night in the month of Ramadan in the year 610 of our era. That night was later named the Night of Power.

The angel told Mohammed that God is one, all-powerful, the creator of the universe. There is a day of judgment for all men. Those who follow the commands of

God are rewarded in a joyous paradise; those who disobey are punished in a frightful hell.

We are further told that Mohammed felt himself possessed by the need to communicate this message. He moved among the people of the town, preaching. He called his faith Islam, after the Arabic word *aslama*, used in the Koran to describe the near-sacrifice of Isaac by Abraham. Scholars say of Islam that it is the religion of complete surrender and submission to the will of Allah. Mohammed was mocked. He warned of doom, spoke of paradise and hell. His wife and a few of his kinsmen were swayed by his passion. One of the kinsmen was named abu-Bakr. Some slaves and members of the lower classes joined his ranks.

He began to preach against the pagan gods. The Umayyad clan were the aristocrats of the Quraysh tribe; their sacred duty and livelihood was the maintenance of al-Kabah, to which pilgrims would flock from everywhere in the peninsula. The growth of Mohammed's following converted their scorn to violence. Followers were threatened, attacked; some fled to Ethiopia.

Mohammed continued to preach in spite of the persecution. He continued to experience revelations. It was during this period that Mohammed is said to have experienced his extraordinary instantaneous journey from al-Kabah to Jerusalem, where he stopped momentarily prior to his ascent—*miraj*—to the seventh heaven. Jerusalem at the time was a Byzantine city, the religious center of the civilized western world and the site of a church that covered the sacred areas of Calvary and the Holy Sepulchre. Its function as a momentary station for this miraculous journey by Mohammed made it the third most sacred city of Islam, after Mecca and Medina.

Almost eleven years after the night in the cave when he experienced his call to prophesy, some members of the Khazraj tribe from the town of Yathrib met Mohammed and were persuaded of the truth of his message. Two years later emissaries of the tribe journeyed to Mecca and invited him to live in Yathrib. The people of Yathrib promised Mohammed and his followers protection. The followers of Mohammed numbered about sixty families.

Over the next two years, the families slipped out of Mecca and made the journey to Yathrib. Apparently Mohammed feared that a mass exodus would come under attack at the hands of his enemies within the Quraysh. He himself arrived in Yathrib on September 24, 622 C.E. That journey is the well-known hegira—*hijrah* in Arabic—and is the year 1 of the Muslim calendar. He left Mecca as a loathed, hated, mocked prophet; he entered Yathrib—I will from now on call it by the name it soon takes on, Medina—as a revered leader, a chief, a powerful arbitrator, a judge, and soon a ruler with religious as well as military and political power.

His group of emigrants was federated with eight major clans from Medina. Jews who were allies of one of these eight clans found themselves included in this arrangement. The clans were called the supporters.

In 624 C.E. Mohammed led three hundred emigrants and supporters in an attack against a summer caravan on the way from Syria to Mecca. The battle occurred about eighty-five miles southwest of Medina. The caravan was protected by a force of over one thousand Meccans. Mohammed proved himself to be as capable with the sword as he was with the word. The Meccan force was defeated. It seems an insignificant razzia, a petty raid in a distant sand-covered corner of the world. But it was the first military victory of Islam and was seen as a miracle and a clear sign from Allah of the truth of His message. In Medina the message in the cave was transformed from a private call to a state religion, a militant Muslim polity.

Ten years went by. The revelations continued. They were committed to memory by professional memorizers. During Mohammed's lifetime verses were set down on stones, palm leaves, on any material that lay at hand. The second successor to Mohammed, the caliph Omar, collected them, and the third, the caliph Othman, published an authoritative version of the work sometime between 644 and 656 C.E. The script has no vowels; variant readings of words are regarded by Muslims as equally authoritative. The work, arranged according to the length of its chapters—the longest come first—lacks chronological sequence. There is apparent universal agreement regarding its literary excellence.

The efforts of Mohammed to persuade the Jewish clans of the region to join him met with failure. To gain their favor he ordered that prayers be directed toward Jerusalem and transformed Friday afternoon into a period of communal gatherings for worship. The Jewish clans persisted in their refusal. He changed the direction of prayer from Jerusalem to Mecca. That marked his break with the Jews. He claimed that Abraham had not been a Jew; that Islam was the true continuation of the religion of Abraham; that Jews and Christians had corrupted the original truth revealed to Abraham by Allah.

In 624 C.E. he besieged a Jewish tribe after a fight in a market had resulted in the death of a Muslim and a Jew. The Jews surrendered and were driven from the city. They were goldsmiths, and they left the peninsula and moved on to Syria. In August 625 C.E. he attacked and defeated the Jewish tribe of Nadir and drove it from Medina. The tribe moved to the oasis of Khaybar, about seventy miles to the north. In the spring of 628 C.E. Mohammed conquered that oasis. The Jews were permitted to continue living there but had to pay a tax of half their produce. That was the year he ended his quarrel with his own tribe, the Quraysh: Muslims and Meccans were now to be treated as equals.

The Jewish tribes attacked by Mohammed had joined his enemies in actively propagandizing against Islam. Jews who had remained neutral were not driven out of Medina.

About two years later, in January 630 C.E., Mohammed led an army of ten thousand men toward Mecca—all the tribes and their allies who had come under the banner of Islam since the year he had journeyed to Medina. There was a minor skirmish. Mecca surrendered. Mohammed entered the city of his birth, smashed its idols—numbering some three hundred and sixty—and forbade pillage. The Kabah was cleansed, purified, and made sacred to Islam; the area around it was declared forbidden, sacrosanct, *haram;* non-Muslims were prohibited from approaching the site of the black stone.

During that same month, January, Mohammed defeated an army of twenty thousand Bedouins in a battle near Mecca. His was now the most powerful army on the Arabian peninsula.

Later that year he concluded alliances with the chief of a Christian tribe and with Jewish tribes in a number of southern oases. The Jews and Christians were taken under the protection of Islam for the payment of *jizyah*, tribute. Only those who were monotheists could pay tribute; defeated pagans were offered Islam or death.

Success in war was for many the measure of the truth of a message. From different parts of Arabia tribes began to send delegates to Mohammed. They made verbal declarations of faith to Islam, paid a *zakah*—poor tax—and allied themselves to Mohammed. They journeyed from as far away as Yemen. The Bedouins came by the thousands.

In March 632 C.E. Mohammed led the pilgrimage to Mecca. When he returned to Medina he took ill. On June 8, 632 C.E., he complained of a severe headache. Later that day he died.

Islam tied together the peoples of the peninsula through faith rather than blood. It transcended tribal allegiances. It offered no priesthood or hierarchy. Wine and gambling were abolished. Idolatry, fornication, bearing false witness, the shedding of blood, exploitation of the widow and orphan, burying alive unwanted newborn girls, deserting one's family—all were forbidden by the words of the sacred book. All Arabians were now either worshipers of Allah or outlaws. The statement of belief in the unity and uniqueness of God and that Mohammed is the prophet of God; personal and communal prayer directed toward Mecca; pilgrimage to the sacred house of Islam in Mecca—the Kabah—at least once during one's life; observance of certain periods of fasting; the payment of a contribution, which later became a tax, to the community or state—these were the five pillars of Islam, the structure of the *Pax Islamica*. About one-third of the peninsula was now united under the banner of Allah. The razzia was forbidden.

Before he died, Mohammed designated his kinsman abu-Bakr to lead prayers in his place. Mohammed left no sons. Few matters would plague Islam more throughout its history than the problem of succession. Muslims would be torn by civil wars and the ruthless slaughter of entire families as the caliphate was transferred from the dead to the living on the points of bloodied swords. In this regard the faith of Allah was little different from that of any other visited upon our species.

Abu-Bakr succeeded Mohammed to the leadership of Islam. He could not be its spiritual successor, for Mohammed was the last of the prophets, the one who had given the world the final true message of God. Abu-Bakr was his caliph, successor, in everything except the function of prophet. He received the oath of allegiance from assembled tribal chiefs.

He proceeded to conquer the remaining two-thirds of the Arabian peninsula for Islam. Within six months his general, Khalid ibn al-Walid, had conquered the tribes of central Arabia. The remainder of the peninsula was quickly subdued. Medina had conquered Mecca; Mecca had conquered al-Hijaz; al-Hijaz had conquered the peninsula.

Arabia was now possessed of a single vast army sworn to the word of Allah as conveyed by his prophet Mohammed. Tens of thousands of tribesmen, who had learned techniques of organized warfare during their conquest of the peninsula, now sensed the power they commanded. Eager to conquer for Islam, hungry for the booty that lay beyond their borders, they turned northward to the green world of the Fertile Crescent. It was the year 633 of our era.

On August 20, 636 c.e., a Byzantine army of fifty thousand men fought an Arab army of about twenty-five thousand men near the Yarmuk River, the eastern tributary of the Jordan. It was a hot day. A furnace wind blew clouds of dust and sand through the air. It was weather made for the soldiers of Islam. The Byzantine army was virtually annihilated. Syria and Palestine were lost to Byzantium. In the spring of 637 c.e., on an eerily similar hot, windblown, dust-filled day, an Arab army defeated a Persian army, and all of Iraq was conquered for Allah.

Omar was caliph then, abu-Bakr having died in 634

C.E. Jerusalem surrendered in 638 C.E. Helena, the mother of the emperor Constantine, had visited the city in 326 C.E. The temple of Venus was destroyed during her visit, and the city was transformed from the pagan Aelia Capitolina to a Christian Jerusalem. Jews were still not permitted to enter the city save on the ninth of Av. Now the aged caliph walked through the streets, visiting the holy places. His beard was untrimmed and his garb was shabby. The Byzantine patriarch of the city remarked in Greek to one of his attendants, "Indeed this is the abomination of desolation mentioned by the prophet Daniel as standing in the holy place."

The Christians had urged that no Jews be allowed to move into the city. The Jews asked Omar for permission to settle two hundred families. The Christian patriarch objected. Omar admitted seventy Jewish families. They were permitted to build a synagogue and an academy. They settled in the quarter southwest of the temple area.

In less than ten years the armies of Islam had broken the Persian empire, brought Byzantium to her knees by reducing her to a tiny remnant of her former greatness, and conquered Alexandria—without burning her libraries. The Arabs had done to Persia and Byzantium what the Teutonic tribes had done to Rome.

In 711 C.E. a Muslim army crossed the narrow body of water separating North Africa from Europe and invaded Spain.

Spanish law at the time regarded the Jews as slaves.

We do not know when Jews first came to Spain. An inscription on a gravestone dated to the third century C.E. has been found in the coastal town of Adra—its ancient name was Abdera—south of Granada, about one hundred fifty miles east of the Muslim invasion site. The period prior to that belongs to folklore and not to history.

The Hebrew word for Spain, Sepharad, apparently comes from the twentieth verse of the one-chapter Biblical book Obadiah: ". . . And the captivity of Jerusalem that is in Sepharad. . . ." There it seems to refer to Sardis in distant Asia Minor. The name subsequently came to be used for the faraway western land we now call

Spain. The Jews of that land and their descendants constitute Sephardic Jewry, one of the two major branches of
the Jewish people. The Muslims called the land Andalus.
The word is connected with the name of the Vandals,
who occupied Spain before the Visigoths.

In the time of Roman rule Jews lived in Spain as pro-
vincials with the same rights of citizenship that had been
granted by Rome to all the inhabitants of the peninsula.
Jews farmed the soil, tended vineyards, possessed olive
plantations, were engaged in commerce. Natives who became Christians appeared unconcerned about dwelling in
the proximity of Jews.

Sometime about the year 305 C.E. a council of Christian clerics assembled in Elvira, a town in Andalusia near
Granada. The main purpose of the council was to formulate ecclesiastical laws that would check worldly influence
on the church and restore discipline to the clerics. Celi-
bacy was introduced. Additional matters were discussed.
Then the council turned its attention to the Jews: Christian women were forbidden to marry Jews unless the Jew
first became a Christian; Jews were prohibited from extending the hospitality of their tables to Christian laymen
and clergy; they could not keep Christian concubines;
they could not bless the fields of Christians. These were
the first laws of any church council against Jews.

Early in the fifth century Spain was invaded by Vandals and Visigoths. The Vandals went on to North Africa.
Under the rule of the Visigoths, Jews and Catholics, as
well as pagans, were subject to the same system of Roman law that had prevailed before the fall of Spain. In
587 C.E. the Visigothic king, Recarred, announced his
conversion to Catholicism. Spain became a Catholic state.

In 589 C.E. the third church council of Toledo ordered
that children born of a marriage between a Jew and a
Christian should be baptized by force. A policy of forced
conversion of all Jews throughout the kingdom was then
initiated. Thousands fled; thousands were converted.
Many of the converted returned to Judaism under a later,
more tolerant ruler.

In the decades that followed, the status of the Jews of
Spain yawed dizzyingly between the extremes of benevo-

lent tolerance and imposition of a choice between conversion or expulsion. The general population appeared to lack the enthusiasm that characterized royal and clerical persecution of the Jews, and so the edicts were difficult to enforce.

In 680 C.E. King Erwig ordered every Jew in the kingdom to accept baptism within a year or be confronted with exile. Nobles too appeared not to share the zeal of their kings on the matter of the Jews, and so the king warned his nobles that they faced heavy fines if they were found helping Jews evade these laws.

The succeeding king reversed the law on involuntary baptism but forced the Jews of the kingdom to sell, at a price fixed by the king, the vineyards, lands, buildings, and slaves which they had purchased from Christians. This policy too would not be carried out successfully.

By then the weary and persecuted Jews of Spain formed a mass of boiling discontent. There were rumors of secret alliances between them and the dreaded Muslims in North Africa. On November 9, 694 C.E., King Egica accused the Jews of treason. Their property was confiscated and all the Jews of Spain were declared slaves and placed in the hands of Christians in different provinces. The Jews were forbidden to practice their faith. Their children were to be taken from them at the age of seven and raised as Christians by special tutors. Many Jews fled the land; many were enslaved. Seventeen years after this edict the Muslims invaded Spain.

To this day no one is able to explain with certainty why that invasion took place. There are legends and frail theories. Historical sources are sparse. Silence surrounds the event like an ocean mist. Some scholars believe it was instigated by a Byzantine officer who went over to the Arab side, knew southern Spain well, and enticed the Arabs into the invasion with promises of spoil. A preliminary raid by a few hundred soldiers in 710 C.E. brought back much booty. But the invasion of the following year is inconceivable unless we assume secret treaties and agreements with a Spanish-Roman populace grown weary of their Visigothic overlords. These natives of the Iberian peninsula are to this day a faceless people about whom almost nothing is known until the tenth century. Were Jews a party to these agreements? There are no hard facts. Given their situation, it would be incredible if they were not.

The invading army was small, about seven thousand men, most of them North African Berbers. Its general, Tarik ibn—son of—Ziyad, a Berber freedman in the service of the Muslim governor of North Africa, achieved inadvertent immortality by landing his forces near a huge rock. The word *jabal* or *jebel* in Arabic means mountain; Jabal Tarik is now more familiarly known as Gibraltar.

In a battle on July 9, 711 c.e., the Muslims destroyed the Visigothic army. King Roderick was killed. Spain was opened to the word of Allah.

The Jews, many of whom were practicing their faith secretly, welcomed the invaders. The Muslims would assemble the Jews of a conquered area and make them the garrison force of captured towns. This occurred in Cordova, Granada, Seville, and Toledo. From a condition of slavery the Jews were abruptly raised to the status of allies of the peninsula's new rulers. The Visigothic nobles had fled northward. Jews took over their abandoned estates. Together with Christians, the Jews would soon be paying the heavy tax levied by Islam against monotheists who did not believe in Mohammed and Allah.

By the end of the summer half of Spain had been conquered. The conquest continued with new armies under new generals. It spilled across the borders of Spain after pushing the Christians into the mountainous region of the north, and was finally brought to an almost natural standstill in 732 c.e., on a Saturday in October. Between Tours and Poitiers, on the soil of France, the Arabs were met and defeated by a Frankish army under Charles Martel. The Arabs withdrew during the night, silently vanishing southward with their tents.

One hundred years after the death of Mohammed, the Arab conquest lost its momentum. His followers were masters of an empire that extended from the borders of Gaul to the edge of China.

The Umayyad dynasty had come to power in 661 c.e. after the last of the original line of orthodox caliphs—all of them in some way connected with Mohammed him-self—was assassinated. The Umayyads ruled over this enormous empire from a magnificent palace in Damascus. These rulers from the deserts of Arabia, descendants of the clan that had once opposed Mohammed, could see the green plain below the city and the far-off snows on Mount Hermon. They would be replaced in 750 C.E. after much bloodshed by the Abbasid dynasty, which would rule the empire from Baghdad, founded in 762 C.E. by the Abbasid caliph Mansur, near the northern rim of the forgotten world of Akkad. Then the caliphate would splinter into distinct and separate caliphates ruling at the same time over different parts of the empire. The Fatimid caliphate would rule in Cairo from 909 to 1171; another Umayyad caliphate would rule in Cordova in Spain from 929 to 1031. During that new Umayyad caliphate Muslims and Jews would become nightingales to a rainbow world of material and aesthetic splendor that still dazzles the eye today as one wanders through the golden cities of southern Spain.

A restless eager wandering had settled upon the peoples of the Mediterranean world. They crowded the port cities. Many Jews were returning to their Spanish homeland, from which they had fled to avoid Visigothic Christian persecution. Others, Jews and Muslims, sought the new opportunities they were certain awaited them in freshly conquered Muslim territory.

One of the wanderers was a Muslim prince named Abd ar-Rahman, the last of the Umayyad royal house. His family had been slaughtered in 750 C.E. by the Abbasid family, which had seized the caliphate from the Umayyads. Declaring an end to the killing, the Abbasids had invited the remaining Umayyads to an amnesty feast. More than seventy princes came out of hiding. During the course of the meal they were massacred and hacked to pieces.

The wanderer, suspicious of Abbasid generosity, had not attended. He was twenty-five years of age, tall and thin, with fair hair and a blind eye. He had wandered in disguise for five years through Mesopotamia, Palestine,

Egypt, and North Africa, at times narrowly escaping capture by Abbasid agents. He wandered to his mother's Berber tribe, the Nafza, in Morocco. There were Umayyads and many Umayyad sympathizers in Spain. Sometime in August 755 C.E. he landed in Spain.

He had in his veins the blood of Umayyad caliphs; the Umayyads and their partisans rallied to him. That winter he led his forces through Málaga and Seville; many joined him.

In May 756 C.E. his army engaged the troops of the governor of Spain in battle near the gates of the ancient Roman wall surrounding Cordova, the capital of Muslim Spain. The governor was defeated. The young wanderer entered Cordova and was proclaimed ruler of Muslim Spain.

That was the beginning of the Umayyad dynasty in Spain. Abd ar-Rahman was then almost twenty-six years old. His wanderings had ceased. He ruled for thirty-two years, from 756 to 788 C.E.

The land continued to be troubled by its many factions. The new ruler was strong, energetic, stubborn. Rebellions were ruthlessly crushed. In the end he became a despot. But his dynasty remained firm, and when he died one of his sons, Hisham I, fought off two brothers and took the throne.

Decades passed. Umayyad rulers held the land intact, successfully subduing the revolts of chieftains and heads of various principalities. From time to time Christian zealots would attempt to stir the Christian masses to rebellion by martyring themselves: they would publicly revile Mohammed, for which the penalty was execution. There was much unrest among the Christians but no rebellion. Many Christians served as government officials.

The Jews of the land were farmers, artisans, laborers, merchants. They adopted Arab names, spoke only Arabic, wrote in Arabic, used Arabic in their liturgy, were Arabic in peripheral matters and Jewish in the core concerns of religion. Their Judaism was that of the Talmud and its laws. They depended almost entirely upon the academies in Babylonia for their sacred texts and for answers to questions of religious law. Heads of communities would send letters to the geonim in Babylonia. The letters would often travel with men who earned their livelihood by carrying messages—scrolls carefully wrapped and sealed in linen—from land to land. Months would pass and the response would arrive. The leaders of the community would gather in the synagogue as the message was unwrapped, opened, and read. At a later time it would be read again and carefully studied, for its language was often the Aramaic of Talmudic law. The scroll would be carefully stored in the synagogue archive.

Scholars estimate that there were about three hundred thousand Jews in Spain. Some southern Spanish cities, like Lucena and Granada, were predominantly Jewish. The land of course had academies of learning and many rabbinic leaders, but they were not comparable in stature with the academies and scholars of Babylonia.

In 912 C.E. Abd ar-Rahman III became ruler of all that remained to the Umayyad dynasty of Muslim Spain: Cordova and its environs. Decades of revolts ineptly handled by previous rulers had reduced the land to a patchwork of warring provinces. The new ruler was in his early twenties. With patience and energy he set about reconquering the land. He was a resolute and daring leader. He proceeded slowly. By 917 C.E. almost the entire land had been reunited. When Toledo, the great former capital, fell to siege and famine in 932 C.E. the land became tranquil. It remained internally at peace all through the remainder of the long reign of this benevolent Umayyad caliph.

In the capital city of Cordova there was a Jewish physician named Hisdai—some scholars vocalize it Hasdai—ibn Shaprut. He had a splendid reputation as a healer. He was also a brilliant medical researcher and had successfully rediscovered the components of an ancient wonder drug known as theriaca, whose secret formula had been lost. He knew Arabic, Hebrew, Latin, and Romance, the dialect of a late form of Latin that would evolve into the language of Spain. He knew Scriptures and other Jewish subjects, and though he himself was not adept at Talmud he had the highest regard for scholars of rabbinic law. When the caliph learned of his medical reputation he invited him to serve as physician at the royal court in Cordova.

There were many physicians in the household of the caliph. It was a glittering world, although the atmosphere was from time to time darkened with oriental intrigue. The Jewish physician, a calm, intelligent, pleasant bachelor in his early thirties, made his way adroitly through the swampy entanglements of the court. Often a caliph would appoint a favored court physician to an administrative post. Abd ar-Rahman III appointed Hisdai ibn Shaprut chief of customs and foreign trade. He proved as successful an administrator as he was a physician. The caliph began to consult the physician on matters of state.

Once he used him on a difficult translation project. The emperor of Byzantium sent as a diplomatic gift an exquisitely illuminated rare medical book containing Greek terms. The book—the *De Materia Medica* of Dioscorides—had been translated into Arabic by Christians at the urging of Abbasid caliphs. But the Christians could not translate the many Greek names of plants and herbs. This Hisdai ibn Shaprut now did, working with a monk sent from Constantinople at the request of the caliph; apparently no one in Christian Spain knew Greek. The work was translated into the idiomatic Arabic of Muslim Spain. The caliph was impressed with the results of his physician's labors. The physician was by then a diplomat and was being sent from time to time on delicate missions to foreign kingdoms.

In 955 C.E. Hisdai ibn Shaprut and another envoy journeyed to the Christian Spanish kingdom of Leon in the north and successfully negotiated a peace treaty with King Ordoño III. Then the duke of Castile agreed to a pact with the caliph. The northern border of Muslim Spain grew silent for the first time in decades. Sometime in the winter of 956 or the spring of 957 C.E. King Ordoño III died. His brother, Sancho I, refused to honor the pact. The border war between Muslim Spain and Christian Spain was resumed.

King Sancho I was known as Sancho the Fat. There were those in his kingdom who looked upon corpulence as an impediment to effective rule—apparently a king may be cruel but not obese. The nobility of Leon began to think him weak-minded because of his obesity. He was deposed and went to live in Pamplona, where his uncle was king. Another prince of the royal house was made ruler in his place.

Sancho's grandmother, Tota, who had once ruled as queen, was enraged. She was a domineering woman with an overpowering impulse to have her grandson rule Leon. There were no physicians in Christian Spain able to cure the illness that had cost Sancho his throne. A suggestion was made that she seek help from the caliph of Muslim Spain, who had under his roof a number of great physicians. This she did, for she loved the power of the throne more than she loathed the Muslims.

The caliph sent Hisdai ibn Shaprut to Pamplona. The doctor undertook to cure the deposed king. But the cure would be protracted and could be best administered Cordova. Would the king and his grandmother consi residing in Cordova for a while as honored guests of caliph? The request was shocking. The physician diplomat was persuasive. Soon the residents of Cordova were treated to the astonishing spectacle of a monarch and queen from Christian Spain accompanied by many attendants coming to the court of the caliph for his aid.

The king was cured. His throne was returned to him. He renewed the peace treaty made by his predecessor with the caliph. It was an extraordinary diplomatic triumph for Hisdai ibn Shaprut.

The physician was a diplomat not only for his caliph but for his own people as well. He was in communication with Jewish communities throughout the world. Wherever possible he used the power of his office to aid Jews. The people, even those in tolerant Muslim Spain, burned with the shame of homelessness and yearned for the coming of the Messiah. Calculations for his coming were made, revised, made again, revised again.

Then Hisdai ibn Shaprut learned of the existence of a Jewish kingdom somewhere in a distant land beyond the Black Sea. He is reported to have sent this letter:

*From Hisdai ibn Shaprut to the king of the Khazars.*

*The kings of the Franks, the kings of the Gebalim, who are Germans, the king of Constantinople and others bring costly presents to the caliph to gain his favor. All their gifts pass through my hands and I am charged with making gifts in return. . . .*

*I always ask the ambassadors of these monarchs who bring the gifts about our breathern the Israelites, the remnant of the Captivity. At length, mercantile emissaries . . . told me that there is a kingdom of the Jews who are called Khazars. . . . Now therefore let it please Your Majesty . . . to command your scribe to send back a reply from your distant land and to inform me fully concerning the condition of the Israelites and how they came to dwell there.*

*When we first heard the fame of my Lord the King and the power of his dominions we lifted up our head, our spirit revived. The kingdom of my lord furnished us with an answer to the taunt: "Every other people has its kingdom, but of yours there is no memorial on earth."*

The authenticity of this letter has been hotly debated by scholars, as is that of the reply:

*From Joseph the king son of Isaac the king, to Hisdai son of Isaac son of Ezra. I wish to inform you that your beautifully phrased letter was given us by Isaac son of Eliezer, a Jew of the land of Germany, who has carried it through Germany, Hungary, and Russia to Khazaria. Know that we are descended from Japhet, through his son Togarmah, the father of all the Turks. The land in which I now live was formerly occupied by the Bulgarians. Our ancestors, the Khazars, came and fought with them. . . . They left while the Khazars pursued them as far as the Danube River. . . .*

*Many generations passed until a certain king arose whose name was Bulan. The kings of the Byzantines and the Arabs who had heard of him sent their ambassadors . . . with the object of converting him to their own religion. But the king . . . sent for a learned Israelite. . . .*

*The king said to the Christian priest: "What do you think? Of the religion of the Jews and the Muslims which is to be preferred?" The priest answered: "The religion of the Israelites is better than that of the Muslims."*

*The king then asked the Muslim scholar: "What do you say? Is the religion of the Israelites or that of the Christians better?" The Muslim scholar answered: "The religion of the Israelites is preferable."*

*Upon this the king said: "You both have admitted with your own mouths that the religion of the Israelites is better. Wherefore, trusting in the mercies of God, I choose the religion of Israel."*

*From that time on the Almighty helped Bulan and strengthened him. Bulan circumcised himself, his servants, attendants, and all his people. Then Bulan brought from all places wise men who interpreted the Torah for him, and up to this day we have been subjec to this religion. . . .*

*I dwell at the delta of the Volga. I guard the mouth of the river and do not permit the Russians, who come in ships, to enter into the Caspian so as to get at the Muslims. I have to wage war with them, or they would lay waste the whole land of the Muslims as far as Baghdad. . . .*

History? Fiction? The yearnings of a stateless people molding folklore out of the vague reports of wandering Jewish merchants, who traveled throughout the world, dealing in silks from China and slaves taken in wars everywhere and furs and swords? Radhanites they were called, probably from a Persian word meaning one who knows the way. One such merchant may have reported the existence of the Khazar kingdom to the well-known Jewish physician in Cordova. But the letters, their style and date of composition remain the subject of serious debate by scholars. The Khazar correspondence is now in Christ Church Library at Oxford and in the University Library at Cambridge.

The kingdom of the Khazars was destroyed about the

second half of the tenth century by the Cumans, a nomadic people who spoke a Turkic dialect and came from
Asiatic Russia.

The Jewish physician worked on in Cordova, earning
the favor of his caliph. Cordova had become, together
with Baghdad and Constantinople, one of the three great
cities in the world. It was a city of parks and fountains,
palaces and mosques. The caliph was a patron of the arts.
His court attracted poets and scholars from all over the
world. The sciences flourished. The city had an academy
for the study of the arts and sciences and free schools for
children. Its population numbered half a million people.
The caliph had a personal bodyguard of almost four thousand Slavs and a standing army of one hundred thousand
men. Commerce and agriculture were abundant. His
treasury overflowed with revenue. He had built, with his
own wisdom and courage, a triumphant land.

He died in his early seventies. Historians inform us that
he left a statement to the effect that he had experienced
only fourteen days of happiness throughout his life.

He was succeeded by his son, al-Hakam II, who ruled
from 961 to 976 C.E. and followed his father's wise domestic and foreign policies. He had a love for books and
would indulge his bibliophilic passion by sending agents
throughout the world to search for rare and important
works. His library numbered four hundred thousand
volumes. He retained the services of the physician Hisda
ibn Shaprut.

The Jews of Muslim Spain looked up the presence of
Hisdai ibn Shaprut in the court of the two Umayyad
caliphs as a sign of the providence of God. The physician
was the unquestioned leader of Andalusian Jewry. He too
had a deep love for culture—that of his own people. He
too was a patron of the arts and sciences, and sent agents
throughout the world looking for books. Those he aided
were Jewish poets and scholars; the books he sought were
texts of the Talmud for the academies of learning in
Muslim Spain.

I marvel at the astonishing turns of history. A wandering Arab prince enters a land and establishes a dynasty that will one day transmit the culture of ancient Greece to Europe and will also enhance that culture by encouraging original research. And so the astrolabe, a simple ancient instrument for navigation, will be perfected by scientists in Cordova and will be used by mariners until the invention of the sextant in the eighteenth century; plane and spherical geometry will be invented; botany and pharmacology will become sciences; a Muslim surgeon named Abulcasis will write a medical encyclopedia that, in its Hebrew and Latin translations, will influence European medicine for centuries. And a Jewish physician, mirroring with wisdom and dignity the love of learning in the hearts of his caliphs, will bring about a flowering of Jewish culture in Spain that will forever alter the nature of Judaism.

Arabs came to Greek culture through the desert tribes that had crossed the borders of Arabia beneath the standard of Islam and conquered the world. Ragged Arab infantrymen and cavalrymen had gazed in stupefied awe at the splendors of the civilizations they had subdued: Persia, Mesopotamia, Syria, Palestine, Egype. The loveliness of Ctesiphon, Damascus, Alexandria, Jerusalem, and other cities dazzled eyes accustomed to a monochromatic world of wilderness and sand. The Arabs brought to their conquests a sharp, ferreting intelligence and a suddenly aroused and challenged latent sense of curiosity.

They dealt briskly with the problems of the Jews, Christians, and pagans they had conquered before turning their attention to the treasures of culture now in their hands. From the monotheistic Jews and Christians Islam demanded tribute and adherence to certain stipulations, though these were frequently not enforced by the caliphs: synagogues and churches could not be taller than a mosque; prayer services were to be conducted quietly; Jews and Christians were to wear some sort of identifiable garb, a shirt or belt, that would distingush them from the Muslim; in matters of law, except where a Muslim was involved, Jews and Christians were autonomous and were to go to their own courts, for the law of Allah was too sacred to be applied to nonbelievers. New Muslims—pagans converted to the path of Allah—obtained full Islamic citizenship—and were the first to enter the arts and sciences, the familiar children of the paganism they had abandoned. In the early years of the Abbasid caliphate, from about 750 C.E. on, converted Muslims began to outnumber those of Arabian descent.

The Arabs had conquered vast territories. The civilizations of those territories conquered the Arabs. The Arabs had little to offer those civilizations save a sacred book and the language in which that book was written and recited—the dialect of Arabic used in northern Arabia during the days of Mohammed. Greeks had once brought enlightenment to Rome. Now Syrians, Persians, Egyptians, and others—as converts to Islam or as Christians and Jews—would bring learning to the Arabs. Arabic civilization did not originate in Arabia or among the Arabs. It was at heart the civilization of Iran and Hellenized Aramaic-speaking peoples who were encouraged to continue their creativity under the rule of curious and culture-hungry caliphs and now had to give expression to their ideas in the language of the conqueror: Arabic.

The language of the Koran and the conqueror became the language of the lands and civilizations that had been conquered. Greek thought was Arabized. Paganism underwent a language journey as caliphs ordered the translation of the literature and science of the ancient world into the tongue of the north Arabian desert. Men from the Arabian peninsula, adherents of a rigorous and demanding monotheistic faith, became the carriers of a culture borne in the past mainly by Greeks and Hellenized pagans. That was the remarkable outcome of this culture confrontation. The desert world of Allah had collided with the Mediterranean world of Zeus—with the relentless logic of the Greeks, their inquisitiveness, their methodical searchings, the controlled zeal with which they had explored frontiers of knowledge for centuries until about 200 B.C.E. when original creativity died in Hellenism. From that time on until the fall of Constantinople in 1453 to Muslim Ottomans, the heirs of the civilization of Greece produced no great poet, political thinker, or scientist—with the exception of Ptolemy. Save for a few poets of stature, the same may be said of Rome. The pagan world seemed dead, and its creativity was carried off to Muslims, Christians, and Jews.

Now, in the closing century of the first millennium, the court of the caliph in Cordova teemed with poets and scientists eager to show their creations to their patron and win his favor. Through this opulent oriental world beneath the sun of southern Spain moved Hisdai ibn Shaprut. He did for his people what he saw the caliph do for Spain. He brought them learning and art.

He appointed a great scholar head of the Jewish academy in Cordova and chief rabbi of Muslim Spanish Jewry. The rabbi, Moses ben Hanoch, had been on a Mediterranean voyage from his community in southern Italy when his ship was captured by pirates. The pirate vessel was in turn taken by naval vessels of the caliph. When Hisdai ibn Shaprut learned of the presence of a Jewish scholar on Spanish soil he had him brought to Cordova. The scholar's profound learning was immediately apparent. The physician prevailed upon him to remain.

The presence of that scholar transformed the nature of Spanish Jewry. He was of such stature that there was no longer a need to turn to the geonim of Babylonia for answers to questions of Jewish law. Spanish Jewish scholars immediately acknowledged the greatness of this emigrant from Italy. Students crowded his classes. Spanish Jewry began to produce its own great scholars. The ties with the Babylonian academies grew weaker. In the end they were gone, and the land stood as a strong adult in the world of Talmudic scholarship. Other communities throughout the dispersion began to develop their own scholars. The Babylonian academies became impoverished and slowly faded.

The physician encouraged poetry and philology, the study of language and the text of the Bible. There were at the time a number of important Arab philologists in Cordova. The sanctity of the Koran and its language had sparked Arab interest in the study of the structure of Arabic. In Christian Europe at this time scholars would gather and debate matters of theology; in Cordova Arab scholars would discuss linguistics.

Jews were caught up in this zeal for words and grammar. A man named Menahem ibn Saruk was born in northeastern Spain. Very early he discovered an interest in Hebrew philology and Bible commentaries. He left behind the economic and cultural poverty of his home and city and wandered southward through Spain. In Cordova he was taken into the home of a wealthy man, the brother of Hisdai ibn Shaprut. He served as the family poet—a custom in those days among the wealthy. Special occasions were marked by poems composed by the family laureate. In time the poet became Hebrew secretary to Hisdai ibn Shaprut. This left him sufficient time to research and write a dictionary of the Hebrew language, a work which pioneered Hebrew philology in Spain. The treatise made him famous, gained him enemies and, for reasons that are not entirely clear—some say he was accused of Karaite sympathies—lost him the favor of his patron. Hisdai ibn Shaprut was capable of despotic action at times. He withdrew his patronage from Menahem ibn Saruk, had him beaten, and ordered that his home be destroyed. The embittered poet and grammarian, lamenting his sudden bewildering loss of favor, returned to his birthplace.

The Jews of Spain esteemed not only the study of the Hebrew language but also the use of the language for poetry. They borrowed for themselves the Arab love for the poet and his work. Poems had lives of their own; once composed they journeyed magically through space and time; rulers and nobles paid well for songs of praise from the pens of poets. The study of language and the creation of poetry were strongly linked in the Arab mind. Now Jews began to sense that link and explored it in the service of Hebrew. The finest Jewish writers in southern Spain would often come together in the home of Hisdai ibn Shaprut. There they would read their latest creations. The physician surrounded himself with Hebrew poets as if to compensate for the chill of his lonely personal life. He provided them with funds, urged them to go on with their creative efforts. One sometimes has the impression he was midwife to poems that in his eyes were the children he himself never brought into the world.

Into Cordova wandered a man who had been born

about 920 C.E. in the North African city of Fez. He had
studied in Babylonia under Saadia Gaon. The fame of
Cordova as a great center of Jewish learning had spread.
He came to Cordova and served as a cantor. In those
days cantors were often poets; they composed liturgical
hymns which they chanted in the synagogue on festivals
and special occasions. It was soon apparent that the new
cantor, Dunash ibn Labrat, was an extraordinary poet.

He revolutionized Hebrew poetry by writing it in Arabic meter. Biblical poetry has forms of its own but lacks
the rhythmic smoothness and polish of metered verse. He
introduced verse structure, transitions, rhetorical flour-
ishes, as well as new themes, poems in praise of patrons,
wine songs with descriptions of the drink, the flowering
garden where the drinking takes place, the singing birds,
the lad serving the wine, the music that fills the air of the
banquet—all of this borrowed from Arabic poetry. This
was new and strange to Hebrew poetry, so the poet would
write of a wine feast and append to it lines of self-protec-
tive but transparently unfelt warning:

*We shall drink among the flower beds hedged with roses*
*And put sorrow to flight with all manner of gaiety*
*Partaking of sweets and drinking from goblets. . . .*
*I chided him into silence: How can you prefer these vanities*
*When the holy Temple, God's footstool, is in the hands of the*
    *gentiles!*

Cordova throbbed with scholars, poets, grammarians.
Sacred and secular verse was composed by the same poets.
Talmudic scholars who had severed their connections with
Babylonia and were now their own masters; academies of
learning filled with students; Bible commentators using
newly developed linguistic tools and searching with honesty into the nature of the sacred text; grammarians exploring the structure of the Hebrew language; poets
singing of God and man and love and wine—that was
Cordova in the closing years of the first millennium.

In southern Spain rabbinic Judaism was exposed to a
happy, warming sun, to aesthetics. It became a golden
tradition, relaxed, and filled with a love for learning all

things. That was what the children did when they went to school. They learned not only to write but to write beautifully; not only Bible, Mishnah, and Hebrew grammar but also poetry; not only Talmud but also philosophy, logic, mathematics, geometry, optics, astronomy, music, natural sciences, and metaphysics. Many studied medicine.

Hisdai ibn Shaprut died about 970 c.e. at the age of sixty-five. Al-Hakam II died six years later and was succeeded by al-Mansur, who was the last of the great Umayyad caliphs in Spain. With his death in 1002 the land began to break apart and the army began to make and unmake rulers. Berbers, Arabs, Slavs, and Spaniards fought one another bitterly for the caliphate. The tenuous unity of ethnic groups held together by the wisdom of Abd ar-Rahman III and his two successors disintegrated into a conglomeration of quarreling petty states. For twenty-one years caliph followed caliph, the puppets of Slavs, Cordovans, Berbers. Anarchy was king in sunny southern Spain.

The Umayyad caliphate came to an end in 1027 when the Cordovans, weary of the chaos, decided to put an end to government by caliph. They abolished the caliphate. The last of the Umayyads was shut in a room with his little daughter, whom he loved. They nearly starved to death before they were released.

Cordova became a republic. It lost its central position in Muslim Spain. The land was once again a crazy quilt of kingdoms. Culture and commerce moved to local Berber and Arab principalities. Jewish courtiers began to appear in various kingdoms. The most famous of them was Samuel ha-Nagid, a rabbinic scholar and an authority in Jewish law, who fled from Cordova and served the small Berber kingdom of Granada as vizier and commander of the army from about 1030 to his death in 1056. Modern scholars regard him as the first great poet of Hebrew Spain. His poetry is filled with accounts of intrigue, treachery, murders, wars, rebellions. He was replaced by his son, Jehoseph, an ambitious and boastful man, who designed and built the Alhambra and was assassinated in 1066.

At about the same time that the Umayyad dynasty

crumbled in the south, the Christians in the north embarked upon the reconquest of Spain. Jewish communities grew tremulous.

In 1066, following the assassination of the son of Samuel ha-Nagid at the hands of jealous Muslims, there was a massacre of the Jewish community in Granada. Survivors scattered to other cities. That was the first persecution of Jews in Muslim Spain. In the north petty Muslim kingdoms were being overrun by conquering Christian armies.

Now poets were the wanderers.

Isaac ibn Khalfon wandered from Cordova, where he had been born about 970 C.E., through the cities of southern Spain, visiting wealthy Jewish families and offering his services as a poet. About fifty of his poems have survived. He wrote joyous poems for festive family occasions and moving elegies for the dead. He wrote love poems and poems about friendship, in emulation of Arabic poets. He wrote in Hebrew about a poet going to his beloved and encountering members of her family who keep watch over her—a theme in ancient Arabic poetry. He wrote of abandoned Bedouin encampments, of the hours he once spent with his beloved amid campfires and silent tents, of the camels upon which the Bedouin depends for his existence. He praised the tribe and, finally, sang the merits and good deeds of his patron. He spent his life wandering. He lived for a while in Granada, where he sat on rugs in courtyards paved with marble amid men dressed in white silk and declaimed in rhythmic verse the uprightness of his host: he fought the wicked, protected the poor, was modest and righteous. Ibn Khalfon was a success in the homes of the wealthy in Granada. They paid well for his poetry.

Solomon ibn Gabirol was taken from Málaga, where he was born about 1020, to Saragossa, where he was educated and orphaned before the age of sixteen. He was quick-tempered and suffered from a serious disease of the skin. He began to write exquisite poetry at sixteen; his genius flowered suddenly. He knew his worth as a poet and was too young and too arrogant to conceal his self-esteem from others. He wrote, "I am the mastersinger and song is my slave. . . . Though I am but sixteen, I have the wisdom of a man of eighty." And he wrote, "I am filled with wrath when I behold fools parading as wise men. . . . They deem their song superior to mine whereas they do not even understand it. . . ." That earned him enemies and a need for further wandering when his patron was killed in a court intrigue.

He left Saragossa and lived for a time in Granada. His patron in Granada was the Talmud scholar, vizier, and warrior Samuel ha-Nagid. The two quarreled when ibn Gabirol criticized some of his patron's poetry. The poet wandered on to Valencia, where he died—some say at the age of thirty, others at the age of about thirty-eight. The German Jewish poet Heinrich Heine called Solomon ibn Gabirol the nightingale of piety.

He sang all through his brief life. He was often ill. Of the twenty books of poetry he boastfully tells us he wrote, only two remain. He was a virtuoso with the Hebrew language. He sang of patrons and friendship, of the inexorable workings of fate and time, of his loneliness in a bustling society which went its own uncaring way in search of material success—all conventional motifs in Arabic poetry. But the full splendor of this nightingale's song is to be heard in his religious poetry. Here the proud poet became the plaintive worshiper, expressing in soaring language, fresh imagery, and complex strophes the deepest fears and yearnings of his soul, his dream for the redemption, his dread over a world that had begun to crumble as the land about him slid into political disintegration and Christian armies began their march of conquest. It is mainly for these poems that he has been remembered and loved by Jews through the centuries.

He wrote,

> *Lord, tell me when*
> *Shall come to men*
> *Messiah blest. . . .*

He wrote,

> *In prayer prone before my King,*
> *I bend to Him my face and knee,*

*My heart His sacrifice shall be,*
*My tear His liquid offering. . . .*

And he wrote,

*Wonderful are Thy works, as my soul overwhelmingly*
*knows.*
*Thine, O Lord, are the greatness and the might, the*
*beauty, the triumph and the splendor.*

And he wrote,

*All realms behold our driven seed,*
*Like wounded doves we fly their hate.*
*All nations hunt us and impede*
*And in the desert lie in wait. . . .*
*Where is that kindness from above,*
*Of which Thy servitors have heard,*
*The boon of Thy peculiar love,*
*For which we have our Father's word?*

There was so much else he wrote, lyrical, poignant, haunting, a nightingale singing to his God for an end to the shame and helplessness of dispersion.

He wrote works of philosophy and ethics. Christians know him best for his philosophical treatise, *The Source of Life*. It was written in Arabic and translated into Latin in the twelfth century by the archdeacon of Segovia and a converted Jewish physician. That was the way many great works in Arabic entered the culture stream of Latin Europe: through the painstaking labors of clerics and Jews.

The title given the translation was *Fons Vitae*. The Arabic original is lost. The name ibn Gabirol became Latinized into Avencebrol, Avicembron, Avicebron. There is no hint of Jewishness in the work. It was studied in monasteries and universities and was reckoned with seriously in the erudite and rarified world of medieval scholasticism. Ibn Gabirol's authorship was announced to the world in 1846 in a learned article by Solomon Munk that appeared in a German scholarly journal. But the book's world view had passed its zenith by then and was no longer the subject of serious Christian theological concern.

Another of these nightingales of Spanish Jewry was born about 1085—some say in Toledo and others in Tudela, a town near Pamplona in the north. His family was learned and wealthy and his childhood was peaceful. His name was Judah Halevi, and he came in time to be known as the singer of Zion.

He was young when he traveled to southern Spain during a period when Jews were caught between the slowly advancing armies of Christianity and the invasion from North Africa by a fanatic Muslim sect called the Almoravides. In 1085 Toledo fell to the Christians. About a year later the leader of the victorious Almoravides attempted to force the Jews of Lucena to convert to Islam. He was placated by a huge bribe. When he died his son appointed to the royal court a Jewish physician whom he sent on diplomatic missions. The fanatics had entered quickly into the hedonism and international maneuverings of civilized life.

The fragmentizing of Spain blurs the picture and makes of it a puzzle map in motion: here a ruler will be tolerant toward his Jews; there a ruler will suppress them. Through this dusty confusion traveled the young poet, entering and winning a poetry contest in Cordova, where he befriended a Granadan, Moses ibn Ezra, one of the finest poets of this golden age of culture and iron age of politics. They spent much time together in Granada amid wealth and culture, and Judah Halevi wrote of wine and love. He met other poets, among them Abraham ibn Ezra from Tudela.

Off in the east Jerusalem was taken by an army of Christian crusaders. The Muslim and Jewish populace was butchered by sword-wielding knights. That was in the summer of 1099. Chroniclers tell of streams of blood flowing through the narrow streets of the city. With the stench of unburied corpses and burned buildings fouling the Jerusalem air, the crusaders assembled in the Church of the Resurrection and chanted *Te Deum laudamus*, praising God for their victory.

When Andalusia fell to the fanatic Almoravides and

the position of Jews in southern Spain began to deteriorate, the poets of Granada scattered. Judah Halevi began to travel. He traveled for the next twenty years. We hear of him in the company of the Jewish vizier Meir ibn Kamniel in Seville and the noted Talmudic scholar Joseph ibn Migash in Lucena. He practiced medicine in Toledo, serving the king and nobility of that new Christian city. Christian kings were kind to their Jews in the early period of the reconquest. Many Jews went from Muslim Spain to Christian Spain to avoid the fanatic conversionist policies of the Almoravides. They were given lands and gardens and homes by the Christian kings, property that had once belonged to Muslims who had fled the Christian advance. The Spanish kings regarded the Jews as an important stabilizing element in newly conquered areas and used them as government officials, courtiers, diplomats. Spanish priests looked upon the Jews as loathsome, despicable, stiff-necked scorners of the true faith who had slain Jesus and were now the rejected of God.

In 1109 Judah Halevi left Toledo and continued his wanderings. During all those years his poetry had gained him fame. He was not only a physician but a merchant as well and needed no patrons for his poetry. His closest friend was Abraham ibn Ezra. They wandered together through Muslim Spain and North Africa.

The years passed. Spain grew turbulent with fanaticism and war. In the late summer of 1140 Abraham ibn Ezra left Spain for Rome, and Judah Halevi left Spain for the land of Israel.

Abraham ibn Ezra lived in Rome for a while, alone and in poverty. Then he wandered to Lucca and Mantua and Verona. He wrote poetry, commentaries on the prophets, works on grammar. He left Italy and wandered through Provence and then up into northern France. He wrote commentaries on the Pentateuch, met scholars, moved through communities like some radiant light falling upon dark corners of Jewish learning. More than a century later people were still writing of his visit. He wrote poetry, astrological works, commentaries on Daniel, Psalms, and the Minor Prophets. His Biblical commentaries are luminous with erudition and honesty—he casts doubt upon the Mosaic authorship of certain passages of the Pentateuch; he is disdainful of philosophers and mystical obscurantists; he seeks the simple meaning of a narrative text but follows the Talmudic sages in their interpretations of legal texts. In 1158, about a decade after the pious mobs of the Second Crusade had ravaged the flourishing Jewish communities and centers of learning in Speyer, Cologne, and Prague, ibn Ezra left Europe and journeyed to London. He continued writing. In 1161 he was in Narbonne. He was old now, and lonely. Sometime in his past he had had five sons, four of whom had died. Some believe the fifth converted to Islam. There are those who believe ibn Ezra's final wanderings took him to the land of Israel, where he died in 1164.

Judah Halevi had arrived in Alexandria in the late summer of 1140. He journeyed along the Nile to Cairo. Jews received him with honor wherever he traveled. The ship he boarded sometime later in Alexandria never left port because of a storm. He returned to Cairo. A few months later he died. Much of his life he had dreamed of reaching the land of Israel and freeing himself of the enslavement of exile. He was buried in Egypt.

His was the sweetest and most poignant of all the nightingale voices of that time—and we know of about fifty Hebrew poets who were his contemporaries in Spain. Few could match the lyric quality of his secular poetry, and none could come near the jeweled fusion of imagery and language that are his most cherished gifts to his people—his odes to Zion, in which he sings in the sweetly sad voice of a poet whose vision of art is his own but whose dreams are those of all his people.

He wrote of love,

> *The night when the fair maiden revealed the likeness*
> *of her form to me,*
> *The warmth of her cheeks, the veil of her hair,*
> *Golden like a topaz, covering*
> *A brow of smoothest crystal—*
> *She was like the sun making red in her rising*
> *The clouds of dawn with the flame of her light.*

And he wrote of love,

> *Would that morning might pursue me with the wind*
> *That kisseth her mouth and swayeth her body;*
> *And would the clouds might bear to her my greeting. . . .*

He wrote of God,

> *Ah, would that I might be a servant of God, my*
> *   Maker!*
> *Though every friend were far from me, yet He*
> *   would draw me near.*

And he wrote to God,

> *My love, hast Thou forgotten Thy resting between*
> *   my breasts?*
> *And wherefore hast Thou sold me forever to them*
> *   that enslave me? . . .*
> *Is there, beside Thee, a redeemer or, beside me, a*
> *   captive of hope?—*
> *O give Thy strength to me, for I give Thee my love.*

He wrote of Zion,

> *My heart is in the east, and I in the farthest west—*
> *How can I find savor in food? How shall it be sweet*
> *   to me?*
> *How shall I render my vows and my bonds, while yet*
> *Zion lieth beneath the fetter of Edom, and I in Arab*
> *   chains?*
> *A light thing would it seem to me to leave all the*
> *   good things of Spain—*
> *See how precious in mine eyes to behold the dust*
> *   of the desolate sanctuary.*

And he wrote of Zion, "I am the harp for all thy
songs: . . ."

Eight hundred of his poems have come down to us. He
also wrote in Arabic a work of philosophy, *The Book of*

*Argument and Proof in Defense of the Despised Faith.* It was translated into Hebrew in the middle of the twelfth century and is known today as *The Book of the Khuzari.* He worked on it for twenty years. The framework of the book is the conversion of the king of the Khazars to Judaism. A Muslim, a Christian, and a Jew debate the merits of their various faiths before the king. Here we have the song of the nightingale not in poetry but in a prose that has influenced the thinking of Jews to the present day.

Yes, the temple has been destroyed and the people is in exile. Yes, nations rise and fall. But the history of the Jews is raised beyond causal laws. That was true of the time of the Bible, and it is also true of the bitter time of the exile. Just as the temple was once the place where humanity could atone for its sins through the sacrifices brought by the Jewish people, so in the dispersion is the Jewish people the very heart of humanity, the servant of God, whose suffering atones for all the sins of the world. No one is left of the ancient world save the Jews; they are sustained by God. To suffer with humility and patience—that is the mission of the Jew in the dispersion. Other peoples of the world take pride in their ability to suffer with patience, but they wish only, in truth, to realize the ideal of the warrior; they measure worth in terms of victories and political success. It is precisely the miserable condition of the Jew that testifies to his mission. The spirit of the Jew works silently. It is like a seed. It must appear to be rotting and dying in order for it to absorb the substance which surrounds it and incorporate it into itself, transforming it thereby into its own being and into a higher level of existence. The covenant is real; it was given to an entire people at Sinai. All the people were witness. Nation, land, and Torah are a unity. Zion is not merely a holy site to the Jew or a point for pilgrimage but the geography upon which creative Jewish history was enacted in the past and will be resumed in the future. . . .

And so he journeyed to Zion to show by example that even a nightingale must give substance to its song. But he died on the way and was buried in Egypt.

The heart cannot leave unfulfilled so powerful a dream,

so poignant a longing. The folk imagination bestirs itself in the face of cosmic injustice and seeks to right the bitter wrongs of the real world. And so a legend grew up around the singer of Zion. He reached the city of Jerusalem—a crusader city now—and as he bowed and kissed its stones and recited the opening words of one of his elegies, "Zion! wilt thou not ask if peace be with thy captive," an Arab horseman trampled him to death. . . .

Many others were wandering at about that time, many. A Jew named Benjamin from Tudela wandered, for reasons unknown to us, from his home in northern Spain to Provence in southern France, where he met scholars and merchants and laborers. He traveled by sea to Genoa, then on to Rome, where he viewed the ruins of the people who had once enjoyed an empire and destroyed the sacred city and temple of God. He journeyed throughout southern Italy and then to Greece, where, he wrote, "The Jews are oppressed and live by silkweaving." He spent a great deal of time in Constantinople and was dazzled by the magnificence of that eastern Christian city. But he was sobered by what he saw of the Jews. "The Greeks hate the Jews, good and bad alike, and beat them in the street. . . . No Jew is allowed to ride on horseback. The one exception is Solomon Hamitzri, who is the king's physician, and through whom the Jews enjoy considerable alleviation of their oppression." Then he wandered through the Greek islands of the Aegean, site of the ancient empire of Athens, and to Antioch, Sidon, Tyre, and the land of Israel. He visited the holy places, entered crusader Jerusalem, journeyed to Tiberias and Damascus, then on to Baghdad. He was admitted to the opulent court of the caliph. He visited Talmudical academies and the exilarch. He wandered through Mesopotamia and Persia and back to Cairo and Alexandria before returning to Spain. He wrote of the Jews of Yemen that they "take spoil and booty and retreat to the mountains, and no man can prevail against them." About the people in Quilon along the southwestern tip of India, he wrote, "The inhabitants are black, and the Jews, too." Of the Jews in the oases of Teima and Khaybar in the northern desert of Arabia, he wrote, "They own many large fortified cit-

ies. . . . They go forth to pillage and to capture booty."
His *Book of Travels* is one of the most important sources
for our knowledge of the second hálf of the twelfth century.

A thirteen-year-old boy named Moses ben Maimon
wandered with his family from Cordova in 1148 after the
city had fallen to the Almohades, another fanatic Muslim
sect from Africa which had driven out the previous
Almoravides with much violence and bloodshed. The
Maimon family spent eight or nine years wandering from
city to city until in 1160 they finally settled in Fez, the
capital of Morocco. In 1165 they left Fez and four weeks
later disembarked at Acre on the coast of the land of Israel. They toured the land, visited Jerusalem, sailed for
Egypt, stayed awhile in Alexandria. The father died in the
land of Israel or in Egypt.

Moses ben Maimon—Maimonides—settled in Fostat, a
suburb of Cairo. There he lived the remainder of his
life—physician to the vizier, leader of the Fostat Jewish
community, and authority of the monumental *Mishneh
Torah* (the words mean repetition of the law) in 1180, an
orderly restructuring of the entire legal literature of the
Talmud, and the *Guide of the Perplexed*, an account of
his personal culture confrontation with classic Greek
thought, his answer to the challenge posed by Aristotle to
all men of faith. Thomas Aquinas would read that response before writing the *Summa Theologica*. We shall
return to Maimonides later when his *Guide* becomes involved in an explosive conflict with a segment of Jewry
contemptuous of Aristotle and all pagan thought.

The Jewish world was in turbulence. The crusader
butchery in Jerusalem had sent a shudder of horror
through Jewry. Muslim historians of that time regarded
the crusades as merely another attack upon Islam by the
Franks or infidels—there was no Arabic term for crusades
until the modern period. But the Jews of that time saw
the establishment of crusader Jerusalem as a deepening of
the shame of exile and an extension of their suffering. The
disintegration of Spain struck Jewry with a special horror,
for many loved that land and regarded it as home. Now

Almoravides and Almohades had darkened the sun of southern Spain with an Arabian desert sandstorm.

From the north, Christian armies continued the reconquest of the land. In 1230 Castile and Leon, two of the kingdoms of northern Spain, were united. In 1236 Cordova fell to the Christians; Seville was taken in 1248. The dreary cycle of Jewish courtiers falling in and out of favor with their rulers was repeated with disheartening regularity. The church grew relentless toward converted Jews who might be practicing Judaism secretly and toward the grating presence of stubborn Jews on the soil of the land who persisted in refusing conversion. A court of inquiry would be established to investigate the lives of suspected secret Jews. That was the Inquisition, imported into Spain from France in 1481.

In 1469 the marriage of Ferdinand of Aragon to Isabella of Castile permanently united these two remaining separate kingdoms of Christian Spain. The army of Castile marched relentlessly southward. Málaga fell.

The only city still in Muslim hands was Granada. It surrendered to siege. The Castilians entered the city on January 2, 1492. I know of no account of the feelings of those Jews who for whatever reason still remained in Granada and now watched the triumphant army of Christian Spain march into the city with its banners and crosses. The crescent of the Spanish Umayyads had been a sun and a song. Beneath that crescent the Jews had remained within the embrace of the ancient covenant and had also reached out to new worlds of beauty and truth. Now the Moorish sultan rode with his queen for the final time from the magnificent red stucco palace, the Alhambra, gazed at the surrounding plain and at the lovely city he had lost, and wept. Eight hundred years of Muslim rule in Spain were at an end.

The crescents were removed and replaced with crosses. The few remaining Granadan Jews would soon be expelled from the land together with all the rest of Spanish Jewry. In a few years the city's Muslims would be forcibly converted to Christianity—against the terms of the surrender agreement. A little over a hundred years later, in

1609, almost the entire Muslim population of Spain would be deported—about half a million people.

In 1499, at the order of the cardinal Ximénez de Cisneros, Queen Isabella's confessor, there took place in Granada a bonfire of Arabic manuscripts. Who was king? Who was not king? In Spain Christianity was king. All the nightingales had been silenced.

# CHRISTIANITY

## Lost in the Enchanted Land

Fires were frequent in ancient Rome. Flames from an overturned oil lamp could swiftly devour a squalid neighborhood. In 64 C.E., during the reign of Nero, a fire broke out amid the shops near the Palatine hill. There was a wind that day, and it blew the flames through the wooden tenements in the level sections of the city, then on up to the hills. The conflagration moved through the crooked streets and narrow winding passageways. "Added to this," writes Tacitus, "were the wailings of terror-stricken women, the feebleness of the aged, the helplessness of the children, the crowds who sought to save themselves or others, dragging out the infirm or waiting for them, and by their hurry in the one case, by their delay in the other, aggravating the confusion."

Nero was not in the city. He returned when the fire began to menace his palace. The palace and everything around it burned. A rumor swept the city: during the conflagration, the emperor had appeared on a private stage and had sung of the destruction of Troy, "comparing present misfortunes," as Tacitus puts it, "with the calamities of antiquity."

The city burned for five days before the flames were brought under control. Then a second fire broke out, this time in the more spacious section of the city. Temples of the gods were destroyed. Of the fourteen districts into which Rome was then divided, three were leveled, four remained untouched, and seven were left with charred, half-burned skeletons of buildings.

The dazed city was swept by a fresh rumor: the fires

had been set at the order of the emperor, who wished to establish a new city and call it by his name.

The half-mad emperor looked about for an acceptable scapegoat. "To get rid of the rumor," continues Tacitus, "Nero fastened the guilt and inflicted the most brutal tortures on a class hated for their abominations, called Christians by the populace. Christos, from whom the name was derived, had suffered the extreme penalty during the reign of Tiberius at the hands of one of our procurators, Pontius Pilate. Temporarily suppressed, this despicable superstition broke out again not only in Judea, where it had originated, but even in Rome, where all things hideous and shameful come together from every part of the world and become popular."

Some known Christians were arrested and tortured. They confessed—to burning the city? to being Christians, which may then have been a crime? We are not told. They named other Christians. There was a mass roundup.

Tacitus tells us that the Christians were convicted not so much of the crime of arson as of hatred of mankind. We are not given the reason for this accusation. It is probable that the Romans of that time looked upon Christianity as a bizarre and blasphemous sect: by denying the existence of the gods and actively preaching atheistic views, Christians might anger the gods and bring disaster upon a city. Such people would be regarded as odious haters of man.

Their execution was made into a sport. Some were sewn into the skins of animals and torn apart by dogs. Some were nailed to crosses or burned. As night drew near, others were used as torches for illumination. The spectacle took place in the emperor's gardens. Nero mingled with the people, wearing the garb of a charioteer. Compassion began to arise for the victims. "It was not," concludes Tacitus, "for the public good that they were being destroyed but to glut the cruelty of one man."

This act of persecution intensified the unpopularity of the emperor and excited pity for the newly formed Christian community in Rome. The founder of the sect, the one called Christos—a Greek word meaning the anointed one and referring to the Messiah—had himself been executed by crucifixion in Jerusalem about three decades before the fires in Rome. Three years after those fires, zealous haters of Rome in the birthplace of Christianity began the rebellion that made a holocaust of Jerusalem and the temple of the Jews.

The name of the founder of Christianity was Joshua son of Joseph. In the Galilean Hebrew dialect of that day his name was probably pronounced Jeshua. Jesus is the ordinary Greek form of the Hebrew name Joshua.

Modern scholars of the Bible study the sacred text of Christianity in the same way as they do that of Judaism in an effort to understand the historical Joshua son of Joseph. Behind the many enigmatic and conflicting traditions and the accretions of later generations, added after Christianity had severed itself from its Jewish beginnings and was increasingly involved in the destiny of Rome, there emerges from an impartial reading of the gospels of Matthew, Mark, and Luke the picture of a Jew who was probably a rabbinical student, a Pharisee, became a preacher and wonder-worker, taught a gentle ethic not unlike that of Hillel, and in the final year of his all too brief life felt himself to be at first a prophet and then the Messiah—and became an apocalyptic Pharisee.

The father of Joshua was a carpenter. His mother's name was Mary—Miriam in Hebrew. He had brothers and sisters. They lived in Nazareth, a town in the Galilee. We know almost nothing of his early years, the years Herod Antipas ruled the Galilee and procurators ruled Judea and the land was turbulent with violence and restless with expectations of the apocalypse, the promised end of days that would bring the Messiah and deliverance from Rome.

When he was about thirty years old Joshua son of Joseph was baptized in the Jordan River by John the Baptist, who was probably a member of the Essenes, Jewish sectarians who lived along the northern rim of the Dead Sea, maintained with care strict rules of purity, asceticism, and separation from what they saw as a corrupted world, and waited for the final war between the sons of light and the sons of darkness that would end in triumph for the God of Israel.

At the moment of baptism, the Holy Spirit descended upon Joshua and a voice from heaven announced that he was the elected one. He wandered off into the wilderness. He remained in the wilderness forty days and emerged transformed. The change in personality from Pharisaic teacher to apocalyptic Pharisee is given literary expression through the enigmatic tale of the mocking temptations of the devil to which Joshua refused to yield. All these events are related in the gospels. The term gospel is the Old English form of the Greek word *evangelion,* which means good news—in this instance, of the birth of the savior. On a Sabbath in a synagogue in Nazareth, at the start of his ministry, Joshua read from a scroll the words of the prophet Isaiah, "The Spirit of the Lord God is upon me, because the Lord has anointed me to bring good tidings to the afflicted. . . ." The Romans used the word *evangelion* when they announced a new caesar or the birth of an heir to the throne.

Joshua spent the following months teaching in the Galilee. He taught the moral precepts of the Pharisaic school of Hillel. When he urged the crowds that gathered about him to love their enemies he was adding his own ideas to those precepts. Scholars have pointed out that Joshua is the only one in the Christian Bible to utter this teaching; it is entirely unique to him.

He did not oppose the written or oral law, though he differed with some on certain details of the law. But much of the law was not yet fixed, and differences of opinion were common then among the Pharisees. He condemned the Pharisees as hypocrites, an accusation the Pharisees themselves hurled at some in their midst; it is found too in the Dead Sea Scrolls of the Essenes. He appears to have shared the doubts of the school of Shammai regarding proselytism. He was a miracle-healer—as were others at the time—but on occasion he would not heal non-Jews. The school of Hillel encouraged proselytism. Nowhere in rabbinic literature is there a law to the effect that a non-Jew may not be healed.

His teachings reveal a profound love for the oppressed,

the outcast. He urged purity of heart, humility; poverty and humility, not pride and possessions, are the marks of the true religious spirit. He promised the kingdom of heaven to those who were poor in spirit, to the meek, to those who mourn; the author of one of the Dead Sea Scrolls assures the humble, the oppressed in spirit, and those who mourn that they will attain salvation.

Passover was approaching. He made a pilgrimage to Jerusalem. He was joined by twelve disciples he had chosen to be judges of the twelve tribes of Israel at the Last Judgment. These disciples were a motley band. Peter and the sons of Zebedee, James and John, were fishermen; Matthew was a tax farmer, the most despicable occupation in the land; all were probably illiterate, with the exception of Matthew, whose work at recording and collecting taxes required the ability to read and write. They were tenuously bound together by love for their master and faith in his promise of the coming redemption.

The city of Jerusalem was crowded with pilgrims from all over the Roman empire. Many of those pilgrims no doubt listened with stunned hearts as Joshua predicted the destruction of the temple and its priests. Others saw him angrily overturn the tables of the dealers in money whose booths adjoined the temple area and who exchanged the foreign currency of pilgrims from outside the land into local coin. Riots were frequent in the city, especially during pilgrimages when the crowds could be stirred up by Zealots. The Sadducean priests were enraged by his prediction.

He spent the Passover Seder—his last supper—with his twelve disciples. They ate together the paschal lamb, the sacrifice that marked the redemption from slavery in Egypt. He recited the benediction over a cup of wine and is reported to have said, "Share it among you; for I tell you, I will not drink again of the fruit of the vine until I drink it new in the Kingdom of God." He recited the blessing over bread and said, "This is my body." The meanings of those words and acts are debated by his followers to this day.

The meal was over. Joshua, accompanied by his disciples, left the city and went to the Mount of Olives. He was arrested by the temple guard in the garden of Gethsemane after being pointed out by one of his disciples, Judas Iscariot. He was taken to the high priest. The circumstances of his arrest are unclear. Why was he betrayed? Why was it necessary for Judas to point him out?

He was held in custody in the house of the high priest. Temple scribes and priests had been called to the house. These were Sadducee members of the committee responsible for the functioning of the temple. The Sadducean high priests delivered him to the Romans. One who pretended to messianism was regarded as an inciter of rebellion. He could be turned over to the Romans without a verdict of the Jewish high court. The priests wanted to be rid of this latest troublemaker, this Joshua son of Joseph. The procurator, Pontius Pilate, had him executed by crucifixion.

The gospels inform us that three days after his crucifixion his tomb was discovered to be empty. His followers, who had disbanded after his death, now believed he had been resurrected and was in heaven.

During his lifetime, as he had gone about the land teaching, many had mocked him. But some had believed him to be the true Messiah son of David. The belief grew stronger after the claim that he was not really dead. He had thought himself also to be the son of man, the manlike judge of the Last Days who appears in the apocalyptic Book of Daniel. He had been a gentle apocalyptic teacher who had loved his oppressed people and his God, and he died on a cross, as had so many others before him. He had lived about thirty years. We know nothing of his physical appearance. In second-century Christian art he is depicted as the Good Shepherd, a beardless young man. Sometimes his hair is cut short and is curly; sometimes it is long. He looks like Apollo. By the fourth century he is bearded—the mark of the philosopher and divine teacher.

With the conclusion of the Passover festival the crowds had thinned and the city had grown less restive. In certain homes small groups of people—all of them observers of the law of Moses—began to meet and talk of Joshua son of Joseph, his teachings, which some had committed to memory, his death, his strange disappearance. Some reported having seen him again. His followers believed he was among them as they spoke of him and joined together in communal meals.

On the fiftieth day after the death of Joshua the disciples were assembled in an attic room when they were suddenly seized by an exaltation of spirit. From that day on they began to preach to the people and reach out actively for converts. The act of baptism marked admission into this new fellowship of faith; it called down the Spirit to cleanse the soul of sin. The Jewish authorities regarded the sect with increasing irritation. "No man should have any dealings with the sectarians," the rabbis warned. "Do not walk among them or enter their homes."

One of the homes in which the Joshua sect met was that of James, whose Hebrew name was Jacob. He was the younger brother of the executed Joshua. He and Peter now led the group. They met to talk of the teachings of their resurrected master, whom they now regarded as the son of man. They expected his imminent return and the coming of the kingdom of God. The years went by.

A Jew named Saul wandered back and forth across the Mediterranean world for much of his life and succeeded in transforming the founder of Christianity into its object of worship.

He began as a Pharisee and earned a living as a tentmaker; like the rabbis, he would accept no fee for teaching the Torah. He had watched with approval the stoning to death in Jerusalem of Stephen, a non-Jewish convert who had predicted the destruction of the temple. "We have heard him say," witnesses had testified against Stephen before the Jerusalem council of elders, "that this Jesus of Nazareth shall destroy this place and shall change the customs which Moses delivered us." At that point Stephen had begun preaching to the assembled throng. Apparently he used the Samaritan scriptures as the basis for his prediction of salvation for those who followed in the path of the dead Joshua and doom for those who did not. The Jews, enraged at this use of the scriptures of pagans for a chastising rod, ran him out of the city and stoned him to death.

After the burial of Stephen, which probably occurred

not very many years following the crucifixion of Jesus, the small group of believers was severely persecuted. Saul joined the persecutors—Jews who had begun to regard this new faith as a serious threat to the ancient covenant with God and reacted to its central teaching with anger. The belief that Joshua son of Joseph was the Messiah meant that Jewish history was at an end and its future as a separate faith would be without meaning. Together with other young zealous Jews and apparently with the approval of the chief priests—so we are told by the author of Acts—Saul broke into the homes of the followers of Joshua and hauled men and women off to prison. Many members of the sect scattered abroad, where they continued preaching the message of their master.

Saul had been raised in the city of Tarsus in Asia Minor. He was a Roman citizen; he could not be flogged without a trial and he could not be executed by crucifixion. He could appeal to the emperor a sentence passed upon him by a provincial court or ruler for a serious offense. While young he had journeyed to Jerusalem and become an ardent Pharisee. Sometime after the burial of Stephen he was sent by the high priest on a mission to the synagogue in Damascus. He was to determine whether or not that synagogue had been infiltrated by members of the Joshua sect.

We are told that Jesus appeared to him in a vision during that journey. Saul became ill and blind. Those who had accompanied him on the journey now led him by the hand to Damascus. He lay three days in a house on a street called Straight and could not eat or drink. He was cured and baptized by Ananias, a member of the Joshua sect in Damascus who had been told in a vision to seek him out. Saul was transformed from a persecutor of the new faith to a disciple of its dead founder.

He went off into the wilderness of Edom and Moab across the Jordan and the Dead Sea, a barren region occupied by the Nabateans, a once nomadic Arabian tribe that had settled there sometime around 300 B.C.E. We are told that he wandered through the wilderness for three years. When he emerged he bore within himself the conviction that he had seen the true Joshua in the flesh, the risen and glorified Joshua. From that time on he believed that the vision gave him the same authority and rank as the earliest apostles, those who had been the first to go out and preach the gospel.

We are told that he preached to the Jews in the Damascus synagogue about Joshua. The Jews were enraged. Some made plans to kill him. He fled to Jerusalem and sought to join the tiny remnant of the Joshua sect whose ranks he had helped reduce. He was greeted with astonishment and cold wariness. He learned of a plot against his life and fled to his birthplace, Tarsus, where he remained a number of years, dormant, silent. He had made no converts. He had even failed to gain the complete confidence of the followers of Joshua. Nothing is known about him during those Tarsus years. He appears to have sunk into oblivion.

A man named Barnabas journeyed from Jerusalem to Antioch. He was a member of the Joshua sect, the only person won over to the words of Saul; he had managed to persuade the Jerusalem group to receive Saul as a disciple after their initial hostile response to his presence in their midst. Now he succeeded in obtaining for Saul a position as teacher in the assembly house of the Antioch followers of Joshua. Then he and Saul were asked by the Antioch group to preach the gospel in areas where it was not yet known. That was the start of the first journey of Saul—or Paul, the Latin form of his name.

He and Barnabas journeyed from 45 to 49 C.E. to Cyprus and various cities in Asia Minor. Paul made it a habit to preach first in the synagogues of the cities he visited. Some synagogues had a special side room for non-Jewish fearers of God, pagans who had accepted the God of Israel but were not yet fully prepared to take on the observance of the law. This was the audience whose hearts Paul now won over—by the tens of thousands, according to some historians—to his vision of the meaning of Jesus.

Little is known about his appearance. He was probably a short man, certainly a passionate man, with a strong personality, obvious qualities of leadership, and an often irksome capacity for preoccupation with details. He was an urban man, fully at home in the cities of the Mediterranean. Nowhere does he write of village life. Christianity came first to urban populations. The Latin word *paganus,* from which we get the term pagan, means a peasant or a countryside dweller; rural populations were slow in accepting the message of the persuasive preacher of the gospel.

He had not known the historical Joshua son of Joseph; his call was from the risen Jesus, the son of God, supernatural, preexistent. He said of the historical Jesus that he was a Jew of Davidic descent, was betrayed, crucified, buried, and resurrected. Worldly standards ceased to be of importance to Paul in his estimate of a man. He had a new vision of the universe; it had been given to him by a supernatural being, not a man who had briefly walked the earth.

He preached a new covenant, one engraved not on stone but on the hearts of men and women. No law can bring salvation to mankind, because all mankind has been corrupted, is eternally mired in sin, as a result of the rebellious act and subsequent fall of Adam. We can be saved only through an act of mercy on the part of God. That act of mercy was indeed shown us when God's son, Jesus, chose to abandon his equality with his Father, was born of a woman, and died on a cross—as atonement for mankind. The entire corrupted cosmos was redeemed through that act; it was crucified and has begun to die; soon the Messiah will come again from heaven. We must prepare for him. By proclaiming faith in Jesus man may be reconciled to God. But it must be done soon, before the coming of the Last Judgment. There is an urgency about the preaching of Paul, a desperate need to convert the world before it is too late. Creed brings salvation; the law deadens the heart. Why is it that many do not respond to this truth? Because God in His mysterious grace has predestined some to be saved and others to be eternally damned—and man can never know the reason. But by choosing Jesus a man reveals he has been chosen by God.

When Paul broke with the Mosaic law, did away with circumcision and dietary regulations as prerequisites for conversion—and at a crucial meeting in 49 C.E. convinced the Jerusalem group of followers to support him at least in the matter of circumcision—he severed forever any future possibility of connection between the rapidly growing new faith and the ancient people of Israel. That Jerusalem meeting, the first church council, was the turning point in the history of Christianity. The infant church broke with its mother and went off on its own. Soon the dietary laws would be abolished; so would the seventh day of the week as the Sabbath, the observance of the festivals, the laws concerning purification. The unwillingness of the Christians to participate in the Jewish rebellions of 67 and 130 C.E. made vivid in the realm of politics what was already clear in the world of faith. All the ties to the long Jewish past were cast off by Paul as he carried his vision on four journeys through the Mediterranean world. Yet he taught that the Jew should be treated with love because he is the brother of the Christian and will one day accept Jesus.

In Jerusalem during the fourth journey he was arrested and charged with preaching that non-Jews should be permitted to enter the temple, a serious breach of the law. Handed over to the procurator for punishment, he invoked the privilege of Roman citizenship and was sent off on a ship to Rome, where he anticipated a quick handling of his case and, at worst, a light sentence.

He lived for two years in a tenement house in Rome under a mild form of house arrest, waiting for his trial. He preached the gospel to all who visited him. He wrote letters. Nero was emperor then.

In 64 C.E.—some scholars think it may have been 67 or 68 C.E.—Paul was beheaded. It is believed that Peter was also martyred in Rome, probably in the scapegoat slaughter of Christians that followed the burning of the city.

In the centuries after Nero, Christianity suffered nine persecutions at the hands of Rome. It seemed an incomprehensible sect. Romans at first regarded its adherents with suspicion: they were thought to be the followers of a crucified rebel; they would not bear arms for Rome. Later they were looked upon with loathing. The people of the empire sacrificed to their many gods and were united religiously by their worship of the emperor. History was dated from the founding of Rome—in 753 B.C.E., according to one ancient Roman historian, or 751 B.C.E., according to another. The Christians worshiped Christ and would not participate in the emperor cult. They believed the world had entered a new historical era since the coming of their founder.

Unlike the troublesome Jews, Christians belonged to no nation and were without roots in a land or history. They claimed that their country was heaven. They lived in densely populated cities but remained aloof from the pagans all around them. They would not eat meat sacrificed to the gods; their sculptors would not carve idols; they would not send their children to pagan schools because the textbooks contained stories of the gods: the poetry of Homer and Vergil. The Roman authorities—emperors, senators, consuls, and governors—gazed upon the flutterings of the early church with, at best, benign contempt and, at worst, violent hostility. Still the sect survived and grew.

During the three centuries that followed the death of Paul, Christianity canonized its sacred writings and, emulating the Jews, created its own Bible. The faith spread through Asia Minor and followed the trade routes to Gaul and Britain. In 177 C.E. a persecution destroyed churches in southern France; raging mobs hurled at the Christians accusations of cannibalism and incest. By the second century there was a Christian church in Celtic Britain.

It was an untidy Christianity in those centuries, loosely organized and noisy with doctrinal strife. It encountered throughout the empire a multitude of cults, doctrines, prophets, teachers, and mystery religions. To this heaving ocean of pagan faiths Christianity now added numerous versions about its own nature and origins—a variety of Christianities—each based upon a different understanding of the events and doctrines out of which the new religion had been born. Christian leaders argued loudly, face to face and by letter and treatise, about the nature of Jesus, his relationship to God, the reasons for the delayed second coming, the notion of pure spirit and corrupt flesh, how to read and understand Scriptures, how to organize the church. Everyone seemed a heretic to someone; but since there was no single dominant church with a set of hard doctrines there could not yet be heresies. Christianity was in a primordial state of being, creative, fluid, mercurial, spinning off sects and doctrines into a pagan world tremulous and glutted to near-death with accretions of gods, priests, astrologers, diviners, demons; with hedonists, cynical nonbelievers, patient stoics, effete aristocrats, and superstitious mobs; with specters of disease, plague, economic instability; and with distant barbarians crashing unceasingly against the borders of the empire.

It seemed a Darwinian world of faith, and it bred strange creatures. One cult worshiped images of Homer, Pythagoras, Plato, Aristotle, Jesus, and Paul. The Roman emperor Alexander Severus, who ruled from 222 to 235 C.E., worshiped with equal reverence in his domestic chapel statues of Abraham, Orpheus, Jesus, and Apollonius of Tyana, a Greek Pythagorean philosopher who lived about 100 C.E. and about whose life we know nothing with certainty.

Into this tumultuous world of gods and cults, uncertainties and fears, came Christianity with its savior god and his resurrection, its emphasis on redemption through faith, its utter certainty about life in the hereafter for those cleansed of sin, its assertion that it alone knew the way to salvation, and the readiness of many of its adherents to accept martyrdom. Slowly, as the decades went by, the organization of the church evolved from a loose structure of self-governing local churches with preachers, traveling evangelists, teachers, healers, and administrators to centralized rule by a bishop, an overseer, in each community. Only one person could conduct the rites of the Lord's Supper, and it was probably out of that sacramental act that centralizing leadership was born. In time the most important of the bishoprics would become that in Rome, center of the empire, site of the martyrdom of Paul and Peter and so many others of the faithful. Doctrinal matters were fought out; some were resolved; others would plague the church for centuries.

In 249 C.E. an army officer named Decius took the throne of Rome. A year later the empire was persecuting

Christians everywhere. Decius sought to unite the Roman world and bring an end to the pervading restlessness and near-anarchy of the time by enforcing the worship of the traditional pagan gods of Rome. He arrested and executed senior clergy. Christians were ordered to make a libation or a sacrifice to the gods of Rome; the emperor did not specifically include himself among the gods. Those who refused were executed or thrown into prison; those who agreed were given certificates. Many fled; many acquired certificates through bribery.

Many were martyred. Tertullian, one of the earliest thinkers of the church, regarded the blood of martyrs as the seed of faith. The victims were mostly clergy and prominent laity. The ordinary Christian who did not parade his faith was rarely touched by Roman persecution.

Decius died in battle in the summer of 251 c.e. The persecution came to an end. Scholars tell us that, in the years that followed, martyrdom came to be seen as a second baptism. It was a baptism not of water but of blood. All sins that had been committed since the first baptism were remitted by this second baptism. Some longed for and openly sought death by martyrdom.

There were other persecutions, but they failed to uproot the church; they were sporadic, half-hearted. People throughout the empire had begun to make their peace with Christianity. Provincial governors preferred to leave the Christians alone; few governors wanted martyrs within their borders.

From 303 to 312 c.e. Christianity suffered its worst and most persistent persecution. It began about the twentieth year of the reign of Diocletian and came as a shock, for the emperor was known as a tolerant man and had a Christian wife. It is generally assumed that the persecution was instigated by the man he had appointed to succeed him, Galerius, whose views on conformity finally proved persuasive. An edict was issued in 303. There were to be no executions. Churches were to be destroyed. The sacred writings of the Christians, their Scriptures, were to be handed over to the authorities and burned.

Other edicts followed after someone set fire to the emperor's palace in Nicomedia in Asia Minor. There was talk about the burning of Rome in the time of Nero. Clerics were imprisoned. They could sacrifice to the gods and gain release or rot in their stone cells. A fourth edict demanded sacrifice and gave death as the alternative. Many were martyred; many sacrificed; many found loopholes and managed to escape the law.

The persecution continued after Diocletian retired in 305 C.E. One hundred Christians died in a single day in Egypt. In the east some provincial governors hesitated to carry out the repressive orders from Rome. Christianity was everywhere in the east now, in the cities, villages, and countryside. Pagans were sickened by the brutalities; sympathy had swung to the Christians. The effort to unite the empire under the old gods was failing. The Roman gods seemed near death.

In 311 C.E., as Galerius lay dying, he made a deathbed statement repenting the persecutions and granting legal recognition to Christians. Another persecution was undertaken in 312 C.E. by Maximinus, successor to Galerius. It too failed.

In that same year, Constantine, a challenger to the throne, met Maximinus in a battle at the Milvian Bridge near Rome. Since the retirement of Diocletian the empire had known nothing but civil war. Constantine's father had been an assistant emperor and had ruled in Gaul and Britain. He had been a pagan monotheist, a worshiper of the Unconquerable Sun. Constantine too worshiped the sun. It is said that he had his soldiers paint the cross on their standards before the battle. Perhaps it was a desperate move by a man who was staking everything on a single military engagement. He sought the help of the Christian God as well as his own; they seemed not too far apart. The armies fought. The victory seemed miraculous, for Constantine's forces had been heavily outnumbered.

He issued coins which depict the sun and the cross. On another coin a cross is destroying a serpent, symbolic of the destruction of paganism by Christianity. On a third set of coins Constantine is in armor and on the crest of his helmet is the cross.

He instituted Sunday as a compulsory day of rest and forbade the construction of pagan temples in his new capital, Constantinople. He rejected paganism but would not persecute its followers. He was not baptized until shortly before his death. Scholars continue to debate the precise date and depth of his commitment to Christianity.

After three hundred years of struggle the new faith had emerged triumphant. The destruction of Jerusalem in 70 C.E. had emptied the city of Jewish followers who might have steered the Joshua sect back to Judaism after the death of Paul. Christianity turned from Judaism and moved into the pagan world. There it met alien cults, strange creeds. Some it absorbed; others it fought. The church polemicized against pagan intellectuals. It said of the Jews that their law was dead and that Christianized pagans had replaced them as the people of God. It vilified their synagogues. It accused them of having put to death its savior—and set the stage for a passion play in which my people has acted the central role for almost two thousand years.

As Rome continued to suffer from civil war and social and economic chaos, Christianity increased its numbers, grew wealthy with donations, built large churches, established major teaching centers in Rome, Alexandria, and Antioch, and developed the thinkers who have come to be known as the church fathers—Clement, Origen, Tertullian, Justin, and others. It helped the pagan mired in a morass of gods to find a path to meaningful faith by offering him one irrevocable choice to salvation, and it showed how the community of a Christian congregation could be an effective embrace against the bitter chill of urban loneliness felt by the peasant who had come to the city seeking work, by the lonely soldier released from the army, the freed slave, the ruined landowner, the pensioner whose fixed income was being devoured by inflation. Christian philanthropy toward strangers, its impulse toward mutual concern, its care of the dead, its acceptance of every person no matter from what tribe, city, or countryside—these were the attractions of the early church to the masses of mankind.

It had a wide embrace. Jews could appreciate its monotheism and rigorous moral standards. Initiates into mystery cults could feel at home in the intimacy of the congregation. Intellectual pagans could learn from Origen to read Scriptures through the screening of allegorical interpretation. Those concerned with doctrine could ponder the concept of the Trinity developed by Tertullian. Those taken by ecstatic religion might hear the words of Clement of Alexandria as he described Christianity in the language of the mystery religions. "Mysteries truly sacred!" he wrote in his *Exhortation to the Heathen*. "O light undefiled! In the flare of torches I behold the heavens of God. Being initiated, I become holy. The Lord himself inducts me. . . . Come if you will and be initiated. Dance in the chorus with angels around the unbegotten and imperishable only true God. . . ."

Christianity was now the religion of the Roman empire. Its ranks swelled. It faced the grime of everyday life rather than the opalescent vision of builders and dreamers. How should it deal with the heretics in its midst? The price of power and expansion was moral laxity. How treat corrupt clerics and kings? How were church and state to fuse into a Christian polity?

Augustine, bishop of Hippo in Africa, one of the Latin fathers, offered answers to these questions. He lived from 354 to 430 C.E. and witnessed the dying years of Rome. At the age of thirty-two, after years of debauched living, he heard a voice from God say repeatedly, "Take up and read; take up and read." The Scriptural passage he turned to by chance told him, "Not in rioting and drunkenness, not in chambering and wantonness, not in strife and envying: but put ye on the Lord Jesus Christ, and make not provision for the flesh. . . ." He became a Christian and spent his life writing and preaching.

The government had the right to suppress heresy, he wrote. The goal of the church was the conquest of the world. It was to absorb and perfect all human institutions and relations. It was to create a total Christian society in which people would not be given the choice whether or not to belong. Violence was permissible in a spiritual cause. It was the sacred responsibility of the church to unearth real and incipient heresy; it was the task of the state to punish those found guilty. Without discipline there would be chaos; man is incapable of resisting the "sheer, sweet taste of sinning."

This and a good deal more in a similar vein was the thinking of this strange man who mirrored the transformation of the now dominant church and was taken up as the theologian of imperial Christianity. He lowered a veil of darkness across the face of classical paganism. And of the Jews he wrote that though they deserved the harshest of punishments for having slain Jesus, they were being kept alive by a providential God in order to serve, together with their Scriptures, as living witnesses to the eternal truth of Christianity.

Augustine lived long enough to see Vandals invade and ravage Africa in 429 C.E., slaughtering priests, torturing monks, burning churches. He died in 430.

The church carried within itself his vision of the world for fifteen hundred years. Often it dominated the voices of piety and saintliness. Early Christianity had expected the imminent coming of Joshua son of Joseph, the Messiah. Pauline Christianity had urged people to prepare for the arrival of the son of God. Augustinian Christianity saw mankind as existing in the final stage between the first and second comings of Christ. It was to be a lengthy stage during which Christianity would subdue the world.

Paganism was in decay. The great classical schools in Alexandria and Athens shut their doors very early in the sixth century. Many pagan temples closed down. Some were burned by Christians.

During the final decades of the fifth century, as Rome lay crushed beneath waves of wandering barbarians, Christianity went forward to Christianize and civilize the tribes which had settled in the vast corpse of the dead empire. Missionaries moved through Provence and the towns along the rich river valley of the Rhine. They built churches and monasteries. They converted whole tribes. They made their way along the old Roman roads and entered the courts of chieftains and kings. They wandered into trade fairs in the large cities and into the marketplaces of villages. Often the messengers of Christ met Jews.

We call those barbaric tribes Germans because that was

what the Romans called them, Germani, applying to all the people along the Rhine-Danube frontier the name of only one tribe—as they had once used the tribal name Graeci to designate all the Hellenes. The Germans called themselves Theut, from which we get the words Teuton and Deutsch. The word Theut means people or folk.

They were one of three nomadic peoples who entered western Europe between the fifth and the eighth centuries. The other two were the Mongols and Arabs. Only the Germans stayed and settled the land—and began the process of creating western civilization.

I gaze at these centuries of confusion and know that I have witnessed them before when Amorites invaded Sumer and Arameans penetrated the Fertile Crescent and Dorians snuffed out the world of Mycenae. Centuries of darkness followed each of those tribal movements. Each time the light returns and we are able to see the new world that has been created on the ruins of the old, we discover familiar elements of the overthrown civilization in the creativity of the new. We may find ourselves listening to a foreign tongue and viewing strange customs. The seminality—the flow of original creativity of the old civilization—is certainly dead. But the forms, the art, and the ideas of that civilization have been absorbed by the newcomers. The great civilizations of our species did not die; what was best in them has remained invisibly alive through the millennia, silent accretions, layer upon layer within and all about us, moving us with painstaking slowness away from the dark magic of our beginnings. The old and decayed world fuses with the young and barbaric one—and renewed seminal creativity occurs. That is what happened once again as these German tribes slowly became sedentary and fused their culture with the civilization of Rome.

Pagan Rome had not died. The legions were dead, but a professional army is one of the most peripheral elements of a culture. The old gods appeared dead—even the immemorial goddess of the private hearth could no longer be worshiped. The church had made bonfires of pagan books and oracles. Pagan temples had been destroyed. But in retrospect we know it all to have been a surface cleansing. The church was far more ruthless to Christian heresies than it was to Roman paganism. Slowly it absorbed and metamorphosed the world of Rome. Idols remained; their names and faces changed, as did their ancient relationship to the forces of nature. Saints took the place of local benevolent deities. Pagan festivals became Christian holidays. Roman Christianity was a creation of the Roman empire through adoption by Constantine and reinterpretation by Augustine. The monastic orders read and preserved the Bible and the rich theological literature created by the church fathers. But in order to study rhetoric, a subject urged by Augustine as a tool for conquest through polemic, the monks read the works of Roman authors. Latin remained alive, the language of prayer and learning and ordinary church discourse. The Roman emperor was replaced in the end by theoretically omnipotent German emperors ruling over a Christianized Roman world. What the Roman church most desired was the restoration of the old boundaries of the empire under the spiritual dominion of the now sanctified center in Rome. The empire of pagan Rome was overrun in 476 c.e., but Roman paganism did not come to an end.

About fifteen hundred years before the fall of Rome, these Germans had begun to migrate southward from the lands we now call Norway, Sweden, and Denmark. By the end of the first century c.e. the region of the Danube was swollen with Germans. We know them under the name Goths. Until about the year 1000 we see in Italy and Gaul the shifting fortunes of these volatile Germans as they seek to settle themselves in this new world. The Vikings who invaded and migrated into this territory in the ninth century were of the same ethnic stock as the Germans. But by then the Germans had been Christianized and their dialects, mixing with Late Latin, or Romance, had begun to create the various languages of the peoples that an eighth-century Spanish chronicler would, for the first time, label with the adjective "European." Until the fourteenth century the fused world of German tribes and Roman Christianity was known as Christianitas, Chretienté—Christendom.

Just as the Fertile Crescent world of today is, if we

turn away from the vanished Sumerians, basically Semitic, so is western Europe, including England, basically Germanic. Vandals, Goths, Burgundians, Lombards, Franks, and others—these were all tribal groupings united by Germanic language and culture.

The German tribes brought to Gaul and Christianity various levels of cultural development. The Franks were violent and barely touched by Roman civilization. Others were at the same stage of development as the people on the Roman side of the frontier. They farmed and traded extensively with Roman merchants and had been early converted to Christianity—Arian Christianity, which held that Jesus was not coeternal with God but had been made by the Father to do His creative work. Jesus was not quite human and not quite divine; he was a demigod. Thus Roman Christianity had to conquer not only pagans of various degrees of culture but also pagans who had been converted to a variant form of Christianity. The Franks had been untouched by Arianism. As had been the case with the invading Amorites, Arameans, and Dorians, the Germans too had no writing. Literacy was tenuously preserved by the church, one of its greatest achievements.

The Germans had considerable skill in metalwork and jewelry and a highly developed folk poetry. The Anglo-Saxon poem *Beowulf* and the German *Nibelungenlied* are remnants of this poetry. *Beowulf* is to the world of Europe what the Homeric epics were to Greece and the Samson cycle was to the ancient Israelites: tales from the semibarbarous heroic age of an infant civilization.

The basic unit of the German tribe was the family, the primitive kindred blood tie. This underwent a change during the invasions. By 600 C.E. loyalties had been transferred from kin to kingship. Allegiance was given to the warrior who was the best fighter and brought back the most booty. The basic unit of the Germans was now the chieftain and his warriors.

The king might claim descent from Woden, supreme god of war, learning, poetry, and magic, who fashioned the earth and the sky from the corpse of the giant Ymir, created the first man and woman from an ash tree and an alder, and, with his wife Frigg and his children Thor, Balder, and Tiw, lived at his court in Valhalla attended by the Valkyries; the king might strut about and act as if kingship were his private property and choose a member of the royal family to take the throne after him—dynasties developed early among some of the Germanic tribes; but wherever original German institutions remained untouched by contact with Rome, the people retained the right to elect their king. This principle often led to chaos as German dynasties rose and fell throughout the centuries of European history.

Blood feuds were common, as was killing that resulted from brawls. Such killing was not considered murder; when you killed a man in a fair fight you might have to reckon with his kinsmen but not with the tribal court. Murder was an act done in stealth; it was an act of killing in which the identity of the killer was uncertain. An individual suspected of murder would undergo a complex procedure of swearing an oath during which a momentary cough or hesitation might condemn him. Or he would be put to an ordeal of hot iron, hot water, or cold water. You grasped a red-hot piece of metal in your hands and released it; your hands were bandaged; three days later the bandages were removed; if the burns were found to be healing without infection you were innocent. Or you put your arm into a cauldron of boiling water; it was then bandaged; if it was healing three days later you were innocent. Or they tied your hands and feet and threw you into a river; if you sank, you were innocent; if you floated, you were guilty—water was a divinity and it would not receive one who was guilty. Everyone believed that divine forces intervened actively in human affairs and would reveal guilt or innocence. If you stood convicted by the ordeal you were immediately hanged by the neck. It appears that death by hanging was introduced into civilization by Germanic tribes. (Most scholars now agree that hanging was not a mode of execution in the ancient world and that wherever the word appears in the Bible it should probably be translated as impalement.)

These were the tribes that shattered Rome. First came the Burgundians in 406 C.E. They settled in the Rhône valley. Then came the primitive Vandals, who cut through France and Spain and went on into North Africa. Then the Goths broke out in 480 C.E., the Visigoths (western Goths) taking Spain and southern Gaul and the Ostrogoths (eastern Goths) settling throughout the Italian peninsula and in Sicily.

The Franks moved southward into Gaul at the start of the fifth century and settled in the region of Paris, colonizing to the north and south and establishing a dynasty known as the Merovingians. In 496 C.E. the Merovingian king, Clovis I, accepted Roman Christianity and was accorded the honorary titles of consul and Augustus. The Franks went on to conquer the rest of Gaul.

In the end, the kingdom included all of today's France and much of the southern half of western Germany. When Clovis I died he divided the kingdom among his sons, who then spent their time plundering each other. Decades of chaos and carnage followed.

By the seventh century about sixty percent of the population consisted of serfs tied to the estates of warring and carousing lords. These serfs lived like the animals that plowed their fields and pulled their wagons—working, breeding, and dying. Perhaps once a year a priest came to them from a distant cathedral and administered the sacraments. There was no parish clergy. The serf lived surrounded by terrifying forces of nature, which he worshiped fervently to ward off their demonic powers. The waters of baptism dried swiftly in this peasant world of fierce superstition and fertility cults. Saints and relics were adopted as additional weapons against angry storms, fearful nights, wild animals, raging diseases, and the relentless misery of existence.

There was no middle class. It had disintegrated in the wake of the economic decline that had resulted from the coming of the Franks and their conquest of Gaul. Towns were depopulated; in 600 C.E. no more than three percent of the people of France lived in urban areas. A town with a population of two thousand people was both sizable and rare.

This was the world which Jews began to enter in some numbers about the start of the eighth century, making

their way across the Mediterranean, then moving northward into the rich valleys, forested hills, villages, towns,
and tribes of Christendom.

There had been Jews in that land in the days of pagan
Rome.

During the dying years of European Jewry in our own
century—the decade of the thirties—a Jewish cemetery
was unearthed in the city of Cologne in western Germany.
It dated to Roman times, Cologne had once been a Roman colony named Colonia Agrippina. Two edicts, issued
by the emperor Constantine in 321 and 331 C.E. mention
the Jews of the city. Cologne was then the seat of the
provincial and military administration. The edicts order
the Jews to accept, together with other Romans, the bur-
densome duties of curia, members of a voting district with
collective responsibility for some aspects of civic life,
which might have included compulsory attendance at the
funerals of near and distant neighbors and the payment of
certain taxes. Nothing more is known about the Jews of
Cologne until the eleventh century, when many of them
no doubt were buried in that cemetery, slain by the pious
mobs gathering for the first Christian crusade against Islam.

There were Jews in the valley of the Moselle in Germany in 888 C.E. and all up and down the Rhineland by
the year 1000. They engaged in agriculture and viticul-
ture. Many were respected international merchants able to
travel with ease across the lines that now divided the
world into two warring powers, Christianity and Islam—
because they could read and write, because they had trade
contacts in both worlds, often fellow Jews, and because
Christians and Muslims trusted them more than they
trusted one another. For a reason not yet clear there were
among these early German Jews few, if any, doctors.

In the city of Avignon in southern France a stamp seal
has been found dating to the fourth century. The seal
contains a menorah with five, instead of the usual seven,
branches. Mute testimony to an inadequately educated
Jew? We do not know. In Narbonne, on the coast of
southern France, a tombstone dated to 687 C.E. was

uncovered. It has a Latin inscription containing three Hebrew words: *shalom al Yisrael*. The words mean peace to the people Israel. They are poorly spelled.

There were Jews in Agde, in southern France, in the year 506 C.E. We know that because their presence is noted in church records. There were synagogues in Paris and Orléans in the sixth century. There were Jews in Marseilles. In 576 C.E. the bishop of Clermont-Ferrand, a town was of Lyon, offered the Jews baptism or expulsion. There were more than five hundred Jews there at the time. About a century earlier the bishop of the town had written some letters in which he mentioned the presence of Jews; these are the oldest written records dealing with Jews in France. Many of the Jews accepted baptism; others fled to Marseilles. Newly Christianized Visigoths dominated southern Gaul from 589 to 711 C.E., and few Jews entered the land at that time. Then Visigothic rule came to an end. Jews began to migrate into the land.

They came from the crowded city slums of the eastern world into which many had been pushed by Muslim conquest. Rich fields had been taken over by Arabs; outlying areas were exposed to pillage by roaming bands of brigands. Palestinian Jewry almost emptied the land after the Arabs took Jerusalem; they had waited for the Messiah, not yet another earthly conqueror; and the land was an economic ruin now, too often fought over, too often plundered. Jews came from Baghdad, Antioch, Damascus, North Africa, Spain, Italy. They went singly or in small groups, five or ten hardy individuals penetrating the green forested land of Gaul, contacting tribes, learning languages, obtaining trade charters—documents of incorporation outlining their rights—from rulers eager to purchase medicaments and spices and to sell furs and slaves. Some Jews came from Byzantium and moved into central Europe through the valley of the Danube; others came by sea to the ports of southern Italy, then up along the towns of the peninsula into Provence or across the Alps to the valley of the Rhine; still others landed in southern France and journeyed up the valley of the Rhône to the Seine and the Meuse. They were along the

Elbe by the tenth century. They were the vanguard of a culture war between Talmudic Judaism and the world of Europe that would result in the second of the two major developments of rabbinic civilization. That war would spin itself out far away from the sunny Mediterranean and Fertile Crescent worlds in which that civilization had been born.

The Jewish culture that would both mirror and be created by that war would come to be called Ashkenazic. The world Ashkenaz appears in the Bible a number of times and seems to refer to a land and a people bordering on the upper Euphrates and Armenia. No one knows how and when it first came to be used of the Jewish community of Germany and northern France. Today the term embraces all of European Jewry north of Italy and Spain, including Jews and the descendants of Jews from Poland, Lithuania, and Russia. It designates the civilization of the Jews who wandered for centuries through the chill world of Europe and is used in contradistinction to Sephardic, the form taken by rabbinic civilization during its encounter with the world of Spain.

In the year 524, during the period of the German tribal invasions of Gaul, only a few pioneering Jews lived in Valence, an important town in today's southeastern France. There was no organized Jewish community in that town until 1323. In 1441 the bishop reminded the Jews of Valence that they were obliged to wear the Jew badge on their garments so that "guests be not regarded as citizens." There were eighteen Jewish families in the town at the time.

Those two Valence dates, 524 and 1441, form an arc of time that begins in light and hope and ends in a dark grandeur of blood, stubborn dreams, and the determination by a suffering people to continue wandering with their own vision of the world. Some of the descendants of those Jews from Valence may have wandered into the gaseous hell invented by some of the descendants of the tribes that tore apart Gaul before and after missionaries converted their warlords to Roman Christianity.

For more than three centuries the German arrivals to

Christianity and the Jewish arrivals to Gaul lived as neighbors, spoke the same language, traded with one another, held public office together, entered each other's homes, followed the same professions and crafts, often had identical names—and neither seemed scarred by this arrangement. Jews and Christians differed only in their religious beliefs and practices. It was a harsh, often cruel frontier world; to the peasant and the warlord there seemed little point to quarrels about matters of belief.

The church, unhappy over this state of affairs, repeatedly warned Christians against close contact with Jews. A din of anti-Jewish legislation arises from the church councils of these and previous centuries. Christian women are not to marry Jews. Christian slaves are not to be sold to Jews. Christian peasants are not to share meals with Jews, accept their food, or observe the Jewish day of rest. The incessant restatement of these and other church laws over so many centuries seems a clear indication to many scholars of the extent to which they went unheeded.

At the church council of Paris in 845-846 C.E., the assembled clerics urged that Jews be prohibited from proselytizing their slaves, be kept from holding public office and from appearing in public around Easter time, and not be permitted to construct new synagogues. These church laws were submitted to the king of France, Charles the Bald, for promulgation and enforcement.

The grandfather of Charles was Charlemagne; his great-grandfather, Pepin the Short, had put an end to the Merovingian dynasty. Charlemagne had savagely conquered, Christianized, and thinly civilized a vast territory. He reinstituted the office of emperor. At his coronation in 800 C.E., his chief religious adviser remarked that of the three highest powers in the world—the papacy in Rome, the emperor in Constantinople, and the royal dignity of Charlemagne—the third was the most important. Charlemagne died and his empire was divided among his grandsons. Louis received the area east of the Rhine—Germany; Lothair was given the middle kingdom—Burgundy and Alsace-Lorraine—and the title emperor; and Charles the Bald took most of what is today's France. Listening now to the request of the churchmen that he accept the recommendations of the Paris church council, Charles the Bald thought the Jews too much an asset to have them ruined by theology. He rejected all the proposals.

Without the consent of the people and the secular state, the church was helpless to enforce its regulations against the Jews. What it sought to do during these turbulent centuries was to prevent the Jews from proselytizing and to encourage them to convert to Christianity. Apparently it had cause for concern regarding Jewish efforts to convert pagans to Judaism. A Jewish master would of necessity convert his slaves to Judaism, else they would be useless to him: Jewish law forbade the eating of food and the drinking of wine handled by non-Jews. There was also the intrinsic attraction of Jewish life, its festivals, days of rest, and celebrations, which did not fail to catch the eyes of hard-working peasants and artisans. A number of high members of the church converted to Judaism during this period: a priest named Bodo from the court of the emperor, Louis the Pious, accepted Judaism in 838 C.E., probably as a result of his contacts with the Jewish merchants who had easy access to the royal court; a cleric named Wecelin; an archbishop named Andreas; and others. Some of these conversions rocked all of Christendom.

The polemical literature of that time is often crude and inflammatory on both sides. In those days the Jews did not hesitate to express themselves bluntly about Christianity and what they regarded as a venal clergy, corrupt papacy, and monastic orders more interested in wealth than piety. A book called *The Life of Jesus,* compiled by a ninth-century Jew out of earlier materials, is a parody of the gospels and a banal and crude account of the ministry of Jesus. About fifty works of Jewish polemical literature—treatises, parodies, poems, dialogues—have survived the heavy hand of later church censors.

Gaul disintegrated politically after the death of Charlemagne. With no one to hold them at the center, the lands that would one day be France and Germany had broken apart into warring principalities. Normans came from Scandinavia, burning and pillaging and settling permanently in the part of France now called Normandy. Muslims raided Provence. Hungarians penetrated Germany. It was like the period of the judges once experienced by the tribes of Judah and Israel—but now there were no judges. The pillaging was not everywhere at the same time, but it was somewhere all the time; one day a band of axe-wielding Vikings might appear in your village and leave some hours later, and it would be a while before the smell of burning and death ceased to thicken the air.

The weakening of secular power should have led to the strengthening of the papacy. But Christendom was in retreat during those centuries. Culture was with the world of Islam. Between 897 and 955 C.E. seventeen popes followed one another in swift succession; the papacy was as much the center of intrigue as the court of a warlord. Church offices were bought and sold. Bishops were appointed by secular rulers and led raiding armies.

There was nothing in this culture to challenge the Jews who settled in the towns of France and Germany as laborers and artisans, worked vineyards, or journeyed along ancient roads as international merchants protected by royal charters against molestation, unlawful tolls, and inequitable procedure in lawsuits. Probably the Jews regarded the world around them with thinly veiled contempt.

From the time of Charlemagne the word Jew had come to convey a picture of a trusted merchant. These Jewish merchants would meet one another at the fairs that were held periodically in Cologne, Champagne, Troyes, and other centers of trade where merchants from all of northern Europe gathered. Dimly—because historical sources are scarce—we can see the Jewish merchants beginning to utilize these fairs as assemblies for the exchange of information about Jewish communities scattered throughout the world. Decisions would be made concerning Jewish life in the land of Ashkenaz: the regulation of business practices; the development of educational and charitable institutions; the establishment of contacts with the secular rulers and their underlings; the raising of taxes; the construction of synagogues; the enforcement of law. The news in one community would here be passed on to all communities. These meetings of Jewish merchants gathered at the fairs were probably the beginnings of organized Jewry in Ashkenaz.

The status of Jews in the period after Charlemagne was fluid; each duchy and county had its own rules. Gregory I, who had been pope from 590 to 604 C.E., and was no doubt one of the greatest popes of early Roman Christianity, had written, "Just as it should not be permitted the Jews to presume to do in their synagogues anything other than what is permitted them by law, so with regard to those things which have been conceded them, they ought to suffer no injury." He forbade forced conversion of Jews. All Christendom accepted his words—and each king and cleric interpreted them as he saw fit. In Toulouse a Jew would be slapped in the face publicly by the bishop every year at Easter time as punishment for the betrayal of Jesus. In 848 C.E. the Jews of Bordeaux were accused of somehow betraying the city to a pillaging band of Danes. The Jews of Sens, a town southeast of Paris, were expelled in 876 C.E. At the fairs the merchants would discuss these occasional outbursts of Christian malice, decide how to help a stricken community and how to seek the favor of this or that cleric or ruler. They would find special delight in debating the wisdom of the various decisions being handed down by the rabbinical scholars who had begun to migrate into the land.

These were not professional rabbis; there would not be a class of professional rabbis in the Jewish communities of the Rhineland until some centuries later. They were scholars, as Hillel and Shammai and Akiva once had been, teachers of Torah who had made their living as merchants or artisans or from vineyards.

The Jews who had come to Gaul beginning in the eighth century had brought with them the tradition of learning and a loyalty to Talmudic law. By the year 1000 the patches of mist covering this community begin to roll away, and we find ourselves gazing at a small Jewish world far from the original home of the Jewish people yet governing itself entirely by the legal system that had been created in and near that home—the Babylonian Talmud.

We have now turned another of our invented corners in

time and entered the present millennium. In the year 1000 panic swept Christendom: this was to be the year of the end of the world and the Last Judgment. Two Saxon scribes wrote the only manuscript of *Beowulf* that has come down to us, probably using material composed by an eighth-century bard. The first Christian is supposed to have reached America—a Viking named Leif Ericson. The Chinese perfected their invention of gunpowder.

There were Jewish communities all through the eastern world—in Byzantium, Mesopotamia, Arabia, Egypt, Persia, India, and China. But the east seemed weary and was no longer the locus of Jewish creativity. There were communities in North Africa and Spain.

During the seventh and eighth centuries there was apparently a thriving Jewish community in southern Italy. Not very much is known about it. We sense its presence through the scholars it sent out to various parts of the Jewish world.

Sometime around the ninth century a number of families from southern Italy migrated to France. Then they moved farther north and west into the river valley of the Rhine. Two rabbinic scholars settled in the city of Mainz, south of present-day Frankfort and downriver from Cologne. The two scholars were Rabbi Moses the Elder and Rabbi Abun the Great. They began to teach. The son of Rabbi Moses the Elder was Rabbi Kalonymus. About a dozen of his written responses to questions of Jewish law have survived. Scholars regard them as the oldest known rabbinic writings of European Jewry, preceding by about twenty-five years the responsa of Rabbi Moses ben Hanoch of Cordova. By the year 1000, when the Jewish community in the Rhine River valley comes sharply into view, the German Christian city of Mainz is host to a flourishing center of Talmudic scholarship which is attracting students from as far away as Italy and Spain.

The greatest of these students was Rabbenu—our master—Gershom ben Judah, who was born in Metz, a city in northeastern France, and lived from about 960 to 1028. He established an academy of learning in Mainz. Students throughout Europe came to this academy, studied there for years, then returned to their communities, where they taught others.

In those days, as in ours, the content of study in a yeshiva, a Jewish academy of learning, was the Babylonian Talmud. You studied the text of the Talmud and the oral commentary on every significant phrase. This commentary had been transmitted for generations from father to son in certain families, some of them able to trace their origins back to the early centuries of the first millennium. The Talmud, which had begun as the oral law, was now written and had an oral tradition of its own. As that commentary had been carried down through the generations it had hardened into carefully chosen words of explanation interspersed between phrases of Talmud. You would read the Talmudic text, listen to your teacher's commentary, memorize it, continue with the next phrase of the text, and then listen and memorize the commentary to that. And the texts were studied not only by the young but also by heads of households—artisans, laborers, and international merchants of power and stature whose lives away from Torah involved them in the often violent world of emperors, kings, counts, dukes, bishops, and archbishops in Germany and France.

Sometime about the year 1000 a synod was called by Rabbenu Gershom of all the scholars of Ashkenaz as well as the leading members of each community. These communal leaders were invariably wealthy merchants. Synods had probably been held before, but this is the first one we know something about. The scholars and communal leaders would meet periodically to enact takkanot, ordinances, new laws, designed to respond to situations unforeseen by the Talmud. These synods emulated the church councils and echoed the ancient kalla gatherings of the Talmudic period in Babylonia.

In order for an ordinance to become legally binding on all Jews of the land, it would have to be adopted unanimously by all who were present at a synod and then ratified by every community. The synod of the year 1000 adopted new laws regarding marriage and divorce. One such law, adopted and later ratified by all the communities of Germany, France, and Italy, forbade polygamy. Another—possibly adopted at a later synod—stipulated that a woman may not be divorced from her husband without her consent. The rabbis and community leaders were giving stern expression to their concern about the possibility of Jews imitating the semibarbarous world in which they lived, where polygamous rulers often discarded their wives on a whim. The synod reenacted the solemn binding stipulation that all Jews were subject to the jurisdiction of local Jewish courts. An individual entrusted with the delivery of a letter, the synod agreed, was forbidden to read it—an important step in the recognition of privacy and individual rights in an age when most men were in vassalage to others, and also a means of preventing the theft of a merchant's business plans.

Other enactments are attributed to Rabbenu Gershom. Newcomers to a community were to be carefully screened. If they could not meet the rigid standards of faith and honest dealing laid down by the local Jewish merchants society and its rabbis they were not to be admitted to the community's religious institutions. Underlying this regulation was the desire to control excessive business competition. In those days all towns, villages, and guilds disliked newcomers. This law forced many Jews to pioneer new areas of the land.

Rabbenu Gershom forbade the hurling of insults at apostates who had returned to Judaism. He prohibited the writing of unauthorized commentaries and emendations in the margins of Talmudic texts because it ruined precious texts patiently transcribed by hand; also, a slight change in the text might lead to confusion and a wrong interpretation of the law.

His attitude toward Christians seems clear: because they prayed to statues, had made a deity of a human being, and believed in the Trinity, they were to be regarded as idol worshipers. But because the Jew was the minority and would be unable to sustain himself without dependence upon Christians, without entering their homes, without offering them hospitality, without selling to them and buying from them, many of the Talmudic laws against associating with pagans were reinterpreted. To give one example, business dealings with non-Jews on

Christian festival days were permitted because "Gentiles outside the land of Israel are not idolaters," an inexplicable opinion held by a single Talmudic authority. But this was an instance of urgent necessity; the alternative was the economic ruin of the Jewish community. Rabbenu Gershom wrote a poem in which he left no doubt about his view of Christianity. "They decree upon us not to call to the Lord . . . to accept the despised idol as god, to bow to the image to worship it. . . ." In the coming centuries very few rabbinic authorities would disagree with this attitude toward Christianity. The lone, clear voice of dissent would be that of Menahem Hameiri, a fourteenth-century rabbi in Provence. "Idolatry has disappeared from most places," he wrote. The prohibition against mingling with pagans does not apply to Christians, who are to be regarded as "restricted by the ways of religion."

Later generations referred to Rabbenu Gershom as "the light of the exile." His liturgical poetry became part of the prayers of all German Jewish communities. One of the cultural landmarks of Ashkenazic Jewry would be this Talmudic legalist who was at the same time a liturgical poet. While the Jews of Muslim Spain were writing works on linguistics, philosophy, highly sophisticated and penetrating Bible commentaries, love songs, wine songs, odes to God and Zion, and enjoying the sun and scent of their southern world, the Jews of Ashkenaz were taking the first steps toward a literature of Talmud and Bible commentaries, sermons, kabbalistic treatises, exalted and mournful religious poetry, law codes, and mystical pietism. That literature would emanate almost entirely from within its own self. There would be little direct culture contact between the small, tight civilization of Ashkenazic Judaism and the vast Christian world surrounding it. Jews regarded the Christians as one of the nations of the world and themselves as the chosen of God, and Christians looked upon Jews as deniers of the true covenant and the killers of Jesus.

About twelve years after the synod of the year 1000, Emperor Henry II ordered the expulsion of all Jews from Mainz. Some thought to save their lives or property by accepting Christianity. Among them was a son of Rabbenu Gershom. Soon afterward the son died, still a Christian. His father mourned him as if he had died a Jew, performing all the rites required by Talmudic law.

One of the disciples of Rabbenu Gershom was Rabbi Jacob ben Yakar, a saintly man utterly devoted to his master. He in turn became the teacher of Rabbi Solomon ben Isaac—Rashi, as he is known, after the acronym formed out of the first letters of his name. Rashi both mirrored and helped create the basic life style of Ashkenazic Jewry. He was a poverty-stricken student, brilliant, too soon married, too soon responsible for a family of daughters. He grew up in Troyes, a town in Champagne southeast of Paris on the Seine. He was born about 1040 to a family of scholars. He entered my life when I was a child and has remained a permanent resident in the Jewish civilization I carry within myself.

He journeyed to Worms, a Rhine valley town south of Mainz, and became a student in the yeshiva of Rabbi Jacob ben Yakar. In that yeshiva were students from the finest families of Ashkenazic Jewry, young men whose fathers were merchants with international reputations. The collective knowledge in the possession of these students was aired in idle gossip as well as in serious discussions centering on Talmudic texts. Their fathers roamed the world and talked at home about the customs of different people; about the ways of sailors, soldiers, farmers, and artisans; about voyages at sea, the crossing of borders, and the excitement of business procedures at trade fairs; about the making of leather and cloth, wine and oil, iron and wood; about the minting of coins, the organizing of caravans, the construction of ships. Many of these merchants owned the ships on which they sailed with the goods they bought and sold. The outside world was real to these students; their fathers were a crucial part of it, connecting separate segments of geography with bridges of commerce. What the young student from Troyes learned and heard in the yeshiva at Worms he would remember and use all his life in his writings.

On occasion he would return to his wife and children in

Troyes, traveling the road that connected the valley of the Rhine to Champagne. This was at a time when a great majority of the people never throughout their entire lives moved more than twenty miles from where they were born. Still that road was crowded with merchants, churchmen, nobles. Here and there new parish churches were being built on property endowed by dukes and counts. You could hear church bells ringing. Christianity had begun to sink roots in the land. A Jew traveling that road would remember the rare occurrences of local persecution and the small French army that had gone off to Spain in 1065 to kill Muslims and had murdered some Jews along the way.

Rashi spent years in that yeshiva in Worms and finally had to give up the life of a student for that of a merchant. He remained in Troyes to manage his family's vineyards and wine production. He held no official position in the town; but it was soon clear to everyone that he was an extraordinary Talmudist and people began to turn to him with questions of law. His daughters married men who went on to become great scholars. I spent years of my life studying the commentaries written by the husbands and sons of the daughters of Rashi—and I return to them often today.

Around Rashi in Troyes there formed a small scholarly circle where the Talmud was carefully studied under his direction. His sons-in-law participated in that island of scholarship; they brought the Torah of the Rhine valley to Champagne. One of their basic efforts was the harmonization of apparent discrepancies in the enormous legal literature of the Talmud.

During the periods of time when he was neither teaching nor overly preoccupied with his vineyards, Rashi wrote the commentaries to the Bible and Talmud that have made him almost as much a part of Jewish life as the texts whose meanings he probed and revealed to centuries of his people.

I do not know if the Talmud would be at all accessible today were it not for the commentary of Rashi. Difficult words and phrases are patiently explained. Complex passages are explored in clear and simple Hebrew. He seems in the room with you, anticipating the problems you will have with the text, waiting for your questions, then answering them briefly, simply, with a clear aversion for convoluted thought. His purpose was to set down the oral traditions and explanations of the text which he had been taught, and to add to them thoughts of his own. He has remained the master commentator of the Talmud, the first one you turn to when the text takes a difficult twist, when you come upon a strange word, or stumble into a passage whose tortuous reasoning is a barely discernible path through a terrain of elliptical phrases, complex cross references, obscure legal principles, and seeming contradictions.

In his commentary to the Bible you will discover that same desire for clarity. But it takes a different form now and seems almost to be directed at another audience—not so much the minds bent over a folio of Talmud but the somewhat less disciplined mentality of the educated common man, the harried artisan, laborer, merchant, who though still a student of the law was more interested in the living people of the Bible, in the literal explanation of the words, in a moral lesson, rather than in the strictly technical structure of the text. When Rashi came upon a word he did not understand he would say, "I do not know what it is." Yet Rashi was a master linguist—though not of the quality of some of the Spanish Jews we have met—and much that is original in the commentary has to do with philological explanations. But often it is less an original commentary than a careful selection by him of teachings from anthologies edited by Palestinian rabbis in the centuries after Judah the Prince. The selection is judiciously accomplished; it has been honed into a lucid, uniform style; Rashi chooses from the vast midrashic literature before him those stories, values, and turns of phrase which he feels will both reflect and reinforce the deepest feelings of the Jews of his time.

His work was not intended as a commentary for uneducated masses. A basic familiarity with the Biblical text and some of its difficulties is an underlying assumption of the work. But this was not a sophisticated Jewry; it was less given to philosophical inquiry than was its Sephardic counterpart. Its beliefs were simple, and Rashi sought to reinforce them through his commentary on the Bible. Israel is the chosen of God, for only Israel accepted willingly the yoke of the Torah while all the other nations refused. Rashi repeats this Talmudic version of election three times at different points in the commentary. Israel is different from the other nations; only Israel studies the Torah, a preoccupation regarded as the highest of religious virtues; Israel is therefore the nation closest and dearest to God. The divine presence rests upon Israel even in the lands of exile; both will be redeemed together at the appointed time, when the righteous will be rewarded and the wicked will be punished. God and Israel are intimately united in a bond of love and mutual dependence, a union inseparable, mystical, eternal.

In Talmudic literature there is a vast spectrum of interpretation concerning the relationship between God and Israel. This careful selection by Rashi of certain aspects of rabbinic thought reflects the specific needs of Ashkenazic Jewry—it required a literature that would explain and justify its existence to itself and a hostile Christianity. It reflects as well the image that Jewish civilization had of itself as the natural continuity of the Talmudic world. There had been no break in history; the covenant had continued intact since ancient times; it was the task of the Jews to follow the commandments, study the law, and wait—wait passively—for the coming of the Messiah, who would lead the people out of bondage, restore the nation and the throne of David, and redeem the world. No love songs here; no wine songs; no evenings in gardens with silk-robed men listening to poets declaim the virtues of a patron. This was a world of church bells, warring kings and counts, proselytizing clerics, and a peasantry of barbarous thugs in vassalage to lords who were often little less than robber barons. It was a Jewish world of simple faith, and Rashi gave it the imagery and vocabulary it required—through his commentary on the Bible. It was copied repeatedly and passed from hand to hand. The first dated Hebrew book was published in 1475, about twenty-five years after the invention of printing; it was the commentary of Rashi on the Pentateuch.

One of Rashi's sons-in-law, Rabbi Meir ben Samuel, was the father of four sons who became the greatest Ashkenazic Talmudists of the twelfth century. The commentary of Rashi gave rise to lively discussion and argumentation in the academies of learning throughout France and Germany. Copies of the Jerusalem Talmud entered Ashkenaz from the south, along with Talmudic works by great Sephardic scholars. Debate grew heated and sharp. Keen minds questioned many of the conclusions of Rashi. Masters and disciples, many of them anonymous, wrote commentaries on the work of Rashi filled with razor-minded and, at times, casuistic reasoning. These commentaries are known as the Tosafot, additions. Their origins, literary style and development, and precise place and time of compilation are among the most difficult problems of scholarly research. Their rapierlike questions and answers, as well as their occasional vein of casuistry, set the tone for all the future generations of Talmudic study.

Outside the small circle of scholars, the world of Christendom was in turmoil. Normans had penetrated into southern Italy and settled in its heel and toe. The Italian cities of Genoa and Pisa took the islands of Sardinia and Corsica from the Muslims. In 1066 Normans invaded and conquered England. Jews followed in the wake of this conquest, the first Jews known to set foot on English soil. On the continent Pope Gregory VII and Emperor Henry IV of Germany were locked in a struggle for power. Christendom depended upon the cooperation of its two swords, the secular and the spiritual, for its delicately balanced existence. For centuries popes and emperors had fought each other for power and domination. The pope possessed the weapon of excommunication and the emperor commanded the powerful armies of Germany. The chaos in Christendom continued.

Early in that century nomadic Seljuk Turks from central Asia had swarmed over the eastern states of the Abbasid caliphate of Islam. They had taken Persia, Iraq, Armenia, and Asia Minor. They were Muslims. They captured Jerusalem in 1070 from the caliphs of Egypt. Their armies now threatened Constantinople. The Byzantine emperor, Alexius Comnenus, made repeated appeals in 1095 for an army of knights to save his kingdom from the heathen Turks.

The pope at this time was Urban II. Appeals to save oriental Christendom had been made before to the people of Roman Christendom and had aroused little enthusiasm. Pope Urban II now conceived a different plan: an appeal to rescue the Holy Sepulchre in Jerusalem from the hands of the Turks, who had closed the city to Christian pilgrims.

On November 26, 1095, at the church council in Clermont, in central France, the pope delivered a stirring speech in which he urged Christians to "enter upon the road to the Holy Sepulchre, wrest it from the wicked race, and subject it" to Christendom. He promised remission of sins and eternal life to all who took up the sword. He offered the assembled lords, who had been brought to the council by their bishops at the urging of the pope, the prospect of their own kingdoms in Palestine. When he was done, his words were greeted with thunderous approval. "Deus vult!" the lords and knights shouted—which means "God wills it!"

Word of the Clermont council spread swiftly. A religious hysteria swept through France and Germany. The grim misery of existence, the oppressive sense of guilt over the burden of sin, the glitter of battle and adventure away from a land whose principalities had become fixed, whose wars had become few—excited the imagination of lord and vassal alike. By the sping of 1096 the land seemed convulsed as peasants hurriedly gathered their crops for the journey to the holy city—instead of harvesting for the coming year—and wagons laden with wives and children began to move southward. They were responding to the command of God. It was the start of the promised second coming of Jesus. The Day of Judgment was close at hand. All through the spring and summer peasants from the north gathered up their belongings and moved through the land. Families joined together into groups; groups became bands; soon a vast swollen pious superstition-ridden host was marching toward the Rhine.

Some had visions. One group was led by a knight, another by a nobleman, a third by a goat with magical powers. They filled the roads and fields and forests of the Rhine.

Jews gazed as outsiders upon this sudden unification of Europe beneath the banner of the cross. No Jew could participate in this Christian crusade. Rumors began to spread. The Jews were secretly aiding the cause of Islam.

As the peasant host made its way southward it began to attack and pillage the Jewish communities along the Rhine. About eight hundred Jews were killed in Worms after days of heavy fighting. More than a thousand died in Mainz. They were buried in ditches. In Cologne the synagogue was destroyed. The Jews were protected by the archbishop, who took them into his castles and dispersed them throughout neighboring towns. Most were found and slain. The peasant mob continued southward, offering Jews apostasy or death. Most chose martyrdom. In all, about five thousand died. Many were saved by local bishops and lords. The communities were devastated. The host moved on, a Christian locust stripping the land of Jews.

In Salonica, which was then part of the empire of Byzantium, Jews and Christians heard of the coming of this host. Many saw visions. The Jews of Byzantium lived on fairly good terms with the Christians. To them the liberation of Jerusalem from the hated Muslims clearly presaged the coming of the Messiah. With the approval of the archbishop and the governor, they stopped their labors, put on their prayer shawls, and waited. I do not know how long they waited.

In the spring of 1097 an army of one hundred fifty thousand men—Franks, Normans, and rabble—met at Constantinople. They began to cut their way southward. Two years later, on June 7, 1099, about forty thousand crusaders stood at the gates of Jerusalem. It seemed to matter to no one that in 1098 Egypt had retaken Jerusalem and declared it once again open to Christian pilgrims. On July 15 the crusaders stormed the city. A massacre followed. Piles of heads and hands could be seen on streets and squares everywhere. The Jews of the city who had somehow lived through the fighting sought refuge in their synagogues. The crusaders burned down the synagogues with the Jews inside. The few who survived the slaughter and the fire were sold as slaves. Jerusalem would remain empty of Jews throughout most of the following century.

In the valley of the Rhine those Jews who had survived the raging mobs of peasants began to rebuild their lives. There had been Jews in Germany now for nearly eight hundred years. Rashi died in 1105, forty-two years before the Second Crusade. The Jews were prepared for that crusade. They bought the protection of bishops and nobles. In the end only about one thousand were martyred.

The Jews had never believed themselves so vulnerable as the crusades now revealed them to be. The suddenly militant feudal world of Christendom—with the serf and vassal knights owing loyalty to their lord and the lord at least theoretically owing loyalty to king and clergy, and all bound to one another by ecclesiastical oaths—this tight Christian world seemed closed to Jews.

They had been international merchants, landowners, and artisans, loosely protected by kings and clerics. Now east and west were linked and there was no need for the special abilities of the Jewish merchant. Christian merchants could traffic in spices and medicaments, for there were no Muslim borders to cross. Eastern civilization moved across the Mediterranean into Provence and the ports of the growing Italian trade cities. Arabic translations of Aristotelian manuscripts made the sea change along with unguents and silks and the Arabian horses that would be crossbred with the puny mounts of knights— themselves poorly nourished men rarely taller than five feet three inches. All through the centuries Jews had been permitted to go about armed—a mark of knightly status in that world. But their weapons were of little help to them against the hordes of superstitious peasants in whom the teachings of the church had begun to sink deep roots and who wished to cleanse their own lands of Jews before they cleansed the Holy Land of Muslims.

The crusades continued for about three hundred years.

They offer us a portrait of Christendom at its best and worst: piety and butchery were intimate companions fused by religious sanction. In 1204 the crusaders sacked Constantinople with horrifying savagery and replaced the Greek emperor with a Latin one; the city was retaken by Byzantium in 1261. In 1212 there was a children's crusade. Thousands of youths flocked to Marseilles. No one seemed to know what to do with them. Ship captains encouraged them to board their vessels and sold them as slaves in Muslim North Africa. By the close of the thirteenth century, when the Holy Land was again in the hands of the Muslims, Christian Europe was a fortress land that was slaughtering heretics within its own borders, the Inquisition had been established in southern France, and the status and nature of Ashkenazic Jews had been entirely transformed. They were looked upon as contemptible usurers and demonic plotters against the world of Christendom.

Those were strange centuries, the centuries of the crusades and those that came afterward. Preachers roamed the land, urging asceticism, poverty, and the imitation of Christ. One preacher would display graphic evidence of the transiency of life by pulling out from beneath his cloak a grinning skull. Some spoke of the healing power of blood. A dry tree is restored to life when blood is poured on its roots. The blood of one cured from a sickness should be used to anoint, and thereby cure, someone who has contracted that sickness. The ultimate sickness, death, can be overcome by the blood of Jesus. Crosses possessed miraculous properties. They sprang up everywhere, in fields and roads and marketplaces. Cemeteries were sacred, as were altar ornaments and images of saints. Demonic imagery—twisted bodies, satanic beings, monstrous heads—surrounded worshipers as they gazed at the ornamentation of their churches. Life was tragic and arbitrary; the ways of God were incomprehensible. The land was obsessed with death, and this obsession would intensify. Crowds of penitents would accompany preachers from town to town. A spectral dance developed, a dance of death, and it was seen often in the towns of the land—a danse macabre, from the Ara-

bic word for gravedigger, *mekaber,* a dancing skeleton
leading away his victims to a gruesome future of putrefac-
tion, dust, and worms. All men, rich and poor alike, were
frail. All men perished.

Epidemics, wars, pillage, and thievery cast a pall across
the land and filled existence with a sense of the pervasive
nature of ill fortune, evil, the power of sudden disaster.
The unseen was real. Malevolent spirits were everywhere.
Bells could frighten off demons. Rings could heal wounds.
Against demons you brought to bear incantations, charms,
sorcery by means of the dead, various forms of divination.
Astrological panic would periodically grip the land; a certain conjunction of planets and stars meant earthquakes,
catastrophes, murders.

Those were the centuries when Ashkenazic Jews
learned how to die for their way of life. Some chose
apostasy when given the choice of baptism or death. But
most believed that the persecutions were the first sign of
the messianic age. Further, converts faced a bleak social
future when they left their immediate world to enter
Christianity; the welcome they might receive from the
church would turn cold on the hostile faces of laymen
who feared economic competition from converts they could
no longer persecute for being Jews. Most Jews regarded
Christainity as idolatry. When the mobs came they would
make every effort to avoid death. No one sought martyrdom. They would fast in penitence for real or imagined
sins. They would seek the protection of bishops and rulers.
They would use their weapons to hold off the mobs. But
when it was clear that defeat was near, they would accept
it as a sign from God that their deaths had been decreed.
There might be a pause in the battle. The men would
gather for a final decision. To let themselves and their
families be taken alive by such mobs was unthinkable.
Jewish law developed a benediction for the act of martyrdom. Fathers would say the words, cut the throats of their
wives and children, say aloud, "Hear O Israel, the Lord
our God, the Lord is one," and commit suicide.

They died without doubting the unfathomable judgment of heaven. They felt themselves linked to the patriarch Abraham and his act of faith when he nearly sacri-

ficed Isaac; in a liturgical poem written during this period Abraham actually sacrifices Isaac—for how could the patriarch have done less than Jewish parents were now doing daily—and Isaac is brought back to life by God. They saw themselves continuing in the tradition of the Pietists who died fighting the Hellenists. It was a charged, passionate choice made with the certainty that the world to come was a living reality and its rewards awaited them when they fulfilled their ultimate duty as Jews.

The accounts of mass suicide written by chroniclers of the crusades make it clear that the Jews who chose martyrdom were fully aware of their actions: they were testifying to the truth and continuing reality of the original covenant and to the cruelty and emptiness of the Christianity that had forced them to such a choice. Martyrdom was an aggressive act of denial, a publicly performed act sanctifying the Name of God. During the heat of battle and before the act of suicide, Jews would shout words of derision about Jesus. Some let themselves be taken alive, agreed to baptism, and then spat on the crucifix, knowing they might be torn to pieces by the infuriated crowd.

In 1171 a new fear entered the demon-ridden world of Christendom. The Jews of Blois, a town in north central France, were accused of ritual murder. People whose aversion for pagan blood sacrifices and the eating of blood dated back to the period of the Bible were now said to have slain a Christian in order to obtain blood for the unleavened bread of Passover and other rituals. Jews, it was whispered, were not human and needed the potency of blood in order to take on and maintain human form. Early Christians had once been accused of using blood; Christian heretics were similarly accused. That was the first blood libel in France; it followed by a few decades the first blood libel in history, which had occurred in Norwich, England, in 1144. There were thirty-three Jews in Blois at the time, men, women, and children. On May 26, 1171, they were burned at the stake. There would be hundreds of blood libels in the coming centuries. Thousands would die. Popes would condemn the accusations and the massacres, but they would not cease.

During those crusade centuries the respected international Jewish merchants passed from the scene. Christian merchants now journeyed between east and west. Guilds had closed themselves to Jewish membership. Jews in possession of capital sought ways of using it to make a living. Roman Christianity had forbidden Christians from lending other Christians money at interest, basing this decision on a verse in the Hebrew Bible and on this passage in the sixth chapter of Luke: "Love your enemies, and do good, and lend, hoping for nothing again; and your reward shall be great. . . ." In the Latin Bible the words "hoping for nothing again" are *nihil inde sperantes* and may well mean something like: lend without giving up hope that your loan will be returned. But Roman Christianity read those words as an injunction against interest loans. Byzantine Christianity apparently had no difficulty with the Hebrew and Latin verses, for there the church itself was deep in the lending business and interest rates were fixed by the government.

Jews were not forbidden to lend money at interest to non-Jews. They entered this unoccupied economic territory and became moneylenders to Christian burghers, artisans, and knights, and bankers to nobles and kings. It was perilous territory, for the repayment of loans was never a certainty—Jews did not have the same status in law courts as did Christians—and persecution or expulsion could bring disaster. Hence interest rates, unregulated at first in most principalities, could be as high as fifty percent a year.

Many Jews remained artisans and small tradesmen. But the Jew who was most visible to the world was the moneylender. The image of the Jew began to change from that of respected international merchant to demonic usurer.

In later centuries, when the church relaxed its ban against interest loans and great Christian banking houses sprang up, the Jews were driven into yet another unoccupied economic territory, the bleak terrain of petty loans to the poor, which neither the church nor any government would then enter. The Jew became the pawnbroker.

All through the twelfth century, that first century of the crusades, Ashkenazic Jewry lived helplessly exposed to the violent anti-Semitism that stalked the land. The dangers extended beyond the mainland and promontories of Europe. In 1190 a mob of English crusaders attacked the prosperous Jewish community of York in the north of England. The Jews took refuge in the royal castle and then committed mass suicide. No one seems to have known what to do with the Jews. They belonged nowhere. The Jewish communities—tradesmen and artisans governed by rabbinic scholars and wealthy families—sought the protection of kings.

The potential income to a royal treasury from the taxes that could be levied against a Jewish community and from a share in its business profits made Jews attractive to kings who were constantly in need of cash for their courts and armies. The status of Jews began to change. By the end of that first century of the crusades, the Jews were *servi camerae regis,* servants of the royal chamber. In Germany—the Holy Roman Empire—the status was explained as a direct outcome of the 66-70 C.E. rebellion against Rome, which had resulted in the destruction of Jerusalem and the enslavement of the Jews to the Romans.

An English law of that period stated, "All Jews, wherever in the realm they are, must be under the king's liege protection and guardianship, nor can any of them put himself under the protection of any powerful person without the king's license, because the Jews themselves and all their chattels are the king's. If, therefore, anyone detain them or their money, the king may claim them, if he so desire and if he is able, as his own."

The Jews were now the protected slaves of kings.

Pope Innocent III, who occupied the papacy from 1198 to 1216, was pleased that Jews were under the rule of Christians and urged the Christain rulers to exercise their power in a way "that the Jews will not dare to raise their neck, bowed under the yoke of perpetual slavery, against the reverence of the Christian faith." In 1215, at the fourth Lateran council, Jews and Muslims were ordered to wear clothes that would set them apart from Christians because "it sometimes happens that by mistake Christians have intercourse with Jewish or Saracen women, and Jews or Saracens with Christian women." Jews were forbidden to hold public office, "since this offers them the pretext to vent their wrath against the Christians."

In 1227, at the council of Narbonne, it was announced that "in order that Jews may be told apart from others, we decree, and we order it most emphatically, that in the center of the breast [of the garments] they shall wear an oval badge the width of which shall be of the measure of one finger and the height one half a palm," and that "during Holy Week they shall not venture out of their homes at all unless because of pressing necessity, and the prelates shall have them guarded from vexation by Christians especially during the said week."

The Jews of the kingdom of Castile in Spain refused to abide by the decree concerning the badge and began to emigrate to Muslim lands. It was pointed out to the king and the pope that this would strengthen the economic power of Islam. The enforcement of the decree was postponed to a more opportune time.

In 1233 an investigation—inquisition—was made by each archdeaconate of Lincoln in England. One of the questions was, "Do Jews live in any place where they did not live before?" Apparently the purpose of the inquiry was to restrict their place of residence. That was one of the early steps in the ghettoization of the Jews.

During that same year the papal Inquisition was officially established. It was directed against the Albigensian sect in southern France. The Albigensians believed that there were two gods, one of evil and one of good, who struggle for victory. Man, a mixture of both, had to strive to attain pure spirituality. They were opposed to procreation because this extended the existence of the human race, which was monstrous and kept the good entombed in evil flesh. They exposed infants and advocated individual and collective suicide. The Roman church aided them in their goals by subjecting them to slaughter. The Inquisition followed Roman church law. You were assumed guilty and had to prove your innocence. Torture was permitted. That Inquisition would one day cross the Pyrenees in search of secret Jews—converts to Christianity who covertly practiced Judaism—in Christian Spain.

The council of Tours decreed, on June 10, 1236, "We . . . emphatically prohibit any crusader or other Christian to dare kill Jews, or to flog them, or to invade their property. . . . For the church tolerates the Jews, since it does not want the death of the sinner, but rather that he return and live." About two decades later the council of Albi decreed against the Jews that "the meat which they prepare privately in their houses they shall not try to sell in the Christian marketplaces. Also, since, in disdain of us, Jews do not use any of our food or drink, we strictly forbid any Christian to use theirs. . . . Also let those Christians be excommunicated who entrust themselves to Jews for medical treatment."

On June 25, 1240, a public trial of the Talmud took place in Paris. In this enchanted land, where a goose was a symbol of magic and a pig could be tried for murder, a book too could be brought to trial. The accuser was Nicholas Donin, an apostate from Judaism. He had urged Pope Gregory IX to destroy the Talmud. It was the source of Jewish stubbornness, he said. The sanctity Jews attributed to it was an insult to the Bible and the prophets. It was filled with foolish errors and contained blasphemies against the church. The courtroom was filled with nobles and churchmen. Four Jewish leaders defended the Talmud. There had been a recent massacre of Jews, and they came with the memory of death in their minds. The judges were an archbishop, a bishop, the king's chaplain, and the chancellor of the recently established University of Paris. The trial went on for several days.

The apostate Donin was a brilliant Talmudist. There could have been little doubt as to the outcome of the trial. The Talmud was condemned. The Jews tried for two years to plead and buy their way out of the impending calamity. On Friday, June 6, 1242, twenty-four wagonloads of Jewish books were publicly burned. Included were the commentaries of Rashi. The Jews smuggled additional copies into Paris. Another trial was held. In 1248 the Talmud was burned again.

Sixteen years before, in 1232, the books of Maimonides were burned in southern France, the aftermath of a violent controversy among Jews.

He had died in Egypt in 1204 and the entire Jewish world had mourned his loss. He was almost seventy years old at his death, and he was buried in Tiberias near the shore of the Sea of Galilee. He is known to Jews as the Rambam, from the acronym built out of the first letters of his name, Rabbi Moses ben Maimon. About twenty-five years after his death a quarrel broke out in Provence concerning the possible heresies in his writings.

Provence is a green and sunny land bathed in the clear light and warmth of the Mediterranean world. In those centuries it was the home of a great school of rabbinic learning where the Talmud was studied together with ancient treatises on mysticism. Its proximity to Islam had brought to its shores books and men from the disintegrating culture of Muslim Spain. Maimonides' philosophical work, *Guide of the Perplexed,* was translated into Hebrew from its original Arabic. The work made its way across the mountains into Christian Spain, which was at the time still engaged in its centuries' long crusade, the reconquest. Many Jews in Provence and Spain who read the book were shocked.

They discovered in Maimonides a man whose reputation as a rabbinic scholar very few dared challenge and who, at the same time, acknowledged without hesitation that "the intellect of Aristotle represents the height of human intellect," and that the writings of Aristotle were the basis of all the sciences. He had not written his *Guide* for the man of simple faith, for beginners in speculation. He was addressing those for whom the validity of the law was established; but they had also studied the science of the philosophers and now they were distressed by questions concerning the law and the books of the prophets. Such a person might be led to renounce the law and be drawn to his intellect, or turn his back upon his intellect and spend his life with imaginary beliefs that would not cease to cause him heartache and perplexity. Neither course is necessary, claimed this scholar—who had been physician to the sultan and his family, to the many rich and poor who crowded his waiting room when he returned home wearily after a day in the royal court, who ate one frugal meal a day and was often at the point of exhaustion, who had been leader of the Jewish community in Cairo and spent his days of rest teaching—neither course is necessary, this rabbi-philosopher claimed, to one who studies the *Guide*.

He knew the dangers of philosphy, was aware that he was writing for the few elitist intellectuals who might be troubled by these questions, and that those of simple faith, the great mass of the people, would react with suspicion at his efforts. He sought to fuse the best in two worlds, the Greek and the Jewish: we accept the tradition, and then attempt to understand it, test and prove its tenets through reason. The rabbinic scholars of France and Spain had different concerns. Dwelling in the heart of a militant Christendom, they were concerned that this little people might be accused of introducing heretical thought through the work of this Jew from across the Mediterranean. There were many among them who were genuinely outraged by certain aspects of Maimonidean thought and felt them to be intrinsically heretical to Judaism. How can one deny the immortality of the individual body and soul and remain a member of the covenant? How dare one say of the sacrificial system that it was merely a step to a higher development of faith? What right does one have to brush away the Biblical descriptions of God through the use of allegory? And why does one bother with the Greeks? What need is there to study the works of a pagan thinker? That was a time when mystical works had begun to penetrate the Jewish world in Christendom. Rabbis felt no need to understand the world scientifically; all the world was a miracle, the working of the God of Israel, filled with His goodness. operating through divine decree, and certain redemption. The notion of a system of laws of nature ordained by God which should be admired by man through reason was absolute heresy. Their mysticism was entirely opposed to the rationalism of Maimonides. One of the greatest among the Spanish rabbis, Nachmanides, wrote with seeming compassion of Maimonides, describing him as a man caught in a culture world not of his own making and attempting to save Jewish souls through his philosophical writing. "They have filled their belly with the foolishness of the Greeks. . . ."

Maimonides was not without fervent supporters in Provence. It was a bitter public controversy, with each side hurling polemics and edicts of excommunication against the other. These are the two essentially irreconcilable elements at the very core of Judaism, the one rational, facing outward toward the world and general culture, eager for all worthwhile knowledge, prepared to enter the marketplace of ideas; the other mystical, facing inward toward its own sources, possessed of its unalloyed vision of Jewish destiny, feeding off its inner strength and rejecting vehemently and with no small measure of contempt any distortion of its vision of reality from civilizations alien to what it sees as the pure essence of Judaism. These two elements at the core of the Jewish tradition, rubbing up against each other, generate the friction and bitterness of controversy and, one hopes, the sparks of creativity.

In 1232 the Inquisition in Provence was informed of the heretical nature of the writings of Maimonides. His books were burned. It is believed that the informants were rabbis of the anti-Maimonidean camp. In Tiberias someone desecrated his tomb.

Pope Innocent III had written that the guilt of the Jews for the crucifixion of Jesus consigned them to perpetual servitude, and, like Cain, they were to be wanderers and fugitives.

The five thousand Jews of England were expelled in 1290; they were taken in by the dukes of central France. The Jews of France, which was then a relatively small circle-shaped kingdom, were repeatedly expelled and allowed to return—until they were finally expelled in 1394; many wandered to Spain.

The Jews of Spain belonged to their kings. In the eleventh and twelfth centuries they were courtiers and tax farmers and went on diplomatic missions. They managed the properties of nobles. Some were moneylenders. Jewish communities were autonomous and paid their taxes directly into the treasury of the king. In Barcelona Jews owned one-third of the estates in the region. There were schools and synagogues and great rabbinical scholars. It was a rich, powerful, educated Jewry—and it all began to disintegrate, beginning with the thirteenth century, as colonization of the land drew to an end and the influence of the church began to outweigh the usefulness of the Jews. Christian Spain was still at war with Muslims in the south, but it was a war only Islam could lose. In 1250 a blood libel struck Spain, directed at the Jews of Saragossa, an inland city between Madrid and Barcelona. The Spaniards had begun to follow the lead set by the persecuting kings and clerics of France.

A major disputation took place in Barcelona in the summer of 1263. The subject was the truth of Christianity and the coming of the Messiah. The disputants were Pablo Christiani—a convert to Christianity who had probably been born in southern France and who was aided by a number of high-ranking clerics—and Nachmanides, whom we met during the Maimonides controversy. The king presided. The room was filled with bishops. Christiani attempted to show how the Talmud itself agrees that the Messiah has appeared, that he was both human and divine, and that he died in order to atone for the sins of mankind. Therefore, he concluded, Judaism has no validity and all Jews should accept the true faith. Nachmanides explained away the meaning given the Talmudic passages by Christiani and argued bluntly about the illogical nature of Christianity. He spoke disparagingly of the death of Jesus. How could the Messiah have come? "From the time of Jesus to the present," he said, "the world has been filled with violence and injustice, and the Christians have shed more blood than all other peoples."

Some of the clerics, infuriated by his words, urged that the dispute be ended. It was interrupted after the fourth day and never resumed. That August the Jews of Spain were ordered to erase from all copies of the Talmud any

unseemly reference to Jesus and Mary. In 1265 Nachmanides was accused of blasphemy. He left Spain and
spent the rest of his life in the land of Israel. In the Old
City of Jerusalem they show you the synagogue where he
prayed; you think of him alone surrounded by angry
faces, defending his faith. That was the last time a Jew
was permitted to speak so openly in a disputation.

About the middle of the fourteenth century the Black
Death reached Spain. Northern Europe was then in a
paroxysm of hysteria over its Jews; they were being accused of poisoning wells. Germany expelled its Jews; they
fled north and east into the cold lands of Slavic tribes. In
the Spanish kingdom of Castile, King Pedro the Cruel,
who ruled from 1350 to 1369, maintained peace, brought
Jews back into the service of the court, and permitted his
royal treasurer, a Jew named Don Samuel Halevi Abu-
lafia, to build a synagogue in Toledo, an exquisite synagogue which has survived the centuries and become a
church and a museum. Samuel Halevi lived in a beautiful
home not far from the synagogue. In 1360 he was suddenly arrested by King Pedro and brought to Seville. The
reason for the arrest is not known. He was tortured to
death. Centuries later El Greco lived in his Toledo home.
Today it is the El Greco Museum. I walked through it
one day and could find nothing in it that tells you it
was once the home of the Jewish treasurer to a Christian
king.

The fortunes of the Jews of Spain rose and fell with the
needs and whims of kings. In the end, the sermons to the
people about Jewish treachery and the warnings and ex-
hortations to royalty were effective. There were mobs and
massacres and martyrdom and conversions. In 1412 the
government of Castile ordered Jews to inhabit separate
quarters in towns and villages. They were to be distinguished from Christians by growing their hair and beards.
There were about thirty thousand Jewish families in Castile at the time. This number does not include the converts, Conversos they were called, many of whom were
secret Jews.

The Inquisition entered Spain from southern France for
the purpose of rooting out these secret Jews. When Isa-

bella of Castile and Ferdinand of Aragon were married in 1469, Christian Spain was united. It employed Jews as tax farmers. The chief rabbi of Castile was also the tax collector for the kingdom. Then, in 1476, the Jewish communities were deprived of the right of criminal jurisdiction; Jewish religious autonomy was at an end. The Inquisition intensified its work, investigating, judging, consigning people to the stake. More than seven hundred Conversos were burned between 1481 and 1488. In the autumn of 1483, Tomás de Torquemada, the queen's confessor, was appointed head of the Inquisition. Terror invaded the land. He moved from town to town, plodding, methodical, inexorable, like the Roman legions of another time. In twelve years the Inquisition discovered and consigned to death by fire more than thirteen thousand men and women who had been converted to Roman Christianity and were practicing Judaism secretly.

With the fall of Muslim Spain there came the hunger for religious unity and the wish to see an end to the faces of strangers. Spain had fought a five-hundred-year-long war against Islam. It wanted itself purified of dross. On March 31, 1492, an edict of expulsion directed against the Jews was signed in Granada. On May 1 of that year Spain began to expel all Jews who would not accept Christianity. About one hundred seventy thousand left the land. They went wandering through Europe, Portugal, North Africa, Turkey. Tens of thousands accepted baptism. The last Jew left Spain on July 31, 1492, the seventh day of the Hebrew month of Av. Spain was officially empty of Jews. Pope Innocent III had triumphed. All the Jews were wanderers, lost in a vast enchanted world.

The family of Torquemada had been Conversos. That is the opinion of most scholars of the Inquisition.

The ranks of the Conversos had grown after a wave of anti-Jewish riots in 1391. The expulsion had added to their numbers. Now, with the Jews gone, there were about three hundred thousand Conversos in the land. They constituted the educated urban middle class of Spain. The wealthier among them married into the Spanish aristocracy.

Spaniards made a distinction between themselves and the descendants of Conversos: those of Jewish ancestry were called New Christians; those who could trace themselves through the generations were called Old Christians. Lower-class Spaniards looked upon the Conversos with suspicion and animosity, and referred to them as Marranos, a word some scholars think means swine. Torquemada was replaced by Diego Deza, friend and patron of Columbus.

After the expulsion, the Inquisition continued to seek out those who practiced Judaism secretly. There had been secret Jews in the land since the time of the forced conversions under the Visigoths in the seventh century. They formed a silent world of their own, risking their lives for what they regarded as the true faith.

Spain was empty of Jewish books. But these Conversos had available to them—as has been shown recently by a scholar—not only the Bible in Latin but also much Talmud, aggadah, Hebrew literature and grammar, Bible commentary, and Jewish history, all of it cited in Latin or in the vernacular in works by Christian theologians, grammarians, scientists, and historians. And through the travels of New Christian merchants, the Conversos were able to maintain contact with Jewish communities beyond the borders of Spain.

Their lives were edged with the constant dread of exposure. A reluctance to eat pork, the lighting of candles on Friday evenings, the observance of certain fast days, the absence of smoke from a chimney on the Sabbath— Jewish law forbids the making of a fire on the day of rest—these were telltale signs of possible secret Jews. Officers of the Inquisition would gather their evidence with painstaking care. The accused individual would be brought before an inquisitional committee and presented with the evidence. The accused would be asked to confess. A refusal would result in detention and further questioning. A defendant might languish for months or years in prison before there would be a trial. If the replies were felt to be unsatisfactory and the evidence warranted conviction, the defendant was tortured. It was all very legal and done with care and deliberation. Torture was administered in order to substantiate what the inquisitors already knew. Everything was set down in writing.

Repentance and punishment took place in a public act called, in Portuguese, *auto-da-fé,* act of the faith. Such ceremonies were held in the main square or church of a city and were attended by dignitaries and crowds. Various penalties might be imposed upon confessed secret Jews: fasting each Friday for six months, or being paraded through the town naked to the waist and carrying an announcement of the offense, or, for men, three years to life in the galleys. Those who would not confess were handed over to the secular authorities and burned alive at a special burning site that was sometimes built outside the town. The property of the convicted person was taken over by the Inquisition. At first the proceeds were given to the king. Slowly most of the confiscated wealth came to reside in the coffers of the Inquisition. That holy office had piety and property as motives for its probings. More than thirty thousand people were slain by the Inquisition: secret Jews, Protestants, secret Muslims, others.

Most of the converts from Judaism remained devout Christians. But Spaniards seemed unable to digest their presence. The Conversos gave Spain much of its extraordinary sixteenth century, the golden age of Spanish civilization. From their ranks came Saint Teresa of Avila, mystic and founder of convents; Fernando de Rojas, author of the first great literary work of the Spanish Renaissance; Diego Laínez, a friend of Saint Ignatius of Loyola and second general of the Jesuit order; Francisco de Vitoria, the greatest jurist of the sixteenth century; poets, humanists, novelists. Most Spaniards found the aristocratic Conversos intolerable.

In 1547 a man of humble, and therefore untainted, origins—an archbishop named Siliceo—promulgated a *limpieza de sangre,* purity of blood, statute and imposed it upon Toledo. In the future only those whose blood was untainted by the blood of Conversos and by official accusation of heresy could be appointed to any ecclesiastical position. In 1556 King Philip II approved the statute. "All the heresies in Germany, France, and Spain," he remarked, "have been sown by descendants of Jews." That was fantasy as far as the Jews of France and Germany were concerned. Strangely, Philip II was himself a descendant of Jews.

The *limpieza* statues spread throughout Spain. Conversos were excluded from guilds and colleges, and could not reside in certain towns. Religious and secular organizations made blood purity a qualification for membership. You had to bring evidence of an unstained genealogy.

This obsession continued through the sixteenth and seventeenth centuries. Communities contended with one another to intensify the harshness of their blood laws. The vaguest rumor of Jewish descent became an irremovable stain. A man's honor depended not on his own accomplishments but on haunting echoes beyond his control. Then Old Christians suddenly found themselves living in dread of a loss of name through hearsay and rumor. No one could prove that his blood had been pure since time immemorial. In the end you established your *limpieza de sangre* by inventing a genealogy, falsifying papers, and bribing witnesses. For centuries the Spanish land devoured itself with its hatred of the Jewish stranger.

I remember standing one day not long ago in the Plaza Mayor in Madrid, an enormous paved square surrounded by stone houses with balconies. It was a bright chilly day. I had read in old reports and in the writings of scholars of an *auto-da-fé* once held there. I saw in my mind the platforms and scaffolding and the festooned apartments in which the king and queen and the royal entourage ate and rested. Awnings shielded the balconies and platforms where royalty and nobility sat watching the proceedings. Archers protected the king. A guard corps maintained order. The crowd was large. Each prisoner held a yellow candle and wore a peaked paper hat. There were forty prisoners. A sermon was preached. The sentences were read. Twenty-four prisoners received penances for various crimes—magic, witchcraft, pacts with demons, bigamy, blasphemy. Nine confessed Judaizers were penanced. Seven prisoners were to be burned at the stake: six condemned Judaizers and a friar convicted of heresy and sacrilege. Those who were to be burned held a green cross in their hands. They were turned over to the secular authorities and led out of the square flanked by soldiers. The crowd hurled at them rage and abuse. The *auto* continued. Prayers were said. The royal choir chanted a psalm. In the evening the seven condemned prisoners, three of them women, were tied to stakes at a distant execution site and burned to death in a huge fire.

There are many fine cafés and shops on that plaza now. There are pigeons and children. An old man was selling toys.

On October 27, 1765, the last Inquisition-instigated burning of a Portuguese secret Jew took place. In 1836 a British traveler met a secret Jew in Talavera, a town in the heart of Spain, a few miles west of Toledo. That Jew was probably practicing Judaism secretly to avoid expulsion; the Inquisition had been abolished in Spain two years earlier.

This is what might have happened to European civilization had it been otherwise between Christians and Jews. . . .

Once upon a time, and a very real time it was, there was a land in which Jews and Christians lived in relative friendship. The friars would preach their Lenten sermons and mobs would go into a frenzy. But tempers would cool swiftly and the Jews would repair their broken windows and venture out to meet their Christian friends, and they would carouse in the streets. It was a brief time: the fourteenth to the sixteenth centuries. It was a small land: from Rome to Milan and from Genoa to Venice, a land of rolling hills and rich valleys and a Mediterranean sky.

The land contained many tiny principalities: the Duchy of Ferrara, Florence, the Republic of Siena, Pisa, the Duchy of Milan, Piedmont, Mantua, Venice. Between these Italian city-states there existed rivalries and competitiveness that sometimes boiled over into war. Small Jewish communities were scattered throughout the land; Jews had been there since Roman times. Now many came as refugees from Germany, France, Spain, and Portugal. They created an international ambiance that quickened thought.

Each of the Jewish communities numbered no more than a few hundred people. At the center of each community were wealthy families who had always been loan-bankers. Their money grew of itself, giving them ample time for leisure and the pursuit of culture. The great Christian merchant-princes of the city-states possessed power and wealth. A conjunction of wealth, learning, and art was beginning to make of this small land a center of cultural splendor.

From the east came Byzantine scholars in the wake of the catastrophic fall of Constantinople to the Turks in 1453. They carried with them the knowledge of the literature of Classical Greece in the original language. The west had possessed that knowledge in translation for two centuries before the coming of the Byzantines. Their arrival intensified an already developing process: now not only the content but also the literature, the words and forms in which the Greeks had expressed themselves, was available to western scholarship. Literary sensitivities were aroused; a heightened sense of aesthetics entered the land.

In the golden years of Florence, when the Medicis ruled and Botticelli, Donatello, Ghirlandaio, and Leonardo da Vinci were transforming the bare walls of churches and palaces into beauty that forever astonishes, Jews moved with familiar ease through the streets and were part of the everyday scene of that magnificent city. Inside the palace of the Medici there gathered for regular study the small group of scholars known as the Platonic Academy.

One day a Jew and a count appeared at the academy. The Jew was Elijah del Medigo, a brilliant scholar of philosophy who knew Hebrew, Greek, and Latin. He lectured in the University of Padua, without official title or publicly recognized position. The count was Giovanni Pico della Mirandola. He was then about twenty years of age; the Jew was about twenty-seven. The count had studied at the University of Padua and there had met the Jew and had commissioned him to translate a series of works on Aristotle. When the young count went to Florence in 1485, he asked del Medigo to join him. The two men became close friends.

The scholar translated a library of philosophical works from Hebrew into Latin for the count. They joined the scholars of the Platonic Academy. The Jew gave public lectures. He held no official position. The two men parted in 1486 and did not see each other again.

The Jew wrote works on philosophy and died young. The count became one of the great scholars of that time. He chanced one day to acquire a copy of the Zohar, a seemingly ancient work by Jewish mystics, and found himself attracted to its lore. The discovery of an unknown Jewish mystical tradition created a sensation in the intellectual world of Christendom and inaugurated serious Christian study of the Kabbalah.

There were other Jews who took part in that Christian encounter with Greek paganism on Italian soil. Judah Abrabanel—also known as Leone Ebreo—wrote the *Dialogues of Love* in 1501. He was a physician. The work was written in Italian and published in 1535, after his death. He too had probably joined the discussions of the Florentine group of Christian humanists. It is a work about love—the love of God filling the universe, emanating from God and reaching to the smallest of creatures. The soul returns to God through the intellectual love of God. It was one of the best-known works of that time. Montaigne read it in a French translation. Giordano Bruno and Francis Bacon were deeply influenced by it. Spinoza had the Spanish edition in his library. Did he derive from it his concept of the intellectual love of God? We cannot be certain.

Another wanderer wrote a book—the greatest work of Jewish scholarship of that age. His name was Azariah de Rossi. He was a physician and he wrote the book because of an earthquake.

The city of Ferrara was jolted by a violent tremor in 1571. The inhabitants fled in terror, the wandering physician among them. He met a Christian scholar outside the city and they fell to talking about a Greek work known as the *Letter of Aristeas,* which describes the events that led to the translation of the Hebrew Bible into Greek. His curiosity aroused, the physician, who possessed an extensive education, began to look into the matter of a supposed Hebrew original of this Greek work. The book that resulted from his researches is called *Meor Enayim,* which means enlightenment to the eyes.

All the literatures of the ancient world, pagan and Hebrew, were his tools as he explored the Bible, the Hellenistic period, the Talmud. He cites the Greek philosophers, as well as Homer, Aesop, and Euclid. He cites the Romans. He cites—astonishingly!—the church fathers and Thomas Aquinas. His method is objective, critical, scientific. He is engaged in a search for truth. He was profoundly influenced by the scholarly methodology of Pico della Mirandola, the disciple of Elijah del Medigo. He went outside his Hebrew sources for facts. He wrote about Philo and brought him back to the arena of serious philosophical regard after an oblivion of fifteen hundred years. He proved that counting the years from the creation of the world and using such a count as the basis for a calendar was a fairly recent tradition; the Talmud had not used such a calendar. He doubted the authenticity of various tales in the Talmud. He made many other claims and discoveries of this sort and it all shocked the rabbis of Italy and they proclaimed a ban against his book. The controversy spread. In Safed, the city of mystics in the Galilee, rabbis signed a proclamation of excommunication against the book. No one would attack the physician, for he led an exemplary religious life. The book lay banned, unread, untaught, for nearly two hundred years until it was rediscovered by sophisticated Jewish scholars of the eighteenth century, who found they were using a methodology similar to that developed by a Renaissance Jew.

Another wanderer, a Converso who came to Italy from Portugal in 1506, wrote a history of the Jews in which he tried to explain the causes of Jewish suffering. His name was Solomon ibn Verga, and his book, *Shevet Yehudah,* a title with so many nuances that it is virtually untranslatable, was a startling insight into a troubled Converso heart. The dispersion is a natural phenomenon not caused by sin but brought about by the laws of cause and effect. He does not accept suffering, rejects the notion of the will of God as the determining factor in history, will not countenance the idea that affliction is a mark of superiority. Jews are hated because people are wrongly educated; they

are taught to hate. The causes of hatred can be removed
if the Jew behaves modestly toward his Christian neighbor
and preaches tolerance and understanding in an effort to
penetrate the wall that has been built between the faiths.
He does not believe in Messiahs and doubts that the redemption is at hand. The book was written in Hebrew
and was widely read and admired. Ibn Verga remained
loyal to his people. He trusted in the mercy of God.

Once upon a time. . . . Not everyone was a scholar
then. Some were artists, though we are not certain of their
names. Jews enjoyed the luxuries of wealth. Women were
fashionably dressed. They walked about bejeweled and
perfumed. All of Italy was densely perfumed then. In
Rome Jews would saunter out of their quarter on Sabbath
afternoons to watch Michelangelo at work on the marble
that would be his Moses. All enlightened people then understood the horns to be a sign of royalty and grandeur
and not the mark of degradation assumed by the ignorant.
Some Jews wore weapons. They gambled at cards and
took to the new game of tennis, which was played with a
hard ball on a hard court. In the summer heat they left
the cities for their country villas. Many enjoyed hunting.
They studied Talmud and read Cicero. Rabbis quoted
Dante and Petrarch in their sermons. Children learned Hebrew grammar and composition, music and dancing, Talmud and Bible. Jews took trips to the land of Israel and
kept careful diaries of their travels. They owned private
libraries, many of the books in Italian and Latin on different branches of knowledge. Many graduated from Italian
universities. Some homes were literary salons for patricians and merchants, rabbis and clerics. People believed
in omens, dreams, visions, alchemy, satyrs. Jewish women
told fortunes in the homes of nobles and prepared love
potions for eager ladies. Everyone wore amulets against
evil spirits. In Venice, where Jews had been admitted in
1516 on condition that they live only in the section of the
*geto nuovo,* the new foundry—in Venice, Jewish singers
and musicians gave musicales in the homes of the nobility.
It was a small, delicately petaled Italian Jewish world,
and it might have yielded a garden of exquisite flowers.
Once upon a time. . . .

In August 1553 the pope condemned the Talmud as a blasphemous work. A month later, on the Jewish New Year, a mountain of Jewish books was put to the torch in an *auto-da-fé* in Rome. In July 1555 a different pope ordered the Jews of the papal states, roughly central Italy, into ghettos. Jews could not own property and had to wear yellow hats. The Jews of Rome were moved to a new quarter of the left bank of the Tiber and a wall was immediately built around the area. By 1612 all the Jews of Tuscany, Padua, Verona, and Mantua lived in ghettos. The walls had two or three gates, which were closed at night. The gatekeepers were Christians. Jews were forced to pay their salaries.

Once upon a time . . . a real and terrible time.

Who was king? Who was not king? In fourteenth-century Europe, rats and plague and death were king.

The rats were black and had silky fur. They lived in houses and ships rather than in fields and sewers. For years they had moved westward along the caravan routes from Mongolia. They carried fleas. The fleas carried the bacillus *Pasteurella pestis,* which they received by biting an infected rat.

This was the bacillus that came on a trading ship from the Crimea to Genoa in the last week of December 1347. It was brought by Italian merchants who had been besieged by a raiding Mongol horde in the Crimea. The Mongols began to die, lifted the siege, and fled. Two days after the ship docked in Genoa plague broke out. Other ships carried it from ports in the Crimea to Constantinople, Venice, and various European shipping centers. Most cities were crowded then, their narrow streets and alleys filthy with refuse and garbage tossed out of windows and with urine and excrement. Black rats came down off the ships and multiplied in the cities. The plague spread through Italy, France, Germany, and the Scandinavian countries. It struck England and Russia. About a third of the population of Europe died of it. The English referred to it as the general mortality. The Germans called it *das grosse Sterben,* the great dying; the French called it *la peste noire*, the black plague. Historians have named it the Black Death.

No one understood what was happening. They could not connect the dying to rats and fleas. People gazed in horror at villages suddenly emptied of inhabitants. Silence shrouded the streets of stricken towns. Dead rats lay along the walls of alleyways and gardens. Carts rolled through dying cities laden with human corpses for mass burial. There was widespread hysteria; some implored God, flagellated themselves, pleaded to be spared; others sank into savagery and licentiousness. People were dying of fever and hideous pustules on the armpits or groin. Many were coughing and vomiting blood. Physicians admitted helplessness. Petrarch wrote that future generations would not believe such events had occurred or know the despair born of terrible and bewildering intimacy with swiftly spreading death.

Everyone sought a cause for the horror. Pope Clement VI referred to the plague as *morbus letalis*, the lethal sickness, regarded it as a punishment for sin, and spoke of "the pestilence with which God is afflicting the Christian people." Others looked about for more tangible explanations. Clearly a demonic malevolence was at the root of this catastrophe. People grew suspicious of strangers. The most vulnerable stranger of all was the Jew. For about a century and a half there had been blood libels and accusations of fiendish desecration of the wafer used in the ceremony of the Eucharist. Jews stole it, stabbed it, burned it, believing it to be the actual suffering body of Jesus and eager to inflict upon it further agony—so it was popularly believed.

A story spread about a Jew who had been given a bag of poison by a rabbi with instructions to empty its contents into wells, cisterns, and rivers. The Jews wanted to poison the world in vengeance for all the centuries of persecution. All of Christendom was in danger of destruction at the hands of the Jews.

In September 1348, Jews in Chillon, on Lake Geneva, were tortured and made to confess to the crime of poisoning wells. Accounts of these confessions under torture were sent to cities in Germany. A number of leading Germans defended the Jews. But the populace was aroused. There were massacres and expulsions. No one knows how many thousands were slain. Six thousand died in Mainz. In Strasbourg, along the edge of today's France, a wooden scaffold was built over a huge pit and two thousand Jews were burned alive. The men were granted permission to wear their prayer shawls.

The slaughter spread deep into France and then to Spain. Pope Clement VI called it "a horrible thing," and ordered that the attacks cease. They went on. In Vienna Jews enlarged their cemetery because they needed additional space in which to bury all who died of the plague.

The dying abated in the middle of 1350, then returned. For about fifty years it came and went in waves. Monasteries stood empty. Armies were depleted. General lawlessness grew pervasive. There were peasant rebellions and violent suppression. The attacks against the Jews continued.

Many Jews migrated eastward into Poland and Lithuania. These were young lands then, fairly recently settled by western and eastern Slavic tribes, among them a tribe named the Polanie, which means field dwellers. The Jews took their books, their belongings, their Yiddish— the language they had developed out of a mixture of Middle German and Hebrew—and their bitter memories of the long centuries of German hatred.

Jews continued to live in Germany after the waning of the plague. They lived in Jewish quarters separated from the Christians. The separation had taken centuries to develop; now, in the sixteenth century, it was general throughout western Europe. They were required to wear special hats and the Jew badge. Some hats were peaked. In many German states Jews could not build new synagogues.

They had always tended to cluster together. Now it was obligatory. Many Jews were grateful that Christians could no longer live in their midst. The challenges of the Christian world, its viciousness as well as its enticements, faded. The tension and aggression of the pioneering centuries weakened and were replaced by apathy; Jews grew indifferent to Christianity. Fourteen hundred years of polemics against Christianity now came to an end.

Some heard of the activities of Martin Luther and thought him to be a rebel against Christianity who was about to become a Jew. Others believed that the violence done by the Reformation to the power of the papacy heralded the coming of the Messiah. Probably those who believed that never read Luther's pamphlet: ". . . Their synagogues should be set on fire, and whatever does not burn up should be covered or spread over with dirt. . . . And this ought to be done for the honor of God and of Christianity in order that God may see that we are Christians, and that we have not wittingly tolerated or approved of such public lying, cursing, and blaspheming of His Son and His Christians. . . ."

The Jews lost interest in Luther. The blood and battles of Reformation Europe touched them only when rulers increased their taxes to finance armies. The Jews earned their livelihood by selling haberdashery, by peddling, money-lending, and pawnbroking. The avaricious among them who would not hesitate to cheat a Christian were repeatedly reminded by preachers of the rabbinic statement, "It is more blameworthy to steal from a gentile than from a Jew, because of the desecration of the Holy Name." They were warned that such practices on the part of individuals endangered the welfare of the community. They were told that one who cheats a Christian will end up cheating a Jew. There were respected business arrangements between Jews and Christians; but on both sides there was also deceit and greed.

Some German cities built walls around their Jewish quarters. The Jews could receive permits to leave their quarters and conduct business elsewhere; but they would return in the evening or for the Sabbath, eager to study a Talmudic text and forget the tumult of the outside world and the hungry grabbing for money which they needed to feed their families. Inside their homes and synagogues and academies, the Jews of Ashkenaz came to regard themselves as intrinsically superior in religious and moral caliber to the murderous world along whose periphery they lived. They believed in their own superior worth not because they had accepted the Torah; rather, they knew the Jews had been given the Torah because they were better to begin with than all the nations of the world.

Many of the ghettos were in large cities and had wide streets. Sometimes the Jewish quarter bordered on rotting slums and the brothel district. Often ghettos were narrow and sunless sections of ancient towns. They could not expand along the ground, for no additional land could be acquired by the Jews; they expanded toward the sky. Floors were added to ancient buildings and blocked the sun.

It was not a gloomy world. There were joyous weddings and parties. The Jews took special delight in Sabbath strolls. On festivals they would walk to a nearby river; the children would watch the fish and the play of sunlight on the water, the men would chat or discuss serious matters of Torah, the women would laugh among themselves and gossip. Purim was the happiest of times, with noisemaking and gift giving and an encouraged flow of strong drink. They cared for the poor and the sick and the dying with an elaborate array of voluntary organizations and charity funds. They collected funds for the Holy Land. It was an autonomous community with its own courts and communal leaders. There were the usual superstitions, the amulets and incantations, the fear of spirits and demons, the concern with astrological portents.

On occasion a wealthy and successful Jew would be asked by a ruler to become his treasurer, his banker, the administrator and supplier for his army. Rulers preferred wealthy Jews to wealthy Christians because they could dismiss the Jews at will and confiscate their property. These court Jews often rose to heights of power and were of great help in times of persecution. Often their good fortune failed and they were swiftly ruined.

The exile stretched on interminably through the sixteenth and seventeenth centuries. There were endless rearrangements of alliances among the nations of the world and constant wars. Distant continents were being carved up by colonizers. In 1663 the Turks declared war on the Holy Roman Empire. In July 1683 they began the siege of Vienna. In 1704 the English took Gibraltar.

Inside the synagogues and study houses of the ghettos a few saintly individuals would sit late into the nights immersed in kabbalistic texts. They learned that the creation had been sundered by an unforeseen breaking of the sacred vessels and by the sin of Adam. The sparks of the Presence had been scattered. Nothing in the world was in its proper place. To gather up the sparks and repair the damage was now the task of the Jew. The exile was like an abandoned garden choked with weeds. The people of Israel was to be the gardener. Dispersion was not only a punishment but also an opportunity. It set before Israel the mission of redeeming the world by separating the sparks from their encrustations of evil. Redemption would not come from the Messiah. The entire people of Israel, through its observance of the commandments and through prayer that took the soul on an ascent to the Infinite One—the people of Israel would restore the cosmos to its original order. This would inevitably bring the Messiah, whose coming would signify that the process of redemption had been completed. They studied and prayed.

Early in the seventeenth century the Frankfort ghetto was plundered by a mob. There were repeated blood libels and accusations of Host desecration. Mystery plays depicted the Jews as Christ-killers, demonic allies of Satan, and bloodsucking moneylenders—the permanent heritage of the enchanted land.

# BOOK FOUR

*Inside Modern Paganism*

# SECULARISM

# Messiahs for a Broken World

On May 31, 1665, the Messiah came.

His coming was unconnected to any specific event of that time. He behaved strangely—broke a number of Jewish ritual laws and engaged in odd sexual acts. No one knew it at the time, but the coming of that Messiah marked not the redemption of rabbinic civilization but the start of its decline.

German Jewry was asleep when he arrived. It was separated from the world around it by the Yiddish it spoke, the beards and sidecurls its men wore, the hair coverings of its married women, its restricted residences, and its small numbers—about fifty thousand individuals as the world turned into the seventeenth century. Degraded and bloodied by clerics, rulers, and mobs, contemptuous of the umbrella culture. Christendom, in which it was embedded, unwilling to encounter alien art and thought and unable any longer to engage in original creativity, the Jews of western and central Europe produced only one thinker of any significance during those ghetto centuries. Rabbi Judah Loew of Prague was a pious ascetic, a Talmudist, and a great mathematician. He is known as the Maharal, the acronym built of the first Hebrew letters of his title and name. He believed God chose Israel for its intrinsic merit. The nations of the world functioned through force; in Israel the soul prevailed. He was a kabbalist.

Rabbi Judah Loew became chief rabbi of Prague and taught in the academy of learning he founded there. He wrote enigmatic works on philosophy and education whose worth has only recently come to be appreciated.

He was held in awe by Jews and non-Jews for his scientific knowledge. He was a friend of the astronomer Tycho Brahe. He knew of Copernicus but would not accept his system because it contradicted that of the rabbis. He disliked Aristotle and Maimonides: intellectual perfection is not the supreme goal of man. The study of Torah enables man to commune with God. The observance of the commandments brings man closer to God.

He wrote that the exile of Jewry was a breakdown in the regularity of the universe. Every nation had a land of its own; every nation had the right to be free; dispersion and enslavement are deviations from the natural order. Messianic redemption is inevitable, decreed by the will of God. He tells us that prior to the redemption "the degradation of Israel will be greater than it ever was." We must not hasten the coming of the Messiah, he warned. He will come, he will come; it is ordained. He knew of the discovery of America. He hoped the ten tribes would also be discovered one day. On occasion he spoke bluntly about the behavior of the Jews of Prague; he would wander through the Jewish quarter of the city in his cloak and full beard and tall hat, a target of the merchant wrath he aroused with his sermons. A later century would attribute to him the creation of a golem, a man of earth and clay which he supposedly brought to life through the magic powers of the Kabbalah. This golem was reported to have saved the Jews of Prague from blood libels through his supernatural abilities. Rabbi Loew lived almost the entire span of the sixteenth century, from 1525 to 1609.

While German Jewry moldered, the Jews of Poland and Lithuania were helping kings and nobles pioneer a new land. These Jews regarded themselves as the bearers of the Ashkenazic tradition. They had begun to migrate from Ashkenaz as early as the eleventh century, but came in large numbers only after the years of the Black Death. There were about twenty-five thousand Jews in Poland at the end of the fifteenth century. By 1648 this number had grown, through immigration and natural increase, to about three hundred thousand, almost three percent of the total population of Poland and almost fifteen percent of its urban population. The theory that much of Polish

Jewry was initially comprised of converted Khazars cannot as yet be satisfactorily substantiated, though it is not to be entirely discounted.

Poland and Lithuania were virtually united by 1600. The territory of Poland extended from the Baltic Sea in the north to the Dniester River in the south, across which lay the Turkish empire; and from the Oder River in the west to the Dnieper and the black earth of Russia. It was a land of lakes and rivers, marshes and hills, and vast stretches of coniferous forests.

The Jews lived in towns and villages, controlled the export and import trade of the king, and ran the domestic fairs. Poland was a static world of wealthy nobles and impoverished serfs. Rulers and nobles sought ways to convert feudal revenues—their portions of a land's produce and a vassal's services—into immediate cash. Collecting these revenues was a difficult and tedious task. Occasionally an agent would be interested in offering a fixed amount of money for these revenues, and the ruler would eagerly accept; the agent would then collect the revenues and keep them for himself, his profit being the difference between what he paid the ruler and what he was able to collect.

It was entirely an accident of history that placed Jewish capital in this economic role. Jews were especially suited for this task not only because of an acquired ability to administer and handle large moneys but also because they were politically powerless and would never interfere in struggles between ruler and ruled. Political stability was crucial to Jewish social and economic existence. The Jew always supported the ruler and noble under whose protection he lived.

Jews administered the lands of the nobility. They were great clothing merchants, dealt in dyes and luxury items. The Jews were in the lumber business; they planted crops; they leased the inns where the peasants dulled their misery with drink. They bred livestock, distilled liquor, and ground grain for flour. They were the lubricant in an otherwise impossible economy of indolent nobles and enslaved serfs, their rights carefully protected by royal charters. They could live where they wished and were permitted to practice their religion openly; only about twenty of the one thousand or so towns in Poland-Lithuania closed their doors to Jews. Many of these closed towns were owned by Christian religious institutions.

The Jews were governed by a council of rabbis and wealthy laymen which met at the great fairs and concerned itself with economic, religious, and security matters; much of Jewry was spread thin in Christian villages and townships.

The Polish Jewish community was entirely regulated by its rabbis in all religious, moral, and cultural matters. Its school system began with the child in elementary school and continued on up to academies of learning where masters and disciples spent their lives with the Talmud and its commentaries. In 1721 twelve years of such higher learning were required in Lithuania after marriage before one could become a teacher of the law and a judge. Jewish presses published prayer books, Bibles, the Talmud, books of Talmudic legends for light reading, and a translation of the Pentateuch into Yiddish with a commentary woven of tales and moral teachings that was enormously appealing to women. Rabbinic civilization reached its zenith with the Jewish world of Poland and Lithuania.

The Jews were a wealthy and powerful autonomous entity within a body of Slavic tribes whose religion was Roman Christianity. Clerics never ceased reminding Polish peasants and nobles of the demonic nature of the Jews. This was a frontier world. Often there was violence. Roads were unsafe. Like everyone else, Jews took easily to their weapons.

Sometime during the early decades of the sixteenth century, Poland annexed much of what is today the Ukraine. The word Ukraine means borderlands—in this case, the forests and fertile meadowlands to the east of Poland. Peasants lived in those borderlands, and cossacks, hosts of swift-moving cavalry squads formed by peasants for self-protection as well as for booty and sheer love of war. The cossacks were cunning soldiers, eager for freedom, capable of enduring fierce heat and cold, hunger and thirst, courageous in war, and fearless in the face of death. They were known for their robustness; few died of disease save in very old age; most ended their lives on what they took to be the altar of fame—death in war. Some cossacks hired themselves out to the Polish army and served as frontier units. Most hated Poles and Jews. The word cossack means independent war adventurer.

The peasants of the Ukraine were of the Greek Orthodox faith. Polish rule over the Ukraine was oppressive— Ukrainian Byzantine culture was contemptible in the eyes of Polish Catholics. The peasants were exploited economically and taxed mercilessly by the Polish nobility. Jews collected the taxes. They moved into the wilderness of the Ukraine, settled in its villages, and served as middlemen for Polish nobles. There were occasional cossack uprisings. Rabbis warned of the danger of tax farming in the Ukraine.

In 1648 a cossack chief, or hetman, named Bogdan Chmielnicki led a mass uprising against the Poles. His possessions had been confiscated by a Polish noble, possibly at the instigation of a Jew. Several thousand cossacks ravaged the countryside, burning towns and villages, slaughtering Poles and Jews. For the Ukrainians it was a war of liberation. For the Poles it was a rebellion. For the Jews it was the calamitous end to a world they had helped pioneer and exploit under the authority of Polish nobles and kings. The Ukrainians were joined by Tartar hordes more interested in booty and slaves for themselves than freedom and justice for the Ukrainians.

The fighting dragged on, sporadic, savage. A letter written during that period recounts the capture of some towns by the cossacks. "They slaughtered eight hundred noblemen together with their wives and children as well as seven hundred Jews, also with wives and children. Some were cut into pieces, others were ordered to dig graves into which Jewish women and children were thrown and buried alive. Jews were given rifles and ordered to kill each other."

In 1654 the Russians entered the war on the side of the Ukrainians. Then the Swedes invaded and devastated northern Poland. Polish historians refer to that period as the deluge.

Jews fought back, often alongside the Poles. Many Jews and Poles fled from the frontier regions into the heart of the country and then found themselves defending interior cities against cossack armies. Jews gazed at the destruction of two centuries of achievement. There were widows and orphans to care for, and slaves to redeem. The slaughter spread and became general as the invading armies ranged throughout the land, withdrew for a time, then came on again. It is estimated that about one-fourth of the Jewish population of Poland died in that rebellion along with tens of thousands of Poles.

About two years before the uprising ended with the peace treaty, signed in 1667, that gave the Russians part of the Ukraine and left the rest in the hands of Poland, word came to the Jews that the Messiah had arrived.

He came as a Sephardic rabbi.

An engraving of him done from life by a Dutchman shows a man with a short beard, roundish features, and pale dreamy eyes. His lips are full and small. He seems dignified, solemn; nothing about his appearance suggests the charisma of messiahship. The index finger of his right hand points to a word or passage on the page of a book. I do not know the name of the book. Perhaps it is the Book of Ezekiel, the thirty-seventh chapter, which tells of the resurrection of the dry, dead bones of Israel. Perhaps it is the Zohar, the compendium of Jewish mystical works written and published in sections by Moses ben Shem Tov de Leon, a fourteenth-century Spanish kabbalist. The Zohar is to Jewish mysticism what the Talmud is to Jewish legalism. The word Zohar means light, illumination, splendor.

Initially its mystical message was for the few who wished to attain the contemplative life in communion with God. There was no messianic element involved in this form of mysticism; the kabbalist, through proper concentration during prayer and the performance of a commandment, experienced an ascent of the soul and united himself to the divine will and the ten stages or attributes of the Infinite One; he thereby achieved personal redemption.

After the destruction of Spanish Jewry and the increasing horror of the exile, Jewish mysticism became wedded to Jewish messianism through mystics who established themselves in Safed. They had come from nearly everywhere in the exile. The nightmarish suffering of their people, the need to understand the nature of the exile, the relationship between the endlessly deferred redemption and a benevolent God, the role of the people of Israel in a murderous world—all of these wrought a radical change in the nature of kabbalistic thought, much of it brought about by a young kabbalist named Rabbi Isaac Luria, who died in 1572 at the age of thirty-eight. He had come to Safed in 1570 from Egypt.

He taught that God, in order to make room for the world, yielded space which His own presence had filled; He went into exile. His attributes, or emanations, or potencies, continued to fill the shapes, the vessels, of worldly appearances. But the vessels proved unable to contain the divine light. They broke. The sparks fell and scattered and were mixed with the dross of earthly existence. The entire cosmos was awry; all was now in one vast exile, even God. Creation itself had gone wrong through a terrible catastrophe.

But the catastrophe could be corrected; the primal flaw could be mended. That was the specific task of Israel. By correcting itself Israel could also correct the cosmic chaos. It could do this through the proper observance of the law. Such observance had cosmic significance: it freed the entrapped sparks, ensured the redemption and the coming of the Messiah. The sparks were now almost free, the kabbalists taught. Soon, soon, the end would come to the darkness.

Some rabbinic authorities tended to regard messianism with suspicion; it possessed a volcanic force that could break the barriers set up by the law. And it could ask a question laden with menacing difficulty for the law: What is the nature of Judaism in a new and redeemed world? But the weary Jewish world was now ready for the Messiah.

His name was Shabbetai, or Sabbatai, Zevi. We are told that he was born in Smyrna, in Asia Minor, on the Ninth of Av, 1626. At the age of eighteen he was ordained as a Sephardic rabbi. His father and two brothers were wealthy merchants. He was strongly attached to his mother.

By the age of twenty he had begun to display alternating moods of depression and elation. Attacked by a fit of melancholy, he would abruptly withdraw from all human contact and live as a recluse. When the melancholy dissipated, he would climb steeply to elation and ecstasy and at times commit acts forbidden by the law of Moses. He would speak aloud the sacred Name of God, pronouncing it in the prohibited manner as it is written and vocalized in the Bible. The people of Smyrna thought him a deranged fool.

During adolescence he had begun to study Kabbalah. He had a lovely voice and a fine musical talent. He would compose songs. In some of his periods of exaltation he spoke of a special revelation granted him by the God of his faith. He was the Messiah, he said. He would sing beautifully. About 1654 the rabbis of Smyrna, angered by his claims and ritual violations, banished him from the community.

He became a wanderer. He journeyed through Greece and Thrace. In Salonika he took a Torah scroll as his bride in a wedding ceremony and was expelled from the city by the rabbis. In Constantinople he celebrated all three pilgrimage festivals in a single week, announced the abolition of the commandments, and uttered a blasphemous benediction: "Blessed art Thou, O Lord our God, who permits the forbidden." He was expelled. He slipped quietly into Smyrna and lived there for a while, deep in melancholy.

In 1662 he set out on a journey to Jerusalem. He reached the city at the end of the year and wandered about the holy places. His mind was clear during this period, and he was a stately and dignified figure. He lived in Cairo for about a year, and the fits of melancholy returned. He married an Ashkenazic girl named Sarah, an orphaned victim of the 1648 massacres in eastern Europe. She was a prostitute, and he took her in emulation of the prophet Hosea. The melancholic state persisted. He felt possessed by demons.

It was brought to his attention that an extraordinary man of God had suddenly appeared in the city of Gaza in the Holy Land. His name was Nathan, and he was reputed to be able to read souls and dispel demons. Shabbetai Zevi journeyed to Gaza.

He arrived in the city in April 1665. Nathan, a young rabbi of flawless reputation, had experienced a vision of Shabbetai Zevi as the Messiah. Tales about the strange Sephardic rabbi had circulated in Jerusalem when Nathan had studied there in 1663. The two men met. Nathan informed Shabbetai Zevi that there was no demon in his soul and that he was indeed the Messiah. His strange acts were expressions of his continued warfare against the realm of the shells, the abyss of evil, the formless golem or matter which could be redeemed only through the special hidden acts of purification and correction performed by the Messiah himself.

The Sephardic rabbi would hear nothing of this and refused to acknowledge the young rabbi's words. They journeyed together to the holy places in Hebron and Jerusalem, then returned to Gaza. There, on May 31, 1665, Shabbetai Zevi was suddenly seized by a sense of elation. Urged on by Nathan, the Sephardic rabbi revealed himself publicly as the Messiah. He was close to forty years old at the time.

Excitement took hold of the Gaza community of Jews. In the weeks that followed, Shabbetai Zevi rode around on horseback, gathering followers. He appointed twelve men to be apostles and judges of the soon-to-be-reconstituted twelve tribes of Israel. A number of leading Jerusalem rabbis regarded it all as dangerous nonsense and banished him from the Holy City.

The young rabbi, Nathan of Gaza—still in his early twenties, ascetic, learned, and above reproach—became the prophet of the new Messiah. He announced the need for mass repentance in order to hasten the coming redemption. He sent letters to various Jewish communities urging fasts and ascetic acts. No rabbi could oppose a call to repentance.

Independent of the events in the Holy Land, a sudden rumor raced through the Jewish communities of Europe: an army of the ten lost tribes of Israel had conquered

Mecca and was marching against Persia. This was in the summer of 1665—before anyone in Europe had yet heard of Shabbetai Zevi.

In the fall of 1665 Nathan of Gaza sent letters to Italy, Holland, Germany, and Poland announcing the Messiah. Four months had passed since the day Shabbetai Zevi had proclaimed himself the Messiah; it is not known why Nathan of Gaza waited so long before writing these letters. Shabbetai Zevi had used those months to journey from Gaza through Safed and on to Aleppo, where a number of Talmudic scholars announced that they believed in him. He went on to Smyrna. Nathan of Gaza had remained behind in the Holy Land.

On a day in early December, during the festival of Hanukkah, Shabbetai Zevi appeared in the synagogue attired in regal garb. He sang the morning prayers ecstatically. He uttered the name of God. His strange behavior, alternating between the dignified manner of the learned Sephardic rabbi and the erratic behavior of the apocalyptic redeemer, attracted many and repelled a few. Poor and wealthy alike, as well as respected scholars of the law, became entranced followers. But there were many who opposed him.

On December 11, Shabbetai Zevi forced his way into the synagogue of his opponents in Smyrna. Before the astonished congregation, he read the Torah portion from a book rather than from the scroll. Then he took the Torah scroll into his arms and sang to it a Castilian love song, his favorite melody, in which he saw profound kabbalistic allusions. He proclaimed himself the anointed one of the God of Jacob. He spoke the name of God and ordered others to speak it too.

A few days went by. The name of the Turkish sultan was dropped from the Sabbath morning public prayer for the welfare of the ruler and in its place was inserted the name of Shabbetai Zevi messianic king of Israel. All through the days that followed people were dancing in the streets ecstatic with joy. Many experienced trances. Prophets wandered about the streets of Smyrna describing Shabbetai Zevi seated on a throne. Commerce ceased. The hysteria was general throughout the Jewish community of the city; rich and poor, learned and unlearned, were caught up in it. On December 30, 1665, Shabbetai Zevi sailed from Smyrna to Constantinople. Letters crisscrossed the world, describing the events in Smyrna, adding fancy to fact and intensifying the fervor. Finally, finally, after fifteen hundred years of shame and wandering—the Messiah had come!

He came to Constantinople and was arrested by the Turkish authorities. They had grown suspicious of his activities, were troubled by the divisiveness his presence caused among the Jews of the empire. Rebels were generally quickly executed by the Turks. But Shabbetai Zevi apparently succeeded in making a considerable impression upon the grand vizier. He was imprisoned in Gallipoli, a Turkish port near the eastern end of the Dardanelles. He lived in a fortress in some comfort—his guards having been bribed by his followers—and was permitted visitors. Among the visitors were the rabbis of Constantinople. He was in a normal state then, his demeanor that of a scholar. The rabbis seemed not to know what to make of him; some went over to his side.

All through the final months of 1665 letters had come from Palestine, Egypt, Aleppo, and Smyrna telling of Shabbetai Zevi and the prophet Nathan. There was messianic fervor throughout Europe. In public processions of joy the Jews carried portraits of Shabbetai Zevi.

Skeptical rabbis maintained a guarded silence, fearful of arousing the vengeful anger of the Sabbatians in their communities. The two most relentless adversaries of the movement were Joseph Halevi, the preacher in the Jewish community of Leghorn, and Rabbi Jacob Sasportas, who resided in Hamburg with no official position and sent forth a steady stream of letters to friends and acquaintances in which he expressed his doubts about the messiahship of Shabbetai Zevi.

Neither Shabbetai Zevi nor Nathan of Gaza was a charlatan. Both were respected and learned rabbis; both regarded their roles as having come to them from God, the one the prophesied Messiah, the other the anticipated prophet who would announce the Messiah's coming. Centuries of isolation from contact with the world had conditioned the people to the belief that the future of the nation and the world depended upon the Jew alone and his cleansing of the mundane through the meticulous performance of the commandments accompanied by the deepest devotion and most focused intent of the heart; at the same time, centuries of expectation, as well as the popular kabbalistic notions that obedience to the law of Moses had cosmic significance and that the coming of the Messiah was the final stage in the redemptive process—all this made possible the frenzied acceptance of Shabbetai Zevi.

News of the Jewish Messiah spread to Christian circles. Pamphlets and broadsheets appeared during 1666 in English, Dutch, German, and Italian. In Poland and Lithuania, on the streets of Pinsk, Vilna, and Lublin, angry Christians watched Jews parade with pictures of Shabbetai Zevi. There were riots. In May 1666 the Polish king forbade these demonstrations.

In Gallipoli, his prison now a royal court as bribed guards looked away, Shabbetai Zevi began signing his letters, "I am the Lord your God Shabbetai Zevi."

Two Polish rabbis visited him in the summer of 1666. After a brief preliminary meeting he sent them to one of his lieutenants in Constantinople. The rabbis asked many questions. At a second audience with Shabbetai Zevi they found him dressed entirely in red. The mantle of the Torah he had with him was red. The Messiah was offering symbolic evidence of his familiarity with the horrors of the 1648 cossack massacres. He promised to avenge the atrocities that had been perpetrated upon Polish Jewry. He sang to them from the Book of Psalms. The rabbis were moved and impressed. In letters to Poland they praised the Messiah Shabbetai Zevi.

About a month after the rabbis left Gallipoli a kabbalist named Nehemiah Hacohen arrived from Poland. He had been summoned by Shabbetai Zevi in one of the letters written by the Polish rabbis. The Ashkenazic kabbalist would not acknowledge the authenticity of the Sephardic Messiah. A preliminary Messiah son of Joseph had to appear and be killed, said the Polish kabbalist, in order for the true Messiah son of David to make his appearance. Shabbetai Zevi's attempts to use kabbalistic texts to prove otherwise left the influential Polish mystic unconvinced. Neither of these two men was even remotely aware of the millennia of Jewish history that echoed through their private controversy. The clans of the house of Joseph, once the most powerful of the northern tribes of Israel, had remained deep in the memory of the people and, in some kabbalistic writings, were assigned a role in the drama of redemption: they would give the people a Messiah who would wage a war of deliverance and be destroyed—as the northern tribes had been; soon afterward, out of Judah, would come the second Messiah, who would unite the people and lead them to victory—as had David son of Jesse, king of the united tribes of Judah and Israel.

The quarrel between the two men dragged on for three days and became increasingly heated. The Polish kabbalist began to feel that his life was in danger. He had heard that nonbelievers had been terrorized and subjected to violence. He informed the Turkish authorities of the goings-on in the Gallipoli prison, converted to Islam in order to avoid possible suspicion of entanglement with the messianists, and fled to Poland, where he immediately reverted to Judaism.

Shabbetai Zevi was brought to Constantinople in a deep state of melancholy. On September 15, 1666, he was tried in the presence of the sultan and given the choice of immediate death or conversion to Islam. He chose Islam and was given a royal pension for the remainder of his life.

His followers would not believe it. The Messiah an apostate to Islam! Nathan of Gaza was told of it that November. It was all a profound mystery, he announced. It would be made clear in time. He left Gaza and journeyed to Smyrna, where he stayed through March and April in the company of followers who had remained firm in their belief in the messiahship of Shabbetai Zevi. Nathan developed the idea that the apostasy of the Messiah was the final stage in the fulfillment of his redemptive mission. He had descended to the very depths of evil, to the realm of the shells, in order to raise up the last of the sacred sparks. The strange actions of the Messiah through the years—his violation of the law of Moses, his licentious heterosexual and homosexual behavior—had been the visible manifestations of his struggles with evil; this apostasy was the final struggle. The Messiah had willingly accepted the shame of this latest of his strange deeds in order to complete the cleansing redemption of the world; he was conquering the realm of evil from within.

The prophet and the Messiah met a number of times in 1667 and 1668. Nathan spent the rest of his life wandering back and forth through the cities of the Mediterranean—Adrianople, Sofia, Kastoria, Salonika—where followers of Shabbetai Zevi persisted in their faith and awaited his return to Judaism.

In the Jewish communities of the Mediterranean and Europe, rabbis who had once been believers silently shed their passionate faith in immediate redemption and would not talk of the strange years when the hope of centuries had seemed so very close to fulfillment. Doubt regarding the accepted wisdom of rabbinic leadership crept into the edges of Jewish thought. The system itself had produced the yearning, had tested and approved of Shabbetai Zevi, and had been found lacking. To reduce the collective shame of the people before the eyes of future generations, communal records containing even the faintest echo of the messianic debacle were removed and destroyed—by order of the rabbis and elders. Silence descended upon the messianic movement of Shabbetai Zevi. But many had written biographical sketches of Shabbetai Zevi and Nathan of Gaza; innumerable letters, tracts, and pamphlets about the messianic movement had circulated throughout the Jewish and Christian worlds—not everything could be suppressed. The researches of Gershom Scholem and others have opened to our gaze the tragic and poignant events in the strange lives of Shabbetai Zevi and his fervent prophet.

Shabbetai Zevi died suddenly on September 17, 1676, the Day of Atonement. He was fifty years old. A little more than three years later, on January 11, 1680, Nathan of Gaza died. Only their followers were aware of their passing.

Small secret circles of these followers persisted throughout the Mediterranean and in Europe—underground Jews, adherents to rabbinic Judaism who met together furtively to speak of their Messiah and to engage in strange behavior, some of it sexual. They wished to sanctify evil and bring the final redemption; sin itself was sacred in a redeemed world that no longer needed the law. The movement lasted about a hundred years and numbered among its members some great rabbinic families.

Few care to talk about it today. Rabbinic and rationalist scholars play down its significance. There had been numerous false Messiahs in Jewish history; none had so affected the total people—so unveiled the volcanic apocalyptic turbulence beneath the rigid surface of rabbinic legalism—as had the movement led by Nathan of Gaza and Shabbetai Zevi.

The people returned to the grim normalcy of the endless exile. But expectations had been too deeply aroused for there now to be an easy resumption of passive suffering. Historians inform us that there was an increase during the eighteenth century of Jewish converts to Christianity. Rabbis, on their guard now against heresies, began to ferret out and excommunicate suspected followers of Shabbetai Zevi in Germany, Italy, Africa, and Poland.

About the middle of the eighteenth century a man named Jacob Frank, who had been born in 1726 in a small town in southern Poland, proclaimed himself redeemer of the Jews. He was a man of great physical strength with an enormous ego, a hunger for power, and unquenchable erotic impulses. During an aimless wandering through Turkey he encountered followers of Shabbetai Zevi. He returned to Poland, declared his intent to mold an army of Jews and create a Jewish kingdom on Polish soil. He was a boorish, ignorant man and preached a blatant disregard for the law. About a thousand people joined him. There were rumors of strange rituals and sexual orgies.

The Frankists—they were regarded by the rabbis and the masses of Jews as followers of the sect of Shabbetai Zevi; the name Frankists came into use in the nineteenth century—these Frankists were excommunicated by an assembly of rabbis that met in the city of Brody in 1756. Still, their mere presence was regarded as a menace to Jewry. Some leaders of the Polish Jewish community thought to rid themselves of the Frankists by having the Christian church burn them at the stake as heretics. The question was put to Jacob Israel Emden, one of the great rabbis of Ashkenazic Jewry. "You will be blessed," he replied, "if you root out evil from your midst. . . ." But he doubted the practicality of the effort: it would be too costly to work through Rome; it would take too long.

In the end Jacob Frank and his followers converted to Christianity and, together with their odd messianism, vanished from Jewish history. They are remembered as yet another embarrassing apocalyptic movement in the gathering eruptions of messianic, antilegalistic zeal that had begun to threaten the second civilization of the Jews.

Some years before the Frankists vanished into Christianity another kind of Messiah appeared—a faith healer who wandered about the peasant countryside of southern Poland dispensing herbs and incantations to Jews and non-Jews in the hills and hamlets of Galicia, Volhynia, Podolia, and the Ukraine. The Ukraine had been divided into two lands by the treaty of 1667. The region east of the Dnieper River had gone to Russia; the right bank, the western Ukraine, remained a Polish possession. There were fewer than one thousand Jews in the Russian sector, most of them leaseholders or involved in trade. They were soon expelled; Russia wanted no Jews on its soil.

The Polish Ukraine with its fertile steppes and richly wooded flatlands remained lucrative frontier territory populated by peasants and dominated by nobles. Jews flocked to it and helped rebuild its ruins. Scholars disagree about the extent to which Jews colonized and pioneered the Ukraine in the period before and after the 1648 uprising. But all appear to agree that in the century following the uprising the Jewish population of the Ukraine—and of Poland generally—increased sharply. All through Europe populations grew in that time.

The Jewry in the west bank of the Dnieper grew in spite of the atmosphere of frontier violence that pervaded the hills and meadows of that fertile borderland. The cossack brotherhood had been disbanded by the Russians and Poles. The land swarmed with Russian soldiers maintained at the expense of the Ukrainians. There were frequent raids from the Russian side of the Dnieper by small bands of *haidemaks,* rebels, made up of Ukranian peasants and cossacks. Poles and Jews would be attacked on the roads, beaten, robbed, sometimes killed, or taken prisoner and sold to the Tatars, who in turn would sell them into slavery to the Turks. These *haidemaks* saw themselves as the proud inheritors of the legacy of Chmielnicki. But they seemed to be out more for plunder than for the cause of freedom and were as troublesome to the Russians as they were to the Poles.

Jews continued as partners of the Polish nobility in the effort to colonize, civilize, and Polonize the peasants along the west bank of the Dnieper. They leased the vast estates of the nobles, operated the inns, collected the taxes. But an irreversible change had settled upon Poland and its Jews as a result of the 1648 cossack uprising. The destiny of both peoples was permanently altered.

The vulnerability of Poland did not go unnoticed by its neighbors. The Polish nobility so prized its privileges and independence that it would permit a single veto to kill the passage of laws and budgets in its assemblies. This effectively paralyzed Polish kings and prevented the raising of large armies. In the end the Polish passion for freedom would result in the disappearance of Poland as a geopolitical entity for more than a hundred years.

For the Jews of Poland the 1648 uprising had initiated a long, slow period of decline from which they never recovered. Migrations out of Poland had begun immediately with the onset of the massacres. Jews had fled westward to Germany and Prussia and southward to Moravia. Their relatives and friends had followed. This flight of some intellectuals from the slayings and dislocations suffered by Polish Jewry was enough to weaken Talmudic scholarship in Poland. In a little over two centuries, as the world of eastern European Jewry became increasingly spectral with the fires of a special hell, that early migration would turn into a tribal inundation that would

wash across the planet and deposit Jews almost everywhere—in Germany, France, England, Palestine, the
Americas, South Africa, Australia. Most of world Jewry
today is composed of descendants of the Jewry of eastern
Europe.

Polish Jewry had received residence rights from kings
that made it independent of city jurisdiction and taxation;
its status was extraterritorial. It was a kind of nation inside a nation; its government was the Council of the Four
Lands, the kahal, to which the various Jewish communities sent representatives when it met periodically at the
great fairs. Its code of laws was the *Shulchan Aruch*—the
words mean set table, an apt title for a work whose brev-
ity, lucidity, and form made it accessible to student and
scholar alike. It had been compiled by Joseph Caro, a sixteenth-century Sephardic rabbi, and augmented by Moses
Isserlis, a sixteenth-century Ashkenazic Polish rabbi, who
had added to it the laws and customs of German and Polish
Jews and had thereby helped make it the authoritative code
of world Jewry. The 1648 Chmielnicki massacres denuded
the Council of many of its great leaders and crippled it
financially. Polish rulers pressed the Jews for increasingly
higher taxes to help finance the wars against the Russians,
Swedes, cossacks, Turks. The devastated Jewish communities could not meet these demands. The Council began
to borrow money from Polish nobles and the Catholic orders. Then it levied a crushing burden of taxes on the
Jews in order to repay these loans. The burden was intolerable, especially for the poor. There was opposition
and bitter quarreling. The Council of the Four Lands and
the Lithuanian Council were to be abolished by the Poles
in 1764; Jews would pay their head tax directly to the
Polish state.

On the surface, during the decades that followed the
massacres and the wars, it seemed Polish Jewry was
recovering from the ravages of the deluge. New towns
were built. Many Jews ceased being moneylenders and
instead borrowed huge sums for business investments.
Academies of learning continued to flourish. But you cannot kill off one-quarter of a people without in some way
breaking its march through history. In retrospect we can

see the dry dead tissue that had begun to form throughout the body of rabbinic Judaism.

Few saw it then. They were aware of course that the Chmielnicki slaughter had behind it economic and political rather than only religious causes. There had been many instances in Jewish history when religion had served as the convenient rationale for the elimination of Jewish economic competition. But rarely had the economic and political elements been more blatant than during the long darkness of the Chmielnicki period. Some Jews accepted the occasional cossack offer to convert to Greek Orthodoxy and were spared death; most Jews fled or fought. The offer was not made to the Poles; they were mercilessly butchered. It was a bloody peasant war, and Jews were simply caught in the middle. Perhaps they wondered how you sanctified the Name of God when you died at the hands of a mounted sword-wielding cossack because you were a tax farmer for a Polish squire. The cossacks slew Poles and Jews indiscriminately. For the first time in Ashkenazic Jewish history it began to seem possible that Jews could die a terrible death not only for the sake of heaven but also for an accident of history. Add to this the failed messianism of Shabbetai Zevi and the tumultuous wanderings of tens of thousands of dislocated people and you have the faint beginnings of the disintegration of rabbinic civilization.

They had fled westward from the advancing hordes of cossacks and southward from the armies of Sweden, sometimes taking to their wagons even on the Sabbath, an act forbidden by religious law. Those who had no means of transportation or would not travel on the Sabbath stayed behind and often died. Thousands went wandering from town to town and from province to province. In those days European towns still discriminated sharply between resident citizens and foreign newcomers. These distinctions were not only social but also legal. You could not simply move from one town to another, settle in permanently, and look about for a way to earn a living. Newcomers were usually barred by law from permanent settlement and from many of the artisan and commercial guilds; there was just so much economic wealth available, and few wished to share it with strangers. Newcomers might be given the right to settle permanently in a new area upon the payment of a considerable sum of money; they could then compete actively for economic opportunities. But the payment of fees for legal residence rights did not always gain the stranger social acceptance. The uprising and the wars, and the subsequent wanderings of refugee populations resulted in class divisions and social stratification—in an alienated and increasingly restless mass of Jews.

Often a Jew would return to his abandoned inn or mill in the Ukraine and find it had been taken over by another Jew. Bitter quarrels and lawsuits would follow. The increase in population intensified economic competition and communal divisiveness. Gazing upon Polish Jewry in the early decades of the eighteenth century, I see a once vital and united people in increasingly desperate disarray. Communal organizations are in the hands of boorish incompetents, for many of the best Polish Jewish families have been slain or have migrated westward. Rabbis seem less inclined to confront the grit of bleak reality and more disposed to remain within the walls of academies and worn folios of Talmud. You can now buy a position of leadership in the Jewish community from your local Polish noble. You can gain admission into an academy of learning upon payment to an instructor. You can purchase a rabbinic position from local authorities. You can no longer be certain that a rabbi is also a scholar: in Lithuania in 1761 all that was required of a man who wished to serve as a rabbi was that he not be under twenty years of age. There are the very rich and the very poor and the alienated in every community. In the Ukraine the Jews are thinly spread throughout the peasant populace, are far from centers of learning, and remain the targets of rebel raids from across the Dnieper.

All through Poland itinerant preachers wander from town to town preaching the importance of Torah study and expounding kabbalistic doctrines about the Other Side, the demonic darkness of the world, and the need to wage endless war against its fearful powers. Of all the doctrines of kabbalistic thought—the retraction of God to make place for the cosmos, the breaking of the vessels, the spilling of the sparks, the means of restoring the world—these preachers chose to deal mainly with the individual Jew's struggle with encrustations of evil, putrescent shells of demonic horror that pulsate with malevolent life, each with a name and nature of its own, each able to be annihilated only when it is precisely known. This Polish kabbalistic preoccupation with the realm of the Other Side was clearly apparent in the period preceding the 1648 disasters.

The kabbalists had calculated that the year 1648 would bring the redemption; instead it had brought Chmielnicki. Nearly two decades later rabbis and kabbalists throughout the Jewish world had proclaimed their faith in Shabbetai Zevi as the Messiah—though the extent of his acceptance by Polish Jewry is still a matter of serious debate among scholars; Shabbetai Zevi had become an apostate. The land had been torn; the people had been savaged. Beneath the surface healing during the early eighteenth century there was much internal bleeding. Vast segments of Polish Jewry, especially the alienated elements in the south and those adrift in the violence-ridden, superstition-filled peasant wilderness of the Ukraine, felt diminishing ties to distant centers of Torah. If the God of the Jews can be approached only through the study of Torah, then He was a distant God indeed to much of Polish Jewry. And among those who did study there was a growing sense of disenchantment with cloistered scholars and shallow-minded communal leaders. The tightly seamed civilization of rabbbinic Judaism in its Ashkenazic manifestation, this tiny Jewish island in a Christian sea, which in the past had been so firm that it needed only the manifest support of people who felt connected to its principles in order for Jewish society to be reconstituted after each deluge—this civilization had been so mauled and was now so filled with splintering discontent that it began to pull apart. The neglected garden of the world, which kabbalists had once thought to weed and plant anew, was now encroaching upon Jewry itself. The Messiah seemed a vague and distant dream overgrown with dry weeds and nettles.

During these first three or four decades of the eighteenth century a pietist reaction set in against the rigid formalism of the Russian church. A similar phenomenon was taking place in Germany, Switzerland, and other parts of Europe. Both banks of the Dnieper became rife with Russian Ukrainian Christian sects—extreme ascetics, flagellants, ecstatics. The Jews of the Ukraine were fully aware of the Christian ferment all around them—the spirit wrestlers, the self-emasculators, the worshipers in long white robes and broad girdles and shirts with wide sleeves, the groups with leaders who were regarded as prophets capable of transmitting their powers to their children, the people who danced, sang, leaped, and whirled as they prayed.

During these decades rumors of odd happenings among the Jews of southern Poland and the Ukraine began to filter northward into the large Jewish urban centers of the land. There were reports of Jews indulging in outbursts of ecstatic behavior as they prayed. This abandonment of emotional restraint spilled over into their everyday affairs; their lives seemed to display a sense of release from entanglement in the earthly realm. Their ongoing ecstatic experiences were singularly at odds with the emotional restraints enjoined by the accepted values of rabbinic Judaism.

Sometime about the middle of the third decade of that century a Jewish mystic and faith healer emerged from the mountains of southern Poland and brought to the alienated elements of Polish Jewry what he believed was a new vision of God and man and a new messianism. He founded the Jewish pietist movement called Hasidism. In so doing, he destroyed the unity of the second civilization of the Jews and the absolute authority of its rabbinic leaders.

He had been an orphan and a bad student. He would flee from school to wander in the woods. His birthplace was Okopy, a small town in southern Poland. Almost everything we know of him has come down to us in oral traditions set in writing more than fifty years after his death. He himself wrote nothing. He was born in 1700 and his name was Israel.

To earn a living, he became a teacher's assistant. He

would gather up the children from their homes and lead them to school. Often he would take them to the woods and teach them to listen to the singing of the birds. He served as a watchman in the local house of study. We are told that in the nights he would sit immersed in kabbalistic works. He seems to have cared little for Talmudic learning—though many of his followers insisted he knew the Talmud well. He married and lived a hermitlike existence with his wife in a hut in the Carpathian Mountains of southern Poland. They dug lime and sold it in the nearby town. From semipagan village women he learned the curative powers of certain herbs. He roamed the heavily wooded hills, deep in meditation.

He became an innkeeper. His wife operated the inn while he moved about the hills. They lived in abysmal poverty. Then they came down from the mountains and settled in a small town. To the people of the town he announced himself as a healer and an exorcist.

Such faith healers were common then and were known by the title baal shem, master of the Name. It was believed that by somehow manipulating and uttering in proper sequence the letters comprising the various names of God they could oust the demons that caused illness. Faith healers were the physicians of the people in Germany and Poland. They wrote amulets. We can trace their beginnings in the sixteenth century. Some were rabbinic scholars; others were kabbalists. During the seventeenth and eighteenth centuries these faith healers came increasingly from the masses. They would attempt to effect their cures by incantations, amulets, prayers, and the use of remedies made from herbs and animal matter. It was believed they could exorcise the demons that entered a person and caused insanity. A variation on the name baal shem was baal shem tov—master of the Good Name. The words baal shem tov form the acronym Besht. Later enlightened Jews regarded them all as benighted or as outright charlatans. Israel was thirty-six years old when he proclaimed himself to be a baal shem.

He became a wanderer. He journeyed through the hamlets and villages of southern Poland, healing the illnesses of innkeepers, laborers, tax collectors, leaseholders. On occasion he ministered to non-Jewish peasants and noblemen. He dispensed salves and ointments, amulets and prayers; he applied leeches; he practiced bloodletting; he performed acts of magic. He would use the income from his wanderings to pay his debts; the rest he would give to charity.

He smoked a pipe, as did most men. He had a fine voice. He loved to tell stories. He slept only two hours a day. He immersed himself in a ritual bath at least once every day and before each attempt at a miraculous cure. He was liked by Jews and non-Jews. We are told he had extrasensory perception; he could read a person's past and predict his future. He was an ecstatic. During prayers he would be seized by uncontrollable enthusiasm. He would dance in a frenzy of joy. Once he claimed that the Messiah had helped him with a particularly difficult cure. He did not receive rabbinic ordination. But his later followers often called him Rabbi Israel Baal Shem Tov—or, simply, the Besht.

He was a charismatic teacher. Wandering through the villages of southern Poland, he taught by word and act the value of feeling in the worship of God. The performance of a commandment was less important to the Master of the Universe than the emotion that accompanied it. He taught that the sparks of divinity which had spilled from the broken vessels during the act of creation now filled the world with sanctity. This was a crucial reinterpretation of the kabbalistic view of the world. Kabbalists believed that the falling of the sparks into the realm of the Other Side had been a cosmic disaster necessitating the task of redemption which was the sacred mission of the Jew. The Besht taught that those fallen sparks infused all of existence with sanctity. No corner of the world was without the presence of the Master of the Universe. The truly pious man experiences God even in the most mundane of acts—eating, drinking, sexual intercourse. Man was not surrounded by swarming hosts of invisible demons, as the scholars and preachers often taught. The world is not full of sin and sinners. One need not seek protection against Satan, wicked spirits, and ghosts through endless study, prayer, penance, mortification, and fasting. No, no, he taught. The Master of the Universe is a compassionate God who loves His people and does not wish them to live in endless dread. He is everywhere, in every blade of grass, in every scudding cloud. He wishes man to be near Him. The fulfillment of even a single commandment, performed with love and intense devotion, is sufficient to bring a man merit. The world can be redeemed through joy. We do not perform the commandments in order to restore the cosmos but to experience the ecstasy that comes from the sense of approaching the presence of God. It is not the mysterious universe outside us that should be the concern of man but the intimate world of our emotions. We are linked to the Master of the Universe through our inner being. It is wrong to weep or fast unnecessarily or to mortify the flesh. To work hard for a living, to labor for material gain—such acts are of value, for they supply us with sustenance, provide for our bodily needs, and help bring happiness into our lives. The Master of the Universe delights in the happiness of His people. Dance—God watches; sing—God hears; be joyous—for God loves His people to be happy. Pray with a full and open heart, for nothing can so bring a man close to the Master of the Universe as can sincere prayer. We have not been placed in this world simply to perform the commandments. No—God needs His people. What good is a king without a nation? The Jew brings the Master of the Universe into this world through his feelings and deeds, through his awareness that all is from God, even sin. What would there be to pray for if the world were empty of sin? And sin is not the horror that Talmudists and preachers make it out to be. If one's gaze should fall upon a beautiful woman—a serious transgression—one need merely recall that her beauty was given her by the Master of the Universe in order to transform a sinful act into one that exalts God. The Master of the Universe knows that His people cannot possibly perform all the commandments. It is inconceivable that He would punish them for their transgressions. Does a loving father punish a stumbling child?

These words found an eager audience among the laborers, innkeepers, and alienated Jews of southern Poland. Here and there some would band together to form their own congregations and talk of the teachings of this gentle and persuasive healer. They would dance and sing and attempt to approach his states of ecstasy. Some among them thought him to be the Messiah, teaching not of the end of days and the return to Zion but of the radiance in ordinary life.

About the year 1745 the Besht ceased his wanderings and settled in the southern Polish town of Medzibosh. He had not created the ambiance of pietism but emerged as its most charismatic figure and now drew to himself many already existing pietist elements. On occasion he would be visited by rabbis from the north. Some were persuaded by his teachings. When he died in 1760 he had around him a small intimate circle of disciples, some of them rabbis and preachers. After six years of uncertainty and inner quarreling, a great preacher from the town of Mezhirech, north of Medzibosh, emerged as the successor to the Besht. His name was Dov Baer. He had many disciples. They began wanderings of their own.

The movement spread rapidly through Volhynia, in which Mezhirech was located, then westward into Galicia and central Poland and northward toward Lithuania. The missionaries sent out by Dov Baer traveled the winter and summer roads of Poland and the dangerous steppes and forests of the Ukraine, preaching the pietism of the Baal Shem Tov. Hasidic communities sprang up everywhere, organized around small prayer groups. It is probably a measure of the aridity of rabbinic civilization that one such Hasidic group was discovered in 1772 in the city of Vilna in Lithuania. Vilna was the stronghold of rabbinism and the home of the greatest rabbinic scholar of that century, Rabbi Elijah ben Solomon Zalman. He was an intellectual recluse, fiercely protective of the law. Any attack on even the smallest detail of the law weakened the entire structure of the Torah and was sinful in his eyes. The Torah was eternal; the study of the secular sciences aided the Jew in his understanding of the Torah; hence, Rabbi Elijah—known also as the Gaon of Vilna—attacked the lack of interest in the sciences prevalent in Talmudic academies. He studied scientific works translated into Hebrew, for he knew no foreign languages. Newton was unknown to him. He was interested in medicine and music. He wrote works on mathematics, astronomy and many commentaries. He disliked casuistry and brought a rigorous, straightforward method of explication to his studies of Talmudic texts. He pruned centuries of liturgical poetry from the prayerbook and introduced congregational singing. On occasion, to remain alert, he would study Talmud with his feet in icy water. He regarded Hasidic ecstasy and enthusiasm, the reports of the miracles and visions of its leaders, as menacing delusions and not unlike the pagan worship of mortal beings. He refused to meet with leaders of the movement who asked to see him. He saw in the Hasidic emphasis on prayer a serious threat to the importance of Torah study. He regarded their adoption of certain Sephardic prayers and their insistence upon the use of specially sharpened knives for ritual slaughter—Hasidim would not eat the meat from animals slaughtered by rabbinically approved slaughterers—Rabbi Elijah of Vilna regarded all these actions as a flouting of rabbinic authority.

He was, of course, correct; the Hasidim were creating their own self-contained communities. In 1772 he issued a ban against their presence in Vilna. Hasidic works were burned. The Hasidim issued a ban of their own and burned a polemical work that had been written against them. A further excommunication against the Hasidim was proclaimed in 1781. "They must leave our communities with their wives and children," it read. "They should not be lodged overnight; their ritual slaughter is forbidden. It is forbidden to do business with them and to intermarry with them or to assist at their burial. . . ." But the movement could not be crushed.

Rabbi Elijah died in 1797. It was rumored that Hasidim danced with joy on his grave.

In 1795 Poland was partitioned among Prussia, Austria, and Russia. About three-quarters of a million Jews lived in Poland at that time, and they constituted something like ten percent of the total population. Poland would not regain its independence until after the First World War.

The partition of Poland further weakened the unity of rabbinic Judaism and resulted in the decentralization of

Hasidism and the subsequent variations in its development. One Hasidic group in Russia, known as the Lubavitcher, restored the emphasis on intellectualism and muted the element of ecstasy. But common to all Hasidic communities was the unique role of the rebbe, the tzaddik, the righteous one, the sacred leader around whom all activity was centered.

These leaders derived their authority from their association with the Besht or with a member of that inner circle who had clung to the Besht, witnessed his ecstasies and meditations, his flights of the soul, listened to his teachings, to his accounts of his visions—and had then experienced in their own beings the rapturous communion with the Master of the Universe, the redemptive uplifting of the divine sparks and the restoration of the soul. Wherever a member of this inner group or his disciples settled, he gathered around himself a circle of fanatically loyal followers.

The tzaddik was the pure soul of their collective being, passionately loved, blindly followed. He was the individual Hasid's numinous link to the Master of the Universe; through the mystical communion of the tzaddik with God, the Hasid too approached the Infinite One. He was to his followers a teacher, moralist, preacher, confessor, miracle-worker, and wonder-healer. He would sing ecstatically the Song of Songs or the opening prayer of the Sabbath eve liturgy. On a Sabbath afternoon, in the gathering dusk of a Polish winter, he would sit at the head of a large scarred table in a dingy house of worship and his followers would crowd around him—laborers, woodchoppers, water carriers, wagon drivers, butchers, merchants—and listen to his words. He might spin a tale with a moral lesson or recount a saying of the Baal Shem or expound upon a verse in the Torah portion of that week—and the bleak and merciless world would slowly dissolve and they would try to cling to him as he ascended stage by stage to the blinding luminosity that often could be hinted at only in silence or by a wordless melody. The tzaddik was able to effect the transformation of the secular into the holy; but it could only be experienced communally; a Hasid could only achieve mystical communion with the Master of the Universe together with his fellow Hasidim by means of collective joy, dance, song, prayer—and attendance upon the tzaddik.

Were you living then in eastern Europe, you might one day have passed a ramshackle building where Hasidim met. You might have looked in upon them and witnessed a ragged rabble seated on benches at an ancient table; and if you were of a rationalist bent of mind and regarded yourself as one of their opponents, a Mitnaged, you might have mocked their pretenses at mysticism, their boorishness, their ignorance of the Talmud, their diluted kabbalism, their familiarity with the brandy bottle and propensity to alcohol-induced joy; or you might have wondered if there was truly something there, intangible but nevertheless very real, as elusive and as vivid as the dreams you knew were lodged deep in the core of your own being.

Hasidim might live miles away from their tzaddik, journeys of many days. Yet they would be linked to him by the tales they would tell one another of his wondrous works, by a recounting of his homilies, by their visits to him on festivals and holy days when all the men of a Hasidic community would join their tzaddik in the ecstasy of prayer, song, and dance while the women remained home with the children; Hasidism—certainly in its beginnings—was a man's world.

The tzaddik—not the local yeshiva-trained rabbi—was the final authority in a Hasidic community. It was to his tzaddik that a Hasid took questions of Jewish law as well as the most intimate matters of life. The tzaddik might or might not be an ordained leader; ordination was irrelevant. The tzaddik might turn to a trained legal authority, but that authority was subservient to the tzaddik. Thus Hasidism succeeded in breaking the absolute authority of the rabbis over the people. Rabbi Chaim of Volozhin, a disciple of the Gaon of Vilna, regarded this attempt by the Hasidim to throw off the yoke of communal authority as a heinous act of social amorality. Another great rabbi, Israel of Zamosc, accused the Hasidim of breaking down the walls of the Torah.

The Hasidim also broke down active messianic hopes

for the redemption of Israel and for an end to the exile. This point is much debated by scholars, but I find it difficult not to believe it is true. The hope for the coming of the Messiah and the redemption did not disappear from the hearts of the Hasidim. They were orthodox Jews. They accepted all of Jewish teaching, including the article of faith about the Messiah: "I believe in the coming of the Messiah; and even if he delays, still I believe." But they placed that coming in a distant future and made it God's work and not their own.

During an ascent of his soul to heaven the Baal Shem encountered the Messiah. The ascent occurred in September 1746. So we are told in a letter written by the Baal Shem to his brother-in-law, who had settled in the land of Israel. When will you come? the Baal Shem asked the Messiah. When your doctrine will be widely known and revealed throughout the world, was the response. And the Baal Shem was bewildered by the answer and greatly saddened by the vast length of time until this could be achieved.

The Baal Shem did not expect the Messiah in his lifetime. That coming was not to be rushed. It was all in the hands of God. In the meantime, the Hasid would cling to the Master of the Universe and thereby destroy the exile from within. It is not the restoration of the cosmos and the hungry desire to bring the Messiah that concerns the Hasid; it is his own personal relationship to God. From its very inception Hasidism stressed the individual soul.

Many Hasidim settled in the land of Israel; their act had little to do with active messianism. They wished to live out their lives and be buried in the land promised by God to the patriarchs, the land of judges, kings, prophets, priests, rabbis, mystics, and saints. Some present-day Hasidim believe that their tzaddik is the Messiah, working patiently to sanctify the mundane normalcy of everyday existence and not to transform reality through an apocalyptic bath of blood. The apocalypse they leave to God. They seem in no rush to witness an end to history. Hasidism neutralized active messianism by returning its explosive clockwork to God.

In the decades that followed the birth of Hasidism

there were among its leaders some of the greatest of saints and the crudest of charlatans. Some wrote books or had their sayings and tales written down by their zealous followers; Hasidism has so far produced a literature of about three thousand works. Some lived among the people, molding them into communities of souls and ending their haunted sense of alienation from Judaism. They trudged on weary legs along frozen or quagmiry roads to bring consolation to their followers, to share a drink with them at a table in a smoke-filled inn, help a blacksmith shoe a horse, take upon themselves their pain, urge them not to despair, to turn their sorrows into joy. One gets the feeling that they would not permit themselves a hard look at the suffering of their people under the Russian czars because they feared they would go mad. Indeed some appeared to waver on the edge of madness; one shut himself away from his people for twenty years, unable to endure the chasm between dream and reality.

Some bridged the chasm by the tales they told; others, by ascents through the words and thoughts of prayers and a contemplation of the letters and an emptying of the mind into the stillness that is the connection with the divine world of thought. They taught their people to pray and sing and love. Some among them used the money given them by the simple ones they led to furnish for themselves sumptuous courts. A tzaddik should live like a king, they said. Why should only the gentiles have kings?

Soon the tzaddikate became hereditary. The revolutionary zeal of Hasidism waned. The spontaneity of its young years faded. It moved closer to traditional modes of Jewish prayer and study. It began to establish its own Talmudic academies in emulation of the academies that were being founded in eastern Europe during the renaissance of Jewish learning brought on by the Gaon of Vilna. It became the implacable enemy of the new ideas and the promise of a better world that washed across Enlightenment Europe.

In 1807 one Hasidic tzaddik, Shneur Zalman of Lyady, urged his followers to spy against Napoleon on behalf of Russia. "If Bonaparte wins," he said, "the wealthy among Israel would increase and the greatness of Israel would be raised, but they would leave and take the heart of Israel far from our Father in Heaven."

Hasidim greeted with suspicion the Napoleonic order to put an end to the ghettos in the lands France conquered. They wanted no part of the godless world of the emerging nation-states. In the second half of the nineteenth century the movement ceased to grow.

The Baal Shem Tov had attempted to bring sparks of light and soul to the weary clay of Talmudic civilization. He gave that civilization its last moment of original creativity at the cost of its first unsuccessful battle against a competing sect within Judaism since the period of the second Jerusalem temple. After three generations of struggle Hasidism was grudgingly accepted as part of orthodox Judaism, though it had its own style of life, separate communities, and some variations in its rites of worship. Now rabbi and rebbe—rabbinic scholar and mystic intermediary—ruled together over the body of religious Jewry. An uneasy truce had been declared between them as they turned to face a common enemy: secularism.

Who was king? Who was not king? Among the Jews of nineteenth-century eastern Europe, rabbis and rebbes were king. Active messianism had ceased. The Messiah was carried off to western Jewry, to scholars, secularists, and Zionists in the world of modern paganism.

It was a Greek world, though it spoke French, English, German, and some Latin. The dark irrationalism at the core of Green paganism was filtered out, as were its pitiless nature gods and lofty Olympian deities. The filtering was done by Voltaire, Hume, Rousseau, Kant, and many others who lived in the eighteenth century and created the Enlightenment. They returned to the foreground of human attention the cool passion for truth, the love of nature, the sense of form, the contempt for blind faith, the regard for individual worth rather than the needs of the tribe—ideas that had bubbled up from time to time in the past through the covering earth of Christian civilization and that had been the best of the gifts of ancient Greece and Rome. This new world soon found itself crowded with Jews, many of them possessed of new fevers of messianism.

*Sapere aude!* Dare to know! Kant borrowed these words from the first-century B.C.E. Latin poet Horace, who lived during the long Roman peace of Augustus, when the arts were eagerly cultivated and the roads and seas were safe and Herod ruled Judea and the concept of the Messiah began to crystallize into an idea about a man, a descendant of King David, who would destroy the rule of Rome, restore the kingdom of Israel, and return dispersed Jewry to Zion. The Messiah would be a charismatic prophet, warrior, judge, king, and teacher of the law. He would appear at the end of human history, redeem and rule Israel, and establish the kingdom of God. No such notion of the Messiah is found in the Bible; there the term simply means the anointed one and refers to David and his dynastic descendants. After the fall of the united monarchy Israelites began to express the hope that the house of David would one day reign again over a reunited Israel and Judah. Then Isaiah had a vision of a future king who would love justice and be endowed with a God-given ability to distinguish right from wrong. This was to be the crucial link between the separate Biblical ideas of a reestablished Davidic dynasty and the Day of the Lord, when YHWH would rule over all the earth. The bitter confrontations with Greece and Rome fused the dream of a future just king to the yearning for a miraculous liberation from the tyranny of pagan rule; and the horror of the expulsion from Spain brought about the frenzied cosmic kabbalistic messianism of Isaac Luria—and then the broken hopes of almost the entire people in the time of Shabbetai Zevi and Nathan of Gaza. Now a new confrontation was about to begin between the Jew and the culture around him. Dare to know! Kant saw in these words the theme of the Enlightenment. Take the risk! We may discover emptiness in the heart of the cosmos. We owe it to ourselves to face the truth.

The men and women of the Enlightenment—in France they were called the philosophes—inherited the classical writings of the Stoics and Epicureans of Greece and Rome that had been preserved by the church. They used that learning to shake themselves free of the trammels of Christianity. Some had a simplistic view of human history: first there had been the river civilizations, the age of dread and myth, the infancy of man; then had come the period of Greece and Rome, that golden time of masterful art and rational thought; darkness had descended with the coming of Christianity, which they regarded as a catastrophic wrong turn in the development of man; now the human species stood on the threshold of a new era that was again resonant with the thought of Greece and Rome and was freeing itself of the chains of revealed religion. They were as contemptuous of Judaism as they were of Christianity. Hume felt that man had the capacity to accept calmly the truths about himself and the world and to face the probability that absolute justice is not built into the starry heavens or the scarred earth.

For the past three hundred years the umbrella civilization of western man has been modern paganism, or secular humanism—secular because it has abandoned the supernatural, humanist because of its emphasis upon classical studies, or the humanities, and its regard for scientific knowledge and the worth of the individual. It is probably the most creative, the most liberated, the wealthiest, most dehumanizing, and most murderous civilization in the history of our species. Among those who have suffered most from its excesses is the Jew. Ironically, Jews helped to mold this umbrella civilization.

The beginnings of the Jewish entry into secularism are bleak and bitter and go back to the seventeenth century. In 1640, about fifty years before the birth of Voltaire, a Jew named Uriel da Costa committed suicide in Amsterdam. He had been born in Portugal into a family of Conversos. The family was of the nobility. His father was a devout Catholic. Da Costa studied in a Jesuit university, became a cleric, and found no sense of salvation in Roman Christianity. He studied the Bible and formed a notion of Judaism that pictured a faith free of oppressive clerics and open to all thought. He converted his family to his version of Judaism. They fled to Amsterdam to escape the Inquisition and practice their new faith openly.

In Amsterdam da Costa discovered a Sephardic

Judaism that was more oppressive than the Christianity he had abandoned. Other Converso families were making that same discovery. In Spain and Portugal they had felt themselves free to criticize openly or secretly the laws, tales, and clerics of Roman Christianity. But they had longed to rejoin the faith of their forefathers. Many went off to the Americas and England, where they soon became influential merchants and bankers, were accepted into the most aristocratic of circles, in time declared themselves to be Jews, and served as the seed beds that would receive future Jewish wanderings. But those who came to Amsterdam found rabbis and communal leaders so fearful of contact with the outside world that all Jewish life and thought was rigidly supervised. These Amsterdam Jews were descendants of refugees from Spain. They remembered all too vividly the stories, told them by parents and grandparents, of how such contact had once proved ruinous to Spanish Jewry.

Da Costa was embittered by the rabbis and what he thought to be their stranglehold upon the Jewish community. He called them the Pharisees of Amsterdam. He wrote a work in which he argued that the doctrine of the immortality of the soul was not Biblical in origin. He was excommunicated and the book was burned.

He lived in Hamburg for a while, returned to Amsterdam, rejoined the synagogue after seeking repentance, and soon afterward began to doubt the divine origin of the law of Moses. Religion was the creation of man, he contended, and so he ceased to be a practicing Jew. Once again he was excommunicated.

He lived on in Amsterdam for seven years, alone, shunned by Jews and Christians. The loneliness became unendurable. In 1640 he asked to be permitted to rejoin the Jewish community. He would have to submit himself to public penance, the elders informed him. He would have to recant his views before the entire congregation.

This he did. He was then given thirty-nine lashes, the customary punishment for certain sins, and made to prostrate himself upon the synagogue threshold. The members of the congregation walked over him. He was a proud, rebellious, angry man in search of a faith that did not exist, adrift in a world that could not yet sustain religious Hapiru who went wandering freely through doctrines in search of truth. He was shaken and tormented by the humiliating penance to which he had been subjected. He killed himself.

Enlightenment thinkers regarded him as a heroic figure in the battle against stone-minded orthodoxy. The Amsterdam synagogue where he did public penance is still in existence: Jews pray in it regularly. Some scholars believe he may have influenced Spinoza.

Like Uriel de Costa, the father of Spinoza fled from Portugal to Amsterdam. Unlike da Costa, he became a wealthy merchant, lived a devout Jewish life, and died a traditional Jew—two years before his son Baruch, then a man in his early twenties, was excommunicated for "abominable heresies" and "monstrous acts"; the words are in the rabbinical pronouncement issued against him on July 27, 1656.

The young man, a brilliant rabbinical student, had studied Talmud, read Maimonides, moved swiftly to the boundary lines of Jewish literature and thought, and found his hunger for learning unsatisfied. You cannot truly cross the frontiers of your own culture until you master the language of another. He began to study Latin in a school opened by a freethinking ex-Jesuit. The Jews around him despised the language, associated it with the hated Inquisition, called it with contempt "the priest's language." He had also turned an open ear to the din of religious controversy in Amsterdam between Conversos and Talmudic Judaism. Then he had voiced doubts concerning the Mosaic authorship of the Pentateuch and about Adam being the first man. For these and similar "evil opinions . . . the council decided, with the advice of the rabbis, that the said Spinoza should be excommunicated and cut off from the nation of Israel."

About sixty years earlier the Italian philosopher Giordano Bruno had argued against all forms of dogmatism, and contended that the way we perceive the world is relative to our position in time and space and that there are as many ways to see the world as there are positions. Therefore, he concluded, we cannot possibly say that this or that postulate is absolutely true and that there is a limit to the progress of human knowledge. For these views the church burned him at the stake in 1600. Now, sixty years later, there were Jews in Amsterdam who wished to kill Spinoza. He left Amsterdam, changed his name to Benedictus—the Latin for Baruch—and finally settled in The Hague in 1670, where he enjoyed the company of a small circle of friends and earned a living grinding lenses that served as aids to human vision.

That was the year his *Tractatus Theologico-Politicus* appeared. The main purpose of the book was its defense of freedom of opinion. He had worked on it for over four years. It went through five editions in a very brief time and made him notorious. It was published without his name on the title page; but it required little wit to recognize the author, for Spinoza's views were by then widely known through letters and word of mouth. He was constantly vilified and accused of atheism. The book was banned everywhere. Booksellers sold it with false title pages.

Spinoza was offered the chair of philosophy at Heidelberg. He pondered the offer for six weeks, then declined it. He preferred solitude and research, he said, to teaching and the probability of dangerous controversy. He lived quietly in the economical lodgings of an artist, doing his own housekeeping, continuing his philosophical speculations, grinding lenses.

All his life he remained an austere and zealous patriot of truth and the country of the mind. He wrote of an immanent, not a transcendent, God; everything is God and aspects of God; all is determined by laws; God is not preoccupied with the affairs of humans; a purposive cosmos is a fiction invented by those unable to comprehend the true nature of the universe. The notion of the will of God is the refuge of the ignorant. To prove the nature of the divine, Spinoza used the procedures of geometry, a creation of the mind, rather than tradition or revelation. Much of the power of Greek thought channeled itself into this self-effacing Dutch Jew who, together with Hobbes, Locke, and a few others of that time, affected forever the way our eyes structure the world—not only the world of

God and nature but also the world of man and one of his most remarkable creations, the Bible.

That was the way Spinoza saw the Bible—as entirely the creation of man. We can interpret it only in the light of its historical background and the intent of its authors; and everyone has the right to make the attempt at interpretation—no prior approval from a higher authority is necessary. A proper history of Scripture requires an understanding and analysis of the Hebrew language and research into the identity of the author of each book. The Bible shows us that the prophets were men with vivid imaginations and a powerful moral sense, basically ignorant men appealing to a primitive people in a prescientific age. They were brilliantly gifted with the ability to instill faith and obedience through story and myth; they were not philosophers; they contradicted each other in their opinions about God; the appeal was to the imagination, not to reason.

The election of the Jews does not mean that they were different in virtue and intellectual ability from other people; it refers only to their monarchy, and it came to an end when the monarchy fell to pieces. The laws of the Bible were applicable only to this monarchic period and should never have been continued beyond it. Nothing can occur in contradiction to natural law, and all accounts of miracles in the Bible must be explained away—as moral tales intended to instruct simple people, or in other ways. The Bible can teach us nothing about those matters on which it makes conflicting statements. Only reason and philosophy can tell us about the essence of God. Nothing of this impinges upon the basic idea of religion: there is one God, who demands justice, desires that mankind live in neighborly love, and forgives penitents. The Bible gives us the foundation for piety; philosophy offers us truth.

He saw in the sages of Jerusalem reflections of the rabbis of Amsterdam and came to the conclusion that the Pharisees had continued to observe the law after the destruction of the Jewish state and the second temple not so much to find favor with God as to oppose Christianity. The scholars of Jewry insisted upon the observance of the Torah only because they wished to continue to rule. Jews have affection for one another and hate all other people; therefore, all other people hate them. Persecution strengthens them; kind treatment may one day bring about their disappearance. He thought it possible that the Jews might eventually return to their own land.

He argued for a rationally governed free society in which "every man may think what he likes and say what he thinks." His ideal state was the merchant community of Amsterdam, where men of many creeds were tolerated; they had only to be willing to maintain public order.

He is the only Jew we know of before the modern period who left Judaism and did not become a Christian. It is no large leap of thought to assume that his critique of the Hebrew Bible is applicable to the Bible of Christianity. He carved out for himself a small secular island in a world that was still an ocean of faith, and he survived, and wrote—though he was not permitted to publish his major work, the *Ethics*—and maintained a lively correspondence with some of the greatest minds of his time, and was regarded with awe and love and hate, and ground lenses for people's eyes, and died quietly of consumption one Sunday morning in February 1677. His *Ethics* appeared after his death along with a selection of his letters, two other philosophical works, and a Hebrew grammar designed to enable his Christian friends to master the language and literature of the people who had cast him out. It is believed that his lens-grinding aggravated his consumption and shortened his life.

A century after his death many of his ideas about truth and freedom were the common coinage of the Enlightenment. Two centuries after his death the new discipline of scientific Bible scholarship was utilizing much of his methodology as it went about exploring the Biblical world. By then the Jewish Enlightenment was a hundred years old. It had developed as an explosive cultural response to the confrontation between Judaism and modern paganism. It was a movement that affected all Jewry; it pulsed with a messianic sense of mission to transform the entire people from stoop-shouldered Talmudists and ghetto dwellers to fully educated and emancipated inhabitants of the sunlight in the new nation-states of western man. Its axiom was the Spinozist rational-philosophical truth that reason was the measure of all things. The edict of excommunication issued against Spinoza has not yet been rescinded.

Now I want to write of the two and a half centuries that began roughly in 1700 and ended about 1950, a breath ago as one measures time in Jewish history. I know of no historian who brackets this span of the Jewish experience, singles it out and deals with it as an entity. But I see a dark and strangely splendid poetry in these centuries.

It began with a tiny apocalypse, the death of an eighteen-year-old girl in Portugal. During the first decade of the eighteenth century more than one hundred people were burned by the Portuguese Inquisition. Then the numbers fell sharply. But from 1721 to 1761 Portugal burned 139 people, most of them women. Another twenty were burned in effigy and over three thousand were penanced. Among those burned in an early decade of that century was the eighteen-year-old girl. Panic-stricken Conversos fled to France, England, Amsterdam, the Americas, where they told tales of numbing horror.

The French political philosopher Montesquieu learned of the girl's death. In a work published in 1748 he directed these words to the Inquisition in the artful form of an argument uttered by a Jew: "We must warn you of one thing: in future ages if someone will dare say that in the century in which we lived the peoples of Europe were civilized, you will be cited as the evidence that they were barbarous; and your image will be such that it will dishonor your age and make your contemporaries the object of hatred."

That was the century in which civilized Europeans could not help noticing the changes that had begun to occur to the Jews. In 1753 an effort was made by the English government to naturalize the civic status of all its Jews; they had been readmitted to England under Cromwell about the middle of the seventeenth century. The attempt aroused anti-Jewish agitation but no violence. It failed but was much talked about in the intellectual circles that graced the salons of Europe. What indeed should be done with these Jews? Yes, all men were free and worthy of equal opportunity. But were Jews to be considered human? Were they capable of being redeemed?

Across the ocean Jews lived in freedom in the English colonies, and that society seemed to be surviving their presence unharmed. They were participating in the American Revolution, had been granted equality even before that land had written its constitution. Europeans knew of this and wondered what to make of it as they wrote and spoke of the dawning spirit of tolerance. Was the Jew to be included in this new world, the bearded, avaricious, unkempt Jew with his arcane, malevolent Talmudism and his noisy synagogues and the stiff-necked prideful otherness he paraded before mankind? Should the Jew be permitted to be himself or should he be granted freedom because it was the only means of improving his nature? Even Montesquieu, publicly a friend of the Jews, vacillated in his published writings between these two positions—and could not shed entirely the dark heritage of the enchanted land. He died in the arms of the church.

The most virulent of Enlightenment anti-Semites was Voltaire. With his beaked nose, thin angular frame, invented nobility, and shrewdly acquired wealth, he moved through the world of eighteenth-century France, possessed of a brilliant, mordant, rapier wit, molding that world with his unbending will, his light and devastating irony, and his quick intelligence, concealing nothing of his loathing of contemporary institutions, his detestation of the church, and hatred of the Jew.

Voltaire's anti-Semitism echoed the familiar rhetoric of the church. Many scholars have claimed that his attack against Judaism was a transparent attempt to undermine the foundation upon which the church erected its edifice. Recently a scholar has argued, with considerable persuasiveness, that Voltaire leapt beyond the church and its teachings about the Jews; that his anti-Semitism was of a far more murderous kind than that found in official church doctrine; that he acquired his hatred of Jews from the same people who taught him the value of freedom and the worth of man: certain Greek and Roman pagans.

The central drama in the history of man, for Voltaire, had not been the period of the Bible but the time of ancient Greece and Rome. He yearned to restore that golden age of true philosophy and culture. European civilization had taken a wrong turn when it had come under the influence of Jewish and Christian ideas; it became infested with an oriental system of thought. The new age of man would return to Europe to its pure origins, reestablish its foundations in Greek and Roman antiquity.

That ancient world had hated the Jew. This stubborn, separate people, worshiping an invisible God, refusing to participate in public rites, in the games, in the cult of the emperor, rejecting the hospitality of others, the food or wine offered as marks of cordiality, flaunting themselves as chosen by their God, abandoning their labor every seventh day—what else could this people be but haters of mankind, slothful, malicious, inherently evil? Voltaire was aware that many pagans had held this notion of the Jew; he took it up as a torch that left a clear trail of malevolence through all his writings.

The Jew of his day was, he believed, identical in character to the Jew of the ancient world. The anti-Semitism of Cicero earned his praise; he added his own anger to the words of the Roman orator: "They are, all of them, born with raging fanaticism in their hearts, just as the Bretons and the Germans are born with blond hair. I would not be in the least bit surprised if these people would not some day become deadly to the human race."

He liked as literature some of the writings of the prophets and a few of the pastroal narratives of the Pentateuch but concluded that the ancient Israelite really had no aesthetic sense, no idea of taste or proportion. Everything in Jewish culture was borrowed from others; the only things that were uniquely Jewish were "their stubbornness, their new superstitions, and their hallowed usury." There was not a page in any of the books purportedly written by Jews that had not been stolen, especially from Homer. The morality of Greece and Rome was cleary superior to that of the Jews.

Voltaire did not charge the Jew with being a killer or rejecter of Jesus; he did not resort to the anti-Jewish position of the Christian civilization he had himself abandoned. He recast the hatred of the Jew, put the new garb of the Enlightenment over the old ideas of Tacitus, Juvenal, Horace, and others: all men were worthy of freedom except the Jews, because the Jews were not of the same species as the rest of mankind. The Jews were corrupt and evil; their very character was twisted; their presence was subversive of true European civilization, because they were the alien, the stubborn hopeless radical other; their nature was unchanging; even if they were to be separated from their religion, their inherent character would remain untouched. He wrote, addressing himself to the Jews, "You have surpassed all nations in impertinent fables, in bad conduct, and in barbarism. You deserve to be punished, for this is your destiny." He saw the Jews as "a totally ignorant nation" possessed of "contemptible miserliness and the most revolting superstition. . . ." But he added, "Nevertheless they should not be burned at the stake."

This feeling of contempt and disgust for the civilization of the Jews was the view of the mainstream of the Enlightenment. Gibbon wrote of the "irreconcilable hatred" of the Jews for mankind; the scholar Jean Baptiste de Mirabaud collected the anti-Jewish views of Greek and Roman writers in a volume that was published in 1769; and Paul Thiry d'Holbach urged Europe to "break the unbearable yoke of the prejudices by which you are afflicted. Leave to the stupid Hebrews, to the frenzied imbeciles, and to the cowardly and degraded Asiatics these superstitions which are as vile as they are mad; they were not meant for the inhabitants of your climate. . . ."

Some men of the Enlightenment believed that the Jew could be remade to fit into the new spirit of man; most were uncertain. After the French Revolution, when the time came to decide for or against the emancipation of the Jew, logic and the hurtling impetus for freedom demanded his emancipation. The forty thousand Jews of France were emancipated in two stages: on January 28, 1790, the Sephardic Jews of the south, many of them descendants of Conversos; on September 27, 1791, the Ashkenazic Jews of the north, whose ancestors had fled to

Alsace and Lorraine from the Chmielnicki massacres. But
the teachings of Voltaire were by then borne on the wind
breathed by the men of the new age. The guillotine of the
Enlightenment removed the absolutism of the past and
substituted its own. All could enter this new bright landscape save the barbarous Jew.

A tragic poignancy hovers over the passionate efforts of
European Jews to penetrate the charged and lighted world
of high culture created by the philosophes. Here was a
world supposedly free of the enchanted years. The Jew
had only to enter it, accept its wisdom and opportunities.
The echoing anti-Semitism would drift off and disappear.
No one at the time seems to have realized that this anti-
Semitism had its source in a resurrected paganism and
that it was settling like a dense, permanent, fructifying
dust upon the anti-Semitism of a weakened but still living
Christianity.

Jews throughout Europe embraced the high culture of
the Enlightenment as their ancestors had once embraced
covenants with YHWH. They could not know that they
were whirling and pirouetting in a pagan danse macabre.

The dance began slowly, a sedate minuet led by the
women in the families of wealthy German Jewish merchants and court Jews and by a young, brilliant German
Jewish thinker who was born in 1729, about the same
time the eighteen-year-old Converso girl was burned at
the stake in Portugal.

The court Jews lived in two cultures. The world of Torah
learning was their highest religious and social value. But
they belonged also to a world of princes and power, of
wealth, weapons, and warring armies. It was their responsibility to supply the prince with money, provide metal for
the mint, provision the army, promote trade and industry.
There were Jews in the courts of Protestant and Catholic
princes throughout the small German states, as well as
Austria, Denmark, and elsewhere, except Catholic
France, where the task of provisioning armies and keeping kings supplied with money was largely in the hands of
foreign Protestant bankers. German court Jews, restless,
hard-working, eager for success, were an instrumentality

of absolutist rulers who were attempting to centralize the power of the state. They worked alongside Christian bankers and contractors. They could not be part of this army of power without cultivating a life style that separated them from the Jews of the ghetto. They assimilated swiftly the manners and dress of German society. They lived with their families in splendid mansions and were in permanent contact with the cultured German aristocracy. The wedding of a court Jew's daughter would almost always find the princely family in attendance. There would be music and dancing and civilized conversation. The men would talk of politics and power. The women would speak of the books then being written by those Frenchmen with the strange ideas about liberty and equality. Jewish women learned French and were among the earliest of conduits to the world of the Enlightenment.

The eighteenth-century Jew was made ready for his entry into this new world by the policies of the absolutist rulers of Germany, Austria, and Russia. Seeking to establish their power over all the different classes in their regimes, these rulers—prince, king, or emperor—reached deeply into the autonomous Jewish communities in their lands, took control of certain internal affairs—such as bankruptcy proceedings and the collection of promissory notes—and also removed from the leaders of the Jewish community their powers of coercion by depriving them of the authority to issue edicts of excommunication. The weakening of church influence, the spread of secular thought, the cultured life style of Sephardic Jews, many of them from Converso families, who emulated with ease—in Amsterdam, England, Italy, France, and elsewhere—the world of the non-Jew, smoothed the path of those Ashkenazic Jews who now wished to infuse the musty ghetto body of the Jewish people with the new ideas emanating from the center of European culture: France.

The dance gradually picked up momentum. Peripheral elements of Jewish civilization were shed in emulation of the periphery of the surrounding culture. Jews shaved their beards and donned the wigs and clothes of their host civilization. The disappearance of dissimilarity in dress led to social acceptance, much card playing, and families joining together to celebrate happy occasions. This cultural contact occurred at first only among upper-class families. But it could not go unnoticed by other classes of Jews. Knowledge of the language of one's land became crucial. A bridge of tolerance was built along the Jewish side of the divide: Jews began to regard Christianity not as idolatry but as the proper and suitable faith of the gentile world.

Now the culture confrontation penetrated to the core of Judaism: some Jews in western and central Europe wondered about the notion of the chosen people, felt a lessening need to observe rabbinic law, became doubtful about the meaningfulness of waiting for the Messiah, and thought more of a messianic age—indeed, perhaps this very age that was clearly soon to be born, this era of fraternity and freedom and civil equality. They began to write in the languages of their various European lands. The writing was different now from that of the past. Jews had created literature out of culture confrontations with Hellenism, Islam, Spain, and Renaissance Italy but had insisted upon the truths of Judaism, upon the revelation, the covenant, the law, and the certain coming of the Messiah. The new writing approved eagerly the basic tenets of the umbrella civilization, its rationalism, its notion of man as the measure of all things, its scorn of supernatural revelation, its deistic concept of God as the creator of the eternal clockwork of the universe and as the future judge of mankind but now unapproachable by man and no longer preoccupied with His creation. These eighteenth-century Jewish men and women—writing in the vernacular or in Biblical Hebrew, which they were attempting to revive; moving with quickly acquired grace through the salons of the aristocracy and the intelligentsia—these were the creators of the movement known as the Haskalah, the Jewish Enlightenment. They mirrored willingly, hungrily, the intellectual fires of France. For them the non-Jewish world was less a locale for business activity than a new landscape for social and aesthetic pleasures. They formed, together with their non-Jewish counterparts, an independent intellectual class unattached to the courts of kings, the families of patrons, the governance of clerics.

The members of this new Jewish intelligentsia were called maskilim, enlightened ones. Their progenitor, the father of the Jewish Enlightenment, was the German Jew who had been born in 1729, a frail man made humpbacked by a childhood disease. His name was Moses Mendelssohn. His father was a Torah scribe in the German city of Dessau. In 1743 Moses Mendelssohn came to Berlin to continue his studies; he had received a traditional Jewish education. He mastered German and Hebrew and gained some knowledge of Latin, Greek, English, French, and Italian. He worked as a merchant in a silk enterprise. He met the German writer Gotthold Ephraim Lessing and through him was introduced into the circles of the German Enlightenment. In 1754, with the help of Lessing, he began to publish works of philosophy.

He lived as a traditional Jew in Berlin. One of his first works was on the nature of beauty and influenced Schiller, Goethe, and Kant. He was an Enlightenment philosopher. He believed in the existence of God and the immortality of the soul, and thought that the revelation at Sinai had been for the purpose of giving the Jews a system of law, a constitution that could serve as an example to all mankind. Judaism was closer to natural religion than was Christianity or any other faith because it was based on practical commandments rather than dogmas and opinions. Throughout the ages Jews had debated matters of belief while acknowledging that observance of the commandments was incumbent upon all Jews regardless of what they believed. Freedom of belief was not incompatible with traditional observance—a tolerant and enlightened view.

German literature was young then; the culture of Germany was dominated by French and Latin. Mendelssohn thought Voltaire shallow. Voltaire never mentioned him. Lessing, Herder, and a few others—poets, dramatists, and philosophers—had adopted German as their literary language. Mendelssohn joined them in their crusade and became so zealous a warrior for the language that he berated King Frederick II of Prussia for a book of poems published in French. "Will the Germans never be aware of their own value?" he asked. In 1761 he was awarded first prize by the Prussian Academy of Sciences for a philosophical essay. One of the two candidates who lost was Immanuel Kant. Mendelssohn achieved renown. He became the darling of the wealthy Prussian Jews and the model for Lessing's hero in the drama *Nathan the Wise*.

A Protestant theologian, John Caspar Lavater, who had known Mendelssohn for years, suddenly inquired publicly why the Jew Mendelssohn did not convert to Christianity. The Jew was shaken by the question. He had thought himself a philosopher in an enlightened world, beyond the need to defend himself against a challenge from a darker age of man. He wrote in polite and restrained fashion of his loyalty to Judaism, which was based on prolonged study and contemplation. Beyond that, he would not engage in polemics—because the Torah had been given only to the Jews and no other people was required to observe its laws; because Judaism was disinclined to missionize; and because he was a member of a minority people whose freedom was tenuous, and he would prefer not to engage the majority religion in a debate. But the polemic between Mendelssohn and Lavater dragged on through the winter of 1769–1770, and when it was finally over—stopped at the insistence of Lavater's Protestant colleagues—Mendelssohn took ill with some kind of nervous disease and was unable to do serious philosophical work for more than seven years.

From the time of that controversy with Lavater, Mendelssohn turned his attention to the Jewish community. He became involved in the anguishing struggle for the civil rights of German Jewry. Most Jews lived in a dismal twilight of degrading inequality, unable to move about or settle freely in cities, locked out of certain crafts and professions. He denied that Jews could not perform such civil obligations as military duty because they were waiting for the Messiah; that dream belonged to the realm of their prayers and would in no way affect their obligations to their country. He himself did not agree with those who advocated a union of all faiths instead of tolerance. Such a union, he said, was for the end of days; he would not transgress the law of Moses in order to obtain civil rights. He knew of the tendency toward separation of church and state in the United States and favored the idea, thereby further undermining the authority of rabbinic leadership. Only the state should have powers of coercion, he wrote. Religion should function only through persuasion.

He was as zealous for Hebrew as he was for German. He disliked Yiddish, which he considered a jargon. He translated the Bible into German and wrote a fairly traditional commentary to the Pentateuch. The rabbis did not care for his translation. He had intended it to be used by the young as an easy path to German culture. Within one generation the Mendelssohn Bible was in the home of nearly every literate Jew in western and central Europe.

He was the living model of the possibility of profound identification between German Jewry and German culture, of the Jewish passion with the German language, of the German Jewish contempt for Yiddish and the closed benighted world of eastern European Jewry. He showed the Jews and the Germans that a Jew could live in both cultures simultaneously. Into his home came the intellectual elite of Germany as well as enlightened Jews who sought his gentle presence, his patience and modesty, his keen intellect and wide knowledge, his wit and warmth. At the same time, he embodied all the contradictions of the Jew who sought emancipation and yet wished to retain his Jewish identity. He was able to overcome this contradiction by the nature of his personality and because of the openness of German intellectual society in the period when he began his philosophical studies. Others would have neither his gift nor his good fortune. He died in 1786 after defending himself in print against the unnerving charge of being a Spinozist.

Now the tempo of the dance quickened. Jewish intellectuals had established a new school in Berlin in 1778. German, French, arithmetic, geography, history, Bible, Hebrew, and the learning of a craft or agriculture—that was the curriculum. These intellectuals knew that the transformation of the Jew from ghetto dweller to active participant in the enlightened world could be effected only through education. The school was an immediate success.

In subsequent years similar schools were founded in other cities along with schools for the training of teachers. Rabbis fought the schools and a curriculum that taught secular subjects and subverted the teaching of Talmud. "We were not all created to become Talmudists," Naphtali Herz Wessely, the pioneer of this new education, responded.

Despairing of the endless attacks by traditionalists, proponents of Haskalah education called for government intervention. Enlightened absolutist rulers issued edicts ordering Jews to send their children to state schools or establish normal schools. Some states insisted that rabbis should have a general education and that philosophy be taught in Talmudic academies. The first rabbinic seminary was established in 1829 in Padua, the city in northern Italy that was a center of Talmudic learning and Haskalah. One of its first teachers was Samuel David Luzzato, a great Talmudist and Hebraist. By then new schools had appeared nearly everywhere that Jews lived in Europe. All the taut coherence of the rabbinic centuries was coming undone in the new messianism of the Enlightenment years.

German Jewry lived in feverish yearning for emancipation. Ghetto restrictions had loosened. Conversion was rife among the Jewish intellectual elite in the decades that closed out the eighteenth century; it was still the only safe-conduct pass into the German world, and scholars estimate that about ten percent of Berlin Jewry took it. Their descendants, great-grandchildren of their children, may have fought in the armies of Hitler.

During those last decades of the eighteenth century enlightened German Jews were certain their efforts would bring about a new kind of redemption for their people. They established a Hebrew journal, a Society of Students of the Hebrew Language, and various other associations to further the spread of their ideas. I see them meeting in the salons of Berlin, talking eagerly of the future, writers, philosophers, teachers, merchants, and their families. They extend aid to one another, care for their sick, undertake the necessary tasks for the burial of comrades and loved ones. They read their writings to each other, perform plays in Hebrew in the privacy of a salon. They were subtly undermining the foundations of traditional Jewish society by substituting their own associations for the old accepted ones.

They feel an increasing identity with the non-Jewish world. As with the outside society, marriage by matchmaking has lost all appeal to these enlightened Jews. It is replaced by romantic love as individuals begin to learn to rely upon themselves. Rabbinic law is no longer their final authority and guide to behavior; they are led now by criteria of taste and feeling drawn from the umbrella civilization.

In the early decades of the nineteenth century dozens of anti-Semitic pamphlets circulated throughout Germany. There were anti-Jewish riots in the summer of 1819. *"Hep! Hep!"* a Bavarian mob shouted, using the cry of herders of goats as it looted the homes and shops of Jews. The process of Jewish emancipation slowed. An intensifying neurotic insecurity settled upon the Jews of Germany as they began a protracted decades-long battle for emancipation. Slowly Germany began to draw them to itself as the legal barriers fell and state after state emancipated its Jews.

What a passion there is in Jews for German culture! They pour into the German world with the same zeal with which their ancestors once conquered Canaan. They write books and plays and works on aesthetics. Their German style is exquisite. They dictate canons of taste. Heinrich Heine—born a German Jew in 1797, educated in a Catholic school—converts to Lutheranism in 1825, becomes one of Germany's greatest poets, lives with a deepening sense of self-loathing for his conversion, begins to study the Bible with care and discovers in it an eternal treasure, "a portable fatherland," and dies in 1856 "a poor, deathly sick Jew."

Rabbis preach in flawless German; synagogues take on the hushed aura of the Lutheran service. Traditionalists cast about desperately for a means of stemming the assimilationist dance, the whirling of the German Jew in the arms of his new beloved. Some rabbis, like Abraham Geiger, urge a radical reform of the faith as the only way to halt the dance; others, like Samson Raphael Hirsch, seek new methods to explain old orthodoxies; still others, like Zechariah Frankel, search for a middle path. These vital religious responses to the anguished struggle for emancipation will be carried to America by immigrants and become the Reform, Orthodox, and Conservative Jewries of the new world.

After the defeat of Napoleon at Waterloo in 1815 and the final liberation of Germany from French occupation, Jews participated zealously in the German march toward the unity and power of a nation-state. They were astounded when they encountered violent anti-Semitism among German university students. In their aggressive hunger for German culture the Jews seemed not to notice the defensiveness of the Germans, the way they were recoiling from this overheated Jewish reentry into creative culture confrontation after centuries of dormancy. Jews appeared unaware that the same elitist Germans who demanded defection as the price of admission into the German world also regarded them contemptuously as turncoats too willing to abandon a decayed faith.

The greatest German Jewish scholar of that century—the century that witnessed the birth of virtually all the contemporary scholarly methodology of western civilization—was Leopold Zunz. He established the foundations of the *Wissenschaft des Judentums,* the Science of Judaism, the study of Jewish history, religion, and literature through rigorous objective criticism and modern methods of research. He wrote prodigiously, attempting to prove to the anti-Semitic German the true value of the Jewish experience. In 1848, as mobs marched through the streets of German cities clamoring for freedom, Zunz repeatedly referred to the revolution as the Messiah. When the revolution failed, many German Jews despaired of this German dance and began a new wandering, to America, taking with them their new ideas about the need for a reformed faith. Hebrew faded as a language for enlightened German Jews: the allure of this brimming bourgeois culture, then at its zenith—with its Kant and Hegel, its

Schiller and Goethe, its scholars, poets, dramatists, composers, journals, newspapers—it was all too dazzling; and their own Jewish learning was too shallow. But the new political parties with their open anti-Semitic platforms are bewildering. How is one to react to *Das Judentum in der Fremde (Judaism Abroad)* by Bruno Bauer, a work that appeared in 1869 and contained all the vile hate that was later to be preached by the Germany of Adolf Hitler? The only possible response is to quicken still further the tempo of the egalitarian dance, show the beloved the depth of our love, convince the Germans that we mean it, with all our hearts, we truly love Germany.

All the old lines of attachment to the Jewish past were dropping away: the yearning for a distant homeland, the loyalty to the convenant, the once shared and remembered history. Western and eastern European Jewries drifted into separate ways during the decades before and after the First World War, the one in a dance with emancipation, the other mired in despotic rule, with emancipation a distant wispy dream. The two Jewries would meet again for the last dance in the sealed chambers of a common destiny.

At the end of the eighteenth century there were roughly two and a quarter million Jews in the world; about two million lived in Europe. Eight decades later there were almost seven million Jews in Europe and an additional half million in other parts of the world. The Jewish rate of population increase had been twice that of the non-Jews.

By 1914 the seven and a half million Jews had increased to more than thirteen million. Among the general population the death rate of infants in the first year after birth was forty percent; among Jews it was less than twenty-five percent.

I have read that the increase in the general population was in part the result of widespread cultivation of the potato—nourishing enough to have kept Germany alive during two world wars—along with the introduction of cotton undergarments, which could be laundered in boiling water. Wool cannot be boiled without shrinking into a clotted, shapeless mass. Before cotton, you were sewn into your woolen underwear for the winter and often your body became a nesting ground for lice and disease. The higher rate of increase among Jews was probably the outcome of ancient traditions of charity, the voluntary associations whose special task it was to minister to the sick, the devoted care lavished upon children, the infrequency of alcoholism and venereal disease. In the years after the First World War there was a decrease in the death rate of non-Jews and a decrease in the size of the Jewish family. At the start of the Second World War there were about fifteen million Jews in the world.

In 1850 about 2,350,000 Jews lived in Russia. Fifty years later that number had risen to five million, despite a flood of Jewish emigration. All through western Europe the process of Jewish emancipation had been completed: France, Holland, and Belgium, by 1831; Denmark, in 1849; Austria and Hungary, by 1867; Italy, by 1870; Germany and England, by 1871; Switzerland, by 1874. Anti-Semitism remained the dark background noise of Jewish life in western Europe, often given a veneer of scientific jargon about the inherent characteristics of Semites and Aryans. Still the Jew was now free; he could vote, run for office, enter freely into professions, join the army. He was a citizen everywhere except in eastern Europe. (In the world of Islam there was no movement by Jews for emancipation. Many Islamic states granted their Jews and Christians various civic rights during the period between the middle of the nineteenth century and the Second World War; almost all took away these rights from the Jews after the establishment of the State of Israel.)

The Russians did not know what to do with their Jews. The principality of Moscow, the core of the future Russian empire, was suspicious of strangers, felt repelled by and attracted to western ideas, regarded foreigners as enemies of the sacred motherland, and shrank from three-quarters of a million Jews it suddenly found within its territory as a result of the partition of Poland. Autocratic czars and czarinas saw the Jews as a problem to be solved only by assimilation or expulsion. But Jews who assimilated would be accused by Russians of trying to take over the motherland and Jews who emigrated would be lamented as a serious economic loss or would be labeled as treasonous revolutionaries. Russia did not know what to do with its Jews.

It did not want them scattered throughout the land and so restricted them to a region, which, by 1815, consisted of twenty-five provinces from the Black Sea to the Baltic, an area of almost a million square miles where the Jews formed about one-ninth of the population. They needed special permits to live in large cities; these permits were granted mainly to Jews involved in the improvement of the Russian economy: bankers, lumber dealers, factory owners, railroad builders. From time to time these magnates would be expelled and sent to live with all the other Jews in the crowded region that has come to be known as the Pale of Settlement. The Greek Orthodox peasants of the region lived in misery. The Russians found it easier to blame the exploitation of the peasants upon the Jew rather than the Catholic nobleman. In the Christian feudal world of Russia the Jew was an alien creature, exposed, despised, hated, feared.

In 1804 the Russians initiated the program of assimilation and expulsion. Elementary, secondary, and higher schools were authorized to admit Jews. The Jews were permitted to open their own schools, but the language of instruction had to be Russian, Polish, or German. Jews could no longer live in the villages, participate in the leasing activity in the villages, or sell alcoholic beverages to the peasants. Thousands of Jewish families were suddenly without a livelihood. The government would permit Jews to settle the land as peasants, become factory workers, or enter the crafts.

Napoleon invaded Russia in June 1812 with an army of five hundred thousand men. Ecstatic eastern European Jews hailed him as the Messiah, hung his portrait on the walls of their homes, and helped provision his armies. On September 14 he entered Moscow. The following day the city began to burn. The fires swept the city until September 19, leaving it a gutted ruin. The Russians had burned their fields and grain in advance of the French troops. Napoleon was without winter quarters or food for his soldiers. He returned to France through the white nightmare of a Russian winter. Less then one-fifth of his army survived.

The expulsion of Jews from the villages of the Pale, halted by the invasion of Napoleon, was resumed in 1822. Nicholas I, czar of Russia from 1825 to 1855, instituted a system of forced conscription of young Jews into the Russian army. They could be taken from the ages of twelve to twenty-five and would remain in the army for twenty-five years. A youth under eighteen would be sent to a military school along with the children of other soldiers. The law applied to the Jewish communities of Lithuania and the Ukraine. Each community was given a quota. No Jewish parents wanted their children to serve under such conditions in the army of this czar. Jews would falsify birth records, conceal their children, or maim them so they would fail the army physical examination. Jews responsible for filling the quotas would be forced to resort to the help of thugs who would snatch the children—to the accompaniment of the screams of parents and neighbors. These children—some younger than the age of twelve—were not likely ever to be seen again. It was a time of horror.

In 1844 the Russian government initiated a candle tax. All candles used by Jews for ritual purposes were to be taxed, including memorial and wedding candles. This tax had been imposed early in the eighteenth century by Jewish communities in Poland whose finances were in ruin as a result of the Chmielnicki swath of blood and the wars with Russia and Sweden. Jews hated the tax, especially poor Jews. It was abrogated in Galicia in 1848. The Russians introduced it in order to finance state schools where Jewish children would be taught in a fashion that would accelerate their assimilation into the Russian world. Each time a Jew bought and burned a ritual candle it helped the government's policy of ridding Russia of Jews. There was also a tax on ritually slaughtered meat.

The schools had been established at the suggestion of enlightened Jews. Books on mathematics and astronomy began to appear. Enlightened Jews thought to improve the plight of their people by having them trained in crafts and agriculture and by opening modern schools. Jewish merchants and physicians who were close to the Russian authorities urged these measures upon the government. But some of these early enlightened Russian Jews became apostates, and the masses of Russian Jews turned their backs upon the Jewish Enlightenment and its program of reform. Only a few entered the new schools. Jews dedicated to the ideas of the Enlightenment would meet in small groups in the towns of the Pale. A fledgling Hebrew literature began to appear: the first Hebrew literary periodical in Vilna in 1841, the first collection of modern Hebrew poems by Abraham Dov Lebensohn in 1824, the first Hebrew novel by Abraham Mapu in 1853. Some wrote stories and articles in Yiddish in order to advance their ideas among the masses. The new generation of enlightened Jews was educated in Russian-Jewish schools. They were aware of the distance between themselves and the traditionalists, especially the Hasidim, whom they looked upon as inhabitants of a world of darkness.

The death of Nicholas I in 1855 and the easing of restrictions against Jews—especially the termination of the dreaded lengthy army conscription—under Czar Alexander II convinced the adherents of the Russian-Jewish Enlightenment that emancipation was now at hand. Certain rights were granted to important Jewish merchants, to intellectuals, physicians, pharmacists, craftsmen; they could now take up residence anywhere in Russia.

In 1861 the Russian peasants were emancipated from serfdom to landowners. Russia began to be penetrated by western science and philosophy. The works of Spencer, Darwin, Mill, Comte, and others were read in German, English, and Russian translations. University students were possessed by positivism. A fever of conviction in the truths of atheism, nature, and socialism swept through the youth of the land and even invaded the Talmudic academies of learning in Lithuania. Students read forbidden books and had visions of a better world than the one in which they now lived. Many young Russian Jews were seized by a messianic belief in the coming transformation of society and joined revolutionary groups. They were hunted, exiled, shot, hanged; they rotted in prisons—for their visions of a new day for the motherland.

In 1874 Jews were accepted as soldiers into the Russian army for a four-year term of service; they could not become officers. Those with Russian secondary-school education were granted deferments. Jews poured into Russian schools.

Now in Russia too the dance began, in slow-motion at first, as the government removed the relentless pressures of the past and Jews began to participate in the culture of the land. They entered the arts. They became journalists, lawyers, dramatists, novelists, poets, critics, composers, painters, sculptors. They seemed suddenly everywhere in the economic, political, and cultural life of the motherland. Some Russians recoiled, among them Fyodor Dostoevski. Even the liberal and revolutionary groups were not enthusiastic about this passionate Jewish participation in Russian life. I know of no Russian poet or novelist—Lermontov, Turgenev, Gogol, Pushkin—who wrote of the Jews in a manner that made of them something more than a caricature that merited revulsion. The most liberal and socialist thinkers of the day—Marx, Bakunin, and others—regarded Jews with open contempt. The Jews were depicted as an alien element poisoning Russian life, a state within a state. But the dance went on. Jewish children gifted with artistic or musical ability were permitted to study in academies outside the Pale and could bring their families to live with them. Violins became the intimate companions of Jewish youths, who were prodded and encouraged by parents eager to break the seemingly endless cycle of poverty and persecution. Russian Jewish cultural life flowered.

The city of Odessa became a major center of the Russian Haskalah. Poets, scholars, novelists, short story writers, essayists—in Hebrew and Yiddish; the city throbbed with Jewish creativity. The dance went on. A little more time, only a little more time—and the anti-Semites would grow silent and full emancipation would be granted to all Jews, and the Jews would show Russia how much they loved the motherland, what patriots they could truly be, how much they could contribute to making Russia a great nation.

At the end of the 1870s there was a famine in Lithuania. Jews began to migrate toward western Europe and the United States.

Then in March 1881 someone threw a bomb that blew Czar Alexander II to pieces. Revolutionaries issued a call for rebellion. There was confusion. Alexander III became czar. A frightened regime rallied the people by blaming Jews for the assassination.

The dance came to an abrupt end in a bloodbath of government-inspired pogroms—a Russian word meaning violent mass attacks—and in the May Laws of 1882. Jews could now live only in townlets. The flood of Jewish students into secondary schools was brought to a stop through the numerus clausus—closed number—which fixed the maximum number of Jewish students who could be admitted to institutions of higher learning: ten percent within the Pale of Settlement and three to five percent outside. More than any other law, this served to embitter and radicalize Jewish youth. Enlightened assimilated Jews were once again seen in synagogues.

The head of the governing body of the Russian Orthodox Church, Konstantin Pobedonostsev, stated clearly the purpose behind the policy of the Russian government regarding the Jews. He voiced the hope that "one-third of the Jews will convert, one-third will die, and one-third will flee the country."

Jews began to flee in a swelling tide.

In 1882 a doctor named Leon Pinsker published a book titled *Auto-Emancipation*. The book appeared anonymously in German. The doctor had a weak heart. He had been one of the proponents of Enlightenment as the answer to the suffering of Russian Jews. The pogroms and the open anti-Semitism of the government brought him to the realization that humanist dreams would not dissipate Europe's hatred of the Jew. In the book he attacked modern western Jews who thought the Jewish dispersion to be a messianic mission to the world; he attacked the traditional Jews who suffered without protest and waited for the Messiah. There is a Jewish problem, he wrote, because the Jew continues to exist as a separate ethnic entity which the world cannot assimilate. The disembodied nature of Jewish existence causes people to fear Jews as they do ghosts. In competition, people will naturally care for their own and discriminate against aliens. Each country has a saturation point regarding Jews; when this point is reached and exceeded, Jews will begin to be persecuted. The only solution was for the Jews to emancipate themselves by establishing a land of their own, a refuge. The land need not be Palestine. . . .

The book exerted a major influence upon the thinking of Russian Jewry and was ignored in Germany. Pinsker joined the Hibbat Zion—Love of Zion—movement organized by Russian Jews, intellectuals and university students, after the 1881 pogroms. Scattered Zionist groups with vague ideologies had begun to form in Russia and Germany about the middle of the century. These groups now fused with the Hibbat Zion movement. At about the same time, other young Jews felt an urgent need for action and left for Palestine to settle on the land, work the soil, get away from the fog of intellectual talk that filled the air of Zionist meetings. Instead, they fought mosquitoes and malaria.

The members of the Hibbat Zion movement did not think Jews could continue to live in Europe. They sought to settle Jews in agricultural enclaves in the land of Israel, then under the dominion of the Ottoman empire, and thought they could obtain the approval of the major powers for this effort. But they had little notion how to accomplish this. They were united in their love of the Hebrew language and their awareness of the sanctity of the land of Israel in rabbinic and kabbalistic thought.

These early struggling agricultural settlements were funded by Baron Edmond de Rothschild. He helped establish Petah Tikvah—the words mean gateway of hope— a sliver of swampland along the margin of the world; that was the first agricultural village in the modern land of Israel. Jews had begun to bring back the song of birds absent for centuries from the swamps and sand dunes of the impoverished promised land.

In 1891 Jews were expelled from Moscow to "purify

the sacred historic capital." In 1894 Nicholas II became czar. He reacted to Jewish participation in the revolutionary movement by encouraging the fulminations of the anti-Semitic Russian press.

On April 6, 1903, Easter Sunday, a pogrom broke out in the city of Kishinev. That year Easter coincided with Passover. The pogrom raged on for two days. Who was king? Who was not king? The mob was king. Forty-nine Jews were slain, five hundred were injured; two thousand families were made homeless. Tolstoy made known his sympathy for the victims. The Russian Jewish poet Chaim Nachman Bialik wrote of the Kishinev pogrom in Hebrew. I shall never forget the first time I read that poem, "The City of Slaughter." I was a young teenager. I could smell the fires and the stench of death. I think it was then that I began faintly to understand, in a way that had never been driven home to me before, the strange destiny of the Jew.

It was during those years of blood and fire that Hebrew and Yiddish secular literature flourished in eastern Europe. There was a Jewish press in three languages: Hebrew, Yiddish, and Russian. A young wandering Jew, Uri Gnessin, wrote of his feelings of alienation, using an interior monologue style that presaged Joyce; an older Jew, Mendele Mocher Seforim, wrote satirical works about small-town—shtetl—Jewish life; a third, Isaac Leib Peretz, a compassionate aesthete, wrote exquisite tales about Hasidim; a fourth, Ahad Ha-Am, wrote in a masterfully wrought essayist's style of the Jewish condition, which he thought to be at a crossroads in history, and urged that Zion become the spiritual center for a renewed people; a fifth, Saul Tchernichowsky, wrote pagan poems about the power of art and his love of Hellenic beauty; a sixth, Sholom Aleichem, wrote warm and humorous tales about life in the hamlets, about boys who were Jewish Huckleberry Finns, about a dairyman who talked to God.

There were others, many others. They were my Hebrew and Yiddish reading as I grew up in the streets of New York, to which the bearded young man who hated Poles and Russians and the lovely young woman who was nearly raped by cossacks—the two people who were to become my parents—had migrated from the apocalypse that was eastern Europe after the Bolshevik revolution and the First World War.

The pogroms in Russia transformed Leon Pinsker and others from enlightened Jewish Russifiers to lovers of Zion. The trial of a Jewish officer in France, accused and sentenced to Devil's Island for a treasonous act he did not commit, transformed Theodor Herzl, a dapper Viennese Jew, from an assimilated and highly sophisticated journalist to the fiery prophet of political Zionism. Bulgarian Jews hailed him as the Messiah.

In Vienna he had written essays and stories. He wrote plays that were successfully produced in German and Austrian theaters. He had received a doctorate in law but had chosen to make writing his career. He became, as he confided in his diary, "a writer of sorts, with little ambition and petty vanities." He knew many languages and traveled throughout Europe. His marriage was not happy. He heard a Paris mob shout "Death to the Jews!" on the day in January 1895 when Dreyfus was publicly stripped of his rank and humiliated. Herzl was then the Paris correspondent of an important Viennese liberal newspaper. He had never thought he would witness such anti-Semitism—not in Paris. He was a writer. He took seriously what he saw and felt.

He felt seized by an idea whose shape he could barely discern. In his diary he referred to it as "a work of infinite grandeur . . . a mighty dream." And he added, "It is still too early to surmise what will come of it. . . . If my conception is not translated into reality, at least out of my activity can come a novel. Title: The Promised Land! To tell the truth I am no longer sure that it was not actually the novel that I first had in mind. . . ."

The idea of writing a novel began to blur. It became instead "a practical program." The process of transformation from an idea about a novel to an idea about the future of the Jewish people was a mystery to Theodor Herzl. "Perhaps these ideas are not practical ones at all and I am only making myself the laughingstock of the people to whom I talk about it seriously. Could I be only a figure in my novel?"

Suddenly he found himself writing a letter to Baron Maurice de Hirsch. The baron was a French Jew who had made a fortune in banking and achieved fame as a philanthropist. Would the philanthropist grant the journalist an uninterrupted hour or two of his time "to discuss the Jewish Question"?

The philanthropist lived in a palace on the rue de l'Elysée. The journalist was passed from one attendant to another. He moved in a bit of a daze through the grand courtyard, up the main staircase, through rooms heavy with the accumulations of wealth.

The philanthropist met the journalist in the billiard room. The journalist pulled out his notes. He wished to present the matter lucidly, he said. He had written down his ideas in advance.

He explained that he had not set out originally to occupy himself with the problem of the Jews. He was a writer and a journalist; he had not concerned himself with the Jews. But his experiences and observations, the growing anti-Semitism he saw everywhere, had compelled him to interest himself in the problem.

"So much for my credentials," he said.

He did not intend to go into the history of the Jews, he said. He wished only to emphasize one point. For two thousand years of dispersion the Jews have been without unified political leadership. "I regard this," he said, "as our worst misfortune. It has harmed us more than all the persecutions. This is why we have inwardly been ruined. There has been no one to train us to become real men. . . . We were pushed into all the inferior occupations, we were locked up in ghettos where we caused one another's degeneration. And when they let us out, they suddenly expected us to have all the characteristics of a people accustomed to freedom."

The journalist went on to speak of the need to unify the Jewish people politically, educate them by offering huge prizes for "striking deeds," for courage, self-sacrifice, ethical conduct, achievement in art and science—for anything great. The moral level of the people would be raised.

The philanthropist said the Jews had too many intellectuals. Jews want to climb too high and that brings all the misfortune.

The journalist said that he had not completed his presentation and had been interrupted. He realized that it was now pointless to go on. He rose to go.

The philanthropist, who was financing a new Jewish colony in Argentina, said that the only solution was emigration.

The journalist responded hotly, "Who told you I do not want emigration? It is all here in these notes. I shall go to the German Kaiser. He will understand me, for he has been brought up to be a judge of great things...."

The philanthropist seemed stunned.

The journalist said, "To the Kaiser I shall say: Let our people go! We are strangers here; we are not permitted to assimilate with the people, nor are we able to do so. Let us go! I will tell you the ways and the means which I want to use for our exodus, so that no economic crisis or vacuum may follow our departure."

The philanthropist asked the journalist where he planned to obtain the funds for this venture.

"I shall raise a Jewish National Loan Fund of ten million marks," said the journalist defiantly.

The philanthropist smiled and called the scheme a fantasy. "The rich Jews will give nothing. Wealthy people are mean and care nothing about the sufferings of the poor." He himself was prepared to hand over everything, he added, provided the others did likewise. He promised the journalist that they would speak again.

The journalist went down the beautiful staircase and through the noble courtyard. He was not disappointed, but stimulated. Once home he rushed to his writing desk.

He kept writing notes to himself on slips of paper. He felt possessed by a supernatural power. "It is working itself out through me," he wrote in his diary. "It would be an obsession were it not so rational from beginning to end."

The slips of paper became the draft of an address he

hoped to give one day before the Rothschild family. He would tell them of his idea for a Jewish state. The gentile world had been roused to envy by the size of the Rothschild fortune. That fortune might one day collapse if its base was not widened. It should be made to serve a sacred purpose. There was only one solution to the Jewish problem. "We are talking about a simple old matter—the exodus from Egypt." The Rothschild fortune should become the financial bedrock for a vast migration and settlement of Jews. Herzl outlined his plan in great detail. He read the address to a close friend, an enlightened doctor and journalist whose opinion he valued. The doctor-journalist informed Herzl that he needed rest and medical care, he was suffering from a nervous breakdown.

Herzl, shaken and depressed by his friend's reaction, wrote impulsively to Baron Hirsch, "For the present there is no helping the Jews. If someone showed them the promised land, they would scoff at him. For they are demoralized. . . . We shall have to sink still lower; we shall have to be more widely insulted, spat upon, mocked, beaten, robbed and slain before we are ripe for the idea. . . ."

Six months had passed since the January day Herzl had heard the Parisian mob scream "Death to the Jews!" In July he resigned as Paris correspondent of his newspaper and became the editor of its influential literary section. He lived in Vienna. He traveled to Berlin and Munich to read the Rothschild address to prominent Jews. He read it to Jews in Vienna, Paris, and London. They would gather in beautiful homes and he would stand before them, a handsome darkbearded figure with a prominent nose, a shock of thick black hair, wearing a demeanor of dignity and sophistication and fixing upon them the dark eyes of a dreamer. They knew of his reputation as a writer and journalist and literary editor of one of the most important newspapers in Europe. They listened to his reading of the address, which lasted about two hours, but would not take his plan seriously. "Today I am an isolated and lonely man," he had written in June, "tomorrow perhaps the intellectual leader of hundreds of thousands. . . ."

He decided to present the plan in a book. He revised

the address, added to it ideas that had come to him during the months he had spent speaking before various groups. The book was published in Vienna on February 14, 1896—a little over a year after the cries of that Parisian mob. It was called *Der Judenstaat—The Jewish State*. That same year it was translated into Hebrew, English, French, Russian, and Rumanian. Since its publication it has appeared in eighteen languages and in eighty separate editions.

It is impossible, he wrote, to solve the Jewish question by assimilation. The Jews had no wish to disappear and gentiles had no desire to host Jews. Only a political solution was possible: establish an independent Jewish state with the consent of the world's great powers. He thought it preferable that the state be in the land of Israel. The state would come into existance based on a carefully preconceived plan. Two groups would have to be established: one acting as the authorized representative of the Jewish people, the other controlling finances and construction. Jewish wealth, large and small bankers, would finance the enterprise.

Orthodox and assimilated Jews in western Europe received the plan coldly. It seemed too unreal, the scheme of a dreamy extremist. The limping Hibbat Zion movement, in tenuous existence for some fifteen years, greeted the book excitedly. Zionist students in Austria and elsewhere urged Herzl to take on the leadership of those Hibbat Zion groups who felt themselves committed to his plan. "Our entire youth, all those who are now between twenty and thirty years of age, will abandon their vague socialistic leanings and turn to me," he had written in his dairy. "They will go forth as itinerant preachers to their own families and into the world. . . ." He agreed and became, in effect, the leader of the Zionist movement.

As he began to move among the suffering, poverty-stricken Jewish masses in eastern Europe, he realized the depth of the people's feeling toward the land of Israel and understood that this feeling could be transformed into messianic political action. From then on, the Jewish state was equivalent in his mind to the land of Israel.

He had a constituency. He became a wanderer for

the tens of thousands of Jews in the Hibbat Zion movement. In April 1896 he was received by the grand duke of Baden, who was the uncle of Kaiser William II of Germany. The grand duke expressed his support of the Zionist cause. Herzl journeyed to Constantinople and, with the help of a Polish diplomat, had an audience with the grand vizier. If the sultan would agree to the creation of an independent Jewish state in the land of Israel, Herzl said, the Jews would raise the money needed to resolve the disastrous financial crisis in which the Ottoman empire now found itself. The offer was rejected. He journeyed to London. The Jewish masses acclaimed him, but Jewish leaders withheld their support. Baron Edmond de Rothschild did not believe it would be possible to organize the Jewish masses for such a plan.

Herzl decided to turn his attention to the masses. On March 6, 1897, at a Hibbat Zion conference, he called for a general Zionist congress. It was to be a national assembly of the Jewish people. Some laughed; others saw it as a gesture of futility. The Hibbat Zion conference, to which had come delegates from Poland, Austria, and Germany, accepted the call. The delegates returned home. Herzl founded a Zionist weekly, *Die Welt,* in order to propagate his ideas.

The First Zionist Congress took place in Basle, Switzerland, August 29 to 31, 1897—about two and a half years after the Dreyfus affair. Herzl insisted that the delegates wear formal attire; he was a man of the theater; he understood the significance of costuming. Life would follow art; the delegates would take themselves and their cause seriously if they were dressed solemnly, formally.

The congress established the World Zionist Organization. It adopted the program of the Zionist movement, Herzl's program. Herzl acted as chairman. He was elected president of the World Zionist Organization. The Jewish people was now his constituency. He predicted there would be a Jewish state in fifty years.

He was a western secular man, a journalist. He understood the insidious nature of diplomacy and the cruelty of power. He knew the language and protocol of kings and diplomats. They might not agree with his plan for the

Jewish people, but he knew they would take seriously his presentation and would come to regard with slowly dawning amazement the growing sense of political power felt by the Jews.

Jewish bankers refused their support. This became the most serious obstacle to his plan, the lack of sympathy he found among Jewish capitalists.

In the fall of 1898 he journey to the land of Israel. Beneath the hot Mediterranean sun he was greeted by Jews who had established the new colonies in the land. He saw tanned Jewish children and men at ease on galloping horses. He saw groves of trees and new houses and grass on sand dunes. He had gone to the land to meet the Kaiser. They met at the Kaiser's tent outside Jerusalem.

"The country can have a great future," said the Kaiser.

"At the moment it is sick," said the political Zionist.

"Water is what it needs, a lot of water," said the Kaiser. "And shade."

"Yes, Your Majesty," said the Zionist. "Irrigation on a large scale!"

"It is a land of the future," the Kaiser said. He had been sitting on his horse. He held out his hand to the Zionist and trotted off. He showed no more interest in Zionism.

Herzl visited Jerusalem. He was sickened by the filth of the old city and the misery and uncleanliness he witnessed in the Jewish hospital. "I am absolutely convinced," he wrote, "that a magnificent new Jerusalem can be built outside the old city walls."

We are now turning another corner in time and entering our own century.

On January 12, 1900, a play written by Herzl opened at the Burgtheater in Vienna. The following day he wrote in his diary, "At the end of the harmless play there was violent hissing, which obviously could not have been caused by this unpretentious comedy. I must not live on Zionism; I am not to live on literature. A problem!"

In 1902 the Ottoman empire offered Herzl Mesopotamia, but not the land of Israel, in return for a sum of money that would alleviate its financial plight. The political Zionist refused the offer.

He published *Altneuland—Old New Land—* a visionary novel in which he depicted the harsh wasteland of Palestine as seen by a Jew and a non-Jew during their trip to a distant island—and then seen again some decades later by the same travelers after the land had become a Jewish state. People have labored cooperatively with the resources of modern science to transform the land into a green world of canals, farms, gleaming cities, trains, roads. Jericho is a winter resort. Old Jerusalem has been cleaned, its streets and alleys paved with new stones. Around the old city there are modern suburbs, with parks, tree-shaded boulevards, institutions of learning, markets, lovely homes. Arabs and Jews live side by side in friendship. The creation of the Jewish state has eliminated anti-Semitism throughout the world. "If you will, it is not a dream," was the motto of the book. "Dream and action are not so far apart as is often thought," wrote Herzl in the epilogue. "All the acts of mankind were dreams once and will become dreams again."

He entered into various negotiations with the British government. The British offered him Uganda—the territory that was once British East Africa, below Egypt and Ethiopia, and that is today's Kenya. Herzl brought the offer to the Sixth Zionist Congress in August 1903. The Zionist movement was nearly torn apart in the ensuing battle between those willing to accept this piece of Africa and those who saw the future of the people only on its own land. The offer would be refused by the Seventh Zionist Congress in 1905.

After the 1903 Kishinev pogrom Herzl visited Russia. He was received tumultuously by the masses and was acclaimed as Herzl the king. They were his people, these eastern European Jews, the army of Zionism. He saw their wretched degradation under the regime of Czar Nicholas II. He continued wandering among kings and bankers. In January 1904 he met with the pope.

"There are two possibilities," the pope said. "Either the Jews will cling to their faith and continue to await the Messiah who, for us, has already appeared. In that case they will be denying the divinity of Jesus and we cannot help them. Or else they will go there without any religion, and then we can be even less favorable to them."

For years Herzl had suffered from a weak heart. His work and his wanderings began seriously to affect his health. "I will have to be patient," he wrote. The movement was not without its bitter inner rivalries: secular Zionists, religious Zionists, socialist Zionists; those who believed any piece of land was acceptable for a Jewish state; those who insisted upon the land of the patriarchs and David and Rabbi Akiva and Bar Kochba. Jewish Bundists—members of the General Jewish Workers' Union in Lithuania, Poland, and Russia, founded in 1897—regarded a non-Zionist socialism as a viable dream, collected strike funds, and organized strikes, May Day demonstrations, and self-defense units against mobs perpetrating pogroms. This was their messianic activity, the liberation of the proletariat from the yoke of the rich bosses. The Bund was the only secular Russian Jewish movement that withstood the force of Zionism. There were those who attacked Herzl's lack of commitment to the Jewish tradition and the Hebrew language. He thought the language of the new Jewish state would probably be German. "Rivalries are beginning," he had written in 1898. "They already want to despose me. . . ."

The controversy over Uganda tore away the last fibers of his health. His heart condition worsened. He caught pneumonia. His heart gave out and on July 3, 1904, he died. He was forty-four years old.

Herzl had established a colonization fund with meager resources and a nebulous international Jewish political organization. Nothing he had done seemed of lasting significance.

Jews continued to colonize the land.

The first wave of immigration, which had begun to enter Palestine in 1881, had made the establishment of agricultural colonies the foundation for the resettlement of the land. These colonists had come from Russia and Rumania, young men and women, and they knew nothing about agriculture beneath the burning sun of the Mediterranean sky. They set up their first agricultural colonies in

1882—Rishon le-Zion, Zichron Yaakov, Rosh Pinah—
and in that first summer the land blazed and the crops
withered. The colonization effort foundered. It was kept
alive through the philanthropy of Baron Rothschild, who
put more than one and a half million British pounds into
the land over a span of fifteen years. These colonies still
exist today—green, large, and well-to-do.

The Turks became wary of the increasing presence of
Jews in the land. In May 1882 they banned further
Jewish immigration into Palestine. Jews entered the land
illegally. By the end of the century the efforts of this first
wave of immigrants began to waver. The children of the
settlers were moving to the cities. The dream of colonization languished in the heat and swamps of the land.

A second wave of immigrants began arriving in 1904,
driven by the shock waves of the Kishinev pogrom. The
failed revolution of 1905 brought a small flood of Russian
Jews to the land. These were hard-working dreamers who
hungered to devote themselves to the renaissance of their
people. Many regarded agriculture and physical labor as
the new driving ideal that would transform the people and
redeem the land. The Jews would reenter history by making the land green.

They organized political parties, established schools, set
up a workers' sick fund. They established a Hebrew press.
Hebrew became the language of the land. Dreamers
sweated in the Mediterranean heat, working the hard soil
with their hands. They formed guard units to protect the
settlements against the raids of Arabs and Bedouins.

Arab opposition to the new Jewish presence had begun
to stiffen around the turn of the century. After 1908 the
Turks permitted the Arabs to acquire weapons. Settlements came under increasing attack. Zionist efforts to negotiate with the Arabs failed. By 1914 there were
eighty-five thousand Jews in the land.

During the First World War the Jewish settlers were
severely persecuted by the Turks. There were expulsions,
jailings, and killings. Some Jews established a spy network
for the British. In September 1917 they were discovered,
arrested, tortured. Jews were crowded into the Galilee by

the Turks, who feared an imminent British invasion. Food was scarce. The Galilee was near starvation.

In an unseen way, the forces set in motion by Herzl slowly began to be felt. The presence of Jews as an international political entity was sensed by the British, who sought the aid of world Jewry in their war effort. On November 2, 1917, England issued the Balfour Declaration, announcing that it looked with favor upon the creation of a Jewish state in Palestine. The land was still part of the Ottoman empire.

The British had invaded Palestine on October 31, 1917. That December, during the festival of Hanukkah, inaugurated by the liberation war of the Maccabees more than two thousand years earlier, General Allenby led a British army into Jerusalem. Pious Jews thought him to be the Messiah.

In 1918 all of Palestine came under British rule. By the end of the war the number of Jews in the land had fallen to a little less than sixty thousand. In the parceling out of booty after the war, Palestine became a British mandate.

The Jewish population began a steady increase during the decade of the twenties—the period of the third wave of immigration, much of it from Poland—despite Arab riots and a slow souring of the British attitude toward Zionism. Jews had entered deeply now into the blood-spattered gladiatorial arena of international geopolitics. I wonder often how those men did it—Chaim Weizmann, David ben-Gurion, and the others—how they made the move from pogroms to diplomacy in a single generation.

On January 30, 1933, Adolf Hitler came to power. He was forty-three years old. Palestine was barely affected by the economic depression of the thirties. More than one hundred thousand Jews entered the land as immigrants from Germany—which had finally put an end to its dance with those of the Mosaic persuasion. They brought light industry and the many skills of German Jewry. Most of Polish Jewry remained in Europe, waiting for the Messiah. Arab riots intensified in the last years of the thirties.

On September 1, 1939, the legions of Germany invaded Poland.

\*     \*     \*

Rivers ran with blood. Beasts roamed the land. Men slew children. People fled from towns for the security of forests. Blood and fire and pillars of smoke concealed the sun and fused together in an immense apocalypse, an *auto-da-fé* that burned the soul of the world.

Who was king? Who was not king? Centuries of Christian and Roman hate were king in the guise of Teutonic pagans. The world was as silent as the Nile had once been. And the wanderings of European Jewry came to an end.

I remember the newspaper photographs, the memorial assemblies, the disbelief in the faces of friends, the shock as news came of death and more death. My parents had both come from old Hasidic families. All had perished—uncles, aunts, cousins, sisters, brother, parents. I remember my father's rage, my mother's soft endless weeping. My father was a follower of the militant capitalist Zionism—the Revisionist party—of Vladimir Jabotinsky, whose disciples organized the underground army of the Irgun under the leadership of Menahem Begin and declared war against British forces in Palestine. He reacted to the Irgun raids with grim and silent satisfaction.

Most of the gentle Jews are dead, he once told me. The gas chambers and ovens have brought a new kind of Jew into the world. Even the Hasidim are no longer gentle.

He had killed Russians during the First World War as a Polish soldier in the Austrian army. Often I would see him clutching his Yiddish newspaper as he read of the day's events, and I could imagine his veined iron hands holding and firing the machine gun he had used in the war.

I was eighteen years old in November 1947 when the great powers in the United Nations granted nationhood to the six hundred thousand Jews then living in the land of Israel—fifty years after its existence as a state had been predicted by the Viennese journalist who had thought to write a novel after a confrontation with an anti-Semitic mob and instead had created the beginnings of what may one day be the third civilization of the Jews.

*    *    *

I am a Jew, an American. Early in this century my wife's father came to America from Russia. He had belonged to a Zionist group. Zionist activity was illegal in Russia after the unsuccessful revolution of 1905. He would meet with his friends in a forest and they would talk of their dreams of a new society in a Jewish state in the land of Israel and of their plans to emigrate from Russia. They would take careful notes of their ideas and plans.

One day his name was spotted on the local police arrest list by a kindly peasant. His father was quickly told. That night the young Zionist began a long underground wandering in unheated trains through the snows of Russia and Poland, past guards whose hatred of Jews had been dulled by fat bribes. A boat from Hamburg brought him to New York—four months after he had left Russia. He never saw his parents again. He was sixteen years old.

His family was one of millions that broke apart in the cataclysm of hunger and hatred that convulsed Europe around the turn of the century. During that time there took place a major westward migration to England and America of European peoples, among whom were to be found eastern European Jews, the parents and grandparents of most of today's American Jewry. With that, there began a chain of events portentous for the history of all Jewry and, perhaps, the world. Many have seen divine guidance in this new wandering of the Jews.

From 1881 to 1914 about two million Jews fled Russia. About three hundred thousand settled in England and built for themselves a small, vital island of Jewry with open bridges to the host culture. Others went to Australia and now live in Melbourne, Sidney, Perth, Adelaide, and elsewhere on that vast continent, feel themselves part of its urban and outback landscape, and worry, together with other Australians, about the distance that separates them from the centers of western civilization. Still others went to Canada when the United States began to close its doors and created great urban centers of traditional Judaism. Some climbed aboard boats that took them to South Africa, discovered an unspoiled, verdant land, settled in, and brought over their families and friends—entire small towns in many instances. They and their children now live in Johannesburg and Cape Town and in other cities of that land, have built a wealthy and highly organized Jewish community, find themselves between the hammer and anvil of that country's growing anguish, and do not quite know where to turn. More than a million and a half Jews settled in the United States. The Jewish population of Russia was quickly replenished by its high birth rate.

The Jews who poured out of the steerage holds of the steamships that crisscrossed the Atlantic found themselves in a land that had already hosted two previous waves of Jewish immigration, one a tiny Sephardic ripple during the colonial period—Stephardim saw themselves as the aristocrats of American Jewry—and another, much larger immigration from Germany in the middle of the nineteenth century.

During the sixteenth and seventeenth centuries the mercantile nations of Europe had carved up the new land for exploitation. In the eighteenth century a revolution had severed the links between settlers and mother country. The land had then gone its own way, tumultuous, frenetic, often coarse, sometimes ruthless, pushing against its frontiers. Colonial Jews had been an exotic minority regarded with some suspicion but never cruelly persecuted. German Jews had not come in sufficient numbers to create a troubling anti-Semitic reaction. They had proved industrious, had introduced into the land the hard-working peddler who brought clothes and books and medicaments to isolated farmers and villagers, and had become storekeepers, international traders, land speculators, clothing manufacturers, financiers. They built Reform synagogues and communities in Pittsburgh, Cincinnati, Cleveland, Albany, Rochester, Syracuse, Boston, Hartford, New Haven, Baltimore, New Orleans, Mobile, Galveston, Indianapolis, Columbus, Chicago, and elsewhere. In 1854, in California, there were ten synagogues. Reform congregations conducted their services mostly in English and professed their total loyalty to America and lack of allegiance to Zion and Jewish law. This second wave of Jewish immigrants began to establish the self-help organizations, foster homes, hospitals, social clubs, literary societies, and fraternal orders that would in later decades give unique configuration to American Jewry.

In the early years of the twentieth century eastern European Jews streamed in a tribal inundation onto the land and settled densely in its great urban centers, most of them in the malodorous tenements—stifling in the summers and freezing in the winters—of New York's Lower East Side, a section teeming with people and pushcarts. There, amid the nightmarish fears of other lonely, dislocated Europeans who were also bereft of their families and without status, sharing the crude intimacies of communal toilets, narrow hallways, thin walls, garbage-clogged air shafts with windows that faced one another from ground floor to roof—amid this noise-filled, dehumanized tenement world, the immigrants slowly settled into their new land and tried to make something of their lives. Many brought with them the religious orthodoxy of their eastern European background; others were socialists, anarchists, actively antireligious. Almost all were very poor. Often they were helped by the uptowners, the wealthy German Jews who wished to see their downtown coreligionists acculturate as quickly as possible, both out of a feeling of compassion and a desire to be spared the embarrassment of having non-Jews identify them as somehow related to these eastern Europeans.

It was this third wave of immigrant Jewry that built the American Yiddish theater, the Yiddish press, established Jewish labor unions, and founded the Orthodox synagogues that blunted the force of Reform Judaism. In time they entered and began to dominate most of the communal Jewish organizations established by German Jews. From their ranks came the religiously moderate masses that made Conservative Judaism the largest of the three American Jewish congregational groupings. Their heavily felt presence evoked an anti-Semitic reaction from some Americans, the "No dogs and Jews allowed here" signs, job discrimination, exclusion from certain clubs and hotels, the anti-Semitism at times coarse and open but most often covertly concealed behind formal courtesies. Henry Ford's newspaper, *The Dearborn Independent,* ranted about the international Jew who was the enemy of Anglo-Saxon civilization, the Jewish Bolsheviks who were set on conquering the Christian world. Some priests and ministers preached anti-Semitism, echoing the early Jewish experience in Spain, Gaul, and Poland. The immigrant generation, as well as the American Jews who had come from Germany, organized to fight anti-Semitism openly in the press and in courts of law and at times through the more concealed methods of economic pressure.

That generation of Jews struggled valiantly with its new world. I marvel at its desperate courage. Many Jews failed; we can read of their anguish in the Yiddish press of the time. Others entered the marketplace and fought their way to success. Still others sensed quickly that an education was often a passage to the American landscape. They entered schools. The American Jewry of today was born in that one generation when the last of the great tribal migrations of our species moved across the cities, hills, and valleys of the new world.

The children and grandchildren of those eastern European Jews now participate in and help mold the Jewish and secular cultures of the land. With little sense of Jewish self-consciousness, many of these Jews are actually creating much of what is today American culture. They feel no reservations and hesitancy on the part of other Americans concerning their presence. There was never the experience in America of a protracted, anguished battle for emancipation, of rights granted and then withdrawn, of twenty-one different sets of laws governing the behavior and status of the land's various Jewish communities, of Judaism as an impossible burden, a monstrous barrier preventing equality and therefore causing deep insecurity and bitter self-loathing, of relentlessly anti-Semitic political parties—as there had been in Germany before and after the rule of Bismarck. American Jewry is in the mainstream of American civilization.

In the decade of the thirties a new wave of German Jewish immigrants fled Hitler, brought literary, artistic, and scientific brilliance to these shores—and intensified the secular Jewish participation in American culture. After the Second World War about 150,000 eastern European Jews entered the United States, almost all of them death-camp survivors. They have sparked a small Orthodox Jewish renaissance in some of the large urban centers of the land. They are reminders of the people's beginnings and a counterpoint to the activity of the secularists. The American Jew mirrors in microcosm the ongoing tension in western civilization between old loyalties and new ideas, the ambivalence reflected in the eagerness to be part of the secular adventure of modern man and at the same time not vanish as a minority group.

The sixteen-year-old boy who fled from Russian police and would one day be my father-in-law somehow managed to live creatively as both secular man and traditional Jew. He labored in the sweatshops of the garment industry during his early years in the United States. Then he took a job as a carpenter in a construction crew. He attended night school and confronted eagerly this new culture. He helped found the Labor Zionist movement in America. These were the socialist Zionists from whose ranks in America and the land of Israel would come David ben-Gurion, Golda Meir, and others. He became a journalist for a Yiddish newspaper. He was a fine writer—in Hebrew and Yiddish. He could write in Russian and English too, but did not publish in these languages. During the First World War he helped organize American volunteers to the Jewish Brigade, which fought in the British army. He would have gone over himself, but he came down with influenza the night before the last boat sailed. He was a short, thin, fragile-looking man and he burned with the strength born of dreams.

When I first met him he was in his sixties and was teaching the Bible in a Hebrew-language parochial school in New York. He was very active in Zionist affairs. It was effortless for me to love him immediately. I would sit with him for hours in the Brooklyn apartment, with the furniture of the twenties and the bookcases crowding the room and the pictures of Bialik and Weizmann and Herzl on the walls, sometimes the two of us alone, at other times together with my wife, who was his younger daughter, and my mother-in-law, and we would talk of the early years of Zionism.

We spoke at length one evening of Moses Hess, an assimilated German Jew of the nineteenth century who had
published philosophical works and many articles and
essays, all on political subjects. He was a socialist and a
follower of Hegel. Then in 1862 he published a book
called *Rome and Jerusalem*. He had noticed a link between the liberation efforts of oppressed nationalities—in
particular the war of the Italians against Austria in 1859
and the writings of Mazzini, the Italian revolutionist—and
the researches in anthropology in which he was engaged.
He was convinced, he wrote, that it was the destiny of
man to put an end to racial domination. All nations would
then undergo a renaissance, including the Jewish nation.
The Jew was the last national problem. There were two
major historical races, the Aryan and the Semitic. The
Aryan race had a dream: it sought to explain and beau-
tify life. The Semitic race too had a dream: it yearned to
moralize and sanctify life. Anthropology had taught him
that of races there is neither inferiority nor superiority,
only variety. History aims at the harmony of nations, the
cooperation of all peoples. The Jews should make every
effort to preserve their identity in the dispersion and
achieve the political restoration of the land of Israel. The
religion would preserve the people. The future Jewish
state would have to be based on land acquired by the entire people; on a legal framework that would enable labor
to proceed fruitfully; and on societies of agriculture,
trade, and industry that would fulfill Mosaic, or socialist,
principles. That was the messianism of this assimilated
Jew, my father-in-law said.

He had come before his time. A secular Amos. No one
listened. Only two hundred copies of the book were sold.
Perhaps I knew that Herzl had read *Rome and Jerusalem*
in the spring of 1901 and had written in his diary, "Everything that we have tried is already in his book. . . .
Since Spinoza, Jewry has brought forth no greater spirit
than this forgotten Moses Hess." Perhaps I knew that.

No, I had not known that.

Perhaps I knew that Hess had been influenced by Zevi
Hirsch Kalischer, a rabbi in Prussia who had written
works urging Jews to abandon the traditional view of the

Messiah and attempt to obtain the consent of the nations for the Jewish resettlement of the land. Perhaps I knew that another early eighteenth-century rabbinic Zionist, a Sephardic rabbi, Judah Alkali, had influenced Herzl's grandfather.

I had known nothing about any of that. I sat for a long time that evening lost in awe over the secret life of ideas.

Often he would tell me of the men he had known, the early dreamers, of Nachman Syrkin, the first ideologist of socialist Zionism, of Shemaryahu Levin, a Zionist writer, and Chaim Greenberg, a later socialist Zionist theoretician. He spoke of Ahad Ha-Am, Ber Borochov, A. D. Gordon, along with other Zionists—the minds who had fashioned the movement that had turned the land green, guided its people through riots and a bloody war of independence, and was now trying to create a viable state out of the grim realities of normalcy. I remember being lost in a deep tunnel of disillusion after a terrorist ambush and a bloody reprisal.

"Dreaming is cleaner than living," he told me gently. "Does that mean we should be without dreams?"

He loved America. Sitting on a living-room sofa or in the kitchen over glasses of tea, we would trade bits of knowledge about American history. During my last year in high school I had been one of a handful of winners in the nationwide Hearst American History Contest. I rode home on the bus staring at myself in the New York *Journal-American*. I had placed very high in a contest in which thousands had participated. "You couldn't come in first?" my father had asked. "Why couldn't you have been first? A Talmudic head should come in first."

I thought I knew American history but there were things my father-in-law knew, especially about the Jews in America, that surprised me. He knew that Jews had been mayors of many frontier towns because often they had been the only literate people around; that in 1915 the Lower East Side of New York City had contained 350,000 Jews in less than two square miles—almost the same number as the entire Jewish populations of Warsaw and Vilna; that when the Jews—sixty thousand workers—had poured out of the factories at the appointed start of the famous 1910 cloakmakers' strike in New York City, the chairman of the strike said it reminded him of the Jews leaving Egypt.

No, I knew nothing about any of those things.

Surely I knew about the first Sephardic Jews who had arrived in New Amsterdam in September 1654 and were labeled a "deceitful race" by Peter Stuyvesant. Twenty-three Jews on a boat fleeing from Brazil where the conquering Portuguese had begun to burn Conversos. Yes, I knew about that. Did I know that there were no Jewish lawyers during the colonial period because lawyers were of low repute then, considered to be corrupt enforcers of bad laws? I said we were making up for that now. He told me of the German Jews who had traveled west on the wagon trains, settling everywhere, opening shops—some of which became the huge department stores we see today—pioneering the land as Jews had once pioneered Gaul and the Ukraine. That was not news to me. He asked me if I knew that in 1700 there were about three hundred Jews in America and that they or their families had almost all assimilated by the time of the Revolution; that there were 6,000 Jews in the country in 1826; 15,000 in 1840; 150,000 in 1860; 280,000 in 1880; and 4,500,000 in 1925, out of a total population of 115,000,000. I said I had read that somewhere.

He had been astonished to discover that sudden growth in the Jewish population, he said softly.

So were a lot of Americans, I said.

He knew the names of the mayors of big cities and of many senators and their voting records. He also knew Talmud and Hebrew literature and was an observant Jew. He had come from a world where the fusion of the sacred and the secular seemed an effortless act.

He was entirely at ease in two cultures and well read in a third, Russian. He loved its great writers and hated its despotism. When Russian Jewry returned to life after the death of Stalin, we talked of it often and his eyes would glow behind his steel-rimmed glasses. He knew Russian Jewry had not died, he said. He had never believed the communists and their tales of the willing disappearance of Russian Jewry.

He thought we could make something of Jewry in America. But it could never be the same Jewry we had once had in Europe. That civilization was dead. Its echoes would continue but its creativity was gone. We would have to create something new. The central idea of Biblical civilization was the covenant, he said. The central idea of rabbinic civilization was the Messiah. He did not know what would be the central idea, the driving force, of this new Jewry. But it would come, he said. Despite the shallowness of American Jewry, its materialism, its ignorance, despite the splintered hopes of secular civilization, the dreariness and loneliness of modern life—perhaps because of all this—it would come. We will do it, he would say repeatedly. Israel and American Jewry will do it together. America does not have the foul smell of Europe; it does not have its history, its centuries of hate. This is a kind land, despite its terrible mistakes and broken dreams. Israel and America will create something new for themselves and the world. "If you will, it is not a dream," he would add, echoing another dreamer from a different time as if to strengthen his own uncertainties.

He knew of the anti-Semitism latent in America like a polluting white noise, barely heard, barely sensed, but always present. We have to be careful, he would say soberly whenever I would mention it. We should take nothing for granted. Who says it will be easy? Where is it written that the world will love us? Those who say America is evil know nothing of Europe. I dream that we can do it, together with Israel—from which the sparks will one day come. He was an educated, rational man, but there were moments when he seemed strangely possessed by the radiant imagination of the kabbalist. Look how our secularists are creating, he once said. Perhaps history will see that as our new beginning.

I am one member of one people confronting these closing decades of the twentieth century. Whether it knows it or not, my people is now engaged in an attempt to create for itself a third civilization. I feel myself part of that venture. I think of Sumer and its rushing rivers, Egypt and its rising Nile, Canaan and its terraced hills and fertility cults,

Greece and Rome, Islam and Christianity, Jerusalem, Babylon, Cordova, Toledo, the Rhine Valley, the Ukraine, Vilna, Odessa, Kishinev. What will Jewry make of itself for the next thousand years?

It is not difficult for Jews to remember the historical traumas of their past: the crusades, the persecutions at the time of the Black Death, the Inquisition, the expulsion from Spain, the degrading ghetto centuries, the Chmielnicki rebellion, the Russian pogroms, the massacres during the First World War, and finally the Holocaust, in which the European branch of Jewry perished—the core, the very heart, of both the sacred and the secular in Jewish life, the branch that produced the great Talmudists with whom I once studied as well as Sigmund Freud, Franz Kafka, Martin Buber, Henri Bergson, Marcel Proust, Albert Einstein. In some future time, eyes will gaze upon us as we have gazed in this book upon worlds of the past. They will say of us either that we used our new freedom—the freedom we sought but were never granted by Europe—to vanish as a people, or that we took advantage of the secret opportunity concealed within the persistent but hidden trauma we are now experiencing—a Jewry and Judaism decisively changed by its confrontation with modern paganism—to reeducate ourselves, rebuild our core from the treasures of our past, fuse it with the best in secularism, and create a new philosophy, a new literature, a new world of Jewish art, a new community, and take seriously the meaning of the word emancipation—a release from the authority of the father in order to become adults in our own right.

Everything seems to be in fragments: Judaism, Christendom, socialism, the secular dream of Hume that man can manage on his own—it is all in pieces around us. We are in an interregnum between worlds, groping about, peering into the future and seeing only our own image vaguely reflected in the dark glass. For many Jews there is a sense of constant struggle with frightening echoes of the past, a wariness that is the reflex of a battered people, a defensiveness after millennia of anti-Semitism, and a fear that once more we might lose hundreds of thousands, perhaps millions, of our people as we compete in the open

marketplace of ideas during this confrontation with secularism. The Jew sees all his contemporary history re-
fracted through the ocean of blood that is the Holocaust.
But there is also a sense of renewal, a forced sharpening
of our self-identity, a feeling that we are approaching
some distant fertile plain, though we cannot clearly make
out the paths leading to it.

This is an early, troubled springtime for the Jewish
people in the United States and Israel, in England,
Canada, Australia, South America, in almost all the non-
European lands to which Jews have wandered in the past
two centuries. The chill of a winter of death is still in the
air.

But Israel is a warmth for Jews everywhere, despite the
failures and disappointments felt when dreams are soiled
by the muck of reality and the weaknesses of human
beings. What a price we have paid for that land: seven
thousand killed in the War of Independence; another
thousand killed in the 1956 Sinai Campaign and the 1967
Six-Day War; three thousand killed in the October 1973
war; hundreds killed by terrorist raids. We offer ourselves
grim consolation: all the wars have cost us less than three
days at Auschwitz.

In the past few years I have wandered back and forth
across oceans. Everywhere I go I meet Jews passionate
with pride in Israel. They fear for her, tremble when her
people are hurt, support her, are not yet certain what sort
of nation-state they wish her to be, are concerned about
the drain upon creative energies and the coarsening of
moral fiber caused by endless military vigilance, and
are dazed with disbelief and joy over an achievement like
Entebbe. From Auschwitz to Entebbe in a single generation.

Yes, most of the gentle Jews are gone. Yes, the Jew is
now solidly inside the affairs of the world. Yes, we are
aware of the resonance of hate that lingers like a stench
upon western civilization. Yes, we will continue to be the
other, to hold our own view of things. Yes, we are a
single people, capable of loving our separate lands as well
as Israel—as one is able to love a mother and a father.
Yes, there will be peace one day. Yes, we will renew our

people. Yes, we touch millennia of precious history when we walk the streets of Jerusalem, and climb the hills, and journey through the sand wastes of the land. Yes, there are flowers to plant, seedlings to nurture, young trees to tend, old earth to nourish, and new earth to put in—a garden of new dreams to bring forth, to add to old covenants and messianic hopes, and to offer to ourselves and to our broken and beloved world. Yes.

# WANDERINGS

World Jewry Today/Map
Bibliography
Index

CANADA - 305,000

UNITED STATES - 5,775,000

CUBA - 1,500

MEXICO - 37,500

VENEZUELA - 15,000

AMERICA
(North, Central, South)
6,700,000

PERU - 5,200

BRAZIL - 150,000

CHILE - 27,000

URUGUAY - 50,000

ARGENTINA - 300,000

WORLD JEWRY TODAY
Approximately 14,260,000

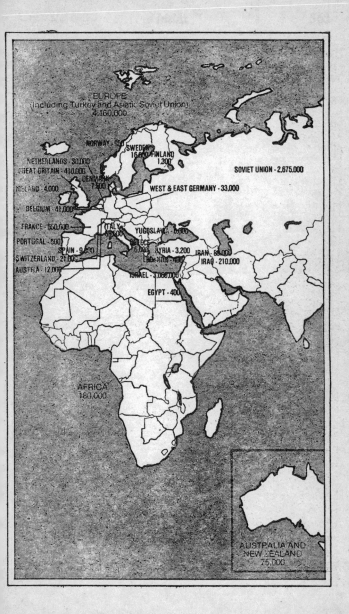

## AMERICA (North, Central, South)

San Francisco - 75,000

Los Angeles - 455,000

Vancouver - 12,000

Denver - 30,000

Phoenix/

Tucson - 32,500

Chicago - 253,000

Detroit - 80,000

Cleveland - 80,000

St. Louis - 60,000

Memphis - 9,000

Dallas/

Fort Worth - 23,000

Houston - 26,000

New Orleans - 10,600

Montreal - 115,000

Toronto - 115,000

Boston - 170,000

New York - 2,000,000

Philadelphia - 350,000

Baltimore - 92,000

Washington - 35,000

Atlanta - 21,000

Miami - 225,000

Cincinnati - 30,000

Rio de Janeiro - 55,000

São Paulo - 75,000

●

## EUROPE (Including Turkey and Asiatic Soviet Union)

Manchester - 35,000

London - 280,000

Paris - 300,000

Zurich - 6,150

Marseilles - 65,000

Stockholm - 8,000

Copenhagen - 7,000

Amsterdam - 20,000

Berlin - 6,000

Leningrad - 165,000

Warsaw - 5,000

Kiev - 170,000

Vienna - 9,000

Budapest - 65,000

Rome - 10,000

Istanbul - 23,000

Tel Aviv & Jaffa - 394,000

Haifa - 210,000

Jerusalem - 266,000

Moscow - 285,000

Bombay - 7,000

Calcutta - 300

Cochin, China - 500

●

## AFRICA

Capetown - 25,000   ●   Johannesburg - 60,000

●

## AUSTRALIA and NEW ZEALAND

Perth - 3,200   ●   Sydney - 28,500   ●   Melbourne - 34,000

# Bibliography

These works were my teachers. I used their words as my medium—much as a painter uses pigments and a sculptor uses clay. I thank the authors for their labors. I read books and monographs in Hebrew, French, German, and Spanish, but I omit almost all of them from this list. I read many other works in English than those listed here, many—but these were the ones through which I wandered repeatedly, extensively, and with most benefit.

Abrahams, Israel. *Jewish Life in the Middle Ages.* New York: Atheneum, 1969.

Agus, Irving A. "Rabbinic Scholarship in Northern Europe" and "Rashi and His School." In Cecil Roth, ed., *The Dark Ages. World History of the Jewish People.* Second series. Vol. 2. Tel-Aviv: Massada Publishing Co., 1966.

Aharoni, Yohanan. *The Land of the Bible: A Historical Geography.* Philadelphia: Westminster Press, 1967.

Aharoni, Yohanan, and Michael Avi-Yonah. *The Macmillan Bible Atlas.* New York: Macmillan, 1976.

Albright, W. F. *The Archaeology of Palestine.* Baltimore: Penguin Books, 1963.

———. *From the Stone Age to Christianity.* New York: Doubleday & Co., 1957.

———. *Yahweh and the Gods of Canaan.* New York: Doubleday & Co, 1968.

Aldred, Cyril. *The Egyptians.* London: Thames & Hudson, 1961.

Alt, A. *Essays on Old Testament History and Religion.* Oxford: Blackwell and Mott, Ltd., 1966.

Altmann, Alexander. *Moses Mendelssohn.* Tuscaloosa, Ala.: University of Alabama Press, 1973.

Arnott, Peter. *The Byzantines and Their World.* London: Macmillan, 1973.

Ashtor, Eliyahu. *The Jews of Moslem Spain.* Translated by Aaron

Klein and Jenny Machlowitz Klein. Philadelphia: Jewish Publications Society of America, 1973.

Avi-Yonah, Michael. *Carta's Atlas of the Period of the Second Temple, the Mishnah, and the Talmud.* Jerusalem: Carta, 1966.

Badian, E. *Studies in Greek and Roman History.* Oxford: Blackwell, 1964.

Baer, Yitzhak. *A History of the Jews in Christian Spain.* 2 vols. Translated by Louis Schoffman. Philadelphia: Jewish Publication Society of America, 1961.

————. *Galut.* Translated by Robert Warshaw. New York: Schocken Books, 1947.

Bainton, Roland H. *Christendom.* 2 vols. New York: Harper & Row, 1966.

Bakir, Abd el-Mohsen. *Slavery in Pharaonic Egypt.* Cairo, Egypt: Imprimerie de l'Institut Français d'Archéologie Orientale, 1952.

Baldson, J. P. V. D., ed. *The Romans.* New York: Basic Books, 1966.

Barcia, José Rubio, ed. *Américo Castro and the Meaning of Spanish Civilization.* Berkeley and Los Angeles: University of California Press, 1976.

Baron, Salo W. *A Social and Religious History of the Jews.* 16 vols. New York: Columbia University Press, Philadelphia: Jewish Publication Society of America, 1952–1976.

Barraclough, Geoffrey. *The Crucible of Europe.* Berkeley and Los Angeles: University of California Press, 1976.

Bein, Alex. *Theodor Herzl.* New York: Atheneum, 1970.

Ben-Sasson, H. H., ed. *A History of the Jewish People.* 2 vols. Cambridge, Mass.: Harvard University Press, 1976.

Benvenisti, Meron. *The Crusades in the Holy Land.* Jerusalem: Israel Universities Press, 1970.

Bibby, Geoffrey. *Looking for Dilmun.* New York: Alfred A. Knopf, 1969.

*The Bible.* Philadelphia: Jewish Publication Society of America, 1917, 1962, 1978.

Bickerman, Elias. *From Ezra to the Last of the Maccabees.* New York: Schocken Books, 1962.

Bloch, Marc. *Feudal Society.* 2 vols. London: Routledge & Kegan Paul, Ltd. 1971.

Blumenkranz, Bernhard. "Germany, 843–1096." In Cecil Roth, ed., *The Dark Ages. World History of the Jewish People.* Second series. Vol. 2. Tel-Aviv: Massada Publishing Co., 1966.

Bouquet, A. C. *Everyday Life in New Testament Times.* New York: Charles Scribner's Sons, 1953.

Bowra, C. M. *The Greek Experience.* Cleveland: World Publishing, 1958.

Bradford, Ernie. *Paul the Traveller.* New York: Macmillan, 1976.

Braude, Morris. *Conscience on Trial.* New York: Exposition Press, 1952.

Braudel, Fernand. *The Mediterranean.* 2 vols. Translated by Siân Reynolds. New York: Harper & Row, 1972.

Breasted, James Henry. *Ancient Records of Egypt.* 5 vols. Chicago: University of Chicago Press, 1906–7.

————. *A History of Egypt.* New York: Charles Scribner's Sons, 1905.

Bright, John. *A History of Israel.* Philadelphia: Westminster Press, 1959.

Burn, A. R. *The Warring States of Greece.* New York: McGraw-Hill, 1968.

*The Cambridge Ancient History.* Vols. 1 and 2, 3rd ed., London: Cambridge University Press, 1970–75. Vol. 3, rev. ed., London: Cambridge University Press, 1976.

Cantor, Norman F. *Medieval History.* New York: Macmillan, 1969.

Cartwright, Frederick F. *Disease and History.* New York: Thomas Y. Crowell, 1972.

Cary, M. *The Geographic Background of Greek and Roman History.* London: Oxford University Press, 1967.

Cary, M., and H. H. Scullard. *A History of Rome.* 3rd ed. London: Macmillan, 1975.

Chadwick, John. *The Mycenaean World.* Cambridge, Eng.: Cambridge University Press, 1976.

Childe, V. Gordon. *New Light on the Most Ancient East.* 4th ed. London: Routledge & Kegan Paul, Ltd., 1953.

Cohen, Gerson D. "The Blessing of Assimilation in Jewish History." Commencement address delivered at Hebrew Teachers College, Boston, June 1966.

————. *The Book of Tradition of Abraham ibn Daud.* Philadelphia: Jewish Publication Society of America, 1967.

*The Columbia Encyclopedia.* 3rd ed. William Bridgwater and Seymour Kurtz, eds. New York: Columbia University Press, 1963.

Cottrell, Leonard. *The Bull of Minos.* London: Pan Books, 1955.

Dawidowicz, Lucy S. *The Golden Tradition.* New York: Holt, Rinehart and Winston, 1967.

Dawood, N. J., ed. and translator. *The Koran.* London: Penguin Books, 1977.

Demsky, Aaron. *Literacy in Israel and Among Neighboring Peoples in the Biblical Period.* Ph.D. dissertation, Hebrew University, Jerusalem, 1976.

Dodds, E. R. *The Greeks and the Irrational.* Berkeley: University of California Press, 1951, 1973.

————. *Pagan and Christian in an Age of Anxiety.* New York: W. W. Norton & Co., 1970.

Dubnow, Simon. *History of the Jews in Russia and Poland.* 3 vols. Philadelphia: Jewish Publication Society of America, 1916–20.

Duruy, Victor. *The World of Legendary Greece.* New York: Leon Amiel Publisher, 1975.

Edwards, I. E. S. *The Pyramids of Egypt*. Rev. ed. London: Penguin Books, 1961.

Elazar, Daniel J. *Community and Polity*. Philadelphia: Jewish Publication Society of America, 1976.

Emery, W. B. *Archaic Egypt*. Baltimore: Penguin Books, 1972.

*Encyclopaedia Britannica*. Chicago: Encyclopaedia Britannica, Inc., 1976.

*Encyclopaedia Judaica*. Jerusalem: Keter, 1974.

Erickson, Carolly. *The Medieval Vision*. New York: Oxford University Press, 1976.

Erman, Adolf. *The Ancient Egyptians*. New York: Harper & Row, 1966.

———. *Life in Ancient Egypt*. New York: Macmillan, 1894.

al Fārūqī Ismaʿīl, and David E. Sopher, eds. *Historical Atlas of the Religions of the World*. New York: Macmillan, 1974.

Finkelstein, Louis, ed. *The Jews*. 2nd ed. New York: Harper & Brothers, 1955.

Flacelière, Robert. *Daily Life in Greece at the Time of Pericles*. New York: Macmillan, 1965.

Flusser, David. *Jesus*. Translated by Ronald Walls. New York: Herder & Herder, 1969.

Frankena, R. "The Vassal-Treaties of Esarhaddon," *Oudtestamentische Studien*, 14 (1965).

Frankfort, Henri. *Ancient Egyptian Religion*. New York: Harper & Row, 1961.

———. *The Birth of Civilization in the Near East*. Bloomington, Ind.; Indiana University Press, 1951.

———. *The Intellectual Adventure of Ancient Man*. Chicago: University of Chicago Press, 1946.

———. *Kingship and the Gods*. Chicago: University of Chicago Press, 1955.

Freehoff, Solomon B. *The Responsa Literature*. Philadelphia: Jewish Publication Society of America, 1955.

Gardiner, Alan. "Attitude of the Ancient Egyptians to Death and the Dead." Frazier Lecture at the University of Cambridge, May 14, 1935. Cambridge, Eng.: Cambridge University Press, 1935.

———. *Egypt of the Pharaohs*. Oxford: Oxford University Press, 1961.

Garraty, John A., and Peter Gay, eds. *The Columbia History of the World*. New York: Harper & Row, 1972.

Gaubert, Henri. *David and the Foundation of Jerusalem*. New York: Hastings House, 1969.

Gay, Peter. *The Enlightenment*. 2 vols. New York: Alfred A. Knopf, 1966, 1969.

Gelb, L. J. *A Study of Writing*. Chicago: University of Chicago Press, 1963.

Gilbert, Martin. *Jewish History Atlas*. New York: Macmillan, 1969.

Ginsberg, H. L. "New Light on Tannaïtic Jewry and on the State of Israel of the Years 132–135 C.E." *Rabbinical Assembly Proceedings.* New York: Rabbinical Assembly, 1961.

Glotz, G. *The Greek City.* London: Routledge & Kegan Paul, Ltd., 1969.

Goitein, S. D. *Letters of Medieval Jewish Traders.* Princeton, N.J.: Princeton University Press, 1973.

Goldin, Judah. *The Living Talmud.* New York: New American Library, 1957.

———. "The Period of the Talmud (135 B.C.E.–1035 C.E.)." In Louis Finkelstein, ed., *The Jews,* 2nd ed. Vol. 1. New York: Harper & Brothers, 1955.

Goldstein, Jonathan A. *1 Maccabees.* Anchor Bible Series. New York: Doubleday & Co., 1976.

Graetz, Heinrich. *History of the Jews.* 6 vols. Philadelphia: Jewish Publication Society of America, 1891–98.

Grant, Michael. *The Army of the Caesars.* New York: Charles Scribner's Sons, 1974.

Grant, Michael, and Don Pottinger. *Greeks.* London: Thomas Nelson & Sons, 1958.

Graves, Robert. *The Greek Myths.* New York: George Braziller, 1955.

Gray, J. *The Canaanites.* London: Thames & Hudson, 1964.

Grayzel, Solomon. *The Church and the Jews in the XIIIth Century.* New York: Hermon Press, 1966.

———. *A History of the Jews.* Philadelphia: Jewish Publication Society of America, 1947.

Greenberg, Moshe. *Hap/biru.* New Haven: American Oriental Society, 1955.

———. "Some Postulates of Biblical Criminal Law." In Menahem Haran, ed., *Yehezkel Kaufmann Jubilee Volume.* Jerusalem: Magnes Press, 1960.

Greenfield, Jonas. *Through the land of the Hittites: a private archaeological exploration through Turkey.* July 1977.

Gurney, Oliver. *The Hittites.* Baltimore: Penguin Books, 1952.

Güterbock, Hans G., and Thorkild Jacobsen, eds. *Studies in Honor of Benno Landsberger on His Seventy-fifth Birthday.* Chicago: University of Chicago Press, 1965.

Guttman, Julius *Philosophies of Judaism.* New York: Holt, Rinehart and Winston, 1964.

Hadas, Moses, *Humanism: The Greek Ideal and Its Survival.* New York: Harper & Brothers, 1960.

Halevi, Jehuda. *Selected Poems.* Translated by Nina Salaman, Philadelphia: Jewish Publication Society of America, 1974.

Hallo, William W., and William Kelly Simpson. *The Ancient Near East.* New York: Harcourt, Brace, 1971.

Hammond, N. G. L. *The Classical Age of Greece.* London: Weidenfeld & Nicolson, 1975.

———. *A History of Greece to 322 B.C.* London: Oxford University Press, 1967.

Hampshire, Stuart. *Spinoza*. Baltimore: Penguin Books, 1962.

Hawkes, Jacquetta, ed. *Atlas of Ancient Archaeology*. New York: McGraw-Hill, 1974.

Hay, Denys. *The Medieval Centuries*. New York: Harper & Row, 1965.

Heaton, E. W. *Everyday Life in Old Testament Times*. London: B. T. Batsford, 1956.

———. *The Hebrew Kingdoms*. Oxford: Oxford University Press, 1968.

———. *Solomon's New Men*. London: Thames & Hudson, 1974.

Hengel, Martin. *Judaism and Hellenism*. 2 vols. Translated by John Bowden. Philadelphia: Fortress Press, 1974.

Hertzberg, Arthur. *The French Enlightenment and the Jews*. New York: Columbia University Press, 1968.

———. *The Zionist Idea*. New York: Atheneum, 1977.

Herzl, Theodor. *Diaries*. 5 vols. Edited by Raphael Patai, translated by Harry Zohn. New York: The Herzl Press and Thomas Yoseloff, 1960.

Hillers, Delbert R. *Covenant*. Baltimore: Johns Hopkins University Press, 1969.

Hindus, Milton, ed. *The Old East Side*. Philadelphia: Jewish Publication Society of America, 1969.

Hitti, Philip K. *History of the Arabs*. London: Macmillan, 1974.

Hopper, R. J. *The Early Greeks*. London: Weidenfeld & Nicolson, 1976.

Hrushevsky, Michael. *A History of the Ukraine*. New Haven: Yale University Press, 1941.

Huizinga, J. *The Waning of the Middle Ages*. New York: Doubleday & Co. 1954.

Hyatt, J. Philip. "The Writing of an Old Testament Book." The American School of Oriental Research, *The Biblical Archaeologist*, VII, 1 (February 1944).

Ibn Gabirol, Solomon. *Selected Religious Poems*. Translated by Israel Zangwill. Philadelphia: Jewish Publication Society of America, 1974.

Jacobsen, Thorkild. Class lectures on archaeology and ancient Mesopotamia. Hebrew University, Jerusalem, January–May 1977.

———. Review of *Lamentation over the Destruction of Ur* by Samuel N. Kramer, in *The American Journal of Semitic Languages*, 58 (January–October 1941).

———. *Toward the Image of Tammuz and Other Essays on Mesopotamian History and Culture*. In William L. Moran, ed., Harvard Semitic Series. Vol. 21. Cambridge, Mass.: Harvard University Press, 1970.

———. *Treasures of Darkness*. New Haven: Yale University Press, 1976.

Johnson, Paul. *A History of Christianity*. New York: Atheneum, 1976.

Joinville and Villehardouin. *Chronicles of the Crusades.* Translated by M. R. B. Shaw. Harmondsworth, Eng.: Penguin Books, 1973.

Jones, A. H. M. *The Greek City.* Oxford: Oxford University Press, 1940.

Josephus. *Complete Works.* Translated by William Whiston. Grand Rapids, Mich.: Kregel Publications, 1976.

Kadushin, Max. *The Rabbinic Mind.* New York: Bloch Publishing Co., 1972.

Karp, Abraham J. *Golden Door to America.* New York: Penguin Books, 1977.

Katz, Jacob. *Exclusiveness and Tolerance.* New York: Schocken Books, 1962.

———. *Tradition and Crisis.* New York: Schocken Books, 1971.

Katzenstein, H. Jacob. *The History of Tyre.* Jerusalem: Schocken Institute, 1973.

Kaufmann, Yehezkel. *The Religion of Israel, From Its Beginnings to the Babylonian Exile.* Translated by Moshe Greenberg. Abridged from original 8 vols. Chicago: University of Chicago Press, 1960.

Kenyon, Kathleen M. *Digging up Jerusalem.* London: Ernest Benn Ltd., 1974.

Klausner, Joseph. *Jesus of Nazareth.* Translated by Herbert Danby. New York: Macmillan, 1959.

Koenigsberger, H. G., and George L. Mosse. *Europe in the Sixteenth Century. A General History of Europe.* Denys Hay, ed. London: Longman Group, Ltd., 1968.

Kramer, Samuel Noah. "Lamentation over the Destruction of Ur." *Oriental Institute of the University of Chicago Assyriological Studies,* 12 (1940).

———. *The Sumerians: Their History, Culture, and Character.* Chicago: University of Chicago Press, 1964.

Langmuir, Gavin I. "Majority History and Post-Biblical Jews," *Journal of the History of Ideas,* 27 (1966).

Laqueur, Walter. *A History of Zionism.* London: Weidenfeld & Nicolson, 1972.

Lasker, Daniel J. *Jewish Philosophical Polemics Against Christianity in the Middle Ages.* New York: Ktav Publishing House, 1977.

Lewis, Bernard. *History.* Princeton, N.J.: Princeton University Press, 1975.

———, ed. *Islam and the Arab World.* New York: Alfred A. Knopf, 1976.

Lewy, Hans, Alexander Altmann, and Isaak Heinemann, eds. *Three Jewish Philosophers.* New York: Meridian Books, Philadelphia: Jewish Publication Society of America, 1960.

Lieberman, Saul. *Greek in Jewish Palestine.* New York: Jewish Theological Seminary of America, 1942.

———. *Hellenism in Jewish Palestine.* New York: Jewish Theological Seminary of America, 1950.

Liebman, Charles S. *The Ambivalent American Jew*. Philadelphia: Jewish Publication Society of America, 1973.

Littell, Franklin H. *Atlas History of Christianity*. New York: Macmillan, 1976.

Lot, Ferdinand. *The End of the Ancient World and the Beginning of the Middle Ages*. New York: Harper & Row, 1961.

McCarthy, D. J. *Treaty and Covenant*. Rome: Pontifical Bibical Institute, 1963.

McKenzie, John L. *Dictionary of the Bible*. New York: Macimllan 1965.

MacMullen, Ramsey. *Enemies of the Roman Order*. Cambridge, Mass.: Harvard University Press, 1975.

————. *Roman Social Relations*. New Haven: Yale University Press, 1974.

McNeill, William H. *Plagues and Peoples*. New York: Doubleday & Co., 1976.

Maimonides. *The Guide of the Perplexed*. Translated by Shlomo Pines. Chicago: University of Chicago Press, 1963.

Malamat, Avram. "The Egyptian Decline in Canaan and the Sea Peoples." In B. Mazar, ed., *Judges. World History of the Jewish People*. First series. Vol. 3. Jerusalem: Massada Publishing Co., New Brunswick, N.J.: Rutgers University Press, 1971.

Mallowan, M. E. I. *Early Mesopotamia and Iran*. London: Thames & Hudson, 1965.

Marcus, Jacob R. *The Jews in the Medieval World*. New York: Harper & Row, 1965.

Margolis, M., and A. Marx. *A History of the Jewish People*. Philadelphia: Jewish Publication Society of America, 1947.

Mattingly, H. *The Man in the Roman Street*. New York: W. W. Norton & Co., 1966.

Mendelsohn, I. "On Corvée Labor in Ancient Canaan and Israel." *Bulletin of the American School of Oriental Research*, 167 (October 1962).

————. "State Slavery in Ancient Palestine." *Bulletin of the American School of Oriental Research*, 85 (February 1942).

Mendenhall, George E. "Law and Covenant in Israel and the Ancient Near East." *The Biblical Archaeologist*, XVII, 2 (May 1954) and 3 (September 1954).

Moore, G. F. *Judaism*. 3 vols. Cambridge, Mass.: Harvard University Press, 1927–30.

Netanyahu, B. *The Marranos of Spain*. New York: American Academy for Jewish Research, 1966.

Neusner, Jacob. *A History of the Jews in Babylonia*. 5 vols. Leiden: Brill, 1955–70.

————, ed. *The Formation of the Babylonian Talmud*. Leiden: Brill, 1970.

————, ed. *The Modern Study of the Mishnah*. Leiden: Brill, 1973.

*The New Cambridge Modern History.* 2 vols. Cambridge, Eng.: Cambridge University Press, 1975.

*The New Testament.* The authorized (King James) version.

Noth, Martin. *The History of Israel.* New York: Harper & Brothers, 1960.

————. *The Old Testament World.* Philadelphia: Fortress Press, 1966.

Oppenheim, A. Leo. *Ancient Mesopotamia.* Chicago: University of Chicago Press, 1964.

Pallis, S. A. *The Antiquity of Iraq: A Handbook of Assyriology.* Copenhagen: E. Munksgaard, 1956.

Parkes, James. *The Conflict of the Church and the Synagogue.* New York: Hermon Press, 1974.

Parrot, André. *Sumer, The Dawn of Art.* Translated by Stuart Gilbert and James Emmons. New York: Golden Press, 1961.

Pfeiffer, Charles F., ed. *The Biblical World: A Dictionary of Biblical Archaeology.* Grand Rapids, Mich.: Baker Book House, 1966.

Prawer, Joshua. *The World of the Crusades.* New York: Quadrangle Books, 1972.

Pritchard, J. B. *The Ancient Near East Supplementary Texts and Pictures Relating to the Old Testament.* Princeton, N.J.: Princeton University Press, 1969.

————, ed. *Ancient Near Eastern Texts Relating to the Old Testament.* Princeton, N.J.: Princeton University Press, 1950.

Renault, Mary. *The Nature of Alexander.* New York: Pantheon Books, 1975.

Ringgren, H. *Israelite Religion.* London: S.P.C.K., 1966.

Roberts, J. M. *History of the World.* New York: Alfred A. Knopf, 1976.

Robinson, Charles Alexander, Jr. *Athens in the Age of Pericles.* Norman, Okla.: University of Oklahoma Press, 1959.

Rostovtzeff, M. *Rome.* Oxford: Oxford University Press, 1960.

Roth, Cecil. *A History of the Jews.* New York: Schocken Books, 1971.

————. *History of the Marranos.* New York: Schocken Books, 1974.

————. *The Jews in the Renaissance.* Philadelphia: Jewish Publication Society of America, 1959. Reprint, New York: Harper & Row, 1965.

Roux, Georges. *Ancient Iraq.* Harmondsworth, Eng.: Penguin Books, 1966.

Rowley, H. H. *Worship in Ancient Israel.* London: S.P.C.K., 1967.

Runciman, Steven. *Byzantine Civilization.* London: Methuen & Company, Ltd., 1975.

Sachar, Howard M. *A History of Israel.* New York: Alfred A. Knopf, 1976.

Saggs, H. W. F. *The Greatness That Was Babylon.* London: Sidgwick & Jackson, 1962.

Sarna, Nahum M. "Paganism and Biblical Judaism." In Stanley M. Wagner and Allen D. Breck, eds., The J. M. Goodstein Lecture Series on Judaica. Denver: University of Denver, 1977.

————. *Understanding Genesis.* New York: McGraw-Hill, 1966.

Savory, R. M., ed. *Introduction to Islamic Civilization.* Cambridge, Eng.: Cambridge University Press, 1976.

Scholem, Gershom. *On Jews and Judaism in Crisis.* New York: Schocken Books, 1976.

————. *Major Trends in Jewish Mysticism.* New York: Schocken Books, 1961.

————. *The Messianic Idea in Judaism.* New York: Schocken Books, 1971.

————. *Sabbatai Sevi.* Princeton, N.J.: Princeton University Press, 1973.

Schorsch, Ismar. *Jewish Reactions to German Anti-Semitism, 1870–1914.* New York: Columbia University Press, Philadelphia: Jewish Publication Society of America, 1972.

Sealey, Raphael. *A History of the Greek City-States, ca. 700–338 B.C.* Berkeley: University of California Press, 1976.

*The Shorter Cambridge Medieval History.* 2 vols. Cambridge, Eng.: Cambridge University Press, 1971.

Sidorsky, David, ed. *The Future of the Jewish Community in America.* Philadelphia: Jewish Publication Society of America, 1973.

Speiser, Ephraim A. "The Biblical Idea of History in Its Common Near East Setting." *Israel Exploration Journal,* VII, 4 (1957).

————. *Genesis.* Anchor Bible Series. New York: Doubleday & Co., 1976.

————. *Oriental and Biblical Studies, Collected Writings of E. A. Speiser.* Edited and introduced by J. J. Finkelstein and Moshe Greenberg. Philadelphia: University of Pennsylvania Press, 1967.

Spiegel, Shalom. *Amos vs. Amaziah.* New York: Jewish Theological Seminary of America, 1957.

————. *The Last Trial.* Translated by Judah Goldin. Philadelphia: Jewish Publication Society of America, 1967.

————. "On Medieval Hebrew Poetry." In Louis Finkelstein, ed., *The Jews.* New York: Harper & Row, 1955.

Starr, Chester G. *A History of the Ancient World.* New York: Oxford University Press, 1965.

Stern, Menahem. *Greek and Latin Authors on Jews and Judaism.* Vol. I. Jerusalem: The Israel Academy of Sciences and Humanities, 1976.

Stobart, J. C. *The Grandeur That Was Rome.* 4th ed. New York: Hawthorn Books, 1961.

Strauss, Leo. *Spinoza's Critique of Religion.* New York: Schocken Books, 1965.

Tcherikover, Victor. *Hellenistic Civilization and the Jews.* Philadelphia: Jewish Publication Society of America, 1959.

Thompson, Thomas L. *The Historicity of the Patriarchal Narratives.* Berlin and New York: Walter de Gruyter, 1974.

Trachtenberg, Joshua. *The Devil and the Jews.* Cleveland and New

York: Meridian Books, Philadelphia: Jewish Publication Society of America, 1961.

——. *Jewish Magic and Superstition*. Cleveland and New York: Meridan Books, Philadelphia: Jewish Publication Society of America, 1961.

Twersky, Isadore. *A Maimonides Reader*. New York: Behrman House, 1972.

Van Seters, John. *The Hyksos: A New Investigation*. New Haven: Yale University Press, 1966.

de Vaux, Roland. *Ancient Israel: Its Life and Institutions*. Translated by John McHugh. New York: McGraw-Hill, 1961.

Weinfeld, Moshe. *Deuteronomy*. Oxford: Oxford University Press, 1972.

——. "Deuteronomy—The Present State of Inquiry." *Journal of Biblical Literature*, LXXXVI, part III (1967).

——. "Traces of Assyrian Treaty Formulae in Deuteronomy." *Biblica*, 46 (1965).

——. "The Worship of Molech and of the Queen of Heaven and Its Background." *Ugarit-Forschungen*, IV (1972).

Weinryb, Bernard D. *The Jews of Poland*. Philadelphia: Jewish Publication Society of America, 1972.

Wellesley, Kenneth. *The Long Year a.d. 69*. Boulder, Colo.: Westview Press, 1976.

Wilson, J. A. *The Culture of Ancient Egypt*. Chicago: University of Chicago Press, 1951.

Winter, Paul. *On the Trial of Jesus*. 2nd ed. Revised and edited by T. A. Burkill and Geza Vermes. Berlin and New York: Walter de Gruyter, 1974.

Wolfson, Harry A. *The Philosophy of the Church Fathers*. Cambridge, Mass.: Harvard University Press, 1956.

*The World History of the Jewish People*. Jerusalem and Tel-Aviv: Massada Publishing Co., 1964–75.

Wright, G. E. *Biblical Archaeology*. Philadelphia: Westminster Press, 1962.

Wright, G. E., ed. *The Bible and the Ancient Near East, Essays in Honor of William Foxwell Albright*. New York: Doubleday & Co., 1961.

Wright, G. E., and F. V. Filson. *The Westminster Historical Atlas to the Bible*. Philadelphia: Westminster Press, 1956.

Yadin, Yigal. *Art of Warfare in Bibical Lands*. New York: McGraw-Hill, 1963.

——. *Hazor*. New York: Random House, 1975.

Yerushalmi, Yosef Hayim. *The Lisbon Massacre of 1506 and the Royal Image in the Shebet Yehudah*. Hebrew Union College Annual Supplements, 1. Cincinnati: Hebrew Union College, 1976.

——. "Professing Jews in Post-Expulsion Spain and Portugal." In Saul Lieberman and Arthur Hyman, eds., *Salo Wittmayer Baron*

*Jubilee Volume.* New York and Jerusalem: American Academy for Jewish Research, 1975.

————. *From Spanish Court to Italian Ghetto.* New York: Columbia University Press, 1971.

# INDEX